The Collected Works of J. Krishnamurti

Volume XI

1958–1960

Crisis in Consciousness

COLLECTED WORKS VOLUME 11

Photo: J. Krishnamurti, ca 1962 by Cecil Beaton

Website: www.kfa.org

Printed in the United States of America

ISBN 13: 9781934989449
ISBN: 1934989444

Contents

Preface

Jiddu Krishnamurti was born in 1895 of Brahmin parents in south India. At the age of fourteen he was proclaimed the coming World Teacher by Annie Besant, then president of the Theosophical Society, an international organization that emphasized the unity of world religions. Mrs. Besant adopted the boy and took him to England, where he was educated and prepared for his coming role. In 1911 a new worldwide organization was formed with Krishnamurti as its head, solely to prepare its members for his advent as World Teacher. In 1929, after many years of questioning himself and the destiny imposed upon him, Krishnamurti disbanded this organization, saying:

Truth is a pathless land, and you cannot approach it by any path whatsoever, by any religion, by any sect. Truth, being limitless, unconditioned, unapproachable by any path whatsoever, cannot be organized; nor should any organization be forced to lead or to coerce people along any particular path. My only concern is to set men absolutely, unconditionally free.

Until the end of his life at the age of ninety, Krishnamurti traveled the world speaking as a private person. The rejection of all spiritual and psychological authority, including his own, is a fundamental theme. A major concern is the social structure and how it conditions the individual. The emphasis in his talks and writings is on the psychological barriers that prevent clarity of perception. In the mirror of relationship, each of us can come to understand the content of his own consciousness, which is common to all humanity. We can do this, not analytically, but directly in a manner Krishnamurti describes at length. In observing this content we discover within ourselves the division of the observer and what is observed. He points out that this division, which prevents direct perception, is the root of human conflict.

His central vision did not waver after 1929, but Krishnamurti strove for the rest of his life to make his language even more simple and clear. There is a development in his exposition. From year to year he used new terms and new approaches to his subject, with different nuances.

Because his subject is all-embracing, the *Collected Works* are of compelling interest. Within his talks in any one year, Krishnamurti was not able to cover the whole range of his vision, but broad applications of particular themes are found throughout these volumes. In them he lays the foundations of many of the concepts he used in later years.

The *Collected Works* contain Krishnamurti's previously published talks, discussions, answers to specific questions, and writings for the years 1933 through 1967. They are an authentic record of his teachings, taken from transcripts of verbatim shorthand reports and tape recordings.

The Krishnamurti Foundation of America, a California charitable trust, has among its purposes the publication and distribution of Krishnamurti books, videocassettes, films and tape recordings. The production of the *Collected Works* is one of these activities.

On Learning, 1958

---　✳　---

It seems to us that a totally different kind of morality and conduct and the action that springs from the understanding of the whole process of living have become an urgent necessity as we are faced with mounting crises and problems. We try to solve these issues through political and organizational methods, through economic readjustment, and through reforms. None of these methods will ever solve the complex human difficulties of existence though they may offer temporary relief. All reforms, however wide and seemingly lasting, are in themselves productive of further confusion and further reformation. Reformation, however necessary, without understanding the whole complex being of man, will only bring about the confusing demand for further reforms. There is no end to reform, and there is no fundamental solution along these lines.

Political, economic, or social revolutions are not the answer either, for they have produced either appalling tyrannies or the power of authority going into the hands of a different group. Such revolutions, at any time, are not the way out of confusion and conflict. But there is a revolution which is entirely different and which must take place if we are going to emerge out of this endless series of anxieties, conflicts, and frustrations. This revolution must begin not at the theoretical and ideational level—which eventually prove worthless—but in bringing about a radical transformation in the mind itself. This can only be brought about through right education, through the total development of a human being. This revolution through right education must take place in the whole of the mind and not in mere thought. Thought, after all, is a result and not the cause. There must be a radical transformation in the cause itself and not in the result. We are tinkering with results, with the symptoms, and we are not bringing about a vital, radical change, uprooting the old ways of thoughts, traditions, and habits. It is with this we are concerned, and only right education can bring this into being.

The capacity to seek and to learn is the function of the mind. By learning we do not mean the mere cultivation of memory and the accumulation of information but the capacity to think clearly and sanely without illusion, to start from facts and not from beliefs and ideals. There is no learning if thought originates from conclusions. Mere acquisition of information, called knowledge, is not learning. Learning implies the love of understanding and the love of doing the thing for itself. Learning is only possible when there is no coercion of any kind. Coercion implies, does it not, every form of influence through affection or threat, through persuasive encouragement or subtle forms of discussion.

Most people think that through comparison learning is encouraged, whereas the contrary is the fact. Comparison brings about frustration, and merely encourages envy, which is called competition. Subtle or obvious forms of persuasion do prevent learning and only bring about fear. Ambition breeds fear. Ambition, whether personal or identified with the collective, is always antisocial. So-called noble ambition is always, in its relationships, destructive.

It is necessary to encourage the development of a good mind that is capable of dealing with the many issues of life as a whole and which does not try to escape from them and so become contradictory, frustrated, bitter, or cynical. And it is essential that it should be aware of its own conditioning, its motives and pursuits.

Since the cultivation of the good mind is one of our chief concerns, it becomes very important how the educator teaches. As the educator is primarily concerned with the cultivation of the totality of the mind and not merely with giving information, he has to impart knowledge or information through every form of discussion, invitation to inquire, and to think independently. Authority, as the one who knows, has no place in learning. The educator as well as the pupil are both learning in this peculiar relationship with each other, but this does not mean that the educator disregards the orderliness of thought. This orderliness is not brought about by mere discipline in the form of assertive statements of knowledge, but if the educator understands that he is cultivating intelligence, there must be naturally a sense of freedom. This freedom is not to do what you like or to think in the spirit of mere contradiction, but a freedom in which the mind is being helped to be aware of its urges and motives which are revealed to the student through his own thought and action.

A disciplined mind is never a free mind, nor can a mind that has suppressed desire ever be free. It is only the mind that understands the whole process of desire that is free. Discipline always encourages, does it not, a movement within the framework of systems of thought and belief. Such a mind is never free to be intelligent. Such discipline brings about submission to authority, or capacity to function within the pattern of a society which demands functional ability, and not the intelligence which has its own capacity. The mind that has cultivated only capacity through memory is as the modern machine, the computer, which functions with astonishing ability and accuracy.

Authority can only persuade to think in certain directions. Thinking in conclusions and being guided along certain lines is not thinking at all; it is merely functioning as a human machine, which breeds thoughtless discontent, bringing with it frustrations, miseries, and so on. And we are concerned with the total development of each human being to his highest and fullest capacity—not to the highest capacity which the educator has in view as a concept, but the capacity to which any one individual may be capable of flowering.

Any spirit of comparison prevents this full flowering of an individual, whether as a scientist or as a gardener. But the fullest capacity of the gardener is the fullest capacity of the scientist when there is no comparison, but when comparison comes in, then there is the disparagement and the envious reactions which create conflict between man and man. Love is not comparative. Like sorrow, it cannot be compared with the greater or the lesser. Sorrow is sorrow, whether it is in the poor or in the rich—as love is.

The fullest development of an individual brings about a society of equals. The present social struggle to bring about equality merely on an economic or some spiritual level has no meaning at all. Social reforms to bring about equality breed other forms of antisocial activities. With right education there is no need for social and other reforms, as envy with its comparative capacities ceases.

We must differentiate here between function and status. Status with all its emotional and hierarchical prestige arises only through comparison of function as the high and the low. When each individual is flowering to his fullest capacity, then there is no division between status and function; there is only the expression of that capacity as a teacher or as a prime minister, and so status loses its sting. The functional or technical capacity is now recognized through having a BA or a PhD after a name; but since we are concerned with the total development of the human being, such an individual may or may not add letters after his name but will have the capacity to take a degree or not, as he pleases. His capacity is not measured by a degree, but he will know for himself his own capabilities. And the expression of his capacity does not bring about that self-centered confidence which mere technical capacity breeds; such confidence is comparative and therefore antisocial. Comparison exists only for utilitarian purposes, but it is not for the educator to differentiate the capacities and give greater or lesser evaluation.

Since we are concerned with the total development of the individual, the student may not be allowed in the beginning to choose his own subjects. If he chooses, his choice will be based on passing pleasures and prejudices and that which is the easiest to do; if he chooses, he will choose according to the immediate needs of a particular society. But when we are concerned with the primary thing and in the cultivation of it, he will naturally come to choose, not the easiest subject to study and pass, but how he can express his capacities to the fullest and to the highest extent. We are concerned in dealing with the many issues of life as a whole with all its psychological, intellectual, and emotional problems. Since the student is helped from the very beginning to look at life as a whole, he will not be frightened of it.

The capacity to deal with any problem as a whole is intelligence. Giving grades and marks to the student does not cultivate intelligence. On the contrary, it degrades the human dignity of understanding. This comparative evaluation cripples the mind—which does not mean that the teacher does not observe the progress of every student and keep a record of it. Parents, naturally anxious to know the progress of their children, will want a report; but, most unfortunately, as they do not understand what the educator is trying to do, they will use the report as a means of coercion in an affectionate or threatening manner to produce the results which they desire and so undo the work which the educator is trying to do. Parents should understand the kind of education that we intend to give. Generally they are satisfied to see their children get a degree of some kind which will assure them of a livelihood. Very few are concerned beyond this. Of course they wish to see their children so-called happy, but beyond this vague desire very few are concerned with their total development. As most of them desire that their children should have a successful career, they either affectionately bully them or frighten them to acquire book knowledge, and so the book becomes very important; with it, there is the mere cultivation of memory that repeats without the quality of real thought behind it.

The difficulty that our educator has to face is the great indifference on the part of the parent to a wider and deeper education, as the parent is only concerned with the cultivation of superficial knowledge which will get his child a respectable position in a corrupt society.

So the educator not only has to educate the children in the right way but also to see to it that the parents do not undo whatever may have been done at the school. Really the school and the home should be the centers of real education and not opposed to each other—the parents desiring one thing and the educator doing something entirely different. It is very important that the parent should be fully acquainted with what the educator is doing and be vitally interested in the total development of his children. It is equally his responsibility to see that this kind of education is carried out and not leave it merely to the teachers whose burden is already sufficiently heavy. This total development can only be brought about fully when there is the right relationship between the teacher, the student, and the parent. As the educator cannot yield under any circumstances to the fancies or the obstinate demands of parents, it is necessary that the parents should understand what the educator is doing and not bring about conflict and confusion in their children.

The natural curiosity and the urge to learn, surely, exist from the very beginning in a child, and this should be intelligently encouraged so that, as he grows, this urge remains vital without distortion and will lead to the study of various subjects. If this eagerness to learn is encouraged at all times, then mathematics, geography, history, science, or biology will not be a problem to the child or to the educator. Learning is facilitated when there is an atmosphere of thoughtful affection and happy care.

Emotional sensitivities can only be cultivated when the student feels that he is secure in his relationship with his teachers. The feeling of being secure in relationship is the primary necessity of children. There is a vast difference between the feeling of being secure and of dependency. Most educators, consciously or unconsciously, cultivate this feeling of dependence and therefore subtly encourage fear, which the parents also do in their own affectionate or aggressive manner; and this dependency shows itself as the authoritarian or dogmatic assertions of what a child should be and should do. With dependence goes always the shadow of fear, and this fear compels the child to obey, to conform, and to accept the edicts and the sanctions of the elders. In this atmosphere of dependency, emotional sensitivities are trampled upon and so can never be cultivated. But when the child knows and feels that he is secure, then the emotional flowering is not thwarted by the fear of insecurity. This security is not the opposite of insecurity. We mean by security the feeling of being at home—not the home from which the child has come, but the home where he can be what he is, where he is not compelled to be or not to be, where he can climb a tree and not be scolded if he falls, where the educator or the housemother or the housefather is concerned deeply with the total welfare of the child—which the child feels at the first impact.

What is important is that the child should feel at the first impact, and not a few weeks or a few months later, that he is at home, completely secure. It is the first impact that is of the highest importance. But if the educator tries various means to gain his confidence and allows the child freedom to do what he likes, then the educator is cultivating dependency and is not giving the child the feeling of being secure, the feeling that he is at home where there are people who are deeply concerned with his total welfare. The very first impact of this new relationship, which the child has never had before, will bring about a natural communication in which the young do not regard the old as a form of threat which is to be respected. A child who feels secure has his own ways of expressing respect which is essential in learning. This respect is denuded of all authority and fear. In this feeling of security, conduct and behavior are not something imposed by the elder, but become a process of learning. And because the child is secure in his relationship with the teacher, with the elder, he will naturally be considerate, and it is only in this atmosphere of security that the flowering of emotional sensitivities can be brought about. In this atmosphere of being at home, of being secure, he will do what he likes, but in the doing of what he likes, he will learn to find out what is the right thing to do—which is not the result of an action of resistance or an action of obstinacy or of suppressed feelings, or a response of an immediate urge.

To be sensitive is to be sensitive to all things about one, whether it be the plants, animals, trees, skies, waters, or the bird on the wing, sensitive to the moods of the people about one and to the stranger that passes by. This sensitivity brings about that quality of uncalculated, unselfish response which is true morality and conduct. So his conduct will be open and not secretive, and being open, a mere suggestion on the part of the teacher is accepted easily without any resistance and friction.

As we are concerned with the total development of the human being and his emotional urges, which are very much stronger than intellectual reasoning, we must cultivate emotional capacity and not help to suppress it. When one is capable of dealing with emotional and intellectual issues, then there will be no sense of fear in approaching them.

Since we are concerned with the total development of the human being, solitude as a means to the cultivation of sensitivity becomes a necessity. As it is necessary to know mathematics, it is also necessary to know what it is to be alone, what it is to meditate, what it is to die—not what is solitude, what

is meditation. And this can only be known by searching it out. And so, there must be a learning of what are the implications of meditation, of solitude, of death. These implications cannot be taught but must be learned. One can indicate, but the learning through what is indicated is not solitude nor is it meditation. But to learn what is solitude and what is meditation as you would learn mathematics, there must be an inquiry, and this inquiry is essentially the way of learning. A mind that is capable of inquiry is capable of learning. But when inquiry is suppressed by superior knowledge or by superior authority and experience, then learning is imitation, and imitation merely produces a human entity who repeats without the experience of learning.

Teaching is not the mere imparting of information but the cultivation of an inquiring mind which will penetrate into the question of what is religion and not merely accept the established religions, churches, and rituals. The search for God, for truth, or whatever name one may like to give to it is true religion, and not the mere acceptance of belief and dogma. Just as the student washes his teeth every day, bathes every day, learns every minute of the day, so also there must be the action of sitting quietly with others or with himself. But when he sits quietly in solitude, it should not be a means of escaping from his boredom or from his everyday activity, and it should not be something unusual but a part of his life. In this solitude which is not brought about by instruction, or urged by external authority of tradition, or induced by those who want to sit quietly but who are not capable of being alone—in this solitude he is also learning to see the implications of all that he has been gathering as knowledge in relation to a life that is not merely acquisitive, self-measured, and self-centered. This solitude helps the mind to see clearly as in a mirror and to free itself from the vain endeavor of ambition with all its complexities of fears and frustrations, which are the expressions of self-centered activity. This solitude gives to the mind stability, that constancy which is not to be measured in terms of time. It is this clarity of mind that is character. The lack of character is the state of self-contradiction.

To be sensitive is to love. The word *love* is not love. And love is not to be divided as the love of God and the love of man. Love is not to be measured as the love of the one or of the many. Love is the capacity to give abundantly as a flower to anyone who cares to take it to his lips, but we are always measuring it in our relationships and thereby destroying it. Love is not a commodity of the social reformer and the social worker; it is not a political instrument with which to create action. When the politician and the reformer use it, they are using the word and so can never touch the reality of it, for love cannot be employed as a means to an end, whether in the immediate or in the far-off. It is the love of the earth and not of the particular field in it. The love of reality is not encompassed by any religion, and when organized religions use it, it ceases to be. Society and organized religions and authoritarian governments, sedulous in their various activities, unknowingly destroy the love that becomes passion in action.

And as we are concerned with the total development of a human being through right education, the quality of love from the very beginning must be nourished and sustained. Love is not sentimentality nor is it devotion. It is as strong as death; it cannot be bought through knowledge. And a mind that is pursuing knowledge for its own sake is a mind that deals in ruthlessness and works merely for efficiency.

So, the educator must be concerned from the very beginning with this quality of love, which is humility, gentleness, consideration, patience, and courtesy. The modesty of courtesy is inherent in the man of good and right education; this enjoins attention to all things about one—the plants, the animals, the way of behavior, and the manner of talking.

This means, does it not, the cultivation of sensitivity towards all things, to care for all things—whether it be a tree or a human being or a piece of furniture or the latest motor—right from the tender age. This emphasis on the quality of love brings about sensitivity and a mind that is not self-absorbed with its ambitions, greeds, and acquisitiveness. Does this not gather about itself refinement, which not only expresses itself as good taste and respect, but also brings about the purification of the mind, and which otherwise has a tendency to strengthen itself in pride? Refinement in clothes, in talk, in behavior, is not a self-imposed adjustment or an outward demand, but it comes with this quality of love. With the understanding of this quality, sex and all the complications and subtleties of human relationship can be approached with sanity and not with excitement and apprehension.

The educator to whom the total development of a human being is of primary importance must be concerned with the implications of sexual urges from the very beginning without arousing the children's curiosity but meeting with their curiosity. As sexual urges play such an important part in one's life, to impart mere biological knowledge or information at the adolescent age may become experimental lust if the quality of love is not felt. Love cleanses the mind of evil. Without all this, mere separation of boy and girl by barbed wire and edicts only strengthens their curiosity and that passion which is bound to degenerate into mere satisfaction. So it is important that boy and girl are educated together rightly.

This quality of love must express itself in doing things with one's hands—gardening, carpentry, painting, handicraft—and through the eyes and ears—as the seeing of trees, the running waters, of the richness of the earth and of the poverty that men have created amongst themselves, and the hearing of birds, music, and song.

We are concerned not only with the mind and the emotional sensitivities but also with the well-being of the physique, and so must give considerable thought to it. For, if the body is not healthy, vital, obviously it will distort thought and make for insensitivity. This is an obvious fact into which we need not go into detail. It is necessary that the body be in excellent health, eating the right food and having sufficient sleep. If the senses are not alert and sensitive, the body will interfere with the total development of a human being. To have grace and control of the muscles, there must be various forms of exercise, dancing, yoga, and games. A body that is not clean, that does not hold itself in good posture, that is sloppy, is not conducive to the sensitivity of the mind or of the emotions. The body is not the instrument of the mind. But the body, the emotions, and the mind make the total human being, and without all of them living together harmoniously, conflict is inevitable. Conflict makes for insensitivity. Mind can control or dominate the body, suppressing the senses and making the body insensitive. Such an insensitive body becomes a hindrance to the full flight of the mind. The mortification of the body is definitely not conducive to search out the deeper layers of consciousness—which is possible only when the mind, the emotions, and the physique are not in contradiction with one another but live together effortlessly without being driven by any concept, belief, or ideal.

In the cultivation of the mind, emphasis should not be on concentration but on attention. Concentration is a process of forcing the mind to narrow down to a point, whereas attention is without frontiers. Concentration is always a limited energy with a frontier or limitation, but when we are concerned with the understanding of the totality of the mind, mere concentration becomes a hindrance, whereas attention is limitless, without the frontiers of knowledge. Knowledge comes through concentration, and the extension of knowledge is still within the frontiers of concentration. Attention, in the sense that we are using the word, can and does use knowledge which of necessity is the result of concentration. The part is never the whole, and adding the many parts together does not make the whole. And knowledge which is the additive process of concentration does not bring about the understanding of the immeasurable. The total is never within the brackets of a mind that is concentrated.

As we are concerned with the whole development of the human being and his mind, attention becomes of primary importance. This attention does not come through the effort of concentration, but it is a state in which the mind is ever learning without a center round which knowledge gathers as experience. Knowledge is used as a means of self-expansion by a mind that is concentrated upon itself, and so such activity becomes self-contradictory and so antisocial.

And as we are concerned with the total development of an individual and therefore with his relationship with another—which is society—emphasis should be laid on attention and not on mere concentration. Learning is only possible in this state of attention in which there is no outer or inner compulsion. Right thinking can only come about when the mind is not bound to tradition and memory. It is attention that allows silence to come upon the mind, which is the opening of the door to that creation. Attention is of the highest importance.

Knowledge then is essential only as a means of cultivating the mind and not as an end in itself. What we are concerned with is not the mere development of one capacity, as a mathematician or a scientist or a musician, but with the total development of the student in which all these things are included.

How is this attention to be brought about? It cannot be cultivated through any form of persuasion, comparison, reward, or punishment; all these are forms of coercion. The elimination of fear is the beginning of attention. Fear must exist as long as there is an urge to be or to become, which is translated as success with all its frustrations and tortuous contradictions. Attention cannot be taught as you can teach concentration, just as you cannot possibly teach how to be free of fear, but we can begin to discover the causes that produce fear and in the understanding of all these causes, there is the elimination of fear. So, attention comes into being when around the student there is the atmosphere of physical well-being, the feeling of being secure, of being at home—of which we have talked earlier—and the disinterested action that comes with love. Love does not compare, and so the torture of 'becoming' ceases.

The general discontent that all of us experience, whether young or old, soon finds a way to satisfaction, and thus our mind is put to sleep. It is awakened from time to time through suffering, and that suffering again seeks some solution which will be gratifying. So in this wheel of satisfaction and dissatisfaction, the mind is caught, and the awakening through pain is part of this discontent. Discontent is the way of inquiry, and there can be no inquiry if the mind is tethered to tradition, to ideals. It is this inquiry that is the flame of attention.

We mean by discontent that state of mind which understands *what is,* the actual, and inquires to discover further. This movement to go beyond the limitations of *what is* is discontent, and if you smother or find ways and means of overcoming discontent, then you

will accept the limitations of self-centered activity and of the society in which you find yourself. Discontent is the lot of most of us, and to overcome it we seek various ways to dissipate it. But discontent is the flame which burns away the dross of satisfaction. Discontent for the little more, for the bigger house, and so on is within the field of envy, and it is envy that sustains this discontent. But we are not talking of envy, the greed for the 'more'; we are talking of discontent that is not inflamed by any desire or experience for the 'more'. This discontent is an unpolluted state which must and which does exist, if it is not allowed to be cheapened through wrong education or through any ideal. When we understand the nature of this discontent, then we shall see that attention is part of this burning flame which consumes the petty and leaves the mind without the limitations of self-enclosing pursuits and gratifications. So attention comes into being only when there is inquiry not based on self-advancement or gratification.

This attention must be cultivated right from the beginning. You will find that when there is love which expresses itself through humility, courtesy, patience, and gentleness, you are already removing the frontiers which insensitivity builds, and so from a very tender age, you are helping to bring about this state of attention. This attention is not to be learned, but you can help to bring it about in the student when there is around him no sense of compulsion and so no self-contradictory existence. Then his attention can be focused at any moment on any given subject, but it is not the concentration brought about through the compulsive urge of acquisition or achievement.

A generation that is so educated will be free from the psychological inheritance of their parents and of the society in which they are born; and because they are so educated, they will not depend on the inheritance of property. This factor of inheritance destroys independence and limits intelligence, for it breeds a false sense of security, giving a self-assurance which has no basis. This false sense of security is the darkness of the mind in which nothing can flourish. A generation which has been educated totally differently, about which we have been talking, will create a new society. For, it will have the capacity born of intelligence, that intelligence which is not hedged about with fear.

As we are concerned with the total development of the student and not of any one particular aspect, attention which is all-inclusive becomes important. This total development is not conceptual—that is, there is no blueprint of the totality of the human mind. The more the mind uses of itself, the greater is its potentiality. The capacity of the mind is infinite.

Since education is not the work of one, but of several together, of the parent as well as the educator, the art of working together must be learned. This working together comes only when each of us perceives what is true. It is the truth that brings us together, and not opinion or belief or theory. There is a vast difference between the conceptual and the factual. The conceptual may temporarily bring us together for monetary or other reasons, but there will be separation when it is only a matter of conviction. If the truth is seen, there may be disagreement in detail but there will be no urge to separate. It is the foolish that break away on some detail, and the detail can never be made into an issue over which there is a dissension. We may come together to work out a concept, an ideal; but these are not factual and need conviction, persuasion, propaganda, and so on; and most of us are used to working together along these established lines of authority.

Working together for a concept, for an ideal, and the action which comes from seeing the truth and the necessity of that truth in action are two totally different activities. Working under the stimulus of authority is not cooperation, whether it is the authority of an ideal or the authority of a person who represents that ideal. You have a central authority who knows or who has a strong personality with certain ideas, and he dominates and forces others, subtly or in other ways, to cooperate with what he calls the ideal. This surely is not working together. But when each of us understands the truth of certain issues, then this understanding of truth brings us together to carry them out in action. This is cooperation. And he who has learned this cooperation because he sees the truth as the truth, the false as the false, the truth in the false, he will also learn not to cooperate—which is as important as to learn to cooperate.

If each one of us sees the necessity that a fundamental revolution in education is essential and perceives the truth of what we have said, then we will work together without agreement or disagreement, without any form of persuasion. Agreement or disagreement exists only when someone takes a stand from which he is unwilling to move, or when he is convinced of an idea or entrenched in an opinion. He brings about opposition, and when such a situation arises, then one or the other has to be convinced or influenced or induced to think differently. Such a situation will never arise when each one of us sees the truth. Then it will not be a mere verbal conviction or an intellectual, reasoned application but an understanding of the truth. If we do not see the truth, then there is contention, agreement or disagreement, with all their distorting and useless effort. It is essential that we work together, for we are building a house together. If one of us is building and the other is tearing down, then the house will not be built. So, we must, each one of us, be very clear that we really understand the necessity of bringing about a new generation which is capable of dealing with the issues of life as a whole and not as separated parts unrelated to the whole.

To work together in this cooperative way, we must meet often together and be alert not to be submerged in detail. Those of us who are seriously dedicated to this understanding have the responsibility of not only carrying out in action all that we have understood but also to see that others come to this understanding. Teaching is the highest profession, if it can at all be called a profession. The art of teaching requires no considerable intellectual capacities but infinite patience and love. Education means, does it not, the understanding of relationship to all things—to money, to property, to people, to nature—in the vast field of existence.

Beauty is not merely proportion, form, taste, and behavior. Beauty is that state of mind which has abandoned the center of itself in the passion of simplicity. Simplicity can only be when there is that austerity which is not the response of calculated denial and disciplined self-pursuit, but that self-abandonment which love alone can bring about. Simplicity has no end. Without all this, we create a civilization in which beauty of form is sought, without the inner vitality and stability of simple self-abandonment. There is no abandonment if there is the immolation of the self in activity, in ideals, in beliefs. These appear to be the larger field, but in reality the self is still working under the cover of different labels. The innocent mind alone can inquire into the immense unknown. But the calculated simplicity of the loincloth or of the robe of a monk can never come near that passion of self-abandonment. From this passion comes courtesy, gentleness, humility, patience—which are the expressions of love.

We know beauty through that which is made or put together—the beauty of a human form or of a temple. We say that tree, that house, that river which is widely curving is beautiful. And because of comparison, we know that which is ugly—at least we think we do. Is beauty comparative? Is beauty that which has been made evident, manifest? We say that a picture, a poem, a face, is beautiful because we already know or feel from what we have been taught, or with which we are familiar, or about which we have formed an opinion. And does not beauty cease with comparison? Is beauty merely a knowledge of the known, or is it a being in which the created is or is not?

We are always pursuing beauty and avoiding the ugly, and this avoidance of the one and the seeking of enrichment in the other must inevitably breed insensitivity. Now sensitivity to both the so-called beautiful and the so-called ugly, surely, is necessary to the understanding or to the feeling of what is beauty. A feeling is not beautiful or ugly, it is just a feeling. It is only when we approach it through our educated and social conditioning that we say this is a good feeling and that is a bad feeling, and so destroy the feeling or distort it. But the feeling that is not given a label as the good or the bad remains intense. It is this passionate intensity that is essential in the pursuit of the understanding of that which is neither the manifested beauty nor the ugly.

What we are insisting upon is the great importance of sustained feeling, that passion which is not the mere lust of the self in gratification. It is this that creates beauty, and since it is not comparable, it has no opposite.

Since we are concerned with the total development of a human being, we must take into full consideration not only the conscious mind but also the unconscious. Mere education of the conscious without understanding the unconscious brings contradiction into human lives, with its frustrations and miseries. The hidden mind is far more vital and vigorous than the superficial. Most educators are concerned with educating the superficial mind, giving it information called knowledge, to acquire a job and to adjust itself to society. So the hidden mind is never touched. All that the educators have done is that they have imposed a layer of technical knowledge and the capacity to adjust to environment.

But since we are concerned with the total development of a human being, we must also understand the state of the hidden mind. This hidden mind is far more potent than the superficial mind, however much it may be educated and however much it may be capable of adjustment. The hidden mind is not something very mysterious. It is surely the repository of the racial memories as religion, superstition, symbol, the tradition of a particular race, the influence of its literature, whether sacred or profane; the collective influence of a particular group, with its own peculiar traditions, aspirations and frustrations, symbols, mannerisms, and food; and the open and hidden desire with its motives and frustrations, its hopes and fears, its hidden sorrows and pleasures, and those beliefs which are sustained through the urge for security translating themselves in various ways. This hidden mind has not only the extraordinary capacity of all this residual past but also the capacity to foresee, near or far, in the future. All this expresses itself through dreams and through various intimations to the superficial mind when it is not wholly occupied with everyday events. The hidden mind is nothing sacred or nothing to be frightened of, nor does it demand the specialist to expose it to the superficial. Only because of the enormous potency of the hidden mind, the superficial cannot deal with it as it wishes. The superficial is impotent to a great extent in its relation to its own hidden. However much it may try to dominate it, shape it, control it, because of its immediate

social demands and pursuits, it can only scratch the surface of the hidden, and so there is a cleavage and contradiction between the hidden and the open. We try to bridge this chasm through discipline, through various practices, sanctions, and so on; but it cannot so be bridged. Because the conscious mind is occupied merely with the immediate—in the sense of the limited present—whereas the hidden has the weight of centuries which cannot be brushed aside by any immediate necessity, the hidden has the quality of deep time. The superficial mind with its recent culture cannot deal with it according to its passing urgencies. So to eradicate contradiction, the superficial mind must understand this fact and be quiescent, which does not mean giving scope to the innumerable urges of the hidden. When there is no resistance between the open and the hidden, then because the hidden has the patience of time, the hidden will not violate the immediate.

It is the hidden, unexplored, and un-understood mind with its superficial which has been educated, that comes into contact with the present—the present challenges and demands. The superficial may respond to the challenge adequately, but because there is a contradiction between the superficial and the hidden, any experience of the superficial only increases conflict between itself and the hidden. This brings about further experience, widening the chasm between the present and the past. The superficial mind experiencing without understanding the inner, the hidden, only produces deeper and wider conflict. Experiences do not liberate or enrich, as we generally think they do. So long as experiences strengthen the experiencer, there must be conflict. A conditioned mind having experiences only strengthens the conditioning, and so increases conflict and misery. Only to a mind that is understanding the total ways of itself can experiencing be a liberating factor.

When there is an understanding of the powers and capacities of the many layers of the hidden, then the details can be looked into wisely and intelligently. What is important is not the mere education of the superficial mind to acquire knowledge—which is necessary—but the understanding of the hidden. This understanding frees the total mind from conflict, and only then is there intelligence.

As we are concerned with the total development of a human being, we must give not only full capacity to the superficial mind that lives in everyday activity but also understand the hidden, for in the understanding of the hidden, there will be a total living in which contradiction, as sorrow and happiness, ceases. It is essential to be aware of the workings of the hidden mind and to be acquainted with it, but it is equally important not to be occupied with it nor to give it undue significance. It is only then that the mind, the superficial and the hidden, can go beyond its own limitations and discover that bliss which is not of time.

Poona, India, 1958

---------------------------------- ✳ ----------------------------------

First Talk in Poona

I think it would be well if we could establish a true relationship between the speaker and the audience; otherwise, there may be a great deal of misunderstanding and misjudgment. Obviously the speaker has something to say, and you have come to listen. What he has to say may have very little value, or it may have significance if one is capable of listening with quiet attention.

It is most important to know how to listen. Most of us do not listen; we come either with a tendency to resist or to refute what is being said, or we compare it with what we have previously heard, or learned from books. In this process, obviously, there is no listening because when you are thinking of what somebody else has said on a subject, your mind is merely going back to various memories—merely trying to compare what is being said with what you have already heard or read. So please, if I may suggest, do follow what is being said.

There are so many terrible things taking place in the world, so much misery and confusion, such decadence, corruption, and evil; and I feel that if one is at all earnest, intent on understanding these human problems, one must approach the matter with a certain serious purpose. What I am going to say may be entirely different from what you know or believe—and I think it will be. I am saying this, not from any sense of conceit or overconfidence, but because most of us, when anything unfamiliar is said, are apt to reject it offhand or to ridicule it. This is especially so with the experts, those who are specialists in some department—the scientists, technicians, lecturers, professors, and so on. They are particularly apt to discard a new approach to our many problems because they divide life into departments and think only in terms of their specialized field. Life's problems are not going to be solved by the specialists. If a man is an economist, he tends to think that all the problems of life will be solved by some economic system which will bring about equality of opportunity for achievement, for gain, and to him every other form of thought, of investigation, of search, seems of secondary importance or not worthwhile.

So, considering all these things, it would be nice, I think, if we could, at least for this hour, listen with a sense of humility, with an attitude of trying to find out what the speaker intends to convey. Afterwards you can question it, discuss it, refute it, or brush it aside. But first, surely, if there is to be any form of communication, there must be a certain understanding, a common ground established between speaker and listener. Listening is very difficult; it is an art. I am sure you have never really listened to anybody because your mind is always occupied, thinking of other things, is it not so? You never actually listen to your wife, to your children, to your neighbor, because your mind is caught up in its own fears and anxieties, in the innumerable preoccupations that arise in the mind and prevent full communication. If you observe yourself you will see how extraordinarily difficult it is to listen to anything, especially to a speaker who is going to say things which you will not like, or which you do not immediately understand, or which seem contradictory. Such things are apt to produce a great deal of confusion, and so you tend to brush them all aside.

So it is necessary to listen with a sense of humility. Humility is entirely different from being humble. Humbleness can be achieved, gathered, cultivated by one who is already full of vanity and arrogance, but humility is not a quality to be acquired; it is a state of being. You are, or you are not, in a state of humility, and we shall discuss all this presently as we go into our many problems in the talks which are to follow. But I am suggesting now that if one wants to learn, to understand what another says, there must be that humility which listens, which does not either accept or reject but inquires. To inquire there must be that state of humility because if you already know, you cease to inquire. If you take a position of agreeing or denying, you put an end to inquiry. Inquiry is only possible when there is a certain freedom of the mind, freedom to go into what is being said, to inquire, to find out. So it is essential that we should listen with a sense of freedom and humility, for only then shall we be able to communicate with each other.

I am not here to instruct you what to do or what not to do, but together we are going to inquire into our many problems. Therefore the thinking should not be one-sided, with you merely receiving. We shall be endeavoring, you and I, to inquire into the whole

problem of human existence, into the whole process of living, of death, of meditation, of conflict, of human relationships. All that we are going into. But first it is essential that the mind that wishes to inquire be somewhat pliable and free, not rigid, not prejudiced, not prone to take a stand from which it is unwilling to move.

Surely it behooves us to make this inquiry, seeing that there is so much conflict and misery, such fearful economic stresses and strains, so much starvation and degradation. Obviously a change is necessary, a radical change. A fundamental revolution is necessary because things cannot go on as they are. Of course if we are earning sufficient money, if we are clever enough to get through life without too much conflict and are concerned only with ourselves, then we do not mind if things go on as they are. But if we are at all inquiring, serious, we must surely try to find out, must we not, how to bring about a change. Because religions obviously mean very little; they only offer an escape. You may go to a guru or a priest, repeat mantras or prayers, follow some doctrine or ritual, but they are all avenues of escape. They will not solve your problems— and they have not done so. The problems still exist, and it is no good running away from them. Whether you go to the temple or retire to the Himalayas to become a sannyasi, it is still a running away.

Throughout the world it is the same problem. Religions have failed and education also. Passing a lot of examinations and putting the alphabet after your name has not solved your problems. No system, educational, economic, political, religious, or philosophical, has solved our problems—which is obvious because we are still in conflict. There is appalling poverty, confusion, strife between man and man, group and group, race and race. Neither the communist nor any other social or economic revolution has solved this problem, or ever will. Because man is a total entity, he has to be taken as a totality—not partially, at different layers of his existence. The specialist is only concerned with a particular layer—the politician merely with governing, the economist merely with money values, the religionist with his own creed, and so on. Apparently nobody considers the human problem as a whole and tackles it, not partially, but wholly. The religious person says, "Give up the world if you really want to solve the problem," but the world is inside oneself. The tears, the innumerable struggles and fears, they are all inside. Or the social reformer says, "Forget yourself and do good," and you may work to forget yourself; but the problem is still there. All the various specialists offer their own remedies, but no one apparently is concerned with the total transformation of man himself. All they offer are various forms of thinking. If you leave one religion and go to another, you only change your mode of thinking. No one seems to be concerned with the quality of thought, with the quality of the mind that thinks.

The problem is enormous, as you and I know fairly well—we have only to observe as we pass down the street, as we get on the bus, as we talk to a friend or to a politician or to a religious person. We can watch this whole process of degradation going on, every form of decline and corruption, a mounting confusion; and surely we can hope to solve it only when the mind is capable of thinking of the problem in a totally different way. There must be a revolution in the mind itself, not merely a change at some partial level of human existence; and with that revolution in our thinking, with that radical transformation of the mind, we can approach the problem wholly. The problem is constantly changing, is it not? The problem is not static, but we approach it with a mind that is already conditioned, that has already taken a stand and ac-

cepted certain sanctions, edicts, values. So while the problem is a living thing, changing, vital, we approach it with a dead mind, and so the conflict increases and the confusion worsens.

So there must be a revolution in thinking, a revolution in the mind itself and not in what the mind thinks about. There is surely a vast difference between the two. We are mostly concerned with what the mind thinks about. The communist is concerned with conditioning the mind to think what it is told, and the so-called religious person is concerned with the same thing. Most of us are concerned with thinking only the thoughts which we already know and have accepted, and these thoughts further condition the mind, obviously. Every thought that you have—as an economist, as a specialist, as a believer in God or a nonbeliever, as a man who pursues virtue or does not—shapes the mind. Your thinking depends upon your conditioning, how you have been brought up, what the pressures of your environment are—religion, society, family, tradition. So if we are at all serious, we shall not be concerned with substituting one thought for another or with sublimating thought to some other level. We must be concerned with the radical transformation of the capacity to think, not merely with the choice of what to think. That is where the revolution should take place, and not at any particular layer of human existence. I hope I am making this point clear. If not, we shall discuss it as we go along. A revolution in the way of thinking is essential—not the choice of what to think or the pursuit of right thought, but a revolution in the capacity itself, in the mind itself. Unless there is a radical change in the mind, you can have no answer to your problems. Do what you will, read any books, follow any authority, any guru, you will never solve your problems unless there is a radical transformation of the mind itself.

What is happening now? You are either a Hindu, a Muslim, a Buddhist, a Catholic, an American, a Russian, or some kind of specialist, and so on; and you approach life with your particular pattern of thinking. The communist wants to solve the problems of life in his way; the Catholic, the Hindu, the Buddhist, in his; so there is ever contention, conflict, bitterness, anxiety, war, which is obviously not the way to solve our human problems. So long as you remain whatever you are, you are not going to solve any fundamental problem. And if you, as a student, specialize to be a scientist hoping science is going to solve everything, it is not going to, I assure you. You may be able to go up into the sky, produce various forms of sputniks, but our problems of human existence are still there—how you treat your wife, how I treat you and you treat me, our ambitions, our greeds, our frustrations, whether there is God, what happens after death, what is meditation, what is virtue, what is the true religious life. Surely all these are our problems, and now we approach them as specialists, as persons conditioned with various hopes, desires, beliefs; and so we never solve them.

Therefore there must be a revolution in the mind. This revolution is not a matter of mere agreement, it is not a matter of conviction, it is not a matter of belief—it must take place. It cannot take place if you believe that there must be a revolution in the mind. That is merely a concept, an ideal, which is worthless. You know there is a vast difference between the word and the verb. The word has very little meaning except as a means of communication, and all thoughts, plans, ideals, concepts, theories, speculations, and the pursuit of them are at the verbal level. If you merely live at the verbal level, it does not bring about a fundamentally new way of thinking. What does bring it about is the verb *being*, not in relation to an idea, but action

itself. Perhaps this is a little bit difficult, but please just listen to it even if only for intellectual amusement. You see, most of us are caught in words, with slogans, ideas, phrases, concepts. These are entirely different from "the verb"—which is not action related to an idea but a state of being, acting. Because the moment you really understand something—which is not just agreeing or being convinced or submitting to pressure, for all these are related to "the word" and do not bring understanding—you act. When there is an understanding which is "the verb," then there is an "acting" which is a state of being. If you think about it a little, you will see the difference between the two, the verb and the word, the doing and the thought of doing, the word *love* and loving. Now most of us are caught in the thought that we should love, as a noble, ideological, perfect thing; that is merely the word. The verb is *loving*, unrelated to any action; it is a state of being, of loving. This is only, by the way, to demonstrate how our minds operate.

Our minds function in words, in concepts, in ideals, in 'what should be', and it is there that the revolution must take place. The mind must be in a state of being, in a state of verb, if one can so put it—not in the state of the word but in the state of the verb. You can see the difference, can you not? To bring into being that state of the verb is the revolution. If you think about it you will see the extraordinary meaning of it, what significance it has—the being and the thought of being.

So our concern then, if we are at all serious, is to bring about a revolution in the mind. I have more or less described, given a significance to that word *revolution* before, and also what we mean by a serious person. Let us examine for a minute or two that word *serious*. Who is serious? And what does that word mean? Who is serious? Are you serious? Is the man who gives up the world and takes the yellow robe serious? Is the man who becomes a social reformer serious? The man who pursues God—is he serious? The man who mesmerizes himself by listening to songs and all the rest of it—is he serious? And the man who completely identifies himself with an idea or who says, "I have taken a vow and I am going to stick to it for the rest of my life"—is he serious? Or the man who immolates himself, who identifies himself with a country—is he serious?

So looking at all the various forms of so-called seriousness, including the insane man who thinks he is sane, are all these people serious? Are all these people really devoted to what they are doing? Surely, that is the test, is it not? Devotion is earnestness, and earnestness is devoid of enthusiasm. The man who is enthusiastic is not earnest; he is just enthused for the time being—as a balloon that is blown up pops and makes a lot of noise. So any one of these who is not concerned with the search for the true in what he is pursuing—such a person is not serious. This is not a mere definition, but if you will examine it, you will see the significance of what is being said.

Surely devotion is not to something, to a god, to a guru, to a picture or some figure. Such devotion is obviously an escape, a running away, trying to forget yourself in something. Whether it is to the country, the state, a picture, or to some idea, such devotion is merely a flight, an escape from the facts of existence. Devotion is something entirely different. Devotion is the capacity to inquire persistently into the ways of the mind because without understanding the mind, whatever you do—whatever you think, or pursue, whatever your ideals, your authorities—has no meaning at all. That is, without understanding yourself, what you do and what you think, or trying to alter what you do and what you think, has little meaning. You understand this, do you not? Without knowing myself, how do I know

what I think is true, how can I know of truth, how can I know of God, whether there is God or there is not? Without knowing myself, what right have I to seek to reform another, or tell another what to do? And would I, even if I knew myself, tell another what to do?

So, without knowing oneself there can be no radical change, therefore no radical action, and therefore no radical transformation in the mind. By knowing oneself I do not mean some superself, the paramatma, the soul—which are merely things you have been told about. To me, without knowing oneself totally, these are all false, they have no reality. After all, if you do not know what you think and why you think, from what source your thought springs and from what background your action comes, whether you believe in God or not has no meaning. Because you have been brought up as Hindus, you believe in God; because your society, your neighbor, your tradition says, "believe"—you believe. But go to Russia and they will say what nonsense it all is; they will brush you off as stupid and regard your action as insane. Whereas he, the Russian, is conditioned also—conditioned to believe that there is no God, to believe that the state is the only right thing to follow. He is conditioned, as you are conditioned. So when you say you believe in God, it has no meaning. Please see how important it is to understand this. Because if you are really seeking God, you must put away all these things, you must put away all your gurus, your knowledge, your tradition, and not follow or accept any authority. That means an inward revolution. And it is only such a man who thinks clearly, who knows his own conditioning, his entire being—not only the conscious, but the unconscious, the totality of his thought—it is only such a man who can inquire if there is or is not truth, God, or whatever name you like to give it. But that means hard work, and nobody wants to work hard, whether at home or in the office or in search of truth; and so we are inefficient, corrupt, and we want to understand truth without work.

Understanding yourself means not the superself, the atma, the superconsciousness, and all that, but understanding the ways of your own reactions, understanding yourself as you are, what you think, why you think, why you do certain things and say certain words. To understand is to be conscious, to be aware of what you are. You will find that it is extraordinarily difficult because most of us are unwilling to understand ourselves. We would rather believe, be told, pushed, persuaded, driven politically, economically, or environmentally. But to watch yourself in all your relationships, whether with your servant, your wife, your husband, or others, to watch yourself when you get into a bus, to be aware when you look at nature, at the trees, the clouds, to watch all your own reactions and to be aware—that, sirs, is real meditation. Then you can go very far. Then you will not create for yourself any illusions.

So there must be the understanding of oneself, and in that there is the revolution. I cannot understand myself if I do not examine myself. When you are angry—at the moment of anger you are not aware of yourself—watch yourself, look at it, and find out why you are angry. Go into it, go into the whole process of anger. I am only taking that as an example. It requires a great deal of thought, penetration, but that is real devotion—not the phony devotion to a guru from whom you are going to get some return; that is just a bargain. Real devotion is to inquire into why you are angry, into the source of your anger, and to understand.

To understand something, surely, there must be neither acceptance nor condemnation. There are many of you here who have heard me for a number of years, unfortunately, because therefore you say, "I know what

he is going to say about this," and so you close your ears. But to find out the whole significance of why one accepts or condemns requires a constant renewal of listening, of understanding. It is not a matter of listening to me only, but of listening to yourself to find out why you condemn, why you have shut yourself off, or why you have accepted. I have said this for a number of years—that if you want to understand something, there must be neither condemnation nor acceptance, but rather you must look at it. There are many who have heard me for ten or twenty years and who say, "I agree with you," but they have not done anything about it. They are at the state of "the word" and not at the state of "the verb." The verb is the doing, not the thought of doing.

So to understand why I accept or reject, why I condemn or compare, requires a great deal of penetration into oneself. After all, why do you accept authority? Why do you accept authority at any level—political, economic, social, religious—the authority of the book or the authority of your own experience? Why do you accept, and why do you reject? Why do you reject communism, socialism, capitalism, or whatever it may be? Don't you see that unless you really know what it is—that drive, that push, the influence which is making you accept or reject, causing you to compare, to justify, identify or deny—you are merely the tool of authority. The man who follows, the man who leads, the man who has ideals, does not know love. The man who follows, how can he know love? He is just following, and the following is enslavement to "the word." And the man who is a leader, who says, "I know and you don't know. I am right and you are wrong"—how can he love? He may identify himself with his country, with an idea, with a reform, and he may lead a most exemplary life of denial and simplicity, but he is full of authority, full of his own knowledge, experience, ideas, and how can such a man know love? Nor can the idealist because he is always thinking of 'what should be'. So, without knowing yourself, what you do and what you think have no reality; your gods have no reality, nor your village reforms which you are doing for various reasons, many of which may be childish, immature, merely respectable.

So in order to bring about a fundamental change in the ways of one's thinking, one must begin with self-knowledge, knowledge of oneself, of the ways of one's own thinking, not with so-called knowledge about God. Knowledge about God is all unreal, false, unless you know yourself. So the religious person is the man who begins with the understanding of himself, not with the leading of a particular life in accordance with some tradition or some book. Surely it is essential to know yourself, to know how to think clearly, without bias, without prejudice, without fear, and therefore to act without fear—which means character. Character is not for the person who merely obeys the law—either the law of society or his own law—but for the person who thinks clearly and whose thought is produced through self-knowledge. Self-knowledge is the knowledge of why you are angry, why you are ambitious, ruthless, sexual, and all the other things which are to be discovered. You have to know about yourself, and the knowing is quite different from merely bringing about a change in the known. I can know why I am angry; we can all know. It is fairly easy, if you know the ABC's of psychology, to know why you are greedy, ambitious, rude, cruel, brutal. But knowing about it and actually understanding it are entirely different. The very process of understanding brings about a change. Because when you understand yourself, there is clarity of thinking, and in that clarity there is character. Character is not produced by following an ideal and sticking to that ideal;

that is merely obstinacy. Character implies clarity, and there is no clarity so long as you do not know yourself, and you cannot know yourself if you are not fully aware of yourself. And in understanding oneself, as we have said, there must be no acceptance or justification of what you are, no excuses, no saying, "I am like this because of my environment," or "I know I am conditioned because I live in a little province and so my mind is provincial," and so on.

To see all this, to be aware of it, to know it, to go into it and see the significance of it requires devotion, endeavor, hard work. Then only can the mind bring about within itself a revolution which will answer all the problems of our life. When you know the source of your problems and the causes of your problems, and when you know that their solution is within your own understanding, then you see that you need not follow anybody; then you have no guru, no authority, no book, no tradition, because you are a light unto yourself. These are not words. I am saying all this because it is so. But you cannot accept it because I say so, for then you become merely a follower, which is an evil thing to be, whether politically or religiously. Whereas, if you begin to understand yourself, to go into yourself profoundly—which requires a great deal of attention, a great deal of devotion—then only will you be able to solve the many problems which confront each one of us.

September 7, 1958

Second Talk in Poona

Last Sunday we gave a general outline of what we are going to consider during these different assemblies, and I propose that I take up a certain point, a certain idea, and work it out fully, go into it in detail. But once again

I would like to point out how important it is that we should establish a communication between us. It is really a fact that I am not talking as to a large group but to each individual, because to me there is no mass, group, class, race, but only the individual—the individual who is capable of thinking independently and therefore of breaking down his conditioning, thus bringing about a creative state of mind. So I am talking to you as though individually and personally. And since you have taken the trouble to come to hear what I have to say, please listen carefully. Do not translate it in terms of your particular vernacular, either local or traditional. When I talk about the understanding of the self, do not translate it into some Sanskrit word, do not make it into something fantastic and say it is self-realization. I just mean the plain "understand yourself," which is infinitely more difficult than understanding the various theories which you have. If you do not want to listen, that is all right, but if you want to hear, please hear properly, and you cannot hear properly if you begin to translate what is being said into your own terminology, into your own ways of thinking. Then you are really not understanding what the speaker has to say.

You have to find out what the speaker has to say before you accept, reject, or criticize. First you have to find out what he means, what he intends. He may exaggerate, he may not give the right emphasis, but you have to take all that in by listening. Then you and I can establish a right relationship. I have something to say which I think will upset the apple cart, the tradition, all those things that you know. But please do not begin, before you have found out what is actually being said, to build a defensive barrier. Keep your reactions to what I have to say until later when you will have the right to criticize, to discard, to accept, or to go into it, as you will. But until then I suggest to you—the individual who is in this room sitting with

me—that you do not quickly react. Listen in a friendly manner, but with a clear mind, not accepting or rejecting or taking what I say and opposing it by quoting some authority—because I do not believe in authorities. Truth is not come at by the process of authority. It must be discovered from moment to moment. It is not a thing that is permanent, enduring, continuous. It must be found each minute, each second. That requires a great deal of attention, a great alertness of mind, and you cannot understand it or allow it to come to you if you merely quote authorities, merely speculate as to whether there is or is not God. You must as an individual experience it, or rather, allow that thing to come to you. You cannot possibly go to it. Please let us be clear on this point—that you cannot by any process, through any discipline, through any form of meditation, go to truth, God, or whatever name you like to give it. It is much too vast, it cannot possibly be conceived of; no description will cover it, no book can hold it nor any word contain it. So you cannot by any devious method, by any sacrifice, any discipline, or through any guru go to it. You must await, it will come to you, you cannot go to it. That is the first fundamental thing one has to understand, that not through any trick of the mind, not through any control, through any virtue, any compulsion, any form of suppression, can the mind possibly go to truth. All that the mind can do is to be quiet—but not with the intention of receiving it. And that is one of the most difficult things of all because we think truth can be experienced right away through doing certain things. Truth is not to be bought any more than love can be bought. And if you and I understand that very clearly from the very beginning, what I have to say will have a very different, a very definite meaning. Otherwise you will be in a state of self-contradiction. You think there is truth, God, a state which is permanent, and you want it, so you practice, discipline, do various forms of exercise, but it cannot be bought. Any amount of devotion, sacrifice, knowledge, virtue cannot call it into being. The mind must be free—it must have no borders, no frontier, no limitation, no conditioning. The whole sense of acquisitiveness must come to an end, but not in order to receive.

If one really understood that, one would see what an extraordinary thing this creativity of the mind is. Then you would really understand how to free the mind so that it is in a state of alert watchfulness, never asking, never seeking, never demanding.

As I have said, I am talking to the individual because only the individual can change, not the mass; only you can transform yourself, and so the individual matters infinitely. I know it is the fashion to talk about groups, the mass, the race as though the individual had no importance at all, but in any creative action it is the individual who matters. Any true action, any important decision, the search for freedom, the inquiry after truth, can only come from the individual who understands. That is why I am talking only to the individual. You will probably say, "What can I, the individual, do?" Confronted with this enormous complication—the national and religious divisions, the problems of misery, starvation, war, unemployment, the rapid degradation and disintegration—what can one individual do about it all? Nothing. The individual cannot tackle the mountain outside, but the individual can set a new current of thought going which will create a different series of actions. He cannot do anything about worldwide conditions because historically events must take their own brutal, cruel, indifferent course. But if there were half-a-dozen people who could think completely about the whole problem, they would set going a different attitude and action altogether, and that is why the individual is so important. But if he wants to reform this

enormous confusion, this mountain of disintegration, he can do very little; indeed, as is being shown, he can have no effect on it at all, but if any one of us is truly individual in the sense that he is trying to understand the whole process of his mind, then he will be a creative entity, a free person, unconditioned, capable of pursuing truth for itself and not for a result.

So, as I have said, that reality which the mind cannot possibly conceive, which it cannot possibly speculate upon or reduce to words, that truth must come to you, the individual; you cannot go to it. After all, it is fairly obvious, is it not, that the individual mind, which is also the collective mind, is narrow, petty, brutal, ugly, selfish, arrogant. How can such a mind invite the unknown? For whatever it thinks must be petty, small—even as its gods are. Your god is the invention of the mind. You may put a garment round it, but its garments are yours; it is your god, but it is not truth, it is not reality. Do what you will, reality cannot be invited; it must come to you. So what is one to do? How is one to experience that something which is not merely created by the mind? That is only possible when the mind begins to understand its own process, its own ways. I am using the word *process* not in the sense of a means to an end. Generally we mean by that word process that if you do certain things there will be a result—if you put oil in the machine, it will run properly; if you follow certain disciplines, make sacrifices, you will get something in return. I am not using the word in that sense at all. I am using the word process as meaning the operation of the mind as it works, not as it searches for a result.

So the mind must come to the state when it is free from all effort, and I want to discuss this evening the whole problem of effort and conflict, and whether there is a state which the mind can reach without conflict in order to arrive at the truth. For it is only when the mind ceases to be in self-contradiction, and therefore ceases to be in conflict, that it is capable of looking and of understanding. It is fairly clear that a mind which is in conflict can never understand anything, and so we want to find out why the mind is in a state of self-contradiction. Surely, if we can understand the conflict within the mind itself, we shall go very far because it will reveal why there is this contradiction within oneself. If we can go slowly, step by step, into that question and if you really follow it, not oppose it, then perhaps you will come to a state of mind in which there is no conflict at all. But you cannot accept my words, for it means that you also must work, not merely listen, that you must become aware of the operation of your own mind. I am only explaining, but it is for you to watch your own mind in operation.

So first of all, why is there conflict in our lives? We generally take it for granted that it must be so, that it is inevitable, that man is born in conflict, and we try to find ways and means to overcome that conflict. In relationships, in politics, or in any other sphere, there is a conflict within, which brings about self-contradiction; outwardly also there is the contradiction between what we feel we should be and what we are. I want to find out why this contradiction exists. I do not accept that it is natural, inevitable, that there is no solution for it, and so we must escape from it. That is immature thinking. I want to understand it, and so I will not escape from it, dodge it, or go to a guru or a cinema. To me, turning to a book, going to a guru, or going into deep meditation when you are in conflict are all the same as taking to drink. But I want to understand if one can remove this inward contradiction. If that is clear we can proceed from there, and please do not say at the end, "Why did you not talk about birth control," or, "I came here to find out

what religion is, if there is a God." A contradictory mind cannot find anything whatsoever of the truth. Just think of it, sirs, how can you, being in contradiction, know anything which is not contradictory? How can you possibly know that state which has no opposites, no divisions, which is the immeasurable? This question you will answer for yourself, and find the truth of it, only when you find out if you can eliminate contradiction within yourself, and that is essential. What you are seeking at present is not the elimination of contradiction, but you are seeking peace for yourself, some state in which the mind will not be disturbed at all. It is like sitting on a volcano and saying, "Let me have peace." There is no meaning to it. So I say: Let us examine what is in the volcano, let it come out, the ugly, the bestial, the loveliness, everything—let it come up and let me look at it, which means that the mind must have no fear. So let us go into it.

Now why is there this state of contradiction in us? Let us begin at the lowest level. I want money, and also I do not want money because I think that it is good to be poor. I am not talking of the man who wholeheartedly says, "I want to be rich"—and goes after it; to him there is no contradiction. He is completely full of energy because he is aggressive, brutal, ruthless, corrupt, violent, he wants money, he wants position; so there is no conflict within. In Hitler, Krushchev, and all the big ones of the world, there is no consciousness of contradiction because they want this thing and go after it, by right means or crooked. We would like to be in that position also, but unfortunately we are not. So we are in contradiction, and so we want a state of mind which will be permanently peaceful, which will have no contradiction. Or take the man who is somewhat insane. To him there is no conflict because he simply says, "I am God," or "I am Napoleon," or he identifies himself with some other belief, and so there is no sense of contradiction. He is what he imagines, and being that, he is full of energy. Have you not noticed such people? They will travel up and down the land, doing this and doing that because they are completely taken up with an idea, they are completely absorbed. And we also would like to be in that state. So, we pursue various ideas until we find something which will suit us, and there we stop. So we must ask again: Why is there in us this contradiction? Contradiction is conflict, is it not? If I am greedy and I do not want to be greedy, there is immediately a state of contradiction in me which brings a conflict; but if I am completely greedy, there is no conflict. Or if I am completely nongreedy, there is no conflict. But why is there this contradiction which, if we are intelligent, if our mind is alert, becomes ever stronger and stronger and is not easily to be got rid of? The stronger, the more active, the more passionate one is, the more energetic one becomes, and the contradiction becomes ever greater until having established a deep, lasting contradiction, we try to escape from it by saying that life is a process of disintegration, disillusionment, and we philosophize indefinitely. Whereas I think this contradiction can be totally removed, not partly but totally. When you love something, when you are interested in something, there is no effort in the sense of working at it. For most of us work is effort; going to the office, doing various things you do not want to do, disciplining yourself means work, which means effort. But if you can go beyond the words we are using to understand this contradiction, you will find a state of being without effort.

Let us look at violence and nonviolence. We are violent, and we say we must not be violent. The nonviolence is the ideal; it is the projection of the mind which feels itself to be violent. So you make nonviolence into an ideal and then proceed to try to transform violence into that ideal. But the nonviolence has no reality! No ideal has any reality, obviously. You do not easily agree with me at first because it is very difficult to eject ideas, ideals from the mind, which means that your mind is so conditioned by ideals that a new idea cannot be received by it. You are as mesmerized by the ideal as the lunatic by his idea. I am not insulting you, but I am just saying how difficult it is for a mind which thinks in habits to consider a new idea. We can see very clearly how ideals are created. I am something—violent, greedy, or what you will—and I want to transform that into the so-called ideal, the opposite. So I create the opposite ideal to what I actually am, and I begin to have an infinite variety of conflicts. I am this, and I must be that—that is the source of conflict. The moment the mind says, "I am not, but I must be," you have begun the whole process of conflict.

Most of you will think that if you do not make an effort, you will go to seed, vegetate, and that if there were no pressure, conflict, compulsion, you would become like a cow. Therefore you bring up your children—as does society, the whole world—geared to the effort to become something, which involves this perpetual movement of conflict. So I can see, can I not, that there must be conflict so long as there is an ideal, and that so long as the mind is concerned with the future, with 'what should be', it is not concerned with *what is*. It is fairly obvious that one cannot have a divided mind—part of the mind thinking of nonviolence and the other part occupied with violence. Therefore you see that so long as there is any kind of ideal in the mind, there must be a state of contradiction. This does not mean that you can merely accept *what is*, and just stagnate. For, here begins the real revolution, if you can put away all your ideals, and how difficult that is! You have been brought up with ideals. All the books, all the saints, the professors, the erudite people, everyone has said that you must have ideals, and that thought has become a habit. It is purely a habit. You are holding on to so many lovely ideals, and when someone comes along and tells you how absurd these ideals are, how they have no reality at all, then, for the mind to really see that ideals have no factual reality, that is to know the truth. Truth is not something away over the hills and mountains. It is the perception of the true in the simple things, and if you see the truth of what we have been saying now, you will break the habit.

But for centuries we have been brought up on ideals, the ideal that you must become something, either the executive, the chief business man, or the prime minister; and if you cannot be any of these, then you turn towards becoming a saint. You are always wanting to become something, either in this world or in the so-called spiritual world. So you have ideals for here and ideals for there. And therefore you have set up a vast field of conflict, which is habit. It has become such a strong, impregnable habit, and you have not thought it out. It is a very difficult habit to break because you are fearful of what is going to happen. Your relationship with people will change; you will no longer easily accept everything that everybody has said. You will begin to question. You might lose your job. So fear steps in and dictates. Fear says, "Do not give up these things because what is going to happen then?" Your wife believes in ideals, and if you give them up there are going to be perpetual quarrels in the house. Who are you to go against the whole authority which has been set up? What right have you to do so? So society smothers you. And unconsciously you are frightened, and you say, "Please, I will only accept these ideals verbally, as I know they have no meaning." But you have not solved the problem of conflict.

Conflict arises, does it not, because man has never tackled the problem of *what is,* ir-respective of 'what should be'. To understand *what is* requires a great deal of attention, intense search, intense inquiry, but to follow an ideal is very easy—and it does not mean a thing. But if you say, "I am violent, and I am going to disregard all the idealistic nonsense about nonviolence and understand the violence," your position is clear. Then the question arises, since you are free of the ideal: Will you no longer seek to change *what is?* Previously the ideal acted as a lever with which you sought to change *what is.* You thought the idea of nonviolence acted as an influence by which you could get rid of violence. That is, having created contradiction through the ideal we hope, through conflict, to get rid of violence. But we have never succeeded in getting rid of violence. It goes on with brutality, outwardly or suppressed, and produces its own results. So can I be left only with violence, not holding on to its opposite also? If so, I have removed one of the causes of conflict, perhaps the major cause.

But to be free of ideals is most difficult, for you may remove them outwardly but still have inward ideals—the so-called inward experience which tells you what to do. You may reject outward authority, and fairly intelligent people have done that, but inwardly they still want to be something, not only the boss of the town or the boss of the school, but they also want to be spiritual, to achieve a state of mind which is at perfect peace. But the desire to be at peace indicates that you are not at peace, so you have to tackle what is actual. So you see the complex nature of contradiction! Though you may consciously say how absurd these ideals are, they are embedded in the unconscious. Your whole race is steeped in ideals; it is not a matter of just removing a few silly ones, but you have to understand the whole process of the mind.

One of the difficulties for most of us is that we do not seem to be able to see the whole. We only see the part. Do not at once say, "How am I to see the whole?" That is not the problem. The problem is that our minds are so small that we do not seem able to take in the whole at one glance. We cannot see the whole mountain, the whole hill, because our minds being small, being petty, are occupied with details, and a collection of details does not make the whole. Please ask yourself why your mind does not receive the truth totally free of the falseness of the whole process of idealization. Must we go through the removal of each ideal, one by one? This would be an enormous task, would it not? Day after day, struggling, tearing them out; it would take years, surely, to go step by step taking one ideal after another and discarding it. So can I not see the whole simple truth that ideals are totally unnecessary? Can I not see the immense significance of it in a flash, and let that truth which I have seen operate?

The truth that a cobra bites and you might die from it, you all know. That is a fact. So what do you do? When you go out into the woods and walk at night, you are naturally very careful all the time. You do not have to say, "I must think about cobras." The fear of being bitten is operating in you. Or in your bathroom you may have a bottle marked poison. The liquid is poisonous and that is the fact. And so, without thinking, your mind is always alert even in the dark, and you do not take the bottle and drink. So you know the truth that the poison in the cobra and the poison in the bottle are dangerous, and your mind is alert to it, not just for one moment, but all the time. Similarly if you can see the truth that ideals have no reality, see it right through, completely, then the perception of the total truth that ideals have no value will begin to operate of itself. You do not have to operate. It will operate.

If you see the truth of that, then you do not have to make an effort to break the ideals one by one. The truth will do it. So the point I want to go into is: Can you not see the totality of the truth of something immediately, as you see the truth that a cobra is poisonous? If you see the truth that conflict must cease, and that conflict is brought about through this division of what I should be and what I am, then you do not have to do a thing. Your conscious mind cannot deal with the imponderable unconscious, but the truth that you have seen will do so. Now has this happened to you? That is, do you see the truth of all this?—not all the implications of it because that is merely a matter of exploration and time. If you feel the truth of it, then for the moment let us leave it aside and tackle the problem of *what is,* because our whole endeavor is to eliminate self-contradiction.

With most people, the more tension there is in contradiction, the more active they are. There is tension in contradiction, is there not? I am violent and I must not be violent; that opposition creates a tension, does it not, and from that tension you act—write a book, or try to do something about it. That is our entire activity at present. You say in India that you are a nonviolent race. God knows what it means! For you are preparing an army and spending 37% of your money on it, I was told. And look what it is doing to you, not only to the poor people, but right through the race. You say one thing and do quite the opposite, why? Because, you say, if we had no army Pakistan would attack, and Pakistan says the same nonsense, and so you keep up this game. Not only in India but throughout the world it is the same contradiction—that we are all kind, loving people and preparing for war! So this nation, this race, the group, the family, the individual is in a state of contradiction, and the more intense the contradiction, the greater the tension, and the greater the tension, the greater the activity. The activity takes different forms, from writing a book to becoming a hermit. So each one of us is somewhat schizophrenic, in a state of contradiction. And not knowing how to get away from it we turn to religion or to drugs or chase women or go to the temple— any form of activity which takes us away from *what is*. We reform the village, but we never tackle this fundamental thing.

So I want to tackle *what is* because if I do not, I see that I will be ever in contradiction. A man at peace within himself needs no gods because then he can go very deeply into himself and very far, where frontiers of recognition have completely stopped, and the frontiers of recognition must end before the mind can receive that which is eternal. Do not just agree because the fact is that it is one of the most difficult things to do and requires tremendous work on yourself. That work is not effort. It becomes an effort, a conflict, a contradiction only when you still want to become something.

So I want to examine *what is,* which is that I am greedy, I am violent. I am examining that, and I see that there must be no contradictory approach to it. I must look at what I am and understand it, but not in relation to 'what should be'. Can I do that? Again you will find that it is one of the most difficult things to do—to examine *what is* without judgment, without comparison, without acceptance, without condemnation, because the moment you condemn you enter the field of contradiction. So can you and I look at violence without introducing the element which creates contradiction, the element of either acceptance or denial. So can I look at my violence? What is the state of the mind that, having eliminated contradiction, looks at that violence? I am left only with that which is actual, am I not, with the simple fact that I am violent, greedy, or sexual. Can I look at it?

What is the state of the mind that looks at a fact? Have you ever really looked at any fact—a woman, a man, a child, a flower, a sunset? What do you do when you look? You are thinking of something else, are you not? You say, that is a handsome man and I must not look at him, or that is a beautiful woman and I wish she were my wife. You never look without a reaction. You look at a sunset and merely say how lovely it is, or that it is not as beautiful as it was yesterday. So you have never looked at it. Your memory of yesterday destroys the perception of *what is* today. How extraordinarily difficult it is for us to look at something clearly, openly, simply! Now let us look at another fact. Why are you listening to me? You are listening to me, obviously, because I have a reputation. You think I can do something for you. You think you must listen to me either because intellectually it amuses you or for various reasons, and so you are not actually listening. What is actually happening is that since what I say contradicts what you think, you do not listen. All you are listening to is what you think you know about me—and you do not really know a thing! What is important is not to know about me but to really follow what is being said, to find out if it has any basis, any reality, any sense, or whether it is nonsense, false. That is the only important thing, and what you think about me personally is totally irrelevant.

So I ask: Have you ever looked at a fact? Please, when you go home really try it, just for fun. If you have a flower in your room, look at it, and see what the mind does; see whether the mind can just look at it, or whether it immediately says, "It is a rose," or "It has faded," and so on. You can, perhaps, look at a flower, at your wife or child, but it is much more difficult to look at yourself totally, to watch yourself without introducing the factor of contradiction or acceptance. Can I just look at my violence without any form of acceptance or denial? You will see, if you try, how extraordinarily difficult it is because the habit comes in and says all kinds of things. To look at a fact, whether a political fact, a religious fact, or the fact of starvation, requires attention, not a state of contradiction. There can be no attention if there is contradiction.

There is starvation in many parts of the world, perhaps not in America, Europe, or Russia, but all over Asia there is. Everybody talks about it, and nothing happens. Why? The communists, the socialists, the reformers, and the big politicians, they all talk about it, all the world talks, and yet nothing happens. The fact is that there is starvation, and another fact is that each group wants the solution of starvation to be according to its own system and says, "My system is better than yours." Because there are national divisions, the manipulation of power politics, this goes on and on. So the fact is that nobody wants to tackle the problem of starvation. They merely want to act in their own way. These are all facts. So can you find out how the mind looks at a fact? Your approach to the fact is far more important than the fact itself because if you approach it rightly, the fact undergoes a tremendous change.

I think we had better stop now, but we will take this up again next time because there is much more involved in this; this is only the ABC and nothing else. And when you ask me to go on and say that you are not tired, I say that you should be tired. If you have been merely accepting what I say, you have not been thinking. It is not a problem to you, it is not operating in you, and that is exactly the point. You listen, but you will tell your child to remember the ideals, and the contradictory process will go on. So it really means nothing to you; if it meant something you would be exhausted. Because this all means a complete revolution.

Next time I am going into the whole question of fear, habit, and tradition, for all these are the factors which prevent you from doing something about the fact. When the mind is

capable of knowing why it cannot look at the fact and frees itself from the accumulated contradictions and conditionings, then the fact undergoes a tremendous change. Then there is no fact. Then you will see that violence has completely gone, been completely wiped away. Then the mind, being free, is no longer in contradiction, and therefore no longer in a state of effort, no longer trying to be something.

September 10, 1958

Third Talk in Poona

The last time we met we were talking about the whole problem of effort—whether through effort there can be any radical change, whether it is possible for a mind which is in a state of self-contradiction to put an end to that contradiction through any form of coercive discipline, through any form of suppression, through any endeavor to overcome it. We have said that a mind in contradiction must be in a state of effort, and we inquired whether inward dissension, inward conflict, could ever produce that change which is necessary if we are to see things clearly and live a peaceful, quiet life. It seems to me that it is important to understand this issue really deeply—that a small, respectable, petty mind must inevitably create contradiction within itself. Life is not petty. We try to reduce life to our own levels of pettiness, but it is too vast, too enormous, too demanding, too urgent. Life presents us with innumerable pressures, challenges, which the petty mind cannot deal with and so, unconsciously or consciously, it creates a state of self-contradiction. Now can such a petty mind, the respectable mind, through any endeavor bring about a state in which there is no contradiction? That is our problem.

Obviously, life's challenge is too demanding, too enormous, too extraordinarily complex to be solved only at any one particular point. It must be tackled totally, as a whole thing. It cannot be tackled merely from the scientific point of view or from the romantic or the so-called religious point of view which, after all, is nothing but a series of dogmas, beliefs, and ceremonies. But the petty mind is caught in all these escapes, and it has reduced its environment to a social condition into which it can fit itself. Surely you and I can see that life is too extraordinarily beautiful, too deep, too profound to be easily comprehended, and yet with my narrow little mind I am trying to meet it. My little mind which is fearful, anxious, acquisitive, violent, has got so many social and religious sanctions according to which it must live, and so there is ever the contradiction between *what is* and what it thinks should be. And having created this contradiction, there is tension, and from that tension, endless activity; and I try to reform that activity instead of understanding the petty mind which creates the contradiction. It is like trying to correct my shadow in the sun; I see that the shadow is very sharp, and so I furiously scratch at the shadow thinking that thereby I am doing a revolutionary thing. But the really revolutionary thing is to bring about a radical change in the mind itself, not in the mere thought which is but a projection of the state of contradiction.

So how is my mind which is obviously very limited and conditioned to transform itself? The mind is conditioned, is it not? All your environment is shaping the mind—the climate, the customs, the tradition, the racial influences, the family—innumerable conscious and unconscious pressures are shaping the mind. You are a Hindu, a Parsi, a Muslim, a Christian, or whatever you are, because you have been influenced by your environment. So your mind is conditioned, and being conditioned you face life, whose challenge is not within time, with your condi-

tioned responses which are always within time. We think the challenge of starvation, the challenge of the appalling inequalities can be dealt with in terms of time because we treat the challenge in terms of our own conditioning. Being a socialist, a communist or what you will, I meet, with my conditioned mind which has been shaped by many influences, a challenge which is itself out of time. All challenges must be out of time. The challenge of life cannot be held within the period of time; for then it becomes the familiar, and therefore I think I can deal with it. When the challenge comes to us, it is never in terms of the known. I will explain, if I can, what I mean.

I ask you—what is God? Being a respectable Hindu or Christian or what you will, you will answer according to your conditioning. But God is something unnamable, unknowable, unthinkable by a conditioned mind; it is something which is totally unknown, but your mind answers according to your conditioning. So the challenge is always reduced to time, and your responses are always within time. Please think about it with me and do not just deny or accept. There is an art in listening, and it is very difficult to listen to something with which you are not familiar. Your mind is always translating, correlating, referring, what is said to what you already know—to what Shankara, Buddha, or someone else has said—and in that process there is no attention. You are already away, off in thought, and if you approve or disapprove you have already ceased to listen. But if you can listen with that attention which is not translating what is being heard, which does not compare, which is really giving the whole of its being to what is being said, in that attention there is listening. I do not know if you have ever tried to listen to somebody with your total being. In that there is no effort; effort and strain mean that you are either trying to get something from the speaker or are afraid, avoiding, resisting, and those processes are not listening at all. So if I may, I most respectfully suggest that you listen to see the truth of what is being said. Truth is not something extraordinary, mysterious, romantic, speculative. Truth is that black is black, that there is a cloud in the sky. To discover what is false and what is true, you have to free the mind from its past traditions, hopes and fears, and look. Truth is something to be discovered from moment to moment, not something that is accumulated.

I do not know if you have ever thought about this whole problem of accumulating, gathering, learning. A mind that has learned is incapable of learning. If I may ask, sirs, what is your reaction to that statement? Because this is not just a lecture where you listen and agree or disagree and then go home and do what you like, but this is an experiment together where, during my exploration, you are watching your own mind. If you so watch your own mind, then I think these talks will have immense benefit, and you will see things happening unconsciously without your demanding it.

So I say a learned mind cannot learn. A mind that has gathered, that has experienced, and that says, "I know," the mind that has studied so much and is so full of other peoples' opinions, ideas, speculations, descriptions—how can such a mind learn? Learning is from moment to moment, but if you learn in order to accumulate and with that accumulation try to direct your life, then you have ceased to live. You have merely gathered and are then projecting what you think life should be. Therefore there is a contradiction between life, which is vast and profound, and your mind, which is caught in its own environmental influences. So we come again to the question of how to free the mind from self-contradiction, because that is one of our major problems. I think this, and I do that. Watch yourself and you will see.

One is full of arrogance, of pride, both of race and of achievement, and at the same time one wants also to have the beauty of humility. So I am in contradiction, which always implies conflict, and to overcome that conflict I exert myself, saying I must put away pride and try to have humility. So I discipline myself, dedicate myself to God and give all my endeavors to what I think is the highest. First I have developed arrogance, pride, and then I offer it to God because I am suffering. That is what we are really doing, is it not?

Now the fact is that contradiction is the very center of the self. I mean by the self not the atma, the paramatma, or any speculative self, which for me has no reality. I am talking of our everyday self—the self which is greedy, the self which suffers, the self which is frustrated in its ambition, which is perpetually worrying, the self which says, "I must achieve, fulfill," yet knows that in the struggle for fulfillment, there is only the shadow of frustration and despair. That self is the reality. So there is this contradiction. I am proud, and at the same time I want to taste the beauty of humility. Of the two, which is real? Surely it is pride. The humility, the what I should be in some imagined future may or may not come into being.

So the problem is how to transform pride without bringing in any contradictory idea with which I hope to remove pride. I feel it is really very important to understand this because we all have this problem of effort—the effort in our work, in our thinking, in trying to change ourselves, the effort to bring about a different society, to resist hate, to get rid of fear, to know of love. Our whole being is a constant effort. There is never a moment of that real feeling which comes to a mind that understands a thing for itself and is not trying to make *what is* into something else. I do not know if you have noticed it, but if there is any pressure, any influence behind your thinking, thought can never fly straight to the truth of a thing. If I think I must do something because someone wants me to do it, then the doing is always biased. The influenced thought can never be a straight thought. If I do something because I am afraid or because I want something out of it, that act is a perverted act; it is not a clean, straight act. In the same way if a thought has any pressure behind it, it must go crooked. So the problem is how to free the mind from this contradiction and how to free the mind from pride. The mind can only free itself from pride when the ideal ceases to be. Because, the ideal is not the fact; the fact is pride. So I have to remove from my mind the whole idea of 'what should be', remove the ideal totally. Then I have only the sense of pride, and I can look at it completely.

One can see that ideals mean nothing. You are not really idealists, you are verbalists. An ideal is merely an escape from doing something actual. I am proud, and I say that tomorrow, later on, I will be without pride. You will never be. So how am I to deal with the fact that I am afraid, that I am proud, that I am arrogant? Because, as I have said, what is important is the individual, not the mass. If the individual changes radically, the mass changes. It is not the other way round. No mass can be creative, produce a picture, write a poem, or anything else. So I am asking you: How will you deal with the fact that you are proud?

Now what is wrong with pride? Why should you not be proud, and what does pride mean? What are you proud of? Of your family, your wealth, your beauty, your character? And if one does not feel proud, one feels inferior, the opposite, and says, "I am a nobody," which is another subtle form of pride. And so one is caught again. So before I begin to inquire why the mind must free itself from pride, I must know what is wrong

with pride. We will come back to it, but let us take something else first.

Most of us have fear of some kind hidden in the corners of the mind—the fear of death, of what the neighbor will say, of losing one's job, or not being able to fulfill. Now why does one want to get rid of fear? Can I think clearly when I am afraid? Obviously not. If I am afraid of what my neighbor is going to say, then I am living according to the ideas of my neighbor because I want to be considered respectable in society. I am afraid of not being respectable, and therefore I comply, conform. So I am always living at a very, very superficial level and at the same time wanting to be conscious of the profound. So there again I bring contradiction into myself. Then I say I must get rid of fear. Have you ever tried to get rid of fear? Let us take the fear of death. It is not just the old people who are afraid of death, the young people are afraid also; everyone in the world is afraid of death, of ceasing to be, even though they may rationalize it. How do you solve that problem? When somebody dies whom you like and you are confronted with death, what happens? You try to console yourself in some belief—reincarnation or the idea of resurrection or some form of rationalization. But fear still exists, and you have just run away from it.

Now if I am to tackle that problem of fear and not escape from it, then I will have to go into the whole question of death—death being an end to what I think has a continuity. I feel I must live on for the next 500 years, or even indefinitely, because thereby I can do something or be something. But the fact is that if I live a thousand years, I shall be the same at the end because I do not change now. So the problem is not death but whether there is such a thing as continuity. Is this not so? Surely, if I can solve the question of continuity, then I shall not be afraid of death. But, what we do now is to try to escape from death by various forms of rationalization, and in spite of my rationalization, I am still afraid. So I see through all the escapes—the radio, the book, the ceremony, the God, the belief—and I see that all the escapes are on the same level and that none is superior to the other. I see that through escape there is no solution, and so I have to find out if there is such a thing as continuity, if there is in me a permanent entity that continues, and if there is anything permanent at all in life.

Do you know anything which is permanent, without change? I would like my relationship with my wife, my husband, to be permanent, continuous; I would like to keep my property forever; I would like to live in a state of perpetual fame, perpetual love, or perpetual bliss and peace, but is there such a thing? Even your properties are now being questioned, and if you have more than so much land, you are heavily taxed. Is there anything permanent? The communists wanted the permanent worship of the state, but they have already had to modify this. There is continuous modification going on everywhere, and it is only the religious mind with its impregnable beliefs that seems impervious to any change. So is there such a thing as continuity or is life a ceaseless change? Surely life is a movement in which there is no permanency. If you look at it carefully, you will see that there is no permanency. There is no permanency even in our thinking, our beliefs, our ideals. Everything you do is uncertain, and you might lose your job tomorrow. So being uncertain, we want continuity, permanency, and so we are back again to the state of contradiction. And it is this contradiction that we must understand because if we could really understand that, we would then be able to approach every problem—pride, fear, death, or whatever it is—totally differently.

Our whole life is geared to contradiction, our whole being is in a state of contradiction, not only the conscious mind, but the unconscious mind, and yet I see that if I am to think clearly, if there is to be any understanding of what is true, the mind must be free, clear. So how is one to be free of contradiction? Can I look at anything without bringing the opposite into it? After all, do I know love only because I know hate? Can I look at this duality completely, understand it fully, go into it with all my being, to understand the truth of it? Are you aware of yourself, of what you are? Surely we know that we are in contradiction, that we say this and do that; you must know of this whirlpool. Then what do you do about it? You try to get rid of it by doing something about it, which means that you are not dealing with the problem itself but trying to cover the problem with another series of ideas. So, without covering the problem with thoughts, can I look at the fact of my pride? Have you tried it, sirs, since I last suggested it? Can you look at a flower without naming it, and can you look at a quality of which you are aware in yourself without trying to do something about it? Have you ever looked at anger without saying to yourself that you must not be angry? If so, you will know how very difficult it is just to look at the fact because the mind is always interfering with the fact by bringing in the memory of 'what should be'. And I say that if the mind can look at the fact without bringing in past experiences, past memories, just being aware of the fact, then that very awareness of the fact changes it totally. The awareness of the fact brings about a cessation of conflict.

If I know that I am a liar, and I do not merely try to change it, saying I must tell the truth, then I can go into the whole question of why I lie. Because I want to know the whole background of my lying, to see the significance of why I lie, I go into it. And I see that I lie because I am afraid. Superficially or very deeply I am afraid of what I have done or said and that you may discover it, or I am afraid of losing my job—endless different things. Now how is it possible to free the mind from fear? If I do anything about it, there is a contradiction and therefore a conflict, an everlasting battle going on. So, let me not say that I must not be afraid, but let me look at the whole process of what has brought about that fear.

Let us take another fact: that we avoid the ugly and cling to the beautiful. Please follow me a little. We think we know beauty because we know the ugly; we know beauty as something manifest, as something expressed. I say this is a beautiful building or an ugly building, but how do I know it is ugly or beautiful? It is because of opinion, because I have been told, is it not? My mind is trained, conditioned, according to tradition as to what is beautiful and what is ugly. Has beauty an opposite? Please do not try to answer, but just listen. Has beauty an opposite, the ugly? If beauty has an opposite, is it beauty?

I may say that life is the false as well as the true and that I know what cold is because I know what heat is, I know pain because I know when there is no pain; there is man and there is woman. The state of duality, which we all know, is inevitable perhaps, but why do we create conflict because of that? The problem we are investigating is not that there is or is not the beautiful and the ugly, but why there is the conflict, the tensions, this enormous amount of worry trying to be this and not to be that? The worry and conflict arise because I want to be this and not that, because this is profitable and the other is not; with the chosen state I want to be identified, and the other I want to put away. So the identification with the one and the avoidance of the other is the whole center of contradiction. And that contradiction cannot be overcome through any form of discipline. Do what you will, follow any system, you will not overcome it. What will free the mind

from contradiction is to tackle the mind itself and find out why the mind attaches itself to the one state and avoids the other. That requires self-knowledge, going into yourself, studying yourself patiently, deeply. But we do not want to do that; we want an immediate result.

So the problem we are going into is not whether in reality there is no man or woman, no evil or good, nothing beautiful or ugly, but why does the mind operate in these divisions. And this means really going into the whole question of what is thinking. Because we always think in this way—that there is beauty and there is the ugly, and I want the one and not the other. So I say to myself, "What is this machinery of thinking which says I must have this and I must not have that, thereby creating contradiction within me?" And I ask, "What is this thing that is thinking?" I am not going away from the main subject, but I am now going to inquire into the question of what is thinking. Have you ever asked yourself that question, or do you just have thoughts? We have never asked, have we, what is thinking; so let us look, let us go into it.

Thinking, surely, is a reaction. If there were no reaction there would be no thinking. I know the sannyasis and the so-called saints do various things in order not to have reactions and therefore destroy themselves, but we are not concerned with that. Thinking is essentially a reaction. I ask you where you live, and you answer without hesitation because you know so well where you live. If I ask you a more complex question, you take time to answer. The gap between the question and the answer is caused by the process of thinking, is it not? Please follow this. So the gap between the question and the answer means that you are inquiring, bringing your memories into operation, and your memory then answers. Then if I ask you a question still more complex, the time interval is greater and in that interval the mind is very active, inquiring, searching through your memories, your records of books and accumulated knowledge, and when it has found what it wants, it gives an answer. If I ask you a very complex question, the interval is much wider, and after searching your mind you say you do not know. Do please listen; it is not a laughing matter. You say, "I do not know," but that is merely a hesitation, an interval in which you are still inquiring, waiting for the mind to find an answer, which means again that the mind is still operating, searching, demanding, waiting, which is all reaction, is it not? All our responses are reactions and that, surely, is clear. That is all we know of the ways of our thinking, that it is reaction, more complex or less complex, more subtle or less subtle, more crooked or more refined. But the whole process of thinking is mechanical. Thinking is merely a reaction to something I know, or which I do not know but I can find out. That is what the computers are doing. They can answer anything you want based on the same principle of association and recollection.

So our thinking now is entirely mechanical, and with that mechanical habit we approach life, which is not mechanical. Life is not just a printing press throwing out news. So with my mechanical thinking I approach life which is not mechanical, and therefore there is contradiction. I try to overcome this contradiction again through the process of thinking, the same mechanical habit, and therefore the contradiction between me and life persists. Now can I approach life in a totally different way?

Let us look at it again. I am inquiring into thinking because it is our thoughts, obviously, which have made this contradiction. There is truth, there is the false, there is the beautiful, and there is the ugly, I am sexual, and I do not want to be sexual, and so on; these are undeniable facts. Thought identifies

itself with the one state and denies the other. So I have to understand the whole process of thinking, not only at the conscious level but at the unconscious level, deep down. That brings out the question of the conscious and the unconscious mind. I ask you: What are you, what does the 'you' consist of? It consists of all that you think, all that you want to be—your ambitions, hopes, fears, the totality of all that is yours. You are the product of racial influences, past traditions, what man has passed on for centuries upon centuries; you are also the superficial, sophisticated, educated mind—the technically trained professor, lawyer, policeman, or whatever your training or lack of training has produced. So you are not only the product of the last forty or twenty years, but also the product of the centuries of the past. You are the totality of all that, but do you know it? I have described all this, and you may now say you know it, but there is a difference between hearing and knowing. That is, you have heard and understood the words I have said, and so you say, "I know it." But there is also another state, which is, that you experience this totality. The experiencing of that totality of what you are is the real knowing; the other is the mere acceptance of the description. Most of us only know in the descriptive sense, not in the experential sense. If you really know yourself in the sense of experiencing the totality of yourself as of the past, then you can break that totality or continue it. At this point you can see, if you will look, how contradiction arises. There is a knowing which is an experiencing of all that you are, which I have just described, and which includes both the conscious as well as the unconscious. But you are not going to experience it because you say that it is too difficult. So one part of your mind says, "I will listen to you and know it all verbally," and the other part says, "I must try and experience that, it must be a marvelous state of experiencing." So you have created a contradiction. You want to experience this totality of your being because you see that the verbal knowing is silly, but you are preventing yourself by not going into it, by being satisfied at the verbal level. I say you cannot free the mind from contradiction until you know the totality of all this. Part of you is the trained or untrained person, but part of you is also the traditional past which tells you to do your duty, to think of God, put on ashes, or whatever you do. All that is there, and you are living at a very, very superficial level. So there is contradiction, and so you have dreams, anxieties, depressions. Until you have gone into your whole background, you cannot possibly be free of this contradiction.

Now, how is one to be totally aware of all this? Must I go through layer after layer analyzing, looking bit by bit into the whole content of myself, like stripping the peel off the onion? That would take all your life, would it not? Your whole mind is conditioned, the totality of your being is conditioned, and whatever you do to get rid of it, you are still within the field of that conditioning. So thought operating upon the conditioned state will not free the conditioned mind because thought is the result, the reaction, to that conditioning. So thought is not the means by which to destroy our conditioning.

To free the mind from all conditioning, you must see the totality of it without thought. This is not a conundrum; experiment with it, and you will see. Do you ever see anything without thought? Have you ever listened, looked, without bringing in this whole process of reaction? You will say that it is impossible to see without thought; you will say no mind can be unconditioned. When you say that, you have already blocked yourself by thought, for the fact is you do not know.

So can I look, can the mind be aware of its conditioning? I think it can. Please experiment. Can you be aware that you are a Hindu, a socialist, a communist, this or that, just be aware without saying that it is right or wrong? Because it is such a difficult task just to see, we say it is impossible. I say it is only when you are aware of this totality of your being without any reaction that the conditioning goes, totally, deeply—which is really the freedom from the self.

Do not immediately translate this into the terms of what you now believe or do not believe, for the whole of that is the self, and thought, which is the reaction of the self, cannot act upon the self without adding to it. Do you not see this? And yet that is what we are doing all the time. Whereas if you see the truth that thought cannot break this conditioning because all thought, analysis, probing, introspection, is merely a reaction to your present state, then you are only aware of the conditioning. In that awareness there is no choice because choice again brings thought into being. Therefore to be aware of this conditioning implies no choice, no condemnation, no justification, no comparison, but just to be aware. When you are so aware, your mind is already free of that conditioning. By simply being aware of the whole process of your conditioning, you will see that you are introducing a new factor altogether, a factor in which there is no identification with or rejection of the self, and that factor is the release, the wiping away of all conditioning. That is why I suggest to you that you experiment until we meet again, that you so observe, and be aware.

September 14, 1958

Fourth Talk in Poona

I would like, if I may, to discuss this afternoon something which may be rather difficult and which I think needs a great deal of understanding and penetration. For most of us everyday living is so oppressive, so demanding and insistent, that whether we are laborers or clerks, professors or what you will, nearly all of our time is taken up with our occupation, and we have very little time in which to think about the wider and fuller implications of living. It seems to me that though one may feel serious, though one may feel dedicated, though one may have some insight into things, nevertheless some time must be given to the whole process of the understanding of the mind—the mind which is not only the reactions, the functioning in association, in memory, but also the mind that is and must be empty and function from that emptiness. It is going to be difficult because inevitably you will translate what is being said into terms of your own experience, your own knowledge, your own tradition, thereby nullifying what you hear. If I say something totally new which you are not able to understand immediately, the mind will translate it into terms of the old. It is like putting new wine into old bottles. We hear something for the first time, and immediately the mind sets going its activity of associating and translates what is being said in terms of its own background, and thereby destroys that which it is hearing.

So it seems to me that it is very important to listen and not to turn to tradition because tradition will not help to bring about clarity. Tradition invariably perpetuates respectability and the respectable mind is far from reality—not that the disreputable mind is any nearer reality. The respectable mind functions in the field of tradition, whether the tradition be ancient or modern, communist, Catholic, Hindu, Buddhist, or whatever it is—which really means that the mind has given itself over to what it has heard or read or been told, and is living according to the sanctions, ideas, and experiences of others. If you are to experience anything new, you must set all that aside, surely, and that is where our difficulty lies. The mind is so stubborn in its demand for certainty that it insists on walking always on the path of safety where there can be no adventure, no risk, no evaluation, no observation or experiencing. So the mind gradually falls into a framework of tradition, and thereby ceases to experience anything other than what it has been conditioned to. But that is not an original experience, and it is only the original experience that really unburdens the mind of its conditioning and enables you to see something for yourself. To see something for yourself will break down the limitations of the mind. Even some flower by the wayside, if you really see it, can do an extraordinary thing to you. It breaks up the pettiness, the habitual grooves of the mind if you can see something original, experience something original.

If you are at all aware of your own thinking, of your own ways of acting, you will find that you have very little, if anything at all, original. The young mind is the deciding mind; the young mind is the mind which is inquiring, searching, looking, experiencing. The traditional mind is the old mind; it is a dead mind even though it can quote all the Vedas, repeat pages from the sacred books. As a race we are very old, and so we have been brought up in this tradition, and we repeat, repeat, and there is nothing original. You have nothing of your own, nothing that is creative. If you are at all creative, it is merely in the scientific field, in the laboratory, and there is not that inner creative state of being which alone can experience something new, something which will solve the problems of the world. But unfortunately this country as well as other countries are burdened with the old mind, and it is extraordinarily difficult to break through tradition and not to think in terms of what Shankara, Buddha, Christ, or your own favorite guru round the corner has told you. To put away all this requires a great deal of understanding of why the mind seeks authority, tradition. Obviously it wants to be secure, but the mind that is secure can never experience newly; it can only repeat, and the repetition is not experiencing. So beware of the persons who quote the Gita or anything else; they destroy your capacity to be creative. The creative individual is a danger to society and so society holds and destroys the individual who is beginning to awaken, to be discontented, searching, experiencing. Authority in any form is evil, and I am using that word without any condemnation. As a cobra is poisonous, so authority is poisonous. You may laugh, but your laughter is an indication that you are brushing it off; you do not really see the poisonous nature of authority. Authority leads you to security, safety; at least you think it does, but it does not—it destroys you.

So for me, as I am talking about all this, there is only the teaching and not the teacher. The speaker is not at all important, and the teaching is only important if you understand and experience; but if you merely repeat or compare, then it is dead. So please remove the person from the teaching so that you can penetrate into what is being said without being influenced. Then you remove all authority and are face to face with the fact of whether it is true or false. But if you introduce the person and his so-called achievement with the looks, gestures, and tradition, then you pervert the teaching. If you really get that one thing—that what is important is what is said and not who says it—then you would see what an extraordinary thing happens to your mind. Then you would find that you would like to see what the truth of the teaching is and whether it is false or real.

That requires real, dispassionate, critical observation, examination.

What I want to discuss is something which through my description you can experience. The description is not the real, but only your experience can be the real. So do not take what you listen to as the real and your experiencing as the unreal.

Now action and reason both bind because action without reason is incomplete, and reason without action is incomplete, and both action and reason, without the understanding of the process of the mind, bind. Is it not so? I may be able to reason most logically, cleverly as any lawyer, but if the background from which my reasoning springs is never touched upon, inquired into, broken into, I am bound by my background. And a man who acts without reason through various mysteries, illusions, delusions, and hallucinations, such a man obviously is also bound and creates mischief. So action and reason both bind unless there is understanding of the ways of the mind. In this world we have to live, which is to act and to reason, but the more clever you are at reasoning and acting, the more mischief you do unless you first understand the whole background of your being, your tendencies, ways of thinking, and conditioning. This seems all so obvious. Most of us are concerned with action, and we want to do things; we cannot sit still or retire into the hills; we feel we have to act, to reform, to bring about a different world, a different state of being, a revolution. And we think that can be brought about by logical, careful reasoning, through the dialectical approach, and all that business. But a really radical revolution has to be brought about by the individual, not by the mass because there is no such thing as the mass. The individual has to understand the whole process of the mind, which means your own mind, not mine. You are not listening to understand me, you are listening to understand yourself, and the understanding of yourself—in which there is both action and reasoning—is meditation. Let us go into it.

First of all, in meditation there is no such thing as distraction. Distraction belongs to concentration. You know how all the so-called religious people throughout the world concentrate; whether they live in monasteries, in caves, go to the temple, or sit by themselves quietly of a morning, to them concentration is very important. But concentration is destructive. Concentration implies distraction, which is the wandering away of the mind. Please watch your own mind. I do not know if you have ever concentrated for any length of time, but if you have you will know what happens. Your mind narrows down, focuses, cutting out every other thought, desire, influence, and is completely absorbed in something. Let us go into that and examine the state of absorption. You must have seen a boy absorbed by a toy; the toy is exciting, new, mechanical, complicated, and he is completely absorbed by it. Is that concentration? Yes because the toy absorbs his whole being, and he is concentrated on it. There the toy is important. With you the book, the word, the mantra, the toy of a Master—a picture, an image—is important, and you hope it will absorb you; and if it does not, you absorb the idea and live in that. Either the image absorbs you or you absorb the image, and live accordingly. If you can be completely absorbed in an idea, legend, myth, and get into some meditative illusion, then you think you have realized truth. But a mind so absorbed in one thing is incapable of seeing the real. Such a mind is a destructive mind; it destroys itself. You begin to see things which are not there, which is hallucination, or you see things which are really there but translate them to suit your own desires, which is delusion.

So if one observes the dangers of concentration, one will see that there is quite a different process of attention which is not concentration. You can never learn through concentration; you can always learn through attention. Attention is never a narrowing down; on the contrary, it is extensive. A mind that is merely concentrating on what you will is not in a state of meditation. There are people who have given twenty years to meditation, and they have come to a point beyond which they cannot go because what they have meditated upon has become their barrier, their prison, and they cannot break through. They see visions, God, this and that, and are very popular as great saints. But what they see is their own projection, their own thought, crystallizing, taking shape, in which they are caught, and we think that is a marvelous thing. It is the most stupid thing, and I am using that word in its dictionary meaning and not in a condemnatory sense.

Can you not see it, experience the truth of it, that concentration is destructive to the mind? The mind is a moving thing, vital, extensive, with tremendous energy; it is the reservoir of that creativeness of which you have no idea; it can penetrate into the most complex and unknown thing; it can go into the unconscious and discover that which is most extraordinary. And yet you force it to a narrow point because you think that is God, the real thing, and thereby you destroy it. Look at all the saints and sannyasis and what they have done to this poor, unfortunate country! They have disciplined their desires, controlled their minds, suppressed every form of beauty, and therefore they have no passion, the living quality, the living fountain of reality.

So if you see the truth of this—that concentration is destructive, is like building a barrier, a wall round yourself—then what will you do? Then you must inquire whether there is a different kind of attention, must you not? But first one must really see that concentration cannot free the mind; on the contrary, it imprisons the mind. Even the schoolboy knows that to learn you must be awake and listening. To learn is not just to repeat from some beastly book to pass an examination. Learning is the sense of understanding, inquiring, searching, for which your mind must be extraordinarily quick, fluid, with the capacity of insight.

So a mind that has the power of concentration, that says it has complete control over thought, is a stupid mind. If that is so, then you must find a way of inquiring which is not merely through concentration. Concentration implies distraction, does it not? The mind takes up a position and says everything else is a distraction. It says I must think about this and exclude everything else. Now to me there is no such thing as distraction because there is no central position which the mind takes and then says, "I will pursue this and not that." So let us remove both the word and the condemnatory feeling of distraction. Please experience what I am saying. Remove that word distraction not merely verbally but emotionally, inwardly. Then you will see what happens to your mind. To us at present there is concentration and distraction, a concentrated outlook and a wandering off. So you see we have created a duality and therefore a conflict. You spend your life battling between the chosen thought and the distractions, and when you can get an hour when you are completely held by an idea, you feel you have achieved something. But if you remove this idea of distraction altogether, then you will find that your mind is in a state of reaction—in a state of association which you call "wandering." That is the fact, and you have removed the element of conflict. Then you are free to deal with the wanderings; you can inquire as to why the mind wanders and not merely try to stop it, to control it.

Then, since you have removed the word, the feeling of being distracted, what is now operating is a mind that is attentive to the wandering, to reaction. Is that not so? I have taken away the feeling of distraction and now my mind is very alert to every movement of thought because it has not taken up a position in which it calls every movement of thought a distraction. I hope you are experiencing as I am talking. So your mind then is in a state of attention, not trying to learn something or to reject, control, or suppress.

Let us inquire into that word *attention*. But I hope it is clear so far. We are trying to understand what meditation is—not how to meditate. If you learn various systems of meditation, that is not meditation; you are just learning a technique. Now I say there is an attention which can become concentrated, but concentration cannot become attentive. So it is important to discover what attention is, and this will help also the student who wants to learn, if he goes into it very deeply. The question now is: Can a concentrated mind learn? Have you ever observed the state of your mind when it learns? I am saying something now, something new is being said, and you are learning about it. We have seen that concentration is destructive, so what is the state of the mind that is learning? It is attentive without compulsion, it is attentive without conformity, without any form of influence, without manipulation, without seeking a reward or avoiding punishment. Are you noticing your own mind? So a mind that learns is an attentive mind in which these other influences do not exist. In that state of attention you learn. That is the only state in which you can truly experience—not in any other state. Now you and I have established, or rather understood, what it means to be attentive, to have that attention in which there is no form of compulsion; so you are attending without effort, are you not, because you are learning. I am not mesmerizing you. I am not trying to put something over on you. You want to find out, you want to learn, and I am forcing you to learn. That is a different matter. We are inquiring into that state of mind which learns, and we realize that that state of mind is attention.

Please go into it and you will see that state has no border, there is no frontier. Does that mean anything to you? Please do not agree with me because it is not a matter of agreement; it is a matter of direct experience. In concentration or absorption—as a devotee is absorbed in whatever he pursues—in that state there is a demarcation. Have you not noticed? When you are concentrating you can almost feel the borders of the mind. All your faculties—emotional, mental, verbal—everything is focused on a certain point, and when there is a focus and no expansion, there is a frontier. A mind which is attentive, which knows what attention really is—which I have described—has no frontier. The mind can come to such a state. Do you understand, sirs? That is an important discovery for you; it is an experience.

I will put it in different words. Our mind is the mechanism of recognition; it is the machine, the record of recognition. You recognize the tree, the light, the temple, the man, the woman, the bird; you know your thoughts, your tendencies, the insults you have received, the hurts you have felt—all these memories are the records of recognition, are they not? So our minds are the process, the mechanism of recognition, and we are always trying to expand this recognition—to know more, to experience more, to read more. This acquisition is all within the field of recognition. Essentially recognition is the center of the self, not the illusory super-self, but the self which is ambitious, vicious, unkind, brutal, which is trying to become a great man, or a saint, or which just wants to be a nobody. It is that center which is expanding through recognition. So the mind can know the frontiers of its recognition. Do

you know that, sirs? Please do not agree because you do not know it. You have never played with it; you have never gone into it. But if you go into it, you will find that you can enlarge the process of recognition, widen the field, the frontier, keep on widening, widening. It is like the conception of the family, the group, the race, the national, and the international feeling—all essentially the same, but vastly expanding.

Now if one understands and experiences the state of attention, then you will find that the mind can go beyond the frontiers of recognition. To put it again differently, the mind functions within the frontiers of the known. I know Poona, Bombay, London, New York; I know my family, my virtues, my tendencies; I know what I want; I know my tradition, that there is God or that there is no God; my memory is all this. So my memory functions in the field of the known. You can enlarge that field and know more and more, indefinitely, which is the endless activity of the clever mind, the erudite mind, the scholarly mind, the mind which knows so much. It has a center from which it goes to the frontier and comes back. It moves in waves but always within the field of the known, and when one talks about the unknown, the unknowable, the unthinkable, this center moves to the frontier and tries to peep over the boundary by speculation, but it is anchored to the known. All its gods are known. Your sacred books have told about it, some poor gentleman experienced it thousands of years ago, and you repeat it and hope to experience it. So you have a center which is hoping to reach something which you think exists; that is, your mind projects what it knows into the future. But however distant thought may go, it is still within the field of the known.

So seeing all this—the ways, the tricks, the subtleties, the cunning processes of thought—how is the mind to break through it all, not taking centuries, many lives, but as a hungry man who wants food immediately. You cannot say to him, "Let socialism come and you will have food"; he wants food now. Likewise the mind must see that in the field of the known, there is no answer. The mind can go up to the frontier of the known, the recognizable, which includes the unknown which it has projected, but it cannot break through. Nor does it want to break through; most people do not want to because the unknown is too dangerous. It is like entering the uncharted seas, you fear you may get drowned. So you say, "I had better remain here and bring the whole world into my narrow heart." So how is the mind to break through?

This is real meditation. You understand, sirs? It was meditation from the moment I began to inquire into tradition and understood putting away tradition because it is the desire for security; then putting away all the teachers, but understanding the teaching; then removing all authority and looking at insecurity; then understanding concentration and its destructiveness; and then discovering, experiencing, a state of mind which is attentive.

Such a mind is not a talkative mind. The attentive mind is not a chattering mind. If you see the beauty of it, if you really experience it, then you can watch your own mind operating. Then the mind watches itself as it functions in tradition and up to the frontiers of the known.

So the inquiry, from when we began until now, is a process of meditation. Meditation is not how to have peace of mind, how to be silent, how to achieve. Those are all immature, childish pursuits. You can take a drug and make your mind absolutely quiet. You can do all kinds of tricks and have peace of mind, but such a mind is still petty, small, narrow. So this whole process, this whole awakening of the mind to itself is meditation.

Any inquiry into the unknown is speculation, and a speculative mind is not an attentive mind. The philosophers, the erudite ones, the theoreticians, the people who say God is this or that, just spin words. So a mind that is attentive has not the virtue of respectability. It has virtue, but not a virtue you can recognize. Its virtue cannot be held, as you cannot hold the wind in your fist. Virtue cannot be held in your mind as a possession, and that is the beauty of it. The moment you are conscious that you are virtuous, you cease to be so, and the mind that ceases to be attentive is no longer a virtuous mind. And an attentive mind which is not absorbed by any toy or belief or idea—such a mind is an empty mind. You look surprised, sirs, and that is because you have not really followed the whole of this inquiry; if you had followed it, which means experienced it, you would see that your mind is empty. Let me put it the other way round.

Now the mind is occupied with thoughts, wandering thoughts, thoughts that come and go ceaselessly, or the particular thoughts which the mind pursues. Is it not so? Either thoughts wander through the mind like a breeze through the house or the mind pursues thoughts. Now I have opened the door onto the attentive mind, but you have to walk through to it. You cannot find it by searching in the mind. The attentive mind is empty—which is not being empty-headed, blank. Only the empty cup is useful, not the cup which is full. A mind that is purged of all those things that we have been talking about, a mind in which there is no conflict, such a mind, being empty, can either receive the unknown or it can remain empty and function from there. If one goes through all this and inquires, experiences, that is the real religious revolution, the only thing that is going to do anything worthwhile in this world—not the communist, the socialist, or any form of revolution. The real revolution is in the mind, and that state of real emptiness is the creative state because that which is empty has no frontiers; it has neither depth nor height. It is this creativity of the mind in the individual that is going to create a new world, and that is the only solution, the only salvation.

September 17, 1958

Fifth Talk in Poona

I should think one of our great problems must be to know what is freedom, and the need to understand this problem must be fairly immense and continuous since there is so much propaganda from so many specialists, so many and various forms of outward and inward compulsion, and all the chaotic, contradictory persuasions, influences, and impressions. I am sure we must have asked ourselves the question: What is freedom? As you and I know, everywhere in the world authoritarianism is spreading, not only at the political, social, and economic levels, but also at the so-called spiritual level. Everywhere there is a compelling environmental influence; newspapers tell us what to think, and there are so many five, ten, or fifteen-year plans. Then there are these specialists at the economic, scientific, and bureaucratic levels; there are all the traditions of everyday activity, what we must do and what we must not do; then there is the whole influence of the so-called sacred books; and there is the cinema, the radio, the newspaper—everything in the world is trying to tell us what to do, what to think, and what we must not think. I do not know if you have noticed how increasingly difficult it has become to think for oneself. We have become such experts in quoting what other people say or have said, and in the midst of this authoritarian welter, where is the freedom? And what do we mean by freedom? Is there such a thing? I am using that word *freedom* in its most simple sense in which is included liberation, the mind that is liberated, free. I want, if I may, to go into that this evening.

First, I think we must realize that our minds are really not free. Everything we see, every thought we have, shapes our mind; whatever you think now, whatever you have thought in the past and whatever you are going to think in the future—it all shapes the mind. You think what you have been told, either by the religious person or the politician, by the teacher in your school, or by books and newspapers. Everything about you influences what you think. What you eat, what you look at, what you listen to, your wife, your husband, your child, your neighbor—everything is shaping the mind. I think that is fairly obvious. Even when you think that there is a God or that there is no God, that also is the influence of tradition. So our mind is the field in which there are many contradictory influences which are in battle, one against the other.

Do please listen to all this because, as I have been saying, unless we directly experience for ourselves, your coming to a talk of this kind has no value at all. Please believe me that unless you experience what is being said, not merely follow the description but be aware, be cognizant, know the ways of your own thinking and thereby experience, these talks will have no meaning whatsoever. After all, I am only describing what is actually taking place in one's life, in one's environment, so that we can be aware of it and see if we can break through it, and what the implications of breaking through are. Because obviously we are now slaves, either the Hindu slave, the Catholic slave, the Russian slave, or slaves of one kind or another. We are all slaves to certain forms of thought, and in the midst of all this, we ask if we can be free and talk about the anatomy of freedom and authority, and so on.

I think it must be fairly obvious to most of us that what we think is conditioned. Whatever your thought—however noble and wide, or however limited and petty—it is conditioned, and if you further that thought there can be no freedom of thought. Thought itself is conditioned because thought is the reaction of memory, and memory is the residue of all your experiences, which in turn are the result of your conditioning. So if one realizes that all thinking, at whatever level, is conditioned, then we will see that thinking is not the means of breaking through this limitation—which does not mean that we must go into some blank or speculative silence. Actually the fact is, is it not, that every thought, every feeling, every action is conformative, conditioned, influenced. For instance, a saint comes along and by his rhetoric, gestures, looks, by quoting this and that to you, influences you. And we want to be influenced and are afraid to move away from every form of influence and see if we can go deeply and discover if there is a state of being which is not the result of influence.

Why are we influenced? In politics, as you know, it is the job of the politician to influence us; and every book, every teacher, every guru—the more powerful, the more eloquent, the better we like it—imposes his thought, his way of life, his manner of conduct upon us. So life is a battle of ideas, a battle of influences, and your mind is the field of the battle. The politician wants your mind; the guru wants your mind; the saint says, "Do this and not that," and he also wants your mind; and every tradition, every form of habit or custom, influences, shapes, guides, controls your mind. I think that is fairly obvious. It would be absurd to deny it. The fact is so.

You know, sirs, if I may deviate a little, I think it is essential to appreciate beauty. The beauty of the sky, the beauty of the sun upon the hill, the beauty of a smile, a face, a ges-ture, the beauty of the moonlight on the water, of the fading clouds, the song of the bird—it is essential to look at it, to feel it, to be with it, and I think this is the very first requirement for a man who would seek truth. Most of us are so unconcerned with this extraordinary universe about us; we never even see the waving of the leaf in the wind; we never watch a blade of grass, touch it with our hand and know the quality of its being. This is not just being poetic, so please do not go off into a speculative, emotional state. I say it is essential to have that deep feeling for life and not be caught in intellectual ramifications, discussions, passing examinations, quoting and brushing something new aside by saying it has already been said. Intellect is not the way. Intellect will not solve our problems; the intellect will not give us that nourishment which is imperishable. The intellect can reason, discuss, analyze, come to a conclusion from inferences, and so on, but intellect is limited, for intellect is the result of our conditioning. But sensitivity is not. Sensitivity has no conditioning; it takes you right out of the field of fears and anxieties. The mind that is not sensitive to everything about it—to the mountain, the telegraph pole, the lamp, the voice, the smile, everything—is incapable of finding what is true.

But we spend our days and years in cultivating the intellect, in arguing, discussing, fighting, struggling to be something, and so on. And yet this extraordinarily wonderful world, this earth that is so rich—not the Bombay earth, the Punjab earth, the Russian earth, or the American earth—this earth is ours, yours and mine, and that is not sentimental nonsense; it is a fact. But unfortunately we have divided it up through our pettiness, through our provincialism. And we know why we have done it—for our security, for better jobs, and more jobs. That is the political game that is being played throughout the world, and so we forget to be human beings, to live happily on this earth which is ours and to make something of it. And it is because we do not have that feeling for beauty which is not sentimental, which is not corrupting, which is not sexual, but a sense of caring; it is because we have lost that feeling—or perhaps we have never had it—that we are fighting, battling with each other over words and have no immediate understanding of anything. Look what you are doing in India—breaking up the land into sections, fighting and butchering—and this is happening the world over, and for what? To have better jobs, more jobs, more power? And so in this battle we lose that quality of mind which can see things freely, happily, and without envy. We do not know how to see somebody happy, driving a luxurious car, and to look at him and be happy with him; nor do we know how to sympathize with the very, very poor. We are envious of the man with the car, and we avoid the man who has nothing. So there is no love, and without that quality of love which is really the very essence of beauty, do what you will—go on all the pilgrimages in the world, go to every temple, cultivate all the virtues you can think of—you will get nowhere at all. Please believe me, you will not have it, that sense of beauty and love, even if you sit cross-legged for meditation, holding your breath for the next ten thousand years. You laugh, but you do not see the tragedy of it. We are not in that sensitive state of mind which receives, which sees immediately something which is true. You know a sensitive mind is a defenseless mind, it is a vulnerable mind, and the mind must be vulnerable for truth to enter—the truth that you have no sympathy, the truth that you are envious.

So it is essential to have this sense of beauty, for the feeling of beauty is the feeling of love. As I said, this is a slight digression, but I think it has significance in relation to what we are talking about. We are saying that a mind that is influenced, shaped, authority-bound, obviously can never be free, and whatever it thinks, however lofty its ideals, however subtle and deep, it is still conditioned. I think it is very important to understand that the mind, through time, through experience, through the many thousands of yesterdays, is shaped, conditioned, and that thought is not the way out. Which does not mean that you must be thoughtless; on the contrary, when you are capable of understanding very profoundly, very deeply, extensively, widely, subtly, then only will you fully recognize how petty thinking is, how small thought is. Then there is a breaking down of the wall of that conditioning.

So can we not see that fact—that all thought is conditioned? Whether it is the thought of the communist, capitalist, Hindu, Buddhist, or the person who is speaking, thinking is conditioned. And obviously the mind is the result of time, the result of the reactions of a thousand years and of yesterday, of a second ago, and ten years ago; the mind is the result of the period in which you have learned and suffered and of all the influences of the past and present. Now such a mind, obviously, cannot be free, and yet that is what we are seeking, is it not? You know even in Russia, in all the totalitarian countries where everything is controlled, there is this search for freedom. That search is there in the beginning for all of us when we are young, for then we are revolutionary, we are discontented, we want to know, we are curious, we are struggling; but soon that discontent is canalized into various channels, and there it dies slowly. So there is always within us the demand, the urge, to be free, and we never understand it, we never go into it, we have never searched out that deep instinctual demand. Being discontented when young, being dissatisfied with things as they are, with the stupidities of traditional values, we gradually, as we grow older, fall into the old patterns which society has established, and we get lost. It is very difficult to keep the pure discontent, the discontent which says, "This is not enough; there must be something else." We all know that feeling, the feeling of otherness which we soon translate as God or nirvana, and we read a book about it and get lost. But this feeling of otherness, the search, the inquiry for it, that, I think, is the beginning of the real urge to be free from all these political, religious, and traditional influences, and to break through this wall. Let us inquire into it.

Surely there are several kinds of freedom. There is political freedom; there is the freedom which knowledge gives when you know how to do things, the know-how; the freedom of a wealthy man who can go round the world; the freedom of capacity, to be able to write, to express oneself, to think clearly. Then there is the freedom from something: freedom from oppression, freedom from envy, freedom from tradition, from ambition, and so on. And then there is the freedom which is gained, we hope, at the end—at the end of the discipline, at the end of acquiring virtue, at the end of effort—the ultimate freedom we hope to get through doing certain things. So, the freedom that capacity gives, the freedom from something and the freedom we are supposed to gain at the end of a virtuous life—those are types of freedom we all know. Now are not those various freedoms merely reactions? When you say, "I want to be free from anger," that is merely a reaction; it is not freedom from anger. And the freedom which you think that you will get at the end of a virtuous life by struggle, by discipline—that is also a reaction to what has been. Please, sirs, follow this carefully because I am going to say something somewhat difficult in the sense that you are not accustomed to it. There is a sense of freedom which is not

from anything, which has no cause, but which is a state of being free. You see, the freedom that we know is always brought about by will, is it not? I will be free, I will learn a technique, I will become a specialist, I will study, and that will give me freedom. So we use will as a means of achieving freedom, do we not? I do not want to be poor and therefore I exercise my capacity, my will, everything to get rich. Or, I am vain and I exercise will not to be vain. So we think we shall get freedom through the exercise of will. But will does not bring freedom, on the contrary, as I will show you.

What is will? I will be, I must be, I must not be, I am going to struggle to become something, I am going to learn—all these are forms of exercising will. Now what is this will and how is it formed? Obviously, through desire. Our many desires, with their frustrations, compulsions, and fulfillments form, as it were, the threads of a cord, a rope. That is will, is it not? Your many contradictory desires together become a very strong and powerful rope with which you try to climb to success, to freedom. Now will desire give freedom, or is the very desire for freedom the denial of it? Please watch yourselves, sirs, watch your own desires, your own ambition, your own will. And if one has no will and is merely being driven, that also is a part of will—being driven is also part of that will, the will to resist and go with it—all that is part of will. Through that weight of desire, through that rope, we hope to climb to God, to bliss, or whatever it is.

So I am asking you whether your will is a liberating factor. Is freedom come by through will? Or, is freedom something entirely different, which has nothing to do with reaction, which cannot be achieved through capacity, through thought, experience, discipline, or constant conformity? That is what all the books say, do they not? Conform to the pattern and you will be free in the end; do all these things, obey, and ultimately there will be freedom. To me all that is sheer nonsense because freedom is at the beginning, not at the end, as I will show you.

To see something true is possible, is it not? You can see that the sky is blue—thousands of people have said so—but you can see that it is so for yourself. You can see for yourself, if you are at all sensitive, the movement of a leaf. From the very beginning there is the capacity to perceive that which is true instinctively, not through any form of compulsion, adjustment, conformity. Now, sirs, I will show you another truth.

I say that a leader, a follower, a virtuous man does not know love. I say that to you. You who are leaders, you who are followers, who are struggling to be virtuous—I say you do not know love. Do not argue with me for a moment; do not say, "Prove it to me." I will reason with you, show you, but first, please listen to what I have to say without being defensive, aggressive, approving, or denying. I say that a leader, a follower, or a man who is trying to be virtuous—such an individual does not know what love is. If you really listen to that statement not with an aggressive or submissive mind, then you will see the actual truth of it. If you do not see the truth of it, it is because you do not want to, or you are so supremely contented with your leadership, your following, or your so-called virtues that you deny everything else. But if you are at all sensitive, inquiring, open, as when looking out of a window, then you must see the truth of it, you are bound to. Now I will give you the reasons because you are all fairly reasonable, intellectual people, and you can be convinced. But you will never actually know the truth through intellect or reason. You will be convinced through reason, but being convinced is not the perception of what is true. There is a vast difference between the two. A man who is convinced of something is incapable of

seeing what is true. A man who is convinced can be unconvinced and convinced again in a different way. But a man who sees that which is true is not "convinced"; he sees that it just is true.

Now as I said, a leader who says, "I know the way, I know all about life, I have experienced the ultimate reality, I have the goods," obviously is very concerned about himself and his visions and about transmitting his visions to the poor listener; a leader wants to lead people to something which he thinks is right. So the leader, whether it is the political, the social, the religious leader, or whether it is your wife or husband—such a one has no love. He may talk about love, he may offer to show you the way of love, he may do all the things that love is supposed to do, but the actual feeling of love is not there because he is a leader. If there is love you cease to be a leader, for love exercises no authority. And the same applies to the follower. The moment you follow, you are accepting authority, are you not?—the authority which gives you security, a safe corner in heaven, or a safe corner in this world. When you follow, seeking security for yourself, your family, your race, your nation, that following indicates that you want to be safe, and a man who seeks safety knows no quality of love. And so also with the virtuous man. The man who cultivates humility surely is not virtuous. Humility is not a thing to be cultivated.

So, I am trying to show you that a mind that is sensitive, inquiring, a mind that is really listening can perceive the truth of something immediately. But truth cannot be "applied." If you see the truth, it operates without your conscious effort, of its own accord.

So, discontent is the beginning of freedom, and so long as you are trying to manipulate discontent, to accept authority in order that this discontent shall disappear, enter into safe channels, then you are already losing that pristine sense of real feeling. Most of us are discontented, are we not, either with our jobs, our relationships, or whatever we are doing. You want something to happen, to change, to move, to break through. You do not know what it is. There is a constant searching, inquiring, especially when one is young, open, sensitive. Later on, as you become old, you settle down in your habits, your job, because your family is safe, your wife will not run away. So this extraordinary flame disappears and you become respectable, petty, and thoughtless.

So, as I have been pointing out, freedom from something is not freedom. You are trying to be free from anger; I do not say you must not be free from anger, but I say that that is not freedom. I may be rid of greed, pettiness, envy, or a dozen other things, and yet not be free. Freedom is a quality of the mind. That quality does not come about through very careful, respectable searchings and inquiries, through very careful analysis, or putting ideas together. That is why it is important to see the truth that the freedom we are constantly demanding is always from something, such as freedom from sorrow. Not that there is no freedom from sorrow, but the demand to be free from it is merely a reaction and therefore does not free you from sorrow. Am I making myself clear? I am in sorrow for various reasons, and I say I must be free. The urge to be free of sorrow is born out of pain. I suffer because of my husband or my son or something else; I do not like that state I am in and I want to get away from it. That desire for freedom is a reaction; it is not freedom. It is just another desirable state I want in opposition to *what is*. The man who can travel around the world because he has plenty of money is not necessarily free, nor is the man who is clever or efficient, for his wanting to be free is again merely a reaction. So can I not see that freedom, liberation, cannot be learned or acquired or

sought after through any reaction? Therefore I must understand the reaction, and I must also understand that freedom does not come through any effort of will. Will and freedom are contradictory, as thought and freedom are contradictory. Thought cannot produce freedom because thought is conditioned. Economically you can, perhaps, arrange the world so that man can be more comfortable, have more food, clothing, and shelter; and you may think that is freedom. Those are necessary and essential things, but that is not the totality of freedom. Freedom is a state and quality of mind. And it is that quality we are inquiring into. Without that quality, do what you will, cultivate all the virtues in the world, you will not have that freedom.

So how is that sense of otherness, that quality of mind to come about? You cannot cultivate it because the moment you use your brain, you are using thought, which is limited. Whether it is the thought of the Buddha or anyone else, all thought is limited. So our inquiry must be negative; we must come to that freedom obliquely, not directly. Do you understand, sirs? Am I giving some indication, or none at all? That freedom is not to be sought after aggressively, is not to be cultivated by denials, disciplines, by checking yourself, torturing yourself, by doing various exercises, and all the rest of it. It must come without your knowing, like virtue. Cultivated virtue is not virtue; the virtue which is true virtue is not self-conscious. Surely a man who has cultivated humility, who because of his conceit, vanity, arrogance has made himself humble—such a man has no true sense of humility. Humility is a state in which the mind is not conscious of its own quality, as a flower which has fragrance is not conscious of its own perfume. So this freedom cannot be got through any form of discipline, nor can a mind which is undisciplined understand it. You use discipline to produce a result, but freedom is not a result.

If it is a result, it is no longer free because it has been produced.

So, how is the mind, which is full of multitudinous influences, compulsions, various forms of contradictory desires, the product of time, how is that mind to have the quality of freedom? You understand, sirs? We know that all the things that I have been talking about are not freedom. They are all manufactured by the mind under various stresses, compulsions, and influences. So, if I can approach it negatively, in the very awareness that all this is not freedom, then the mind is already disciplined—but not disciplined to achieve a result. Let us go into that briefly.

The mind says, "I must discipline myself in order to achieve a result." That is fairly obvious. But such discipline does not bring freedom. It brings a result because you have a motive, a cause which produces the result, but that result is never freedom, it is only a reaction. That is fairly clear. Now, if I begin to understand the operations of that kind of discipline, then in the very process of understanding, inquiring, going into it, my mind is truly disciplined. I do not know if you can see what I mean, quickly. The exercise of will to produce a result is called discipline; whereas, the understanding of the whole significance of will, of discipline, and of what we call result demands a mind that is extraordinarily clear and "disciplined," not by the will, but through negative understanding.

So, negatively, I have understood the whole problem of what is not freedom. I have examined it, I have searched my heart and my mind, the recesses of my being, to understand what freedom means, and I see that none of these things we have described is freedom because they are all based on desire, compulsion, will, on what I will get at the end, and they are all reactions. I see factually that they are not freedom. Therefore, because I have understood those things, my mind is open to find out or receive that which is free.

So, my mind has a quality which is not that of a disciplined mind seeking a result, not that of the undisciplined mind which wanders about, but it has understood, negatively, both *what is* and 'what should be', and so can perceive, can understand that freedom which is not from something, that freedom which is not a result. Sirs, this requires a great deal of inquiry. If you just repeat that there is a freedom which is not the freedom from something, it has no meaning. So please do not say it. Or if you say, "I want to get that other freedom," you are also on the wrong track, for you cannot. The universe cannot enter into the petty mind; the immeasurable cannot come to a mind that knows measurement. So our whole inquiry is how to break through the measurement—which does not mean I must go off to an ashram, become neurotic, devotional, and all that nonsense.

And here, if I may say so, what is important is the teaching and not the teacher. The person who speaks here at the moment is not important; throw him overboard. What is important is what is being said. So the mind only knows the measurable, the compass of itself, the frontiers, ambitions, hopes, desperation, misery, sorrows, and joys. Such a mind cannot invite freedom. All that it can do is to be aware of itself and not condemn what it sees; not condemn the ugly or cling to the beautiful, but see *what is*. The mere perception of *what is* is the beginning of the breaking down of the measurement of the mind, of its frontiers, its patterns—just to see things as they are. Then you will find that the mind can come to that freedom involuntarily, without knowing. This transformation in the mind itself is the true revolution. All other revolutions are reactions, even though they use the word *freedom* and promise utopia, the heavens, everything. There is only true revolution in the quality of the mind.

September 21, 1958

Sixth Talk in Poona

As this is the last talk, I am going to cover as much ground as possible. Most of us, I think, from childhood to maturity and even up to the grave are accustomed to being told what to do and what to think. Not only the society about us, but all our religious books, our governments, everybody tells us what to do and what to think, and it would be a great mistake if you expected the same thing from the speaker, because what is important is to find out for oneself what one thinks and from that find out what to do. It is essential, surely, to know oneself—not the self which is supposed to be beyond consciousness, which is described in various books, and so on, but the self that is within the limitations and the frontiers of consciousness. In the understanding of that everyday consciousness, in the unrolling of that extraordinary map, in venturing on the ocean of the unfolding self and seeing its whole significance, comes right action, which is true vocation. But if one does not know the ways of one's own mind, the ways of one's own thought, if one does not perceive the first reaction to every challenge, the first movement of thought to form a demand, if one leaves that first movement of the mind unexplored, unquestioned, without discovering the cause of the responses, then we shall be utterly lost in the verbal and theoretical activities of the mind.

Most of us are concerned with action, with what to do. There is so much sorrow, misery, and starvation, and what can the human being who is conscious of all this do about it? Is he to leave the reformation entirely to the government, or should he, as an individual, join an organization which will bring about a little more order, a more equal distribution of land, a little more happiness and beauty in life? That is one of our problems, is it not? Has true religion any relation to reformation? Has the really

religious man any relationship with politics and government? Or must he concern himself entirely with all the implications of that word *religion?*—which is not the same thing at all as organized religion, belief, dogma, ritual, the reading of sacred books, and doing nothing about it. All that is merely verbal enjoyment. The problem is, is it not, that one sees the misery in this world, the unemployment, the starvation, the appalling state of things, and what is one to do? Should one join a group to bring about reformation or is that the function of the government? Please, I am not asking you to do anything. We are just examining the whole problem of action because most of us want to do something in this world either in a limited, narrow sense or in a wider sense. To do something about it is a human, instinctual response, but there is a great deal of confusion which I am briefly exploring now—which does not mean that you must follow any of the things I say because to be a leader or a follower destroys human relationship. Neither a leader nor a follower can bring about a mind that is capable of affection, of love.

So one of our problems is action. We see this misery about us, and what should we do? Should one join a group to bring about reforms, or should one see to it that the government makes such laws, restrictions, and edicts as will bring about a right reformation? And why do the people who are dedicated to some kind of reform join hands with the politicians? Is it because they think that by joining hands with the government they can accelerate reformation, or is it because they are trying to fulfill themselves through reforms and through politics? Helping to bring about a reformation in society gives us an opportunity to expand ourselves, does it not? It gives us a chance to become important. Then we are somebody, in the religious as well as in the political field. But is that the function of the truly religious man? I hope you understand the question, sirs. It is the function of the government to pass laws against corruption, to see that there is no starvation, no war, no extremes of wealth and poverty, and when the government does not do it, is it your responsibility, as an individual, to see that there are politicians to do all this? Why should you or I take an interest in politics? I am not suggesting that you should dissociate yourselves from voting and all that business, but is it the duty of the religious man to enter the field of politics, which is concerned only with immediate results—to build a dam, to bring hydro-electric current all over the country, and so on? Is it the duty of the religious man, is it his job, his vocation, to enter into that field?

Now we want to do both, don't we? We want to be serious or so-called religious, and we also want to dabble in politics. So I am trying to find out what is the real function of a religious man. We know the function of the politician—not the crooked man, but the right kind of politician. It is his job to see that certain things are done, carried out, and that he himself is incorruptible. But what is a religious man, and if he is really religious, will he take part in politics, in the immediate reformation? Let us go into the question of what we mean by religion and the religious man. Obviously we do not mean the man who goes to the temple three times a day, nor the man who repeats a lot of words, nor the man who follows some doctrine like the savage gathering to himself all kinds of beliefs. And surely he is not a religious man who repeats what Shankara has said, or Buddha, or Christ; he merely spins words. Such a mind is a diseased mind. The religious man is he who, realizing his conditioning, is breaking through that conditioning. Such a man does not belong to any religion, he has no beliefs, follows no ritual, no dogma because he sees that dogma, ritual, belief are merely conditioning factors, the influences of

the society around him. Whether he lives in Russia, Italy, India, America, or anywhere else, the environment is conditioning him and influencing him to believe or not to believe. But the religious man is he who, through self-knowledge, begins to discover his conditioning and to break through it; and the breaking through is not a matter of time.

Now what do we mean by time? Sirs, I am describing but it is for you to experience, so do not say to yourself that you will listen very carefully in order to see whether Shankara, Christ, or Buddha says the same thing. We are discussing, you and I, as two individuals trying to find out for ourselves, and if you compare what you hear with what you have read, then you are not listening, then you are not experiencing as we go along. We are trying to discover what it is to be religious and whether the religious man is concerned with time as a means of arriving at virtue or as a means of conquering his disabilities, his afflictions. In examining this process of time, which is the distance between what we are and what we want to be, we say time is necessary. We say time is essential to cultivate virtue, time is necessary to free the mind from its conditioning, time is required to travel the distance from an idea to another idea, to the ideal. The distance from a point to a point, that is what we mean by time, whether it is chronological or psychological—chronological time means needing a whole lifetime or many lives, and psychological time means the 'I will arrive', 'I will be' state of mind. The 'will be' is time, is it not?

So, is time necessary in order to understand, or is understanding something that is immediate, something unrelated to time? Surely, if you are really listening, then time ceases. I do not know if you have ever experimented with the question of time. If you have, you will realize that all understanding is in the immediate present, and by the present I do not mean in opposition to the past or the future, but a mind that is completely attentive with an attention that has no causation, that does not wish to arrive somewhere. So I am trying to uncover that instantaneous understanding of the conditioning of the mind, and in that understanding break through the conditioning. That is what we are examining. I realize that my mind is conditioned by society and I want to know if time is necessary to break through that conditioning. Is time necessary in order to see, to understand something? Will I understand after two hours or by the end of the day or after many days, or do I understand something immediately? We generally think that time is necessary in order to understand. We rely on progress, we say, "Give me time, give me opportunity. Let me use discipline, grow, become, and at the end I will understand." That is the traditional, the religious, and the so-called human approach. And I ask myself if that is so. Is understanding really a matter of time, or is it a matter of the immediate present? If it is a matter of the immediate present, it means that the mind must be free of the idea that it will understand in the future. After all, when it says, "I will understand," the "will" is the time period. Now during that time period what actually happens? You go on in your own sweet way, do you not, carrying on with all your pleasures and pains because you really do not want to understand; but when you do want to understand, then the action is immediate. Please, this does not require time in which to think if what is said is true or not, but it requires a certain state of attention. I do not know if you have ever thought what we mean by yesterday, tomorrow, and today. In chronological time we know that yesterday was Tuesday, but it means also all the content of yesterday, and the memories, the experiences, the pleasures and unhappiness of the many, many yesterdays which condi-

tioned yesterday. And what do we mean by tomorrow? We mean all the past passing through today into the future which is somewhat modified, but which has the same content as yesterday. That is what we mean by yesterday, today, and tomorrow; yesterday, with all its struggles, efforts, and miseries, passing through today and coming to tomorrow, which is the future. And what is today? Is today merely a passage of yesterday to tomorrow?

Please, sirs, do listen, and you will see it. Is today merely the passage of yesterday through this thing called today and going on to tomorrow, or is today something entirely different? Is there not the timeless today, the feeing that today is dissociated with the past or with the future? But you cannot dissociate from the past if you are not dead to the past. If you carry the burden of yesterday through today and on to tomorrow, then there is no ending of yesterday. Then you only know a continuity, not an ending. I do not know if you have ever tried dying to something, ending. Have you ever tried dying to a pleasure? I know you have tried dying to sorrow, to a worry, to an unpleasant, irritating problem, but you have never died to a pleasure, have you? It is this pleasure of wanting, wanting to be different tomorrow, which is the reason for our continuity from yesterday through the present to tomorrow; it is as simple as that. So, is it possible to die to yesterday? Can I not die today to my property, my desires, my virtues, my ambitions, and all the petty little activities, put them away from me completely? Have you ever tried it? I am afraid you have not, and yet you talk in apprehension about dying in old age, whereas if you die to yesterday, there would be no fear of death in the tomorrow because there would be nothing to carry over to tomorrow of those things to which you are clinging. If you have really listened to this, you will have experienced that state of mind which is dead to yesterday.

Unfortunately most of you are being stimulated by me, but if you really do die to the past, even for a second, then that experience is the perceiving of something true, and that will act. As a poison will act of itself in your body, so the truth will act as a poison unless there is action in relation to that perception.

So a religious man, as I was saying, is concerned with freeing the mind from conditioning through self-knowledge, and we say that time is necessary to break the conditioning because the conditioning is not only at the conscious level but also at the unconscious level where there is the residue of the racial, family, and general human experience. Now must one go through all that process, or is there a way of really breaking through and understanding it immediately? That is the real crux of the problem. I say that there is a way of doing it immediately and that there is no other way. The desire for another day is the allocation of time for the mind to continue merely playing with the idea of being free from conditioning. To realize that the mind is conditioned and is a prisoner in that conditioning requires attention, and it is that attention, that immediate perception which frees the mind. Such a man is not concerned with reforms, for all reforms are within the field of time. So I am talking of the man who is not concerned with bureaucracy, administration, and all the immediate reforms and edicts but who is concerned—however much he may make a mistake—with truth, whose primary interest is that. Such a mind has no authority either over somebody else or over itself. It is not out to guide people, it is not out to tell people what to think, whether there is a God or no God. Such a mind is concerned with helping man to free himself from his own conditioning, and I say such a man is a religious man. You may ask, what has such a man to do with society which needs reformation, purgation? I say that the religious man will be the most important fac-

tor because he is the revolution. It is not that he will bring about a revolution but that he himself is in a state of revolution. I leave it to you to think out the difference.

Most of us see all these things either clearly or in confusion, but we can see that to extricate oneself from conditioning raises the problem of fear. Is it not so? Fear is something which exists not by itself but only in relation to something else. I am afraid of public opinion; I am afraid that someone might discover my foolishness; I am afraid of death, of losing my job, of not being an important person. And it is this feeling of fear which creates confusion in the mind, nothing else. Being confused, we try to solve the problems which the confusion has created. Instead of going to the cause, we try to reform the effects, whereas if we examine it very closely, we will discover that the cause and the effect are not separate. The cause is not here and the effect over there; cause-effect are always together. So confusion or the lack of clarity of thought is brought about by fear.

Let us look at it again. What is the cause of confusion? Take a very simple thing. I must act, and I want to do good in the world. I know that the government is supposed to do good in the world, but I myself want to be religious, and I also want to be powerful, saying I want to help. Actually I want a Rolls Royce, and all the rest of it, do I not? So ambition, wanting to fulfill, is the cause of confusion not only in the religious but in the political field as well. The search for fulfillment is the cause of fear and confusion. Confusion does not come suddenly out of the sky; it comes because of various causes. So as our minds are confused, what is the cause of it? If one were able to think clearly, there would be no sense of confusion. If my mind were very clear, not clear about something, but in a state of clarity, there would be no confusion. I hope you understand the difference between the mind being clear about something and being clear in itself. So, out of the cause comes confusion; the confusion does not come first and then the cause. We are talking about fear, and I say that fear comes because we want to fulfill. I need not describe what I mean by fulfillment—the sense of my family, self-importance, being the big fish in a little pond, the powerful politician, the great saint, using any avenue through which I can expand myself. And so long as I want to be the chief man in the little town, there is always the fear that you will want to be the same. And so we begin to compete, and I am always anxious, and all the rest of it. So fear begins. So long as there is the desire to be something, there must be fear, and that fear causes confusion. I do not say it is the chief cause, but it is one of the causes.

I am going to examine what we mean by fear, but please do not merely listen to the words. You know what you are afraid of, do you not? You are afraid of losing your job, of your wife becoming ill, or you love someone and that person does not love you, or you fear death. If you are at all alert, you can see for yourself what you are afraid of. Please watch your own fear as I describe it. Now what do we mean by fear? Let us take death for an example. What does fear of death mean? It means I am afraid of the future, I am afraid of what might be, I am afraid of coming to an end. That fear exists in time. The thought of tomorrow and of me not being something in the tomorrow, the future, brings fear. That is, thought creates fear by thinking of tomorrow. Is that not so? I am a dishonest man, and I cover it up because I do not want you to discover it, and I am afraid you might. I am afraid that you might see through me sometime—which is again in the future. Fear is of time. Whereas, if I can say, "Yes, I am dishonest, and I do not mind your discovering it now"—then I abolish

time, and there is no more fear. There is only the fact. When I know the fact, there is no fear. But in being confused about the fact, and in trying to change the fact into what I think it should be, according to my fancy, fear begins. If I know I am a liar, a greedy man, there is no fear. It is so. But if I try to cover up a lie and try to be something else, then fear begins. Therefore the desire to change without understanding the actual fact, without looking fully at the fact but merely wishing it to be something else, that is the beginning of fear—in which is involved time and the desire to achieve. So you have fear which causes confusion. Unless you eradicate fear you cannot be free of confusion. Understanding fear implies understanding the process of the mind, the self, and how it creates the thing called time. Which means that thought creates time. I am not talking of chronological time in the sense of the train going at 9:30. I am talking of the process of fear, of the self that creates time in order to be something in the future, and in that process there is frustration and sorrow. And in order to escape from that sorrow, you invent all sorts of nonsense, myths, and live in a state of illusion and fear.

So we come to the point, which is: Can the mind look at the fact without the desire to change the fact? I am greedy, I am envious—envy is a part of greed, is it not? Can I look at the fact that I am envious? Please, sirs, look at it. Do not merely listen to me, but look at the fact, if you can. Then you will see how extraordinarily difficult it is to look at anything, to know that you are violent, to know it in the sense that you see that you are violent. When you do not compare, condemn, or justify yourself with regard to it, is there not understanding of the fact and therefore a fundamental change in the fact itself? That is, I am violent. Can I look at it without any sense of avoidance, can I attend to it? I have explained before what I mean by attention. Attention is not of time, it is not saying, "I must attend," or "I will cultivate it," which requires time. But the mind that says, "I must see this thing," acts, looks. When you are really interested in something, when your whole life depends on it, you give complete attention.

So the mind that is capable of freeing itself from its conditioning is really freeing itself from the known, is it not? The mind is put together by the known, in which there is suffering, pleasure, and the desire for fulfillment. The mind is all that; it is the result of time. The mind works within the field of the known. These are obvious psychological facts. Thought can only function in the field of the known because thought is the result of the known, the reaction of the past, of experiences which have been stored up. The mind is the bank of memory, of associations, and from that there comes the response. The response is thinking.

So thinking is within the field of the known, and within that field and from that field, it tries to find out what the unknown is. That is impossible. I sit here and wish to know what is beyond that hill. Someone sees it and describes it, and I sit here and read books about it and say it is Buddha, Shankara, Christ, and begin to speculate. So all knowledge is within the field of the known, and from that center you try to move into the unknown. You cannot. You cannot invite the unknown, the immeasurable, that which is inconceivable, into the known. That is why the mind must free itself from the known, the known being all the memories, the experiences, the pains, sorrows, desires, and the will—all the psychological accumulations. Then you will see that freedom from your conditioning is not a matter of time. Conditioning is to be broken through immediately. Understanding is in the present only, in the immediate. And there is no understanding because you are not giving your

full attention. Do not say, "How am I to give full attention?" for then you are barking up the wrong tree. Then you will seek a system which will cripple the mind further. No system is going to free the mind, but what will free the mind from its own knowledge is the understanding of the immediate reaction to a challenge. If I ask you, "Do you believe in God?" your response is immediate. Go into that response. Find out why you answer that way. If you go into that one response, you will uncover the whole thing. If you would understand *what is,* that which is immeasurable, it is essential that the mind be free from the known—the known of Shankara, Buddha, Christ, the known of every book, every thought, every experience. The mind must be empty, but not vague, blank, mesmerized into vacancy. The mind must be purgated of all the past, not only of its sorrows, but also of its pleasures, and that means enormously hard work—much harder than the practice of any discipline in the world. Because it requires attention from moment to moment so that the mind does not accumulate. You see a beautiful sunset and there is a tremendous feeling of loveliness, and the mind holds on to that experience as an accumulation. And if you are not attentive, you have given soil for that experience to take root and abide. Therefore it becomes of the known. Unless there is full attention, every experience engenders the soil in which it can abide.

This attention you will not get through any practice, through any meditation. It is there, if you are interested, if you have eyes to see, if you say, "I must find out." Then you will see that such a mind is the unknown. All this I have been talking about is not a theory, it is not something for you to learn and repeat. It is something for you to go into. It is a field in which you have to work; you cannot learn from me. There is no teacher, no guru for this. You have to see,

you have to suffer, you have to travel the unknown sea by yourself, in yourself, and that
requires enormous work, it demands attention, and where there is attention there is
love.

September 24, 1958

Madras, India, 1958

--- ✳ ---

First Talk in Madras

I think it is quite important, if we are to understand each other, that we establish the lines of right communication between ourselves, because if we do not have the means of communion with each other, we shall never come to a full comprehension of what we are talking about, or be in any position to agree or disagree. I think it is fairly important to find out for ourselves what we mean by listening. Are we only capable of really listening to another when something is urgently demanded of us or when circumstances force us to do so, when there is a necessity? If we see that all our life depends on definite understanding, then we are wholly all there, and we listen with eager attention, and then between the speaker and the one who listens there is established a right communication. Obviously you are here to listen to something, and I want to say something, but how are we to establish the right communication between yourself and myself? It is really very important, so please do not just brush it aside and say, "Well, talk, and we will see if we can understand." I do not think it is quite as easy as that because what is important is not only what I have to say but also how you listen to what I have to say, if there is to be real communication.

If you translate what I say in terms of your own ideas and opinions, or according to your own prejudices and conditioning, obviously there is no communication. Then you are listening to your own opinions, to your own ideas. So if you want to listen, it is essential, is it not, to first find out what the speaker has to say. You must find out if what he has to say is logical, reasonable, sufficiently clear to be applicable to the problems with which one is confronted, or whether he speaks from a particular prejudice and argues from that point of view to a certain conclusion, and so on. But it seems very difficult to listen because I have talked for over thirty years, here and all over the world, and apparently it seems as if it is almost impossible to communicate what I have to say. It is quite a phenomenon.

So what prevents the understanding of what another says, and can you and I understand each other? For most of us listening is merely a habit, is it not? You come to a meeting and you listen, but what actually takes place when you are listening? First of all you have certain opinions about the speaker, certain conclusions, he has a reputation of some kind, you like his face or you dislike this or that, so you are listening, really, not to him but to what your opinions are about him or to what you think yourself. If you watch yourselves, your own way of listening, you will soon find out that actually you are not listening at all; one is translating what one hears according to what is most convenient to hear, what one wants to hear, and so on. So there is a barrier, and when you say you are listening, you are really not listening at all.

So I feel it is very important for us to remove that barrier. And I assure you that it is one of the most difficult things—to be able to listen to another without any of these mental interruptions, without any form of translation, interpretation, comparison; just to listen. Then we shall establish a communion with each other; then we will get at the heart of the matter and not merely argumentatively stick at words. So I hope we can listen to each other in that way because I think that in the true act of listening, there is a miracle. If I know how to listen to what another has to say, then I go beyond the words, then I capture his meaning. But I must first listen; then I can agree or disagree, then I can see the falseness or the truth in what he says. So I must have the capacity not to project my own ideas, my opinions, my conclusions, my experiences, for these act as a barrier to that comprehension. So if I may suggest, please listen in that manner if you can. It is one of the most difficult things; it is an art.

You cannot learn to play a violin in a day, and similarly you cannot listen rightly immediately because you have never listened before. I don't know if you have ever tried to listen to anybody—to your wife, your husband, your neighbor, to a politician, to an authority—have you ever really listened? If you try you will find out how extraordinarily difficult it is. In listening you will begin to discover whether what is being said is false or true, you will find out from what source or from what background the speaker is talking, what is the fullness of his thought, whether it has reason, intelligence, and sense, or whether he is merely projecting his own prejudices, his temporary reactions.

Listening does not demand concentration; when you concentrate there is no understanding; when you concentrate you are forcing yourself to listen, are you not? You listen only when there is a sense of freedom, when the mind is relaxed, observing. Then there is a possibility of learning. What I have to say is not merely the communication of certain information, knowledge, but if we can learn, then we shall be able to face all our problems. Then we shall be able to learn about the problem. I feel that we have got so many problems in life that unless we learn about these problems, we shall never be able to resolve them. We have to learn, not how to meet the problem, but about the nature of the problem itself.

Now what is the state of the mind that learns? That is, if I have a problem—economic, social, religious, they are innumerable—and if I know how to learn about a problem, then I can resolve the problem. But if I come to the problem with a mind that already desires to resolve it in a certain way, or if the problem has innumerable complications and side issues which I do not follow, then I shall not be able to meet it fully. I can only meet it when I am capable of learning all about it. I don't know if I am explaining what I want to say.

I hope you see the difference between a mind that accumulates knowledge and a mind that learns. Learning is a living process; it is not an additive process. I am going to go into this very carefully, and you will see presently that a mind that accumulates knowledge cannot learn. To learn, the mind must be free, capable of swift movement, but a mind that is accumulating is not capable of swift movement; it has a fixed point from which it moves. You will see, as we go along, that to understand the problems of our existence we must approach the matter totally. I am using that word *totally* to indicate that our approach must not be through departments, not as a technician, an engineer, a scientist, a lawyer, a scholar, a politician, and so on, but we must approach life as a whole because life is all these things. Life is earning a livelihood, life is the constant battle in relationship, life is beauty as well as ugliness, life is the sense of adjustment to all things. So to approach a problem we must come to it totally, not as a specialized entity. That being so, let us look at what is taking place in the world, because what you are, the world is, from what you think, you create the world; you are part of the world, not separate from the world; your problems are the world's problems—the world being your neighbor and the neighbor being he who is next door or ten thousand miles away.

Now what is taking place in the world, what is actually happening? There is overpopulation, there is overorganization, there is mass communication. Through these things the human mind is being controlled. When there is overpopulation, inevitably there is confusion with a curtailing, conditioning, limiting of thought—which is what is happening in India. There is overpopulation in this country, and so there is enormous confusion, deterioration, corruption; and to control this corruption, this deterioration, there must inevitably be a dictatorship controlling the mind of man. And over-organization also tends to bring about control of man and his thought; and through mass communication—the radio, newspapers, politicians, television—you are being influenced and therefore controlled. So through every channel of existence, every channel of perception, we are being shaped, conditioned, controlled. Society, religions, books, newspapers, magazines, organizations—whether they are spiritual or not spiritual—economics, politics, everything is influencing man and shaping him according to certain ideas, opinions, concepts. I do not know if you are aware of all this. If you are at all thoughtful, you must be aware of what is taking place, not only in Russia or in China, but throughout the world. What you think—as a Hindu, Buddhist, Christian, Catholic, and all the rest of it—is really conditioning your mind to a particular type of thought, habit, symbol, activity, and social relationship. That is obvious, is it not? That is so natural that we accept it as inevitable. It is an irrefutable fact that what you think, what you feel is shaped by your environment. Everything—books, teachers, environment, food, climate—shapes your thought, and as society becomes more and more organized, the conditioning of the mind is deepened. This is a fact whether you like it or not.

When you realize that fact, then the question arises as to what place the individual has in relation to that process of conditioning. Please, we are not arguing about this; we are trying to learn about it—about the fact that you are influenced by everything, by the past and by the present which creates the future. In relation to that fact, where is the individual? Is there an individual at all? It is very important to discover this, very important for each one of us to learn about it, to learn whether you are really an individual or merely the expression of conditioned thought, influenced through the centuries and therefore thinking in a particular way so that the individual has really ceased to be altogether. I hope you see the point.

The dictators want to eradicate free thought, not only the dictators in Russia or in China, but the dictators in this country and everywhere, because the moment you are able to think for yourself, you are a danger to society, according to their point of view. And so education, religion, social influences, radio, and television tell us what to think, and we repeat their opinions, arguments, and counter arguments. You read the Gita or the Bible and you repeat, or you read Marx and you repeat, taking sides, agreeing or opposing.

So, seeing all this, is there an individual at all? If there is not, then how is an individual to be created? I do not know if I am communicating what I want to say. I feel we are not individuals at all. Though you may have a different body from another, a different face, a different form, you are the mass. You are a communist, socialist, capitalist; you belong to certain categories, professions, callings. You have certain functions, and you identify yourself with those functions or with the job, the capacity, and you cease to be an individual. Obviously, to be an individual there must be freedom, total freedom which means an action which is not the reaction of a conditioning. I hope you follow this.

Now what is freedom? We only know the freedom from something, do we not? Freedom from anger, slavery, oppression, freedom from the wife, the husband, and so on. We only know the freedom from something in order to be something else, do we not? I only want to be free of my anger to be something different. That is all we know about freedom. So freedom is a reaction, is it not? That is, I am a prisoner and I want to escape. The wanting to escape is a reaction from being a prisoner, and that reaction I call freedom. So, as far as we are concerned, freedom factually is a reaction. But surely freedom in itself is not a reaction. If it is, it ceases to be freedom. Please think about it and do not say, "You are talking nonsense," but let us find out about it, learn about it.

So seeing what is taking place in the world, we realize that the individual has ceased to exist, and the question is how is the individual to be created anew? People see the need for this. The reformers, the socialists, many people say we must create a society which will produce a new type of individual, we must create the environment which will bring about such an entity. Perhaps I am oversimplifying it, but all reformers, all social revolutionaries have said, "Let us create an environment which will produce the individual who will be free and therefore creative." To me that is a false ideal altogether. Because if the individual is merely the product of environment, then however magnificent, however orderly, however beautiful the society may be, the individual will still only be a made-up thing, a result. He may be more clever, more kind, and this and that, but he is still essentially a product, and therefore he ceases to be an individual. If you observe, the real individual is never a slave to the environment, he dominates it or he leaves it and goes away; he is not a plaything of environment and environment does not shape his thinking. We see that, but we say that they are exceptions, and leave it at that. That is merely a good excuse. It is a way of not really tackling the problem—to say that those people are exceptions, God-sent, or whatever it is, and that we are not capable.

So the reformer has not solved the problem and never will. He is concerned with the reformation of society to produce the right individual, but the right individual is not the product of society; he is totally free of society. He dominates, breaks through the conditioning of his environment; he acts upon society; society does not act upon him.

So seeing all this—seeing how the mind is shaped by every social, religious, and economic influence, seeing that with every form of dictatorship there is tyranny, and also seeing that the social reformers, the economic revolutionaries hope by creating the right environment to produce the right individual—seeing all this, do you not ask yourself how a right individual can come into being, an individual who is not the plaything of circumstances? Perhaps this is the first time you have asked yourself this question, and if you are really inquiring into this, what is the answer? I hope you understand the problem because unless you are very clear about the problem, your answer will not be clear.

Perhaps I can put it differently. Our minds are conditioned; that is a fact. There are multitudinous ways of being conditioned and the mere reformation of that conditioning will not bring about the true individual. Every well-organized, efficient society must condition thought, and whether they do it brutally or with kid gloves, it is the same thing; they must condition thought. So seeing all this, how is one to be an individual? Because if you are not an individual, there cannot be a creative society.

You see, if you are not an individual you are bound to create more confusion, more sorrow, more problems for yourself and for society—which again is an obvious fact. So how are you to become an individual, how are you to be the individual who is not driven by circumstances, who is not influenced by society, who is not controlled by the politician, and all the rest of it? How is such an individual to come into being? If that were your problem, how would you set about it? If you are interested in this, as you must be since you are supposed to be intelligent, supposed to be concerned with religious matters, with society, and so on, how will you tackle this problem? How will you be that individual? This is really a very important question because it is only such an individual who will find reality, it is only such an individual who will find if there is God, or no God, it is only such an individual who will be free of time and who will discover the immeasurable. Others can talk about the immeasurable, God, the timeless, and all the rest of it, but they only deal in words. What they say has no meaning because they are like so many parrots merely repeating what they have been told.

So our problem is the mind. The mind which is conditioned, which is shaped, which is the plaything of every influence, every culture, the mind which is the result of the past, burdened with innumerable memories, experiences—how is such a mind to free itself from all this and be a total individual? I say it is only possible when there is serious, earnest study of oneself—the self being not the atma or some so-called higher self because those again are just words. I am talking of the self of everyday existence, the self that gets angry, the self that is ambitious, that gets hurt, that wants to be seen, that is very keen, that says, "I must be secure; I must consider my position," and so on. That is the only self we have. The higher self, the super-atma is only an ideology, a concept, an unreality; and it is no good going after unreality, for that leads to delusion. I know all the sacred books talk about the super-atma, whatever that is, and for the man who is caught in the daily self, it is a marvelous escape. The more he speculates, the more he writes about it, the more religious he thinks he is. But I say that if you can go into the self which we all know, the self of everyday movement, then through that self-knowledge, through careful analysis, careful observation, you will find that you are capable of breaking away from all influences which condition thought.

Another thing is that thought, by the very thinking process, conditions itself. Is it not so? Whatever thought you have affects the mind, and it is necessary to understand this. Whether the thought is good or bad, ugly or beautiful, subtle or cunning—whatever thought it be, it shapes the mind. So what is thinking? Thinking, surely, is reaction—the reaction of what you know. Knowledge reacts, and we call it thinking. Please observe it, sir, and think it out; we will go into it again and again. If you are alert, aware of your own process of thinking, you will see that whatever you think has already shaped the mind; and a mind that is shaped by thought has ceased to be free, and therefore it is not a mind that is individual.

So self-knowledge is not a process of the continuity of thinking but the diminishing, the ending of thinking. But you cannot end thinking by any trick, by denial, by control, by discipline, and so on. If you do, you are still caught in the field of thought. Thinking can only come to an end when you know the total content of the thinker, and so one begins to see how important it is to have self-knowledge. Most of us are satisfied with superficial self-knowledge, with scratching on the surface, the ordinary ABC of psychology; it is no good to read a few books on psychology, scratch a little, and say you know. That is merely applying to the mind what you have learned. Therefore you must begin to inquire as to what is learning. Do you not see, sir, the relationship between self-knowledge and learning? A mind that has self-knowledge is learning, whereas a mind that merely applies acquired knowledge to itself and thinks it is self-knowledge is merely accumulating. A mind that accumulates can never learn. Please do not agree with me, but observe. Do you ever learn? Have you found out yet whether you learn anything, or whether you just accumulate information?

I said just now that without self-knowledge there is no individuality, and I have explained what I mean by individuality, the individual. I say that without self-knowledge there is no individual. You have heard that statement, and what is your reaction to it? You say, do you not, "What do you mean by that?" That is, you say, "Explain and I will either agree or disagree with you," and you say afterwards that you have learned something—but is that learning? Is learning a matter of agreement or disagreement? Can you not inquire into that statement without agreement or disagreement? Surely you want to find out if that statement is false or true—not whether you agree or disagree. No one cares if you agree or disagree, but if you find out for yourself whether that statement has truth in it or not, then you are beginning to actually see, to learn.

So a mind that agrees or disagrees, that comes to a conclusion, is not capable of learning. That is, a specialized mind is never a creative mind. The mind that has accumulated, the mind that is steeped in knowledge, such a mind is incapable of learning. To learn there must be a freshness; there must be a mind that says, "I do not know, but I am willing to learn. Show me," and if there is no one to show, it begins to inquire of itself. It does not start from a fixed point and move to another fixed point. That is what we do, isn't it? We come to a conclusion, and from that fixed point we think more and move to another conclusion. And this process we call learning. But if you observe you will see that you are tied to a post and merely move to another post, and I say that is not learning at all. Learning demands a mind that is willing to learn but not in order to add to itself. Because the moment you are engaged in adding to yourself, you have ceased to learn. So self-knowledge is not a process of addition. What you are learning is about the self, about the ways of the mind. You are learning of its cunningness, its subtleties, its motives, its extraordinary capacities, its depth, its vastness; and to learn you must come to it with enormous humility. A man who has accumulated knowledge can never know humility. He may talk about humility, he may quote about humility, but he has no sense of humility. The man who learns is essentially humble.

So we have this problem of bringing about the true individual. Such an individual cannot be created except through self-knowledge, and you have to learn about the self. There cannot be any condemnation of what you find and there cannot be any identification with what you find, for any identification, justification, or condemnation is the result of accumulation, and therefore you cease to learn. Please do see the importance of this. It may sound very contradictory, but it is not. If you will observe you will see how necessary it is to learn, and to learn there must be a sense of complete humility, and there is no humility if there is condemnation of what you see in yourself. Similarly, if you see something good and identify yourself with that, then you cease to learn. So a mind that is capable of learning is the true individual mind, not the mind that has accumulated. At present we are all the time adding to our accumulations.

For instance, have you ever examined what experience is? Observe, sirs, do not just listen to me but watch your mind and go into it as I am talking. When you say, "I have had an experience," what do you mean by that? Experience means, does it not, a sensation, a reaction which is recognizable. I recognize that I am having a pleasurable experience or a painful one. I recognize it because I have had a similar experience before. So the previous experiences condition the present experience. It is not a fresh experience. If it is a new experience, it is immediately recognized and translated and put into the old. So, every experience conditions the mind because all experience is recognized by means of previous experience. So, experience is never a liberating factor.

While the whole world is developing technicians, specialists, with every thought shaped and conditioned, there is no possibility of anyone being an individual. The possibility of being an individual comes only when you begin to understand and learn about yourself, not through books because the self—what you are—cannot be understood through someone else. You have to observe it yourself, and you can observe it with clarity, with strength and purposive directive-

ness only in relationship. The way you behave, the way you talk, how you look at a flower, a tree, the way you speak to a servant, the movement of your hands, your eyes—everything will show, if you are at all aware, how your mind works, and the mind is the self. It can invent the super-self or it can invent the hell, but it is still the mind.

So, unless the mind understands itself, there is no freedom. Freedom cannot come by accumulation. You have to learn what an extraordinary thing the mind is. It is the most marvelous thing we have, but we don't know how to use it; we only use it at certain levels, specialized self-centered levels. It is a magnificent instrument, a living thing of which we still know very little. We only know the superficial stretches, the thin layers of consciousness, but we do not know the total being of the mind, the extraordinary depths; and you cannot know it merely by speculating about it. You can only learn about it, and to learn you must give total attention. Attention is different from concentration. Concentration merely narrows the mind, but attention is a state in which everything is.

So, what is of importance for a religious man is not the repetition of what he has learned from books or the experiences which his conditioning has projected, but his being concerned with the understanding of himself—without any delusion, without any warping, without any twist—to see things in himself as they are. And to see things as they actually are is an enormous task. I do not know if you have ever done it. I do not know if you have ever observed anything without coloring it, without twisting it, without naming it. I suggest you try, for a change, to look at what you call greed or envy, and see how difficult it is to look at it because the very word *greed, envy,* carries with it a condemnatory significance. You may be a greedy man, an ambitious man, but to look at ambition, the feeling, the sensation, without condemning it, just to look at it requires, as you will see, extraordinary capacity.

All this is a part of self-knowledge, and without self-knowledge, do what you will, reform, have every kind of revolution, super-leaders, super-politicians, you will never create a world in which the individual becomes a total being and so can influence society. So if you are interested in this, then we will go into it very, very seriously. But if you only want to go into it superficially, please do not come; it is much better not to come. It is far better to have a few people who are really serious than many who are followers. What is necessary is earnestness, an earnest mind that begins to inquire within itself. Such a mind will find for itself that which is real.

October 22, 1958

Second Talk in Madras

I think it would be good if we could—you and I—quietly by ourselves, as two human beings together, talk over our problems. I think we should get much further if we had that feeling, than by thinking of this as an audience being addressed by a speaker. That is, if you and I could go into some corner, a quiet room, and explore our problems, I think we would get very much further, but unfortunately that is not possible. There are too many people and time is very limited. So one resorts to a large audience, and invariably one has to generalize, and in the process of generalization, the particularities, the details have to be omitted, naturally. But for most of us the generalities seem to have very little significance and the particular problem, the particular issue, the particular conflict seems all-important. One forgets the wider, deeper issues because one is forcibly faced with one's own little everyday problems.

So in discussing, in talking together, I think we must bear in mind both these issues,

not only the general, but also the particular. The wider and deeper issues escape most of us, but without understanding these, the approach to the little problems, the petty trivialities, the everyday conflict will have very little meaning. I think we must see this very clearly right at the beginning—that if one would solve the everyday problems of existence, whatever they may be, one must first see the wider issues and then come to the detail. After all, the great painter, the great poet is one who sees the whole—who sees all the heavens, the blue skies, the radiant sunset, the tree, the fleeting bird—all at one glance; with one sweep he sees the whole thing. With the artist, the poet, there is an immediate, a direct communion with this whole marvelous world of beauty. Then he begins to paint, to write, to sculpt; he works it out in detail. If you and I could do the same, then we should be able to approach our problems—however contradictory, however conflicting, however disturbing—much more liberally, more wisely, with greater depth and color, feeling. This is not mere romantic verbalization but actually it is so, and that is what I would like to talk about now and every time we get together. We must capture the whole and not be carried away by the detail, however pressing, immediate, anxious it may be. I think that is where the revolution begins. Please bear in mind that I am not talking as to a large audience but that I am talking, if I may respectfully say so, to you, to each one. And I hope we can understand that first principle of the immediate and the fundamental issue.

After all, we have many problems, not only the individual, personal problems, but also the collective problems, as starvation, war, peace, and the terrible politicians. I am using the word *terrible* in the verbal sense and I am not condemning them. They are superficial people who talk of these problems as though they can solve the whole thing in a nutshell. And our own personal problems are the problems of relationship, of our job, of fulfillment and frustration, of fear, love, beauty, sex, and so on.

Now, what happens with most of us is that we try to solve these problems separately, each one by itself. That is, I have a problem of fear and I try to solve it. But I will never be able to solve it by itself because it is related to a very, very complex issue, to a wider field, and without understanding the deeper problem, merely to tackle the particular trouble—one corner of the field instead of the whole—only creates more problems. I hope I am making this point clear. If we can establish that—you and I as two people in communication with each other—then I think we shall have resolved a great deal because, after all, understanding is that, is it not? What does it mean, to understand something? It means, does it not, to grasp the significance of the thing totally. Otherwise there is no understanding, there is only intellection, merely a verbalization, the play of the mind. Without understanding the totality of your being, merely to take one layer of that being and try to solve it separately, in a watertight compartment unrelated to the totality, only leads to further complications, further misery. If we can really understand that, really feel the truth of it, then we shall be able to find out how to tackle our individual, immediate problems.

After all, sirs, it is like this. You never see the sky if you are looking through a window; you only see part of the sky, obviously. You must go outside to see the whole vast horizon, the limitless sky. But most of us view the sky through the window, and from such a narrow, limited outlook, we think we can solve not only one particular problem but all our problems. That is the curse of society, of all organizations. But if you can have that feeling of the necessity of the comprehension of the whole—whatever that whole is, and we will go into that—then the mind has already a different outlook, a different capacity.

If that is very clearly established between you and me, as two individuals, not as a listener and a talker, not as a guru and a disciple—all that nonsense is wiped away, at least so far as I am concerned—then we can proceed. So what is the issue, the wide, profound issue? If I can see the totality of it, then I will be able to tackle the detail. Now I may put it into words, but the word is not the thing. The word *sky* is not the sky, is it? The word *door* is not the door. We must be very clear to differentiate between the word and the fact, the word and the thing itself. The word *freedom* is not the state of freedom, and the word *mind* is not the actual thing, which is really totally indescribable. So again, if you are very clear that the word is not the thing, then we can proceed with our communication. Because I want to convey something to you and you want to understand, but if you merely hold onto the words and not to the significance, then there is a barrier in communication.

So, what is that thing which, being understood, being explored, having its significance fully grasped, will help us to unravel and resolve the detail? Surely, it is the mind, is it not? Now when I use that word *mind*, each one of you will interpret it differently according to your education, your culture, your conditioning. When I use the word mind, obviously you must have a reaction to that word, and that reaction depends upon your reading, your environmental influences, how much or how little you have thought about it, and so on. So what is the mind? If I can understand the workings of that extraordinary thing called the mind, the totality of it, the feeling, the nature, the amazing capacity of it, its profundity, width, and quality, then whatever its reaction—which is merely the product of its culture, environment, education, reading, and so on—I can tackle it. So what we are going to do, if we can, is to explore this thing called the mind. But you cannot explore it, obviously, if you already have an idea about it. If you say, "The mind is atma," it is finished. You have stopped all exploration, investigation, inquiry. Or if you are a communist and say that the mind is merely the result of some influence, then also you are incapable of examining. It is very important to understand that if you approach a problem with a mind already made up, you have stopped investigating the problem and therefore prevented the understanding of the problem. The socialist, the capitalist, the communist, who approaches the problem of starvation, does so with a system, a theory, and so what happens? He is incapable of making a further examination of the problem. Life does not stop. It is a movement, and if you approach it with a static mind, you cannot touch it. Again this is fairly clear, is it not, so let us proceed.

When I use the word *mind* I look at it without any conclusion; therefore, I am capable of examining it, or rather, the mind, having no conclusion about itself, is capable of looking at itself. A mind that starts to think from a conclusion is not really thinking. It is asking an enormous thing, is it not, for the mind to examine a problem without any conclusion. I do not know if you see this—that with most of us thinking starts from a conclusion, a conclusion that there is God or no God, reincarnation or no reincarnation, that the communist system will save the world, or the capitalist. We start from one conclusion and go to another, and this process of moving from conclusion to conclusion we call thinking; and if you observe it, it is not thinking at all. Thinking implies a constant moving, a constant examination, a constant awareness of the movement of thought, not a fixed point from which to go to another fixed point.

So we are going to find out what this extraordinary thing called the mind is, because that is the problem and nothing else. It is the mind that creates the problem; it is the thought, the conditioned mind, the mind that is petty, narrow, bigoted, which has created beliefs, ideas, and knowledge, and which is crippled by its own concepts, vanities, greeds, ambitions, and frustrations. So it is the mind which has to be understood, and that mind is the 'me', that mind is the self—not some higher self. The mind invents the higher self and then says it is only a tool for the higher. Such thinking is absurd, immature. It is the mind which invents all these avenues of escape and then proceeds from there to assert.

So, we are going to find out what the mind is. Now you cannot find out from my description. I am going to talk about it, but if you merely recognize it through the description, then you are not knowing the state of your own mind. I hope you understand this. Now, I say the state of the mind is beauty, and that without knowing beauty, without the full comprehension of the feeling of beauty, without having beauty, you will never understand the mind. I have made that statement and you have heard it. Then what happens? Your mind says, "What is beauty?" does it not? Then you begin to argue with yourself, to find words so that through a definition you may feel the beauty. So you depend on words to evoke a feeling, is that not so? I am inquiring what this extraordinary mind is, which is the product of time, the product of many thousands of years. Do not jump to the idea of reincarnation. The mind is the product of many yesterdays, is it not? It is the result of a thousand influences, it is the result of tradition, it is the result of habit, it is put together by various cultures. It knows despair and hope. It knows the past, it is the present, and it creates the future. It has accumulated knowledge, the sciences of technology, of physics, of medicine, and countless other pursuits; it is capable of extraordinary invention. It is also capable of inquiring beyond itself, of searching for freedom and breaking through its conditioning. It is all these things and much more. And if the mind is not aware of itself, of the extraordinary complexities, merely concentrating on any detail, on one particularity, will destroy the totality.

Please, I hope you are listening with care because if you do not listen rightly, you will go away and say, "What on earth has he been talking about?" But if you listen rightly, which is an art, you will already have discovered what an extraordinary thing the mind is. It is not a matter of finding it out afterwards, but in the very course of listening you are discovering this mind. There is all the difference between being told what an astounding thing the mind is and making the discovery for yourself. The two states are entirely different. When you say, "I know hunger," you have directly experienced it, but the man who has never experienced hunger can also say, "I know hunger." The two states of "knowing" are entirely different; the one is direct experience and the other is descriptive knowledge.

So, can you experience directly the quality of this amazingly complex mind—the vastness of it, the immensity of it? It is not limited to a particularity, as the mind of a lawyer, prime minister, or cook, but it is everything—the lawyer, the prime minister, the cook, the painter, the man who is frightened, jealous, anxious, ambitious, frustrated—it is all that. And it is the mind that is creating the problem, according to the environmental influences. Because of overpopulation in this country, because of the caste system, because of starvation and the rest of the business, the problem of employment has become immediate, important. And so the mind, this complex thing, because of

pressure, because of the immediate demand, responds only at a certain level and hopes to solve the problem at that level. And the man who is not concerned with the immediate, immense problem of starvation, of war, escapes into some other form of immediate problem. But what is required is to investigate this whole totality of the mind. And to do that, what is essential is freedom, not authority. I think it is really very important to understand this because it is authority which is destroying this unfortunate country. Do not say, "Are not the other countries being destroyed too?" They are. But you and I are concerned for the moment with what is here, and this country is idolatrous. There is, here, the worship of authority, and the worship of success, the big man. Look at the way you treat your cook and the way you treat the man who is successful, the cabinet minister, the man who has knowledge, the saint, and all the rest of it. So you worship authority, and therefore you are never free. Freedom is the first demand, not the last demand of a mind which says, "I must find out, I must look, I must inquire." For the mind to investigate itself, to investigate the problems of its own making, to investigate that which is beyond its own limitations, it must be free at the beginning, not at the end. Now if you really feel that, if you see the necessity of it, there is an immediate revolution. Revolution is not the doing what you like because you imagine you are free, but revolution is the seeing the necessity that the mind must be free. Then it is capable of adjustment through freedom, not through slavery, not from authority. Am I making myself clear?

Let us look at it again. Because of overpopulation, over-organization, and common communication, because of the fear of losing a job, of not being up to the mark, and because of all the pressures of modern civilization with its amazing technology, and the threat of war, hate, and all that, naturally the mind is confused, and so it seeks an authority—the authority of a Hitler, of the prime minister, the guru, the book, or the commissar. That is what you are doing, and therefore you are authority-bound, idolatrous. You may not worship a statue, a thing made by the hand, but you worship the man who is successful, who knows much or has much. All that indicates an idolatrous mind which is essentially the mind crippled by an example, by the hero. The hero means the authority, and a mind that worships authority is incapable of understanding.

Now let us look at this extraordinary field of the mind, look at what it is capable of. The sputniks or the rockets—it is all the mind. It is the mind that slaughters, kills thousands because of its dogmas, as the churches and dictators have done. It is the mind that is afraid. It is the mind that says, "I must know if there is a God or not." And to understand this mind you must begin with freedom. But it is extremely difficult to be free because the mind which wants to be clear is, at the same time, afraid to be free. After all, most people want to be secure, secure in their relationships, secure in their jobs, secure in their ideas, in their professions, in their specialties, in their beliefs. Watch your own mind and see what is happening—you want to be secure, and yet you know you must be free. So there is a contradiction going on. The mind which says there must be peace and yet creates and supports war is schizophrenic, in contradiction. In this country you talk about peace, nonviolence, and yet you are preparing for war. There is the mind that is peaceful and the mind that is violent, and so in the mind there is conflict.

So the first thing for all inquiry, for all new life, for all understanding and comprehension is freedom. But you do not demand freedom, you demand security. And the moment you want physical security, you plan to create it—which means you establish various forms of authority, dictatorship, control, while at the same time you want freedom. So the conflict begins within the mind. But a mind which is aware of its conflict must find out which is of primary importance—freedom or security. After all, is there such a thing as security at all? You may want it, but is there such a thing? Events are showing that there is no such thing as security. Yet the mind clings to the idea. If the mind demands freedom first, then security will follow, but if you seek security first, you will never have freedom, and so you will always have different forms of conflict, misery, and sorrow. Surely all this is obvious.

So to understand the quality of the mind and its immensity, there must be freedom—freedom from all conditioning, from all conclusions—because it is only such a mind that is a young mind. And it is only the young mind that can move freely, investigate, be innocent.

Then, it seems to me, beyond freedom is the sense of appreciation of beauty. So few of us are aware of the things about us. The beauty of the night, the beauty of a face, of a smile, the beauty of the river and of the cloud radiant at sunset, the beauty of moonlight on water; we are so little aware of this extraordinary beauty because we are so insensitive. To be free, sensitivity is essential. But you cannot be free if you are crowded with knowledge. No mind is sensitive if it is burdened with knowledge.

And I think the other thing beyond freedom is—to use a word which unfortunately is connected with such absurd sentiment and wishy-washiness—love. Love has nothing to do with sentiment. Love is hard, in the sense that it is crystal clear, and what is clear can be hard. Love is not what you think of as love. That merely becomes a sentiment.

If we could understand, feel our way into this, we should see that freedom, beauty, and love are the very essentials for discovery— not knowledge, not experience, not belief, not belonging to any organization. Not being anything is the beginning of freedom. So if you are capable of feeling, of going into this, you will find, as you become aware, that you are not free, that you are bound to very many different things, and that at the same time the mind hopes to be free. And you can see that the two are contradictory. So the mind has to investigate why it clings to anything. All this implies hard work. It is much more arduous than going to an office, than any physical labor, than all the sciences put together. Because the humble, intelligent mind is concerned with itself without being self-centered; therefore, it has to be extraordinarily alert, aware, and that means real hard work every day, every hour, every minute. And because we are not willing to do that, we have dictatorships, politicians, gurus, presidents of societies, and all the rest of the rubbish. This demands insistent work because freedom does not come easily. Everything impedes—your wife, your husband, your son, your neighbor, your gods, your religions, your tradition. All these impede you, but you have created them because you want security. And the mind that is seeking security can never find it. If you have watched a little in the world, you know there is no such thing as security. The wife dies, the husband dies, the son runs away—something happens. Life is not static though we would like to make it so. No relationship is static because all life is movement. That is a thing to be grasped, the truth to be seen, felt, not something to be argued about. Then you will see, as you begin to investigate, that it is really a process of meditation. But do not be mesmerized by that word. To be aware of every thought, to know from what source it springs and what is its intention—that is meditation. And to know the whole content of one thought reveals the whole process of the mind.

Now, if you can move from freedom, then you will discover the most extraordinary things of the mind, and then you will find that the mind itself is the total reality. It is not that there is a reality to which the mind goes, but the mind itself, that extraordinary thing, when there is no contradiction within itself, when there is no anxiety, no fear, no desire to be successful—then that mind itself is that which is eternal, unnameable. But to speculate about the eternal without understanding the whole process of the mind is just childish play. It is an immature game which scholars—whom you worship—play. So it would be good if you and I could really go into this without any dramatic heroism, without any spectacular rubbish, but as two human beings interested in solving the problems we have, which are also the problems of the world. The personal problem is not different from the world problem. So if you and I can go into it with humility, knowing our states, tentatively inquiring, then you will find that without your asking, without your inviting, there is that which is not controllable, which is not nameable, to which there is no path. Then only, as you begin to inquire, you will see how extraordinarily easily you will be able to solve your problems, including the problem of starvation which is so enormous. But you cannot tackle it if you have not understood the mind. So please, until we meet next time, do watch your mind, go into it, not merely when you have nothing to do, but from the moment you get up to the moment you go to bed, from the moment you wake up until you go back to sleep. Watch as you talk to your servant, to your boss, your wife, your children, as you see the bus conductor, the bus driver, watch as you look at the moon, the leaf, the sky. Then you will begin to find out what an extraordinary richness there is—a richness not in knowledge but in the nature of the mind itself. It is in the mind, also, that there is ignorance. The dispelling of ignorance is all-important, not the acquisition of knowledge, because the dispelling of ignorance is negative while knowledge is positive. And a man who is capable of thinking negatively has the highest capacity for thinking. The mind which can dispel ignorance and not accumulate knowledge—such a mind is an innocent mind, and only the innocent mind can discover that which is beyond measure.

October 26, 1958

Third Talk in Madras

I wonder what is the function, the meaning of a talk like this? It would be very interesting, I think, if one could ask oneself that question and find not a superficial answer, not a convenient answer, but the deep, true response to a question of that kind. If we looked very deeply into ourselves, I think we would find, almost invariably, that we want to get something. We come here to listen to somebody who has something to say because we think that perhaps it will help us, enlarge our comprehension, and so on. But I am wondering if that is the right purpose. I am asking myself—and I think you should ask yourselves also—whether one wants to be influenced to think in a certain way. Because I think if one starts with that intention—to get something, to be influenced—you and I will not meet; we will not be able to communicate with each other. I certainly do not want to influence you at all, in any manner, to think this way or that because I think that is immature, that is merely propaganda, and we can leave that to the politicians, the communists, and the other brainwashers. I do not want to influence your thinking or your action one way or the other, and if you come with the intention of being influenced, then you and I won't meet. But I think this talk will have a significance if we can find out why the mind allows itself to be influenced, and why our whole culture, society, environment, education is a series of influences all of which condition the mind. It is a fact, is it not, that everything is influencing us—what we eat, what we read, the newspapers, cinemas, radio, political speeches, books—everything is influencing us consciously or unconsciously. We are being influenced much more unconsciously than consciously. The mind may quickly read through something because it is occupied with something else, but what you have read soaks in, seeps in, and remains. This is also a form of propaganda, perfected advertising, so that your mind unconsciously conforms to a pattern of ideas, thoughts, suggestions. With all this we are fairly familiar.

Now why does this happen? Why is it invariably that the mind gets conditioned, shaped, and having been shaped, has then to be broken down? After all, that is what is happening; our entire culture, the whole challenge of life is met by that process. There is a conditioned state, then a challenge, then a response according to the conditioning, and then a modification of our conditioning as a result of the challenge. That is what is actually happening in the world, is it not?

Please, as I said the other day, this is not just a talk. We are communicating, you and I, communing with each other, thinking aloud. It is not a matter of merely listening and then going home, agreeing or disagreeing. Understanding does not come through agreement or disagreement. One cannot agree or disagree about a fact; you can only agree or be convinced if I am asserting something or giving an opinion. But what we are doing is actually examining a fact, and we must be very clear that to examine a fact does not demand that you should agree or disagree with it.

It is a fact that the mind is influenced, to an extraordinary extent, profoundly, is it not? Environmental, religious, social, cultural, climatic, dietetic influences condition the mind; the challenge comes to it and it responds according to its capacity. Its capacity is invariably limited, inadequate, and therefore there is a conflict between the challenge and the response. And if the response is not adequate, full, deep, then the entity in whom the culture, the race, is embodied gradually disappears. This is what has happened throughout history, and it is happening to all of us every day. So why is the mind a slave to environment, a slave to culture? Because a mind so conditioned must obviously be broken. That is, I cannot remain a Hindu, go to the temples, go to some saint, and so on; it becomes impossible because the movement of life is constantly breaking the patterns down. Every culture has been broken—the Roman, the Greek, it is a historical fact—because it can no longer respond to the challenge adequately. So they all go under. But our whole tendency is to conform to a culture and, having conformed, when the challenge comes I do not respond. I say I must remain a Hindu, or a Muslim, a Christian, Catholic, or communist, and so there is a continual battle of adjustment between myself and the challenge, myself and a new idea, myself and a new perception of what life is. This is what is actually happening, is it not? There is no argument about it, there is no opinion about it. This is actually happening now in India. The whole Western culture, all the things the West has brought here—parliamentarianism, militarism, scientific investigation, and so on—these things have come, and they have brought a challenge. The West has imposed part of its culture upon Indian culture, and the Western being more potent, more dynamic, this culture is gradually going under. Though you may put on *namams,* do puja, carry on in the old way, the end of it is inevitable. The more dynamic destroys the weaker, and either we conform to the new pattern or we are destroyed. And what generally happens is that we are destroyed because the other, being stronger and more vital, conquers. That is precisely what is happening.

Now we want to find out why the mind allows itself to be influenced. Have you ever asked yourself this question? It is not a question of a good influence or a bad influence, but of any kind of influence because one can see that the mind is shaped by every thought, by every action and reaction. Whether the reaction is conscious or unconscious, the mind is being shaped; it is being conditioned by every influence around us. Now why is that? One can see the obvious fact that if you do not conform to the pattern of society, of a particular culture, you are broken by the society, the culture throws you out. You depend on the pattern for your livelihood, for your family, your marriage, and all the rest of it. So I am afraid that if I do not conform, if I do not allow myself to be influenced, if I become a revolutionary, then I shall be outside the pale, regarded as a malcontent, a person who has no balance. So being afraid—of losing the job, of not having stability, security, a reasonable sense of well-being—the mind allows itself to be influenced, to conform. Again, this is an obvious fact that through the fear of insecurity, we conform. We have played this game all the time for centuries.

So I see that conformity, imitation, adjustment are absolutely necessary for so-called survival. But I also see very clearly that a mind that is only seeking survival can never be creative. Please, I hope you are following all this, not merely intellectually because words and intellect are of no avail in this. It is the man who feels, however weakly, however tentatively, gropingly, that breaks through. So we are asking: In this world of adjustment, in this world of constant conformity, is there a mind that breaks through and is creatively revolutionary? I think it is a valid question, and I hope that you are asking it. Must the mind always proceed in conformity, little by little breaking away and conforming, conforming and breaking away, endlessly? In that process there is no revolution at all, and therefore there is no creative release. Or has the breaking through nothing to do with adjustment? Please, I am thinking aloud. I feel that the release into the unknown, from which there is a new outburst of creative thought—that release is not progressive. Technique is progressive, but not the new élan, the new creative release which discovers something fresh, unlimited. After all, the technician, the specialist, along whatever line, is never the creative person. He does not discover something entirely new. He may more and more perfect the technique in this and that, but it is only the really creative mind that can break through totally and really discover whether there is God, and so on. It is not the progressive, calculating, knowing mind, the technical mind, the specialized mind that can discover—and I am using the word *discover* in its enormous sense, not in a petty, little sense of some new invention. This release, this discovery is what I am concerned with, and I think it means the really religious mind. The religious mind is not the phony mind that goes to the temple, repeats, and conforms. That is not religion at all. To me religion is the full perception of this progressive and immoral virtue, if I may use the term, which leads to mere respectability and pettiness of mind, from which there is no release. After all, if your mind is not precise, clear, clean, strong, vital, how can it break through all conditioning? A confused mind cannot possibly break through.

To break through, certain qualities are obviously necessary, but do not let us give emphasis to those because if you can first see

the necessity of breaking through, then you will have the vitality to do so, and at the same time you will establish the virtues—which will not be intellectual but actual.

Let us look at it again. I am asking myself: What is a true revolution? Because obviously the communist revolution is not a revolution. It is a reaction. All the previous revolutions, all forms of religious revival are still nothing but reaction. The petty little mind has a reaction, and we get very thrilled about it. To me that is not religion at all. Because, as you can see, such revolutions only throw up a new form of conditioning for the mind. Then what is true revolution? I don't know if this is an important question to you. I think it should be, if I may say so. Because the way we are going—little by little cultivating a few virtues, reforming a bit here and a bit there, reading a few sacred books, attending a few classes, meditating or praying every morning, repeating words—all this, to me, has no meaning at all. It is merely self-improvement or self-adjustment to a pattern. A religious mind cannot adjust to a pattern, so it is this breakthrough that is so important.

I wonder if we understand each other? Because I feel, if I may point it out, that if you can really listen to me, really listen, then you will see the breaking through for yourself. You will break through; you cannot help it. What is destructive of understanding is the positive assertion of opinion, and the positive assertion of opinion is all that we have, is it not? All the sacred books, all that the politicians say, all the things you believe are merely positive assertions of opinion, and a mind so filled is incapable of listening. It can argue, but argument, however logical, however sane, however correct in the realm of conformity, has no place when you want to find out about something entirely new. Therefore if you want to listen, you cannot bring all that in. First you must listen, as you would listen to a piece of music. Later you can say you like it or do not like it, but first you must be in a state of mind that is capable of reception. Such a mind says, "I will listen to you; I will go into it, I will not argue, bring up all my opinions, experiences, and knowledge and smother you with them; I will first listen."

Now, if you can so listen, then I feel the thing is done. I don't know if you have ever listened to anybody. Actually we are always throwing up defenses; we seldom listen. What I am saying is neither pleasant nor unpleasant, so there need be no defense. I am just stating a fact; you will decide later if you like it or not, but first you must listen. Propaganda and listening are entirely different processes. The propagandist, political or religious, does not want you to actually listen. They merely want to emphasize your prejudices, your opinions, your particular tendencies, and so on. I want you to listen with all your attention, and having listened, to bring to bear all your critical capacity, all your doubts, your inquiries, the whole vitality of your mind.

So I am asking you: What is this total revolution in the quality of the mind?— which is not merely a shaping of the mind to a new series of ideas. Can you listen in such a way that you feel the quality of this revolution, which is not additive but a total breaking through the environmental conditioning? I am doing my best to explain something which is very difficult to explain. It is like saying to a man, "Listen, and keep quiet." And to that he says, "What am I listening to, and why should I keep quiet?" But it is only a mind that will keep very quiet—not with enforced quietness, not with a disciplined quietness—that can listen in order to understand. Such a mind is totally attentive without any compulsion.

What I am saying is this—that there is a revolution which is not a reaction, which is not additive in the sense that by adding many, many details of knowledge, the whole problem will be resolved. By putting many spokes together you can never make a wheel; you must have the feeling, the perception of the wheel first and then the spokes are useful. So this breakthrough is not a matter of ideation, of breaking through one form of conditioning to another form of conditioning. You see, our thinking, if you examine it very closely, is a movement from the known to the known, is it not? Just watch your own mind. The known is the conclusion, the experience, what you have thought, the idea, and so on, and you move from the known to the known. After all, the so-called religious person has his idea of what God is, what truth is, what this or that is; he has moved from previous knowledge to the present knowledge, and he calls it progress. All revolutions come about in this way also. Examining the facts of the known, reacting to them, and creating a new pattern is called a revolution, a new society, utopia, but it is merely moving from the known to the known. With this process we are familiar.

Now the revolution I am talking of, or feeling my way into, is not this at all. It is the perception, the understanding of the totality of the known, and leaving it, not carrying it on. The mind, being aware of its own content, of its own store of knowledge, by its own self-critical capacity, seeing its own movement from the known to the known, from conclusion to conclusion— leaves it all and makes a jump, as it were, into the unknown. But if you ask, "How am I to jump into the unknown?" you have already stumped yourself because then you are back in the pattern of wanting to know the way, the path, the method. There is no such thing. The moment you say what am I to do, what practice, what virtues, what action will bring about this jump, this breakthrough, you have merely made a breakthrough into another known. You are again asking to be led from the known to the known. The moment you ask for a prescription for breaking through the known, you have not left it. I say you must be fully aware of the known. You must be fully aware of the whole operation of the mind, know all its intricacies, the way it reacts, both the conscious and the unconscious which is hidden, concealed. If I know myself totally, completely, know all the tricks, the deceptions, the subtle maneuverings of the mind in order to be secure, to be this or that, when I know all that and yet I do not find any release—then the mind leaves it alone. Therefore self-knowledge is essential.

To break through, the mind must know the operations of itself like a mathematical problem. The real mathematician, I am sure, thinks of a problem most acutely, in detail; with profound inquiry he searches for a true way out, and he does not find it. So he leaves it, and suddenly, as he gets into a bus or as he walks, the whole thing is shown. But it is essential that I know this whole content of myself, why I think as I do, why I am influenced, what is the purpose of this extraordinary mind. I must inquire not intellectually but with feeling. There is verbal inquiry and there is inquiry with feeling. The verbal inquiry is mere curiosity or merely concerned with adjusting, conforming, changing. Such a mind is not a feeling mind. With most of us the intellect, the capacity for words is very strong. All our education, social upbringing, religious reading, religious dictums and disciplines are only on the verbal level. I do not know if you have noticed it, but they have no feeling. As you read the Bible, the Gita, or the Koran, they themselves are just paper with words printed on it, but you bring the feeling to these words, the words themselves have no feeling. So this inquiry into the whole process of the mind requires not a verbal intellection, but there must be a feeling with it.

I wonder, sirs, if you have any feeling about anything? Have you any strong feeling about anything? Do please look at the question, play with it a little, and you will see. Apart from the small feelings for self-improvement, self-interest, the petty, little worries and hopes, have you any strong, vital feeling about anything? And if you have, how soon it is translated into petty action! Am I making myself clear? Unless you are passionate, with intense feeling, self-knowledge means nothing at all. Then self-knowledge is merely a further instrument for the exploitation of yourself and your neighbor. That is why it is very important to find out if you have feeling. Do please ask yourself seriously and earnestly if you have a strong feeling about something—or are we all so dead, so respectable, so petty, so bourgeois that we never have a strong, burning feeling? See whether it is really vital or only petty. I know you get frightfully angry if your neighbor throws something over your wall, and occasionally you are a little passionate, sexually, but is that all? I mean passion in the sense of the total abandonment of oneself, because out of that comes true simplicity—not the calculated simplicity of the loincloth. So if the mind itself can be fully aware of itself with the greatest of feeling, then you will see that you can let go, then you will see that you can break through. The feeling is in itself disciplinary, whereas all the so-called religious people have destroyed their feelings, disciplined their desires out of existence. Their gods are cheap gods to whom they come with nothing. But the mind with intense feeling, deep inquiry—not throttled feeling—will begin to create its own discipline. The mind which is confused, disorderly, influenced, can never be a clear instrument to search itself out. Whereas the very intensity of the feeling of inquiry into yourself will release the conditioning, break the conditioning.

Unfortunately, I am talking Greek because none of you has tried any of this. You see, I am trying to say so much in one talk. What I want to say is this: The mind is conditioned, whether you recognize it or not. And must you go through all the layers of the conditioning, analyze it all, dissect it, or is there a way of breaking through right away? I think there is. I say that if you are aware that the mind is conditioned, and if you are aware that a conditioned mind, whatever it does, whatever its gods, rituals, ideations, virtues, is still limited, conditioned—then you will see that it can break through. But you must first grasp the totality of that, feel the whole implication of it without going into detail. You know it is like seeing the whole vast horizon, the beauty of it, the vitality, the purity, the distance, and the nearness of it. The mere depth of feeling, when you are aware of it all, will act. But this is not a trick; this is not some mysterious experience or poetic imagination. If I can realize that my mind is petty, that my gods are petty, my Gita, my Koran, my Bible is petty, the temples I build, the stupid images which have no meaning except the meaning the petty mind gives to them; if I realize without despair, without cynicism, that my whole life and thoughts are petty—then the very truth of that realization makes the mind completely still, completely quiet; and it is necessary to be quiet to break through. You can repeat some words and mesmerize yourself into quietness but you might just as well take tranquilizer pills. But when you see the vastness of your conditioning, it is like seeing something enormously beautiful, a splendid sky. At the sight of itself, so completely conditioned, knowing itself so, the mind becomes totally still—not only the conscious mind but the unconscious also. Then you will find that creative release takes place—not because you want it, but because that is the movement of life.

October 29, 1958

Fourth Talk in Madras

There is a tendency, is there not, to reduce most things to formulas and to try to live according to those formulas. We think that if we could find a right formula for education, for a good way of living, and for understanding the beauties of the earth, we would solve our problems. A formula according to which we can live is what most of us are seeking, are we not?—the good formula, the formula that is capable of adaptation, the formula that will stand the test of reason, of life. To me, any formula of that kind not only destroys the full significance of life and is irrelevant, but also makes a man most irresponsible and superficial. We think that by following a formula—for peace, for meditation, for discipline, for reaching a particular ideal, and so on—we become very responsible, very earnest, very serious. I very much question such a mentality because I feel that such a person is not really earnest; he is merely copying, following, ridden by authority. A follower, surely, is never an earnest person, and it is only to the earnest that life reveals itself, not to the follower of a formula. Life is for the earnest, and the earnest one is not he who merely seeks an escape from conflict and sorrow, from the various problems, accidents, and incidents of life. The earnest man has not a ready-made solution with which he approaches life's problems. The one who is really earnest is he who inquires, who tries to investigate for himself into the whole problem of existence, and who does not merely live according to the ideas of some philosopher, psychologist, or religious savior. The moment you follow anybody, you cease to be really earnest. But unfortunately, all our tendencies, our education, our inward fears, the accidents of life, the sorrowful impacts—all these tend to harden the mind, and the mind which has become hardened and which is then merely seeking a way out is not, I feel, an earnest mind.

It seems to me that it is very important to have the quality of earnestness, but without striving for it, if you know what I mean. You cannot strive to appreciate the beauty of a sunset; to appreciate the beauty of a sunset, what is required is a great deal of intelligence, of sensitivity, alert visual perception of trees, birds, clouds, nature, including human beings and also oneself. You cannot suddenly decide to appreciate the lovely radiance of a cloud. It does not happen that way. To see the beauty of it, not merely visually but to have this whole sense of beauty—which is never static, which has no formula, which you cannot be educated to appreciate—requires hard work. You may read literature about it, read what the poets have written, see all the picture galleries, go to the museums, but to really see something and feel the loveliness of it requires an enormous amount of inward work.

In the same way, to be really earnest requires not a striving to be earnest, which is most silly, but it requires the understanding of one's own capacity, of one's own endeavors, of the significance of one's own activities and search. This means being aware of the words one uses, of one's feelings, gestures, observation of the gossip, and all that. To be aware in order to change these things, to correct them, is to make yourself even more impregnable to life. To look at a sunset and say, "I must be awfully serious to see the beauty of it," has no meaning, but if you watch and are aware of the beauty of a leaf on the roadside, the beauty of a passing face, and also the corruption, the ugliness, the sordidness, then with that sensitivity, if you look at the sunset, it has a meaning, a depth, it has its own significance and is its own poem. In the same way I think earnestness is essential for any man, and especially for one who is trying to find out what is true, what is the meaning of this existence. But unfortunately for most of us, earnestness merely means frightful endeavor, great struggle, constantly trying to be serious when one is actually superficial.

I think this constant endeavor to be something, to become something, is the real cause of the destructiveness and the aging of the mind. Look how quickly we are aging, not only the people who are over 60, but also the young people. How old they are already, mentally! Very few sustain or maintain the quality of a mind that is young. I mean by young not the mind that merely wants to enjoy itself, to have a good time, but the mind that is uncontaminated, that is not scratched, warped, twisted by the accidents and incidents of life, a mind that is not worn out by struggle, by grief, by constant strivings. Surely it is necessary to have a young mind because the old mind is so full of the scars of memories that it cannot live, it cannot be earnest; it is a dead mind, a decided mind. A mind that has decided and lives according to its decisions is dead. But a young mind is always deciding anew, and a fresh mind does not burden itself with innumerable memories. A mind that carries no shadow of suffering, though it may pass through the valley of sorrow, remains unscratched. And one must have such a mind. It is obviously essential because to such a mind, there is life—not the life of superficiality, not the life of enjoyment, though it may also know enjoyment, not the life of getting, losing, gaining, being fretful, you know the whole business of our existence, burdened with knowledge.

Now one sees the necessity of it, surely. As I am talking you must feel that one must have this quality of a fresh, uncontaminated mind capable of real perception, of immediate perception, which I will go into presently. And seeing the necessity of it, we ask, "How am I to get it, what examinations, what subjects have I to take, what meditation, what discipline should I practice, what sacrifices must I make, in order to get it?"—these are the questions that one asks. I do not think such a young mind is to be acquired. It is not a thing that you can purchase through endeavor, through sacrifice. There is no coin to it and it is not a marketable thing, but if you see the importance of it, the necessity of it, if you see the truth of it, then something else takes place, and that is what I want to convey, if I can, in this talk. It is not a matter of how to get it because all the processes, all the forms of self-discipline, all the various ways in which the mind subjugates itself in order to get something, they all cultivate this mountain of memory which merely burdens the mind and makes it old, decrepit, useless. But if you can see the necessity of a fresh mind, if you can get the impact of the implications of it and not merely ask how to get it, then the process of thinking is entirely different, is it not? If you say, how am I to get it, then your whole approach is entirely different; then there is no instantaneous perception, no timeless understanding.

I wonder if we understand anything through time? Do I understand anything tomorrow, the day after tomorrow, a year later, or ten years later? Is understanding a matter of time? Is seeing something as true, real, or is seeing something as false a matter of time, or of instant perception, the instant being out of time? It must have happened to you, surely, that you have seen something immediately. That sense of immediacy is out of time—time being yesterday, today, and tomorrow. And can we not in the same way see the necessity, the urgency, and the extraordinary vitality of a young mind? I am not using that word *young mind* as something which is in time. The young mind is out of time; it is innocent, fresh, and if you see the truth that there must be such a mind, then your whole approach to life is entirely different, is it not? Let me put it the other way around. Perhaps we can get at it differently.

Why does the mind grow old? It is old, is it not, in the sense of getting decrepit, deteriorating, repeating itself, caught in habits, sexual habits, religious habits, job habits, or various habits of ambition. The mind is so burdened with innumerable experiences and memories, so marred and scarred with sorrow that it cannot see anything freshly but is always translating what it sees in terms of its own memories, conclusions, formulas, always quoting; it is authority-bound; it is an old mind. You can see why it happens. All our education is merely the cultivation of memory; and there is this mass communication through journals, the radio, the television; there are the professors who read lectures and repeat the same thing over and over again until your brain soaks in what they have repeated, and you vomit it up in an examination and get your degree and go on with the process—the job, the routine, the incessant repetition. Not only that, but there is also our own inward struggle of ambition with its frustrations, the competition not only for jobs but for God, wanting to be near Him, asking the quick road to Him. All this constant striving, struggling, with the disappointments, sorrows, grief, and unresolved problems are eating our hearts out, and on top of that we try to acquire so-called wisdom through books, which is all nonsense. We have the innumerable schools of wisdom, which again is sheer rubbish.

So, what is happening is that through pressure, through stress, through strain, our minds are being crowded, drowned by influence, by sorrow, consciously or unconsciously. If we are conscious of it, we can try to brush it off, but the unconscious, the deep racial contradictions, the impressions from various cultures quarreling with each other, the disappointments, all this, surely, is making the mind old. All these memories, and they are after all only memories, are dulling the mind, and as we grow older our memories take a deeper hold, and we look back to the happy days or look forward to some future. So surely the major factor in this deterioration is this constant usage of the mind in the wrong direction. We are wearing down the mind, not using it.

So we have seen the major factors which are causing the mind to become dull, insensitive, impregnable to new ideas, new visions, a new quality. It is essentially a thing of time, and time is always in terms of the past, present, and future, something limited. Is it not so? Can we go into it? It is really an extraordinary subject. There is chronological time—yesterday, today, and tomorrow; your train goes at a certain time, and so on. Chronological time is not important, so let us leave it aside. Now what is time? Is there time to a mind that is unscathed? Is there time to a mind that has experienced but is out of it again? But there is time to a mind that has experienced and retained a memory based on pleasure or pain or whatever it is. The mind is, after all, by its very nature, its very construction, by its whole process of education, a product of time. All that you are, your mind, is the result of time in the sense that from your youth, from the moment you were born, until now, you have acquired, learned, experienced, suffered, traveled, seen, had innumerable experiences, all in relation to time. And such a mind, being the result of time, always thinks in terms of duality, or along a particular direction as a specialized entity.

I hope you are listening to me, not as to a talk to which you feel you must listen, however boring, but listening to see if your own mind is not working in the way described, using the speaker only as a sounding board, as a mirror in which to watch your own mind. Otherwise, what is said has no meaning.

What we are trying to find out about is time. The mind is the result of time, of many yesterdays, and the experiences, the shocks, the sorrows, the pleasures, the problems, the enjoyments, the things that one has learned have been carried over to today and then again on to tomorrow, modified but continuing the same process. And such a mind, rooted in time, now asks, "Can I find something which is beyond the mind; is there the eternal, is there something which is timeless and, if there is, what is one to do?" But the moment you say, "What is one to do?" you have already brought in the whole process of time. So we know now what time is, psychologically, inwardly. It is the sense of continuity, the sense of being, or not being, or of becoming. All becoming is of time, and that is all the mind knows.

Now is there a state, a living, an inquiry—whatever you like to call it—which is not the projection, the result of time, which is not within the shadow of time? Cannot the mind die to time and see something totally new, instantly? The dying to the past is the birth of the immediate present. The words *immediate* and *present* are not of time though they both indicate a relation to time. When we say "the present," the mind immediately thinks of the past or the future, and when we say "immediately" or "now," it is again related either to the past or the future. But can one not think or rather feel a sense of the now, the immediate present, in such a way that the sense of the past and the future—all the things one has known, experienced—drop away like the leaves in autumn? For in that state the mind is fresh, timeless. But this means, does it not, that the mind must be really free of all mass influence, of all inherited culture, of all tradition, of all the things it has known, experienced, rejoiced in. It means to break with it instantly, not progressively, for progressively is still in time.

Sirs, what we are talking about is one of the most difficult things. As I have said, truth is something that is seen not in time but from moment to moment. It has no continuity, no abiding place. Wisdom cannot buy it, and no experience can give it to you. You must die to everything you know—your Masters, your gurus, your wisdom, your societies, everything. For knowing is within the field of time. The young mind is not accumulative; it is the old mind that has accumulated and is accumulating. The old mind must die, and how is this to happen? And when I say "how" I am not talking of a method. One sees, does one not, that to understand anything, it must be immediate or not at all. The immediate may be in the tomorrow, but it must still be the immediate. I do not know if I am making myself clear because it is so subtle; it is not a thing to be put in black and white, not a thing to be made into a conclusion and stamped upon the mind.

Understanding is not of time. Perception is immediate. Perception of the full significance of sorrow, for instance, is immediate—not the explanation of sorrow, not the cause of sorrow. One can explain, show the cause, but the understanding of it, the feeling of it, the freedom from it is not a matter of time at all. Look, sirs, for the greater part of our lives, sorrow is our constant companion. We shed tears because we have not succeeded or because we are this when we think we should be that. We are constantly frustrated; there is death, there is old age, there is disease, there is attachment to a person or to an idea. We know the innumerable avenues of sorrow, the small, petty little sorrows and the enormous grief. There is the constant beating we receive from the boss, the domination of the wife, the husband, and there is death. We all know what sorrow is—the deep wound which can never heal and which, if touched, makes us weep our hearts out. It is the lot of all of us—the young, the old, the powerful, the dictators, they all know this agony. Then the mind begins to analyze, to dissect, to es-

tablish certain sanctions, formulas, and it tries to carry out those denials saying, "This is right and that is wrong, I must do this and I must not do that." And in that battle, frustration, misery, there is again everlasting conflict. It seems that whatever we touch brings this sorrow.

Now obviously, to be free from it is not a matter of time. To wipe away the wound completely, not merely intellectually, verbally, but deeply, inwardly, is not a matter of time. All the conscious and unconscious wounds one has received through life—the insults, the flatteries, the memories that burden and crowd the mind, the longings and frustrations, hopes and despairs—these cannot be healed through time. They can be covered; you can put a lid on them, a wax layer, but they cannot be wiped away through time. If you try to do so, then you are back in formulas—reincarnation, what to do and what not to do—you are again caught in the same ugly business of struggle, everlasting despair and hope.

Obviously there must be a way out—to walk out of it, like shedding your clothes, never turning and looking back—like a cloud disappearing before a strong wind. I think there is such a way. But that way can never be found if you cling to the old, obviously. You must let it all go, not knowing the other. You understand me, sirs? If you think you know the other way—how to wash the mind clean—then you are not letting go. Whereas if you do not know the other, but see the falseness of time as a means of healing, as a means of liberating oneself from sorrow, if you see that the whole process of thinking in terms of memory is false, then your mind is not looking in any direction; therefore, being free, it is capable of seeing, perceiving, instantly.

I do not know if I am making myself clear. Let me put it differently. Have you ever tried dying to a pleasure? We want to die to sorrow, but have you ever tried to die to any pleasure? Have you ever tried dying to a pleasure voluntarily, not forcibly? Ordinarily when you die you don't want to; death comes and takes you away; it is not a voluntary act, except in suicide. But have you ever tried dying voluntarily, easily, felt that sense of the abandonment of pleasure? Obviously not! At present your ideals, your pleasures, your ambitions are the things which give so-called significance to life, but they have no significance at all. It is the 'you' who is giving significance to them. Life is living, abundance, fullness, abandonment, not a sense of the 'I' having significance. That is mere intellection. If you experiment with dying to little things—that is good enough. Just to die to little pleasures—with ease, with comfort, with a smile—is enough, for then you will see that your mind is capable of dying to many things, dying to all memories. Machines are taking over the functions of memory—the computers—but the human mind is something more than a merely mechanical habit of association and memory. But it cannot be that something else if it does not die to everything it knows.

Now to see the truth of all this, a young mind is essential, a mind that is not merely functioning in the field of time. The young mind dies to everything. Can you see the truth of that immediately, feel the truth of it instantly? You may not see the whole extraordinary significance of it, the immense subtlety, the beauty of that dying, the richness of it, but even to listen to it sows the seed, and the significance of these words takes root—not only at the superficial, conscious level, but right through all the unconscious.

So if you are able to listen in that way, you will see that it is enough, in itself. You don't have to do a thing because the very act of listening fully is like a seed in the earth, in the womb—it has life and that goes on.

So, can one see now that understanding is not a matter of time, that perception is not the result of a conclusion, an explanation? You can have a million subtle explanations of why you suffer, but the explanation of sorrow is not the ending of sorrow. But if you can see that sorrow can end, not in time, but in dying to it—without any thought of reward, without any explanation—as you can die also to pleasure, then you will see that time has very little meaning to an earnest man. Then life is a thing to be lived in immediate fullness. I do not know if it has ever happened to you—to see a firefly and, in that, the whole universe of light, of truth, of beauty. This is not merely a romantic, poetic idea, but to feel that way means that the dross of memory has been washed away—which does not mean that you forget where you live, become loony. But the identification, the attachment, the crippling effect of experience upon which the mind lives, sustains itself, grows decrepit, and deteriorates—all that is washed away. It must often have happened to you, sirs, that you have been hurt by an insult, by something someone has done, your husband, your wife, or whoever it is. And can one not die to the wound, without reason, without calculation, without any need to forgive? In understanding there is no need for forgiveness. Can one not die to it totally, so that the thing is gone? If you are listening to me and not just being mesmerized, surely you must have seen already that the mind—which is put together by time—can die to itself.

Probably you have never experimented with this, but if you will do so, then you will see that all perception, all understanding is out of time, and that is liberation—the liberation from time. It is like love. Love is not of time. You do not say, "I loved yesterday, or I will love tomorrow." Love is timeless, and when you so love, there is no future or past. That which is full, complete, is not bound by time or separated by space. So if you have really heard this, just a little, it is enough. The seed, if it is true, will have its own momentum. All that the mind has to do is to keep clear of the debris. But even to listen requires a certain attention. Attention is not of the mind; attention is love. After all, you give your whole heart and listen fully to somebody whom you love. Love is not of the mind, and its quality is timeless.

We know none of these things, unfortunately, and so our mind rules. Our mind governs our conduct, our way of life, and so our behavior is based merely on habit, on so-called morality. A merely moral mind will never know truth. It is only the man who is sensitive, who is always losing, never accumulating, only such a man can understand, and that understanding is out of time.

November 2, 1958

Fifth Talk in Madras

I think it would be very interesting if we could find out for ourselves if there is any teaching at all, and if there is a teacher. Most of us think we learn from life, and we give a particular significance to life. We say we learn through the various experiences, incidents, and accidents of life. We accumulate experiences, and this accumulation further conditions our thinking and all future experience. So we say we learn from life, and we give significance to life. The greater the significance we give it, the more rich we think our life is in pursuit of that significance. I do not know if you have noticed how most of us crave to give to life a significance; we say life must have a purpose, must have an end gain; otherwise, what do we live for? These questions invariably arise, do they not, from the desire to establish a fuller, deeper, wider significance. And also we say we learn from life, and this gathering

is called knowledge or experience. So either we are satisfied with gathering knowledge, experience, and enriching that accumulation, or else we try to give significance to life. So we are always seeking a purpose, a significance, a meaning.

Now, is there a meaning to life at all, in the sense of a significance which we can grope after, and is there a teaching and a teacher in life at all? There is, of course, a teacher in the mechanical sense, in a school, for those who are seeking specializations, special techniques, and specialized knowledge, such as mechanics. All such knowledge, surely, is a process of acquiring and storing up a technique and utilizing that memory for the purpose of a livelihood. But I am asking myself whether there is anything to be learned from life, and if there is anyone who can teach me about life. Someone can teach me the mechanical process of living, but I can also see that so long as we are accumulating knowledge, we do not seem able to go beyond the limitations of that knowledge. Obviously we must have knowledge— know some mathematics, how to run cars, airplanes, how to do a job, and all the rest of it—and for that there must be teachers. But can there be "teaching" apart from that? And if there is no teaching apart from that kind, then what is the function of a talk like this? This is really quite an important question if you will put it to yourself. One can learn dancing, to play the violin, or how to read and write, how to fly a machine, how to go to the moon, and all the rest of it, and obviously, for that one must learn from somebody. But are we learning from this talk, and what do we mean by learning? If I say I am learning to drive a car, that is very simple—I am accumulating knowledge, and the more I drive, the more expert I become, until without much thought I can drive. There knowledge is necessary. To apply a technique I must store up knowledge. So are we learning here, in that mechanical sense? Do you learn from the Gita or the Bible, and what is it you learn? How to interpret or how to conform your life to what is said, is it not so? That is again mechanical. That is, you think that there you might find a significance to life which means that life in itself has no meaning except for the significance you choose to give to it.

Please let me here remind you, if I may do so without boring you, that you are not just listening to a talk by someone else. We are journeying together, if we can, into the whole problem of living. I am not teaching you, and you are not learning from me. All that business is too immature, puerile. But what we are trying to do is, really and actually, to experience this inquiry into the whole process of learning and to discover if the mind can free itself from the limitation of knowledge and experience, or learn something which is beyond the field of knowledge. I will try and go into it a little because I want, if I can, to talk presently about what we mean by creation.

So, what do we mean by learning? Or is there no such thing at all apart from the mechanical learning? Surely there is no learning because one can see very clearly that all experience only conditions further experience; all experience makes the next experience mechanical. For instance, when one has had an experience of a sunset, of anger, of greed, or this or that, that experience leaves a residue in the mind, does it not? The mind is that residue; it is not a separate thing, it is the mark of that experience. Then I immediately translate that experience in terms of previous experience. So every experience is translated, modified, and given significance by the mind. All experience is really a mechanical process, the mind translating it according to its desires and memories, calling it pleasurable or painful,

enriching or not enriching, sorrowful or beautiful.

So one can see that there is learning where mechanical things are concerned, and one can also see that so-called learning from experience or from a teaching is again a mechanical conditioning of the mind. And is there any other form of learning? Can I learn anything from you other than in those two categories? One can see, can one not, that those two categories are mechanical; the learning from experience is a little more subtle, but it is still within the field of habit—habit being memory. Then is there any other form of learning?

You are listening to me, and I wonder why? Is it in the hope of learning something, to find a purpose in life, to clarify your problems, or to enrich your memories? Or is it that without using that word *learning* we are both in a state of attention in which we are seeing things very clearly? I hope you understand what I mean. In that state of attention you do not learn—you are merely attentive. It is the mind which is not attentive that tries to learn, that wants to be taught, and this process merely cultivates memory. And then it becomes mechanical and establishes habits—habits of thought, habits of ideas, habits of values. So we want to find out what is this attention which is not accumulative because the moment the mind is the machine of accumulation, it ceases to be attentive. Then it is merely functioning mechanically, which most of us want because it is much easier to live that way. It is like laying down rails and running on them for ever and ever because it is not disturbing. So our mind is always cultivating habits in order to be secure. In order to be secure we try to learn—from the teacher, the book, from this and that—and that learning is a process of establishing habits. If you watch your own mind, if you are aware of yourself, you will see that this is so. We want to be secure in all circumstances—in our ideas, our jobs, our experiences, our emotional states, and so on. We want a permanency which means, actually, a continuity of habit. And is there any other form of learning, or is there only attention?

You see this question is important because they are doing extraordinary things, chemically, to our bodies. You can take various forms of pills—pills to bring the mind to great attention, pills that make the mind extraordinarily alert, pills that stimulate an astonishing intensity of perception, of bright colors and tremendous effects. So chemically the mind can be made into whatever it wants. You can get into almost any state emotionally, or so-called spiritually, or with that extraordinary sense of alertness to everything about you. It is said that one can wipe away the unconscious, too, through a chemical process. These things are being done, and with the mind so controlled by chemistry—and you don't have to just accept my word for it—then where does this inquiry, this liberation, the search for something beyond the mind, the urge towards God, the eternal—where does it all come in? If I can make my mind stop worrying through some pill, be extraordinarily attentive for the moment in which it is operating, surely I have solved a great many difficulties. I can produce various forms of experience that way, see visions, and so on.

So, knowing all this, one asks, "Is there such a thing as eternity? Is there such a thing as truth? Is there such a thing as being beyond the reaches of the habit-ridden mind?" Because, you know, one can be made to believe anything; they have pills for that also. So beliefs, knowledge, experience, have very little meaning any more since you can be made to believe anything. Taking all this into consideration, looking at it all with a really profound inquiry, with a sense of wanting to find out, of feeling one's way into

the unknown, is there any learning at all? Or is there only a state of attention which is not induced by any pill? You can make yourself attentive by a pill or by various means, and it again becomes a habit.

So since mechanically you can remove conflict, get complete relaxation through a pill, then what is the function of the mind? Are we merely to live adjusting ourselves to our environment, going to our job and not getting worried because one has taken a pill? This is actually taking place. If the mind can be induced to have no worries, to be quiet, peaceful, silent, to forget the past, then what is the function of the mind? Is the mind to be merely a plaything of pills, not only pills from a bottle, but the pills of habit, of memory, of experience? If one can break through all that, then what is the function of the mind?

Surely one can only ask that question when one has broken through, when you have, through self-knowledge and very careful observation, broken through. When you have thrown off certain habits of thought, certain attitudes and certain beliefs, even then the mind can be made more intense in that freedom by a pill. Knowing of all these extraordinary things which are going on in the chemical world in relation to the human organism, one naturally asks oneself if there is reality, God or whatever it is, or is all that mere invention? Is it the mere desire of the mind to escape into some permanent, everlasting, irrefutable security? Because that is what most of us want—to be led to that state. And how is the mind to purge itself of all these ideas, these habits, these mechanical and chemical things and find out if there is truth? Can I learn to look at reality and understand its significance, or can I not learn anything about it at all? Or can the mind only perceive reality without being able to translate it into action? I do not know if I am making myself clear. I am afraid I am not.

You see, I have been thinking a great deal about what is creation. When I say "thinking," let us be clear about that. For most of us, thinking is merely reaction. Thought is merely the reaction of what you know; thought is the result of your experience, of your conditioning. So there is no thought which is free. But I use the word *thinking* as meaning investigating. And I have been thinking what this creation is, which is not mere talent, gift, or the ability to invent. What is this creative state without which the mind will always be bound to a world of mechanics, of habits? Let me put it differently.

Our lives are mechanical, a movement from the known to the known, and in that there is no creation, there is no sense of that immense, immeasurable state which is beyond the reach of the mechanical mind. Without the awareness of that, without the perception of that, without being attentive to that, life must remain mechanical. So how is a mechanical mind to break through itself and realize, feel the other? Obviously all limitation must go; all thought must cease because thought is merely the response of memory, the response of knowledge; it is still within the field of the known. So I see that thought must cease, the limitation must be broken through, there must be no sense of having a purpose, and the mind must be astonishingly active without being active *about* something. Because most of our minds are active about something. The mind must be extraordinarily attentive. I see that these things are necessary, essential and that they cannot be brought about through any inducement, through any pill, through any trick of belief, mode of conduct, or way of virtue—which are all habit-forming.

So, how is the mind to be aware of all these mechanical habits and not be caught in them? How is the mind to purge itself of the known without any inducement? Sirs, you may not have put all these questions to yourself, but I am putting them to you so that you can answer them for yourself. Because it is only such an inquiring mind that can perceive instantly, for a timeless second, that which is immeasurable. It is there, always there, timelessly. But the mind can never find it because it only knows about learning, which is accumulation; it only knows habit, which is of time. And whatever it thinks is still within the field of time. So how is the mind to drop all this? I hope you understand what I am asking, sirs, because unless this takes place, do what you will, have a perfect social state, a perfect welfare state, a perfect organization, it is like having a marvelous house without anything inside. And that is what we are becoming—good minds, healthy bodies, stimulated emotions, all controlled by pills, and not being able to go beyond that.

So, how is the mind to allow that thing to come to it? Obviously the mind cannot go to it. It must come, and how is it to come? You cannot invite it, you cannot make a habit of it, you cannot sacrifice yourself for it, or make yourself into this or that to get it. It must come; and the "how," in the sense of by what conduct, by what path, by what system, by what process of thinking—is not the problem. You see, to put this question seriously to yourself, you must be aware, totally, of the full implications of the question. Knowing all the habits of the mind, knowing that you can do anything now with the mind through drugs which will have no aftereffects, then surely you see that such a mind, which has been influenced, cannot possibly receive that which has no measure, which is nameless. And yet without that other, it is like having a perfect body, a beautiful mechanical mind, which is but an empty shell. So how is that unknown to come? You cannot induce it; you cannot buy it through any means. It is too vast, immeasurable, and so fleeting that the mind cannot capture it. It cannot be held within the field of time.

Do please listen to this. How is the mind, which has established borders, frontiers, to break through those frontiers? How is the mind which functions only in the habits of knowledge—how is it to cease instantly, not in the future? I hope you are actually listening—not listening to learn something which you can think about when you get home, for then you will never discover. Because thinking about it in the future is merely to be caught in time again. But if you can listen now, very simply, then your mind will see for itself that the very question contains its own answer. You do not have to seek an answer—the question is the answer.

Creation is something which the mind cannot use. It cannot use it to paint, or write a poem, or make an invention, or have visions. It is far beyond all that. The mind, on the instant, must be free for that extraordinary thing to take place.

So, sirs, what is important is the state of full attention in which there is no border, no frontier, no limit. All concentration is based on limitation—but not attention. When there is that attention which is not induced in any way, then you will see that it is the limitless. But it cannot be captured by the mind, nor can the path of time lead you to it. Seeing all this—and there is much more to it—seeing this whole extraordinary process of the mind, then all that the mind can do is—as in front of a magnificent mountain, as in front of anything that is really beautiful—to be wholly attentive and verbally, intellectually in thought, completely silent. It is in that state of attention that there is no question. Therefore that which has no time, is.

So, sirs, that is why I feel so strongly that a revolution in the quality of the mind is necessary. Not merely a change of ideas, thoughts, and beliefs, but a revolution in the quality of the mind itself. This quality of the mind cannot be learned, cannot be cultivated, can be seen only on the instant and forgotten on the instant, cannot be accumulated. But once the mind sees this quality, this revolution in itself, then it will never lose it. That is why it is very important not to be merely respectable, not to be petty, but to cease all this activity, to break away from this terrific weight of respectability—which does not mean to become disreputable. To break through everything, on the instant, so that the mind lives all the time in a state of noncontinuity—that is full attention.

November 5, 1958

Sixth Talk in Madras

I think it would be worthwhile and interesting to go into the whole problem of the word, the symbol, and the name. Words play a very important part in our lives. The symbol, the name has extraordinary significance for us, and perhaps if we could break through the significance by understanding the whole content of the mind, which is so filled with words, symbols, and names, then perhaps we should be able to understand the whole process of thinking. Because I feel that if we do not know how to think rationally, sanely, with deep insight as well as with reason, our thinking will not lead us very far; and further, to go beyond reason, we must first know the whole process of reasoning. One cannot just skip it and say it is not important. One must know the root of reasoning. One must know what is the conditioning from which all reasoning takes place. I am not talking about verbal reasoning but the reasoning based on actual experience, actual living. If we can proceed from there, I think we can go very deeply into the investigation of the whole problem of what is the 'me', and the whole field of thought.

But to go very deeply, I think we must begin with the word and see how extraordinarily effective a word is, and how we confuse the word and the meaning and the significance of our feelings. I feel it would be good if we could understand, each one of us, what an extraordinary importance words have, neurologically as well as physically, in the ways of our thought, the ways of our action, the way of our living. It seems to me that unless we can break through the barrier of words and free thought from words, we shall not be able to find out who the experiencer is and if it is possible to free the mind from all experience. It sounds odd and crazy, but we will see what it means as we go along.

I do not know if you are aware of the role words play in your life. First of all, we know that the word is not the thing. The word *tree* is not the tree; that is obvious. And the word *time* is not the whole field in which time, as yesterday, today, and tomorrow, exists; time as distance, time as progress—the word is not all that. So we must be able to dissociate the word from the thing, and to dissociate the word from the feeling which the word evokes. I do not know if you have ever tried it yourself as an experiment—to dissociate a feeling from the word. Take the word *love,* and the actual feeling. Does the word awaken the feeling; or does the feeling come first and then the word, the symbol? Unless one has experimented very carefully with this for oneself, one's thinking will be very limited; one only functions upon the verbal level otherwise. So it seems to me that it is very important to see how the word, the name, the symbol gives shape to thought because all words, symbols, names shape our thinking. The word *India*—if you are an Indian and feel very sentimental about it, if you are nationalistic and all that nonsense—gives immediately an emotional surge; an undefined, sentimental, unrelated feeling is aroused by

that word. It awakens in you the picture of India, the map, the country, the sea, the dirt, the squalor, the beauty of the mountains, the rich sunsets, and the division of the people, their callousness, the superstitions, the traditions—the whole thing. Obviously the word arouses an extraordinary feeling. The word is not the feeling, but you give significance to the word and it takes hold of you. The word *Christ,* the word *Buddha*—how immediately it has significance, neurologically and biologically. So, too, the word *meditation.* How, immediately on hearing it, the mind takes a posture, the mind assumes a certain attitude; that word reawakens certain memories from childhood, from what you have read, from tradition, and you at once have thoughts of what you must or must not do. So each word awakens and shapes the mind; the thought shapes the mind.

After all, that is the whole process of propaganda. Unless the mind is able to dissociate the word from the feeling and investigate the feeling freed from the word, you will ever be a slave to words; therefore, you will be a slave also of tyranny, of propaganda, of all the religious rackets. Take the word *guru*—what an extraordinary significance it has for you; at once you become reverential. I do not know if you have noticed it, but the word *Brahmin* to an anti-Brahmin is something terrible, and the word *Russian* implies at once a political belief. I am just indicating the extraordinary slavishness of the mind to the word.

Then the question is: Can the mind free itself from the word? And, is there thinking without the word, the symbol? After all, unless you are able to dissociate the word from the feeling, you do not know what you are. Take the word *atma*—that is a favorite word of all the religious, phony people. By using that word they think they have solved everything. But to find out whether it is a fact, whether it has any reality, one must first be free of all the emotional significance we give to that word. Then you can investigate it; then you can think very sharply, and such thinking has significance.

So if the mind can dissociate the word from the feeling, then the mind can investigate what it actually is. Is the mind merely a series of words which we have accumulated—with all their significances, conscious as well as unconscious—or is the mind different from the word? Is there a mind without the word? Is there a thought without the symbol? I do not know if you have ever thought along these lines, but I would like to inquire into it very deeply with you to see if the mind can be free from the word and, when it is free from the word, what is the state of the mind? And, is the observer who examines the mind merely another series of words? And when thought is freed from the word, is there thinking? I do not know if I am making myself clear, but unless one goes into this very seriously—inwardly, deeply—self-knowledge will have very little meaning.

So, what is the self?—bearing in mind what we have seen previously, that the word must be separated from the thought, the feeling. I think it is very important to go into this because if I do not know what I am actually, if I do not know the source of my thought, why I act this way or that, why I have beliefs, ideals, ambitions, why I struggle ceaselessly, if I do not know the source and cause of all this, obviously whatever I think, whatever I do is merely an addition or a subtraction on the periphery. If the quality of the mind itself is to undergo a tremendous revolutionary change—the quality, not the layers, the thoughts, the activities, but the quality of the mind itself—if there is to be a revolution at the very center and not at the periphery, then I must understand all this, I must understand myself.

Obviously we must change, but not through environmental influences, not through slogans, not through propaganda, or mechanistic devices conditioning the mind from outside. Because if the mind is to have within itself a new quality, then the mind must understand all this, be aware not only of the conscious, everyday state, but also of the unconscious, where perhaps words have much more significance than in the conscious mind. For in the unconscious are stored up all the traditions, the racial inheritance, the years of thought, the conclusions, hopes, and fears. To understand this extraordinary thing called the mind—which is infinitely capable and yet so petty, narrow, deadly—the mind must be aware of itself, of its own conditioning.

So, what is the mind? Let us begin, not with the mind, but with the self which we say we must know. There must be self-knowledge, must there not? There must be a total comprehension of oneself, not merely a peripheral understanding of some immediate superficial response. I say there must be such a comprehension, and if we investigate very carefully the whole process of thinking and the verbal response, if we can go into it very deeply, then we will see that a revolution in the quality of the mind is immediate—immediate in the sense of being stripped of time. I hope you are following all this and not merely learning a few phrases to quote back to me when we start again. Because if you could seriously consider what is being said, not merely hear it, but apply it in the sense of being aware through my description of yourself, of how your own mind is working—then I think we shall be able to go very far.

So, what is this self which has such an extraordinary importance? Do not say that it is not important, that the only important thing is the higher self, and all that nonsense. Because if it had no importance, we would not be fighting for jobs, we would not be killing each other, we would not be ambitious, frustrated, unhappy in this whole field of isolated agony and loneliness. So, sirs, what is the 'me', the 'you'? Do not bother about how it began and where it will land, but actually, what are you now? A few possessions, a house, a bank account if you have one, a name, a form, certain tendencies, a certain temperament, your fears, hopes, ambitions, achievements, some technical knowledge, the know-how for living in this world—you are all that, are you not? But you want to add to it that you are also something which you call the atma or the higher self, the eternal, the spiritual entity. But again that is in the field of thought, is it not? Since you can think about it, it is related to thought and therefore still within the field of time. I hope you understand this. One cannot think about something one does not know—the immeasurable, the timeless—can one? There is no measurement for it; it is outside the field of thought. One can speculate, spin a lot of theories about it, but theories are not actualities.

So what I can think about is related to time; it is not out of time. Surely this is fairly clear, is it not? Being a Hindu you can think about God because you have been told certain things. The communist does not think about God because his symbol is the state, which is his God. So your God is the product of your own thinking and therefore not real. If you really feel that to be so, to be true, then your God has no meaning whatsoever. Then you can start to find out if there is a God or not. That is fun; that inquiry has vitality, depth, fullness, vigor, but just to repeat that there is God and go to the temple, or whatever you do, has no meaning; it is deadly, unreal, a devitalizing existence. As you know, this is what is happening in this poor, unfortunate country; we are dying to beauty, dying intellectually, artistically, morally, in every way because we are living at the verbal level which has no meaning at all.

So the self is the 'me' with all its memories. There are the memories at the superficial, conscious level where we add techniques, modern science, and so on, and below that is the unconscious with all the causations, the sexual urges, the perversions, fears, racial and family inheritance, the gods, beliefs, ideals, the culture of centuries—all that is the 'me'.

Now is that 'me' merely a word? Do you understand what I am asking, the meaning of my question? Say you call yourself a Hindu, a Brahmin, a Christian, a Buddhist, or whatever it is; is what you are merely a word dissociated from your consciousness? Or does the word signify your consciousness? Or has the word Hindu, Brahmin, Buddhist, Christian no meaning at all? Are you not just aware of yourself as consciousness? Do you follow what I mean? I do not want to take more examples or we shall get lost; we must be able to think generally, abstractly, then we can come to the particular. If you can grasp the significance of the total statement, then you can work out the details for yourself. After all, sirs, we are not only the full, rich past coming into contact with the present—in which the Western culture is imposing itself on the Eastern—we are creating action. But is all this merely a series of words?

Let me put it differently. What is the instrument of your investigation? It is thought, obviously, is it not? When you say, "I will look, I will investigate," what do you mean? Do you look verbally, using words all the time, or do you say to yourself, "I know the danger of words, but I will just look." Can you look without words? Probably this seems too abstract, but I don't think it is if you are following what I am saying. We say we want to investigate the 'me', to have self-knowledge, but obviously it is essential to find out what the instrument is with which we examine, investigate. Are you investigating yourself by means of a series of words or symbols? That is actually what you are doing. You have an idea of the self, a picture, a symbol of the self, and with another series of words you are investigating. But cannot the mind look at itself without any symbol, without any word? Can I free the mind from the word, from the thinking? Thinking is the response of memory, a series of words, is it not? There is in memory a kind of bank of associations, and from that I respond. Take a very simple thing. I ask you something with which you are very familiar, such as where do you live, or what is your name. Your response is immediate because you are so familiar with the question and the answer—it is automatic. The mind does not need to set going the motion of thought; the response is instantaneous. But if I ask you a question a little more complex, there is a gap before you can respond. In that gap is the process of thinking, investigating, which is memory taking time to find the reply. So the interval between a challenge and the response is time, and in that time thought is taking place. The greater the lag between the question and the answer, the more the thought process is working. That is simple; you can experiment with yourself and see it happening. Whether the response is automatic or delayed, it is always the response from memory, from the bank of words.

Now please do watch yourself as you listen. Because I am asking you now a question. When you think, what is taking place? Are you thinking in words, in symbols? And is there such a thing as thinking without words, without symbols? Is there such a state? You see I want to go into it further, more deeply, but I cannot if you are not following, going along with me.

I say to myself, "Am I merely a collection of words?" For if I strip myself of name, of property, of certain things I may have, what am I? Have you ever gone into it? If you have ever gone into yourself, stripped yourself of your specialties, your knowledge, your ambitions, the hundreds of things that one has, what then are you? You must surely, in moments, have experienced that sense of complete isolation, loneliness. Now is that state merely verbal, is that acute loneliness merely verbal? Or is it actual? Please listen carefully. If it is actual, then is it possible to look at it, investigate it, without a word? It is possible, is it not? Then, if you have removed the word, is not investigation only, that state? Obviously, if you remove the word, then the investigator is not somebody apart from that agony, that complete self-isolation. So there is no observer when the word is not used. I do not know if I am making myself clear. Let us take something closer, nearer. I am angry. At the moment of that intense adrenal flow into my blood when I am angry, there is no awareness or consciousness of a separate 'me' who is angry. There is only the state of anger. A second afterwards there is self-identification with that state, and then I say, "I am angry." Now if you do not identify yourself with that state, if you free the mind from the word *anger,* what then? Does it continue? Sirs, I hope you are following this, if even only a little bit. I am not playing intellectual gymnastics, but if one can do this, it means an extraordinary, radical change in the quality of the mind.

The word anger has great sociological and moral significance. The word itself is condemnatory. And that word you give to a feeling automatically, and so you never investigate the feeling itself. You are incapable of investigating it because you have already invested it with a verbal significance. So, can you free the mind from the word and look at the feeling? Is it anger that is there when you take away the word?

So we begin to see what an extraordinary significance the word has. If you have ever experienced loneliness, you will know the terror, the agony, the despair, the incommunicable state in which the mind finds itself. But if the mind can free itself from the word, then you are able to look at it without verbalizing. Then your looking brings into being an entirely different state.

Seeing all this, what is the experiencer, the observer, the thinker, to whom experience, knowledge, is so important? What does that word *experience* mean? Is it again only a word, or an actual state of experiencing in which there is no separate experiencer? I am afraid I am putting too many things into one basket all at once, but unless you go through all this very profoundly, you will find that the experiencer always separates himself from the experience, and therefore the conflict between the two false things will always exist, which is the most destructive thing to the mind and the main cause of our deterioration. I am going on quickly and I hope you will keep pace.

Is there experiencing without the experiencer? Obviously not. Unless I am aware that I am experiencing, there is no experiencer. When I separate myself from experience and am aware that I am experiencing, then I say I like this experience and I do not like that; this is pleasurable, that is not pleasurable. Then I seek the one and avoid the other. So my mind has divided itself, is in a state of contradiction, caught in the duality of pleasure and no pleasure, and I spend my life in that way everlastingly until I die. So I want to find out if there is experiencing without the experiencer. That may sound crazy, but it is not. Because I see that so long as I am conscious that I am experiencing, I divide it all up as pleasurable or painful and pursue the one and avoid the other, thereby creating endless conflict. I also see that conflict of any kind, outward or inward, is deadly to a

mind that wants to be alert, healthy, vigorous, vital. So the question is: Can there be experience without the experiencer? Which is the same question as: Can there be thinking without the word? Please do not answer; it is not a question of agreeing or disagreeing; you have to go into it.

When I go into that question very deeply, I see that there can be a state of experiencing without the experiencer and in which there is no experience at all. This is not a state of insensitivity, of death, of a mind which has been anesthetized, but the state of a mind which is completely awake, totally aware of itself because it has completely understood the whole content of itself and all the processes which I have described. When such a mind is totally comprehending itself and knows all the intricacies of itself, then you will find there is a state which is not experiencing at all. So long as there is awareness of an experience, there must be a division between the observer and the observed, and therefore conflict. So you have to find out whether there is such a thing as thinking without words, if there is an experiencing without the experiencer, and if there is a mind that is fully awake without experiencing, without knowing experience.

Now when the mind is not experiencing but is fully awake, such a mind alone can discover that which is beyond. But, you see, these are words. It is very interesting, what is taking place now. I want to communicate something to you, I want to tell you something, but I can only tell you something of which you know. I cannot tell you of something you do not know. I want to, but you only know the experiencer experiencing, with all the struggle. You do not know the state of experiencing only, without the experiencer translating the experience according to his memory. And you certainly do not know—though some of you may—the state where there is no experiencer at all. I want to tell you about it, but see the difficulty! There are no words to describe it; no symbols to cover it. For it, your holy books have no meaning; they are dead.

So I say that to go through all this profoundly in yourself, that alone brings a new quality to the mind, that alone is the true revolution. Then there is the creative mind; that is creation. So you see how important it is to have self-knowledge, not the platitude, but actual self-knowledge, not the verbal approach, but the actual comprehension of the whole state of your being. If you go into it, you are bound to come to this point where you are able to think without the word, where there is an experiencing without the experiencer, where there is only a state where there is no experience. How can something which is totally alive, which is light, experience? To know of that, the whole problem of thinking must be gone into, and then you will see the extraordinary beauty of it, the depth, the riches that are really there. Such a mind does not need gods, rituals, ceremonies, a country, or books. To such a mind the whole thing from beginning to end is a way of meditation, a way of living.

November 9, 1958

Seventh Talk in Madras

I think almost all serious people must have thought a great deal about the necessity of bringing about a radical change in the quality of the mind. We see, as things are in the world, that there is no fundamental alteration or change in the human mind. Of course, through pressure, economic and social, through various forms of religious fear, through new inventions, and so on, there is change, but this change is always peripheral, on the outside, and obviously such change does not bring about a deep, radical change in the quality of the mind. You must have noticed that society always follows a pattern, certain formulas, in the same way as every individual follows certain concepts, ideals, always moving within the pattern. You must have noticed it not only in yourself and in society but in all our relationships, and you must have wondered how to bring about a deep, lasting, integrated change, so that the interaction between the outer and the inner does not bring about corruption. I do not mean anything mysterious by the ''inner.'' It is the inner quality of the mind that I am talking about, not inward things which the mind imagines and speculates about. All society, all human existence is a matter of this interrelationship between the outer and the inner which is constantly fluctuating and always modifying. And if I may, I would like to talk about the possibility of a radical change because I think it is very important. After all, we are social entities and we must live by action. Life is action. One cannot just sit and speculate; neither can one merely carry on with the corruption because, as we know, it only breeds contradiction within ourselves and everlasting torture and struggle.

So how is the mind to change? How is there to be a radical change in the total consciousness, not only on the upper levels of the mind, but also at the deeper levels, and not along a set pattern? Following a pattern is not a change at all; it is merely a modified continuity of what has been. How is one to really change the quality, the substance of one's consciousness totally? I do not know if you have thought about it, or are you merely concerned with outward changes which are brought about by every form of social and economic revolution, every new invention? If we are concerned with a total change of consciousness, of the quality of the mind, then I think we must think negatively because negative thinking is the highest form of thinking, not the so-called positive thinking. The positive is merely the pursuit of a formula, a conclusion, and all such thinking is limited, conditioned.

I hope you are listening rather than just hearing because I want to go into something rather difficult, if I can, and I hope we shall be able to proceed with it together. But if you are merely hearing and not listening, then you will be caught at the verbal level and words then become over-significant. Words are only the means of communicating something. So I hope you are going to listen without any desire to understand mere ideas. I have no ideas because I think they are the most stupid things; they have no substance, no reality, they are just words. So I hope you are listening in the sense of trying to see the problem—just to see it, not to struggle to understand it or resolve it, but to see this extraordinary complex problem which we have—the problem of bringing about a total change in consciousness, in the mind.

As I was saying, negative thinking is the highest form of thinking. We never think negatively; we think only positively. That is, we think from a conclusion to a conclusion, from a pattern to a pattern, from a system to a system—that I must be this; I must acquire some virtue, follow this or that path, do certain disciplines. The positive thinking is always in the grooves of our own conditioned thinking—I hope you are watching your own mind, your own thought—and that way only leads to further limitation of the mind, to narrowness of the mind, to pettiness of action; it always strengthens the self-centered activity. Negative thinking is something entirely different, but it is not the opposite of positive thinking. If I can understand the limitations of positive thinking, which invariably leads to self-centered activity, if I can understand not only verbally, intellectually, but as the whole process of human thinking, then there is a new awakening in negative thinking.

Most of us are attached to something—to property, to a person, an idea, a belief, an experience—are we not? You are attached to your family, your good name, your profession, your guru, to this and that. Now, this attachment invariably breeds suffering and conflict because the thing to which you are attached is constantly changing, obviously. But you do not want the change; you want to hold on to it permanently. So, being aware that attachment breeds sorrow, grief, pain, you try to cultivate detachment. Obviously both attachment and the cultivation of detachment are positive ways of thinking. Detachment is not the negation of attachment; it is merely attachment continued under a different verbal garb. The mental process is entirely the same, if you have ever noticed it. For instance, I am attached to my wife. In that there is pain, struggle, jealousy, frustration; and to escape from all that, I say, "I must be detached, I must love in an impersonal manner"—whatever that may mean—"I must love without limitation," and I try to cultivate detachment. But the center of my activity in attachment or detachment is exactly the same thing. So, our thinking which we call positive is a conflict of the opposites or an endeavor to escape into a synthesis which again creates an opposite. Take communism—it is the antithesis of capitalism, and eventually through struggle the communists hope to create a synthesis, but because it is born of the conflict of opposites, that synthesis is going to create another antithesis. And this process is what we call positive thinking, not only outwardly, socially, but inwardly also.

Now if one understands the total process of all this, not only intellectually, but actually, then we will see that a new way of thinking comes into being. It is a negative process unrelated to the positive. The positive way of thinking leads to immaturity, to a mind that is conditioned, shaped, and that is exactly what is happening with all of us. When you say you want to be happy, you want truth, God, to create a different world, it is always in terms of the positive—which is to follow a system that will produce the desired result, and the result is always the known, and it becomes again the cause. Cause and effect are not two different things. The effect of today will be the cause of tomorrow. There is no cause, isolated, which produces an effect; they are interrelated. There is no such thing as a law of cause and effect, which means that there is really no such thing as what we call karma. To us, karma means a result with a previous cause, but in the interval between the effect and the cause, there has been time. In that time there has been a tremendous lot of change, and therefore the effect is never the same. And the effect is going to produce another cause which will never be merely the result of the effect. Do not say, "I do not believe in karma"; that is not the point at all. Karma means, very simply, action and the result, with its further cause. Sow a mango seed and it is bound to produce a mango tree—but the human mind is not like that. The human mind is capable of transformation within itself, immediate comprehension, which is a breaking away from the cause, always.

So negative thinking is not thinking in terms of patterns because patterns imply a cause which will produce a result which the mind can manipulate, control, and change. With that process we are all very familiar. What I am trying to convey is a negative thinking which has no causation. This may all sound too absurd, but we will go into it and you will see. We will approach it differently.

Most of us are discontented, are we not? We are discontented with our job, with our wife, husband, children, neighbors, society, or whatever it is. I want position, I want money, I want love. We know all this. Now discontent with something is positive, but discontent in itself is negative. I will explain. When we are discontented, what is actually taking place? If I am discontented with my job, with myself, what is happening? I want to find contentment through this or through that. So the discontent is canalized until it finds something which will be satisfactory, and then it fades away. That is what we call positive action—to find something which will make us happy. But without the flame of real discontent—not discontent with something—life has no meaning. You may have a marvelous job, an extraordinary brain, get degrees and be able to discuss, quote, but your discontent has merely taken the shape of cleverness, and there you are completely sterile. You started with discontent, and at school perhaps you were very good, but as you grew that discontent became stratified into cleverness or into some form of technique, and there you are satisfied because you feel you have capacity and can function. That again is positive thinking. Whereas negative thinking is just to be in a state of discontent, and such a mind is a very disturbed mind. It is not satisfied, and it is not seeking satisfaction because it sees that satisfaction leads only to that positive action which we all seek. To find a way to be satisfied everlastingly means to be dead. And that is what you want; you call it peace of mind and say, "For God's sake give me some corner in this universe where I can die peacefully." So the positive action leads always to death. If you can see that, then you will see that a negative way of thinking is taking place. Therefore the negative way of thinking never starts with a conclusion because one sees where conclusions lead.

So the negative way of thinking is the maintenance, the sustenance of the quality that is discontent—discontent in itself, not with something. Please do not get caught at the verbal level but see the significance of this. But we must understand that positive thinking is conditioned thinking and that there is no change in that; there is modification but no radical transformation. Radical transformation is only in the negative thinking, as we saw in relation to attachment and to discontent. This positive thinking leads only to a dull mind, an insensitive mind, a mind that is not capable of reception, a mind that thinks only in terms of its own security—either the security of the individual or of the family, group, or race, which you can observe very clearly in world politics.

After all, this earth is ours, yours and mine. This earth which is so marvelous, so beautiful, so rich, is ours to live on happily without all this fragmentation, without being broken up into different fields called England, Germany, Russia, India. Yet we are battling to keep up the separation. Nobody thinks of this whole world as ours, nobody says, ''Let us do something together about it.'' Instead, we have this fragmentary way of thinking which we call positive, or we pursue some idea of internationalism, which is equally silly. If I can see that, then there is a different approach, a different feeling of the mind, whether it be the Russian or the German or whatever mind it is. Then there is no such thing as the nonsense of patriotism; there is the love of the earth—not your earth and my earth, you cultivating your little field and I cultivating mine, and quarreling over it, but it is our earth.

Now when we see that this positive way of thinking is destructive, then the negative way comes into being. To think negatively there must be sensitivity—sensitivity both to the beautiful and to the ugly. The man who is pursuing what he calls the beautiful and avoiding the ugly is not sensitive. The man who pursues virtue without understanding that which is not virtuous, merely avoiding it, is invariably insensitive. Please think this out with me, feel it out, and you will see. So appreciation of the beauty of a tree, a leaf, the reflection on still waters is not sensitivity if you are not also aware of the squalor, the dirt, the way you eat, the way you talk, the way you think, the way of your behavior.

Under this tree it is very beautiful, very quiet, there is lovely shade and light, and just outside there is that filthy village with all the squalor and dirt and the unfortunate human beings who live there, but you are not aware of it. So we are always wanting beauty, truth, and God, and avoiding the other, and that pursuit is the positive and leads to insensitivity, if we are not aware of the other. And the positive way of erecting buildings for dances, having special schools for dancing, all that business becomes a personal racket, satisfying to the mind that is only thinking positively. Creation is not positive, ever. Creation is the state of mind in which there is no positive action as we know it.

So, radical transformation takes place in the mind only when there is this negative thinking. As I said the other day, the thinking that we know of is always in words or symbols. I do not know if you have noticed that there is thinking without words, but that thinking is still the result of the positive word. I will explain. You always think in words, symbols, do you not? Please look. The word, the symbol becomes very important to thought. It is the basis of all our thinking; there is association through memory and the memory is a picture, a word, and from that we proceed to think, again in symbols, words. That is all we know, and also if you are very alert, aware, you can see that there is thinking without the word, without the symbol. I am not going to give an example because then you will get lost, so please capture the significance, for negative thinking is not related to thought-with-the-word. Unless you see this, you will not see what follows. I am thinking aloud; I have not worked it out at home and then come here to speak it out. So please see this, not merely verbally or speculatively, but actually experience that thought functions in words, in symbols, and also that thought functions without the word and the symbol. Both these are positive ways of thinking because they are still in the realm of the opposites. Let me put it differently.

You must have watched your mind, how vagrant it is, how it wanders all over the place, one thought pursuing another. When you try to examine one thought, another comes in. So the mind is full of this movement, the agitation of thought. The mind is always occupied with thought. Thought is the instrument of the mind, so the mind is never still. Do not at once say, "How am I to make the mind still?" That is all too immature, stupid, because it means again a positive following of some pattern. So, realizing the incessant activity of the thought-producing mechanism, through memory, through association, being aware of that, cannot the mind empty itself of this mechanism? Do not ask how, just listen, because understanding is instantaneous; it is not a process which will ultimately get you a mind emptied of thought. If you see the positive, destructive way—of the mind's activity of producing thought and being controlled by it and then trying to empty the mind—if you can see the falseness or the truth of it, then you will also see that the mind can empty itself of itself, of its limitations, of its egocentricity, of its self-centered activities. Please go with me a little.

The mind is perpetually active, producing and controlling thought. It realizes that and says, "I must be quiet," but that generally means quiet through control, which is again positive, destructive, and limiting. But you can see if you go a little further that the mind can be emptied of thought, can free itself from the past, not be burdened by the past. It does not mean that memories are not there, but they do not shape or control the mind. Now all that is still positive thinking. If you see the falseness of it, the mind will invariably go further, which is, the mind then is not the slave of thought, but it can think what it wants. I do not know how to put this. As I said, I am thinking aloud with you, and you will have to excuse me if I try different ways of putting it.

I do not know if you have ever tried to think without being a slave to thought. With most of us the mind is a slave to thought—it pursues thought, contradictory thought, and all the rest of it. If you perceive that and empty the mind, it can then think, freed from thoughts associated with memory; and if you go further into it, you will see that the mind which is free—not in the sense of the opposite of slavery, but free in itself—then that mind, emptied of memory, can think in a negative way. Then you will see that the mind, being completely empty of systems, formulas, speculations, thoughts associated with memory, experiences, and so on, can perceive that there is a state in which there is action in this world, not from fullness, but from emptiness.

You see we are acting now with full minds, overcrowded minds, minds that are incessantly active, in contradiction, struggling, adjusting, ambitious, envious, jealous, brutal, or gentle, and so on. You follow? We are acting on that level. The mind, being full, acts. That action can never produce a new mind, a new quality of mind, a fresh mind, an innocent mind—and it is only such an innocent, fresh mind that can create, that is in a state of creation. The mind sees that, and if the mind can empty itself, then the action that is born out of emptiness is the true positive action, not the other. That is the only true, positive, creative action because it is born out of emptiness. If you have done any painting, written a poem, a song, you will find the deep feeling comes out of nothingness. But a mind that is crowded can never feel that nothingness and can therefore never be sensitive.

One sees that there can be a radical change in the quality of the mind, which is absolutely necessary now because the present society is a dead society, reforming itself through various forms of anesthesia and pumping activity into itself. If you as an individual are to change fundamentally, radically, deeply—and therefore change society—then this whole thing that I have described must take place. Then beauty has quite a different significance, as has ugliness, because beauty is not the opposite of the ugly. An ugly face can be beautiful. But such beauty is not conceived by the mind that has avoided ugliness.

So if you have really listened and do not try to do anything about it—because whatever you do will be so-called positive and therefore destructive—then it is enough. It is to see something lovely and leave it alone, not try to capture it, not take it home and smother it by thought.

If you have seen for yourself, not through my persuasiveness, not through my words, my influence, if you have felt the beauty, the extraordinary quality of the mind that is empty, then from that emptiness there is a new birth.

It is this new birth which is needed, not the going back to Mahabharata, Ramayana, Marx, or Engels, or revivalism. The mind that is really creative is the empty mind, not the blank mind or the mind that merely wishes to be creative. It is only the empty mind that can understand this whole thing— the extraordinary process of thought and thought emptying itself of its own impetus. Then you will see that there is a radical, deep change which is not brought about by influence, circumstances, culture, or society. It is that mind which will create a new society. And the moment it creates a new society, that society is already in corruption. All societies are in corruption because that which

is created is ever dying. Therefore, recognizing that no society, no tradition, no knowledge is permanent, we can see that the mind which is empty is creative, is in a state of creation.

November 12, 1958

Eighth Talk in Madras

It seems to me that most of us are so desirous of being intellectually clever, getting to be so technically trained—which is all a cultivation of the mechanical habit of the mind—that religion plays a very superficial part in our lives. But however clever, however erudite, however capable in the expression of his ideas a man may be, he is never really satisfied with his own cleverness, and he invariably turns to something he thinks is deeper; he begins to inquire, to search because his intellect obviously does not satisfy him wholly. So he turns to religion. Either he becomes a Catholic, where he finds safety, where his intellect can no longer tear things apart, or he turns to some form of Buddhism or Hinduism or what you will. This is what is actually happening right throughout the world. Religion, being thought of as something mysterious and having a quality of "otherness" about it—the intellectual seeks to take shelter in that "otherness" and is satisfied by the belief. And for the rest of us who are not highly intellectual—though we may be very clever verbally, which perhaps is the same thing—religion implies tradition or a revivalism, attending certain ceremonies, going to churches, going to temples, and so on. Being able to quote a lot of platitudes, which really have no meaning, gives us a feeling of religiosity. But surely reality, truth, or whatever it be is not to be caught through any of these methods, nor by a petty mind, however clever it is. Because a petty mind, whatever its activities, whatever its gods, whatever its virtues, visions, formulas, conceptions, and speculations, must invariably remain petty, small, narrow, limited. I think that is fairly obvious, though one may not admit it to oneself. Actually it is a fact that a small mind cannot see beyond the limits of its own frontiers; it cannot go beyond the frontiers of recognition.

So, living within the field of recognition—which I will go into presently—our gods, our realities are always within the time limitation, always something to be achieved through various forms of discipline, control, suppression, or sublimation. I do not know if you have noticed how your own mind operates. If you have, you are bound to have observed how extraordinarily limited the mind is. You may be a technical expert, a high-ranking executive, a bank manager, or a clerk, but behind the façade of technical knowledge there is a vast field of discontent. And this discontent soon takes the form of seeking to become very religious, sanctimonious, or tearful; and such a mind being petty, small, narrow, limited, obviously its expression, its search for God, for truth is very, very limited. If you ask the savage or the primitive man what God is, he will express it in very limited, narrow terms, such as the worship of the elements. And if you go higher in the scale of so-called civilization, culture, you will find man's gods are equally limited, based on what he has been told or what his little field of search has revealed. So the petty mind always functions within the field of its own recognition. Is not that so with most of us? Our virtues are standardized, our norms are defined, our activities respectable, our whole outlook is limited to the recognized and the respected. If you watch your own mind—and I am not insulting you by saying you have a petty mind—you will see that it functions only within the frontiers of recognition, that which you can recognize. It expresses simplicity in terms of the loincloth; its passions, affections, hates, its drive and power are always recognizable, associated with what is considered respectable by the majority. Is it not so? If you watch yourself, you will see that you are always functioning within the field, the frontiers, the barriers of recognition and so always within the realm of time. Our gods, our virtues, our loves, struggles, aspiration, and goodness are all very limited and narrow.

Now most of us are unwilling to see that. We either blame society or our education or say that circumstances have forced us to be as we are, and we refuse to acknowledge honestly to ourselves that our own mind is petty. But a mind that functions only within the field of time, that is, the yesterday, today, and tomorrow, is obviously a petty mind. Whether the "yesterday" travels backwards indefinitely, or the "tomorrow" travels forward indefinitely, or the "today" be limited to the present—it is all within the field of time and therefore very narrow. The man who wants to become the manager, the boss, the whole process of seeking power, the ambition, however seemingly noble, extensive, ideological—all this is within the field of time and therefore petty.

Please do listen to all this and not merely hear it intellectually and casually agree or disagree or rationalize it away. Because if you actually listen, you will see the workings of your own mind like the ticking of a clock; you can hear it, see it, observe it if you are sensitive enough to feel the motion, the action of your own mind. It is a fact, whether one acknowledges it to oneself or not, that we try to modify ourselves, recreate society, bring about some revival, or pursue some new set of ideas, but always within that recognizable field of the mind. Our Masters, our gurus, our visions are all recognizable, and therefore there is nothing new. That which you recognize can never be new. Whatever you recognize, you have already known.

And that which is known has already been established in the past, which is memory, which is of time, and therefore it is the old.

So, the very serious man who really wants to understand this whole problem of existence must obviously put the question to himself as to how to break this barrier, which is not only of the conscious mind but of the hidden, deeper layers of consciousness which again, if examined very deeply, is still within the field of time and recognition. I am using the word *recognition* in its very simplest form. I recognize you because I have met you previously; otherwise, obviously, I would not know you. I am using the word in that sense.

To the petty mind—even though it be intellectual and therefore functioning more cleverly within the field of recognition—to the petty mind there is nothing new. It functions always within the known, even though it calls it the future. All the social workers, the reformers, the seekers of a utopia, the communists, anti-communists, socialists, capitalists, they are all working within the field of recognition, in the field of the norm they have established, which is always based on time. So none of them can bring about a true revolution. A fundamental revolution means something totally new, and we need such a revolution because all other forms of revolution—economic, social, or religious—have failed. They are all really only the antithesis of what has been, a reaction from what has been.

So, seeing this extraordinary process of the mind in ourselves, and in the intellectual people, in the visionaries, in the social workers, and in the so-called saints, we must have asked ourselves how to break this narrow, petty, traditional mind. The scientific mind is also a traditional mind and functions in the field of recognition. The scientist is not going to bring about a revolution; he will invent new methods or ways of living, but

they will only create new circumstances to which the mind must adjust itself, and therefore it is not a revolution. You can use refrigerators, fly in a jet, or go to the moon, but the mind is still petty, narrow.

Seeing all this and being aware of this whole process, how is the mind to break through, break right away from the pettiness? I do not know if you have ever asked yourself that question. And when you do, how do you reply, what is your response? If you are not too bored with the question, if you really want to find an answer as you want to find food when you are hungry, then how do you go about it? Surely, to break anything, to bring about radical action there must be passion. Feeling strongly about something brings its own action, does it not? If I felt strongly about the squalor in the streets, the dirt, if I felt urgently, intensely about it, I would do something. I would create an organization which will do something about it. I would not sit down and intellectually rationalize the squalor and leave it to somebody else to tackle. If one feels something deeply one acts, does one not? But unfortunately we have disciplined our feelings. We have been told for centuries that desire is wrong, that it leads to sorrow, that one must be free of desire, and then one will find God—a dead God, generally. Whatever it is you find—obviously a dead mind will find nothing worth finding. It is only a living mind that will find.

For centuries people have said, "Destroy, control, shape, subjugate desire," and society—which after all is only the interaction between individuals—has helped to maintain and sustain the suppression of all feelings. You dare not have strong feelings because if you have a very strong feeling, you may do something vital, you may be a dangerous entity, a dangerous citizen. So you begin to suppress, control, shape your feelings to the edicts of society, or else you try to sublimate, that is, try to find some way of escaping from the violent tortures of strong feeling. This is what we do, is it not? So, gradually we destroy all feeling except the very, very superficial feelings of a little sex, earning a livelihood for the family, for the very narrow circle, and so on. So our minds, which are petty, reduce all feelings to the same level, and yet without passion—I use that word because, though you may not like it, I think it is the right word—without passion you cannot do anything vital.

What does that word *passion* mean? I would like to go into it because I think it is very important. Most people, here and elsewhere, though they are frightfully active superficially—creating new mills, more dams, more scientific inventions—if you observe, you will find that all over the world most people are dead. It is only the dying that are corruptible, not the living. And being dead—though not altogether dead, obviously—how is one to revive? We still have a flicker of some emotion, a flicker of an aspiration, a spark of ambition, but it is so very small. You all want to take the next step on the ladder of success, and how are you to break out of such narrowness and be made anew? That is the problem, is it not? I do not know if you have thought about it at all. Legislation will not help. Obviously there is going to be more legislation, more planning, more state welfare from the womb to the tomb, and in that process the mind will become more and more trapped. So seeing all this, what is one to do?

Obviously there must be passion, and the question is how to revive that passion. Do not let us misunderstand each other. I mean passion in every sense, not merely sexual passion which is a very small thing. And most of us are satisfied with that because every other passion has been destroyed—in the office, in the factory, through following a certain job, routine, learning techniques—so

there is no passion left; there is no creative sense of urgency and release. Therefore sex becomes important to us, and there we get lost in petty passion which becomes an enormous problem to the narrow, virtuous mind, or else it soon becomes a habit and dies. I am using the word *passion* as a total thing. A passionate man who feels strongly is not satisfied merely with some little job—whether it be the job of a prime minister, or of a cook, or what you will. A mind that is passionate is inquiring, searching, looking, asking, demanding, not merely trying to find for its discontent some object in which it can fulfill itself and go to sleep. A passionate mind is groping, seeking, breaking through, not accepting any tradition; it is not a decided mind, not a mind that has arrived, but it is a young mind that is ever arriving.

Now, how is such a mind to come into being? It must happen. Obviously, a petty mind cannot work at it. A petty mind trying to become passionate will merely reduce everything to its own pettiness. It must happen, and it can only happen when the mind sees its own pettiness and yet does not try to do anything about it. Am I making myself clear? Probably not. But as I said earlier, any activity of a petty mind, a small mind, a restricted mind, however eager it is, will still be petty, and surely that is obvious. A small mind, though it can go to the moon, though it can acquire a technique, though it can cleverly argue and defend, is still a small mind; whatever its activities are, it is a small mind. So when that small mind says, "I must be passionate in order to do something worthwhile," obviously its passion will be very petty, will it not—like getting angry about some petty injustice or thinking that the whole world is changing because of some petty, little reform done in a potty, little village by a potty, little mind. If the little mind sees all that, then the very perception that it is small is enough; then its whole activity undergoes a change.

Look, sirs, so long as I do not acknowledge that I am blind, everything I do is disastrous. But if suddenly, being blind, I acknowledge it, what happens? I develop totally new tendencies, new ways of perception, do I not? My touch becomes much more sensitive; I apprehend anything that is very close to me; a totally new set of reactions is set going; all my consciousness becomes astonishingly sensitive and acute. And most of us are blind, asleep, petty, narrow; and if we could only acknowledge it, not merely intellectually, verbally, but actually see it—without falling into despair which again is the process of the small mind that ever climbs towards hope and drops back into despair—then we would see that a totally new set of reactions comes into being. And do you see what happens then? That recognition brings into being humility. Not the humbleness of a mind which says, "I see I am petty and I wish I were big"—that is merely the extension of vanity. I am talking of the mind that actually sees that all its actions are petty, and immediately there is a sense of humility. Humility is not a thing to be cultivated. A mind that cultivates humility merely makes itself humble; it is like a cloak it puts on, and behind the cloak there is vanity.

So when I recognize that my mind is small and that whatever it does will still be small, when I know that, when I feel it, when I perceive the significance of what is being said now, then my mind is humility. And that is essential, for then begins real learning. Because, the mind that has learned cannot learn. How can a mind which is burdened with learning, how can a mind which has accumulated knowledge be free to climb the mountain? It can climb only when it has unburdened itself, and the moment the mind unburdens itself of what it has learned, it is learning.

So the very perception of the pettiness of one's own mind which works and functions only within the field of recognition, that very perception is a breaking-through, and at that very instant there is humility and therefore the action of learning. And you cannot learn if there is no passion, and there can only be passion when there is complete self-abandonment. I hope you follow this. You cannot be passionate if you do not abandon yourself, obviously. That is, if there is not complete self-forgetfulness, complete self-abandonment, complete self-abnegation of this time element, which is the self, then there is no passion. The very essence of humility is self-abandonment. So in this sense of humility there is the passion to learn, not to accumulate learning—that is nothing, that is merely to be an encyclopedia—but the passion to find out, to inquire, to search, to understand; and such passion can only come when the 'me' is absent. You do have such passion when you are vitally interested in something; you totally forget yourself when you love somebody. And I do not mean the love that knows jealousy, the love that knows hate, the love that is occupied with itself, the stupid sense of sympathy that wants to do good. Love never wants to do good. Love never wants to reform. It is a thing that is eternal, and you cannot capture it within the net of time.

So there cannot be humility if there is no passion to learn, and passion does not come into being unless there is self-abandonment. When there is self-abandonment, there is simplicity, there is austerity—not the cultivated austerity of the mind that says, "I must only have one meal a day, only possess two loincloths" and makes a public exhibition of itself. And you will see that the simplicity of self-abandonment is extraordinarily rich. In the so-called simplicity of fasting, prayer, discipline, and controlled austerity, there is no richness, there is no beauty, there is no sensitivity. But to the mind that knows passion through self-abandonment, there is a simplicity of enormous, boundless, endless riches. Such a mind is infinitely sensitive, and such a mind is a creative mind; it is free from conflict. And there is no self-abandonment, with all its beauty and riches, unless there is self-knowledge. If you do not know yourself—if you do not know what you think, what you feel, what your ideas are, what the sources of your motives are, why you think this, and why you do that—if you do not know how your mind operates, obviously you cannot abandon yourself. You may chip off one or two pieces, cut out the things you do not like from this total consciousness, but that is not self-knowledge. To understand yourself you must be aware of the way you talk, your gestures, your approach to another, your fears and ambitions, your joys and fleeting loves. To know all that—not as an accumulation of knowledge, but to see it as it actually happens every day and watch it—in that total awareness there is self-abandonment. Then only there is passion.

Sirs, you cannot come to truth empty-handed. Truth will not come to you if you have suppressed all your feelings, all your emotions, if you have tamed them all, made them respectable. Nor must you be a sinner. Perhaps the sinner is nearer because he is active, he has feelings. You must be extraordinarily rich in your emptiness. Now you are rich only in the dead ashes of virtue, of struggle, in your little aspirations, ambitions, and frustrations; yet, laden with all of that you want to find God. You cannot, obviously. Only to the mind that is completely empty, that is not seeking, not demanding, not asking, only to such a mind reality comes—not the reality of the Upanishads, the Gita, or the Bible, none of that. Those are words, platitudes, they have only the meaning which your little mind gives them. One must empty the mind of all thought, for thought is of time; one must empty the mind of all knowledge of the yesterday, of all experience, so that the mind is made fresh, new, young, innocent, and yet totally empty. It is only the empty mind, which is void, that can be filled.

But that means hard work. It is hard work to realize that one's mind is petty, small. It is hard work to observe this fact, to face it, to grapple with it, not trying to escape from it. It is much harder work than going to your office or passing an examination because it demands constant alertness, constant awareness, watching every minute to see your petty, little actions. And most of us are unwilling to work hard, and therefore the Bible or the Gita gives a very good escape, and we think that by quoting them, we become very religious; or else we take up social work and escape there. None of these things will bring reality. It is the mind which has abandoned its pursuits that is rich in its emptiness and therefore quiet; only such a mind knows silence without the recognition of silence, and only to such a mind the immeasurable comes.

November 16, 1958

Bombay, India, 1958

---　✳　---

First Talk in Bombay

Communication is at all times quite difficult, and especially so when one is concerned with the very complex problem of living and the extensive implications of one's daily activities. To talk about that and to communicate all the implications involved in the process of living is very, very difficult. If you want to communicate an idea to someone else, that in itself is quite complex, but it is more particularly so when one is dealing with what we call life. Life includes, does it not, every act of living, every subtlety of thought, the nuances, differences, the struggles, the joys, the extensive depths of thought, and to communicate all this is extremely difficult, especially when most of us are not used to thinking along this particular line.

I want to say something to you, and for you to listen to what is being said requires, naturally, a verbal comprehension. You have to understand English, the actual words, so that there is communication at the verbal level, and the verbal level then leads to the intellectual comprehension of what is being said. Through the medium of words, what is said is conveyed to the intellect. Then the intellect either rejects or accepts what is being said. But before it accepts or rejects, naturally it must weigh, balance, reason, exert its capacity to discover what is false and what is

true, and that takes time, and in the meanwhile the speaker has gone on with a new set of ideas, a new thought, and so you are left behind and it is difficult to catch up with what he is saying. You are always behind and he is always going ahead, and communication becomes extremely difficult.

So, there is communication at the verbal level, there is communication at the intellectual level, and also there is communication at the emotional level; and the emotional level is much easier. When one appeals to emotions it is comparatively easy for you to be carried along on that wave of sensation.

The problem of communication is extraordinarily difficult, and one must realize the difficulty and be able to pierce through the words because then only is there communion. Communication leads to communion and communion means sharing, partaking. This is not a discourse on what to do or what not to do; it is an experiment in communing with each other. We are going to commune with each other at all levels—verbal, intellectual, emotional—and therefore it means partaking, sharing with what the speaker is saying. This does not mean that you must agree or disagree. One can only agree or disagree with ideas and opinions. When you are dealing with facts—facts which reveal truth—there is no agreement or disagreement. The sharing comes in when you and I can see the fact, and see the truth or falseness in the fact. And in the process of this communion with each other, I hope we shall be able to discard that which is false and see very clearly, very precisely that which is true. The perception is as important as action. To me, perception is equal to action.

What I am going to speak about now and in the coming talks is not a matter of ideas, of dealing with opinions, conclusions, and all the intellectual accumulations of the mind in order for you to refute or accept. What we are doing now is to share together, commune with each other about the whole process of life. And life is so extensive; in it is involved work, pleasure, sorrow, death, joy, meditation, the whole process of thinking, following, fear, the accumulations of memory, the responses of memory, as well as the extraordinary beauty of the evening when clouds gather towards the sunset over the horizon. All that is life. Life is not just the small section of your personal joys, your own little family, your particular ambitions, your sexual pleasures, and so on. Life is all the laughter of the world, all the tears, sorrows, miseries, toil, conflicts, struggle, and the extraordinary delight of seeing something beautiful. All that is life, and we must partake of that, commune with each other about it, but not theoretically, speculatively, or abstractly, not quoting from some idiotic or so-called sacred book. That has no value. We are dealing directly with life, not with ideas about life, and there is a vast difference between the two. We are not dealing with ideas or theories, we are dealing actually with life—the life that covers this full earth, the life of everyday existence, the life of our toil, our ambitions, our deceptions and corruption. This is a fact, and if we approach it with opinions, ideas, or theories, we shall not see the fact. Merely to collect opinions about the fact has no value at all, obviously.

So, being very clear as to what we are going to talk about, our relationship with each other must also be established. In a large audience like this, it seems almost impossible to single out the individual and talk to the individual, but that is what I want to do. I want to talk to each one of you as an individual, not as a part of a large audience with many different ideas, many opinions, many conclusions. If you and I, as two individuals, can commune with each other at all levels—intellectual, verbal, emotional—then we shall be able to understand each other. Surely that is the act of understanding, is it not? When with all our being, not just one broken part of ourselves, we listen to each other, then there is communion. So can you listen with all your being—intellectual, verbal, emotional, physical—with all your senses, all your feeling for beauty and all your awareness of evil? For then there is communion, then there is an understanding.

But the difficulty is, is it not, that we have never listened like that to anything. We listen only partially to the song of a bird; we look only partially at the moon; we never really look at a tree or a flower—we glance and pass by, thinking of other things. We never look at something totally, with complete fullness, but it is only then that there is communion. So, what we are going to talk about requires total attention with all our being. If you listen merely verbally, intellectually, obviously there is no communion; neither is there if you merely react emotionally. Then you are throwing up the barrier of sensation or the barrier of words, opinions, or ideas, and so there is no comprehension. If you want to understand something, you must give your whole being to it—your body, your mind, your heart, everything—and then only is there the possibility of complete understanding. But that is a very difficult thing to do because most of you have reserves of accumulated opinions, conclusions, ideas, experiences, what you have learned, your stored-up hurts and pleasures—and all these act as barriers. So what we are going to do is to examine these barriers, not only the conscious barriers, but the unconscious ones also, because they prevent total comprehension.

As I said, I am talking to you, the individual, because I think it is very important that you should find out for yourself the ways of your thinking, the ways of your feeling, how you react, because it is urgently important that there be an individual. As we can see in the world, individuality is being totally crushed out. We will go into what I mean by the word *individual* and what you mean by it, a little later on. We must first see what is happening throughout the world, how the powers-that-be are trying to capture the mind. That is what is taking place everywhere—a getting hold of the mind. Religions have done it—the Christians, Catholics, Buddhists, Hindus, Muslims, and so on. They have captured the mind and implanted in it certain ideas, opinions, beliefs, and doctrines, certain conceptions of what is true and what is false, and what God is. They have captured the mind, which is an obvious fact. If you will observe your own mind, you will see that you are either captured by your particular religion or you are captured by a political slogan or by a particular system of thought, and so on. And throughout the world, as one can observe, the different governments through various means are capturing the mind so that the individual has really ceased to be.

You are not really an individual, are you? You are merely a collection of ideas and opinions implanted by a religion, a political party, by books, newspapers, and propaganda of all kinds; you are just a series of ideas, a series of memories. We can see also that in this world there is overpopulation, over-organization, and mass communication, and that these three things are destroying the in-dividual because they destroy freedom. We do not realize these extraordinarily subtle things which are going on around us. In a country like this which is overpopulated, there is endless suffering, starvation, and poverty; so, obviously there is a revolt against the system and a demand for a new system that will satisfy and that will give food, clothing, and shelter. And so you get mass communication and from that, control of your mind. So through various processes—conscious and unconscious—through subtle propaganda, psychological pressures, the mind is being captured, as it has been captured before. But now it is done much more expertly, more cunningly, as they know all the tricks of psychology, and the psychologists are helping to show the powers-that-be how to capture the mind of man. I do not know if you as an individual are aware of all this. Do not say, "Yes, but what can I do about it?" Perhaps you cannot do anything about it, but first, what matters is, are you actually aware of it?" Perhaps you will never ask what to do about it because you will do the right thing if once you are aware of what is taking place actually. You never ask what to do when you face a dangerous snake. The trouble is that you do not see the extraordinary things that are going on in the world, the effort that is going on to capture the mind and make the mind a slave to certain systems of thought, to certain religions, to certain patterns.

So our problem is, is it not, how to release the individual energy. Because obviously, when your mind is not free, there is no release. That is why one merely functions in habit with a certain set of ideas, with certain fixed opinions and conclusions, repeating the same words, looking at life the same way, pursuing the same enjoyments and falling into the same despairs. You know the routine pattern, and obviously the mind becomes a machine doing the same thing over and over again. Such a mind cannot have a creative revolt. What is actually wanted now is not more scientists, more agriculturalists, more bridge builders, engineers, and technicians—though, of course, you will have them because at a certain level they are obviously necessary—but what the world actually needs is individuals who are explosively creative, who are not merely mechanical, repeating endlessly, imitating the same thing over and over again. That is why this country is dead. Though you may have new machines, dams, factories, and plans for more and better food, inwardly you are dead. Because you are not an explosive individual, therefore all the forces around you tend to make your mind slavish to a particular pattern of thought. And so, religious, economic, and political tyrannies abound.

One of the chief difficulties is that you and I have never given thought to the discovery of what an individual actually is. I am not talking of the individual as opposed to the community, or of the rugged individual who just barges ahead from ambition; but can we find out actually what we mean by an individual and find out whether it is possible for the mind to free itself from all these compulsions and influences, and be free? Obviously if the mind is not free, there is no possibility of creativeness; you will merely continue to act as a machine. So is it possible for you, the single human being, actually to discover for yourself what it is to be an individual—that is, to find out if the mind can be free?

In the past your mind identified itself with certain ideals, like "Freedom for India"—for which you sacrificed yourself, went to prison, and did all kinds of things. Nowadays you will probably not do that kind of thing any more because not only have you seen what ideals lead to—how people who went to prison could not get jobs—but you have seen the falseness of such ideals, have you not? So you will no longer pursue a leader who

promises all kinds of absurd things because your mind is beginning to think, to look, to watch and inquire. All over the world ideals, sacrifices, utopias are beginning to disappear from the thoughtful, intellectual mind.

So, seeing what is actually taking place in the world, the problem is, is it not, to find out for oneself clearly, very deeply, if the mind can be free. And one can only find that out by first recognizing that the mind is a slave to society, the product of a particular culture. Look, sirs, you may be a bridge builder, an engineer, a scientist, a pen pusher—but whatever it is you are, it is your whole life, is it not? You may have a few little pleasures, a few worries, a family, sex, and so on, but most of your life you are a technician of one kind or another. Now, when you remove that technique and when your mind is freed from your little worries, what are you? Nothing at all, are you? You are an empty shell. And, being an empty shell you are frightened, so you run after gurus, read books, go to a cinema, turn on the radio, or do a hundred other things. Inwardly you are bursting with ambition even though you are caught in routine, and it is all destroying your mind.

So what is necessary, obviously, is to free the mind. And you cannot free your mind if you do not first understand it. That is an extraordinarily arduous task, but that is real meditation. That is real discipline because to understand the whole process of the mind demands attention, and the attention is, in itself, discipline. You do not have to impose a discipline on the mind in order to be free. Without freedom you can never find out what is true or what is false; without freedom you can never find if there is God or if there is no God. Of course you can speculate, you can believe that there is God or that there is not, but that is all immature, totally infantile. But for the mind to inquire into this whole problem of freedom and all the implications of freedom, to discover, to find out for yourself, you have to give your whole being to it; and you cannot give your whole being to it if you are not free. So the mind must be free, and that requires self-knowledge—to know yourself, to know all the reactions of the mind, to know what you think and the sources of your thought—not speculating, not asserting that there is the atma or the higher self, which is only another escape. To actually find out about yourself—about your ambitions, your greed, your envy, vanity, struggle, cruelty, the thoughtless acts, the way you talk, the way you look at people—to know the whole of that is very difficult. It means constant alertness, constant watchfulness; it means knowing why you identify, why you condemn, why you judge. This does not mean you have to analyze yourself because analysis does not reveal the truth. What brings about perception is to actually experience what you are.

Look sirs, you believe, do you not, that there is God. If you are a proper, respectable, petty Hindu or Christian, you believe in God because you have been taught to believe from childhood. Now to find out is quite a different matter. It has nothing to do with belief, it has nothing to do with books or what you have been told. To discover if there is reality, man must be free from the ideas he has about truth, about God. And to be free from that idea, you must first examine why you have that idea, you must look. When you look at it ardently, eagerly, the explanation is there, the answer is there. I will show you what I mean, and I hope I can make myself clear.

Most of us want security—economic, social, ideational—and if it cannot be found, then we try to find security at another level, the level of beliefs. We assert that there is some permanent entity called God, and we take comfort, solace, security in that idea. Why do we do this? Because inwardly we want something that will be enduring; inwardly we are poverty-ridden, empty, so we put all our thoughts, our devotion, our love, our hopes on this thing called God. Whether the idea is real or unreal, we do not inquire because it satisfies, it gives us a sense of safety. So we never examine what we do and why we do it, but just accept it because inwardly we want to be completely secure.

Now if you see that, if you understand it actually, without analyzing, then you have understood the fact that the mind seeks security, and also that there is no such thing as security. Then the mind is free, and only then can the mind discover if there is God, if there is truth. But that requires arduous work, does it not? For you who believe in God, it is hard work to be free from that belief, is it not? Because if that belief goes, where are you? You are lost, you are miserable, you are like a leaf driven by the wind, and you want a refuge. Whether the refuge has any reality, you do not inquire, and so you have all this confusion about gurus, saviors, paths, systems—the misery of all that enslavement. So you see all that, actually, because I have explained it, whether you like it or not. Without deep analysis you can see it at a glance, swiftly; but you cannot see anything at all if you merely cling to a belief, to a conclusion. So, what I am suggesting is that in order to find out if there is truth, if there is reality, if there is something which is beyond the measure of the mind, the mind must first be free.

If you go very deeply into yourself—and the ultimate depth is the whole universe—then you will discover that which is timeless. If you take one thought, one single thought and go into it to the end, completely, wholly, with all your being, then you will come to that which is timeless—because in the process of delving deeply into yourself, the mind is freeing itself. That means that you have to be aware of your thoughts all the time. But most of you, unfortunately, are so occupied with your daily living that you have no time for anything else; you are too tired at the end of the day. So you think you will find reality by swallowing a tablet, a belief, which is only a tranquillizer that will put you to sleep. And society wants you to be asleep because society does not want a dangerous man, society does not want an explosive revolutionary. The economic revolutionary and the social revolutionary—they are merely reactionaries. They do not consider the whole of man; they only take a part and make the part the most important. The part is useful, but emphasis on the part, giving the part the significance of the whole, will never bring happiness to man.

So, that is one of our difficulties, is it not, to see the whole truth—not just a leaf, a branch, but the whole tree. If once you see the totality, then you can look at the particular. But if you examine the particular without the perception of the whole, then it has no meaning—and that is exactly what is taking place in the world. The village reformer, the scientist, the bureaucrat, the technician, the politician—they are all concerned with the little reform, with the immediate, with the part, and they are making an awful mess of the world. The world is the whole earth, with its vastness, its riches, its beauty—in which every little field is included, the fields called Russia, America, England, India, and so on. But without seeing the totality of that, merely to concentrate on one little field and get very excited about it leads to destruction.

So our problem is, is it not, how to see the whole. I hope you understand, sirs, what I mean by the whole. I mean the whole of man, the totality of man, not only his little comforts, the security of his house, but the totality of his struggle, his ambition, his frustrations, his joys and miseries. To see all that and go beyond that requires deep attention. I am sure you have never seen anything totally. You have never looked at a flower

with all your being, have you? You have never really looked at your wife, your son, your neighbor—with all your being. You either look at your wife physically or as a useful being in the kitchen, as someone to bear your children, or as a comfort. Your whole time is taken up by the office, by earning your bread and butter. Your whole life is broken up into sectional fragments, and every society, every system, every group is trying to solve the problems which the broken pieces have created. And that process only gives rise to more problems. Do please be aware of this and you will see how simple it is.

All the politicians and the reformers are concerned with the improvement, the betterment, of the fragments and not of the whole. And that is what you also want because you are so immediately concerned with your bread and butter, your security, your frustrations, and your little joys. So a mind that is so broken up, that is in fragmentation—how can such a mind see the whole? You understand, sirs, what I mean? You think partially, do you not? You think in fragmentation—your job, your family, your house, your nation, do you not? You never think of the earth itself, our earth, of which India or your country is just a little, colored part. You never think of man, you think of 'me'. You think of your wife but not of the woman. You think of a virtue, of nongreed, but you do not think of the totality of virtue, its actual significance.

So all our thinking is in fragmentation, and can such a mind, which is broken up, which is in pieces, see the whole? If you understand my question, how will you answer? Now, you see, we are communing with each other, we are partaking together in the understanding of the problem. You are not now merely hearing my words but we are actually partaking in this problem together. So you are not waiting for an answer from me, waiting for the solution; we are together sharing the problem. Am I making myself clear? The problem is this: How can a mind which is fragmented, broken up, which works in unrelated sections—it thinks of God and kicks the servant, it wants to be kind and is unkind—how can such a mind see the whole? I am sure you have never put this question to yourself before, but now you are asking yourself, and what is your first reaction?

The first reaction, I think, is how to bring the fragments together, is it not? You think that by putting all the fragments together you can make the whole. You think you can gather the broken pieces and put them together and integration will take place. But integration will never take place that way because the entity who is gathering and examining these fragments is a broken entity. Please follow this, sirs. The mind that says, "I must bring all these broken pieces together and make them integrated" is itself only a fragment; it is not the whole mind, is it? When you see the truth of that, then what takes place? You see we are trying to communicate with each other, and unless you are experiencing as I am talking, it has no value at all.

So, your being is in fragments, and the mind is also another fragment. Now what are you going to do? What is your reaction? I am talking to you, the individual, and I hope you are examining your own mind, examining your life, looking at the whole of it—your wife, your child, the society, your ambition, your quarrels, your worries, your vanities, your joys—all the little bits, fragments, broken pieces, and how you give emphasis to one piece and neglect the others. This is actually your life, is it not? I am talking about your individual life. Now, how is such a life, all broken up as it is, disintegrated, how is that life, that mind to see this enormous wholeness—life as a whole? Because unless you see the totality, there is no answer to the fragment. Surely it is very

important for you to understand this. Unless you see the totality of your life, the whole of it—in which joy, pleasure, anger, distress, misery, struggle, everything is included, and unless you see the whole of this earth as one and not just the piece called India or whatever it is—your search to find an answer from the fragment will have no meaning; it will only lead to more misery. It is only the man who sees the whole who has an eternal answer. The capacity to see the whole is reality, is God, is everything in the universe.

So how is a broken mind to see the whole? First we must see the truth that a mind broken up can never see the whole. The village reformer, the politician, the technician, the guru, the seeker after truth are all, as you know, broken parts, each functioning in his own limited way and trying to give importance to the part; they will never see the truth. They all have partial answers, but the partial answer is most destructive. The total answer is only found by a mind which is not in fragmentation.

If you see that a total response is the only answer, then you will no longer fight over all the things you now fight over—your family, your position, your authority, your land, your country. So then you have discovered something, have you not?—that integration cannot take place by putting all the fragments together; that the fragments, though relatively important, are not the total answer; that all the sayings of the guru, the teacher, all beliefs are giving importance to the little fragments when they have no importance at all. So you cease to be a follower—which is a marvelous thing, a glorious thing. Therefore you are beginning to see the quality of the mind which is free. You are beginning to experience, to feel the quality of the mind which sees the place of fragments but does not give the fragments all-importance. So your mind is already freeing itself from the fragmentations. I hope you are following with your whole being so that you see and can say, "By Jove, how true it is!"

When you see a beautiful moon, when you see the lovely sunset, you do not argue about it; your whole being is with it completely. And the same when you see the truth of this. When you approach it with your whole being—there it is. When you see that through the fragment there is no answer, when you really feel it deeply, as when you look at the sunset, at a beautiful flower, a lovely face, a bird on the wing—then what happens?

So what is necessary is not the struggle of putting the fragments together but seeing the truth that the fragments hold no answer. And to see the truth of that means giving yourself totally to it. In giving yourself totally to something, you are acting as a whole being—which you do when you see something as true. So the perception of truth demands passion, intensity, an explosive energy, not a mind that is crushed through fear, through discipline, through all the horrors of cultivated virtue; those are all the partial pursuits of the broken mind. When you see this thing, then your whole being is in it. Only the mind that is passionate, that knows the passion of freedom, such a mind alone can find that which is measureless.

November 26, 1958

Second Talk in Bombay

The act of learning needs humility. A mind that has accumulated a great deal of knowledge, that thinks it knows, is incapable of learning because it is full of conclusions, opinions, prejudices, beliefs, and dogmas; and such a mind has no humility. One needs a great deal of humility in order to learn. It is essential that there be a sense, a feeling of humility, but humility is denied when the mind is merely functioning as a machine that is gathering knowledge, gathering experience,

information in order to act, in order to function. Such a mind is never learning. Life is not a conclusion; it does not move from one fixed point to another, from one experience to another; it is altogether too vast, it is a living thing, really immeasurable by the mind. And to learn about life one needs an abundance of humility, but humility is denied when the mind is merely gathering. That gathering, that accumulation becomes the distorting point from which it functions, from which it thinks, from which it acts. I do not know if you have ever noticed the workings of your own mind. If so, you will have seen that the moment it has gathered anything—experience, knowledge, information, an idea of any nature—then in it there is a peculiar quality of aggressive accumulation. The man who asserts that he knows obviously does not know, and obviously he has no humility. But humility is not a thing to be cultivated; if you do cultivate it, it becomes mere humbleness which is nothing more than the opposite of vanity and arrogance. Humility is not a product of the mind, but in the very act of learning, which is a constant process, a never-ending process, in that state there is humility. Humility is not a cloak you can put on, a garment you can wear at your convenience.

So it seems to me that learning is astonishingly difficult, as is listening also. We never actually listen to anything because our mind is not free; our ears are stuffed up with those things which we already know, so listening becomes extraordinarily difficult. I think—or rather, it is a fact—that if one can listen to something with all one's being, with vigor, with vitality, then the very act of listening is a liberative factor, but unfortunately you never do listen, as you have never learned about it. After all, you only learn when you give your whole being to something. Even when you give your whole being to mathematics, you learn; but when you are in a state of contradiction, when you do not want to learn but are forced to learn, then it becomes merely a process of accumulation. To learn is like reading a novel with innumerable characters; it requires your full attention, not contradictory attention. If you want to learn about a leaf—a leaf of the spring or a leaf of the summer—you must really look at it, see the symmetry of it, the texture of it, the quality of the living leaf. There is beauty, there is vigor, there is vitality in a single leaf. So to learn about the leaf, the flower, the cloud, the sunset, or a human being, you must look with all intensity.

If you can listen in the same way, not only to what is being said, but to everything around you—the cry of a child, the sound of the rolling waves coming in, the noise of the airplane overhead—then out of that deep listening will come an enormous comprehension. Comprehension is not born out of gathering, out of an accumulation of information. Comprehension is always instantaneous. You and I are communicating with each other about a subject which is very difficult. I would like to tell you something, not in the sense of a lecturer giving instructions to you as to what to do and what not to do, that would be too absurd—but cannot you and I, as two individuals, look into this problem together? The speaker may explain, see more of the subtleties, the nuances, the difficulties, but if you do not listen with your whole being, you will not be able to follow, then there will be only a verbal meaning, and words do not satisfy a hungry man.

So you and I will go into this together. You are not going to learn anything from me, you are not going to gather something here and go away with it because if you do that, it will be merely an accumulation, something which you store up to remember. But as I am talking, please listen with your whole being, with your full attention, with eagerness, as you would listen to something which you

really love—if you ever do love. Because here you are receiving no instructions and you are not a pupil. You are learning an art—and I really do mean that. We are learning together and therefore the division of the teacher and the disciple has completely gone. It is immature thinking to regard somebody as a teacher who knows and yourself as one who does not know. In that relationship both lack humility and therefore both cease to learn. This is not just a verbal expression, a temporary statement, as you will see for yourself if you listen without merely looking for instructions as to what to do and what not to do. Life is not understood through a series of instructions. You can apply instructions to a dynamo, the radio, but life is not a machine; it is an ever-living, ever-renewing thing. So, there is no instruction—and that is the beauty of learning. The mind that is small, instructed, taught, only strengthens memory—as happens in all the universities and schools where you merely cultivate memory in order to pass examinations and get a job. That is not acquiring intelligence. Intelligence comes when you are learning. In learning there is no end, and that is the beauty of life, the sacredness of life. So you and I are going to learn, to explore, think together, and communicate with each other about action.

To most of us life is action, and by action we mean something which has been done, is being done, or will be done. Without action you cannot live. Action does not mean only physical movement, going from here to there; there is also the action of thought, the action of an idea, the action of a feeling, of environment, of opinion, the action of ambition, of food, and of psychological influences—of which most of us are totally unaware. There are the actions of the conscious mind and the actions of the unconscious mind. There is also, is there not, the action of a seed in the earth, the action of a man who gets a job and sticks to it for the rest of his life, there is the action of the waves beating on the shore, the action of gentle weather, of rain; there is all the action of the earth and of the heavens. So action is something limitless. Action is a movement both within and out of time. I am thinking aloud with you; I am exploring. I came here with one thought, action, and I want to discuss it with you, go into it, explore it gently, slowly, quietly, so that you and I understand it together.

But when you merely reduce action to, "What am I to do? Should I do this and not do that? Is this right, or that?" then action becomes a very small thing. We do, naturally, have to act within time; I do have to stop at the end of the hour; one has to go to the office, the factory, take meals, at a certain time. There must be action in time, and that is all we know, is it not? You and I really do not know anything else except action which is recognizable and within the field of time. By time we mean yesterday, today, and tomorrow. Tomorrow is the infinite future, yesterday is the infinite past, and today is the present. And the conflict between the future and the past produces a thing which we call action. So we are always inquiring how to act within the field of time, of recognition. We are always asking what to do, whether to marry or not to marry, whether to yield to temptation or to resist, whether to try and become rich or seek God. Circumstances, which are really the same as time, force me to accept a job because I have a family and I have to earn, and so there is all the conflict, turmoil, and toil. So my mind is caught in the field of action within time. That is all I know, and each action produces its own result, its own fruits, again within time. That is one step, is it not, to see that we are caught in the action of time.

Then there is the action of tension. Please follow this because we are examining it together. There is the action born of the ten-

sion between two opposites, which is a state of self-contradiction—wanting to do this and doing totally the opposite. You know that, do you not? One desire says, "Do this," and another desire says, "Do not do it." You are feeling angry, violent, brutal and yet a part of you tells you to be kind, to be gentle, nice. For most of us action is born out of tension, self-contradiction. If you watch yourself you will see it; and the more the struggle, the contradiction, the more drastic and violent is the action. Out of this tension the ambitious man works ruthlessly—in the name of God, in the name of peace, or in the name of politics, of his country, and so on. Such tension produces great action; and the man who is in an agony of self-contradiction may produce a poem, a book, a painting; the greater the inward tension, the greater the activity, the productivity.

Then, if you will observe in yourself, there is also the action of will. "I must do this and I must not do that. I must discipline myself. I must not think this way. I must reject, I must protect." So there is the positive and the negative action of will. I am just describing, and if you are really listening, you will see that an action of real understanding takes place—which I am going to go through presently. The action of will is the action of resistance, negatively or positively. So there are varieties of action, but most of us know the action of will because most of us have no great tension since we are not great. We are not great writers, great politicians, or great saints, so-called; they are not really saints at all because they have committed themselves to a certain form of life and therefore have ceased to learn. We are ordinary people, not too clever. Sometimes we look at a tree or a sunset and smile happily, but for most of us action is born of will; we are resisting. Will is the result of many desires, is it not? You know, do you not, the action of will—"I feel lazy and I would like to lie in bed a little longer, but I must discipline myself and get up; I feel sexual, lustful, but I must not, I must resist it." So we exercise will to produce a result. That is all we know; either we yield or resist, and yielding creates its own agony which presently becomes resistance. So we are everlastingly in battle within ourselves.

So, will is the product of desire, wanting and not wanting. It is as simple as that, do not let us complicate it—leave that to the philosophers, the speculators. You and I know that will is the action that is born within the field of two opposite desires, and our cultivation of virtue is the cultivation of resistance. Resisting envy you call virtuous. And that is going on always within us—a desire producing its opposite and from the opposite a resistance is created, and that resistance is will. If you watch your own mind you will see it. And as we have to move in this world, we exercise this will, and that is all we know, and with this will we say we must find out if there is something beyond. With this will we discipline ourselves, torture ourselves, deny ourselves— and the more you are capable of denying yourself, the more saintly you are supposed to be. All your saints, your gurus, and gods are the product of this denial, this resistance; and the man who can follow ardently, deny-ing everything, following the ideal he has projected—him you call a great man.

So when you look at this life of action— the growing tree, the bird on the wing, the flowing river, the movement of the clouds, of lightning, of machines, the action of the waves upon the shore—then you see, do you not, that life itself is action, endless action that has no beginning and no end. It is some-thing that is everlastingly in movement, and it is the universe, God, bliss, reality. But we reduce the vast action of life to our own petty little action in life, and ask what we should do, or follow some book, some sys-tem. See what we have done—how petty, small, narrow, ugly, brutal our action is. Please do listen to this! I know as well as you that we have to live in this world, that we have to act within time, and that it is no good saying, "Life is so vast, I will let it act; it will tell me what to do." It won't tell us what to do. So you and I have to see this ex-traordinary phenomenon of our mind reduc-ing this action which is infinite, limitless, profound, to the pettiness of how to get a job, how to become a minister, whether to have sex or not—you know all the petty little struggles in life. So we are constantly reduc-ing this enormous movement of life to action which is recognizable and made respectable by society. You see this, sirs, do you not?— the action which is recognizable and within the field of time, and that action which knows no recognition and which is the end-less movement of life.

Now the question is this: Can I live in this world, do my job, and so on, with a sense of this endless depth of action, or must I, through my petty mind, reduce action to a functioning only within the field of recogni-tion, within the field of time? Am I making myself clear?

Let me put the thing differently. Love is something which is not measurable in terms of action, is it not? I do not know if you have ever thought about it. You and I are talking together now face to face and we are both interested in this and want to find out. We know what this feeling of beauty, of love is. We are talking of love itself, not the ex-planation of love, not the verbal expression. The word *love* is not love. Though the intel-lectual mind divides it into profane love and sacred, divine love, all that has no meaning. But that beauty of feeling which is not ex-pressible in words and not recognizable by the mind—we know that thing. It is really a most extraordinary thing; in it there is no sense of the 'other', and the observer is absent; there is only the feeling. It is not that I feel love and express it by holding your hand or by doing this or that act. *It is.* If you have ever had that feeling, if you have ever lived it, if you have understood it, expressed it, nurtured it, if you have felt it totally with all your being, you will see that with that feeling one can live in the world. Then you can educate your children in the most splendid manner because that feeling is the center of action, though within the field of time. But not having that feeling, with all its immensity, passion, and vigor, we reduce love merely to the "I love you" and function only within the field of time, trying to catch the eye of another.

So you see the problem. Love is something that knows no measure, that cannot be put together by the mind, cannot be cultivated, something which is not sentimental, which has nothing to do with emotionalism and nothing whatsoever to do with good works—the village reform, and so on. When you have that feeling, then everything in life is important, significant; therefore, you will do that which is good. But without knowing the beauty, the depth, the vigor of it we are trying to reduce love into something which the mind can capture and make respectable. And the same applies to action, which we are now trying to understand.

Action is an endless movement which has no beginning and no end and which is not controlled by cause and effect. Action is of everything—the action of the sea, of the mango seed becoming the mango tree, and so on. But the human mind is not a seed, and therefore through its action, it becomes only a modified reproduction of what it was. In our life there is the constant pressure of circumstances, and although the circumstances are always changing, they are ever shaping our lives. What was, is not; what is, can be broken. So can we not sense, feel, this enormous action of life which ranges from the movement of the little worm in the earth to the sweep of the infinite heavens? If you really want to know what this extraordinary thing is, this action, then you must go through it, you must break through the barrier of this action in time. Then you will know it, then with that feeling you can act, you can go to your job and do all the things that are recognizable within the field of time. But from within the recognizable field of time, you cannot find the other. Do what you will, through the petty you will never find the immeasurable.

If you once really saw the truth of this—that a mind functioning within the field of time can never understand the eternal, which is outside of time—if you really saw that, felt it, then you would see that a mind which speculates about love and divides it up as carnal, profane, divine, or sacred can never find the other. But if you can feel this astonishing action—the movement of the stars, the forests, the rivers, the ocean, the ways of the animals and of human beings—if you can know the beauty of a tender leaf in spring, the feeling of rain as it drops from the heavens, then with that immense feeling you can act within the field of recognition, within the field of time. But action within the field of time can never lead to the other. If you really understand that, not verbally, intellectually, if you really feel the significance of it, grasp it, see the extraordinary beauty and loveliness of it, then you will see that the will has no place in this at all. All action born of will is essentially self-centered, egocentric, but such action will disappear totally when you have understood it fully, when you have really felt yourself moving in it, with your mind wholly in it. Then you can see that there is no necessity for will at all; there is a quite different movement. The will then is like a knotted piece of rope; it can be undone. That will can be lost; but the other cannot be lost, it cannot be increased or decreased.

So, if you are listening with your whole being, learning with your whole being, which means feeling deeply, not merely listening to words intellectually, then you will feel the extraordinary movement of learning, of God—not the god made by the hand or by the mind, not the god of the temple, mosque, or church, but this endless immeasurable thing, the timeless. Then you will see that we can live with astonishing peace in this world; then there is no such thing as temptation, no such thing as virtue, because virtue is merely a thing of society. The man who understands all this, who lives it, is orderly, inwardly at rest; his action is entirely different, much more effective, easier, and clearer because there is no inward confusion, contradiction.

So, a mind that holds to conclusions is never humble. A man who has learned is carrying the burden of his knowledge, but a man who is learning has no burden and therefore he can go to the top of the mountain. As two human beings, you and I have talked of something which cannot be captured through words; but by listening to each other, exploring it, understanding it, we have found something extraordinary, something that is imperishable. Life reduced to the 'me' clinging to life is perishable, but if you can see that extraordinary life from the beginning to the end, if once you have gone into it, felt it, drunk at its fountain, then you can live an ordinary life with utter newness, you can really live. The respectable man is not living—he is already dead—and life is not a thing to be invited by the dead. Life is to be entered and forgotten because there is no 'me' to remember the living of that life. It is only when the mind is in a state of complete humility, when it has no purpose for its own little existence, when it does not move from a point to a point, from experience to experience, from knowledge to knowledge—only such a mind which is totally, completely, wholly not-seek-

ing knows the infinite beginning and the infinite end of existence.

November 30, 1958

Third Talk in Bombay

In all forms of communication words, naturally, are very important. They become more so when you are dealing with abstract and rather complicated problems because each one will translate every word according to his own understanding of it. So it is very difficult when one wants to deal with the extraordinary problem of life, with all its complexities and subtleties. Words become really significant if we can keep to their dictionary meaning and also allow ourselves to go beyond the mere definition, beyond any mere conclusion which a word may convey.

Take for example the word *freedom*. Each one will translate it according to his own particular necessity, demand, pressures, and fears. If you are an ambitious man, you will translate that word as something necessary in order to carry out your ambitions, fulfill your desires. To a man who is bound to certain traditions, freedom is a word to be afraid of. To a man who indulges himself in all his fancies and desires, that word conveys the possibility of further indulgence. So words have an extraordinary significance in our life, and I do not know if you have ever realized how deep and profound the significance of the word is. The words *God, freedom, communist, American, Hindu, Christian,* and so on—these words influence us not only neurologically, but they verbally vibrate in our being, bringing out certain reactions. I do not know if you realize all this and, if you do realize it, you will know that it is very difficult to free the mind from the word. As I want to talk over with you a very complex problem, I think we should come to it with the hesitancy and the clarification of a mind that not only understands the words and their significance, but which is capable also of going beyond the word.

One can see what is happening throughout the world at the present time. Wherever there are tyrannies, freedom is denied; wherever there is the powerful organization of the church, of religion, freedom again is denied. Though they use this word *freedom,* both the religious and the political organizations refuse that freedom. Also one can see that where there is overpopulation, freedom must inevitably decline, and wherever there is overorganization, mass communication, freedom is denied. So seeing all this, how is an individual like you or me to interpret freedom? Living, as one has to in this world, in a society which is completely bound to organizations, in which technicians are very important, the mind becomes a slave to a certain form of technique, to a method, to certain ways. So at what level, at what depth do we translate that word freedom? If you walked out of your office, that would not mean freedom; you would merely lose your job. If you drove on the wrong side of the road, the policeman would be after you and your freedom would be curtailed. If you do what you like, or if you get rich, the state will control you. All around us there are sanctions, laws, traditions, various forms of compulsion and domination, and all these are preventing freedom.

So if, as a human being, you would understand this problem, which is a real problem, then from what depth are you inquiring? Or are you not concerned at all? I am afraid most of us are not concerned; what we are concerned with is our daily bread, our families, our little troubles, jealousies, ambitions, but we are not concerned with the wider, bigger problems. And the mere concern for the solution of the problem will not produce a remedy. You might find an immediate remedy, but that will only produce other problems, as one well knows. So at what level, from what depth do you respond to the word freedom?

One must also realize, surely, that the word is not the thing. The word *truth* is not the truth. But for most of us the word is sufficient; we do not go beyond the word and investigate what lies behind the word. Do please consider this. The very word *Muslim* prevents you from looking at the human being who represents that word. The nervous response and the psychological response to that word is very deep, and it evokes in you all kinds of ideas, beliefs, prejudices. But if one could think very deeply, it will become obvious that one must separate the word from the actual thing. A great deal of misunderstanding in our relationships lies in the wrong significance we give to words. Therefore it is very important that you and I, as two individuals, establish right communication so that we understand each other on the same level at the same time. I do not know if you have noticed it, but when you love somebody, communication between the two of you is immediate. Similarly, if we can establish such communion, then I think we shall be able to explore this very complex problem. The great difficulty in establishing communication is the word, and you and I must pierce through the word and go beyond if we are to commune with each other, to share, partake in the problem which we are going to unroll, uncover, discuss.

The problem is the mind. Now, when I use the word *mind* it may mean to me something entirely different from what it means to you. You have never thought about what the mind is, you have never explored the whole content of the mind. The mind is obviously a state, a being, a fullness, a depth, a vastness, but all those words do not indicate the actual state, they are merely descriptive words, and the state is not the word. I hope you are following. It is not very difficult, but you and I must be clear as we go along. So we must examine how to approach the mind. Is the mind the brain, and is the mind separate from the brain, is the mind a product of the brain? Please look at it. Please investigate with me.

We can see that the brain is the response center for sensations. Nerves carry sensations to the brain, and the same nerves carry the impulse of both pleasure and pain. That brain, through sensations, begins to differentiate between hot and cold, pleasure and pain, and so on. From that differentiation thought arises. The process of thinking is the reaction of memory, and memory is part of the mind. I am going to explain very carefully, so please follow. I am bitten by a snake, there is a sensation which is painful, and there is the memory. So thereafter I am always frightened of snakes. Part of the brain has retained that memory, so whenever I see a snake, I quiver. Or, I ask you where you live. You are familiar with the question and your response is immediate; you do not have to think about it. The nerves carry that question to the brain, and the brain, having stored-up memories of where you live, responds immediately with the answer. If I ask you a question which is a little more complex, then there is a gap between the question and the answer, a time interval. In that interval the brain looks into memory and takes a little time to find the answer. So in that gap, during the time interval, the process of thinking is going on. Is that not so? I ask you what you want. You want so many things that you hesitate. Before you answer you look around, search, investigate, and that investigation causes the gap because you are thinking what you want. Then I ask you a still more complicated question, and what happens? Please watch your own mind. Again the words set up the vibration of the

question and the brain responds with the message, "I cannot find an immediate answer; I must look further into memory." So during that interval you are thinking rapidly and the gap between the question and the answer is much wider. And if I ask you an extremely difficult question, then, after many seconds of searching in memory, you finally say, "I do not know." But that "I do not know" means, does it not, that you are still looking around, expecting an answer, waiting for an answer either from yourself or from somebody else. Now there is a state of "I do not know" in which there is no looking around, no waiting for an answer, but we will come to that presently. First we must understand the process of thinking. It is a challenge and a response, is it not? If the challenge is familiar, the response is immediate; if the challenge is not a familiar one, the response takes a little time, and during that time you are thinking, which means that the whole mechanism is set going—not only the verbal vibrations but also memory—and then you answer. That is what we are doing all the time, is it not?

Memory is stored-up experience, tradition, the accumulation of knowledge, and memory is always accumulating and always responding. You see a person whom you recognize and you respond, but if you don't know the person there is no recognition, no response. This is not a complicated thing, it is very simple, as you can observe if you watch your own mind. We can see that this so-called brain responds to many forms of sensation, and obviously it must be extraordinarily sensitive, alert, vital, strong if it is to respond to every reaction and action. Most of us do not respond with sensitivity because the brain, through worry, conflict, excesses, indulgences, and so on, has been made dull. Only a little part of it functions.

So we see that the process of thinking is the response of memory, which is acting all the time like a machine. So one asks, "What does freedom mean?" I hope you understand this question and that I am making myself clear. If my whole mind is the result of time, the result of tradition, of various cultures, experiences, conditionings, always having the background of the family, the race, the belief, always functioning within the field of the known—then where is freedom? If I am moving, as I am, all the time within the limits of my own mind, which is full of memories and the product of time, how is the mind to go beyond itself? The word *freedom* to such a mind means nothing, does it, because it only turns freedom into another demand, saying, "How can I be free?" Please follow this carefully and you will see. I realize, consciously or unconsciously, that mine is a very narrow life; there is perpetual anxiety, struggle, fear, misery, sorrow, and so on; and so I say, "I must be free, I must have peace of mind, I must escape from this limitation." This is what each one of us is demanding. Outwardly, under the various tyrannical governments there is no freedom; you are told what to do and you do it, and inwardly the same problem continues. Here, in a so-called democratic country, you are more or less outwardly free—more or less— but inwardly you are a prisoner, and you are asking this question about freedom. The greater the organization of a church or of a society, and the greater the efficiency and the means of mass communication, the greater is the conflict and turmoil. So we are always in a struggle with our environment and within ourselves. Struggle is going on perpetually and there is contradiction and misery: "My wife does not love me, I love someone else, there is death, I believe, I do not believe"— there is ever turmoil and restlessness, as with the sea.

Have you ever watched the sea? There are certain days when the wind is quiet, there is no breath of air, and the sea reflects the stars.

There is a tranquillity, a breathlessness, a sense of peace, but beneath there are deep currents, deep movements; its waters cover an enormous area and actually it is never still; it is ever moving, moving restlessly; every breath that comes shatters the quietness, the stillness. So also is the mind. We are eternally restless, and becoming aware of that, we say, "Give me peace. Let me find God. I want to escape from this misery and to find out if there is an everlasting peace, bliss." That is all we want, and that is why we are in such a frightful struggle, such a tension of contradiction, one desire battling against another. Ambition breeds frustration and emptiness, and then this desire to fulfill again brings the shadow of frustration. It is no use my merely describing our state—we are aware of it, are we not?—from the state of confusion, turmoil, misery, grief, to the state of a sense of passing joys, of occasionally looking at the sky and saying, "How beautiful, how wonderful!" and occasionally knowing the feeling of love. But it is all temporary, fleeting, it is all in a flux. So the mind says, "Is there not a permanent state of peace?" and it proceeds to invest an idea of God, of truth, with permanence. And all the religions encourage this investiture of an idea with permanency. Every religion in the world says that there is a permanency, a bliss which you must seek, and that there is a way to it. They say there is a path from turmoil to reality. You understand, sirs? The moment you are seeking a state which will be permanent, you must find a way to it—a belief, a method, a system, a practice. Now to me there is neither a permanency nor a method. There is no method to discover reality. Let us go into it and see.

I am full of fear—fear of death, fear with regard to love, fear of public opinion, fear of so many things. I am aware that I am anxious, fearful; and so I say I must find a method which will help me not to be afraid.

That is what we are all concerned with, is it not? So I go to someone who says there is God, there is bliss, and he tells me what to do in order to get it, and I accept that there is a method, a way, to get from here to there. I want to explore that idea, but if you really examine it, you will see that it has no meaning. So you and I are going to look at it together, but you cannot look at it if you are holding on to the idea that there is a way, if you are mesmerized by a method, a system, or your tradition of centuries. To throw all that off and examine the thing differently demands a great deal of energy, a great deal of vigor. We are not now examining whether there is a permanent state of bliss; we are examining the thing called the "way," the method to get from greed to nongreed, from fear to no-fear, from jealousy to nonjealousy, from transiency to permanency. In other words, we want to know how to get from point to point in a specified direction. Is that not so? Now if I want to become an engineer, there is a specified direction, there is a method—I have to study higher mathematics and so on, and I know the way I must proceed. If I want to learn a language, I know I will have to study the first lesson to the fifteenth and so on. That is, in learning a technique I move from a point to a point and during that time interval I am learning, and at the end of a certain period, I know it. That is very simple to see—that in technical things there is a movement from the known to the known. Similarly, all your religious books and teachers tell you that you can go from the point of turmoil to the point of bliss, and that there is a way from transiency to permanency. They say you must believe, practice, meditate, resist evil, exercise control in order to get from this point to that point— which means taking a specified direction to what you think you know to be bliss. In the same way as you know the state of turmoil, so there is said to be a specified direction to bliss, and to arrive there you must practice.

Now what is involved in this process? First of all, is bliss a static thing, a fixed state that does not move? You can go to your house because your house is fixed, but is bliss, reality, God, or whatever you like to call it, a static state or a moving thing, a living thing, a struggling thing that cannot be fixed? The desire to find a fixed, static state is the outcome of my turmoil, my misery, is it not, and so out of my confusion I create a thing called the "permanent," and then say I must find a way to it.

And what do we mean by a method, a practice, a discipline? To me, every form of discipline corrodes the mind, destroys intelligence, limits thought, narrows down this extraordinary capacity of the mind. I am not asking you to accept this, but as we are trying to communicate with each other, I am telling you how I see it and I hope you are looking at it also. What does the word *discipline* mean? It comes from a Latin word which means "to learn"—not to control, not to subjugate, not to compel, but to learn. You cease to learn when you compel yourself, but if you understand, for instance, that you must know all about fear, that you must not merely resist fear, control it, or find a method of escaping from it, then in examining the fear you are learning about it. Therefore no discipline is necessary. I do not know if I am making myself clear. We say we want to know all about fear, so we have to examine it, we have to learn what is involved, at what depth the fear is. Fear must be in relation to something; it cannot exist by itself. Consciously or unconsciously I am afraid of something; so I have to examine, to explore, and in the process of learning all about the fear, there is a total cessation of fear—not merely an arriving at the opposite of fear, called courage, but a total cessation of fear.

But to understand that requires a great deal of thought, a great deal of inquiry.

Now I am going briefly to examine fear. First of all, I am afraid, let us say, of death. What do I mean by fear of death? After all, I do not know anything about death; I do not know if there is continuity or not; I do not know anything about the unknown; all that my mind is used to is the process of functioning within the field of the known. So I am afraid of something which I do not know. Is that not so? You are afraid, are you not, of the tomorrow, of losing your job, of somebody being ill in the family, of the future uncertainty, of the unknown. You know very well, do you not, that feeling of fear, that anxiety, that gnawing sense of uncertainty, but you have never actually looked at it, have you? You have never said to yourself, "Let me look at it." Now, how does one look at fear? First of all you must separate the word from the fear, from the feeling, must you not, because the word blocks you from looking at the state. I hope you are following all this because if you are really interested and are looking at it, you will be totally free from fear, from jealousy, from greed—the things the mind is caught in. If you go through it, you will see that the mind will be completely free from all this struggle, but you can only do it if you can go beyond the word. So first I must recognize that there is fear, then I must be aware that I must not escape from it into some conclusion—go to the temple, the guru, take a drink, turn on the radio, read a book. All those escapes have to stop, not from compulsion, but because you really want to learn, to understand, and you cannot learn about something if you run away from it, which is obvious. So I come to the point of no escape from fear. Then I am left only with the word *fear* to indicate the fear. And can I now separate the word from the actual state?

Now if you can do that, if you are really capable of understanding that the word is not the thing, that the word *fear* is not the fear; if you can separate it, then you will see that the feeling you have is entirely different. Then you will have approached it for the first time; for the first time you will have freed the word from the feeling. Therefore your mind is capable of discerning the feeling, of going into it, absorbing it, understanding, learning.

So the mind frees itself from the method, the "how," from this movement to a specified point. The specified point means a distance, it means time, that you will eventually get there; but life is not a fixed point, reality is not fixed, it is a living thing like the waters of a river. You cannot take a handful of water and say it is the river; the river is the whole movement from the beginning to the end. Likewise reality cannot be held; life cannot be imprisoned, and it has no direction.

So there is no method. Do what you will, practice all the idiotic things, repeat the word *om*, and exercise from morning to night, you will never capture this immeasurable thing. Those things only mesmerize the mind, making it dull and stupid. But if you want to learn about the mind, then you will see that the very learning brings its own subtle form of attention. Learning has no beginning and no ending, and life is that learning of the self, the 'me', learning endlessly, never accumulating, never posing, never struggling. Then you will find, as you do this, that the mind becomes totally empty of the known, and then there is creation.

December 3, 1958

Fourth Talk in Bombay

Most of us are concerned with the immediate action, are we not?—what to do, what to think, what should be done—and we concentrate on that demand and give our whole thought to it. And this concern for immediate action becomes our chief problem. "Should I do this or should I not do it, or what must be done?" So we spend a great deal of energy in concentrating on the immediate. This concentration surely begins from the center of a certain desire, a certain urge, demand, or motive, does it not, through trying to solve the immediate problem. If you observe you will see for yourself that when you are concentrated on an immediate problem, the demand for the solution of that problem and the process of concentration come always from a center. There is a center which narrows down the whole field of attention, from a certain point to a certain point. That is what happens, is it not? I have to do something, and I bring my whole thought to bear upon it, but the coming together of thought on a point is the outcome of a center of motive, a center that demands a solution according to pleasure and pain, according to vanity, according to frustration, and so on. That is what is happening all the time; there is always a center from which concentration takes place. So concentration becomes a process of exclusion, a gathering together of all thought to a certain point. That is what you do when you have to study, when you have to do a job. You say you must concentrate, and all thought is brought to a certain point and from there you act.

I think there is a difference between concentration and attention. Attention is awareness of the whole field of thought; attention is extensive; it has, if you observe, no frontier, no limitation. Attention is an awareness of the whole, and in that state, when you give attention to any problem, then you are able to observe the whole field of thought and also comprehend the implications and significance of the problem. Whereas concentration narrows down all thought to a certain point and so is an exclusive process. So,

invariably our action, being born of concentration, is limited; and in that state of concentration, there is no attention. But when there is attention—in that extensive sense of the mind being without a frontier—there can also be concentration. The little does not hold the big, but the big can hold the little.

Now when you are paying attention to what is being said, you are listening not only to grasp the meaning of the words but listening also to find out what the speaker means, to see the wider implications, to go behind the words, beyond the intellectual level. But that wholeness of attention and comprehension is denied when there is concentration with a motive.

You know, when you appreciate beauty, it is really being in a state which is proportion, symmetry, color, shape, movement, and a living quality. Not only is the intellect very alert and sensitive, but there is a state of wholeness of attention and feeling. But if you are merely concentrating on the appreciation of something beautiful, then there is no real feeling of beauty. I hope I am making myself clear because I think it is very important to understand this. For I feel that without the sense of beauty, one cannot possibly understand what is true. Truth is not merely an idea or an intellectual concept, a formula; it is a state of being. It is a state of mind that comprehends totally, not a mind that is concentrated with a motive upon an idea. I feel it is very important and urgent to feel this quality of beauty, which is not the denial of the ugly or the opposite of the ugly. All opposites are the outcome of a motive in a state of concentration, whereas beauty is a state of mind in which there is an attention which has no boundary. I am only putting into words what most of us occasionally do feel. You know how, when you say of something, "How beautiful, how lovely!" your whole being is in that; in those words there is real feeling, and your mind is not just concentrated on an idea of what you consider to be beautiful.

I feel that a mind which is not capable of seeing and feeling totally the beauty of the earth, the sky, the palm tree, the horizon, the beauty of a line, a face, a gesture, will never comprehend that extraordinary thing which is beauty and freedom. For most of us freedom is merely the opposite of bondage, therefore merely a reaction. But to comprehend the feeling, the beauty, the loveliness, that extraordinary state which is not the opposite of bondage, requires a mind that is capable of seeing the totality of something. Most of us, surely, have lost or have never had real feeling. Our education, our way of life, our daily habits, traditions, customs have deprived the mind of feeling. If you observe, go into your own mind very diligently, you will find that feeling itself has no motive—the feeling for a tree, the sense of appreciation of a rich man driving a beautiful car, the sight of the villager starving, struggling, toiling day after day. If there is feeling, then from that feeling itself there is an action which is much more comprehensive, much more potent than the intellectual action of the do-gooders and the reformers because in it there is understanding, a feeling for both the ugly and the beautiful—but not as opposites. To have such feeling is essential if we are to understand this whole process of our existence and our ways of thinking. It means comprehending the depth, the width of life and also this extraordinary thing called the self, the 'me'. To understand this 'me', this self, with all its joys, its struggles, its pains, intentions, hopes, fears, ambition, envy, jealousy, and so on, there must be deep feeling, not mere intellection. You know, when you have a feeling for something, you see much more sharply, much more intelligently and clearly. I do not know if you have noticed it, but when you love somebody, or when you see something rather extraordinary about someone, you become

much more intelligent, sharp, alert, do you not? There is a sharpness and alertness from concentration, but in that there is no feeling, no affection.

If one can really grasp this, not merely intellectually or verbally, but actually, seriously, then when you see something—a tree, a boy, a girl—with this quality you can also be aware of the whole content of the mind, not merely the superficial, the obvious, conscious mind, but the unconscious with all the innumerable struggles, the racial inheritance, the motives and experiences and stored-up knowledge. From that fullness of awareness and feeling you will see a totally different process of action taking place.

Perhaps I am talking about something of which you have had no experience, and probably you will tell me to be practical and come down to earth and tell you what to do and not to do, and not be vague. But you see the difficulty is that unless you see this—unless you see the whole sky, the beauty of the night, of the morning, and the evening, you can never do anything worthwhile under the heavens except your petty little activities of daily existence. Unless you grasp this whole thing, your existence will remain miserable, sorrowful; but with the perception of this enormous thing called life, with the feeling for it, you can come to the practical with precision, with clarity, with depth. But most of us are merely concerned with immediate profit, with immediate results, the immediate pleasure or pain. So it seems to me it is very important in the pursuit of the understanding of the self that there be this feeling. But most of our feelings are dead because when you see every day the same poverty, the same squalor, the same misery and struggle, and the same customs and habits, the mind gets dull, deadened, insensitive, and it becomes very difficult to feel. So, if I may, I would like to go into something which, if we can understand it very deeply, will help us to realize this feeling—the feeling which is quite different from sentimentality, from emotion, tears, and devotion. If we can get this feeling, then the heavens will open.

If I may deviate for a moment, I would like to make it clear that I am talking to you as an individual. You and I, as two friends, are really concerned with life, with all the turmoil that human beings go through, and so we are talking about this because we are interested. I hope you are not merely listening to me or trying to learn from me. You will learn only by observing yourself while I am describing. But if you are carried away and depend on the verbal description, then you are merely hearing without learning. If you are listening—which is an act of attention, not concentration—and directly experiencing your own state, then you will see that an extraordinary feeling of the love of learning comes into being which is not the learning from a book, from a talk. That kind of learning is merely knowledge; it is dead, it has no meaning, it is only the cultivation of memory, and memory is not intelligence. If you and I can really listen, learn, you will see the turmoil of feeling arising; I am using that word *turmoil* in the right sense—a bubbling, a release of fullness without which there can be no understanding.

To get back to our inquiry, I would like you to investigate with me into the problem of attachment because it is very important to understand it. You are attached, are you not, either to things, to people, or to ideas. You are attached to things—a car, some property, a dress, or whatever it is, or you are attached to a person—your wife, your child, your friend; or you are attached to an idea of God or no God, of the state, of reincarnation. Now what does this attachment mean? One can understand to a certain extent being attached to a watch or a house, even though they are dead things, but the attachment to a person or to an idea is much more compli-

cated. Attachment seems to me to be invariably to dead things. The attachment to the wife, the husband, the son—is it to a living thing or really to a dead thing? Are you attached to a living person or the picture you have made of a living person? And is not that picture a dead thing? We are inquiring, going into it together. What are you attached to? Not the living person, but the idea, the memory of the pleasures and experiences you have had from that person. Please follow this—can you be attached to a river? You may have a picture, a memory of a particular river you know of, but you cannot be attached to living waters; the river is moving swiftly, it is in a constant state of movement, and what you are attached to is a picture which the word *river* awakens—somewhere where you had pleasure, amusement, a quiet evening by the riverside, but you cannot be attached to the movement of that water. If we follow this carefully we are going to find out how through attachment we are destroying feeling, because all our attachment is to dead things. You can never be attached to a living thing any more than you can be attached to the river, to the sea, because the living thing is moving, eternal, in a state of continual motion. So when you say you are attached to your son, your daughter, your husband, if you can very carefully look within yourself, you will see that you cannot be attached to a living person because that person is constantly changing, moving, in a state of turmoil. What you are attached to is your picture of that person. For instance when I say I am attached to my son, it is because through him I immortalize myself, through him I become prosperous, I expect him to keep up my name. I say I may have been a failure, but he will be successful, he will be more ambitious than I have been, and so I identify myself with him—the "him" being a picture. But the picture is a dead thing! So look what the mind is doing—it is creating pictures and attaching itself to dead things!

And when you say you are attached to an idea, what are ideas? Look, sir, you are a Hindu, a Parsi, a Muslim, a Christian, a Buddhist, an atheist—whatever you are, you have that idea firmly fixed in your mind, as it is firmly fixed in the mind also of the socialist, communist, or capitalist. But ideas can never be living things—they are conclusions, reactions, dogmas impressed on your mind from childhood through propaganda, compulsion, education, and various forms of communication. And have you not found how astonishingly difficult it is to free the mind from an idea? To free the Hindu mind from reincarnation, karma, and all the rest of it is almost impossible. So again you can see that a mind attached to an idea is attached to a dead thing, as a conclusion is a dead thing, and a belief also. So you are attached to a dead thing, but it is very difficult to cease being attached because we do also love people. But where there is attachment can there be love? Or is love something vital, creative, moving—a feeling which cannot exist together with what is dead? How arduous and difficult it is to see this fact! It requires a great deal of insight, a great deal of energy and comprehension to see that the mind is everlastingly attaching itself to dead things and that such a mind is itself dead. Being of the dead, we are functioning only in the field of the burning-ghat. Therefore how can one have feeling?

So you begin to see that love knows no attachment. That is a hard thing to swallow, but it is a fact. And because our minds are so attached to dead things, problems arise. Then we try to cultivate detachment—which is attachment in a different cloak and therefore still in the field of death. Do observe in yourself how dead we are, how we have destroyed the bubbling feeling. The earth is not a dead thing, but when you are attached to something you call "India," which is just a symbol of a small part and not the earth itself, then you are clinging to something which is dead. Therefore your nationalism is merely a flirtation with death; it has no depth, no vitality. But the feeling for the earth itself—not my earth or the Russian, American, or English earth—that has a living quality.

So can we not understand, feel, see, that where there is attachment there is death? After all, when you are doing the same thing every day, getting up at the same time, repeating the same routine, going to the office, and so on, it becomes a custom, a tradition, a habit, and so your mind becomes dull. You may pass a lovely sunset or sunrise, a single tree alone in a field, and no depth of feeling is aroused because habit has taken the place of feeling, and your mind becomes attached to habit and objects to being shaken. The mind objects to change, and so the mind is destroying itself through its own attachments to dead or dying things.

Now if you have really understood all this, not merely verbally or intellectually, but if you feel deeply with me that this is really a very serious thing, then you will see that you can go to the office, take a bus, function in everyday life with a different quality, a new quality of mind. After all, you cannot stop doing your regular jobs, living your daily life; now it is a routine to which you are attached. And when you are attached to the fountain that holds the water, you cannot move with the living water. To see the truth of this requires not only insight, clarity of thought, precision of mind, but also the sense of beauty. If you have understood, you will see that attachment has no meaning any more. You do not have to struggle to be free of it; it drops away like a leaf in the wind. Then your mind becomes extraordinarily alive, sharp, precise, no longer confused. But without understanding all this, you will merely say, "Let me have it," or "I have something I must do." You are attached to action and you want the immediate answer. You have to decide what to do tomorrow, and that is much more compelling, much more urgent to you than this inquiry, than this search, than the feeling of this whole quality of comprehension, understanding, beauty, and love. So your actions are always leading to death—death being confusion, misery, suffering, and toil. If you see a man who only wants immediate action, immediate solution, what can you do for such a man who is pursuing death and insists on doing it? I am afraid most of us are like that. That is why the people of this country are inwardly dead. Though they may build dams for irrigation, industries, lessen population, feed people better, and all the rest of it, it is like the superficial structure of a beautiful house with no one living in it. That is what is happening. Technology is an art, but we have reduced it to a mechanical thing.

So if you and I have really truthfully and honestly asked ourselves how to awaken this feeling, then we shall have seen that any form of attachment is a dead thing, and that this deadly quality of attachment—to things, to people, and to ideas—invariably leads to the grave. In perceiving this you will see that your desire for immediate action has an answer at a totally different level, and the answer will be true, and it will be practical.

I hope I have made myself clear because for most of us the day-to-day action of habit has become all-important, so that we never see the horizon but are always doing something. You can only have the explosion of feeling when you understand this whole process of yourself and your attachments. If you can explore, examine, look into this thing called attachment, then you will begin to learn, and it is learning that will break up the dead things; it is learning that will give the feeling to action. You may make a mistake

in that action, but that mistake is a constant process of learning. To act means that you are trying to see, to find out, to understand, not merely trying to produce a result—which is a dead result. Action becomes very small and petty if you do not understand the center, the actor. We separate the actor from the action; the 'I' always does that and so becomes a dead thing. But if you are beginning to understand yourself, which is self-knowledge, which is learning about yourself, then that learning is a beautiful thing, so subtle, like living waters. If you understand that, and with that understanding act—not with the action of thought, but through the very process of learning—then you will find that the mind is no longer dead, no longer attached to dead and dying things. The mind, then, is extraordinary; it is like the horizon, endless, like space, without measure. Such a mind can go very deeply, and become that which is the universe, the timeless. From that state you will be able to act in time, but with a totally different feeling. All this requires not chronological time—days, weeks, and years—but the understanding of yourself, which can be done immediately. You will know, then, what love is. Love knows no jealousy, no envy, no ambition, and has no anchorage; it is a state in which there is no time, and because of that, action takes on a totally different meaning in our daily existence.

December 7, 1958

Fifth Talk in Bombay

Most of us are too occupied to admit the need of change. The mind is incessantly active, in a turmoil, occupied with this and that, with the innumerable problems of life, not only the external, but the inward also, and this constant occupation, both in the conscious and the unconscious, does not allow a change to take place. It seems to me that it is very important to go very deeply into this question of change because with the onrush of events, with the conflicting and contradictory environmental influences, with the pressures of social upheavals and the establishment of tyrannies, military dictatorships, and so on, change merely becomes an outward adjustment. So the question is: Is there change at all? If so, at what level do we change? And what do we mean by change? You and I obviously see that there must be some kind of change, not only in governments, in the economic and social structures, but also in the way of our living, in the way of our thoughts and aspirations. In all these things there must be some kind of revolution, some kind of change. Is it merely continued modification that is needed, or is there a need for a change which is totally different, which is not merely within the field of time?

I shall go into this, if I may, this evening. It seems to me that all the changes that take place under pressure, under influence, under social revolutions are in fact no change at all; they are merely adjustments to the environment. And that is what is happening all the time, constantly. A new government, a new social order, a new way of thinking comes into being—through propaganda, through various forms of mass communication—and because of the pressure we automatically adjust ourselves to it. That is what is actually going on in the world, and this striving to adjust, this struggle to conform, this incessant urge to yield, to follow, obviously wears down the mind, and in that process we think we are changing.

Now, how do you change? What makes you say, "I must change. I must no longer do this or that"? I do not know whether you have ever considered this. If you feel envious, jealous, or ambitious, or whatever it is, what makes you seek to put an end to it—if you ever do? I do not know if you have ever examined it, or whether you just go on with it—sometimes exploding, sometimes with jealousy dormant, but always simmering, always there. And if you want to change radically, to uproot jealousy altogether, then how do you proceed?

Most of us depend upon circumstances to bring about a change, but the fundamental situation always remains the same; circumstances may vary, but the state of jealousy is always round the corner and the cause of jealousy is ever there. One may cover it up, one may run away from it through various forms of discipline and denial, but essentially it is there and, given a new situation, it will arise again. You must have experienced this very often. Now what makes you or me change? And what do we mean by that word *change?* And is the mind capable of changing when it is occupied? Most of our minds are occupied, are they not? The mind is always occupied in the sense of being continually concerned with the daily activities, earning a livelihood, with social problems, with sex, with amusement, with what the neighbors say, with the decrees of the government. If you are rich, you are concerned with hiding your money from the tax authorities, and so on. Usually your mind is occupied, whether you are conscious of it or not. The mind is in a perpetual state of turmoil, always occupied with something, and when a problem is put to it—like this problem of change—it then begins to occupy itself with that problem. Is that not what happens, and what is happening now? I am putting to you the problem of what you mean by change, and at what level do you change, and what compels you to change, and your mind says, "By Jove, here is a problem. I must look at it, I must occupy myself with it." But a mind that is occupied with a problem, looking into it, revolving round it, analyzing it, forcing it along this way or that—such a mind will not allow any change.

I think change comes about in a totally different manner, and I would like to go into it with you. Change implies a movement from one point to another point—towards an idea or a particular desire. There is either the social revolution, which is from a given condition to a new condition, or there is the feeling that I am greedy and I must change to nongreed, I am violent and I must become nonviolent, which is again a process from a given point to another point, from one quality to another quality. That is what we call change, is it not? I hope this at least is clear between you and me, so that we are thinking together precisely and clearly on this point. I am ignorant and I must become learned, enlightened; I am miserable but I must try and be happy; I am in turmoil and I must find peace. So this movement is a change from something to something. Now what does this involve? Surely it involves time, does it not? There must be not only chronological time but psychological time. That is, to move from one point to another implies distance, an interval, a gap which must be covered by thought, by activity, which requires chronological time as well as the psychological time of "I will do it one day" or "I really must be different." I hope I am making that point clear, that whatever change is required, whether outwardly in social conditions or inwardly, time is involved. And so you say time is necessary.

Now what do we mean by time? It involves not only the interval, the movement from one point to another point, but it also involves, does it not, the movement from the present to the tomorrow, to the future. We always think in terms of time because our whole mind is based on time, is the result of time, is it not? You existed yesterday, you exist today, and you will exist tomorrow if no accident takes place. So you are always functioning, are you not, within that field of time. We are always thinking in terms of

what has been, what is, and what will be. And within that field of time, we say we must change. But in that field is there change at all, or is there only the conflict between *what is* and 'what should be'? After all, I cannot change the mind in an instant, nor can I change society because there are too many contradictory urges at work, too many opposing desires, too many laws, regulations to control and shape mass activity. All that structure cannot be overthrown totally in an instant, by tomorrow. All the reformers and revolutionaries try to bring about change, either violently or gradually, but they all require time. And when I say to myself, "I was; I am," and "I shall be," I also am caught in time. So I am asking myself whether the element of time is the factor, the catalyst, the force that brings about change, or whether a totally different thing, a different element altogether is needed to bring about change. So long as I am changing in the field of time, I am still functioning within the field of my own thought. The 'what I should be', 'what I am', and 'what I must not be' are all within the field of my own consciousness, is it not so? When you have been angry or jealous, you begin to discipline, correct, control, but it is always the 'you' that is controlling, making an effort not to be angry: Always it is the self that is operating, and the self is obviously in the field of time. The self is the field of time. Am I making this too difficult? I do not think so because, after all, most of us do function that way. A constant battle is going on within us, wearing us out in the process. So I am asking myself whether a change is possible, since change within the field of consciousness is no change at all. It is like merely putting on a different mask: I may no longer be angry, but the element of the 'me' that has controlled the anger is still there. So how is change to be brought about? Because I see that so long as I think in terms of time, there is no change. I do not know if

I am conveying the significance of the fact that so long as I am thinking of changing, I must resort to time. Time is a very difficult thing to understand because all striving implies time and self-consciousness, and in that field is there ever real change, or is change something entirely outside the field of time?

Let us put it differently. Without learning about yourself—yourself as a social entity, an economic entity, an individual—obviously there can be no radical change. What you do without knowing yourself is merely alteration, adjustment to a certain pattern. So without knowing yourself there can be no radical transformation. Now, is learning about yourself a matter of time? Can you know the entirety of yourself on the instant, or is it a matter of time—slowly analyzing, exploring, dissecting, examining? In that process, if you miss any particular angle, any particular layer, your conclusion, your examination will not be clear, it will be perverted. It would be an endless process, would it not, a process in which any slightest mistake would lead to further confusion. So the question is: Can I know myself immediately? Can the mind learn of its entire process, its whole depth, discover its vastness, its extraordinary richness, on the instant?

Before we go further, I think that you should listen differently. You are listening now, are you not, to see how you can transcend time and so bring about a change. I have pointed out that in the field of time there is no change at all, that a mind which struggles to be nonenvious is still envious, and then I have asked if one can learn about oneself totally without the process of analysis. I am now asking how you are listening to me. Are you asking yourself how to get that change which is radical? If so, you are back in the field of time, are you not? Or are you listening to me and learning without that barrier of time? Am I making the problem clear or more difficult? Probably more

difficult because this is a very complex problem, and if you have not followed inwardly, then you will find what I am going to say now much more difficult.

Silence, the movement of silence is the only field in which there is a change; that is the only constant state from which change can take place.

Look, sirs, the problem is this: I see that social influences, pressures, environment, bring about certain changes in me; a quarrel with my wife necessitates a certain adjustment. And throughout my life I keep on adjusting, constantly changing superficially, but inwardly I am the same, and the problem is how am I to change deeply, without influence, without compulsion, without a motive—because a motive implies time. I see I must change because I know I am dull, stupid, envious, anxious, fearful, and every pleasure is vanishing, and I want to change so radically, so totally, that my mind is new. If that is your problem also, then we are in relationship, we can commune with each other, and we must establish that relationship in order to understand what we are exploring and what we are going to discover. If you only change under pressure, under influence, then you will find that you are merely adjusting, imitating, conforming, and obviously that is not change. Behind it all the entity is still the same.

That very word *change* implies, does it not, to change from this to that, so now let us eliminate the word change and ask: How am I to exist in a state of constancy which is invariable, which is not merely a permanent state?

You see, sirs, we must differentiate between the permanent state and that which is constant. The state of permanency—wanting to be immortal, wanting to have permanent peace, joy, bliss—that is what most of us actually want, is it not? And can we get it? Or, is there a state which knows no change at all, in which there is always a quality of freshness, a newness, a sense of being? Change implies an impermanency which is seeking permanency. But there is a state without any change, in which there is a quality of shadowless movement—a movement which has no time in the sense of being this and becoming that. So how is the mind to move from this state to that? All our activity is based on the impermanent trying to become the permanent—politically, economically, socially, and psychologically. I can also see very clearly that there can be a state of mind in which there is no change at all, but it can only come about when the mind is motionless and stable. Such a motionless state is a still mind, not a dead mind, and it knows neither impermanency nor permanency. It is a mind that is completely quiet. Such a mind does not demand change, and all its action springs from that silence. That is the only state in which the weariness, the conflict of the worrying mind completely ceases. So, is it possible to move from here to there, but not in time?

Let me put it differently. I know hate, I know jealousy, ambition, and so on, and I can control hate, discipline it, but I see that that is an entirely different thing from the mind that never knows hate, that has never tasted hate because it is innocent, fresh, of a completely and totally different quality. Can the mind instantly be that which knows no hate? After all, the hating mind cannot know what love is. So how is hate to cease on the instant, totally, so that there is the other state where there is only love? That is the complete, radical change. And how is this miracle to take place? We say that the miracle can only take place by the grace of God or by some mysterious means. If you say that, it will never happen. To bring about this miracle, first we must be very clear that

there is no change in terms of time, only a process of putting on a different mask.

Let us attack it from another point of view. Are you ever conscious of being silent? Have you experienced silence? If you have experienced silence, then it is not silence, is it? If there is an observer observing silence, then it is the projection of the experiencer—the experiencer wishing to be in a state of silence. Therefore it is not silence. Reality can never be experienced; if you do experience reality, then it is not reality because then there is the division between the experiencer and the experience. That division signifies duality and all the conflicts of duality. So silence can never be experienced.

If you really understand that, if you are listening and learning the fact that silence can never be experienced, then what is the state of the mind that has no experience of silence, that *is* silence? I begin to see that a mind which is silent is not conscious that it is silent. So also with humility. If you are conscious that you are humble, then that is not humility. If I am conscious that I am holy, spiritual, I am not; if I am conscious that I know, then I am ignorant. If I am conscious that my mind is silent, then there is no silence. So silence is a state of mind in which there is the absence of the experiencer. Can you listen to me in that state of silence, being unaware that you are silent?

Sirs, this requires a great deal of energy, a great deal of precise thinking, but if you have thought very, very clearly, observed yourself very deeply, sharply, with such clarity that no shadow is left, then you will see that the mind has a quality of silence in which time and the movement of time have ceased; all question of change has totally ceased because there is no demand and no need for change.

This is one of the most difficult things to convey because words cannot describe it. If you are merely waiting to experience it, you will not; you will only wait and wait. But if you have examined deeply the whole problem of change, the whole movement of going from one state to another, from one point to another, if you have gone into it very, very deeply, grasped it, understood it, and abandoned it—in which abandonment there is neither hope nor despair—then there is a state of mind which is silence, and that silence is not recognizable by the mind because all recognition is a process of experience. So, change implies only a movement in time, and that movement is like cutting the air with a sword—it does nothing, it merely produces a lot of activity. But when you understand the whole process, the implications and the significance of change, and thereby let it drop away from you, you will see that the mind is in a state of silence in which all movement of time has ceased, and that new movement of silence is not recognizable and therefore not experienceable. Such a state does not demand change; it is in eternal movement, and therefore beyond time. Then there is an action which is right, which is true, always and under all circumstances.

December 10, 1958

Sixth Talk in Bombay

I wonder why one gives importance to thought? To us, thinking has become very important and significant. The more subtle, the more cunning, the more complicated it is, the more we give it importance, and I am wondering if thought has any deep, fundamental significance at all. Do we live by thought? Do we conduct our life by thought? Does ideation—the ideal—play any deep significant part in our life, or do we think casually, are our ideas superficial, our thoughts not very deep? And can thought go very deep, or is it always superficial? I think

it will be very interesting if we can go into this whole problem and find out if a religious life is dependent on thought. By a religious life I do not mean going to the temple, the church, the dogmas, beliefs, rituals, and all the rest of it. All those are obviously social conveniences and of very little meaning. But is thought conducive to a truly religious life? Does thought unfold the beauty, the depth of a really deep religious feeling? Is thought the instrument for the discovery of what is true? If not, then what part does thought play in all our seeking?

If we could, you and I, really think this out, slowly, deeply, then perhaps we would be able to discover the true significance of life and not give that enormous importance to thought. Perhaps we shall also be able to find out that there is no right or wrong thinking, but that thought itself is very superficial.

Thought is really a reaction, is it not?—a reaction to any given problem whether it be a problem of mathematics, physics, or a problem of relationship. What we call "thinking" is always a reaction between the problem, the challenge, and the response, is it not? And thinking, as one sees if one looks, is the collected experiences stored as memory and responding to any challenge. The whole of one's background of experience, of knowledge gathered and accumulated through everyday experience, becomes the immense reservoir of memory, and that memory responds, either in a verbal manner or in an emotional manner or intellectually.

I hope you are listening to me not as to a talk or discourse but as though you and I were two people together, talking over the problem and trying to find out the true significance and worth of thought.

To me, thought is not the instrument of real discovery; thought is not the instrument which explores, that is capable of discovering or examining. And if you and I are going to understand each other, to communicate, commune with each other about the significance of thought, we must both be capable of looking without accepting or rejecting, without defending or taking anything for granted. What you and I are going to do is to examine thought, not verbally or intellectually, but looking at it as a fact. I do not know if you have ever looked at a fact without clouding that fact with an opinion. I feel that if we can look at this complicated thing called "thought," neither giving our opinion nor expressing our prejudices by saying it is necessary or not necessary, but by merely observing it we shall be able to explore the whole content of thought, the whole machinery of thought.

Thinking, surely, is superficial; it is the response of memory, the collected experiences, the conditioning; and according to that conditioning, which is our background, thought responds to any challenge. Thought is always bound to this collected experience, and the question is: Can thinking ever be free? Because it is only in freedom that one can observe, it is only in freedom that one can discover. It is only in a state of spontaneity, where there is no compulsion, no immediate demand, no pressure of social influence that real discovery is possible. Surely, to observe what you are thinking, why you think, and the source and motive of your thought, there must be a certain sense of spontaneity, of freedom, because any influence whatsoever gives a twist to observation. With all thinking, if there is any compulsion or pressure, thought becomes crooked.

So can thought ever set man free, set the mind free, and is freedom the essential necessity if one is to discover what is true? There are two different types of freedom—the freedom from something or the freedom to fulfill, to be something; and there is freedom, just freedom. Most of us want to be free from something—free from time or free

from a relative, or else we want to be free to be fulfilled, to express ourselves. All our ideas of freedom are limited to those two—the freedom from something or the freedom to be something. Now both are reactions, are they not? Both are the result of thought, the outcome of some form of inward or outward compulsion. Thought is caught in that process; thought seeks freedom from tyranny, freedom from a corrupt government, freedom from a particular relationship, freedom from a feeling of anxiety, and in freeing oneself, one hopes to be able to fulfill oneself in something else. So we always think in terms of freedom from, or freedom to be, to fulfill. And it seems to be that thinking of freedom only in those two categories is very superficial.

So, is there a freedom which is not merely a reaction, in which there is neither a movement from nor a movement to be? And can such a freedom be captured, engendered as an idea by thought? Because if you are merely free from something, you are not really free, and if you are free in the sense of being fulfilled, in that there is always anxiety, fear, frustration, and sorrow. Can thought free the mind so that sorrow and anxiety have ceased altogether? Surely, as with love, real goodness is not cultivated by thought; it is a state of being, but that state cannot be brought about by the mind which says to itself, "I must be good." So, can one find out by searching through the various channels of thought what freedom is? Can thought uncover the true significance of life, unfold reality? Or must thought be totally suspended for reality to be?

Let me put it differently. You are seeking something, are you not? If you are a so-called religious person, you are seeking what you call God, or else you are seeking more money, more happiness, or you want to be good; you are seeking the expression of your ambition. Everyone is seeking something.

Now what do we mean by seeking? To seek implies that you know what it is you are seeking. When you say you are seeking peace of mind, it must mean either that you have already experienced it and want it back, or you are projecting a verbal idea which is not an actuality, but a thing created by thought. So search implies that you have already known or experienced what you seek. You cannot seek something which you do not know. When you say you are seeking God, it means you already know what God is, or else your conditioning has projected the idea that there is a God. So, thinking compels you to seek that which thought itself has projected. Thought, which is superficial, thought, the result of many experiences which have been gathered and which form your background—from that thought you project an idea and then you seek it! And in your search for God you have visions, you have experiences which only strengthen the search and urge you on to follow the projections of your background. So, searching is still the motion of thought. One is in conflict, in turmoil, and in order to escape from that turmoil, thought begins to project an idea that there must be peace, that there must be permanent bliss, and then it proceeds to seek it. This is actually what is taking place in each one of us. One does not understand this miserable existence, this everlasting chaos, and one wants to escape to a permanent state of bliss. Now that state is projected by the mind, and having projected it, thought says, "I must find help to get to it"—and so follows the methods, the system, the practice. Thought creates the problem, and then tries to escape from the problem through various systems in order to reach the projected idea of a permanent state. So, thought pursues its own projection, its own shadow.

Now, the question is, really: Can the mind suspend thinking and face everyday experience from a different quality of mind?

This does not mean to forget or neglect collected memory, collected experience. Technicians, bridge-builders, scientists, clerks, and so on are, of course, needed, but is it possible—realizing that thinking is not the solution to our problems—to suspend thought and observe the problem? I do not know if you have ever tried really to look at a problem without the agitation, the turmoil, the restlessness of thought. Thinking creates a series of motions of restlessness, of anxiety, of demand for a solution, and have you ever tried to sink thought, to suspend thinking and just observe the problem? Please try it, sirs, as I am talking. Listen so that you can look at the problem without the agitation of thought.

You have many problems—problems of relationship, of family, problems of your work, your responsibilities, problems of your social, environmental, or political life—whether they are immediate, pressing, or remote. Take any one of those problems and look at it. You have always looked at it, have you not, with a certain agitation of thought which says, "I must solve it. What am I to do? Is this right or is that? Is this respectable or not possible?" and so on and on. And with this restless thought you examine the problem, and obviously, whatever solution you find through that restlessness is not a true answer and only creates more problems. That is what is actually taking place with each one of us. So can you look at the problem, suspending your thought? Thought is the result of collected experiences, and their memories respond to the problem, but can you suspend thought so that for the moment your mind is not under pressure, not under the weight of a thousand yesterdays? It is not merely a matter of saying, "I will not think." That is impossible. But if you see the truth that an agitated mind that is merely responding according to its conditioning, its background, its accumulated experiences cannot resolve or understand the problem—if you see the truth of that fact totally, then you understand that thought is not the instrument which will resolve our problems.

Let me put it differently. It seems that whatever man can do, an appropriate electronic machine can do also. It is being discovered and will be perfected in a decade or two that what a human mind can do, the machine can do also, and quite efficiently. It will probably compose, write poems, translate books, and so on. And chemically they are making drugs to give comfort, peace, freedom from worry, tranquilization. So you understand, sirs, what is going to happen? Is the machine to take over your work and probably do it better, and is the drug to give you peace of mind? There are certain drugs you can take to make your mind extraordinarily quiet so that you won't have to go through disciplines, controls, breathing exercises, and all those tricks. So the petty mind, the shallow mind, the limited mind which only thinks an inch from itself, will have no more worries, it will have peace. But such a mind is still petty; its frontiers are recognizable and all its thoughts are shallow. Though it is very quiet through taking pills, it has not broken down its own limitations, has it? A petty mind thinking about God, going from one graven image to another, uttering a lot of words, murmuring a lot of prayers, is still a petty mind. And that is the case with most of us.

So how can thought, which is always superficial, always petty, always limited, how can that thought be suspended so that there is no frontier at all, so that there is freedom—but not the freedom from something or the freedom to be something? I hope you understand the question.

You see, one can forever improve oneself—one can think a little more, apply oneself to self-improvement, be more kind, more generous, this or that, but it is always

within the field of the self, the 'me'. It is the 'me' that is achieving, becoming, and that 'me' is always recognizable as a collection of experiences, memories. And the problem is how to resolve, to break down the frontiers of the 'me'. When I say "how," I do not imply a method but an inquiry. Because, all methods involve the functioning of thought, the control of thought, the substitution of one thought for another. So when you merely have methods, systems, disciplines, there is no inquiry.

Seeing all this—that thought is the result of memory, of collected experience which is very limited, and that the seeking of reality, God, truth, perfection, beauty is really the projection of thought in conflict with the present and going towards an idea of the future, and seeing that the pursuit of the future creates time—seeing all this, surely it is obvious that thought must be suspended. There must be something, surely, which thought cannot capture and put into memory, something totally new, completely unknowable, unrecognizable. And how are you, with the restlessness of your thought, to understand that state?

Is understanding a matter of time? Will you understand this tomorrow by thinking about it? You know how, if you have a problem, thought investigates it, analyzes it, tears it to pieces, goes into it as much as it can, and still has no answer because it is always with the anxiety of the problem. Then it gives it up, lays it in abeyance, and because thought has dissociated itself from the problem so that the problem is no longer pressing on the mind, consciously or unconsciously, then the answer comes. It must have happened to you.

So can we not see through this whole business of thinking? You know how you worship the intellectual man who is full of knowledge, which is nothing but words and ideas, but who is still living on the superficial level. Have you observed how instinctively you are attracted to a man who says, "I know"? So, seeing all this, the question is: Can thought be suspended? If you have understood the problem, then as I begin to explore it further, you will be able to follow.

There is the problem of death, the problem of God, of virtue, of relationship; there is the problem of the conflict we are in, the job, the lack of money; there is the problem of poverty, starvation, and the whole misery of despair and hope. You cannot solve these problems one by one; it is impossible. You have to solve them totally, as a whole thing, not little by little; otherwise, you will never solve them. Because in solving one problem as though it were dissociated from the others, you merely create another problem. No problem is separate, isolated. Every problem is related to another problem, superficially or deeply, so you have to comprehend it totally. And thought can never comprehend it totally because thought is partial, is fragmentary. So how is the mind to solve the problem? You cannot solve it as though it were isolated; you cannot find a solution through an intellectual abstraction; you cannot solve it through accumulated memories; you cannot solve it by escaping to the temple, or to alcohol, or to sex or anything else. It must be comprehended totally, understood totally, and this can happen only when there is the suspension of thought. When the mind is motionless and still, the reflection of the problem on the mind is entirely different. When the lake is very quiet, you can see the depth of it, you can see every fish, every weed, every flutter; similarly, when the mind is completely motionless, one can see very, very clearly. This can only take place when there is a suspension of thought, not in order to resolve the problem, but to see its significance, its fragmentary nature; and then thought of itself becomes quiet, motionless,

not only at the conscious level but profoundly.

That is why self-knowledge is essential, why it is essential to learn about yourself. And you cannot learn about yourself if you do not look, or if you look with a mind that is full of accumulated knowledge. To learn, you must be free. Then you can look at the problem not merely from the surface; then every issue, every challenge is responded to from a depth which thought cannot reach.

A motionless mind, a still mind, is not decayed, dead, corrupt, as is the mind which has been made still by a drug, by breathing, or by any system of self-hypnosis. It is a mind that is fully alive; every untrodden region of itself is lighted up, and from that center of light it responds—and it does not create a shadow.

December 14, 1958

Seventh Talk in Bombay

I wonder why you come to these talks. If it is merely to try to confirm your own particular theory about life or to try to find another theory which is superior, more subtle, then I think these talks will have very little meaning. Because what we are trying to do here, if we can, is to break through the curtain of theories and become intelligent. We have so many problems, at all levels of our being—physical, psychological, intellectual, and so on—and obviously no theory is going to solve any of them. The theory always brings about conformity, but the understanding of the fact frees the mind and brings about intelligence, an enlightened way of living. This enlightened way of living is obviously denied when the mind is ridden by theories, ideologies, formulas, or intellectual conceptions. I think—and I am saying this in all humility—that the function of these discourses here is to awaken, if possible, this intelligence so that you as an individual will be able to meet the various situations in which you find yourself with enlightenment, with clarity, with a sense of deep inward understanding.

So if you and I are clear on this point, that we are really trying to break through this wall of darkness, the wall of theories, beliefs, dogmas, and superstitions, then, in the breaking through we shall awaken that intelligence which is an enlightened comprehension of the whole process of living. Then these discourses will have meaning, real significance. But if we merely translate what is said into a formula, a theory, then we shall miss the whole point of all this. Ideas, however refined, however cunning, however subtle can never solve the problems of our existence; no dogma, no new or old system will ever resolve the intellectual, psychological, and physical problems of our life. What we need is the application of enlightened intelligence to our everyday living, and that requires a great deal of insight, a great deal of deep inward inquiry. Obviously there is no deep inward search if we merely function according to a particular formula or theory—whether capitalistic, socialistic, or religious. That merely leads to conformity. But unfortunately most of us are caught in theories, in formulas, in systems of thought. We first have a system of thought and then try to fit the fact to that system—which is an impossibility. This is invariably what we do. We accept some theory and to that theory, to that belief, to that dogma we try to conform, which obviously leads to a most absurd way of living.

So you and I, as two individuals who are caught up in the stream of life of which we are part—with our turmoils, anxieties, fears, our passing affections and joys—can we not understand our problems, apply our minds to them and sharpen the mind through application? But not in a cunning way, which is

what most of us want—to survive at any cost through various forms of political and business cunning and cunning in relationships. Because I feel that if we could become sensitive to this extraordinary thing called life, not merely seek to translate life according to our own particular pattern of thought, but be sensitive to the whole process of life—to nature, to people, to ideas—then perhaps we can discover what is true and what is false.

That faculty of sensitivity is, of course, intelligence, is it not? Intelligence is the capacity to be deeply sensitive to all the movements of life. You cannot continue to live fragmentarily, individually, in segregation—as a businessman, a financier, a politician, a religious person, a communist, or this or that—because you are a total being with extraordinary faculties. To be alive, alert, to be sensitive to this movement of life is the only true intelligence, and when one is so intelligent, then one can apply that intelligence totally to any action at any level. So it seems to me that it is essential to be sensitive to life, sensitive to the ugly, to the beautiful, to the heavens, to all the untrodden regions of one's own mind and to the restlessness of one's own mind—with its demands, sorrows, and inward anxieties. We are not trying to find an answer to the problem but rather to be sensitive to the problem, and with that sensitivity, which is intelligence, we can then understand the problem and therefore resolve it. There is no answer to the problem at any level, but there is a resolution of the problem if there is sufficient intelligence, sufficient sensitivity to the problem itself. But unfortunately, most of us seek solutions, seek an answer, and therefore we never are sensitive to a problem because when the mind is seeking an answer, it is obviously running away from the actual problem. But through sensitivity intelligence is awakened, and then you can deal with the problem, whatever it be. All the paraphernalia of ritualism, belief, and all that stupid nonsense has no meaning if one has the faculty of sensitivity to the whole process of living, and this sensitivity is denied when the mind merely functions in habit. Most of our minds do function in habits of thought—conclusions we have arrived at, our experiences, some peculiar state which we have known; these become our habits and we function from them.

Now if I may digress a little, I hope you are listening not merely intellectually or merely to the verbal significance of the words because then you are not applying what you hear, then you are not capable of learning. Here you and I are trying to learn together and in this inquiry there is neither the teacher nor the taught. Life is not a process of being taught by a teacher. Everything has to be learned. A dead leaf in a dirty street, if you can look at it with sensitivity, has enormous meaning. You can learn from that dead leaf because it has lived, has seen the spring and the summer, and it knows death. One can learn from everything, every incident, every experience, from every gesture, every look, every word. So I hope that you and I are listening to each other in that manner. That requires humility; a mind that knows no humility cannot learn, it merely acquires information. Such a mind is really arrogant in its own knowledge; it accumulates, becomes cunning, but it can never learn. Though I am doing the talking, I hope you are listening in that state of mind which is learning—learning about your habit of thought, which is imitation, conformity, respectability, pettiness of mind. It is that mind which is insensitive to life. It is that petty mind which creates problems, and it is still the same mind which seeks an answer to its problem and therefore increases the problem. It is about that mind that we have to learn.

If you have observed your own mind you can see how extraordinarily quickly it falls into grooves of thought. You can see, can you not, how the mind is conditioned to function along certain lines, to establish so-called good habits and to avoid evil habits. Now, there is no good habit or bad habit, there is only habit, and it is habit which makes us dull, stupid, heavy, without sensitivity to the challenge of life. You know, this is what is happening to all of us, is it not? We want to establish habits so that we do not have to think any more. We want to establish a good habit so that we can function automatically, like a machine. And as machines have no sensitivity, so obviously the mind that functions in habit has no sensitivity. A bureaucrat who has lived for thirty or forty years signing papers, how can he be sensitive to life? He functions with a limited mind, and all specialists, technicians, and the rest of us are in the same state; we learn a job and live in it. So the problem is how to die to habits, and I want to discuss this very deeply, leading to the problem of death.

I want to discourse on this whole problem of death, but you and I will not be able to understand that problem if we do not first understand the mind that creates habit, the mind that creates a center from which it functions. That center is the 'me', is it not? That center is the self with its accumulated, organized experiences from which it acts and thinks, from which it loves, and from which it hates. It is that center—which is obviously the organized experience of habit, thought, knowledge—which functions, and that center is not separate from thought, from the self. There is only the thinker who creates the self. And I feel that if you and I do not fully understand this center of habit, of imitation, and if that center is not broken, dissolved, then we shall never understand what death is.

I would like to go into that, think aloud about it with you—or rather not "think" but discourse upon it. But if you merely listen without really observing, without being aware of your own center—the center of anxiety, of suffering, the center that wants to love and does not know how to, that is seeking some kind of fulfillment, some kind of happiness, joy, some form of physical or psychological survival—if you are not aware of all that, which is essentially a bundle of imitations from the yesterday, then my going into this problem of death will not answer your questions. As I have said, there is no answer to any problem, there is only an understanding of the problem. Likewise there is no answer to death, but only the understanding of death—the extraordinary depth of it, the beauty of it, the vastness, the newness of it—and that very understanding brings about a wholly different state of mind which will make you free of the fear of death and the sorrow of death. But the fear of death, the fear of loneliness, and that aloneness which comes with the understanding of death—all that will not be understood if you do not intelligently comprehend the implications of habit, of imitation, of conformity, of respectability.

Now, how is this center to be dissipated? I am using the word *how* not in the sense of finding an answer or a new system, but merely to start an inquiry into the problem. I want to know how to break this center, not merely continue that center in a different way under the communist regime, the socialist regime, the capitalist regime, or some other regime with the innate suffering, pain, and sorrow. I want to understand it, to break it, and I see that time is not the solution. This lengthening of the future is not the solution; the continuity of what has been is not the answer. I hope you understand what I mean. One realizes, doesn't one, that this center is the self, the 'me'—that craves, that wants, that is seeking power, position, prestige, that has this constant nightmare of struggle, adjustment, pain, sorrow, and fleeting joys, all of which is wearing us out at all levels of our existence. So I am asking: How is this center to be broken? We say time, many future days will solve it, or we believe in reincarnation. But that is merely giving what has been a modified continuity in the future, is it not? There is still the survival of this center, is there not, with all its anxieties, problems, fears, the residue of imitation, of habit. So the question is: Is it possible to die to that center now?—not in the future, not waiting until you are old and worn out, and bodily death comes. Am I putting the problem clearly? Sirs, can I die to myself now? After all, death is the great negation, and all negation at that deep level is sacred, is profound. That is why negative thinking is the greatest form of thinking and so-called positive thinking is really only a continuation of imitation, conformity. So I am asking you how to die—how to die to a habit. You understand, sirs? The habit of ambition which you know—can you die to it? Everyone is ambitious, from the greatest leader to the poorest man in this social structure. You want to be something, to become something, do you not? And the struggle, the pain, the frustration, the ruthlessness and cruelty that is involved—you know it all, and still you want to fulfill. Now can one die to that habit of thought? Not tomorrow, but can the urge cease on the moment? Because, surely, the moment it ceases the mind becomes astonishingly sensitive, and in the cessation of that particular habit, there is enlightenment. That enlightenment is awakened by the intelligence which comes when you see the whole implication of ambition. I am taking ambition as an example, but there is also envy, greed, pride, and also virtue, which I am going into presently. Can one die to all this? Because, if you cannot die to it, obviously you will have continuity—continuity of sorrow and death—and then death is a fearful thing. After all, virtue also is a form of continuity, the perpetuation of what you think is good, true. Virtue, to you, is a positive state and virtue, which is the cultivation of an opposite, implies continuity. If you are violent you cultivate nonviolence and pursue that ideal day after day. You practice, subjugate your mind, but obviously all that is merely the continuity of a certain idea, a certain thought, that is all. The continuation of a particular idea which you call virtue is merely conformity to a certain pattern which society demands. Real virtue is the complete cessation of ambition, of envy, of greed, of pride—not the transforming of one particular feeling into another kind of feeling. The cessation of habit, in which there is no continuity of what has been—that alone, surely, is virtue. To cease totally, to have no pride at all is utterly different from being conscious of pride and cultivating humility; cultivated humility is merely the continuation of pride in a different form. But the cessation of pride, totally, on the moment—surely, that is possible.

Look what is happening everywhere! Everyone is ambitious, from the highest to the lowest. And once a man gets into a position he can hold, he will not relinquish it; he says that for the good of the country, for the good of the people, for the good of society, he must stay in office. You know all the verbiage. Do not say, "If I am not ambitious, what will happen to me?" You will find out, surely, what will happen if you cease to be ambitious. You will have a different life altogether. You may or may not fit into this rotten society, but you will have understood; there will be a state of virtue that knows no tomorrow. Virtue is a state of being, on the instant, and in that there is great depth of beauty. So you must die to all your yesterdays. But that becomes a theory, a mere statement if you have not really understood the whole problem of the mind that has accumulated, if you are not aware of your own habits, of your own prejudices, ambitions,

frustrations, joys, and sorrows. If you are not aware of all that, then the mere statement that you must die totally to all the yesterdays has no meaning. You may repeat it, pass it on, but it will have no meaning. Whereas if you can take one thought, one habit that occurs to you and die to it, then you will see that dying is something quite different from anything you have known.

If I can die to my pride, if I can die to my ambitions, if I can die to all the injuries I have received, the insults, the despairs, the hopes and fears that I have nourished for so long, then my mind is no longer thinking in terms of time; then death is not merely at the end of existence, then death is at the beginning as well as at the end. This is not a theory, this is not a poetic statement; if you repeat it, it has no meaning, but if you die to one of your habits—any habit—just die to it, just drop it, as a leaf falls away naturally, automatically, then you will notice that in that very dying a new breath comes into being, a new way of existence. It is not that you will replace death by another way of existence, but the very dying to the habit brings about a new, creative living. Please, sirs, do listen as I am talking and apply it—not when you get home, not as you wait for the bus, not looking for the moment of tranquillity, but now. Can you not die now to something? Can you not die to your dislike of somebody, to your fear of somebody, to your beliefs— which is much more difficult, because your guru, your belief gives you hope, a future. But if you can die to your own despair, then there is no need of a guru, which means there is no need for hope, no need for the tomorrow. To die to despair is the negation of death; it is a state of the greatest creativeness.

Then there is the further problem of what it is that continues in our daily existence. We are all concerned, are we not, to know if there is some form of continuity after death.

You hope, many of you, that you will reincarnate, make yourself perfect, become more and more of value—which means climbing the ladder of success. If you are a nobody in this life, you hope you will be somebody in the next life. There is always this problem of continuity. Now what is it that continues in this life, and why do you cling to that continuity? Why does the mind hold on to, attach itself to that form of what has been? You understand the question, sirs? You are afraid of death, and so you say you will continue hereafter. Now before you look into the future, can you not question the present? What is it that continues? What is it to which you cling? To your position as a clerk, a minister, a priest, a businessman—the deceiving, dishonest, corrupt individuality? Is that what you are holding on to? Your family, your property, your name, is that what you are clinging to? And all this you want to continue after death? Good God! All that is nothing at all, is it? Your name, your property, your ideas, experiences, joys are all changing, moving, and in them is uncertainty, fear, and despair. So is that what you want to continue? And is there a continuity of all that; is there a continuity of anything, or does everything naturally die? The mind refuses to accept death now, does it not, but surely that which continues can never be creative, can never find that extraordinary state of mind that is creation. Obviously, what continues is only that which has been, modified in the present in order to proceed to some future, and such a continuity—with all its implications of sorrow, failure, hope, and despair—is merely the continuity of the center, the 'me', the self which invents the super-self, the atma, and all the rest of the theories.

Can that continuity come to an end now, not just wait for death from accident, disease, or old age? I do not know if you have thought of this problem at all. The traditional approach obviously does not uncover the problem. So really the question is whether the mind with all its memories, organized experiences, can die to its memories and not merely become dull, stupid, incapable of creativeness. Can we not die to memory so that memory does not influence the mind—even though we retain it factually? Because if you factually forget yesterday, you cannot survive, you cannot live. But when yesterday influences today—as it does with all of us—then you lose the sensitivity, the profundity of the real dying to the yesterday.

If you have really listened to all this, then you are learning about death, that death is now, not in the future. The beauty of death is in the present, and because it is negative, a positive approach can never discover it. But when the continuity of what has been comes to an end, then a new quality of mind comes into being; though it has the accumulated knowledge of a thousand yesterdays, yet the mind is dead to all that and so is fresh, new, innocent. But if you ask, "How can I get that innocence?" you are asking a most silly question. There is no method, no system; systems, methods, disciplines, virtues give only a continuity of what has been, modified. It is only in dying that there is a creative mind. One can see also that the stronger the mind is in its egotism, in its self-centered activity, the more energetic, violent, struggling the self is. And obviously it will continue because the mind is different from the brain. Though the mind is the result of the brain, it is free of the brain, as thought is free of the brain. Thought continues as a vibration which may manifest itself afterwards, but that again is a form of continuity and that continuing entity can never be creative, can never know this extraordinary state of creation. So, sirs, what this world needs at the present time is not more technicians; there will be more technicians, but at their level they are not going to solve the human problem. They may build more dams, better roads, better means of communication, bring about more prosperity, a better way of living—which of course is essential—but that is all. In all this we have denied religion because for most of us life is mainly a physical matter. Through technology you may be going to have perfect physical living, but that is not the answer to our fundamental problems.

So what is required is a mind that is in a state of creation, not in a state of continuity. And creation can be really understood, learned about, known, experienced, only in the state of death. Creation is reality, creation is what you call God—but the word *God* is not that creation; the word is only a symbol, it has no meaning. Repeating about God, praying to God, going to temples, churches, has no meaning. But if you die to all the words, to all the symbols, then you will find out for yourself—without reading any book, without going to any guru, without any ritual, without any support—you will find that state of creation in which everything exists. But you cannot comprehend that state by any amount of repetition of the word. That state comes only when you die to your ambition, to your anxiety, to your corruption. Then you will see that in that state of death which is negation, there is a totally different state of the positive, which is creation.

December 17, 1958

Eighth Talk in Bombay

I would like to talk this evening about meditation, but to go into it really deeply one must see that meditation is not something apart from daily existence; it is intimately connected with our daily activities, our daily thoughts, with our conflicts, our passing pleasures and joys. It is not something which you do in a quiet room all by yourself, unre-lated to the daily movement of life. To really go into it deeply I think one must begin by understanding the problem of influence.

I hope that you, as an individual, are not being influenced in any way by these talks because to me, influence—unless one fully comprehends its significance—is a poison. It conditions, deteriorates, and perverts the mind. And there are so many influences, are there not? There is the climate, the food you eat, the very thoughts you have, the pressures, your education, the newspapers you read, the churches, temples, and there is the influence of the family, the influence of the husband over the wife and the wife over the husband, and also the influence of centuries of tradition. Everything about one is influencing the mind, shaping one's thought, consciously or unconsciously, and one is not aware of these influences. To be aware of all these many influences and to be free of them is the process of meditation. But this requires a deep, an enormous understanding because with a shallow mind, a petty mind, sitting down to meditate is obviously just a process of murmuring, muttering, a repetition which has no meaning at all.

To understand this whole problem of influence, the influence of experience, the influence of knowledge, of inward and outward motives—to find out what is true and what is false and to see the truth in the so-called false—all that requires tremendous insight, a deep inward comprehension of things as they are, does it not? This whole process is, surely, the way of meditation. Meditation is essential in life, in our everyday existence, as beauty is essential. The perception of beauty, the sensitivity to things, to the ugly as well as to the beautiful, is essential—to see a beautiful tree, a lovely sky of an evening, to see the vast horizon where the clouds are gathering as the sun is setting. All this is necessary, the perception of beauty and the understanding of the way of meditation, because all that is life, as is also your going to the office, the quarrels, miseries, the perpetual strain, anxiety, the deep fears, love, and starvation. Now the understanding of this total process of existence—the influences, the sorrows, the daily strain, the authoritative outlook, the political actions, and so on—all this is life, and the process of understanding it all, and freeing the mind, is meditation. If one really comprehends this life, then there is always a meditative process, always a process of contemplation—but not *about* something. To be aware of this whole process of existence, to observe it, to dispassionately enter into it, and to be free of it is meditation.

So I would like, if I may, to talk about all this; but first, if I may suggest, do not be mesmerized by that word *meditation;* do not immediately take up a posture, mental or physical, do not take up a special attitude because a mind that takes up a posture, an attitude, can never be in a state of meditation. Meditation is really the uncovering, the unfolding of the extraordinary process of the mind with all its subtleties, its wanderings, its superficial actions, and its deep movement of which the conscious mind is not aware at all. The total comprehension of all this, and the entering into it, is meditation.

Now I hope you understand that I am talking to you as an individual, not as to an audience. You and I are quietly, freely, dispassionately trying to understand this thing called life. And if we are to explore together, you cannot be influenced or take up an attitude which has been influenced. You have to listen, which means, really, to learn. If you take up an attitude, you cease to learn; if you say you already know what meditation is, then you cease to learn about meditation; if you say, "I have meditated all my life and I have had visions, I have had clarity, I have had experiences, and that is good enough for me," then you have already ceased to meditate, ceased to learn. Meditation is not a finality; the beauty of meditation is that it is unending; it is an eternal thing. Also, it would be a misfortune if you are merely persuaded by me to think this way or that. But if you are aware of the influences about you, including mine, aware so that you know what you eat, what you think, what you read, and how it is always shaping the mind, then you will see that in spite of all the influences that are pressing upon you, you will break through. I think it is very important to understand this at the beginning because our life is lived in the valley of despair, with hope as the ideal, the utopia, the thing to be gained, the thing for which one strives, disciplines the mind. We are everlastingly climbing this steep hill called hope and falling back into the valley of despair—despair because of lack of fulfillment, the feeling of inferiority, the sense of hopelessness, loneliness, of not 'being', not 'arriving'. Between these two states we exist. We accept hope and make a philosophy of it, weave our life around it. All the religions of the world are based on hope—some call it resurrection and others give it a different name, but always this sense of hope exists in us both outwardly with regard to success and inwardly with regard to spiritual riches.

And there is also this sense of despair. I do not know if you have ever felt very strongly the sense of despair, of hopelessness, complete loneliness, the misery of not being recognized by society, the feeling of complete uselessness, that the individual does not count at all. After all, historical processes are going on—wars, revolutions, violent changes, economic pressures, social upheavals—in which the individual has no voice at all. The tyrannical powers, communistic or whatever they be, totally prevent individual thinking. And when you perceive all that, when you are caught up in it, then there is despair. So you make a philosophy of despair, which is to accept things as they are and make the best of them, which some call materialism. Or else, when you are hoping, struggling to arrive, to achieve, it is called spirituality. Both are in the same valley; they are two sides of the same coin, and we live in that state. Our heavens, our gods, our rituals are the promise, the reward, the hope of a better existence. And so we live either very superficially in hope or equally superficially in despair.

Now the question I should like to ask is whether you have ever felt, very deeply, the sense of despair, the sense of complete loneliness when there is no answer, no relationship to anything—without the mind seeking any escape, without the mind seeking any explanation. I think this is an important question to ask oneself because usually we turn to explanations, do we not, we seek the cause thereof, we say it is karma, it is this or that. And we build around our despair a philosophy which merely takes us to the opposite state of hope. And we accept that state because for most of us hope is an enormous incentive for action—the hope that you will get a lot of money, the hope that there is a God who will protect you, who will help you—you know the whole racket of all that. So either there is a philosophy of despair or a philosophy of hope, or else you just accept things as they are, and exist. That is what most of us are doing, just existing. Though we spin a lot of words, though we talk about ideals, goodness, beauty, truth, and all the rest of it, they are just superficial reactions, words, but what we are actually doing is merely existing. Very few want to be away, free from both despair and hope. They both represent a process of time, do they not?—not only chronological time but psychological time. Despair wants to come to an end, which is in time, and hope wants to arrive somewhere, also in time.

So there is despair, there is hope, and there is merely existing—not being concerned with anything, carrying on from day to day, thoughtless, not caring any more, not investigating—that is what most of us are doing. We are just existing, rotting in our jobs, rotting in our family life, rotting in our search for money, position, knowledge, and so on. We talk about God, truth, and all the rest of it with an acceptance of things as they are. That is the actual state for most of us. There is always the ideal, the hope to arrive, and if you are a very strong, vital person you will struggle, you will push to get somewhere. And if you are a little more vital, clear, you will also see the despair, how hopeless the world is, how little we change, and how every revolution, every war destroys in the name of peace, in the name of love, in the name of utopia.

So our life is caught in this valley of tears, and how is the mind to break away from it all, to become alive? Because this state is death, obviously. Hope, despair, and the acceptance of things as they are, these states surely indicate death, do they not? Because in these states the mind is decaying, burdened down, crowded by time. If you observe your own mind, you will see that this is what is actually taking place; we are caught in hope, despair, or just existing; it is a fact. Now, how is the mind to break away from all this? Surely meditation is the process of breaking away. Meditation is not in order to have peace, for how can a mind that is not free have peace? This everlasting search for peace of mind is sheer nonsense. The rich man with a full bank account talks about it, and the man who is in misery also talks about it. But there is peace only in freedom.

So, in the realization of these states of despair, hope, and mere existence, one must surely ask oneself whether the mind can break through all this. I hope you understand the questions, sirs? Always we are asking,

"What am I to do? Where am I to look for help? On whom can I depend? What system must I follow?" That is our everlasting cry, not only when in tears of despair, but beneath our smiles we are asking, asking.

Surely the first thing to realize is that nobody is going to help you—nobody. One has to stand completely alone. After all, when one sees how crowded the mind is with alternation of hope and despair, how the mind is bound by tradition, by knowledge, by every influence known and unknown, being possessive, possessed, and dispossessed; when you begin to investigate, understand all that, you will find, will you not, that the mind must be alone, uncontaminated, untouched, become innocent, fresh, new. Now how is this to come about?

First of all one can see that any practice, any discipline, any habit, good or bad, merely brings about the continuity of either despair or hope. Is that not so? You practice, you discipline—what for? You sit meditating in the morning, perform various rituals, repeat words, prayers—what for? Because you hope, do you not, to bring about tranquillity of mind, you hope to arrive somewhere, you hope to understand, and so you repeat the Gita or the Bible or whatever you do in order to quiet the crowded mind—which is hypnotizing the mind by words. Again you are caught in the web of hope. You can see, can you not, that every system of control in order to arrive at a psychological result obviously implies the perpetuation of hope, and therefore there is always despair lurking behind. So, how are you to break through, to be free? Because it is only in freedom that there is peace. Peace is a byproduct, as virtue is a byproduct; it is not an end in itself, it is a secondary issue. But if the mind can understand and be free, then there is peace. How is the mind to be free? I am using the word *how* not in the sense of inquiring what system to follow, what discipline to follow, but in the sense of inquiring into freedom, into the realization of the fact that the mind must be free. That is the first essential perception. But that freedom is denied when there is prayer. The power of prayer is within the field of time, and a mind that is seeking, begging, supplicating, obviously is not a free mind. By the power of prayer you can probably get what you want, but what you want is so petty, trivial because it is still within the field of hope and despair. So, prayer is not meditation, but seeing the truth about prayer and therefore being free from prayer is meditation. Also, the repetition of words is merely a process of hypnotizing the mind; you obviously do become still if you constantly repeat a word or a sentence, but you make the mind dull thereby, and in that there is no freedom. But the understanding of the process of the mind being made dull by repetition, by habit, by ritual, and the understanding of the psychological desire to be secure through the repeated word—that is meditation.

At this point the problem becomes much more complicated, for we must examine both the meditator and the meditation. And you have to listen, if I may suggest, very carefully. One must listen not merely in order to repudiate or accept, but to learn. A mind that is eager to learn does not accept or deny; it listens to find out. The problem of meditation and who is the meditator requires a great deal of penetration. Now, who is the meditator, the thinker, the 'I' who says, "I must meditate"? What is the entity which experiences and then says, "I have had an experience"? You observe, and there is the thing observed; there is the thinker, and there is the thought. Now what is the thinker? Please do not answer by quoting authority; do not say that Shankara, Buddha, Christ has said this or that. A man who quotes has ceased to be intelligent; when you merely repeat from memory, you have ceased to think. We are trying to understand and to go into something for ourselves, and therefore the moment you quote, you have stopped thinking, looking, understanding, learning. Distrust people who quote. They are merely recording machines, gramophones, and they use knowledge as a means of self-expansion. So please listen to learn, because in examining the thinker together, we are going to come upon this extraordinary thing called fear. Without understanding fear there is no meditation. Meditation is the understanding of the whole process of how fear comes into being.

Now what is the thinker? It is the name, the form, and the brain that responds, is it not? This brain, through reactions and repeated stimuli, creates the mind; the mind is related to the brain, as the brain is related to the mind; they interact upon each other. But the mind is independent of the brain; and thought, though it depends on the brain, is also independent of it. I ask you where you live; you hear the question and a series of reactions take place in the brain, and then you remember where you live and tell me. So there is the name, the form, the brain. The brain creates the mind and the mind is related to the brain; there is an interaction going on all the time between the two. But yet the mind is independent, different from the brain, and it is the mind that is the center of the 'I', the thinker. It is this mind—which is the outcome of the brain—that thinks, that says, "I remember; my name is this; I live there; I have this job; I feel pain." So the thinking process is the result of the brain, and the thinking process creates the center from which you say, "I know, I do not know; I am happy, I am unhappy." That center is the bundle, the residue of all memory, of all experience, of all traditions, of the conscious as well as the unconscious. All that consciousness, which is the mind, is related to the brain. Between the two there is a con-

stant interaction, and yet the mind is independent, separate from the brain though related to it.

So, as long as there is this center in consciousness—the observer who is accumulating, and the observed—there must be conflict. Please understand this; I will go into it. So long as there is a thinker, an experiencer and the experienced, the observed, there must be a conflict between the two. That is so, is it not? I have experienced pleasure, and I want more; I have experienced pain, and I do not want any more; I am evil, and I must be good; I want to fulfill, and there is frustration. So there is a constant strife, struggle, endeavor between the experiencer and the thing that is experienced. This center is greedy and so it says, "I must not be greedy," and so there is conflict. We all know this, do we not? And it is this struggle which is wearing out the mind; it is this constant battle going on in the field of the mind which is the deteriorating, distorting, deadening factor. So what is the mind to do? In the mind there is this dual process going on of the observer and the observed, and therefore the conflict, the pain, the whole business of sorrow, misery, hope, and despair. Everything centers round this entity, the thinker, the observer; and so long as that center exists, there must be sorrow because the center is the shadow-maker. And that center is created by thought, which is the reaction of memory—memory being also part of the brain—so they are all interrelated. Now the question is: How to die to that center? How to dissipate it so that the center is no longer the shadow-maker, no longer the entity who says, "I suffer; I wish I could be happy"? For then consciousness, awareness, has no center, and yet the brain is capable of receiving impressions, translating, acting. I hope you understand the problem, sirs. I hope I am making it clear. So long as there is the thinker and the thought, so long as there is the experiencer and the thing being experienced, there must be the deteriorating factor of conflict, and through conflict you can produce nothing, through conflict there is no creation. There is creation only when the mind is totally quiet. The brain may have problems, the brain may work out a lot of things, but the solution to the problem which the brain has can only take place when the mind—which is related to the brain—is in a totally different state in which there is no center, when it is motionless. And that state of motionless mind is not a thing to be gathered, captured, arrived at by your brain. The cunning brain will say, "I must get that state and everything will be all right," but the cunning brain can never know it. Whereas the realization that so long as there is strife in any form, there must be a center of unconsciousness which is creating all the confusion, all the misery, the travail and toil—the realization of that, the feeling of that, the total comprehension of it, brings to the mind an extraordinary state of awareness in which there is no center, and therefore no frontier. Such a mind is completely aware, fully enlightened, every untrodden region of it is known, and therefore it is completely quiet. In that state there is no experiencer.

If you have followed, step by step from the beginning of this discourse, if you have gone into it, if you have really felt it with me, understood, not accepted, but seen the truth of it as you went along, then you will find there is an irrefutable, real, true state of mind which is without the center.

Then a problem arises which is really much more complicated—the problem of what this state is, what is the mind that experiences this complete motionlessness? If there is no center which recognizes the motionless state of the mind, how do you know such a mind does exist? Please, sirs, understand this question because it is very deeply related to your daily living; it is not something remote,

beyond the hills, beyond the ocean. If you understand this, you will understand your daily relationships, your daily activities, your daily thoughts; then you will approach life in a much more significant way, more vitally. After all, you only know an experience because you have already experienced it; you know pain because you have experienced pain. So there is an experiencer who has experienced pain and recognizes it as pain.

Now the question is: If there is no center in consciousness, only a state of awareness in which there is no border, no frontier, no time—because it is something beyond time, eternal, incorruptible—then how does the mind know that such a state exists? If it cannot be recognized, how can one know it exists? This is not a puzzle, sirs, but please understand this, watch your own mind when a problem like this is put to you. It is something which you do not know, which you have never experienced, and therefore the experiencer can never touch it. What an experiencer can experience is only that which he recognizes, and recognition only comes because you have a memory. Therefore this state of awareness without a frontier, without a center, is something which cannot be experienced by the experiencer. Then what is it which knows it exists? Now watch, sirs, look at it. Do you know the state of love when you say, "I love"? If you have already experienced love and there is an experiencer who says, "I love you," then it is no longer love. Let us put it differently. Where there is the perception of beauty, there is no desire. When you see something very beautiful, the immediate perception of it drives away all desire. Have you not noticed it? A beautiful person, a tree solitary in a field against the sky—in the beauty of that perception there is no desire. Desire comes much later, when I say, "I want to go back and look at it again. I would like to see that face again." Then the whole process of desire starts; then the process of time comes in. Now if you understand that, then you will see that there is a state which is not experienceable by the mind as the experiencer, the center; and that state is timeless, not something which is continuous.

So the whole of this discourse, from the very beginning to now, is meditation. The understanding of the ways of the mind is the uncovering of the self, not the gathering of knowledge about the self. I am not talking about the superself, there is no such thing; that is an invention of the mind in its desire to be secure, to be immortal. All that we actually know is this valley of tears in which we live with despair and hope, and out of that we invent a heaven, a permanent self, and so on; all that is unreal. But to understand this whole process requires great perception, keen attention, a real understanding of oneself, taking every thought and looking at it, going into it. If you can go into even one thought completely, to the end, then you will find out about the thinker and the thought, and that state of mind in which there is no center. All this is meditation, and if you do not understand all this, your life will remain shallow, empty, miserable, and do what you will—read any book, follow any teacher—you are still in the valley of darkness. It is only when you begin to understand this total process that there is a freedom in which there is silence and peace.

December 21, 1958

Ninth Talk in Bombay

We are all aware, surely, of the inexplicable inequalities in the world, of great wealth and extreme poverty, of extensive misery, of the appalling human endeavor which seems to lead nowhere. This strife and toil is in all our lives up to the moment when we die. We are aware of all this and in our despair, in our misery, in our constant struggle, we turn to something which we call God, to some belief, support, or dogma. And I would like to talk over with you, if I may, this thing called religion. But before we go into it, I think we must be very clear of the division between the word, or symbol, and the feeling, the fact. The word is one thing, and the fact is another, and that is very difficult for most of us to realize. The word is never the actual thing, and it needs very precise thinking not to confuse the word, the symbol with the fact. Knowledge is one thing and love is another; perception is one thing, and to know is another thing. Knowing is not feeling, and what you feel can never be expressed in words. Words, symbols are merely a means of communication. But the word, the symbol does not signify the actual thing one feels. So there is a division between the word and the fact, between knowledge and love, between knowing and feeling, and I think it is very important to understand this. If we are to communicate with each other clearly, we must be aware of the difference between the symbol and the fact.

As I have been saying during all these discourses, the individual is of the highest importance—even though society, religion, governments do not recognize that fact. You are very important because you are the only means of bringing about the explosive creativity of reality. You yourself are the environment in which this reality can come into being. But you will have observed that all governments, all organized religions and societies, though they assert the importance of the individual, try to obliterate the individual core, the individual feeling because they want collective feeling, they want a mass reaction. But the mind that is merely organized according to a certain pattern of belief, weighed down by custom, by tradition, by knowledge, is not an individual mind. An individual mind can only be when you deliberately, knowingly, with feeling put all these influences aside because you have understood their significance, their superficial value. Then only is there an individual creative mind.

It is extraordinarily difficult to separate the individual from the mass, and yet without this separation reality is not possible. So the true individual is not the individual who merely has his own name, certain emotional responses, certain customary reactions, some property, and so on, but the true individual is he who is endeavoring to cut through this confusion of ideas, through this morass of tradition, who sets aside all these and tries to find the reason, the core, the center of human misery. Such a one does not resort to books, to authority, to well-known custom, but casts all these away and begins to inquire—and he is the true individual. But most of us repeat, accept, comply, imitate, obey, do we not, because for us obedience has become the rule—obedience in the home, obedience to the book, obedience to the guru, the teacher, and so on; and with obedience we feel there is security, safety. But actually life is not safe, life is never secure; on the contrary, it is the most uncertain thing. And because it is uncertain, it is also profoundly rich, immeasurable. But the mind in its search seeks safety and security, and therefore it obeys, complies, and imitates; and such a mind is not an individual mind at all.

Most of us are not individuals though we each have a separate name, a separate form, because inwardly the state of mind is time-bound, weighed down by custom, tradition, and authority—the authority of the government, the authority of society, the authority in the home. So such a mind is not an individual mind; the individual mind is outside of all that, it is not within the pattern of society; the individual mind is in revolt and so is not seeking security. The revolutionary mind is not the mind that is in revolt. The revolutionary mind merely wants to alter things according to a certain pattern and such a mind is not a mind in revolt, a mind that is in itself discontented.

I do not know if you have noticed what an extraordinary thing discontent is. You must know many young people who are discontented; they do not know what to do; they are miserable, unhappy, in revolt, seeking this, trying that, asking questions everlastingly. But as they grow older they find a job, marry, and that is the end of it. Their fundamental discontent is canalized, and then misery sets in. When they are young their parents, teachers, society, all tell them not to be discontented, to find out what they want to do and do it—but always within the pattern. Such a mind is not truly in revolt and you need a mind in real revolt to find truth, not a conforming mind. Revolt means passion.

So it is very important to become an individual, and there is individuality only through self-knowledge—knowing yourself, knowing why you imitate, why you conform, why you obey. You obey through fear, do you not? Because of the desire to be secure, you conform in order to have more power, more money, or this or that. But to find what you call God, to find whether there is or is not that reality, there must be the individual who is dead to the past, who is dead to knowledge, dead to experience; there must be a mind that is wholly, totally new, fresh, innocent. Religion is the discovery of what is real, which means that you have to find and not follow somebody who says he has found and wants to tell you about it. There must be a mind which receives that reality, not a mind which merely accepts reality verbally and conforms to that idea of reality in the hope of being secure.

So there is a difference between knowing and feeling, and I think it is very important to understand this. With us, explanations are sufficient, which is, "to know." We say, "I know I am ambitious; I know I am greedy; I know I hate,'' but such knowing is not being free from the fact. You may know that you hate, but the actual feeling of hate and the freedom from it is an entirely different thing from the pursuit of the explanation of it and the cause of it, is it not? That is, to know that I am dull, stupid, and to be consciously aware of the feeling of my dullness and stupidity are two entirely different things. To feel implies a great deal of vitality, a great deal of strength, vigor, but merely to know is only a partial approach to life—it is not a total approach. You may know how a leaf is constructed, botanically, but to feel a leaf, smell it, really see it, requires a great deal of penetration—penetration into oneself. I do not know if you have ever taken a leaf in your hand and looked at it. You are all town-dwellers and you are all too occupied with yourselves, with your progress, with your success, ambitions, jealousies, your leaders, your ministers, and all the rest of the nonsense. Do not laugh, sirs. It is tragic because if you knew how to feel deeply, then you would have abundant sympathy, then you would do something, then you would act with your whole being; but if you merely know that there is poverty, merely work intellectually to remove poverty as a government official or village reformer without the feeling, then what you do is of very little importance.

You know, passion is necessary to understand truth. I am using the word *passion* in its full significance because to feel strongly, to feel deeply, with all your being, is essential; otherwise, that strange thing called reality will never come to you. But your religions, your saints say that you must not have desire, you must control, suppress, overcome, destroy, which means that you come to truth burned out, worn out, empty, dead. Sirs, you must have passion to meet this strange thing called life, and you cannot have passion, intense feeling, if you are mesmerized by society, by custom, if you are entangled in beliefs, dogmas, rituals. So, to understand that light, that truth, that immeasurable reality, we must first understand what we call religion and be free of it—not verbally, not intellectually, not through explanations, but actually be free because freedom—not your intellectual freedom but the actual state of freedom—gives vitality. When you have walked through all this rubbish, when you have put aside all these confusing, traditional, imitative things, then the mind is free, then the mind is alert, then the mind is passionate; and it is only such a mind that can proceed.

So let us, as individual human beings, because it is you and I who are concerned, not the mass—there is no such thing as the mass except as a political entity—let us find out what we mean by religion. What is it for most of us? It is, is it not, a belief in something—in a superhuman divinity who controls us, shapes us, gives us hope and directs us—and we offer to that entity our prayers, our rituals; in its name we sacrifice, propitiate, pray, and beg, and we look to him as our father to help us in our difficulties. To us, religion is not only the graven image in the temple, the letters in the mosque, or the cross in the church, not only the graven image made by the hand, but also the graven image made by the mind, the idea. So to us, religion is obviously a means of escape from our daily sorrow, our daily confusion. We do not understand the inequalities, the injustices, death, the constant sorrows, struggles, hopelessness, and despair; so we turn to some god, to rituals, mass, prayers, and thereby hope to find some solace, some comfort. And in this process, the saints, the philosophers, the books weigh us down with their particular interpretation, with custom, with tradition. That is our way of life, is it not? If you look into yourself you would agree, would you not, that that is a general outline of religion. It is a thing made by the mind for the comfort of the mind, not something that gives richness, fullness of life, or a passion for living. So we know that, but here again knowing and feeling are two different things. Knowing the falseness of organized religion is one thing, but to see it, to drop it, to put it all away—that requires a great depth of real feeling. So the problem—for which there is no easy answer—is how to drop a thing, how to die to it, how to die to all these explanations, all these false gods—because all gods made by the mind and the hand are false. No explanation is going to make you die to it. So, what will make you die to it, what will make you say, "Now, I drop it"? We generally give up something in order to get something else we think is better, and we call it renunciation. But surely that is not renunciation. To renounce means to give up, not knowing what the future is, not knowing what tomorrow will bring. If you give up, knowing what tomorrow will bring, then it is merely an exchange, a thing of the market; it has no value. When physical death comes you do not know what is going to happen next; it is a finality. In the same way, to die, to give up, put aside totally, deeply, all that we call religion, without knowing what will be—have you ever tried this? I do not know if it is a problem to you, but it must surely be a problem to any man who is alert, who is at all aware, because there is such immense injustice in the world. Why does one ride in a car while the other walks? Why is there hunger, poverty, and also immense riches? Why is there the man in power, authority, position, wielding his power with cruelty? Why does a child die? Why is there this intolerable misery everywhere? A man who asks all these questions must be really burning with them, not finding some stupid cause—an economic, social, or political cause. Obviously the intelligent man must turn to some-

thing much more significant than mere explanatory causes. And this is where our problem lies.

So the first and most important thing is not to be satisfied by explanations, not to be satisfied by the word *karma,* not to be satisfied with cunning philosophies, but to realize, to feel completely that there is this immense problem which no mere explanation can wipe away. If you can feel like that, then you will see that there is a revolution in the mind. Usually if one cannot find a solution to misery, one becomes bitter, cynical, or one invents a philosophical theory based on one's frustration. But if I am faced with the fact of suffering, that there is death, deterioration, and if the mind is stripped of all explanations, all solutions, all answers, then the mind is directly confronted with the thing itself; and curiously, our mind never allows that direct perception.

So there is a difference between seeing and knowing, feeling and loving. Feeling and loving does not mean devotion; you cannot get to reality through devotion. Giving yourself up emotionally to an idea is generally called devotion, but it excludes reality because by giving yourself up to something, you are merely identifying yourself with that thing. To love your gods, to put garlands around your guru, to repeat certain words, get entranced in his presence, and to shed tears—you can do all that for the next thousand years, but you will never find reality. To perceive, to feel, to love a cloud, a tree, a human being, requires enormous attention, and how can you attend when your mind is distracted by knowledge? Knowledge is useful technologically, and that is all. If a doctor does not know how to operate, it is better to keep away from him. Knowledge is necessary at a certain level, in a certain direction, but knowledge is not the total answer to our misery. The total answer lies in this feeling, this passion which comes when there is the absence of yourself, when you are oblivious of all that you are. That quality of passion is necessary in order to feel, to understand, to love. Reality is not intellectual; but from our childhood, through education, through every form of so-called learning, we have brought about a mind that is sharp, that competes, that is burdened with information—which is the case with lawyers, politicians, technologists, and specialists. Our minds are sharpened, made bright, and that has become the most important thing to keep going; and so all our feeling has withered away. You do not feel for the poor man in his wretchedness; you never feel happy when you see a rich man driving in his beautiful car; you never feel delighted when you see a nice face; there is no throb when you see a rainbow or the splendor of the green grass. We are so occupied with our jobs, our own miseries that we have never a moment of leisure in which to feel what it is to love, to be kind, to be generous—yet without all this we want to know what God is! How incredibly stupid and infantile! So it becomes very important for the individual to come alive—not to revive; you cannot revive dead feelings, the glory that has gone. But can we not live intensely, fully, in abundance even for a single day? For one such day covers a millennium. This is not a poetical fancy. You will know of it when you have lived one rich day in which there is no time, no future, no past; you will know then the fullness of that extraordinary state. Such living has nothing to do with knowledge.

Our problem is how to die to everything that we know so that we can live, to die to the injustices, the pleasures, and the pains. I do not know if you have ever tried to die to something. I assure you that it is only when you die that there is a fresh mind, but you cannot die if you are not passionate. It is only the empty mind that is rich, not the mind that is full of knowledge, beliefs, experiences, hopes, and despairs—such a mind is worn out, such a mind is not a new mind; it is an experienced mind, and an experienced mind can never learn. It is only the empty mind, the mind that is dead to the past, to everything, that is rich because such a mind, being passionate, can receive, and therefore knows what it is to love.

Sirs, have you ever really felt deeply the inequality of life—why you have and another has not, why you are gifted and the other is not? If you have really felt it passionately, then you will know that love knows no inequality. To see the man who rides in an expensive car, and enjoy what he enjoys, without envy; to see also the beggar at the roadside and feel for him in his wretchedness—this is to know love, and that there is no answer to inequality except love.

Religion, after all, is the discovery of love, and love is something to be discovered from moment to moment. You must die to the love that you have known a second before in order to ever know anew what love is. And love can only come into being when there is this passion of feeling. Then, out of that feeling there is action, and that action will not bind you because love never binds. And so religion is not the thing that we have now, which is a miserable thing, a dark thing, a deadly thing. Religion implies clarity, light, passion; it implies a mind that is empty and therefore able to receive that immeasurable, incorruptible richness.

December 24, 1958

Tenth Talk in Bombay

This will be the last talk and I wonder—not what each one has got out of listening, but—to what depth, to what extent each one has really gone into himself and discovered something for himself. It is not merely a matter of what has been said or what will be said, but rather whether each one, out of his own earnest endeavor, has uncovered the extraordinarily complicated process of the mind, how far each one of us has discovered the ways of consciousness, how deeply one has experienced for oneself the things we have been talking over. It seems to me that the mere repetition of words or of what you have read only puts the mind to rest; it makes the mind sluggish. An earnest mind is not one that merely repeats, either from the sacred religious books or from the latest equally sacred books on Marx, on capitalism, socialism, or psychology. Mere repetition does not open the door to direct experience. To speak from direct experience, from direct understanding, and direct knowledge is quite a different thing, for then there is an authenticity, a depth to what one has thought and felt. One who merely repeats from memory or from what he has learned, heard, or read, surely is not a serious person. Nor is he serious who indulges in theoretical, abstract thinking. An earnest man, surely, is he who goes within himself, observes things about his own sorrow and misery, is sensitive to starvation, degradation, wars, and injustice, and from the observation of the external begins to inquire within. Such a man is an earnest man, not he who is merely satisfied with explanations, who is everlastingly quoting, theorizing, or seeking a purpose of life. The man who seeks a purpose of life merely wants a significance for his own living, and the significance he gives will depend upon his own conditioning. But the mind which, through the observation of everyday incidents and relationships, everyday activities and challenges, begins to inquire, goes more and more within itself and uncovers the hidden. Because after all, that is where the essential fundamental change has to take place. Though innumerable outward changes are obviously necessary—putting an end to wars, and so on—the only radical change is within.

So one of our major problems is: What makes one change? What makes the mind which is traditional, conditioned, in sorrow, jealous, envious, ambitious, what makes such a mind drop all those things and be fresh, new, clear? If you change because of pressure—pressure of new inventions, of legislation, of revolution, of family, and so on— surely such a change, which has a direction, is no change at all, is it? That kind of change is merely an adjustment, a conformity to laws or to a pattern of existence, and if you have noticed it within yourself, change through compulsion, through anxiety, is the continuity of what has been before, modified, is it not? I think it is very important to understand what it is that makes a man change totally. Technological knowledge obviously does not bring about an inward transformation; it may alter our point of view, but it does not bring about that inward transformation in which there is no struggle, but in which there is an enlightened, active intelligence.

I wonder if you have ever asked yourself what it is that makes you change. Of course, if the doctor tells you that if you continue to smoke cigarettes it will give you lung cancer, through fear you may abstain from smoking. The pressure of fear or the promise of reward may make you stop a certain activity, but is that a real change? If through pressure, through fear you change, modify, adjust, that is not transformation, it is merely the continuation of what has been in a different form. So what will make you really transform yourself? I think such transformation comes not through any endeavor, any struggle, any pressure of reward or punishment, but it comes about instantaneously, immediately, spontaneously, when there is a comprehension, a perceiving of the whole. I am going into it, but as I have been saying, mere listening to the words will not help you to learn about what is being said. One has to see the totality of human existence, not only a section; one has to see and feel the whole depth of existence, of life, and when there is such a comprehension, in that state there is a total change, a total transformation. Now we change only in fragments—controlling jealousy or envy, giving up smoking or eating too much, joining this group or that group to bring about some reform—but they are all segments, fragments, unrelated to the whole. Such activity, unrelated to the perception of the whole, obviously must lead to various forms of maladjustment, contradiction, and strain. So our problem is really how to see, how to comprehend and feel the totality of life, be with it, and from there act wholly, not fragmentarily.

Let me put it differently. I do not know if you have noticed it in yourself, but most of us are in a state of contradiction, are we not? You think one thing and do another, you feel something and deny it the next minute—not only as an individual, but as a race, a group. You say you must have peace and talk about nonviolence, and all the time you are inwardly violent, and you have the police, the army, the bombers, the navy, and all the rest of it. So there is contradiction in us and outside of us. And the greater the contradiction, the greater is the tension, until the tension ultimately leads to neurotic action and therefore an unbalanced mind. As most of us are in a state of self-contradiction, we live perpetually in tension and strain, and from that tension there is unbalanced activity. And if one realizes this tension of contradiction, then one tries to bring about an integration between two opposites, between hate and love for instance, and one only produces something which is nonrecognizable, which you call nonviolence and all that stuff. But the problem is to see the central fact that the mind is in contradiction within itself and not try to obliterate the contradiction by giving strength to one of the opposites.

So, when you see that the mind is in a state of self-contradiction and know the stress and the tension of it—the pain, sorrow, misery, and struggle—when you comprehend, perceive, understand the whole process of the mind in a state of contradiction, then such a total understanding brings about quite a different state and quite a different activity. After all, if you perceive the whole, vast sky merely through a narrow window, your vision is obviously unrelated to the wide heavens. Similarly, action born of self-contradiction is very limited, giving rise only to pain and sorrow.

I wish I could make it clear, this feeling of the whole. To feel the quality of India, the quality of the whole world—not as a Parsi, Hindu, Muslim, not as a socialist, communist, or congressman, not as a Russian, Englishman, German, or American, but to feel the total suffering of man, his frustrations, his contradictions, his miserable, narrow existence, his aspirations—to have such a feeling, such a perception is to bring about the total transformation of the mind.

Let me put it differently. Governments, societies, every form of pressure and propaganda say you must change. But there is a constant resistance to change and so there is a conflict between the actual and the ideal. The actual and the ideal are contradictions, and we spend our lives from childhood to the grave struggling between the two, never coming to the end of something, never coming to the end of attachment but always pursuing detachment. In attachment there is pain, and so we cultivate detachment. Then the problem arises of how to detach oneself, and this brings in the practicing of a system which, if you think about it, is all so silly. Whereas if you can understand the whole process of attachment and the whole process of detachment, what is implied in both, then you will never be either attached or detached; there is a totally different state, a real transformation of the mind. After all, you are attached only to dead things because you cannot be attached to a whole thing, a living thing, like living waters, can you? You are attached to your picture of your wife, your husband, and the picture is only the memory. You are attached to the memory of certain experiences, pleasures, pains, which means you are attached to the past, not to the living present, not to the woman or man who is at present endeavoring, struggling. Attachment is obviously to dying things and to the dead; you are attached to your house; the house is not a living thing, but you give life to it from your desire to be secure, which is a desire of the dead. Attachment is invariably not to the living, not to the present, but to the past, which is of the dead. And without understanding that, we are trying to become detached, and what does it mean? Detachment from what? Not from the living thing because you have never held it; but you are trying to be detached from a memory, from what you think, which gives you pain. You do not radically change. So you are caught between attachment and detachment. Whereas if you really go within yourself very profoundly and find out what the root cause of your attachment is, you will find that it is obviously the desire to be comfortable, to be safe, and so on; then you would also understand the whole process of the cultivation of detachment and the implications of detachment. The understanding of both, completely, is the process of self-knowledge. If you go into it very deeply as a means of uncovering your own comprehension, then you will find that there is the intelligence which will respond; then you will see that there is not a change, but transformation.

Looking at this world with all its anxieties, its wars, its slow decay, surely most serious people want earnestly to find a means, a way by which the mind is not a mechanical entity but is ever new, fresh, young. But you cannot have such a fresh mind if you are everlastingly in conflict. Hitherto you have accepted conflict as the way of life, have you not, but when you begin to understand the total process of the way of struggle, then you will see that there is actual transformation and that the mind is no longer caught in the wheel of struggle.

Let me put the problem differently, sirs. Being simple is essential, but simplicity for most of us is merely expressed in outward things. You think you are simple, saintly, and virtuous if you have only a few things, only a loincloth. A loincloth is not a symbol of simplicity of mind, nor does it indicate the understanding of the extensive richness, the liveliness, the beauty of life. But you have reduced all that to the loincloth level, and that is not simplicity. And a mind that is burdened with knowledge, with erudition, with information is not a simple mind; the electronic computers now can quote you almost anything—it is merely a mechanical response. And a mind that is constantly groping, wanting, searching, burning out desire and at the same time desirous, is not a simple mind. Please listen to all this, sirs; learn about it as I am talking because if you really follow this, you will see that what will come out of this is true simplicity. But first you must see what is not simplicity, and obviously the man who is caught in ritual, perpetually repeating, calling on the name of God, and doing so-called good is not a simple man. Then what is simplicity? The simple mind is the mind that transforms itself, the simple mind is the result of transformation. The mind that says, "I must be simple," is a stupid mind, but the mind that is aware of the extensiveness of its own deceptions, its own anxieties, its own illusions, aspirations, and all the turmoil of desires—such a mind is simple. Being totally aware of all that—as one is aware of a tree or the heavens—there comes this extraordinary simplicity. I am using the word *simplicity* to denote innocence, clarity, a mind which has abandoned itself. A mind that is calculating, becoming virtuous, a mind that has got an end in view which it is everlastingly trying to pursue—such a mind is not abandoning itself. It is only out of total self-abandonment that simplicity comes, and to be completely aware of the extensiveness of the illusions, fancies, myths, urges, and demands of the mind is self-knowledge. It is the full understanding of existence as it is and not as it should be. But that beauty of simplicity does not come into being if there is no self-abandonment, and abandonment means, surely, the dropping away of all conditioning, as a dead leaf falls away from a tree; and you cannot die to something if you are not passionate. To die means the feeling of coming to a point or state beyond which there is nothing; a state of mind in which, with all the cunning tricks and speculation, do what you will, you can proceed no further. In that state there is neither despair nor hope, and the whole question of search has come to an end. A total death has come into being; and if you do not die, totally, to the past, how can you learn? How can you learn, sirs, if you are always carrying the burden of yesterday?

I do not know if you have ever inquired into yourself as to how to be free of the yesterday, the thousand yesterdays, the thousands of experiences and reactions and all the turmoil of restless time? How is one to be free of all that so that the mind becomes extraordinarily quiet, simple, innocent? Such a state is only possible if you understand the totality of your existence—what you do, what you think, how you are absorbed in your daily activities, your job, the way you speak to your wife, your husband, the way you treat your so-called inferiors, the way you educate your children, and so on. If you regard your attitude in all that as merely a temporary reaction, some-

thing which can be got over, adjusted, then you have not understood the totality of life. And I say that in the understanding of the totality of oneself, there is a transformation which is immediate and which has nothing to do with the restlessness of time. You may take time in the investigation, but the transformation is immediate. Do not confuse the process of time and transformation. There is time in the sense that there is a gap between what I am saying and your listening. The vibration of the word takes time to reach your ear, and the nervous response as well as the brain response takes a split second. Though it may take time for it to travel to your brain, once you understand all of what is being said, there is a complete break from the past. Revolution is not from the outside but from within, and that revolution is not a gradual process, not a matter of time.

So transformation of the individual can take place only when there is a total comprehension of the ways of the mind, which is meditation. To understand oneself is a process in which there is no condemnation, no justification, but just seeing what one is, just observing without judging, without checking, controlling, or adjusting. The perception of what one is, without any evaluation, leads the mind to an extraordinary depth, and it is only at that depth that there is transformation; and naturally action from that depth of understanding is totally different from the action of adjustment.

So I hope you, as an individual, have listened to these talks not merely to gather information, to be intellectually amused, excited, or emotionally stirred, but have learned about yourself in the process and therefore freed yourself. Because from the beginning of these talks until now, we have been speaking about the actual, everyday state of the mind, and if you disregard it and say you are only interested in God, in what happens after death, then you will find that your God and your "after death" are only a set of speculative ideas which have no validity at all. To find what God is, if there is a God, you must come to it with a full being, with freshness, not with a mind that is decayed, burdened with its own experiences, broken and dwindled by discipline, and burned up with desires. A mind that is really passionate—and passion implies intensity and fullness—only such a mind can receive that which is immeasurable. That immeasurable cannot be found except as you dig deeper and deeper within yourself. Your repetition that there is the eternal is child's talk, and your seeking the eternal has no meaning either, for it is unknowable, inconceivable to the mind. The mind has to understand itself, to break the foundation of its learning, the frontiers of its own recognition, and that is the process of self-knowledge. What you need now is an inward revolution, a totally new approach to life, not new systems, new schools, new philosophies. Then, from this transformation, you will see that mind, as time, ceases. After all, time is as the sea which is never still, never calm, everlastingly in motion, everlast-

ingly restless, and our minds, based on time, are caught up in its movement.

So, only when you have totally understood yourself, the conscious as well as the unconscious, only then is there a quietness, a motionlessness which is creation. And that stillness is action, true action. Only, we never touch it, we never know it because we are wasting our energy, our time, our sorrow, our endeavor on things superficial.

So the earnest man is he who through self-knowledge breaks down the walls of time and brings about a motionless state of mind. Then there is a benediction which comes into being without invitation; then there is a reality, a goodness which comes without your asking. If you crave it you will not get it, if you seek it you will not find it. It is only when the mind has understood itself totally, comprehended itself widely so that it is without any barrier and is dead to everything it has known—then only reality comes into being.

December 28, 1958

New Delhi, India, 1959

* * *

First Talk in New Delhi

It seems to me very important that we should first establish between ourselves right communication and understanding. For most of us, communication is merely at the conscious, at the verbal or intellectual level, and it is very difficult really to understand anything when communication is limited to that level. I think there is a form of communion which comprehends not only the conscious but also the unconscious level, and also goes further, beyond that; and there is real communication or communion, it seems to me, only when there is complete harmony between these three. Behind the conscious or verbal understanding of the significance of the words, there is an unconscious comprehension which is not merely verbal; and there is also a form of communion which goes beyond all that and which has no symbols, no words or phrases as a means of communication. It is the total integration of these three that makes possible a complete understanding of anything, is it not? To put it differently, I can understand something totally, fully, completely, only when I think with my whole being, which includes the conscious, the unconscious, and a state which lies beyond both and is not expressible in words. When there is this total comprehension, this total approach, there is surely complete communion between two human beings.

I think it is very important to establish this state of communion between ourselves. But the difficulty is that most of us merely accept verbally or intellectually what is convenient, and reject what is not, and on that level we dispute. This is what most of us do. But to go deeper, beyond the verbal level, beyond the level of words and symbols, requires much more attention, much more insight, a greater quality of awareness. And it seems to me that if we comprehend and communicate merely at the verbal level, these talks will have very little meaning. It is very easy to talk and argue about certain ideas, but we are not dealing with ideas. Ideas do not bring about a really fundamental change in the quality of the mind. Ideas influence us, they give a certain activity to the mind, but fundamentally, deeply, they do not change the quality of the mind; and it is surely very important that there should be such a change—a radical transformation in the quality of the mind. For it is only in bringing about a revolution in the quality of the mind itself that we can resolve the many problems that we have.

I hope that we now understand each other. There is no teacher with something to be taught. I think we must be very clear on this point—that the speaker is not the teacher, nor are you the disciple. If you put yourself in the position of a disciple, of a man who accepts or rejects, who wants a particular comprehension in order to resolve certain problems, I am afraid you will be disappointed. The true relationship between you and the speaker is one of understanding; it is a relationship in which we are both learning, and if you merely accept or reject what is said with a sanctimonious, religious attitude, you obviously cease to learn, and therefore communication between us is impossible. What we are trying to do, surely, is to understand the main problems of life—to go into them, to learn about them, and to see all the reactions of the mind in relationship to everything. If we do not learn about ourselves directly and are merely eager to be instructed, then instruction is not a process of learning, but only the accumulation of knowledge, which does not solve our problems. What does solve radically and fundamentally our problems is a mind that is capable of inquiring, searching, learning. When you and I as two human beings talk things over together, inquiring, searching out, then our relationship is entirely different. Then you do not accept or reject; then the speaker is not on a pedestal and you are not down below, and we are both learning.

To be capable of learning, the mind must obviously put aside all that it has learned, which is extraordinarily difficult. To learn, the mind must be in a state of freedom. We are in a state of freedom when we want to find out, when we want to know, when we want to understand or discover something; but that freedom is destroyed the moment we begin to interpret what we discover in terms of our conditioning, in terms of our established morality, our environmental influences, and so on.

So, may I point out that these talks will be utterly useless if we do not from the very beginning establish the right relationship between you and me. After all, what is important is not society but the individual who creates society, the individual who thinks, who feels, who suffers, who is probing, questioning, asking. So you and I as individuals are inquiring, and through this process of inquiry, we are going to learn.

But learning ceases when there is the accumulation of learning. And it is a most difficult thing to really be in a state when the mind is learning because it demands a sense of complete humility, does it not? If one wants to know something deeply, inwardly, that very urge to know presupposes a mind that is really humble; but we are not humble, and that is our difficulty.

Humility is necessary in order to learn. But humility is not to be cultivated. The moment you cultivate humility, you are cultivating the field of arrogance, and the humility which that field produces is false. But if we really begin to inquire, to probe, to ask questions, then there is humility because in that state of inquiry the mind does not assume anything; it does not accept any authority, it has no tradition and is not bound by knowledge. Surely a mind that is humble has no authority in itself through its own acquisition of knowledge, nor does it accept the outside authority of a teacher. This deep sense of humility is essential to the process of learning. The truly humble mind is not weighed down by learning, by experience, by a knowledge of the sacred books. The man who is always quoting is not humble. The man who has read a great deal, and whose burden is knowledge, has no sense of humility.

So it seems to me of the utmost importance that from the very beginning we establish between us, you and I, a relationship in which you are not looking to be guided, or hoping to have your problems solved by another. There is no solution to any problem apart from the problem itself, and it would be well if we could really understand this deeply, fundamentally. There are no solutions;

there are only problems, and the resolution of each problem lies in the problem itself. That much you and I should understand right from the start. We have innumerable problems at all levels of our existence—social, economic, intellectual, moral, sexual. There is the problem of death, the problem of what is true, of whether there is God, and the problem of what this whole business of life is all about. Having a problem, we always seek a solution, which means that our attention is not on the problem, but away from the problem in search of a solution. If you and I can simply understand this one thing, that the solution of a problem lies in the problem itself, then we shall pay tremendous attention to the problem.

Do please give your mind to what is being said. I know you have problems of every kind because everything that the human mind-heart touches, it makes into a problem—which is a terrible thing. Having made problems, we want solutions, so we go everlastingly in search of them. We go from one career to another, from one teacher to another, from one religion to another until we find what we think is a solution—and that becomes our curse because it is not a solution at all. It is a deception, and so the problems multiply.

Now, you and I together are going to uncover the problems, understand them, but that is possible only when there is communication between us, not only at the verbal level, but also at the unconscious level, which is extraordinarily important. Because any fundamental change comes about, surely, not through decision but only when there is deep comprehension of the full significance of the problem—which is not a matter of decision.

What we intend to do during these talks is to establish right communication with each other as two individuals, and then proceed to uncover our many problems. In the under-standing of one's problems as an individual, the mind will be free because the individual is the totality of the mind—the conscious, the unconscious, and the untrodden regions beyond.

After all, your mind is made up of what it has learned, of certain modern techniques which help you to survive, and there is also, in the unconscious, the residue of the past, of tradition, of innumerable influences, impressions, compulsions, fears. In addition to all this there are the conscious urges, the ambitions, frustrations, and conflicting desires which create a wide chasm of self-contradiction.

So the transformation of the individual is of the highest importance because what you are, the world is. You as an individual must bring about a radical change in yourself, for what you think, your mode of activity and relationship, your ambitions, your frustrations, your miseries—all this produces the world about you; and unless there is a transformation in the quality of the mind itself, mere tinkering on the periphery, which is called revolution, whether communist or any other, will never bring about a fundamental change. The individual may adjust himself to a particular environment; he may become a communist, a socialist, a capitalist, or whatever it is, but inwardly, deep down, he will still be the same. That is why we must be concerned with the transformation of the individual at the core. But that requires a great deal of attention, a great deal of penetration, insight; it means that the mind must go beyond tradition in an ever-deepening inquiry, which is a delving into self-knowledge; and as this demands great energy, we prefer to quote the sacred books, or go to a guru, or belong to some so-called religious society, thinking all this is going to free the mind, but it is only perpetuating our misery.

It seems to me that we must be concerned with the process of learning, and we can learn only when we die to all the things of yesterday. It is only the new, fresh mind that learns, not the mind that is burdened with the accumulations of the past. So our problem is to understand ourselves. Without understanding oneself there is no possibility of understanding what is true and what is false, or of finding out if there is something eternal, immeasurable. Unless there is full comprehension of ourselves, life is merely a constant flux without much meaning. So self-knowledge is essential.

I know you will all nod your heads at this statement that you must know yourself, for it has been repeated ad nauseam for ages, but really to go into oneself and observe the whole structure of the mind requires an immense aloofness from every thought and every feeling. Because, after all, thought and feeling are the reactions of the mind, and to know myself I must be aware, without condemnation or judgment, of my reactions in relationship to all things. I must see my responses—the unconscious as well as the conscious—to people, to property, to ideas; otherwise, I do not know myself. I must not take these reactions for granted, or merely accept them verbally, intellectually, but actually be aware of every reaction; and this requires enormous attention.

I do not know if you have ever tried to be aware, not only of your reactions, but of the causes behind them—which is not introspection, for it does not concern the self at all. It is rather the uncovering of the self, the direct experiencing, through inquiry, of the whole structure of the self. To inquire into yourself there can be no authority; no psychologist, no guru can teach you. To know the extraordinary subtleties of the mind, its contradictions, its urges, its ambitions, frustrations, and miseries—to know all that, there must be no sense of condemnation or judgment of what

you see. There must be mere observation, which is extraordinarily difficult.

I wonder if you have ever observed anything really—a fly or a picture or a sunset or the beauty of a leaf or the moonlit waters on a still night. Perhaps you have never really perceived these things. Most of us have not because the moment we see something, we immediately give it a name, cover it with a symbol, translate it in terms of what we know—which are all distractions preventing direct perception. To see something without naming it, to observe it totally, is possible only when there is no comparison, that is, when the mind is really quiet, silent in its perception.

To find out about oneself, such a mind is necessary—a mind that is capable of looking without interpreting, without condemning, without justifying. Try that sometime, and you will find out how extraordinarily difficult, how arduous a thing it is. Our tradition, our education, all our moral and religious training has conditioned us to condemn, to justify, to cover up, not to penetrate. There can be penetration, deep insight, only when your mind is capable of observation without being distracted by any process of evaluation, and unless you know the source of your thinking, you have no basis for thinking at all. Then you are merely a machine, repeating certain ideas, predetermined thoughts.

So, to penetrate deeply into yourself is not introspection; it does not give strength to self-centered activity but begins to open the door through which you will be able to perceive the whole process of your own mind. And if you go into it very deeply, dying to everything that you have discovered in the process of understanding, you will find that involuntarily, without any compulsion or discipline, the mind comes to a state of quietness, a state of alertness; and it is only then that a radical revolution takes place.

In all these talks you and I are going to discover the ways of the mind; we are going to find out how it is conditioned, shaped as a Hindu or a Muslim, a Parsi or a Christian, a communist or a socialist, and see how it holds on to certain beliefs, to certain ideas or aspirations. We are going to learn about all that so that our minds are liberated through direct perception, and then we shall have a totally different relationship with society. We cannot exist in isolation, and it is only in relationship that we discover what we are.

We have so many problems that our life is crowded with them. We know life only as a problem, and we never see life as a whole—this extraordinary vastness of a mind that has no barrier, that is not in bondage to experience. We do not know the quality of the mind that is illimitable, eternal. That is why it is very important for each one of us to learn how to listen.

Now, listening is a very difficult thing to do. Most of us never listen. We hear, but we do not listen. Surely, listening implies no interpretation. If I say something, you may listen, but you cease to listen the moment you interpret what you hear according to your background. Whereas, if there is no interpretation, no evaluation, but an actual listening with your whole being, then you will find in that very act of listening there is a mirror in which you see for yourself what is true and what is false—and that is the beauty of listening.

Just as you have never looked at anything—at a flower, at a star, at a reflection on the water—with your whole being, so you have probably never listened to anything with your whole being. To listen with your whole being is to listen with your conscious mind, with your unconscious mind, and with your body—that is, with all your senses fully awakened. It is only when you listen in this manner that you are able to discern that which is true, and the truth about the false.

That is all the mind needs, isn't it?—the capacity to see what is true in ourselves and about ourselves.

To perceive what is true, there must be a total giving of oneself to the thing. If in listening to music you are capable of paying total attention, the music has quite a different meaning. If you are able to give your whole being to a problem, the problem is not. The problem exists only when there is contradiction within ourselves. This inner contradiction can be dissolved only through self-knowledge, and the self is revealed only in relationship with the one or with the many.

All this demands, surely, a tremendous alertness, and everything about us tends to put us to sleep. One of the drugs that puts us to sleep is obviously knowledge. A mind that knows can never learn. Another drug is tradition—not only the tradition of centuries, but the tradition of yesterday, the tradition that says, "I know; I have experienced." Knowledge, tradition, and the experiences that one gathers, both the good and the bad, the joyous and the sorrowful—all these contribute to put the mind to sleep. And it is only the alert mind, the mind that is constantly questioning, asking, looking into itself and all its activities—it is only such a mind that can discover what is true. Truth does not demand belief, truth is not the result of experience, truth is something that you perceive directly; but this is possible only when the mind is innocent, not burdened with a thousand and one problems. To die to all that is the beginning of wisdom.

What you and I are trying to do in these talks is to look into ourselves and uncover the many layers of our consciousness. If you do not do that and merely listen to a series of words, you will find that these talks will have very little meaning, and your coming here will be a fruitless thing. But if you follow and directly experience what is being said through the observation of your own mind, then together we can go very far. In penetrating deeply within yourself, you will find that the mind becomes completely motionless, spontaneously still and free. That state of quietness is not the result of any discipline; it cannot be brought about through any yogic practice. It is the outcome of understanding oneself. Such a mind is essential to the understanding of the totality of life. Only such a mind can find out what is true, whether there is God.

Most of us are caught in some form of sorrow, turmoil, travail, and we can resolve it only through understanding ourselves—"ourselves" being the conscious as well as the unconscious. The more you understand yourself, the more subtle and beautiful you will find the mind to be, and without understanding yourself there is no reality. You may quote the sacred books and affirm your belief in God, but it is all just words without much meaning. What is essential is self-knowledge. To know oneself is not to talk about the atma, the super-self, and all that business, which is just an invention of the mind. To know oneself is to know the mind that invents the super-self, that seeks security, that is everlastingly wanting to be settled, undisturbed, reassured. To know all that through direct observation brings about a spontaneous tranquillity of the mind. And it is only the tranquil mind, the mind that is still, motionless—it is only such a mind that knows the tremendous activity of being totally alive.

February 8, 1959

Second Talk in New Delhi

I would like, if I may, to talk over with you the problem of action. By action we generally mean what we do or think we should do under given circumstances, the question of what is the right course to take,

and whether a particular action is justified or not. Most of our thinking is concerned with what to do. In the political and economic fields, in our personal relationships, and in the world at large, we are all primarily concerned with what is right action. And I would like, if I may, to talk over with you, not what is right and what is wrong action, but the totality of action, for if we can get a feeling of the action that is total, that is not self-contradictory, then perhaps we shall know or be able to feel our way through any particular action.

But it is very difficult, I think, to get a feeling of the totality of something. After all, to get the feeling of a tree, it is no good merely examining a leaf or a branch or the trunk. The tree is a totality, the hidden as well as what is shown, and to understand the beauty, the loveliness of a spreading tree, one must have a feeling of the totality of it.

In the same way, I think one must have this feeling, this inward comprehension of total action. If we look at ourselves, we will see that in our relationships, in our governments, in every department of our living, there is not a total action but many separate, unrelated actions. The government does one thing unrelated to our personal existence, the businessman does something else unrelated to the action of the government, and the individual says, "I am a communist; I am a Catholic," and so on. Each one is concerned with action according to a particular system or within a limited sphere, hoping that such action will cover the whole field. So there is always a contradiction, not only in the individual, in you and me, but also in our relationship with society, with the government, and with others.

Now, what is total action? You and I—you as an individual and I as another individual—are talking this over. I am not laying down the law. I am not saying, "This is right and that is wrong," but together we are going to find out what is this extraordinary action which is total and therefore not contradictory in itself.

All our responses have their opposite responses, have they not? If you observe you will see that every desire has its own contradictory desire. The moment we desire something, there is the shadow of an opposing desire, so our action always creates a contradiction, an opposite response.

Now, is there an action which is total, which does not create a contradiction, and which is not merely the continuance of a particular form of activity? We are going to find out; we are going into it very hesitantly and discover the truth of the matter for ourselves.

After all, the function of a speaker is not merely to give you ideas—at least I do not think so—because ideas never really change human beings. One idea can be opposed by another idea. The very idea of total action creates an idea opposite to it. But if we can put away mere ideas and think together, feel together, proceed, investigate, question together, then perhaps we shall get the feeling of a total action which is not self-contradictory because that which is total cannot have within it something opposed to itself.

This is a very complex problem, and like all complex problems, it must be approached very simply, which is the way of learning. To learn, the mind must be in a state of inquiry, and the mind is not inquiring when it makes a decision and starts from there. If I have a conception of what is right and what is wrong action, I have already made a decision, and such a mind is incapable of learning the truth about action. Though it may be very active, it is really a dead mind. There is no movement of learning for the mind that has already learned; there is no experiencing for the mind that is burdened with past experiences. I do not know if you understand this, or if I am making myself clear.

You see, the difficulty is that most of us are used to similes, examples, illustrations. If I could give you ten examples, you would think you had understood—but really you would not have understood. Examples and illustrations are most deceiving. They prevent you from really thinking, inquiring. An example can be offset by a contradictory example, and in arguing about the examples, we shall get lost. Whereas, if we can capture the totality of action, the feeling of it, then we shall be able to work it out in detail in our daily existence. But that requires enormous attention, and a great deal of insight. Most of us are unwilling to give our complete attention to a problem of this kind, and we would rather be excited or amused by discussing examples.

What you and I are trying to find out is whether there is a total action that will cover the whole field of our existence. I say there is—but not dogmatically. I say there is a total action which will cover every department of our existence—governmental, economic, social, and the whole field of human relationships. But you cannot come to it, you cannot comprehend the feeling, the beauty, the subtlety of it, if you approach it from a particular point of view. Therefore there must be a letting go of your communism, of your Hinduism, of your conception of action according to the Gita, the Bible, the Koran, or your latest guru. All that must be wiped out in order to find the total action which will respond to every challenge.

As I was saying last time, it is very important to know how to listen because most of us never listen at all. Listening is in itself an action of liberation—it frees the mind. But when you do listen, what actually happens? If you observe your own mind, you will see that you are comparing what is being said either with what you know or with some authority whom you respect. You are always comparing or interpreting, aren't you? Therefore the mind is not in a state of listening at all. To listen you must give your total attention, and total attention is denied when you are comparing or interpreting. When you say that you see a correspondence between what is being said here and the teachings of Shankara or Buddha, that is a lazy man's way of listening. But if you really want to learn the truth about yourself, then you are bound to listen without comparing, without a calculated interest. And I say in that very act of listening without comparison or interpretation, you will discover for yourself that in the state of learning the mind is not accumulating. But when the mind has learned, it obviously ceases to learn because it is always interpreting the new in terms of the old.

So listening is an extraordinary thing because if you are really capable of listening, it frees the mind from all influence. Then the mind is clear, sharp—and such a mind is necessary to find out what is true.

This question of action, of what to do, is an enormous problem, and if we merely listen consciously, at the intellectual or verbal level, we shall enter the field of argumentation: "I am right, you are wrong; I quote you this, you quote me that," and so on indefinitely. That is why it is important to communicate with each other at a much deeper level, unconsciously. I think fundamental change takes place only at the unconscious level. Change at the conscious level is based on a decision, and decision will always produce its own contradiction.

Please follow this a little bit patiently. Action born of choice is based on a decision, and such action is self-contradictory. I decide to do something. That decision is the outcome of choice, and choice always contains its own opposite. Therefore the action of decision is a contradiction, inwardly as well as outwardly. There is an action which is not of choice, not of decision, and in such action there is no contradiction, but that requires a great deal of inquiry into oneself.

Now, this is not a matter of acceptance or denial. Don't immediately say to me, "I disagree with you," or "You are utterly right," because that would have no meaning. What matters is for you to see the truth that action born of choice, of decision, will inevitably produce a self-contradictory reaction. If you decide to do something, your action is born of choice, and that action will invariably create its own opposite; therefore, you are caught in contradiction. So what are you to do? I say there is a total action in which there is no contradiction at all. But to understand that, one must go into the unconscious, and it is there that we shall have to commune with each other. Do you understand? I hope I am making myself clear. I see that I am not.

Most of us are concerned with what to do, what kind of legislation to enact, what kind of reform to carry out, and all the rest of it. But I say that is not important; put that aside for the moment and concern yourself with total action which is not self-contradictory. If you can find out what total action is, then you will be able to act truly in a particular direction. Do you understand?

Let us say that I do not know what to do as a governmental official or in the family or as a citizen who is not committed to any particular party or system. But before I ask what I am to do, I say to myself, "There must be a total action, an action which is whole, which does not contain the seed of self-contradiction." To understand the tree, I must look at the whole tree and not be concerned with a particular leaf. If I want to understand life, I must understand the whole depth, breadth, and height of it, and not approach it through a particular system, belief, or ideology. Similarly, I must put aside for the moment the particular act, and be concerned with the comprehension of total action.

Sirs, life isn't any one particular thing. Life isn't just the bureaucratic system of New Delhi, life isn't just the communist system or the capitalist system, life isn't just tyranny or self-contradiction. Life is all these things, and far more; it is the daily relationship of conflict, of misery, of struggle and travail. Life is birth and death; it is meditation, inquiry, and all the various subtleties which the mind invents. Life is enormous, immeasurable by the mind, and you think you have understood life when you are able to dissect a tiny part of it. You say, "Yes, I know life," but you don't know life as long as your whole concentration is given to one section or department of life.

In the same way, what matters is not the immediate act but the inquiry into the totality of action, so I say: Put aside the immediate act. But you are not going to put it aside. The pressure is much too great. You have to do something tomorrow; you have to act. So the conscious mind is perpetually occupied with immediate action, like a machine that is constantly in motion. You never say, "I will put this all aside and find out."

So you and I are now inquiring at the unconscious level; therefore, communication is entirely different. It is not verbal, it is not mere analysis, it is not a process of giving examples; it is like feeling your way under water. You can't assume anything, you can't be dogmatic or assertive; you must be negative. That is why negative thinking is tremendously important. Negative thinking is the highest form of thinking—but let us not go into that for the moment.

I hope you are following all this. If not, we will discuss it another time.

You and I are communicating at the unconscious level, where there is only the act of listening and not the listener who says, "What shall I do?" Leave the "what to do" to the conscious mind. We are going to inquire unconsciously into the totality of action—which does not mean that one goes to sleep; on the contrary, it is quite an extraordinary state of attention.

Now, let us differentiate between attention and concentration. Concentration, being a focusing of the mind, is limited, but attention is not. The conscious mind can be concentrated at its own level, but the unconscious can only be attentive, not concentrated. Am I making this clear? Sirs, don't immediately say yes. I mustn't ask that question, for you are apt to say it is clear because you want to proceed. I can proceed, but you will merely remain on the verbal or conscious level, and therefore you won't be able to proceed. You and I must proceed together, or not at all.

So we are inquiring negatively into the totality of action, which means that the mind is not concerned with decision; it is not for the moment concerned with what to do, the immediate action. Let me put it around the other way.

The conscious mind is always concerned with the immediate question of what to do. All politicians are concerned with what to do; therefore, they are not concerned with the totality of action. At the conscious level there are and must be decisions, but those decisions are based on choice, which is the action of will, and therefore they become self-contradictory. Seeing the psychological truth of this, I begin to inquire negatively, which is the only approach to the unconscious. There cannot be a positive approach because the positive approach belongs to the conscious mind. The unconscious is enormous; it is like a vast sea where there is a perpetual movement, and how can you approach that enormous depth with a positive idea? To learn, there must be a negation of the positive. There is no learning at the conscious level; there is only the acquiring of knowledge.

As I said, sirs, this is a very difficult question. Concentration is exclusion, and what you exclude is always waiting to come in. Attention is a negation of concentration because there is no exclusion, and that is the way one must approach the unconscious. That is the way you and I are going to communicate, which means that we are not concerned with the immediate decision and the activity based on that decision. We are inquiring negatively into the whole field of the unconscious, in which there is an action which is not self-contradictory.

So, what have we done so far? We have seen that to understand something, there must be a total feeling, which is love. Love is a total act; it is a feeling of wholeness in which all the senses are fully awake, the mind completely at rest, and in which there is no contradiction. To comprehend the beauty of a tree against the sky, there must be a feeling of the totality of the tree, and that feeling is denied when you merely concern yourself with a leaf. But when you get the feeling of the totality of a tree, then you can be concerned with the leaf, with the branch, with the flower.

As we are concerned this evening with action, we are inquiring into the totality of it, and you can approach it only negatively, not with a desire to know what is the right thing to do. If that much is clear, we can proceed, but I'm afraid it is not clear because most of us have not thought about this at all. We have only thought about what to do, what is right, what is profitable, what will give us more power, influence—which means that we are always calculating, self-interested, and therefore always self-contradictory. And there we remain, hoping to find a way to integrate our self-contradiction, but we never find it because at that level there is no end to self-contradiction.

It is very difficult not to be a communist, a socialist, this or that, and to inquire into what is total action. Most of us are committed to something or other, and a man who is committed to something is incapable of learning. Life never stands still; it does not commit itself to anything; it is in eternal movement. And you want to translate this living thing in terms of a particular belief or ideology, which is utterly childish.

So what we are trying to do is to feel out the totality of action. There is no action without the background of thought, is there? And thought is always choice. Don't just accept this. Please examine it, feel your way into it. Thought is the process of choosing. Without thought you cannot choose. The moment you choose, there is a decision, and that decision creates its own opposite—good and bad, violence and nonviolence. The man who pursues nonviolence through decision creates a contradiction in himself. Thought is essentially born of choice. I choose to think in a certain way. I examine communism, socialism, Buddhism, I reason logically and decide to think this or that. Such thought is based on memory, on my conditioning, on my pleasure, on my likes and dislikes, and any action born of such thought will inevitably create contradiction in myself and therefore in the world; it will produce sorrow, misery, not only for me, but for others as well.

Now please listen quietly, and don't say yes or no. Is there an action which is not the result of influence, which is not the result of calculated self-interest, which is not the result of past experience?—and I have explained how the burden of accumulated experience makes the mind incapable of experiencing.

Is there an action which is not the outcome of choice, of ideation, of a decision, but is the total feeling of action? I say there is. As we are living now, the government does one thing, the businessman does another, the religious man, the scholar, and the scientist each does something else, and they are all in contradiction. These contradictions can never be overcome because the overcoming of a contradiction only creates another tension. The essential thing is for the mind to understand the totality of action, that is, to get the feeling of action which is not born of decision, as one might get the feeling of a lovely sunset, of a flower, or a bird on the wing. This requires an inquiry into the unconscious with no positive demand for an answer. And if you are capable of not being caught up in the immediacy of life, of what to do tomorrow, then you will find that the mind begins to discover a state of action in which there is no contradiction, an action which has no opposite. You try it. Try it as you go home, when you are sitting in the bus. Find out for yourself what is this extraordinary thing, an action which is total.

You see, sirs, the earth is not communist or capitalist, it is not Hindu or Christian, it is neither yours nor mine. There is a feeling of the totality of the earth, of the beauty, the richness, the extraordinary potency of the earth, but you can feel that total splendor only when you are not committed to anything. In the same way, you can get the feeling of total action only when you are not committed to any particular activity, when you are not one of the "do-gooders" who are committed to this or that party, belief, or ideology and whose actions are really a form of self-centered activity. If you are not committed, then you will find that the conscious mind, though involved with immediate action, can put aside that immediate action and inquire negatively into the unconscious where lie the real motives, the hidden contradictions, the traditional bondages, and blind urges which create the problems of immediacy. And once you understand all this, then you can go much further. Then you will be able to feel—as you would feel the loveliness, the wholeness of a tree—the totality of

action in which there is no opposite response, no contradiction.

This is not the integration of action with its opposite, which is nonsense; on the contrary, it is the understanding of the totality of action which comes when the mind is capable of not being centered in the immediate activity. To be centered in the immediate activity is concentration. Awareness or attention is not centered in the immediate activity, but in that attention the immediate activity is included. So there is a totality of action only when the mind is capable of inquiring deeply from moment to moment and is not merely concerned with the immediate. Then the mind penetrates; it asks fundamental questions. Because its inquiry is fundamental, its action is anonymous, and being anonymous it has no contradiction, no opposite.

February 11, 1959

Third Talk in New Delhi

This evening I would like, if I may, to talk over with you the whole process of the mind. To most of us, apparently, thought is very important; but thought, even though it shapes our actions and our lives, will have very little meaning unless we understand the ways of the mind.

Before I go further, I would like to ask you what is the purpose or significance of your coming here? It is a valid question, I think, and one which you will have to answer for yourself. What is the motive, the intention of your coming? On that will depend your understanding of what is going to be said. If you come merely out of curiosity, obviously you will be little satisfied and will go away rather more confused than before. But if you come, not just to hear what the speaker has to say, but in order to understand yourself, then I think these talks will have some meaning. But to understand oneself requires a great deal of attention, not only while we are here, but also when we go out into the ways of our daily existence; for it is in our everyday relationships that we find the mirror in which to see ourselves as we are.

So let us be very clear about our intention in gathering together here this evening. You are not going to learn anything from the speaker. To me there is neither the teacher nor the taught; there is no leader and no follower, no guru and no disciple; there is no path to reality, no system or discipline that can bring about the realization of that extraordinary thing which we call the real, the eternal, the immeasurable. No organized religion can lead you to it. And if you have come here with the hope of being led to happiness, to peace of mind, you are not only going to be disappointed but more confused than ever.

So as an individual you must be very clear about why you are here. The man who follows any path, any system, any teacher, or who belongs to any organized religion is merely an imitator and not an individual who is trying to understand the whole field of human existence. Living is a very complex process, and to understand it demands extraordinary attention, a detailed perception, a precision in thinking; so, obviously there can be no following, there can be neither an easy acceptance nor a casual denial. If that much is very clear between you and me as two individuals, then together we can proceed. But if you have come here merely to juggle with words, or intellectually to be amused, or cleverly to refute what is said, then I think you will miss the significance of the whole thing.

If one asks oneself very clearly, "Why have I come?" that very question will begin to unravel the process of one's own mind. After all, the mind is the only instrument we have. It is the mind that perceives, that

thinks, that calculates, that desires, that communicates, that penetrates, that creates its own blockages, that tries to fulfill itself and finds frustration, misery; it is the mind that is ambitious and ruthless, affectionate and sympathetic; it is the mind that knows pleasure and pain, love and hate, that takes delight in beauty. So unless we understand this extraordinary thing called the mind, we shall have very little basis for rational, clear, and perceptive thinking.

Thinking plays a very large part in our life, does it not? It covers almost the whole field of our existence. That is why it is so important to understand the mind, from which thinking emanates. The mind is the source of our thought, of our feeling, of our perception, our awareness; it shapes our relationship with society, with nature, with each other. So without understanding the mind, any change we bring about in our thinking will have very little meaning.

Now, in this talk and in all the talks to follow, what we are trying to do is to unravel this thing called the mind. It is not our intention that you should be influenced to think in a particular direction—and it is very important for you and me to understand this. All influence, good or bad, is pernicious because it enslaves the mind. Influence is mere propaganda. The constant repetition of certain phrases creates belief, which is not thinking. To me any influence, whether pleasant or unpleasant, and however subtle or shrewd, is a form of compulsion. So again let us be very clear that you are not being mesmerized by me; your mind is not being influenced to think in a certain direction.

It is very important, I think, that we understand this. Influence, which is propaganda, is being exerted on the mind all the time. Newspapers, magazines, books, the speeches that are given by television and radio—all this and everything else that goes to make up our environment is urging us to think in a certain direction, and consciously or unconsciously we either resist or accept it.

Please don't just listen to me, but watch your own mind in operation. I am only describing the operation of your own mind, how influence twists and perverts your thought. There is not only conscious influence, which is called education, but also unconscious influence, the influence of which one is not aware, and perhaps this is much more potent than the conscious influence. If I directly tell you to do something, you may or may not do it, depending on my authority, my power of persuasion, and on your willingness or otherwise to accept what I say—which is a conscious influence. But the unconscious, where there is no means of defense, is much more easily penetrated by subtle suggestions, ideas, arguments; and influences on that level are apt to affect the mind much more. I do not know if you have observed this. And there is the whole weight of tradition, the modern as well as the ancient, that shapes the mind gradually, unknowingly.

So one has to be alert at all these talks not to be influenced, not to be hypnotized into accepting what is said—which does not mean that you must reject it. What we are trying to do is to understand the process of the mind, and you cannot understand the mind, the whole extent and depth of it, if you merely accept or reject. You and I together are trying to understand the mind, go into it, uncover all the various aspects of it, and not merely confine ourselves to one particular part. We are exploring and therefore discovering; and what you discover for yourself matters much more than anything you may hear from me. But you are not really listening if you are prejudiced, if you are argumentative, if you merely reject or accept, for then you remain at the verbal level; therefore, you cannot explore, you cannot discover the movement, the extraordinary subtleties of the mind. I may point out to you many things, but unless you directly experience them, you cannot possibly understand the process of your own mind.

If you are really alert, you will see that there is no guru, no path, no system or belief that can lead you to truth. There is only the exploration of the process of your own thinking. When once you begin to know the ways of your mind and see what it is that lies behind your thought—why there is fear, why you seek security, and all the rest of it—then you will never again follow anybody.

That being clearly understood by you and by me, let us ask ourselves: What is the mind? When I put that question, please don't wait for a reply from me. Look at your own mind; observe the ways of your own thought. What I describe is only an indication; it is not the reality. The reality you must experience for yourself. The word, the description, the symbol, is not the actual thing. The word *door* is obviously not the door. The word *love* is not the feeling, the extraordinary quality that the word indicates. So do not let us confuse the word, the name, the symbol, with the fact. If you merely remain on the verbal level and discuss what the mind is, you are lost, for then you will never feel the quality of this astonishing thing called the mind.

So, what is the mind? Obviously, the mind is our total awareness or consciousness; it is the total way of our existence, the whole process of our thinking. The mind is the result of the brain. The brain produces the mind. Without the brain there is no mind, but the mind is separate from the brain. It is the child of the brain. If the brain is limited, damaged, the mind is also damaged. The brain, which records every sensation, every feeling of pleasure or pain, the brain with all its tissues, with all its responses, creates what we call the mind, although the mind is independent of the brain.

You don't have to accept this. You can experiment with it and see for yourself.

I ask you where you live, which is a question with which you are familiar. The air waves striking upon the eardrum cause an impulse to be sent to your brain, which translates and responds to what it hears according to its memories, and you say, "Sir, I live in such and such a place." The response of the brain is also the response of the mind according to its conditioning. The mind is not only the result of the brain but also of the time process—the time process being both external or chronological, and inward or psychological, inside the skin as it were, which is the sense of becoming something. So the mind is the result of the brain and of time, and it is made up of both the conscious and the unconscious, the surface and the hidden.

Now, the mind is controllable through education, is it not? That is what is happening throughout the world. The communists get hold of the mind through so-called education, through brainwashing, and so control it. That is essentially what all organized religions do. You are a Hindu or a Parsi, a Muslim or a Buddhist because you have been brought up as one; your parents, your tradition, your priest, your whole environment, all help to condition your mind in that way.

So the mind is being influenced all the time to think along a certain line. It used to be that only the organized religions were after your mind, but now governments have largely taken over that job. They want to shape and control your mind. On the surface the mind can resist their control. You will become a communist only if it pays you. If you think you will find God through Catholicism, you will become a Catholic, not otherwise. Superficially you have some say in the matter, but below the surface, in the deep unconscious, there is the whole weight of time, of tradition, urging you in a particular direction. The conscious mind may to some extent control and guide itself, but in the unconscious your ambitions, your unsolved problems, your compulsions, superstitions, fears, are waiting, throbbing, urging.

So there is a division in the mind as the conscious and the unconscious, the open and the hidden; inwardly, deeply, there is a contradiction. You remain a Hindu and cling to certain superstitions even though modern civilization says they are nonsense. You are a scientist, and yet you marry off your son or daughter in the old traditional way. So there is in you a contradiction. There is also a contradiction in thought itself, in desire itself. You want to do something, and at the same time you think you should not do it. You say, "I must," and "I must not."

This whole field of the mind is the result of time; it is the result of conflicts and adjustments, of a whole series of acceptances without full comprehension. Therefore we live in a state of contradiction; our life is a process of endless struggle. We are unhappy, and we want to be happy. Being violent, we practice the ideal of nonviolence. So there is a conflict going on—the mind is a battlefield. We want to be secure, knowing inwardly, deeply, that there is no such thing as security at all. The truth is that we do not want to face the fact that there is no security; therefore, we are always pursuing security, with the resultant fear of not being secure.

So the mind is a mass of contradictions, oppositions, adjustments, emotional reactions, conscious as well as unconscious, and from there we begin to think. We have never explored the depths of our own consciousness, but merely act on the surface. We believe or do not believe; we pursue what we think is profitable; we compel ourselves to do something, or we argue, drift. This is our life. And in this state the mind is seeking God. Being unhappy, miserable, self-contradictory, the mind says, "I want to find reality."

But you can perceive what is real only when the mind is not in a state of self-contradiction. Whether you believe or do not believe in God has very little importance. Actually, it is of no importance at all because in your life it is just a matter of convenience, of tradition and social security. You are conditioned to believe in God, as the communists are conditioned not to believe. It is conditioning that makes you call yourself a Hindu or a Buddist, a Muslim or a Christian. Your moralizing about God or truth and your quoting of the various scriptures has very little significance because the moment you discover for yourself that your mind is conditioned, that whole structure will collapse.

Being afraid, the mind finds security within the field of its own thought, convictions, and experiences; it builds a haven of refuge through belief and wards off the movement of life. This is the actual fact, whether you acknowledge it or not. The haven of refuge which the mind creates and remains within is the 'me' and the 'mine', and every form of disturbance that might shake the foundations of this refuge, the mind rejects.

Seeing that thought is transient, the mind creates the 'I'-process, the 'me', which it then calls the permanent, the everlasting, but which is still within the field of the mind because the mind has created and can think about it. What the mind can think about is obviously within the field of the mind, which is the field of time; therefore, it is not the timeless, the eternal, though you may call it the atma, the higher self, or God. Your God is then a product of your thought, and your thought is the response of your conditioning, of your memories, of your experiences, which are all within the field of time.

Now, can the mind be free of time? That is the real problem. Because all creation takes place outside the field of time. All profound thinking, all deep feeling is always timeless. When you love somebody, when there is love, that love is not bound by time.

But the conditioned mind, surely, is incapable of finding out what lies beyond time. That is, sirs, the mind as we know it is conditioned by the past. The past, moving through the present to the future, conditions the mind; and this conditioned mind, being in conflict, in trouble, being fearful, uncertain, seeks something beyond the frontiers of time. That is what we are all doing in various ways, is it not? But how can a mind which is the result of time ever find that which is timeless? All it can do is to mesmerize itself into a state which it calls the timeless, the real, or make itself comfortable with certain beliefs.

To find reality, the mind must transform itself; it must go beyond itself. And unless the mind is capable of receiving reality, it cannot resolve the innumerable problems that confront us in our daily life. It can adjust itself, defend itself, it can take refuge temporarily; but life is all the time challenging the defenses that you so sedulously build around yourself. The house of your beliefs, of your properties, of your attachments and comforting ways of thinking is constantly being broken into. But the mind goes on seeking security, so there is a conflict between what you want and what life's process demands of you. This is what is happening to every one of us.

So the mind is the result of time, it is caught up in conflict, in discipline, control; and how can such a mind be free to discover what lies beyond the limits of time? I do not know if this problem interests you at all. Everyday existence, with all its troubles, seems to be sufficient for most of us. Our only concern is to find an immediate answer to our various problems. But sooner or later the immediate answers are found to be unsatisfactory because no problem has an answer apart from the problem itself. But if I can understand the problem, all the intricacies of it, then the problem no longer exists.

Most of us are concerned, I think, with how to live in this world without too much conflict. We want what we call peace of mind, which means that we do not want to be deeply disturbed. That is why we accept the immediate answers about death, about sorrow, and so on. But these problems cannot be understood, nor can there be the cessation of conflict until one begins to comprehend the whole process of the mind. When you begin to inquire into the mind, you will make the inevitable discovery that the limits or frontiers of the mind are defined by that which is recognizable, and that these frontiers of the mind can never be stormed, so thought can never be free. Thought is merely the reaction of your experience, the response of memory, and how can such thought ever be free? Freedom means, surely, a state which has no beginning and no end; it is not a continuity of conditioned thinking based on experience with all its memories.

So thought, which is the response of memory, of accumulated experience, of one's particular conditioning, is not the solution to any problem; and I think for most of us this is a bitter pill to swallow. Thought can never fly straight because it is always influenced, it is always motivated, attracted, and that attraction is based on our conditioning, on our background, on our memory. So thought is merely mechanical. Please, sirs, do see the significance of this. Machines are taking over more and more of the functions of the human mind. The electronic brain, which can do much better work in certain areas than you and I can, is based essentially on association, memory, experience, habit, which are also

the ways of the mind; and through association, memory, experience, habit, you can never come to that which is free.

It is of fundamental importance, then, to be aware—not only at the conscious or surface level, but also at the deeper, unconscious level—of this extraordinary thing called the mind, with its frontiers of the recognizable. And can this mind—which is the result of time in both the chronological and the psychological sense—with all its demands, with all its variances and influences, be creative? Because that is what is needed, surely—a mind that is not merely productive or inventive, but in a state of creativeness which is not the product of the mind.

I do not know if I am making myself clear. This is a difficult thing to go into, and it will mean very little unless you have followed what has been said this evening—followed it, not just verbally, but at the same time watching your own mind.

In what we call thinking there is always a thinker apart from the thought, an observer different from the observed. But it is thought that has produced the thinker; there is no entity as the thinker who produces thought. Thought, which is the reaction of memory, produces the thinker. If there is no thinking, there is no 'I'—though this is contrary to what you have always been told. You have accepted the idea that there is a permanent 'I'—which you call the atma, the higher self, and all the rest of it—that produces thought. To me this is sheer nonsense—it does not matter what the books say. What is important is for you to find out the truth of the matter for yourself. As long as there is this division of the thinker and the thought, as long as there is an experiencer who is experiencing, the mind is held within the frontiers of the recognizable and is therefore limited. It is caught in the process of accumulation, attachment, and is therefore in a state of perpetual self-contradiction.

So in the mind there is this division of the experiencer and the experienced, the observer and the observed. Knowing this fact and recognizing its own limitations, how is the mind to go beyond itself? Because it is only when the mind goes beyond itself that there is creation. Creation cannot take place within the field of the experiencer and the experienced, the thinker and the thought, because in that field everything is in a state of conflict; there is confusion, misery. As long as there is the experiencer and the experienced, the thinker and the thought, there is a division, a contradiction, and hence a ceaseless struggle to bring the two together, to build a bridge between them. As long as that division exists, the mind is held within the frontiers of the recognizable, and what is recognized is not the new. Truth cannot be recognized. What you recognize you already know, and what you know is not *what is*.

Now, how is the mind to free itself from the known? For only in the state of unknowingness is there creation, not within the field of the known. Being the result of time, which is the known, how is the mind to die to the known?

Sirs, there is no answer, there is no system by which you can make the mind new, fresh, young, innocent. As long as the mind is functioning within the field of the known, it can never renew itself, it can never make itself totally free. So please listen to the question, and let the seed of the question penetrate into the unconscious; then you will find the answer as you live, as you function daily.

How is the mind to free itself from the known? It is only in that state of freedom from the known that there can be creation, which can then be translated as inventiveness, as the creativeness of an artist, as this or that—all of which is irrelevant, it has only social significance. God, or truth, is that state

of freedom from the known; it has nothing to do with your ideas about that state. The man who is seeking God will never find God. The man who practices a discipline, who does puja and all the rest of it, will never find out what is true because he is still working within the field of the known. It is only when the mind is dead to everything that it has experienced, totally empty of the known—not blank, but empty, with a sense of complete unknowingness—it is only then that reality comes into being.

February 15, 1959

Fourth Talk in New Delhi

This evening I would like to suggest that we talk over the question of change and revolution; but before we go into it, I think it is very important to understand the relationship of the individual to society. The first thing to realize is that the problems of the individual, his sorrows and struggles, are also those of the world. The world is the individual; the individual is not different from the society in which he lives. That is why, without a radical transformation of the individual, society becomes a burden, an irresponsible continuity in which the individual is merely a cog.

There is a strong tendency to think that the individual is of little importance in modern society, and that everything possible must be done to control the individual, to shape his thought through propaganda, through sanctions, through the various means of mass communication. The individual himself wonders what he can do in a society which is so burdensome, which bears down on him with the weight of a mountain, and he feels almost helpless. Confronted with this mass of confusion, deterioration, war, starvation, and misery, the individual not unnaturally puts to himself the question, ''What can I do?'' And I think the answer to this question is that he cannot do anything, which is an obvious fact. He can't prevent a war, he can't do away with starvation, he can't put a stop to religious bigotry, or to the historical process of nationalism, with all its conflicts.

So I think to put such a question is inherently wrong. The individual's responsibility is not to society, but to himself. And if he is responsible to himself, he will act upon society—but not the other way round. Obviously the individual can't do anything about this social confusion, but when he begins to clear up his own confusion, his self-contradiction, his own violence and fears, then such an individual has an extraordinary importance in society. I think very few of us realize this. Seeing that we cannot do anything on a world scale, we invariably do nothing at all, which is really an escape from the action within oneself which will bring about a radical change.

So I am talking to you as one individual to another. We are not communicating with each other as Indians or Americans or Russians or Chinese nor as members of any particular group. We are talking things over as two human beings, not as a layman and a specialist. If that much is clear between us, we can proceed.

The individual is obviously of the greatest significance in society because it is only the individual who is capable of creative activity, not the mass—and I shall explain presently what I mean by that word *creative*. If you see this fact, then you will also realize that what you are in yourself is of the highest importance. Your capacity to think, to function with wholeness, with an integration in which there is no self-contradiction—this has an enormous significance.

We see that if there is to be any real change in the world—and there must be a real change—then you and I as individuals will have to transform ourselves. Unless there is a radical change in each one of us, life becomes an endless imitation, ultimately leading to boredom, frustration, and hopelessness.

Now, what do we mean by change? Surely, change under compulsion is no change at all. If I change because society forces me to change, it is merely an adjustment according to convenience, a conformity brought about by pressure, by fear.

Most of us change only under compulsion, through fear, through some form of reward or punishment. Psychologically, this is the actual fact. And when we are forced to change, it is merely an outward conformity, while inwardly we remain the same. I may change because my family or the society in which I live influences me to do so, or because the government requires that I act in a certain way; but this is only an adjustment, it is not change, and inwardly I am still greedy, envious, ambitious, frustrated, sorrowful, fearful. I have outwardly conformed to a new pattern; I have not changed radically within myself. And is it possible for me as a human being to be in a state of continuous change, revolution, which is not the result of any compulsion or promise of reward?

Surely, anything I do because of compulsion, fear, imitation, or reward is within the field of time, and it breeds habit. I do the thing over and over again until habit is established, and this habit is within the field of time. So there can be no real change, no revolution, within the field of time; there can only be adjustment, conformity, imitation, habit. Change requires a total perception or awareness of all that is implied in imitation, conformity, and this total perception frees the mind to change radically. I am just introducing it to you, so that you and I can think it out together.

As I said, any form of change through compulsion is no change at all, which I think is fairly obvious. If you force your child to do something, he will do it through fear, but there is no understanding, no comprehension of what is involved. When action is born of fear, outwardly it may appear to be a change, but actually it is not.

Now let us find out if it is possible to understand and free the mind from fear so that there is a change without effort. All effort to change implies an inducement, does it not? When I make an effort to change, it is in order to gain, to avoid, or to become something; therefore, there is no radical change at all. I think this fact must be very clearly understood by each one of us if there is to be a fundamental change.

If we are well-off and have a good job, if we are fairly well-to-do, most of us are contented and do not want anything changed; we just want to carry on as we are. We have fallen into a certain habit, a certain comfortable groove, and we want to continue in that state of endless limitation. But the wave of life does not function in that way, it is always beating upon and breaking down the walls of security which we have built around ourselves. Our desire to be secure right through, psychologically as well as physically, is constantly being challenged by the movement of life, which like a restless sea is always pounding on the shore. And nothing can withstand that pounding; however much one may cling to inward security, life will not allow it to exist for long. So there is a contradiction between the movement of life and our desire to be secure; and out of this comes fear in all its various forms. If we can understand fear, perhaps in the very process of that understanding, there will be the cessation of fear, and therefore a fundamental change without effort.

What is fear? I do not know if you have ever thought about it. We are going to examine it now, but if you merely follow verbally what is said and are not aware of your own fear, then you will not understand and will not be free of fear.

After all, these meetings are intended not merely to stimulate you but to help to bring about a change in the quality of the mind. That is where there must be a revolution—in the quality of the mind itself. And that revolution can take place only if you are aware of your own fear and are capable of looking at it directly.

Fear is a sorrowful, a dreadful thing, and it is always following most of us like a shadow. One may not be aware of it, but deep down it is there: the fear of death, the fear of failure, the fear of losing a job, the fear of what the neighbors will say, the fear of one's wife or husband, and so on. There are fears of which one is conscious, and fears of which one is unaware. I am not talking about a particular form of fear but of the whole sense of fear, because unless the mind is free from all sense of fear, which is not to cover it up, thought cannot function with clarity, with perception; there is always apprehension, confusion. So it is absolutely essential for the individual to be free from fear in all its forms.

Now, how does fear arise? Is there fear when you are actually confronted with the fact? Please follow this closely. Is there fear when you are face to face with the fact of death, let us say? Surely, when you are directly confronted with the fact, there is no fear because in that moment the challenge demands your action and you respond, you act. Fear arises only before or after the event. I am afraid of death in the future. I am afraid of what may happen if I become ill—I may lose my job. Or I am afraid at the thought of what has already happened, or what nearly happened. So my fear is always linked to the past or to the future, it is always within the brackets of time, is it not? Fear is the result of my thinking about the past and of my thinking about the future. If you observe very carefully you will see that there is no fear of the present. That is because, when there is full awareness of the present, neither the past nor the future exists. I do not know if I am making myself clear on this point.

Knowing that I shall die in the future, I am afraid of death, of what is going to be. I have seen death in the past, and that has awakened in me fear of what is going to happen in the future. So my mind is never fully aware of the present—which does not mean that I must live thoughtlessly in the present. I am talking about an awareness of the present which is not contaminated by past fear or future fear, and which is therefore limitless.

This is very difficult to understand unless you experience for yourself what I am talking about—or rather, unless you observe the actual arising of fear. Fear comes into being only when thought is caught in the past as memory, or in the future as anticipation. So time is the factor of fear, and until the mind is free of time, there can be no radical wiping away of fear. It sounds complicated, but it is not. We are used to resisting fear, to disciplining ourselves against it. We say that we must not think about the past or the future, that we must live only in the present; therefore, we build a wall of resistance against the past and the future and try to make the best of the present, which is a very shallow way of living. If that is clear, let us look again at the whole process of fear.

Being afraid, how am I to resolve fear? I may resist fear, I may escape from it; but resistance and escape do not wipe away fear. How then am I to approach fear, how am I to understand and resolve it without effort? The moment I make an effort to be free of fear, I am exercising will, which is a form of resistance, and resistance does not bring understanding. So this habit of effort must go— that is the first thing I have to realize. My mind is caught in the habit of condemning, resisting fear, which prevents the under-

standing of fear. If I want to understand fear, there must be no resistance, no defense-mechanism in operation with regard to that particular feeling which I call fear. And then what happens? What happens when the mind is free from the habit of resisting or running away from fear through reading books, listening to the radio, and through the various other forms of escape with which we are all familiar? Then, surely, the mind is capable of looking directly at that feeling which it calls fear.

Now, can the mind look at anything without naming it? Can I look at a flower, at the moonlight on the water, at an insect, at a feeling, without verbalizing it, without giving it a name? Because verbalizing, giving a name to what is perceived, is a distraction from perceiving, is it not?

Please, sirs, I hope you are actually doing this, experimenting to find out whether you can look at your fear without naming it. Can you look at a flower without giving it a name, without saying, "It is lovely. It is yellow. I like that flower. I don't like that flower"—without all the chattering of the mind that comes into operation when you look at something? Try it and you will find that it is one of the most difficult things to do. This chattering of the mind, this verbalization in terms of condemnation or admiration, is a habit that prevents direct perception.

So you are now aware of your fear; you know you are afraid. Can you look at it without condemnation or acceptance? Are you looking at it through the focus of the word *fear,* or are you aware of that feeling without the word?

Sirs, let us take another example. Most of us are idolatrous—which means that the symbol becomes extraordinarily significant. We worship not only the idol made by the hand, but also the ideal created by thought. Now, an idolatrous mind is not a free mind. An idolatrous mind can never think clearly, perceptively. The man who has an ideal is obviously not very thoughtful. I know it is the fashion to have ideals; it is the respectable escape from the actual fact, and that is why ideals become all-important. But however much you may pursue the ideal of nonviolence, for example, the actual fact is that you are violent.

So the idealistic mind is idolatrous; being violent, it worships the ideal of nonviolence and thereby lives in a state of self-contradiction. The ideal of nonviolence is merely the mind's reaction against its own violence; and if it is to be free of both, the mind must be aware of the fact of its violence, but not in relation to the opposite, which it calls nonviolence. Then one can look at violence, observe it with one's whole being, which is not to condemn it or say that it is inevitable in life.

Now, are you aware of your fear in that way? Are you aware of the feeling without the word? That is, can you look at the feeling without verbalizing it, which is really to give your whole attention to the feeling, is it not? There is then no distraction, no verbal screen between you and what is being observed. That is true perception, surely—when the mind is not chattering but sees the fact entirely, without the word coming in between.

This observation of fear without verbalization is in itself discipline; it is not a discipline imposed upon the mind. I hope this is clear because it is very important to understand it. The observation of fear is in itself discipline. You don't have to exercise discipline in order to observe. The exercising of discipline in order to observe prevents observation; it blocks perception. But when you see the falseness of disciplining the mind to observe, that very perception brings its own discipline.

If you want to understand something, if you want to understand fear, you must obviously give your whole attention to it. Do not say, "How am I to give my whole attention without discipline?" That is a wrong question which will receive a wrong answer. First see the truth that to understand your fear, you must give it your whole attention, and that there can be no attention as long as you run away from fear or condemn it. This condemnation and escape is a habit which you have fallen into, and habit cannot be wiped away by any discipline. The disciplining of the mind to wipe away habit merely creates another habit. But in observing fear without verbalization, without condemnation or justification, there is a spontaneous discipline from moment to moment—which means that the mind is free from the habit of discipline.

I wonder how many of you are following all this? Perhaps you are too tired at the end of the day to follow it consciously, but if you just listen without a conscious effort to listen, I think you will find that listening is in itself an astonishing thing. If you listen rightly, a miracle takes place. The man who knows how to listen without effort learns much more than the man who makes an effort to listen. When one listens easily, effortlessly, the mind can see what is true and what is false; it can see the truth in the false. So listen to what is being said, even though you may not be able to follow it consciously, through direct experience. After all, the deep, fundamental responses of human beings are anonymous. It is not that I am telling you something which you then understand, but when the mind is in a state of listening there is an understanding which is neither yours nor mine; and it is this effortless understanding that brings about a fundamental revolution.

To go back, fear exists only within the brackets of time, where there is no real change but merely reaction. Communism, for example, is a reaction from capitalism, just as bravery is a reaction from fear. Where there is freedom, which is the absence of fear, there is a state which cannot be called bravery. It is a state of intelligence. That intelligence can meet problems without fear, and therefore understand them. When a mind that is afraid is confronted with a problem, whatever action it takes only further confuses the problem.

So, freeing the mind is the action of intelligence. There is no definition of intelligence, and if you merely pursue a definition, you will not be intelligent. But if you begin step by step to find out precisely what you are afraid of and why, then you are bound to discover that there is a division between the observer and the observed. Please follow this a little bit, sirs; I am only putting it differently.

There is the observer who says, "I am afraid," and who is separate from the feeling which he calls fear. If, for example, I am afraid of what the neighbors might say, there is the feeling of fear and the 'me' who is the experiencer, the observer of that feeling. As long as there is this division between the observer and the observed, between the 'me' who is afraid and the feeling of being afraid, there can be no ending of fear. The ending of fear comes about only when you begin to analyze and examine very carefully the whole process of fear, and discover for yourself that the observer is not different from the observed. There is fear because the observer in himself is afraid, so it is not a matter of being free from the fear of a particular thing. Freedom from the fear of something is a reaction and is therefore not freedom. When I am free from anger, that freedom is merely a reaction from anger, and therefore it is not freedom. When I am free from violence, that freedom is again only a reaction from violence. There is a freedom which is not freedom from something, and which is the highest form of

intelligence, but that freedom can come into being only when one goes very deeply into this whole question of fear.

Now, let us look at another problem, which is this: Why do we have ideals? Is it not a waste of time? Do not ideals prevent the perception of what actually is? I know most of you have ideals: the ideal of nobility, the ideal of chastity, the ideal of non-violence, and many more. Why? Do they really help you to get rid of *what is?* I am avaricious, acquisitive, envious, let us say, and I have the ideal of renunciation. Now, why should I have that ideal at all? We say the ideal is necessary because it will act as a lever, as a means of getting rid of avariciousness. But is that so? Surely, the mind can be free of greed, or whatever it is, only when it applies itself to the problem, and not when it is distracted by an ideal. That is why I say the ideal is utter nonsense. Being violent, the mind pursues the ideal of nonviolence, which is a vast mechanism of escape from the actual fact of violence. It is a self-deception. It has no validity at all. What has validity is violence and one's capacity to examine it. To pursue the ideal of nonviolence, all the time struggling within oneself not to be violent, is another form of violence.

So what matters is not the ideal, but the fact and your capacity to face the fact. You cannot face the fact of your anger, your violence, as long as you have an ideal because the ideal is fictitious, fallacious; it has no reality. To understand your violence, you must give your whole attention to it, and you cannot give your whole attention to it if you have an ideal. Idealism is merely one of the habits that we have, and India is drowning in this habit. "He is a noble man; he has ideals and conforms to them"—you know all the nonsense we talk. The simple fact is that we are violent, and it is only when we look at our violence without justification or condemnation that we can go into it. The moment one's mind ceases to justify or condemn violence, it is already free to examine the structure of violence.

Fear expresses itself in different forms. There is not only fear as despair but also fear as hope, and most of us are caught in the chasm between the two. Being in despair, we run to hope; but if we begin to understand the whole process of fear, then there is neither hope nor despair.

Sirs, I do not know if you have ever tried pursuing virtue to its limit and examining it without acceptance or rejection. Try it sometime—try pursuing and looking at virtue without justifying or condemning it, and you will find that you come to a point in the understanding of virtue which is not merely a social convenience or conformity to an idealistic pattern. You will come to a point when the mind is free from the whole idea of virtue, and therefore faces a state of nothingness.

Again, sirs, please listen before you agree or disagree; just listen, and let the words sink into your unconscious.

The mind is at present cluttered with ideas, is it not? The mind is the result of experience; the mind is fearful; it knows hope and despair, greed and the ideal of non-greed. Being the result of time, the mind can function only within the field of time, and within that field there is no change. Change there is merely imitation or reaction, and therefore it is not a revolution.

Now, if the mind can push more and more deeply into itself, you will find that it comes to a point when there is complete nothingness, a total void, which is not the void of despair. Hope and despair are both the outcome of fear, and when you have deeply pursued fear and gone beyond it, you will come to this state of nothingness, a sense of complete void which is not related to despair. It is only in this state that there is a revolution, a radical transformation in the quality of the mind itself.

But this state of nothingness is not an ideal to be pursued. It has nothing to do with the inventions of the mind. The mind cannot comprehend it, for it is much too vast. But what the mind can do is to free itself from all its chattering, from all its pettiness, from all its stupidities, its envy, greed, fear. When the mind is silent, there is the coming into being of this sense of complete nothingness which is the very essence of humility. It is only then that there is a radical transformation in the quality of the mind, and it is only such a mind that is creative.

February 18, 1959

Fifth Talk in New Delhi

This evening I would like to talk about what is confusion and what is clarity. But before we go into that, I think we ought to understand for ourselves what is the intention of these talks. It would be a great pity if we listened merely to find answers to our problems. As I have often pointed out, and I hope you will not mind if I say it again, there is only the problem, there is no answer; for in the understanding of the problem lies its dissolution.

So I think it would be wise to listen, not in order to find an answer or to receive instructions, but to discover for oneself, in the very process of listening, the truth about confusion and clarity.

Most of us are satisfied with descriptions, with answers, with explanations, and we think we have found a solution to our problems. That is why we are so eager to repeat, to quote, to explain, to formulate. But all those things, to me, are barriers to comprehension. A man who quotes is obviously incapable of clear thinking. He relies on authority for his thought. But even though there is in the world every form of authority seeking to drive man in a particular direction, there are more and more individuals who are aware of the problem, and who have not only discarded authority but are trying to discover for themselves the whole significance of living.

Now, either we give a meaning to life, or we are living. The man who gives a meaning to life, who seeks what he calls the goal of life, is obviously not living. He wants to find something of greater significance than the very fact of existing and living, so he creates a utopia, a speculative formulation of what life should be, and according to that formula he guides his life.

That is exactly what I don't propose to do. We have innumerable problems, some of them quite suffocating, and they are there to be understood, not from any particular point of view, but as part of the total process of living. There are people who perceive the problems of life and who want to resolve them according to certain beliefs and dogmas, either religious or politico-economic; they look at the discords and horrors of man's existence only from that narrow point of view, and they think that through some form of belief or legislation they can bring about a transformation in the world. And there are scientists who are only concerned with the exploration of matter and going upward into the sky. All these people are approaching the problems of existence from a particular point of view, are they not? They are all breaking up into segments the process of living. But living, surely, is a total process; it is not a matter of departmental behavior. At present the individual is one thing in the government and something else in his private life; he is an economist or a communist or a businessman, and that has nothing to do with his hunger for reality, his longing to find out the truth of death, of

meditation, of all the extraordinary things that comprise life.

So I think it would be a very great pity if you as an individual were to listen to all this with a fragmented mind, with a partial or specialized mind. Life is not fragmentary, and it must be approached totally, fully, and as deeply as possible.

What is important, it seems to me, is to understand this vast ocean of life with its immeasurable loveliness and reality, its shallowness and great depths, its joy, its misery, its strife and pain. The struggle to earn a livelihood, the sense of despair, of utter hopelessness, the mistakes and accidents, the deep delving into oneself through meditation and discovering that reality which is beyond time—all this is life, and to see the full significance of it, the mind must be very clear. There must be no shadow of confusion. The mind must be capable of exploring every untrodden region of its own being without accumulating what is discovered because the mind that accumulates obviously cannot go very far. I am not being rhetorical but merely factual. When the mind is burdened with a great deal of experience, how can it experience anything new? It is the mind that is young, fresh, innocent, the mind that is always moving, that has no accumulation of experience, no refuge—it is only such a mind that can understand life as a totality.

To have this extraordinary perception of the immensity, the immeasurableness of life, our minds must be very clear, very precise. And precision of the mind is not a matter of following instructions; it does not come about through discipline or obedience. Precision comes to the mind only when one understands this whole process of confusion in which most of us are living. Most people—from the biggest politician to the poorest clerk who goes on his bicycle every day to repeat some ugly routine of business—are confused, and without understanding what it is that brings about this sorrowful state of confusion, the search for clarity is merely an evasion, an escape.

Very few of us are willing to admit that we are wholly confused. We say, "I am partly confused, but there is another part of me which is very clear, and with this clarity I am going to clear up my partial confusion." Or, if you admit you are totally confused, you say, "I shall go to somebody who will tell me what to do to clear up my confusion." But when you choose a guru or a leader to help you, you are choosing out of your own confusion; therefore, your choice is bound to be equally confused. (Laughter) Don't laugh, sirs, this is actually what is happening in the political world, and also in your so-called religious life with its gurus, beliefs, philosophies, and disciplines; it is happening in all the ways of your existence. Being confused, you turn to someone who promises to clear up your confusion. So dictatorships appear; ruthless systems of exploitation come into being, both political and so-called spiritual.

So first of all, we have to realize that confusion can never be cleared up for us by another, and this is a very difficult thing for most of us to face. The mind does not want to see the fact that there is no one who can help it to be clear. But as long as you are confused, your choice of a leader or a guru is the result of your confusion; and if you are not confused, you will not create the leader, the guru, the hierarchical system of authority.

The simple fact is that the mind is confused. If you really look at your own mind, you will see that you are in a state of confusion politically, religiously, and in every way. You don't know what is the right thing to do, whom to follow, or whether to follow anyone at all. Specialists contradict other specialists. The communists, the capitalists, and the various religious sects are all working against each other. So the mind is con-

fused, and whatever it chooses or decides to do in its confusion is bound to bring about still further confusion, further conflict and misery.

Now, why is there confusion? I am going to inquire into it, and please listen to what is being said without rejecting or accepting it. Just listen as you would listen to anything worthwhile. First see the truth that a mind that chooses out of confusion can only breed further confusion. That is one fact. Another fact is this: that when the mind says it is only partially confused and thinks there is a part of itself which is clear—the higher self, the atma, and all that business—it is still totally confused. The mind that says, "There is a part of me which is not confused," is deceiving itself. If there were any part of you which is very clear, obviously that clarity would wipe away all confusion. Where there is clarity, there is no darkness; there is only clarity. So it is sheer nonsense to think there is part of yourself, a spiritual essence, which is clear, and that only the material world is in a state of confusion. That idea is an invention of the mind which prevents you from looking at the fact. The fact is that there is only confusion, so you must be aware of this fact and not deceive yourself.

What brings about this state of confusion? Essentially, it is the urge to be different from what you are, which is encouraged by educational and other influences that make you think you must have ideals. Where there is an urge to be different, there is an endless process of imitation, which means following the pattern of authority. Please see the truth of this. When you desire to be different from what you are, you begin to follow, you have standards, formulas, ideals, which means there is a contradiction between what you are and what you think you should be. Just observe this contradiction in yourself. Do not accept or deny what I am saying, for that would be very silly—if I may use that word without any derogatory significance. Surely the moment you want to be different from what you are without understanding what you are, you have set in motion the process of self-contradiction; and this very self-contradiction is the way of imitation. If you are lazy, for example, you have the ideal of not being lazy, and you strive to live up to your ideal; and in that very striving you have established the pattern of imitation.

So there is an inward going and an outward going. The outward going you call materialistic, and the inward going you consider to be spiritual. But the man who goes inward in the sense of pursuing an ideal, who struggles to change himself through discipline, and all the rest of it—the mind of such a man becomes a battlefield of contradictory desires, does it not? Psychologically, inwardly he has established the pattern of imitation, of authority, and he struggles to live according to that pattern. So your inward going is really as materialistic as your outward going—materialistic in the sense of being profitable. Outwardly you want more power, a better position, greater prestige, you want more land, more possessions; and inwardly you want to be something other than what you are. So both are a form of self-interest, self-perpetuation.

These are facts; they are not my invention. I am merely exposing the facts. You probably won't like it because you think you are a religious person, and therefore you will discard all this. But if you are capable of examining yourself very clearly, precisely, impartially, you will see that there is this desire to be different, both inwardly and outwardly; hence, there is imitation and the creation of authority and therefore an endless contradiction between *what is* and 'what should be'. This state of self-contradiction is the beginning of confusion.

Now, there is an inward going which is not motivated by the desire to be different,

and therefore it does not create the self-contradiction which breeds confusion. That is the true inward going—seeing the fact as it is without trying to change it. To see the fact that one is lazy, that authority in various forms dominates one's life—to see this fact and not try to alter it, not say, "I must not be lazy; I must be free from authority," is surely of the greatest importance because it does not create the opposite and bring about the confusion of self-contradiction. But simply to perceive the fact is an extraordinarily difficult thing to do because our minds are always comparing, always desiring to change *what is* into something else.

Take authority, for example. When you are aware that you are being compelled, pushed around, when you know that you have to obey, what happens? There is also a movement of the opposite, is there not? That is, you feel that you must be free. So in the very fact of obedience, there is the contradiction of that obedience. This contradiction is inevitable as long as you do not understand the whole process of authority—not why you must keep to the right or the left side of the road, which is obvious, but why there is the authority of the guru, why you treat a particular book with such extraordinary reverence, and all the rest of it. If you really go into it, you will see that the mind wants to be certain, secure; it wants to be led, guided, so that it will have no struggle, no pain, no feeling of aloneness. As long as the mind does not see this fact and merely seeks clarity, inwardly or outwardly, there is bound to be authority; and that authority is the result of your confusion, which is the outcome of self-contradiction.

So one begins to see that every desire has its own equal and opposite response. Do you understand? Am I making myself clear? Surely, desire creates its own opposite. In other words, all desire is self-contradictory. I desire to be good, to be kind, to be affectionate, and at the same time there is the desire to be violent, to be angry, to be jealous, and all the rest of it. The very urge to be something creates the opposite desire, does it not? No?

Sirs, let me put it in a different way. Can you have a desire without its opposite? Surely not. I want to be kind, and yet I am brutal; I want to be nonviolent, and I am full of violence. So desire is contradictory in itself—which does not mean that there must be no desire at all. On the contrary. If you observe yourself as we go along, you will see that something quite different comes into being—not a mind that is desireless.

Confusion arises where there is the urge to be different. That is an important fact to discover for oneself. And it is also important to see the truth that every desire has its own opposite.

Now, seeing the truth of something is an immediate perception; it is not a disputatious, analytical approach in which you finally say, "Yes, I understand." Perception of what is true takes place when the mind is in a state of real inquiry, which means that it is not defending nor is it on the offensive. You can see the truth as the truth, the false as the false, and the truth in the false, only when your mind is very clear and simple, that is, when it is uncluttered with thoughts, with experiences, with its own hopes and fears. To see the truth of something, the mind must be fresh, innocent, which is really a state of self-abnegation.

I was saying that there is confusion when there is self-contradiction, which arises with the desire to be different, and the desire to be different sets going various systems of imitation and authority. You must see the truth of this for yourself—not by my persuasion, for then you don't see it at all, and you will again be persuaded or influenced by somebody else. There is no good influence; all influence is evil, just as all authority is; and

the more absolute the authority, the more absolute the evil. So it is of the utmost importance for you to see the truth of this for yourself—that there is confusion when there is self-contradiction, which is born of the desire to be different, and this desire breeds imitation and authority.

Now, if you see that simple fact, then the question arises, "Must there not be the understanding of what I am?" And the understanding of what you are is the real inward-going; it is not a reaction to or the rejection of outward-going. But you do not know what you are. You think you are the atma, the higher self, this or that; whereas, you are actually the result of innumerable influences, of tradition, of various environmental pressures, and so on. The fact is that you are conditioned by the culture in which you were born. Just as a communist is conditioned not to believe in God at all, to say it is sheer nonsense, so you are brought up and conditioned as a Hindu, and you believe accordingly.

To find out what you are requires the comprehension from moment to moment, not only of the outward influences which have molded your life, but also of the subtle influences and urges of the unconscious, of which you are generally unaware. What you are is not static; it is moving, changing all the time. It is never a permanent state, and in the perception of that impermanency there is no contradiction. I do not know if you see the truth of this. What you are is never fixed, permanent. You would like it to be permanent, you would like to be able to say, "I am the ultimate spiritual self, which is permanent," because in that "permanent" state you think you will have found happiness, security, God, and all the rest of the business. Whereas, to see what you are at each moment and to pursue what you see to its fullest depth and width is the true inward-going, and this true inward-going will never create self-contradiction and confusion because there is complete abandonment at each moment of what has been observed, experienced, learned. It is the mind that has assumed a position, that has experienced and says, "I know," that wants to be different—it is only such a mind that creates self-contradiction and therefore confusion.

You are obviously the result of influence. Your mind is being influenced all the time by the newspapers, by the radio, by speeches, by your wife or husband, by society, by traditions, dogmas, beliefs. You are influenced by what you eat, by what you wear, by the climate you live in, by the daily routine you follow, and so on. But to know all this, to be aware of these innumerable influences from moment to moment without acceptance or rejection is to begin to be free of them because, obviously, a mind that is very alert is not easily influenced. It is the mind that is unaware of itself, that is crippled by tradition, held in the bondage of time—it is only such a mind that is always being influenced.

To see at every moment what actually is requires a perception, an alertness, an awareness in which there is no accumulation because *what is* is constantly changing. Today you are not what you were yesterday; what you were yesterday has been modified by a series of events in time. Thought moves from point to point in time; it is never absolute, never fixed, never the same. *What is* is never static. Therefore you don't have to introduce the idea that you must be different. The very perception of the fact of *what is* is sufficient; it brings about its own movement of change, which is the transformation of *what is*.

So a mind that is confused, yet seeks to become clear, creates a contradiction in itself and thereby increases its own confusion; and whether it goes outward or inward, a confused mind builds up systems, disciplines, contradictions, compulsions, which only breed further misery. The man who goes outward you call materialistic, and the man who turns inward you call spiritual; but they are both self-contradictory. Whereas, there is a true inward-going which is not a reaction, not the opposite of outward-going. It is the simple perception of *what is*, and this is very important to understand.

Sirs, what happens when a mind that is lazy becomes aware of its own laziness? It immediately says, "I must discipline myself not to be lazy. I must get up early every morning. I must do this; I must not do that." Now, laziness is an indication of a disciplined mind. The mind that disciplines itself is lazy. (Laughter) Sirs, don't laugh it off; just see the truth of it. Becoming aware that I am lazy, I force myself to get up early every morning, to take exercise, to sit quietly in so-called meditation, and all the rest of it. Now, what has happened? I have merely set going another habit of thoughtlessness. Thoughtlessness is the very essence of a lazy mind. When you see that you are lazy and force yourself not to be lazy, that very forcing breeds contradiction and further confusion. The fact is that you are lazy. Look at that fact, go into it, uncover all the factors that are making you lazy. Don't try to change the fact, but watch laziness in operation, be aware of it from moment to moment. Then you don't have to discipline yourself. The mind is alert every minute to see when it is lazy, and such a mind is not a confused mind.

So there is confusion only when there is an outward-going or an inward-going which becomes a contradiction. Perception is neither inward-going nor outward-going; it is seeing things as they are at every moment without prejudice, without color, without evaluation. Only then is there clarity. Such a mind has no untrodden regions, either on the surface or inwardly, because it is so alert, so watchful, so aware that its every movement is perceived, examined, and understood.

All that I am saying is that a clear mind is a perceptive mind. The more there is true perception, in the sense of self-knowledge, the deeper that perception penetrates within—but not in terms of time. When there is self-knowledge, which is a perceiving of the continuous movement of *what is,* not only at the conscious level but deep down in the unconscious, then you will find that there comes a state which is not measurable by the mind. The mind is then extraordinarily clear; it has clarity without a shadow, and only such a mind is capable of receiving what is true.

February 22, 1959

Sixth Talk in New Delhi

May I suggest that we talk over together this evening the question of what is self-knowledge. It is a rather complex problem, and like many other problems of life, it has no final answer. Most of us easily accept the explanations of self-knowledge which we hear from another or read in psychological or religious books, and it would be a great pity if we merely remained at that level. Instead, let us this evening see if we can penetrate into the depths of our own consciousness, which is to experience directly the total process of our own thinking and feeling, the totality of our hopes and our fears.

Before we go further, I think it is important for you to be aware of how you are listening to what is being said. I shall try to go into this whole question of self-knowledge, but if you merely listened to the explanations and were satisfied with words—that, it seems to me, would be a most fruitless thing to do. It would be like a hungry man listening to a lot of words and explanations about the harvest or the preparation of food, hoping that his hunger would thereby be satisfied. Actually, most of us are in that position. We are

not hungry in the deep sense of the word; we are not really eager to understand the whole process of the mind, the totality of our own thoughts and feelings. That is why we are so easily satisfied by explanations and approach our many problems at the explanatory level; and I think that both the man who merely explains and the person who is satisfied with explanations are living very superficially.

Do explanations ever resolve any vital problem? I may explain to you the falseness of nationalism—its corrupting, destructive, and deteriorating effect—but though you may see the validity of such an explanation, it obviously does not free you from nationalism. The fact is that you enjoy the feeling of being nationalistic; you like belonging to a particular group—it is profitable to you both emotionally and economically. So explanations never bring about understanding, they never really solve any vital problem. A dentist may tell you that taking too much sugar is very bad for your teeth, and he may even show you a great deal of evidence in support of his statement, but you like sugar, and you go on taking it in large quantities. So explanation is one thing, and direct action is quite another. Either you are merely following the words, the explanations, or in the very process of listening, you are directly experiencing what is being described—which has much more significance, far greater validity, greater vitality than being satisfied with words.

So let us be very clear about where explanations end and real perception or experiencing begins. You can go only so far with explanations, and the rest of the journey you must take by yourself. Most of us are not willing to take that journey because we are lazy and easily satisfied with the obvious, which is always the explanation. But the vitality of direct action, experience, lies beyond the explanation, however obvious or subtle it may be.

That is why it is very important to experience directly the things that we are talking about and not merely stop at the verbal level. I think it would be really fascinating if we could go into this whole problem of self-knowledge and find out what is the real basis of our thinking, the basis of all our actions, of our very being. If one can inquire into this step by step, in minute detail, and directly experience it, then I think one will go very far. After all, to go far one must begin near, and the near is the 'me', the self, this whole process of the mind. You may be a scientist or an engineer and master the technology of space travel, but the real journey is inward, and that is much more difficult, much deeper and more significant than mechanically going to the moon. The immeasurable is still within oneself.

So it is very important to comprehend where the verbal or intellectual explanation ends, and direct perception or experiencing begins. Explanations can never lead to reality. However satisfactory the explanation may be, it cannot give you the understanding that is born of direct perception, direct experience.

If you realize this very clearly, then you will never be satisfied with explanations, you will never quote, you will never turn to the authority of the Gita or the Bible. You may read as a mere intellectual amusement, but direct experience is worth infinitely more than what is taught in the books. A living dog is better than a dead lion. All the heroes in the books are dead lions, and their authority is disastrous. What you directly experience and know for yourself is far more valid than the explanations of all the various authorities, whether ancient or modern.

With that in mind, let us inquire into the process of self-knowledge. Like a signpost, I am merely pointing the direction. The signpost is not important at all. What is important is the man who is journeying. The speaker is not a guru, he is not an authority, he is not a guide. One has to take the inward journey alone—not as a reaction away from outward things, but as the inevitable process of trying to understand. The outer must lead to the inner, that is, to an understanding of the whole process of existence, in which there is no division as the outer and the inner.

To understand the whole process of existence, outwardly as well as inwardly you must comprehend the ways of your own thinking; you must find out why you think what you think, which is to see the source of your thought. Without the discovery of that source, you have no real basis for inquiry, for action. Your action now is based on habit, on routine, on discipline, on your particular conditioning. There is an action which is entirely different from the habitual action of routine, of discipline, of conditioning; but such action comes only through self-knowledge, and that is why it is so necessary to understand oneself.

Now, what do we mean by knowledge? When we say, "I know," what does it mean? I know you because I have been introduced to you. Having once met you, a picture of you remains in my mind, and when we meet again I recognize you. So knowing is a process of recognition, and we recognize through the background of past experience, which means that knowing is cumulative, additive; knowledge can be added to. And when we say, "I must know myself," we think the self is something stationary, static, fixed, and therefore recognizable. Or we have been told what the self is and have come to certain conclusions about it, and from that background we begin to recognize the self. So knowing is always a process of recognition, without which there is no knowledge. Knowledge is additive through recognition. This may seem complex, but it is actually very simple.

Knowing is one thing, and understanding is another. Knowing implies accumulation; it is a process of recognition through past experience. Each new experience is conditioned by and adds to previous knowledge. So knowing is additive, whereas understanding never is. When you say, "I know you," you know me only from the background of a previous, static experience. You know me by my features, by my name, by what I have said to you, or by what others have said to you about me, and so on. All that knowledge is of yesterday. Since then I have undergone many experiences, many varieties of influence, and I may have changed tremendously. But you retain the memory of yesterday, and from that background you judge me today. So you say, "I know you," when in fact you do not know me at all, but you find it very convenient to say, "I know you," and move on.

Perhaps I am not making myself clear. Unless you understand this one simple thing, it is going to be very difficult for you to see the significance of this whole movement of self-knowledge.

When the mind says, "I know," all that it knows is what has happened yesterday or at some other time in the past. With that knowledge it approaches the present, but the present is changing from moment to moment. So the mind can never say, "I know," and this is very important, psychologically, to understand. The man who says, "I know," does not know. You can never say, "I have found truth," because truth is moving, living, dynamic; it is never still, never static, never the same; and that is the beauty, the splendor of truth.

To understand this thing called the 'me', the self, you must come to it without saying, "I know," without accepting any authority. All authority is dead, and it does not bring about this creative search. Authority can guide you, shape you, tell you what to do

and what not to do, but all that is still within the field of knowing; and burdened with the known you cannot follow that which is living, vital, moving. So the mind that sees the truth of this and wishes to inquire into itself will never say, "I know"; therefore, being in a state of constant movement, it is able to observe that which is also never the same. This is the beginning of self-knowledge. I do not know if I am making myself clear.

Look, sirs, the self as we know it is a limited thing, but it is also living, moving, and a mind that is conditioned, bound by tradition, a mind that says, "There is a higher self and a lower self," and all the rest of it—such a mind cannot possibly understand the self. I am not using the word *self* in any significant spiritual sense; I mean by that word the self which functions daily, which thinks, feels, invents, hopes, wants, and is caught in conflict, the self which is biased, which speculates, judges, seeks.

Is all this too difficult? I hope not. If it is, you can skip it, and perhaps I can put it differently.

We know the self as the 'me' which has property, which has qualities, which has certain relationships, which is conditioned by a particular culture, by the many environmental influences, by the books it reads, the philosophies it studies, the techniques it learns. The mind which is jealous, which knows love and hate, hope and fear—all that is the self. The self is not only at the superficial level, it is not only the conscious mind functioning in our daily activities, but it is also the unconscious mind, which functions at a much deeper level. The totality of that consciousness is the self.

Now, from that center, which is the self, all our thinking begins. Where there is a center, there is also a circumference, a frontier. The center is the conscious as well as the unconscious thinker who knows, and the frontier is that which he seeks and which is also within the field of the known. So there is the thinker and the thought, the experiencer and the experienced, the observer and the observed. Don't accept or deny this; rather follow it, not just verbally, but through the explanation actually see how your own mind is working.

I want to know myself. Why? Because without knowing myself, I have no ground upon which to build anything. I do not know whether my thoughts are valid, whether I am living in illusion, whether I am deceiving myself; I do not know why I struggle, why I have certain habits, and so on. Without knowing myself I am incapable of seeing clearly. So I must know myself, which means that I must understand my own mind. I must be aware of every reaction, of every thought, without any sense of condemnation or justification. I must be in a state of inquiry, which means looking at every thought, every feeling without prejudice, without the background of previous experience which says, "This is good, that is bad; this I must keep, that I must discard."

All this is obvious, is it not? If I want to understand my son, I have to be aware of him as he is, study him without condemnation or comparison; I have to observe him when he is playing, when he is crying, when he is overeating, and so on. In the same way, if I want to understand myself, I must watch myself, without judgment, in the mirror of relationship; I must be aware of what I say to you and how you react to me; I must observe how I talk to my servant, how I talk to my wife or husband, how I treat the busman and the coolie; I must know what I feel, what I think, and why. I must see the whole process of my thinking and feeling. This does not demand discipline at all. When you discipline yourself to observe, the discipline prevents you from observing because discipline then becomes your habit. Where there is a real concern to find out, there is a constant obser-

vation which does not require the habit of discipline.

So this is the first thing to realize—that it is absolutely essential to know yourself; otherwise, you have no basis for thought at all. You may be very erudite and have a big position, but that is all nonsense as long as you do not know yourself, because you will be walking in darkness.

To understand yourself there must be an awareness, a watchfulness, a state of observation in which there is not a trace of condemnation or justification, and to be in that state of observation without judging is an extraordinarily arduous task because the weight of tradition is against you; your mind has been trained for centuries to judge, to condemn, to justify, to evaluate, to accept or deny. Don't say, "How am I to get rid of this conditioning?" but see the truth that if you want to understand yourself, which is obviously of the highest importance, you must observe the operation of your own mind without any condemnation or comparison.

Now, why do you compare, why do you condemn? Isn't that one of the easiest things to do—to condemn? If you are a capitalist, you condemn the communist, just as the communist condemns the capitalist. If you are a devout Christian, you obviously condemn Hinduism, or Islam, because it is the easy thing to do—to condemn and get on with it. Condemnation is really a reaction, and it is one of the indications of a lazy mind.

The same is true of comparison, is it not? Can a mind that compares ever understand? Sirs, don't agree or disagree, but watch yourself. When you compare your younger son with his older brother, do you understand the younger boy? And in the classroom, in so-called education, is not the sensitive child destroyed by comparing him with those who are older or more clever? Surely, comparison is also one of the indications of a slack mind, a thoughtless mind, a mind that is inherently lazy; and such a mind can never understand.

The next question is: What is thinking? Surely, what we call thinking is a reaction of memory, of one's conditioning. If I ask you a question with which you are familiar, your response is immediate because the mechanism of memory operates instantly. There is no gap between the question and the answer. If I ask you a much more complex question, then between the question and the response there is a gap, a lapse of time during which the mind is looking in the storehouse of memory, going over all the things it has learned to find an answer. Surely, that is what we call thinking—the response of memory.

Now, memory is always conditioned, is it not? You are conditioned as a Hindu, a Muslim, a communist, a capitalist, or whatever it is, and when I ask you a certain question, you reply according to your conditioning. If you are a devout Hindu and I ask, "Do you believe in God?" you will say yes because for centuries you have been educated, conditioned to believe. And if the same question is put to someone who has been conditioned not to believe in God, he will say, "What nonsense are you talking?" So all our thinking, from the most superficial to the most complex, is a response of memory according to its conditioning.

The mind that says, "I am going to inquire into myself," is already conditioned; it is conditioned as a Hindu, a Buddhist, a Christian, this or that. It is only in understanding this conditioning that the conditioning can be broken down. And obviously it must be broken down. It is absurd to be a Hindu, or a Christian, or a communist, or a socialist. We are human beings, and to solve the problems of life, we must approach them as human beings, not as members of these conflicting groups. No system, no belief or ideology is going to solve our human problems. Starvation is a human problem,

and we must tackle it together, not divided as capitalists and communists. Systems are no good at all in solving the basic problems of life; they only further condition our minds, which are already conditioned by tradition, by environmental influences, and so on.

Now, how is the conditioned mind to resolve its conditioning? Do you understand the question? You are conditioned as a Hindu, let us say, and you are totally unaware of that conditioning because you live in a society where practically everybody is Hindu and you have accepted it, so you never question it at all. But now someone is telling you that your mind is conditioned, and you have begun to see that it is true, so you say, "How am I to be free from this conditioning?"

Sirs, freedom from a particular conditioning is still a conditioned state, is it not? Please follow this. To be free from something is a reaction; therefore, it is not freedom at all. I will show you what I mean. Merely to free myself from nationalism is a reaction because I want to be something else. My conditioning gives me pain, sorrow, and I say I must be free from it in order to be happy, that is, in order to be something else. In other words, I free myself from something in order to be in a more gratifying state, which is obviously a reaction; therefore, it is not freedom. Freedom is not born of reaction; it is a state of mind in which there is no desire to be or not to be something.

If you see the truth of that, then the next question is: What does it mean to be free of conditioning? It means, surely, not freedom from something, or freedom to be something, but seeing the fact as it is. Let us say I am conditioned as a Hindu. I do not want to be free from my conditioning; I want to see it. And the moment I see it as it is, there is freedom, not as a reaction. I do not know if I am making myself clear on this point. I don't want to take examples because examples can be refuted by other examples. But what is important is to think of it negatively, because negative thinking is direct thinking.

You see, there is positive thinking and negative thinking. Positive thinking is deciding what to do, how to break down one's conditioning by practicing a system, a method, a discipline. In practicing a method or a discipline in order to be free of conditioning, one has merely introduced a further conditioning, a new habit. That is positive thinking. Whereas negative thinking is to look at the fact of one's conditioning, and see the truth that no system or discipline can bring freedom from conditioning.

Sirs, many of you practice nonviolence, you worship the ideal of nonviolence, you everlastingly preach nonviolence. That is the positive approach, which you know very well. But the truth is that you are violent, and the negative approach is simply to perceive that truth. To perceive the truth that you are violent is enough in itself. You don't have to do anything. The moment you act upon violence, you have introduced the fictitious ideal of nonviolence.

I don't know if you see this. Let us say I am greedy. That is a fact, and I know it. I don't want to change greed into nongreed; to me that has no meaning because I see that becoming nongreedy still has the qualities of greed. All becoming is obviously a form of greed. The mind is aware of the fact that it is greedy, and it also perceives that any move on its part to change greed is still within the field of greed. This very perception of *what is* is the resolution of it.

So the inquiry into the self must begin with a negative approach because you don't know what the self is. You may think you know the self as a greedy man, as this or that, but the self is being influenced, it is undergoing constant change, and to understand it you must approach it, not positively, but negatively, obliquely.

Most minds are conditioned, and the breaking down of that conditioning does not come about through any resolution or determination, through any practice of discipline. It comes about only when there is a negative approach to one's conditioning. The mere perception of *what is* is enough in itself. Follow this and you will see why. When you understand the negative approach, which is to see the truth of it, its uselessness, its fictitious nature, then your mind, which is greedy, is no longer caught in the fictitious process of trying to become nongreedy. Therefore it is free to look at *what is,* which is greed; and because the mind is free to look at greed, it is capable of dissolving greed. Try this the next time you are angry or violent. Don't condemn it, don't say it is right or wrong, but look at it. Just to look at the feeling, without naming it, without condemning or justifying it, is an extraordinary thing. The very word *anger* is condemnatory, and when you look at the feeling without naming it, the verbal association with that feeling through the word *anger* ceases.

Go along with this, sirs; don't accept or reject what is being said, but just follow it whether you understand it or not.

To understand the whole process of the self, there must be a negative approach because the conscious mind can never go consciously into the deep unconscious. You may be a great technician outwardly, on the conscious level, but inwardly, in the deep layers of the unconscious, there is the everlasting pull of the racial, instinctual, traditional responses; there all your ambitions, your frustrations, your hidden motives and fears are rampant, and you have to understand all that. To understand it, you must approach it negatively. The positive approach is always within the field of the known. But the negative approach frees the mind from the known, and therefore the mind can look at the problem anew, afresh, in a state of innocency.

Then you will discover that the self is not only the seeker but also the process of seeking, as well as that which is sought. The seeker is seeking peace of mind, and he practices a method by which to find what he seeks. The seeker, the seeking, and the sought are all one and the same thing. When the seeker seeks what he wants, which is peace of mind, it is still within the field of the known. His seeking is a reaction from the conflicts of life, so the peace he is everlastingly pursuing is a projection of the known. Whereas, if the mind, seeing for itself the fictitiousness of that pursuit, is not concerned with peace at all but with understanding its own conflicts, and therefore approaches them negatively, then there is the beginning of self-knowledge.

The understanding of oneself is a constant, timeless process. There is no end to self-knowledge. The moment you see the truth that the understanding of oneself is limitless, your mind is already freed from the known and therefore able to penetrate into the unknown. A mind that is tethered to the known can never move into the unknown. All your Gods, your Bibles, your Gitas, your Marxist books will not lead you very far. To go far you must begin near, which is to see that a mind hedged about, bound by the known, cannot proceed into the unknown.

The unknown is the total negation of the known; it is not a reaction from the known. So there must be an end to the game of the seeker and the sought. In other words, there must be an end to all seeking. Then only is there something new. All profound discoveries are made in this state, not when the mind is pursuing a projection of the known. It is when the mind ceases completely to move in the field of the known, when it does not project the known into the unknown—it is only then that there is the coming into being of an extraordinary state of creative newness which has nothing to do with the

known. That is truth, that is reality, that is God, or whatever name you care to give it. But the name is not the thing.

So one must begin near, which is to empty the mind of all the things it has known—inwardly, psychologically, not factually. You cannot forget where you live, that would be amnesia. But you have to wipe away, in the psychological sense, all that you have known as a man of experience, as a man of knowledge, as a man who has read, read, read, and who is controlled by what is known—all that must come to an end. What is known has always a center, and therefore always a circumference, a recognizable frontier. The frontier ceases only when the center ceases. Then the mind is unlimited, not measurable by man.

February 25, 1959

Seventh Talk in New Delhi

This evening I think it would be worthwhile to talk over the very complex and intricate problem of time and life, and to see in what way they are related to each other. To do this one needs a very precise and penetrating mind, a mind that is not caught up in conclusions, in speculative theories, and is therefore capable of listening, which is really experiencing. But most of us have theories about time, about love, about death; we are full of speculative ideas and are satisfied to remain on the verbal or speculative level. We are like a man who is always ploughing and never sowing. And it seems to me that if one would experience, one must have the capacity to listen with one's whole being, as one does when one is really interested in something. Then, perhaps, listening is experiencing.

Now, to experience something directly, one must have a mind that is tentative, hesitant, that does not start from a conclusion or take a stand. Surely, to unravel a problem like death or time or love, it is essential to approach it with a sense of humility, with great hesitation, with a certain tenderness—if one can use that word without sentimentality. It is only then, I think, that we shall be able to experience the truth or the falseness of what is going to be said. One must perceive the false as well as the true; otherwise, there is merely acceptance or denial. If one is capable of perceiving what is true and what is false, then experience has an extraordinary significance. It is an immediate response to challenge; there is no question of saying, "I will think about it, I will go home and meditate upon it," which actually prevents the immediate response. Without perception there is no immediate response, and perception is really quite simple. One perceives, and that is all. There is no argumentation, no speculation, no system of thought. Either one sees or one does not see; one comprehends or one does not comprehend. He who does not comprehend will never come to comprehension by thinking about it, by seeking explanations. To seek explanations is to remain at the verbal, explanatory level. A man who actually experiences something does not seek an explanation. His own perception awakens the explanation.

And so, when we are discussing, talking over together any serious problem, it seems to me that one must have the intelligence, the tenderness to perceive what is false and what is true. Such perception is very difficult for most of us because our minds are stuffed with so many ideas, cluttered up with so many conclusions, traditions, beliefs, and they are whirlpools of self-contradiction. But I think it is possible to discover for oneself what is false and what is true if one is aware of one's own conditioning and says, "I know I'm conditioned, and I'm not going to let the influences of that background interfere with my perception." Perception comes when

there is humility, a sense of hesitancy, of tenderness, not when there is dogmatic assertion or denial, or mere acceptance.

We are going to talk over together, as two individuals who are really concerned, the problem of death, of time, and that extraordinary thing called love. To really comprehend these things, we must feel our way into them as into an unknown realm, a region where the mind has never trodden, and this requires a delicate touch, a sensitive approach. That sensitivity is denied when you have an attitude of assertion or denial, which is obviously immature, the reaction of a thoughtless mind. So whether you are young or old, whether you are a technician with a good job or a coolie or a mother with many children, I would suggest that you approach these questions, which concern us all, without seeking an answer; for, as I said, there is no answer, and if you expect an answer at the end of the talk, you will be disappointed. But what you and I can do, as two individuals, is to explore the problem. It is much more important to explore than to discover. What matters is to keep on looking, examining, perceiving, without saying, "I have found." The man who has found, has really not found; the man who says he knows, never knows. So it is with an attitude of learning, of feeling it out together, that you and I as two human beings are going to look into the problem.

I do not know if you have ever thought about death or time or that state which we call love. But before we begin to inquire into what is death, we must first know what life is—not life at any particular level, not the life of a scientist or a parliamentarian or a housewife or a businessman. These are all included in examining what life is in our own daily existence. Without knowing what our living actually is, we can never find out what is the significance of life. So let us very carefully, advisedly, look into what we call living.

What is our living? What is the life we live from moment to moment, from day to day, from year to year? It is a constant strife, is it not? We ceaselessly struggle to adjust ourselves to society, to our neighbor, to our wife or husband, to the government, to the culture in which we live. There is an endless battle between ourselves and the environment, a constant turmoil of embitterment, routine, drudgery, and boredom. We are forced to do things which we cordially dislike, so there is a contradiction, a series of conflicts and associations which strengthen memory. From this memory we act, we function. Most of us are not real human beings but mere functionaries, and we have no time to think about these things so we say, "I will think about serious things when I retire."

The politician who goes in for government is not concerned with man; he is concerned with policies, systems, status. The writer is concerned with verbal expression, with competing, struggling to get ahead and make a name for himself—and therein lies the seed of his frustration. The man who hasn't arrived wants to arrive, the man who has little longs for more—these and many other conflicts make up the life we know from day to day. There is a passing joy, a love that soon withers, a sensation that becomes routine, a sense of utter boredom; our life is narrow, petty, shallow, and memory as experience overshadows it all. These are obvious facts of our daily existence, and at the end of it there is the inevitable: death. Death is the ending of everything that we have known, everything that we have experienced, and we are frightened of that ending. Fear is related to time in the sense that the mind foresees the ending of all that it has known, and therefore projects the known into the future from the background of the past. Death is the unknown, and facing the unknown, the mind seeks the continuity of all that it has known.

So our life is a series of events with their causes and effects in the field of time. That is, I lived, yesterday, with all its pleasures, passing joys, conflicts, sorrows, struggles, and with that burden of yesterday I live today, which obviously colors the mind of today, and this in turn shapes and distorts the mind of tomorrow. We know only this continuity, do we not? I know I lived yesterday; I know that today I am responding inadequately to certain challenges, and therefore suffer; and I know that tomorrow—if nothing happens, if there is no accident, if the sky does not fall on me—I shall carry on in the same pattern: going to the office, continuing with my struggles, my likes and dislikes, having the little pleasures of sex, going to the temple, and so on. Our life is a constant movement in the field of time, which is called continuity. That is all we know.

Have you been observing your own life, your own mind, and not merely listening to my description? If while listening you are watching your own mind, you will see that what is being said is true. You cannot refute, deny, or accept it. It is simply a fact. A little pain, a little pleasure, the vanity of achievement, abiding sorrows, deep frustrations, ambitions that can never be fulfilled, envy, jealousy, the fear of emptiness, loneliness, the fear of destruction—this is our life, the only life we know. We live and function within the field of the known.

Memory is the known. If you had no memory of yesterday and no memory of today, then obviously there would be no memory tomorrow. But the mind is not capable of freeing itself from memory because it is itself the result of memory, and its functioning is within the field of time. So memory—the memory of every experience, of every thought, of every reaction—is a state of continuity, and that is what you are. If you say you are the atma, the permanent soul, or the higher self, it is still within the field of the known because you are merely repeating what you have been taught. You have read about the atma and you like the idea—it satisfies you, it gives you a certain comfort because life is transient and you hope there will be something permanent.

That is why the mind creates the concept of a permanent God, a permanent spiritual essence, a permanent state of peace. But all this is still within the field of the known. It is the reaction of the known to the unknown—death. The mind that has continuity is in perpetual fear of death because death is an ending, the ending of the physical. So the mind says, "I have worked, I have suffered, I have experienced, and there must be a future for all that I have gathered; there must be some form of continuity." If my son dies, I say, "He must live still, and I must meet him again." I want to meet him exactly as I knew him, never perceiving that life is a movement, a constant change. My only concern is to perpetuate that which I have known. All knowledge is based on the known. There is no knowledge of the unknown, however much you may speculatively translate the unknown in terms of the known.

The mind is a mechanism which by its very nature produces through memory the sense of its own continuity. This continuous mind knows there is an ending, so it believes in reincarnation or clings to some other belief that offers hope of self-perpetuation. This is what we do; this is a fact in our everyday experience, is it not?

Now, why are we so frightened of the coming to an end of all the things we have known? What is it that we have known? What do you know except your struggles, your miseries, your little pleasures and vanities, the appalling pettiness of your own thinking—"my wife, my house, my children, my possessions"—the turmoil and travail of your daily existence? That is all most of us know, and we are frightened to let it go. So

time plays an enormous role in our life—not only chronological time as yesterday, today, and tomorrow, but also time in the psychological sense of fulfilling oneself, arriving, becoming something. Tomorrow has great significance for us because tomorrow is the ideal—tomorrow I shall be nonviolent, tomorrow I shall have a sense of love, humility, tomorrow I shall achieve greatness, tomorrow I shall reach God, tomorrow I shall find out what is true and know how to live. We are always becoming something within the field of time. The verb *to become* has assumed extraordinary importance. If this verb is wiped away from the mind, there is then only a sense of being, which is timeless. But you cannot experience that state unless you feel out, perceive for yourself the significance of becoming. A man who is becoming is not living, and therefore he is in constant fear of death. The man who is living is free of becoming, and for him there is no death.

So time is the measure of the mind, and such a mind can function only within its own measure; it cannot function beyond its own measure, which is the measure of man. Within the field of time there is always fear—fear of death, fear of ending, fear of the future, the unknown. I do not know what is going to happen tomorrow—I may fail, I may lose my job, my son may die. I am well today, but tomorrow I may be ill. The very thought of tomorrow is the awakening of fear. I have known illness, I have suffered, and with that memory I live today in fear of tomorrow. So the beginning of fear is the knowledge of time, which is after all the state of a mind that has continuity.

Cause and effect are a continuous process within the field of time. A cause is never static, nor is the effect. What was an effect becomes the cause of still another effect. Follow all this, sirs; see it in your own life. The cause becomes an effect, and the effect becomes a cause. There is no fixed cause with a fixed effect, except perhaps in the case of seeds. An acorn can never become a mango; it will always become an oak. Cause and effect are fixed. But the mind is not fixed; it is not static, and that is the beauty of the mind. In the interval between cause and effect there are various influences at work, subtle pressures and trends which change the effect, and that effect undergoes further changes; it is again shaped and modified in the process of becoming the cause of still another effect. With the mind there is no fixed causation which produces a fixed result.

So one discovers that the mind can change abruptly the moment it perceives the falseness of continuity, in which there is always the fear of death. When the mind is earnestly seeking to understand the whole problem of death, time, and love and is therefore fully aware of the innumerable causes and effects which are pushing it in various directions, it can change suddenly—tomorrow it can be totally new, completely transformed. This is true revolution—not the economic or social revolution, but the revolution of the mind that perceives death and time as a continuous process in which there is no resurrection, no renewal. What is continuous cannot be renewed. It is only the mind that has come to an end abruptly, not speculatively, not through discipline or any form of self-hypnosis, but through seeing precisely *what is*—it is only such a mind that can go beyond the clutches of death.

Sirs, have you ever tried to die to your pleasures and to your sorrows? As a withered leaf falls off a tree and is blown away by the wind, have you ever let your pleasures, your sorrows, your anxieties just drop away and die? Have you ever tried it? Most of us have not because we want to carry that burden to the end of our life, and beyond. We hate somebody, and we want to keep on hating him; we say he has done us an injustice, or

we offer some other explanation and carry on as before. Or having had a marvelous experience of great delight, great loveliness, we want to live in the memory of it. We also want to live in the state of ambition, which is really the state of envy. After all, ambition is envy. A man who is not envious is not ambitious.

But our society is based on envy, on jealousy; it has sanctified the words *ambition* and *competition*. And is it possible to die to all that? Try dying to your vanity, and you will find it a most extraordinary experience. Don't ask what will happen. Just try it. When death comes, it wipes your mind away. There is no hope; it is a finality, an absolute ending. In the same way, one can die to vanity without explanations, without a motive, without a cause. Try it and you will discover the extraordinary state of a mind that has left everything behind, that has unburdened itself of all the things it has known. If you can die in this way to the continuity of time as memory, then you will be able to meet that extraordinary thing called death, not at the end of your life, not through old age, not through some disease or accident, but while you are living, vitally alert, fully conscious of your whole being. When you have died to your vanity, to your ambition, to your petty demands, then you will discover what death is. And you will find that death is not a thing about which you can hold beliefs or speculate; it is totally the unknown.

But for most of us the unknown is a fearful thing because we cling to the known. The known is the factor which holds us. I know you and you know me. If I am your wife, you know me, you have lived with me, you have had pleasure from me; you think in terms of "my house, my wife, my job," all of which is the known, within the field of time. And can you die to all that? If you cannot die to it, what happens to your mind? What happens to the mind which knows continuity? Do you understand the question? If I cannot die psychologically to my house, to my properties, to my wife, to my children, if I cannot free my mind completely from everything I have known, what happens? Obviously one cannot forget the facts of everyday life, the way to one's house, the techniques one has learned, and so on. But cannot the mind die to the psychological implications of vanity, of power, of position, of prestige, to all the things that it has inwardly held most dear and which are also part of memory?

Sirs, if you cannot die to all the past and breathe the fragrance of the new, then obviously your mind has become respectable, which is what most of us are. We are respectable in a society which is based on envy, with its false moralities, its imitated virtues, its empty talk of nonviolence and peace. A respectable mind is an imitative mind, and what happens to such a mind? Is it a mind at all, or merely a repetitive recording machine? Do think about it, sirs, give your attention to what is being said. Such a mind obviously continues as a recording machine which is essentially not different from the millions of Indians, Chinese, Russians, Americans, or what you will that make up the society to which it belongs. It is this petty, small, limited mind that continues, and you hope to preserve that continuity, you hope to live again, so you believe in reincarnation, in life after death, or in some other form of survival. But it is only the man who perceives the recording machine in operation and dies to that whole process of continuity—it is only such a man that lives anew.

Let us look at it the other way. Are you so very different from your neighbor? You have a different form, a different name, a different job or function, but inwardly are you so very different from the so-called mass? I am afraid you are not. And the ministers, the great of the land—what are they? Strip away their position, their cars, their caps, and all the rest they put on and they are just like you or another—recording machines continuing in the world of time, seeking power, position, struggling, enjoying, suffering. The man who is envious may be driven to the top by his envy, by his desire for position and power, so that in history he lives on, but he is still within the field of time. It is only the mind that is dead to time, dead to the known—it is only such a mind that can find out what love is.

Now, sirs, love is not sentiment, love is not devotion, love is neither carnal nor sacred, neither profane nor pure. It is a state of being, and you cannot divide it. You cannot say, "I love one and I do not love the other." Have you ever taken a leaf in your hand and looked at it, a leaf that has just fallen on the dirty road where thousands of people have walked and polluted the ground with their spittle? If you can feel that leaf, you will know how to love.

Sirs, don't take notes; experience what is being said, feel your way into all this. Because love is an extraordinary thing, is it not? We have divided it into the love of God and the love of man. To me that is an irreligious thing to do. There is only love.

But a mind that is sentimental, a mind that is jealous, envious, ambitious, a mind that is nationalistic, provincial—such a mind will never know what love is. There is no right and wrong when there is love, for when you have that feeling, then love can do what it will. But that is an extraordinary state of being because most of us only know continuity in time, the fear of death, and the love which is smothered by jealousy. That is all we know, and we never let go of the known. Holding with one hand to the known, with the other we grope after the unknown. We are not purely materialistic, but neither are we really inquiring into the unknown, so we are miserable human beings with sorrows that do not pass away and joys that are soon withered by time.

Dying is from moment to moment, and on a mind that is dying, no influence leaves its mark. Such a mind offers no soil for experience to take root, and therefore it is always young. But this state of being is possible only when the mind is dying every day to everything it has known, to every experience, to every memory, to every pleasure, to every sorrow. You can never ask how to die, any more than you can ask how to avoid death. The leaf just drops off the tree. When there is dying, there is loving. Without dying, love becomes hate, jealousy; and no belief, no temple, no sacred book is going to save you from the fear of death. What liberates the mind from the fear of death is dying from day to day, and only then is there the timeless state of love.

March 1, 1959

Eighth Talk in New Delhi

May I suggest that we talk this evening about the mind in meditation, which is a most complex and subtle problem. If one does not know what meditation is, true meditation, I think one misses everything in life. It is like being in a prison where you see only the wall opposite you and know only the limitation, the pain, the sorrow, and all the petty little things that make up your life of confinement. So it seems to me that meditation is a very direct and intimate problem for each one of us because it requires the approach of a mind in meditation to understand the whole movement of life.

But to share this investigation into the mind in meditation is quite a difficult problem in itself. Sharing implies interest, does it not, on the part of the people who are listening; it means observing and partaking in the

thing we are talking about. If I say to you, "Look at the flower, how beautiful it is!" you can share the beauty of the flower only if your mind is at rest and therefore in a state of observation. To put it differently, your own mind must be capable of meeting the other mind on the same level at the same time; otherwise, there is no sharing of that experience. We cannot share something in which I am interested and you are not. I may point out, describe, explain, but there is no sharing unless you meet me on the same level of observation and with the same intensiveness, the same feelings of the heart.

This is not a rhetorical statement; it is an everyday fact. You may say to your friend, "Do look at that marvelous sunset!" but if your friend is not interested in the beauty of the sunset, you cannot share it with him. Similarly, the sharing of any problem with your wife, with your husband, with your neighbor, requires a communion in which there is a mutual and immediate perception of the same thing.

Now, let us see if we can together feel the importance of meditation, and also perceive the beauty, the implications, the subtleties of it. To begin with, that word *meditation* has a very special significance for you, has it not? You immediately think of sitting in a certain posture, breathing in a certain way, forcing the mind to concentrate on something, and so on. But to me that is not meditation at all. To me meditation is entirely different, and if you and I are to share this inquiry into what is meditation, you will obviously have to put aside your prejudices, your conditioned thinking about meditation. That is true, I think, whether we discuss politics, or a particular system of economics, or our relationship with each other. Such a talk, such a discussion or exchange, to be of any value, must be a process of sharing; but there is no sharing if either of us starts from a conclusion, from a fixed point of view. If you are given to a particular form of so-called meditation and the other is not, there can obviously be no sharing. You must let go of your prejudices and experiences, and he must also let go of his, so that both of you can look into the problem and find out together what is meditation.

If you and I are to share and understand this problem, which is a very subtle and complex one, it is essential that you not be mesmerized by what I am saying. If you merely accept or reject it or interpret it in your own way instead of trying to find out what lies beyond the explanation, then there is no sharing, no real communion. So it is very important to approach this problem intelligently.

Now, don't let us seek a definition of intelligence. A specialist may be very clever in his chosen field, whether it be electronics, mathematics, science, economics, or what you will, but as long as he looks at life from that narrow, limited point of view, he is obviously not intelligent. To be intelligent, the mind must be capable of dealing with the whole of life and not just with a certain part of it.

Being an economist, a scientist, a businessman, a housewife, this or that, you may reject all this and say, "What has meditation got to do with my life? Meditation is all right for the sannyasi, for the man who has renounced the world, but my function requires that I live in the world like any ordinary man, so what has meditation got to do with me?" If that is one's approach, then one is merely perpetuating one's own dullness, one's own insensitivity, one's own lack of intelligence. We are talking about human beings, not just about their various functions. I hope you see the difference. Whatever may be the specialized function of a particular human being, we are talking about the total human being himself. But if you regard life merely as a matter of function and cling to your particular status in that function, then you will obviously never meet the whole problem of existence. And it is the capacity to meet this problem totally that constitutes the very essence of intelligence.

It seems to me that it is only a mind in meditation that can affect fundamentally all our actions, our whole way of living. Meditation is not reserved for some hermit in the Himalayas, nor for a monk or a nun in a monastery; and when it is, it becomes an escape from life, a denial of the reality of living. Whereas, if you and I as two human beings, not as specialists, could find out what it means for the mind to be in the state of meditation, then perhaps that very perception would directly affect our actions and our whole way of life in confronting the many complex problems of modern existence.

Now, what is meditation, and what is the state of the mind that is capable of meditating? Who is the meditator, and what is it that he meditates about? There is the meditator and the meditation, is there not? And surely, without understanding the meditator, there can be no meditation. A man may be able to sit in what he calls profound meditation, but if his mind is petty, conditioned, limited, his meditation will have no meaning at all. It will be a form of self-hypnosis—which is what most of us call meditation. So, before asking how to meditate or what system of meditation to follow, it is very important, isn't it, to understand the meditator.

Let me put it in a different way. A superficial mind may be capable of quoting word for word various scriptures, but it does not thereby cease to be superficial. It may sit entranced by the object of its devotion, it may repeat mantras, it may try to fathom reality or seek God; but being in its very nature a shallow mind, its so-called meditation will be equally shallow. When a petty mind thinks about God, its God is also petty.

When a confused mind thinks about clarity, its clarity is only further confusion.

So it is very important to find out, first of all, what meditation means to the entity that wants to meditate. In what most of us call meditation, there is, is there not, the thinker, the meditator who wishes to meditate in order to find peace, bliss, reality. The meditator says, "If I am to find that reality, that bliss, that peace which I am seeking, I must discipline my mind," so he takes, inwardly or outwardly, a posture of meditation. But the mind is still petty, still confused, still narrow, prejudiced, jealous, vain, stupid; and such a mind, in seeking or inventing a system of meditation, will only be further limited along the lines of its own narrow conditioning.

That is why I say it is very important to begin by understanding the meditator. A monk in a monastery may spend hours in contemplation, in prayer; he may gaze endlessly upon the object of his devotion, whether made by the hand or by the mind, but such a mind is obviously committed, conditioned; it is seeking salvation according to its own limitations, and though it may meditate until doomsday, it will never find reality. It can only imagine that it has found reality and live in that comforting illusion—which is what most of us want. We want to build castles in the air, find a refuge where we shall never be disturbed, where our petty minds will never be shaken.

So, without understanding the mind that is meditating, meditation becomes merely a process of self-hypnosis. By repeating the word *om* or any other word, by reciting a mantra, or running through the alphabet a sufficient number of times, you can create a rhythm of sound which will mesmerize your mind, and a mesmerized mind becomes very quiet, but that quietness is still within the field of your own pettiness. Unless one deeply understands the thinker, the meditator,

there is always a division, a gap between the meditator and that upon which he meditates, and this gap he is everlastingly struggling to bridge.

What matters, then, is to perceive one's own mind in operation—not as an observer, not as an entity who is looking at the mind, but for the mind to be aware of its own movement. I do not know if I am making myself clear.

When you look at something, there is always the observer, is there not? When you look at a flower, you are the observer, and there is the flower. The thinker is apart from the thought, the experiencer is separate from the experienced. If you watch yourself, you will see there is always this division of the observer and the observed, the 'I' and the 'not-I', the experiencer and the thing that is experienced.

Now, one of the problems of meditation is how to eliminate this gap which separates the experiencer from the experienced because as long as this gap exists there will be conflict—not only the conflict of the opposites, but also the conflict of a mind that is everlastingly struggling to achieve an end, to arrive at a goal. So how is one to bring about that extraordinary state of mind in which there is only experiencing and not an experiencer?

Sirs, what happens when you sit very quietly and try to do some kind of meditation? Your mind wanders all over the place, does it not? You think of your shoe, of your neighbor, of your job, of what you are going to eat, of what Shankara or the Buddha or the Christ has said, and so on. Your mind drifts off, and you try to bring it back to a particular focus or central issue. This effort on the part of the thinker to control his thoughts is called concentration. So there is always a contradiction between the thinker and his wandering thoughts, which he tries everlastingly to pull in and force along a particular groove. And if you do succeed in forcing all your thoughts into a chosen pattern, you think you have achieved a marvelous state. But that is obviously not meditation; it is not the awakening of perception. That is merely learning the technique of concentration, which any schoolboy can do.

Concentration is a process of exclusion, resistance, suppression; it is a form of compulsion. The schoolboy who forces himself to read his book when he really wants to look out of the window or go out and play is said to be concentrating, and that is exactly what you do. You compel your mind to concentrate, and so begins the contradiction between the observer and the observed, the thinker and the thought, which is a state of endless conflict. Becoming aware of this conflict in yourself, you say you must get rid of it, and so you seek a system of meditation—a procedure with which we are all very familiar, especially in India where almost everyone practices some system of meditation.

Now, what does the practicing of a system of meditation imply? Let us think it out together. It implies, does it not, that through a method, a practice, a system, you will arrive at a certain point which you call peace or liberation or bliss. You want to realize God, and you practice a system to bring about that realization. But no system can ever lead you to what you say you want because your mind is crippled by the system. From the sannyasi downwards and from you upwards, this is actually what is taking place.

Any system implies a movement from the known to the known, and the known is always fixed. When you say, "I want to reach peace," the thing you are striving after is a projection of what you think peace should be; therefore, like your house, it is fixed, it cannot move away, and a path or a system may lead you to it. But reality is a living thing, it is not fixed, it has no abode, and therefore no system can lead you to it. If you once really perceive the truth of this, you are free of all the gurus, of all the teachers, of all the books—and that is a tremendous liberation.

So our problem is, is it not, to experience the fact that the thinker and the thought are one, that the observer is the observed; and if you have ever tried it, you will know that this is an extraordinarily difficult thing to do. It does not mean identifying oneself with the observed. Do you understand, sirs? You can identify yourself with an individual. You can identify yourself with the image in the temple, to which you do puja and feel a tremendous emotion which you call devotion. But such identification still maintains the one who identifies himself with something. We are talking of an entirely different state in which there is no identification, no recognition, no experiencer apart from the experienced who creates contradiction by trying to identify himself with the experienced. There is no experiencer at all, but only experiencing.

You may identify yourself with the object of your devotion, but there is still a duality. You think of yourself as an Indian because you have identified yourself with a colored section of the map called India—which the politicians have exploited, and which you also would like to exploit. But the fact is that this, like every other form of identification, maintains the entity who has identified himself with something.

If you see this fact, then the next question is: Is it possible for the mind to bring about a state in which there is only experiencing without the experiencer? Let me put it differently. Every minute of the day the mind is receiving impressions. It is like a sensitive photographic film upon which every incident, every influence, every experience, every movement of thought is leaving an imprint. Whether we are conscious of it or not, that is what is actually taking place. Burdened with these imprints of past experiences, the mind meets the new in terms of the old. In other words, there is always the past meeting the present and creating the future.

Now, can the mind receive impressions and not be marked by them? Do you understand, sirs? Let me put it very simply. You are insulted or flattered, and this has left a mark on your mind; that is, the insult or the flattery has taken root in the soil of the mind. Now, have you ever experimented to see if you can receive insult and flattery so that afterwards your mind is completely unmarked by them? Innumerable experiences, piled one upon another, are leaving their chaotic and contradictory impressions on the mind like scratches on the surface of memory. And can the mind experience anew, without these scratches? I say it can, and that only then is there the coming into being of a state in which there is thinking without the thinker, experiencing without the experiencer, and therefore never a contradiction.

If you observe your own mind in what you call meditation, you will see that there is always a division, a contradiction between the thinker and the thought. As long as there is a thinker apart from thought, meditation is merely a ceaseless effort to overcome this contradiction.

I hope all this is not too abstract and too difficult, but even if it is, please listen. Although you may not fully understand what is being said, the very act of listening is like planting a seed in the dark soil. If the seed is vital, and if the soil is rich, it will produce a shoot; you don't have to do a thing about it. Similarly, if you can just listen and let the seed fall in the womb of the mind, it will germinate, it will flourish and bring about an action which is unconsciously true.

Another problem in meditation is that of concentration and attention. Concentration implies, as I pointed out earlier, a restriction, a limitation; it is a narrowing, exclusive process. When the schoolboy concentrates, he excludes the desire to look out of the window and says, "This is an awful book, but I must read it in order to pass the examination." That is essentially what we all do when we concentrate. There is resistance, a narrowing down of the mind to a certain focus, which is called concentration.

Now, attention is altogether different. Attention has no frontier. Please follow this closely. A mind in the state of attention is not limited by the frontier of recognition. Attention is a state in which there is complete awareness of everything that is taking place within and about one, without the border or frontier of recognition which exists in concentration.

Sirs, for God's sake, do listen to what I am saying; experience what I am talking about. Don't take notes. Would you take notes if someone were telling you he loves you? (Laughter) You laugh, but you don't see the tragedy of it. The difficulty with most of us is that we want to remember, we want to have the recognition of what has been said, and we store it away in memory or put it down in a notebook so that we can think about it tomorrow. But when someone is saying he loves you, do you take notes? Do you look the other way? It is the same thing here; otherwise, these meetings are useless. Empty words have no meaning at all. So listen to what is being said, and if you can, experience it—but not as an experiencer.

I was pointing out the difference between concentration and attention. In concentration there is no attention, but in attention there is concentration. In attention there are no borders to the mind. When you are in the state of attention, you hear what is being said, you hear the coughing, you see one man scratching his head, another yawning, another taking notes, and you are aware of your own reactions. You listen, you see, you are aware; there is an attention in which there is no effort. Effort exists only when there is concentration, which is opposed to attention. In the state of attention, your whole being is attentive, not just one part of your mind. The moment your mind says, "I must have that," there is concentration, which means that you are no longer in the state of attention. Concentration arises with the craving to have or to be something, which is a state of contradiction.

Just see the truth of this. In attention there is a total being, whereas in concentration there is not; it is a form of becoming. A man who is becoming must have authority; he lives in a state of contradiction. But when there is simple awareness, an effortless attention without an end to be realized, then you will find that the mind has no frontier of recognition. Such a mind can concentrate, but its concentration is not exclusion. Don't say, "How am I to get that state of attention?" It is not a thing you can "get." Just see the truth of this—that in the state of attention the mind has no border; there is no recognition of an end to be gained or achieved. Such a mind can concentrate, and that concentration is not exclusion. This is one of the things to be discovered by a mind in meditation.

Then there is the problem of the many contradictory thoughts that arise in the mind. The mind is vagrant, restless, flying endlessly from one thing to another. That is the lot of most people, is it not?

Now, why does the mind do this? Surely, the mind does it because in its very essence it is lazy. A mind that is vagrant, crowded with thoughts, a mind that goes from one thing to another like a butterfly, is a lazy mind; and when a lazy mind tries to control its wandering thoughts, it merely becomes dull, stupid.

Whereas, if the mind is aware of its own movement, if it sees all its thoughts as they arise one after another, and if it can take any one thought, good or bad, that comes along, and pursue that thought to the very end, then you will find that the mind becomes extraordinarily active. It is this activity of the mind that puts an end to the vagrancy of thought—but not through control or by force. Such a mind is tremendously active, but its activity is not that of a politician or an electrician or a man who quotes books; it is an activity without a center. The mind that is driven by ambition, that is chasing its own fulfillment, is not active in this sense at all. But if you can take one thought and go into it fully, ravishingly, delightfully, with your whole being, you will find that your mind becomes extraordinarily active; and there must be this activity, this precision of the mind.

Our next problem is that the mind is the result of time, the result of the known. All that you have experienced—your memories, your conditioning, everything that to you is recognizable—is within the field of the known, is it not? The mind thinks from the known to the known; its movement is always within the field of the known. And it is of the utmost importance for the mind to free itself from the known; otherwise, it cannot enter into the unknown. A mind that is bound by the known is incapable of experiencing that state in which there is complete stillness without deterioration. It is only when the mind has understood the known at the unconscious as well as at the conscious level, when it has understood and therefore freed itself from the desires, the ambitions, the hates, the flatteries, the pleasures, everything that it has collected—it is only then, in this liberation from the known, that the unknown comes into being. You cannot invite the unknown. If you do, what you experience will again be the result of the known; it will not be the real.

So the mind in meditation is in a state of awareness without the center of recognition, and therefore without a circumference; it is attention without a frontier. The mind in meditation is that which has freed itself without effort from the known. The known has fallen away as a leaf drops from the tree, and so the mind is motionless, in a state of silence; and such a mind alone can receive the immeasurable, the unknown.

March 4, 1959

Ninth Talk in New Delhi

This evening I would like to think aloud about action, religion, and the nature of beauty. It seems to me that they are all related, and that to be concerned only with action or with religion or with the nature of beauty is to destroy the fullness of action, which then becomes merely an activity. If we are to go very deeply into the question of what is action, I think we must also consider religion and the nature of beauty as well as the quality or sensitivity of a mind that feels and appreciates what is beautiful.

For most of us action becomes a routine, a habit, something that one does, not out of love or because it has deep significance for oneself, but because one has to do it. One is driven to it by circumstances, by a wrong kind of education, by the lack of that love out of which one does something real. If we can go into this whole question, I think it will be very revealing, for then perhaps we shall begin to understand the true nature of revolution.

Surely, true action comes from clarity. When the mind is very clear, unconfused, not contradictory within itself, then action inevitably follows from that clarity; we need not be concerned with how to bring about action. But it is very difficult, is it not, to have undisturbed perception and to see things, not as one would like to see them, but as they actually are, undistorted by one's likes and dislikes. It is only out of such clarity that the fullness of action takes place.

Clarity is of far greater significance than action. But our minds are ridden by systems, by techniques, by the desire to know what to do. The "what to do?" has become very important; it is our everlasting question. We want to know what to do about starvation, what to do about inequality, about the appalling corruption in the world, and about our own sorrow and suffering. We are always looking for a method, a means, a system of action, are we not?

But how to find clarity is obviously a much more significant inquiry because if one can think very clearly, if one has perception which is not distorted, which is direct, complete, then from that clear perception, action follows. Such clarity creates its own action. But people who are dedicated to various systems are always at loggerheads with each other, are they not? They cannot work together. Each interprets the problem in terms of the system to which he is committed, according to his particular conditioning and self-interest. I do not know if you have ever noticed how most of us divide ourselves into groups, parties, and systems, and commit ourselves to certain conclusions. Any such commitment, surely, does not bring clarity. It brings only enmity, opposition. But if you and I approach our human problems, not with commitments, conclusions, and self-interest, but with clarity, then I think these problems can very easily be solved.

So the real problem is the mind that approaches the problem, and may I suggest that we not merely listen to what is being said but go into ourselves and find out in what manner the mind is confused. If we ask how to clear up our confusion, it will only bring about the cultivation of another system. To actually see that the mind is confused has far greater significance, surely, than the question of action, of what to do. We have to live in this world, we have to act, we have to go to the office and do a hundred different things;

and from what sort of a mind does all this action come? I can describe the background of the mind, but I think it will have very little significance if you do not relate what is being said to your own mind. Most of us think that self-knowledge is merely a matter of information, the accumulation of various explanations as to why the mind is confused, and we are easily satisfied by explanations. But really to understand oneself, one has to put away all the explanations and begin to explore one's own mind—which is to perceive directly *what is;* I must know that I am confused, that I am committed, that I have a vested interest in some system, ideology, or belief, and see the significance of it; and surely, that very perception is enough in itself. But that direct perception is prevented if I am satisfied merely to explain the various causes of my confusion.

It seems to me that the real revolution is not economic, political, or social, but the bringing about of this new quality of the mind which is always clear. And when the mind is not clear, what matters is to perceive directly the cause of confusion without trying to do something about it. Whatever a confused mind does about its confusion, it will still be confused. I do not think we see the significance of this. All that most of us are concerned with is how to clear up our confusion, how to wipe away our darkness. But simply to perceive that the mind is confused is in itself enough. Try the experiment with yourself, and you will see. There is no answer to a confused mind; there is no way out of its confusion because whatever way it finds, it will still be confused. Whereas, if the mind is vitally aware of and fully attentive to its confusion, if it sees that it is muddled, that there is a distortion, that there is a vested interest—this in itself is enough. It brings about its own action, which I think is the real revolution. Because it approaches the

problem negatively, such a mind acts positively. But when the mind approaches a problem positively, it acts negatively and therefore contradictorily.

Do think it over and you will see the truth of this. After all, no amount of argumentation, persuasion, or influence, no promise of reward or threat of punishment can make you see the true as true, the false as false, and the truth in the false. What is needed is the simplicity that looks directly at things as they are—and that is the new quality of mind which is really a revolution. Problems may appear to be positive, but they cannot be solved through a positive approach because problems are always negative; therefore, they must be approached negatively.

Sirs, take the problem of starvation. How do we approach it? The communists approach it through one system, the capitalists through another, while the organized religions have conflicting systems of their own. Surely, the problem of starvation, like every other human problem, must be approached negatively; no system is going to solve it because each man will fight for his particular system in which he has a vested interest. You can see this happening right now in the world around you. Whereas, if the mind frees itself from the system and approaches the problem negatively because the problem itself is negative, then from that negation will come a positive action. Then there is no quarrel between you as a communist and me as a capitalist, or between you as a Hindu and me as a Christian or a Muslim, because we are both concerned not with the system but with the problem. In the problem there is no vested interest, whereas in the system there is, and it is this vested interest over which we are everlastingly quarreling.

Now, just to see the truth of this brings clarity, and out of that clarity there is action.

And I think it is the same with every problem because all problems are negative, and you must approach them negatively, not with a positive mind. To be free from greed or envy or jealousy or ambition, you must approach it negatively and not say, "How shall I get rid of it?" The direct perception of what is negative brings clarity.

I am afraid one has to think a great deal about these things—not think, but rather feel one's way into them because thoughts never lead to a fundamental revolution, ideas never bring about a radical change in the quality of the mind. Ideas, thoughts, only lead to conclusions, and out of these conclusions there are vested interests. A mind that starts with a conclusion has altogether ceased to think. After all, what we call thinking is merely a reaction, isn't it? It is the reaction of one's background, of one's memory, of one's knowledge. Therefore, thinking is always limited, conditioned. But direct perception is never conditioned. You can perceive directly the fact that you are envious, for example, without having to think about it, and that direct perception has its own action. But once you begin to think about why you are envious, to find reasons for your envy, to explain it, to condemn or justify it, to look for a way to be free of it, then that whole process prevents direct perception, which is the negative approach to what you call envy.

Perhaps you will reject all this because the mind tends to reject what it hears for the first time as something new. But I think it would be a pity if you merely rejected it, saying, "You don't give us a system of meditation, a method by which to do this or that." I think a mind that pursues a system or a method and functions within it is essentially a lazy mind. It is so easy to function in a system; the mind can operate like a cog in a machine; it doesn't have to think. Whereas, in approaching a problem negatively, you have to be alert; it requires an extraordinarily attentive mind. And I think this is the only real revolution because it does not create enmity and vested interests, while systems, ideas, conclusions always do.

Now, with the clarity of direct perception let us look at what we call religion. Surely, a religious mind is not a believing mind. Belief is positive, and a mind that believes in something can never find out what is real.

After all, what is the religion which you profess? You believe that to find God or whatever you may call it you must discipline your body, control your mind, destroy every form of desire. You would go to that which you call holy with a mind that is crowded with beliefs, desecrated by superstition and fear. You worship the symbol instead of discovering what is real, so the symbol becomes all-important. You pray, and your prayer is supplication, begging something for yourself or your family from what you call God. It is a thing of the marketplace. If you beg, your bowl may be filled. If you ask for a refrigerator, you may get a refrigerator. If you ask in prayer for peace, you may find what you call peace, but it is not peace.

So you have made of religion a refuge, an escape, a meaningless thing. You seek reality through constant discipline of the body, through suppression or control of every desire. You approach what you call God with a mind that is worn out, hopeless, in despair, with a heart that is dry, fearful, ugly. The man who repeats a lot of phrases, who reads the Gita from morning till night, or who denies himself everything and takes the sannyasi's robe—do you think such a man will find the real? Surely, one must set out to discover reality with a fullness of heart, with all one's sensitivities highly developed, with a mind that is rich—rich in clarity and not in experience, rich in the perfume of real affection.

Religion is not that which you now call religion; it is not in the book, it is not in the mantra, it is not in the temple, it is not in the graven image, whether made by the hand or by the mind. It is something entirely different. To find out what religion is, the mind must go to it with an extraordinary fullness because it is empty, and it is only then that reality can come into being. This is a complete reversal of everything that you have been taught, and that is why it is very difficult for you to see the truth of it.

For centuries it has been said that you must be desireless, that every form of desire towards any object must be thwarted, cut off. Whereas, I say desire is not to be suppressed, cut off, thwarted, controlled, but to be understood. Control, suppression, is a form of laziness. To understand desire with all its subtleties, with all its promptings, with all its drive and energy, requires constant watchfulness, a mind that is extraordinarily alert and capable of delving deeply into itself, not only at the conscious level, but at the unconscious level as well. The conscious mind is the positive mind; it has learned, it has experienced, it has gathered, and it wants to translate everything in terms of its own self-interest. The unconscious, on the other hand, is the negative mind, and you cannot go to it positively. It is only when the conscious mind is quiet, undisturbed, that it is able to receive the hints and intimations of the unconscious. That is the way of dreams.

It is not a positive assertion or denial that brings about clarity, but this whole process of understanding. If, as you listen, you go into yourself and observe your own mind, which I hope you are doing, you will find that out of such listening there comes the clarity of understanding. A mind that is clear because it understands itself can deal with desire, but a mind that is lazy, and therefore suppresses, controls, shapes desire, will always live in a state of self-contradiction. I do not know if you have noticed that when a desire is controlled, shaped, driven, suppressed, it reacts, and hence we live everlastingly in the conflict of duality.

Sirs, do listen to what is being said, and as you listen, watch your own mind. It is what is being said that is important, and not the speaker, because what is being said is true; and being true, it is anonymous. It has nothing to do with the speaker.

If, as you listen, you are aware of yourself, observing the movement of your own thoughts, you will see how desire is forever creating its own opposite, which means there is a division, a contradiction in the mind; and out of that contradiction you seek God, you fashion saints and idols for your worship. Whereas, if you do not oppose desire, but go into yourself and really begin to understand your jealousy, your sexual urge, your ambition, your feeling of envy, and every other form of desire; if you observe and are aware of it totally without accepting or denying it, without saying it is bad or good—which is to approach it with a mind that is negative and therefore capable of perceiving directly—if you can do that, then you will discover that God is something entirely different from the God of your seeking. It is the unhappy mind, it is the confused, fearful mind that seeks God. The mind may think it has renounced the world, but if it is still burning with desire, its renunciation is merely a form of self-advancement; its vested interest is now belief in the idea which it calls God. Whereas, if you begin to understand this whole process of the self, the 'me', with its desires, its ambitions, its subtle urges, then you will see that belief is a hindrance to reality, for belief creates authority; and a mind bound by authority will never find out what is real.

So religion is not of the church or the temple; it has no dogma, no belief, no practice. A religious man is one who is inquiring ceaselessly into himself. A politician is not a religious man, though he may call himself one, because he is concerned with a particular result which becomes his vested interest. Only the mind that is in a state of negation will find reality because it is only such a mind that is capable of seeing the false as the false and the true as the true.

Just as the mind must be sensitive, uncommitted, to perceive directly what is true, so it must be open, sensitive, to feel the nature of beauty. Most of us say, "That is beautiful," or "That is ugly," because we have the memory of what is beautiful and what is ugly according to the tradition, the education, the culture in which we were brought up. But surely, like love, beauty has no opposite. A mind that has this extraordinary sensitivity to beauty is sensitive also to that which is ugly, and does not compare. I do not know if you have ever been aware of your own feelings, of your own reaction when you suddenly see a sunset or a tree in full bloom against the sky. At that moment, surely, you are not noticing whether it is beautiful or ugly, but there is a total response in which the thinker is absent—which means, does it not, that the mind has completely abandoned itself. I hope you are following this.

Perhaps you have never experienced that state of mind in which there is total abandonment of everything, a complete letting go. And you cannot abandon everything without deep passion, can you? You cannot abandon everything intellectually or emotionally. There is total abandonment, surely, only when there is intense passion. Don't be alarmed by that word because a man who is not passionate, who is not intense, can never understand or feel the quality of beauty. The mind that holds something in reserve, the mind that has a vested interest, the mind that clings to position, power, prestige, the mind that is respectable, which is a horror—such a mind can never abandon itself.

To perceive the nature of that which is called beauty, the mind must completely come to an end, but not in despair. It must be very simple because only a simple mind can see what is true. But the mind cannot be made simple through discipline. The sannyasi who wears a loincloth, who takes only one meal a day and feels virtuous about it is not simple. Simplicity is a state in which the mind has no consciousness of itself as being simple. The moment you are conscious of your humility, you have ceased to be humble. The moment you are conscious of your non-violence, you are full of violence. The ideal and all the practices and disciplines to achieve it are a self-conscious process, and therefore not virtue.

Do look at all this because your minds are ridden with this sort of thing; you are slaves to it. You may agree with what is being said, but you will fall back into your old ways. It is not a question of agreement, it is a question of perception. Once you perceive for yourself the truth of the matter, you can never go back to the nonsense of ideals and disciplines. This is not being said to make you believe or disbelieve, or to create a new dogma. But you must be intense in perceiving the significance of every thought, every feeling that you have, and out of that intensity comes clarity; and clarity creates its own discipline—you don't have to practice a discipline.

Sensitivity to beauty is not just a matter of seeing beauty as manifested in a painting, in a tree, or in a poem. It is the feeling of beauty, and like the feeling of love, it is not merely in the expression, in the word, in the holding of a hand. That feeling, which is extraordinary, creates its own action. For the man who knows what love is, who is in the state of love, there is no sin, no evil. Do what he may, it will be essentially right. In the same way, a mind that perceives is very simple, and it is simple because it perceives; and that very perception creates its own action. It is only such a mind that can come to the state of total abandonment—which is not a gradual process in time. Just to see the truth of that is enough. Such a mind does not seek truth; it does not go to the temple or to the sacred books; though it is active, it is not concerned with action. Because it has been through an inward revolution which has brought a new quality to it, such a mind can wait in negation to receive that which is eternal.

If one observes, one can see within oneself the past, not merely one's own past, but the whole past of humanity. After all, we are the result of centuries of human existence, with its chain of thoughts and experiences, joys and sorrows. But to inquire into and to break through all that requires a negative approach; the mind must be capable of approaching everything through negation. Don't translate ''negation'' as the equivalent of some Sanskrit word and put it by, but actually experience it. The moment you begin to translate, compare, you have gone away from the fact; you are living in the memory of what you have read or heard, and therefore you are dead. Whereas, if you are directly experiencing, then the mind is astonishingly clear, precise, unburdened, and therefore its action is revolutionary. It is only such a mind that can receive the benediction of reality.

March 8, 1959

Tenth Talk in New Delhi

This is the last talk of the present series, and if I may I would like to talk about ignorance, experience, and the mind which is in the state of creation.

But before we go into all that, I think it is very important to understand the relationship between you and the speaker because if that relationship is not clearly understood, even after these several talks, it will lead to a great deal of confusion. The speaker is not important at all; he is merely the voice, the telephone; but what is said, when one is in the process of learning, has an immense significance. If you give importance to the speaker as a teacher, you are merely creating a following, and thereby you are destroying yourself as well as what is being said. Both the follower and the teacher are a detriment to the process of learning, and when one is intent on learning, there is neither the teacher nor the follower.

I think it is also important to understand that I am not talking to you as an individual who is opposed to society, or as one who belongs to this or that group. To me there is only the human being, whether he lives in India, in America, in Russia, in Germany, or anywhere else. So I am not talking to you as an Indian with a particular system of beliefs, but together we are endeavoring to find out what this whole process of living is all about.

This is our earth; it is not the Englishman's or the Russian's, the American's or the Indian's; it is the earth on which we live, you and I. It does not belong to the communist or the capitalist, the Christian or the Hindu. It is our earth, to be lived on extensively, widely, and deeply; but that living is denied when you are a nationalist, when you belong to a party or an organized religion. Please believe me; these are the very things that are destroying human beings. Nationalism is a curse. To call oneself a Hindu or a Christian is also a curse because it divides us. We are human beings, not members of a sect or functionaries in a system. But the politician, the man who is committed to a conclusion or a system in which he has a vested interest will exploit each one of us through our nationalism, through our vanity and emotionalism, just as the priest exploits us in the name of so-called religion.

But in considering these things together, I think it is very important for each one of us to understand that hearing is one thing, and listening, which brings action, is quite another. You may superficially agree when you hear it said that nationalism, with all its emotionalism and vested interest, leads to exploitation and the setting of man against man; but to really free your mind from the pettiness of nationalism is another matter. To be free, not only from nationalism, but also from all the conclusions of organized religions and political systems, is essential if the mind is to be young, fresh, innocent, that is, in a state of revolution; and it is only such a mind that can create a new world—not the politicians, who are dead, nor the priests, who are caught in their own religious systems.

So, fortunately or unfortunately for yourself, you have heard something which is true; and if you merely hear it and are not actively disturbed so that your mind begins to free itself from all the things which are making it narrow and crooked, then the truth you have heard will become a poison. Surely, truth becomes a poison if it is heard and does not act in the mind, like the festering of a wound. But to discover for oneself what is true and what is false, and to see the truth in the false, is to let that truth operate and bring forth its own action.

It is obviously of the greatest importance that as individual human beings we understand for ourselves this whole process of living. Living is not just a matter of function and status, and if we are content to be mere functionaries with a certain status, we become mechanical, and then life passes us by. It seems to me that if one does not really participate in life, take to one's heart the fullness of life, then the mind becomes petty, narrow, full of the dogmatic beliefs which are now destroying human beings.

If that is clear, let us inquire into the question of ignorance. What is ignorance, what is knowledge, and what is wisdom? Surely, all knowledge is within the field of time, and a mind that pursues knowledge is bound by time, limited to the field of the known. The things one knows, the facts one has gathered, the technique one has acquired, whether it be bridge building, accounting, or what you will—it is all within the field of the known.

Now, knowledge is always operating in human relationships, is it not? I know you, and you know me; I know how to write, how to talk, how to do this or that, all of which is born of memory—memory which has been acquired, stimulated, educated. The mind functions from this background of memory which is called knowledge. Knowledge may be indefinitely extended, it may be made wide, deep, certain, encyclopedic in its scope, but while socially useful, it is still within the field of ignorance. Knowledge does not wipe away ignorance. No amount of your reading the Gita, or any other books, will wipe away ignorance.

So, what is ignorance? A man may be very erudite, he may be skillful in the laboratory, or efficient as a bureaucrat, or a great builder of dams and bridges; but if he does not understand himself, he is essentially ignorant. If I am unaware of the way I think, the way I feel, if I do not see my own unconscious motives and hidden demands, if I do not know why I believe, why I am afraid, what are the sources of my ambition and frustrations, if I do not uncover and understand all that is within myself, then however high I may build the superstructure of knowledge, it will inevitably become the means of destruction.

Ignorance is the state of a mind that has no comprehension of itself. You may quote the Gita, the Bible, the Koran, or whatever book you hold sacred, but if you don't know yourself, the quotations will have no meaning. The clearing away of ignorance lies in the understanding of oneself—not the higher self, not the paramatma and all the rest of the superstructure which the mind has built in order to escape from its own pettiness, but the self which is operating every day and which is torn by ambition, frustration, jealousy, envy, hate, fear. It is surely the understanding of this whole process from moment to moment that brings about that state of mind which may be called wisdom. So wisdom has nothing whatever to do with knowledge. Knowledge and ignorance go together; one flows into the other, and ignorance is strengthened by experience.

Please do listen to what is being said, and don't brush it aside. Just listen, even if you don't quite understand. You may understand the word, the phrase, the symbol; but the word, the phrase, the symbol is not the real. If you realize this, then perhaps you will begin very hesitantly to feel your way into the meaning behind the words, which is to inquire into yourself. And after all, that is the function of this meeting—not to impose on the mind any idea or belief, but to help us to think out together the fundamental problems of life.

So you, as a human being, and I, as a human being, are learning. I am not, as you know, a saint or a teacher sitting here on the platform and telling you what to do because there is no authority when we are both learning. Learning ceases when there is acceptance of authority. What is important is to listen with a mind that is inquiring, a mind that wants to discover what is true and what is false. But most of us listen with an opinion, with a belief. When we approach a fact, we have opinions about the fact, and therefore the fact never operates on the mind. So may I suggest that you listen to find out for yourself what is true and what is false. Do not wait for someone else to tell you because no one else can.

As I was saying, ignorance is strengthened by experience because experience is cumulative, additive. Experience is essential at one level as function, but experience which is

cumulative in the sense that it strengthens the mind in its center of self-interest only furthers ignorance, and that ignorance becomes what we call knowledge.

If you watch the operation of your own mind, you will see that it is always translating the new in terms of the old, that is, in terms of previous experience, which in turn is the result of your particular culture, of your beliefs, of your education, of your conditioning. So experience is never a liberating factor. Experience only strengthens the center of ignorance. You may have a vision of Christ or Krishna, for example, but that experience is the result, is it not, of your background as a Christian or a Hindu; and the experience further strengthens the background, the conditioning, the belief. So experience is obviously not a means of liberating, freeing the mind. After all, experiencing is a process of pain and pleasure, sorrow and joy, denial and acceptance. That is all we know. That process of experiencing is going on all the time, and without understanding it, the mind will never come to that state in which it is fully active, but in which there is no experiencing.

I do not know if you have ever noticed that the mind is capable of perceiving without experiencing. When you suddenly see a lovely tree expanding into the sky, what happens? You experience it, that is, you name it, you say, "What a beautiful tree; I must admire it." That is what most people do, consciously or unconsciously, when they see a beautiful thing; they experience it. But if you just perceive a sunset, a lovely flower, or the splendor in the grass, there is no experiencing. It is not that you identify yourself with what is seen, but it is a state in which there is neither the observer nor the observed, a state of pure perception without interpretation, without the recall of memory. That is the liberating factor, for it frees the mind from the past.

In function, experience is necessary. I am not a mechanic if I have no experience with machines. I am not a gardener if I do not know the soil. Experience teaches me about the things I have to do in discharging a certain function. But experience is destructive; it is a deteriorating factor when it becomes a tradition in terms of which everything is translated. That is what is happening the world over, and particularly here in India where everything is bound by tradition and you are a big man if you can write a commentary on the Gita.

So experience is destructive when it becomes merely an additive process. Do please listen to this. A traditional mind is a dead mind; it is limited to the field of the known, which is the field of function and status. It is only the mind that is in a state of attention, in a state of perception, which means that it is not experiencing or translating in terms of the old—it is only such a mind that is fresh, young, innocent, and therefore creative.

In knowledge there is ignorance, and experience is binding; but the understanding of oneself—which is to know the whole process of oneself, the unconscious as well as the conscious, the hidden as well as the open—frees the mind, it makes the mind fresh, young. The young mind is always moving, changing, deciding; it is always approaching the frontier of itself and breaking through. But the mind that has experienced and is acquiring further experience, though this is valuable at a certain functionary level, is never a fresh mind; it is never eager, new. The communist mind, or the capitalist mind, or the mind that thinks in terms of a sovereign political state—how can such a mind be young? How can it make decisions that are new, decisions not based on old ideas?

Without understanding oneself, without uncovering and fully comprehending the hidden ways of one's thought and desire, the hidden want, there will always be hate, pride, fear. So let us look at this hidden want.

I do not know if you have ever gone deeply within yourself. To do that, surely, you must put aside all explanations, all conclusions about yourself, all the knowledge you have acquired about the self. Only a free mind is capable of inquiring, not a mind that is tethered to some conclusion, belief, or dogma.

If you have ever inquired very deeply into yourself, you are bound to have come upon that state which we call loneliness, a sense of complete isolation, of not being related. As a human being, you must at some time have felt that desperate, agonizing, despairing sense of isolation, from which consciously or unconsciously we are always running away. In our flight from the reality of that extraordinary sense of loneliness, we are driven, are we not, by a deep urge that is everlastingly seeking fulfillment through books, through music, through work and activity, through position, power, prestige.

If at any time you have felt that sense of utter loneliness, or if you have ever consciously, deliberately allowed yourself to be aware of it, you will know that you immediately want to run away, to escape from it. You go to the temple, worship a god, plunge into perpetual activity, talk everlastingly, explain things away, or turn on the radio. We all do this, as we well know if we are at all conscious of ourselves.

Now, to realize that escape in any form will never satisfy this deep urge for self-fulfillment, to see that it is insatiable, a bottomless pit, you must be aware of it totally, which means that you must see the truth that escapes have no reality. You may escape through God or through drink, but they are both the same; one is not more sacred than the other. You have to understand this hidden urge and go beyond it, and you cannot understand and go beyond it if you have not tasted that extraordinary loneliness, that darkness which has no way out, no hope. Hope comes into being when there is despair. A mind is in despair only because it is frustrated in its hope. To understand this deep urge, this hidden want, you must perceive it totally, as you might perceive a tree or a lovely flower. Then you can go beyond it; and once beyond it, you will find there is a complete aloneness which is entirely different from being lonely. But you cannot discover that state of complete aloneness without understanding the deep urge to fulfill yourself, to escape from loneliness.

All this may sound unusual, unreal, and perhaps you will say, "What has this got to do with our daily living?" I think it is intimately related to your daily living because your daily living is a misery of frustration; there is an everlasting striving to be, to become something, which is the real outcome of this deep urge, this hidden want. On the surface you may practice discipline, control your mind, do your puja, meditate, go to the temple, read the Gita, talk about peace, or what you will, but it is all nonsense as long as you do not understand the hidden want that is driving you.

So that state of aloneness is essential because our minds are worn out with constant effort. What is your life? You are constantly trying to be this and not to be that, striving everlastingly to become famous, to get a better job, to be more efficient; you are making endless effort, are you not? I wonder if you have ever noticed what a miserable existence we have, always striving to be something, to be good, to be nonviolent, ceaselessly talking about peace while indulging in political emotionalism and preparing for war. Our life is one of strife, turmoil, travail, and a mind in that condition can never be fresh, young, new. Surely, seeing all this, one must have asked oneself whether such effort is necessary to live in this world. There may be a

different way of living altogether, a way of living without effort—not at the lowest level, like a cow, nor like a human being who is forever doing what he likes, but at the highest level, a level where there is no effort.

But you cannot say, "How am I to realize that state of mind in which there is no effort?" because the very desire to acquire that state is another form of attachment, and all attachment is to things that are dying, or dead. You are attached to the dead, not to the living. You are attached, not to your wife who is a living human being, but to the wife of pleasurable memory. You cannot be attached to the living, moving river; you are attached to the pleasure of having seen that river, which is a memory, a dead thing.

There is a way of living which is completely effortless. Please, sirs, I am not asking you to accept this. It has nothing to do with acceptance or denial. You simply don't know it. All you know is effort, strife; you are perpetually driving yourself to be or not to be something, and your aggressive pursuit of your own ambitions, with its tensions and contradictions, is the outcome of this hidden want. You cannot remove this hidden want by mesmerizing yourself. You have to look at it, and you cannot look at it as long as you are escaping. You can look at it only when you come to it completely without fear because it is the fact. Don't dictate what the fact should be; let the fact tell you what it is. Most of us come to the fact with an opinion about the fact, with knowledge, with belief, which is an immature, a childish thing to do. You must come to the fact with innocency, with a fullness of heart, which is humility. Then the fact will tell you what it is.

This hidden want is extraordinarily deep and subtle, but if you are able to look at it without any opinion, without any fear, then you will discover that you can go beyond its darkness to a state in which the mind is totally alone and therefore no longer the result of influence. This aloneness is the state of attention.

As I said the other day, attention and concentration are two different things. In this aloneness, which is the state of attention, there is no shadow of concentration. Being alone, uninfluenced, not caught in opinion, the mind is completely attentive; it is motionless, silent, utterly still. But you cannot make the mind still. You can mesmerize the mind by repeating certain phrases, or quiet it by prayer, but that is not stillness—that is death. It is like putting the mind in a straightjacket to hold it still—and therefore the mind decays.

What is essential is to understand this deep, hidden want, which is always changing—and that is the beauty of it. You think you have understood it, only to find that it has moved somewhere else. So one has to pursue this hidden want down all the dark corridors of the mind. Then there comes that aloneness which is attention, and which is really a motionless state. I am not using that word *motionless* in opposition to activity. A mind that is motionless, still, is not a dead mind. It is an active mind, it is activity itself because it is still, and only such a mind is creative—not the mind which paints, dances, or writes books. That is merely the outward expression of a mind which may not be creative at all. A mind may have the gift of writing; it may catch an occasional vision of something and express it in a poem or on canvas, but creativity of the mind is entirely different. The mind that is in a state of creation is really perfectly still, and only such a mind can receive the immeasurable. To know the real, the imperishable, the measureless, the mind must be silent, in a state of complete humility; and the mind has no humility as long as there is the deep, hidden want.

March 11, 1959

Madras, India, 1959

---------- ✳ ----------

First Talk in Madras

It seems that communion is a very difficult art. To commune with one another over the many problems that we have requires listening and learning, which are both very difficult to do. Most of us hardly listen, and we hardly learn. To commune with each other, which is what these meetings are intended for, requires a certain capacity, a certain way of listening—not merely to gather information, which any schoolboy can do, but rather listening in order to understand. This means being critically aware of all the implications of what is being said, as well as observing very carefully your own evaluation of what is being said. During the process of evaluating what you hear, obviously you are not listening because the speaker has already gone beyond your idea, your opinion, your fixed thought. You have already stopped listening, and so communion becomes very difficult, especially when there is a large audience. When two or three are gathered quietly in a room, then it is possible to talk over together the meaning, the semantic significance of the word. But when one is talking like this to many people, it becomes almost impossible for us to commune with each other, to share with each other the many problems that must obviously confront every thoughtful man.

It seems to me of the utmost importance that we do listen in order to learn. Learning is not merely the accumulation of knowledge. Knowledge never brings perception; experience never flowers into the beauty of understanding. Most of us listen with the background of what we know, of what we have experienced. Perhaps you have never noticed the difference between the mind that really learns and the mind that merely accumulates, gathers knowledge. The mind that is accumulating knowledge never learns. It is always translating what it hears in terms of its own experience, in terms of the knowledge which it has gathered; it is caught up in the process of accumulating, of adding to what it already knows, and such a mind is incapable of learning. I do not know if you have noticed this. It is because we are never capable of learning that we pass our lives in sorrow and misery, in conflict and calumny; and hence the beauty of life, the vast significance of living, is lost. Each hungry generation destroys the coming generation. So it seems to me very important that we commune with each other quietly, in a dignified manner, and for that there must be a listening and a learning.

When you commune with your own heart, when you commune with your friend, when you commune with the skies, with the stars, with the sunset, with a flower, then surely you are listening so as to find out, to learn—which does not mean that you accept or

213

deny. You are learning, and either acceptance or denial of what is being said puts an end to learning. When you commune with the sunset, with a friend, with your wife, with your child, you do not criticize, you do not deny or assert, translate or identify. You are communing, you are learning, you are searching out. From this inquiry comes the movement of learning, which is never accumulative.

I think it is important to understand that a man who accumulates can never learn. Self-learning implies a fresh, eager mind—a mind that is not committed, a mind that does not belong to anything, that is not limited to any particular field. It is only such a mind that learns.

Do please experiment with what is being said as we go along. I would like to consider with you the vast and complex problem of freedom, but to inquire into that problem, to commune with it, to go into it hesitantly, tentatively, requires a very sharp, clear, and incisive mind—a mind that is capable of listening and thereby learning. If you observe what is taking place in the world, you will see that the margin of freedom is getting narrower and narrower. Society is encroaching upon the freedom of the individual. Organized religions, though they talk about freedom, actually deny it. Organized beliefs, organized ideas, the economic and social struggle, the whole process of competition and nationalism—everything around us is narrowing down the margin of freedom, and I do not think we are aware of it. Political tyrannies and dictatorships are implementing certain ideologies through propaganda and so-called education. Our worship, our temples, our belonging to societies, to groups, to political parties—all this further narrows the margin of freedom. Probably most of you do belong to various societies; you are committed to this or that group, and if you observe very closely, you will see how little freedom, how little human dignity you have

because you are merely repeating what others have said. So you deny freedom, and surely it is only in freedom that the mind can discover truth, not when it is circumscribed by a belief or committed to an ideology.

I wonder if you are at all aware of this extraordinary compulsion to belong to something? I am sure most of you belong to some political party, to a certain group or organized belief; you are committed to a particular way of thinking or living, and that surely denies freedom. I do not know if you have examined this compulsion to belong, to identify oneself with a country, with a system, with a group, with certain political or religious beliefs. And obviously, without understanding this compulsion to belong, merely to walk out of one party or group has no meaning because you will soon commit yourself to another.

Have you not done this very thing? Leaving one ism, you go and join something else—Catholicism, Communism, Moral Rearmament, and God knows what else. You move from one commitment to another, compelled by the urge to belong to something. Why? I think it is an important question to ask oneself. Why do you want to belong? Surely it is only when the mind stands completely alone that it is capable of receiving what is true—not when it has committed itself to some party or belief. Please do think about this question, commune with it in your heart. Why do you belong? Why have you committed yourself to a country, to a party, to an ideology, to a belief, to a family, to a race? Why is there this desire to identify yourself with something? And what are the implications of this commitment? It is only the man who is completely outside that can understand—not the man who is pledged to a particular group or who is perpetually moving from one group to another, from one commitment to another.

Surely, you want to belong to something because it gives you a sense of security—not only social security, but also inward security. When you belong to something, you feel safe. By belonging to this thing called Hinduism, you feel socially respectable, inwardly safe, secure. So you have committed yourself to something in order to feel safe, secure—which obviously narrows down the margin of freedom, does it not?

Most of us are not free. We are slaves to Hinduism, to communism, to one society or another, to leaders, to political parties, to organized religions, to gurus, and so we have lost our dignity as human beings. There is dignity as a human being only when one has tasted, smelled, known this extraordinary thing called freedom. Out of the flowering of freedom comes human dignity. But if we do not know this freedom, we are enslaved. That is what is happening in the world, is it not? And I think the desire to belong, to commit ourselves to something, is one of the causes of this narrowing down of freedom. To be rid of this urge to belong, to be free of the desire to commit oneself, one has to inquire into one's own way of thinking, to commune with oneself, with one's own heart and desires. That is a very difficult thing to do. It requires patience, a certain tenderness of approach, a constant and persistent searching into oneself without condemnation or acceptance. That is true meditation, but you will find it is not easy to do, and very few of us are willing to undertake it.

Most of us choose the easy path of being guided, being led; we belong to something, and thereby lose our human dignity. Probably you will say, "Well, I have heard this before; he is on his favorite subject," and go away. I wish it were possible for you to listen as if you were listening for the first time—like seeing the sunset or the face of your friend for the first time. Then you would learn, and thus learning, you would discover freedom for yourself—which is not the so-called freedom offered by another.

So let us inquire patiently and persistently into this question of what is freedom. Surely, only a free man can comprehend the truth—which is to find out if there is an eternal something beyond the measure of the mind; and the man who is burdened with his own experience or knowledge is never free because knowledge prevents learning.

We are going to commune with each other, to inquire together into this question of what is freedom and how to come by it. And thus to inquire, there must obviously be freedom right from the start; otherwise, you cannot inquire, can you? You must totally cease to belong, for only then is your mind capable of inquiring. But if your mind is tethered, held by some commitment, whether political, religious, social, or economic, then that very commitment will prevent you from inquiring because for you there is no freedom.

Do please listen to what is being said and see for yourself the fact that the very first movement of inquiry must be born of freedom. You cannot be committed and from there inquire, any more than an animal tied to a tree can wander far. Your mind is a slave as long as it is committed to Hinduism, to Buddhism, to Islam, to Christianity, to communism, or to something it has invented for itself. So we cannot proceed together unless we comprehend from the very beginning, from now on, that to inquire there must be freedom. There must be the abandonment of the past—not unwillingly, grudgingly, but a complete letting go.

After all, the scientists who got together to tackle the problem of going to the moon were free to inquire, however much they may have been slaves to their country, and all the rest of it. I am only referring to that peculiar freedom of the scientist at a research station. At least for the time being, in his laboratory, he is free to inquire. But our laboratory is our living; it is the whole span of life from day to day, from month to month, from year to year, and our freedom to inquire must be total; it cannot be a fragmentary thing, as it is with technical people. That is why, if we are to learn and understand what freedom is, if we are to delve deeply into its unfathomable dimensions, we must from the very start abandon all our commitments and stand alone. And this is a very difficult thing to do.

The other day in Kashmir, several sannyasis said to me, "We live alone in the snow. We never see anybody. No one ever comes to visit us." And I said to them, "Are you really alone, or are you merely physically separated from humanity?" "Oh, yes," they replied, "we are alone." But they were with their Vedas and Upanishads, with their experiences and gathered knowledge, with their meditations and *japas*. They were still carrying the burden of their conditioning. That is not being alone. Such men, having put on a saffron cloth, say to themselves, "We have renounced the world," but they have not. You can never renounce the world because the world is part of you. You may renounce a few cows, a house, some property, but to renounce your heredity, your tradition, your accumulated racial experience, the whole burden of your conditioning—this requires an enormous inquiry, a searching out, which is the movement of learning. The other way—becoming a monk or a hermit—is very easy.

So, do consider and see how your job, your going from the house to the office every day for thirty, forty, or fifty years, your knowledge of certain techniques as an engineer, a lawyer, a mathematician, a lecturer—how all this makes you a slave. Of course, in this world one has to know some technique and hold a job, but consider how all these things are narrowing down the mar-

gin of freedom. Prosperity, progress, security, success—everything is narrowing down the mind so that ultimately, or even now, the mind becomes mechanical and carries on by merely repeating certain things it has learned.

A mind that wants to inquire into freedom and discover its beauty, its vastness, its dynamism, its strange quality of not being effective in the worldly sense of that word—such a mind from the very beginning must put aside its commitments, the desire to belong; and with that freedom, it must inquire. Many questions are involved in this. What is the state of the mind that is free to inquire? What does it mean to be free from commitments? Is a married man to free himself from his commitments? Surely, where there is love, there is no commitment; you do not belong to your wife, and your wife does not belong to you. But we do belong to each other because we have never felt this extraordinary thing called love, and that is our difficulty. We have committed ourselves in marriage, just as we have committed ourselves in learning a technique. Love is not commitment, but again, that is a very difficult thing to understand because the word is not the thing. To be sensitive to another, to have that pure feeling uncorrupted by the intellect—surely, that is love.

I do not know if you have considered the nature of the intellect. The intellect and its activities are all right at a certain level, are they not? But when the intellect interferes with that pure feeling, then mediocrity sets in. To know the function of the intellect and to be aware of that pure feeling without letting the two mingle and destroy each other require a very clear, sharp awareness.

Now, when we say that we must inquire into something, is there in fact any inquiring to be done, or is there only direct perception? Do you understand? I hope I am making myself clear. Inquiry is generally a process of analyzing and coming to a conclusion.

That is the function of the mind, of the intellect, is it not? The intellect says, "I have analyzed, and this is the conclusion I have come to." From that conclusion it moves to another conclusion, and so it keeps going.

Surely, when thought springs from a conclusion, it is no longer thinking because the mind has already concluded. There is thinking only when there is no conclusion. This again you will have to ponder over, neither accepting nor rejecting it. If I conclude that communism or Catholicism or some other ism is so, I have stopped thinking. If I conclude that there is God or that there is no God, I have ceased to inquire. Conclusion takes the form of belief. If I am to find out whether there is God, or what is the true function of the state in relation to the individual, I can never start from a conclusion because the conclusion is a form of commitment.

So the function of the intellect is always, is it not, to inquire, to analyze, to search out; but because we want to be secure inwardly, psychologically, because we are afraid, anxious about life, we come to some form of conclusion to which we are committed. From one commitment we proceed to another, and I say that such a mind, such an intellect, being slave to a conclusion, has ceased to think, to inquire.

I do not know if you have observed what an enormous part the intellect plays in our life. The newspapers, the magazines, everything about us is cultivating reason. Not that I am against reason. On the contrary, one must have the capacity to reason very clearly, sharply. But if you observe, you find that the intellect is everlastingly analyzing why we belong or do not belong, why one must be an outsider to find reality, and so on. We have learned the process of analyzing ourselves. So there is the intellect with its capacity to inquire, to analyze, to reason and come to conclusions; and there is feeling, pure feeling, which is always being interrupted, colored by the intellect. And when the intellect interferes with pure feeling, out of this interference grows a mediocre mind. On the one hand we have intellect, with its capacity to reason based upon its likes and dislikes, upon its conditioning, upon its experience and knowledge; and on the other, we have feeling, which is corrupted by society, by fear. And will these two reveal what is true? Or is there only perception, and nothing else? I am afraid I am not making myself clear. I will explain what I mean.

To me there is only perception—which is to see something as false or true immediately. This immediate perception of what is false and what is true is the essential factor—not the intellect, with its reasoning based upon its cunning, its knowledge, its commitments. It must sometimes have happened to you that you have seen the truth of something immediately, such as the truth that you cannot belong to anything. That is perception: seeing the truth of something immediately, without analysis, without reasoning, without all the things that the intellect creates in order to postpone perception. It is entirely different from intuition, which is a word that we use with glibness and ease. And perception has nothing to do with experience. Experience tells you that you must belong to something; otherwise, you will be destroyed, you will lose your job, or your family, or your property, or your position and prestige.

So the intellect, with all its reasoning, with its cunning evaluations, with its conditioned thinking, says that you must belong to something, that you must commit yourself in order to survive. But if you perceive the truth that the individual must stand completely alone, then that very perception is a liberating factor; you do not have to struggle to be alone.

To me there is only this direct perception—not reasoning, not calculation, not analysis. You must have the capacity to analyze; you must have a good, sharp mind in order to reason, but a mind that is limited to reason and analysis is incapable of perceiving what is truth. To perceive immediately the truth that it is folly to belong to any religious organization, you must be able to look into your heart of hearts, to know it thoroughly, without all the obstructions created by the intellect. If you commune with yourself, you will know why you belong, why you have committed yourself; and if you push further, you will see the slavery, the cutting down of freedom, the lack of human dignity which that commitment entails. When you perceive all this instantaneously, you are free; you don't have to make an effort to be free. That is why perception is essential. All efforts to be free come from self-contradiction. We make an effort because we are in a state of contradiction within ourselves, and this contradiction, this effort, breeds many avenues of escape which hold us everlastingly in the treadmill of slavery.

So it seems to me that one must be very serious, but I do not mean serious in the sense of being committed to something. People who are committed to something are not serious at all. They have given themselves over to something in order to achieve their own ends, in order to enhance their own position or prestige. Such people I do not call serious. The serious man is he who wants to find out what is freedom, and for this he must surely inquire into his own slavery. Don't say you are not a slave. You belong to something, and that is slavery, though your leaders talk of freedom. So did Hitler, so does Khrushchev. Every tyrant, every guru, every president or vice-president, everyone in the whole religious and political setup talks of freedom. But freedom is something entirely different. It is a precious fruit without which you lose human dignity. It is love, without which you will never find God, or truth, or that nameless thing. Do what you will—cultivate all the virtues, sacrifice, slave, search out ways to serve man—without freedom, none of these will bring to light that reality within your own heart. That reality, that immeasurable something, comes when there is freedom—the total inward freedom which exists only when you have not committed yourself, when you do not belong to anything, when you are able to stand completely alone without bitterness, without cynicism, without hope or disappointment. Only such a mind-heart is capable of receiving that which is immeasurable.

November 22, 1959

Second Talk in Madras

This evening I would like to talk over with you the rather complex problem of sorrow. Sorrow is not just a matter of wanting something which one cannot get. It is deeper and much more subtle than that, and to understand it requires a great deal of inquiry, penetration. As I was saying the other day, understanding is not the result of intellectual perception. Understanding does not come by thinking things over. I want to understand this whole process of sorrow, with all the pain, the anxiety, the fear, the extraordinary heaviness and despair involved in it. I want to understand it, and merely thinking about it, reasoning about it, seeing different aspects of it, and coming to a conclusion will never bring about the total understanding that liberates the mind from sorrow. It is only when your whole being, as it were, invites sorrow, when it is open to the significance, the inwardness, the subtleties, the purity, the extraordinary movement of sorrow—only then, I feel, is there total understanding. If one is capable of this total understanding, which means that one is listening to sorrow, learning about sorrow, then I think the miracle takes place. To be free of sorrow is to give one's heart totally and entirely to the problem. But we very rarely give our hearts to a problem; we give only our minds, our thoughts. Thought alone will never resolve any vital human problem. We can think about the problem, and we must. We can also play with words, indulge in arguments, come to conclusions, and quote authorities, which is what most of us do, but this will not help us to open the door to understanding and thereby free the mind from the turmoil and entanglements of sorrow.

I do feel that sorrow can be ended. There is an ending to all sorrow, but the ending of sorrow begins with the understanding of sorrow. In the beginning is the end, not in thinking it over and then having sorrow come to an end eventually. At the very beginning is the ending because the end and the beginning are one; they are not two different things.

Most of us are held in some kind of sorrow, whether it be the petty little sorrow of a schoolboy or the equally petty sorrow of an adult who is caught in the conflict of his wants, his anxieties, his hates, his fears, his ambitions, his frustrations and fulfillments. Being caught in all this, we think in terms of a beginning and an ending; we do not see that in the very beginning of the understanding of sorrow is the ending of sorrow. I think this fact must be grasped, not just intellectually or verbally, but with love, with a sense of completely seeing the truth of it—which is not acceptance. The moment you merely accept something, there is its opposite, the denial of it. That is one of our difficulties—we either accept or reject or play in between. But if we actually see that in the beginning is the ending, if we perceive it as a fact, feel the truth of it totally, with all our

being, then we shall understand sorrow and not merely escape from sorrow.

After all, sorrow is the state of a mind which is in contradiction with itself—"I want" and "I don't want." The mind is driven by compulsions, desires; it struggles in the grip of ambition, with its fulfillments and frustrations. There are innumerable contradictions in our life, both inward and outward. In our speech, in our behavior, in our thoughts and feelings, there is a constant state of self-contradiction, and the tension, the pain, the turmoil of this self-contradiction is what we call sorrow.

I do not know if we are at all aware of this state of contradiction in ourselves. I think most of us are aware of it only when it reaches a crisis. Then we are thoroughly upset, and we want to find a way out of it, so we seek a method, a system, an escape. But we are not aware of our everyday state of self-contradiction. We do, or are forced to do, a certain job, and we really want to do something else. The life we lead, socially and economically, is not the life we would like to lead. In our relationships there is an element of compulsion, and we are subject to innumerable self-contradictions. I do not know if we are aware of all this. If we are aware of it, we bring it all to a head and act. But if we are not aware of this state of contradiction in ourselves, it goes on quietly smoldering until a tension is built up which eventually bursts into flame and either drives us into a neurotic state or forces us to find a temporary solution. Or there is a total understanding of all the hidden wants, a grasping of the whole significance of self-contradiction, and hence the ending of it.

Now, I do not know which it is you actually do, or whether you are even aware of your self-contradictions. Your tradition of centuries as a Hindu, which requires you to put ashes on your forehead and all the rest of it, meeting the pressure of the modern world creates a contradiction in you. You want to lead a spiritual life, whatever that may mean, and at the same time there are the demands of your daily life, and you are inwardly torn by innumerable desires. I wonder if you are aware of these contradictions in yourself. I think you should be because the moment you begin to be aware of yourself, it stirs up all the hidden corners of the mind, which most of us do not know—and do not wish to know because we do not want to be disturbed. We want to carry on with our traditions, and we also want to lead very modern lives. We go to a modern office and function there, and when we return home we are orthodox Hindus, Muslims, or whatever it is we are. We never face in ourselves this contradiction—the contradiction of authority and freedom, of leadership and the deep urge not to obey but to find out for oneself.

We must all have tasted this extraordinary contradiction in our lives; we must be somewhat aware of it, but unfortunately we never bring it to a crisis and for a very simple reason—because a crisis would mean action, something would have to be done about it. We are not willing to bring our self-contradiction to that boiling point when we have to act, and so we lead tortuous, contradictory lives, pining away for some haven where we hope we shall be at peace.

Please really listen to what I am saying and do not take it as a lecture which you attend and then go home and carry on as before. I am describing the state of your own mind. If you do not wish to listen, then do not come here, and that is the end of it. But since you are here, you are being driven to listen, even though the mind obviously resists listening. It wants to find an answer, a way out, but there is no answer, there is no way out of contradiction. Any way out of contradiction is the creation of another contradiction. One has to understand contradiction totally, go into it deeply, and feel one's way through it.

I have said that sorrow is a state of contradiction which becomes acute when something vital happens in your life—when your son dies, when your wife or husband turns away from you. It becomes acute when, seeking fulfillment, you find that in the shadow of fulfillment there is always frustration. You love, and you are not loved in return. You want to be good, and you are not. You pursue the outer, hoping to find the inner, or in pursuing the inner, you struggle to reject the outer. This is your actual state, is it not? In your life there is a ceaseless contradiction.

Now, why does this contradiction exist? Please do not give me an answer, a verbal explanation or definition because that is not going to solve the problem. You know all the definitions, all the answers, but you are still in sorrow. So mere explanation does not dissolve sorrow. Yet how easily we are satisfied with explanations, and that is the curious part of it. I wonder if you have noticed how quickly words, explanations, satisfy most of us. This indicates a peculiarly shallow mind, does it not? But we are now considering a problem which has no answer of that kind. There is no answer to sorrow. There is no way out of sorrow. Do what you will—go to church, mesmerize yourself with mantras, stand on your head, run away—nothing will free you from sorrow. What will put an end to sorrow is the understanding of sorrow.

So, why does contradiction exist in us? I want something, and I cannot get it. I want to become a great man, and on the way to becoming great, I find many temptations, many trials, many despairs, frustrations. In fulfillment there is the constant shadow of pain. So I ask myself—and may I suggest that you also should ask yourself—why is there this inner contradiction? Don't you think contradiction exists because the mind is capable of choice? I choose to go to the right instead of to the left. That very choice implies an attraction towards the left. If there were no attraction, I should not have to choose. Choice exists, surely, between two ways of action, two ways of thinking, living. That is fairly simple. The way of action I choose is for the purpose of fulfillment. I have a compulsion to fulfill myself in a certain direction—as a minister, as a writer, as a poet, as a singer, or through the family, begetting children. In that very process of choosing, there is the opposite.

Have you ever noticed yourself acting without choice? Has it ever happened to you that you have performed an action in which there was no choice at all? Surely it must have happened. You do something totally, completely, without thought, without the distraction of the intellect; your whole being, emotionally and intellectually, is there. Has this not happened to you? Perhaps rarely, but it does happen. At such moments, you know action in which there is no choice, hence no contradiction, and therefore no sorrow. Do not ask, "How am I to know that action? How am I to reach that choiceless state?" The very question, "How?" creates a contradiction.

I think the mind that seeks a system by which to understand something is a most stupid mind. It is all right to use a system as an engineer, as a mechanic, as a technician, or a scientist because you are dealing with mechanical things. But life is not mechanical; it is an imponderable thing, limitless, fathomless. Only a very superficial mind wants an answer to a problem that has no answer. When such a mind finds an answer, the answer reflects its own superficiality, and with that it is satisfied.

I am certainly not complaining, I am not irritated, I am just pointing out that there is no answer to sorrow, and this, I think, is an extraordinary thing to realize. What matters is to perceive the ways of sorrow. Out of choice there is contradiction, conflict, and therefore sorrow. After all, if we did not

have to choose, if there were no conflict, we should not have the problem of sorrow. But this does not mean that one must be contented, satisfied, and lead a comfortably bovine life. One has to grasp the inward significance of this. Where there is contradiction, there is effort; and where there is effort, there is choice. Choice implies the lack of totality of action. Only when you give to something your mind, your heart, your whole being—it is only then that there is no sorrow, because there is no contradiction. It is not a state to be arrived at by meditation or through awareness or through self-knowledge or through quoting various texts. The whole process of sorrow has to be understood.

What do we mean by understanding? What do we mean by perception? Surely, perception is a timeless state. As long as the mind is as it is now—the result of time, the residue of many thousands of yesterdays in relation to the present—sorrow cannot be understood. The mind is the result of time; it is the instrument of time, and with that instrument we are trying to understand or to dispel a problem which is itself the product of time.

Look, sirs, there is sorrow. We all feel the shadow of sorrow, so we find ways and means to get rid of it, to escape from it. We say, "Let us reason about it; let us bring together all the facts," and so on. This is the process of the mind, the intellect, which is obviously the result of time—time in the sense of what has happened, what one has learned, experienced. With this instrument we are trying to dispel sorrow. But sorrow itself is the product of time. I do not know if I am making this thing clearer or more obscure.

You say, "To understand sorrow I need time to think about it. I must grow in understanding. To be free of sorrow, I must practice a system until I arrive at a state in which my mind will no longer be disturbed." These are all steps in time, are they not? And through this process you are trying to dispel sorrow, the product of time—which is impossible. You need a totally new factor, a different quality, another dimension, and that is perception—perception in which there is no time at all. You see it instantaneously. But that requires astonishing attention; it requires all your vitality. The mind, being totally gathered, precipitates itself upon the problem and sees the depth, the width, the beauty of the problem. But unfortunately, your mind is not really attentive because you have been to the office, you have your quarrels, you have a miserable existence, you are driven as a slave by society, which grinds you down. So when you listen, you are tired out, and how can you give complete attention? I do not think you have ever given complete attention to anything. If you had, you would not be doing what you are actually doing. You would not be a clerk wanting to become the manager, or a politician wanting to be the governor or some other glorified person. You would not belong to any group, to any nationality, to any party, to any organized religion.

So I would suggest that the ending of sorrow is not a matter of evolution, a matter of growth, a matter of development. The truth about sorrow is to be perceived in the immediate. Surely, you have on occasion perceived something which has struck you so forcibly that it has altered your whole way of thinking. That something you have seen is the truth—and the truth brings its own action, its own revolution. You do not have to do a thing about it. That is why it is very important to perceive the truth of any problem.

Our problem is not sorrow and the ending of sorrow, so much as it is the fact that the mind is caught up in tradition, in the ways of mechanical thinking. That is really our problem. When the mind is free from all that, then one can look at sorrow. I wonder if we are at all aware of how tradition surrounds us, of how the mind is bound by tradition? Social tradition is very superficial, and one can throw it off as one throws off an old garment, but there is also tradition of a different kind, which is much stronger, much more profound, and that is the tradition of experience. I do not know if you are aware of how experience shapes the mind. Experience does shape the mind, does it not, sirs? And what is this experience? Surely, it is the reaction of the past to the present. The present is a challenge, and I respond according to my conditioning, according to my culture, according to my education—all of which is the past. This response of the past to the challenge of the present is experience; therefore, experience can obviously never be new, and that experience only strengthens the past. Experience, which is the response of the past to the present, only strengthens the past, so experience is never a liberating factor. On the contrary, it is a binding factor. I hope I am making myself somewhat clear.

We are all familiar with the idea that experience is necessary. Experience is necessary in dealing with mechanical things. I need experience to drive a car; I need experience to run a factory, to be a foreman, to work at a technical job. I can't do these things without experience. But is experience necessary for a mind that wants to perceive? Take a simple example. One wants to know what is reality, God, or truth, that something which is not measurable by the mind. Everybody fundamentally wants to know this; it does not matter who they are or what they call themselves. The atheists, the communists, the Catholics, the Hindus, the Muslims—everybody wants to find out this one thing because without it, life is empty. All the prayers, rituals, ideologies, ambitions, family quarrels, mean nothing without it. And everybody repeats what their gurus or the saints or their leaders have said. In this matter they have said, "You must grow in experience; you must practice this discipline, follow these teachings, and ultimately, in the long distance of time, you will attain the truth." I do not believe all that; to me it is all nonsense because through time you are hoping to capture the timeless, which is an impossibility. You have to go behind and find out how to liberate the mind from the enslavement of experience.

Do listen; this is very important. And it is quite difficult to understand because you have never thought about it at all. Great seers have always told us to acquire experience. They have said that experience gives us understanding. But it is only the innocent mind, the mind unclouded by experience, totally free from the past—it is only such a mind that can perceive what is reality. If you see the truth of that, if you perceive it for a split second, you will know the extraordinary clarity of a mind that is innocent. This means the falling away of all the encrustations of memory, which is the discarding of the past. But to perceive it, there can be no question of "how." Your mind must not be distracted by the "how," by the desire for an answer. Such a mind is not an attentive mind. As I said earlier in this talk, in the beginning is the end. In the beginning is the seed of the ending of that which we call sorrow. The ending of sorrow is realized in sorrow itself, not away from sorrow. To move away from sorrow is merely to find an answer, a conclusion, an escape; but sorrow continues. Whereas, if you give it your complete attention, which is to be attentive with your whole being, then you will see that there is an immediate perception in which no time is involved, in which there is no effort, no conflict; and it is this immediate perception, this choiceless awareness that puts an end to sorrow.

November 25, 1959

Third Talk in Madras

It would perhaps be worthwhile to talk over together the rather complex problem of action—not a specialized action in relation to a particular problem, but action as a whole. We are not here concerned with political action, or with whether you should choose a particular job, or with what you should do under certain circumstances. I think such an approach to the problem of action is invalid because we always seem to get lost in the part and are therefore incapable of tackling the problem as a whole. So if it is possible, I would like to consider, rather hesitantly, this question of action, of what to do.

Are we not faced with this problem, all of us, in different ways? But we unfortunately translate it in terms of what to do in a particular set of circumstances, what to do when a challenge arises, and so on. Surely, action born of choice is partial; it is never total, and our problem is how to capture the significance, the meaning of total action, and not be caught in a particular form of action demanded by society. If we can be very clear in our approach to this problem, then I think we shall find the right answer. But most of us invariably put wrong questions and get wrong answers, which only creates further problems.

So, what is total action? If one understands the totality of action, one will respond rightly to a particular demand, but to respond to a particular demand without this understanding only creates further confusion. If I act merely politically, without completely understanding the totality of action, such partial activity itself breeds contradiction. That is the case with most of us. Being caught in a network of special ideas, we try to solve our problems through partial action, which only increases and expands our problems.

Then what is total action? It is action in which there is no contradiction, is it not? And such action must obviously come about without effort because effort is the result of contradiction. I would like to go into this problem and understand it as much as possible within this given hour.

But before we go into the question of total action, must we not inquire into the present action of the individual in relation to society, in relation to an organized political group, in relation to everything that is going on about us? What is the action of the individual at present, and what can he do when society is crushing him, perverting his thinking, so that he has no freedom? The more society is organized, the more ruthless it is with the individual. We see this happening in different parts of the world. The communists have no place for the individual; though they talk about his ultimate freedom, the individual is completely destroyed. It is essentially the same with the organized religions. Though they talk about the individual attaining salvation, the individual is conditioned according to a particular creed, whether it be Catholic, Muslim, Hindu, Buddhist, or what you will.

So the encroachment of society upon the individual is constantly increasing, and his margin of freedom, his clarity of thinking, is becoming very narrow. I do not know if you are aware of this. You must be. And being aware of it, what are you to do? I am merely putting this question so that we shall begin to think it out together. What is the individual to do, under present circumstances, in his relationship with the family, with society? What is he to do with regard to religion? Should he join the overwhelmingly organized communist society? Surely, the moment you join an organization, you are already a slave to that organization. To fight a Hitler or to fight the communists, you have to employ the same methods which they use. We all know this. And what is the position of the individual who is confronted with all these things? Most of us are just swallowed up because to struggle against the pressure of society would involve a great deal of discomfort and uncertainty; it would mean a revolution in the life of the individual. To break away from the habit of belonging to something requires immense clarity in thinking because clarity in thinking is character. Without such clarity, there is no character, no individuality.

Now, what is the nature of total action? I think, tentatively, that there are two ways of action. One is action from a center, and the other is action which has no center. Most of us act from a center—the center which is made up of knowledge, of experience, the center which is conditioned according to the culture, the religion, the economic status in which we have lived. When you go to the factory or to the office, when you carry on your business, when you perform ceremonies, rituals, when you worship what you call God—in all this you are consciously or unconsciously acting from the center of knowledge, of tradition, of experience. That center can be controlled; it can be strengthened or weakened by a carefully organized society. I may leave Hinduism and become a Catholic or a communist, but whatever I do, that center will always remain; only the technique, the coating, has changed.

I am not saying anything very strange. This process is obviously taking place in each one of us. As a Hindu you think in a certain way. If you become a communist you will think in a different way, but your thinking is always from the center of conditioning. All self-conscious exertion to achieve arises from that center, which is also made up of ambition, fear, envy, hate, of the desire to do good and the desire to be good. So we are functioning from that center all the time—or rather, that center is functioning all the time because the mind is not different from that center. The thinker is the thought; the thought is not apart from the thinker. The center is the process of thinking according to a certain pattern, thinking according to our conditioning as Hindus, Buddhists, Christians, communists, or what you will. As long as that center is functioning, obviously there must be innumerable contradictions, conflicts; there must be fear, hope, despair. Out of the desire to fulfill ourselves and to avoid frustrations, we invent many illusions, myths, which we dignify with such words as *God, truth.*

There is, I feel, an action which is not the outcome of a center. But that action can be known only when one does not belong to any society, to any nationality, to any organized religion—which means that one is capable of withstanding all the influences of the group, of society. This, it seems to me, is the only hope for the individual in a world where communism is spreading and where organized religion, which is fighting communism, is also spreading. After all, the Roman Catholic Church is a highly organized religious body, and it is fighting communism, which is also highly organized, and which is its own religion. These two—communism and organized resistance to communism—are spreading. So what is the individual to do? To belong to any group, to any religious or political organization implies the functioning of a center, of a conditioned mind.

I do not know, sirs, if I am making myself clear. If not, we can discuss this point again later on.

That center, from which most of us function, is made up of knowledge in different forms—knowledge as technique, knowledge as experience, knowledge as tradition, knowledge as memory of the things we have been told. It is essentially a center of habit, a center of authority. That center is authority itself. So I think we should examine the whole process of knowledge and authority.

A mind that is a slave to knowledge is bound by authority. Please think it over as I am talking to you and do not wait until you

go home. The mind that has accumulated knowledge of what to do, what to think, or how to think; the mind that has merely acquired the technique of a professor, of a mechanic, of a priest, of a bureaucrat—such a mind is obviously a slavish mind, bound to its own knowledge. It is never free. The mind is free only when it is aware of its authoritarian knowledge and puts it aside. Then it can use knowledge without being enslaved by knowledge.

But this is an extremely difficult thing to do. Knowledge gives us a sense of functioning in society with stability, with clarity; it gives us a feeling of certainty, a sense of security; so knowledge breeds authority, and we worship authority. We worship the man who knows, the professor, the guru, the writer of books, and so on. But the mind that is inquiring, that is seeking to understand what is freedom, cannot be a slave to knowledge.

If you observe your own mind in operation, you will see how extraordinarily difficult it is to be free of past experiences, previous thoughts, established habits. I do not know if you have observed and have tried to understand yourselves in this way, but if you have, then you will know how arduous it is to free the mind from the pattern of yesterday. Yesterday may be tradition, it may be your own experience, it may be what you have read, what you have gathered, what you have listened to, what you have learned. Essentially it is based on the opinions, the ideas of others—on what Shankara, Buddha, Christ, Marx, or Stalin has said. This yesterday has already set going a momentum; it has established a pattern which has become your authority, and unless this momentum of yesterday, which has created in your mind a pattern of authority, is understood, you are blocked in the pursuit of self-knowledge. You cannot proceed further because authority, whether political or so-called religious, makes the mind a slave; it cannot think freely, it cannot be totally aware.

When knowledge becomes the core of authority, it is very difficult for the mind to be free of authority. The electronic brain can perform certain functions much faster and far more efficiently than the human mind, but it is not free. It cannot think of something new, it can only function in accordance with what it has been taught to do—and that is exactly the situation with the human mind, except that in the case of the human mind, there is hope of freedom, of freshness, of newness. But the freshness, the newness cannot come into being as long as the mind is unaware of and does not understand the binding quality of authority, of knowledge.

Knowledge is a peculiar thing, is it not? We not only know the past, but we also know the future, or think we do, because the past projects itself through the present into the future. The communists, like the organized religious people, claim to know the future, and they are willing to sacrifice the present generation to achieve that future, the ultimate and perfect utopia. They are slaves, not only to the past, but also to their projected future.

Now, realizing that our minds are crippled, that we are not free either from the past or from the projected future, should we not ask ourselves whether there is action which has no center? But first of all, is it possible for one to communicate to another the significance of such action? I am speaking English, and you understand the English words, which have a certain meaning, so we understand each other to some extent at the verbal level. But surely the significance of total action is communicable only when you and I go beyond the verbal level. Mere description cannot bring about understanding; on the contrary, description perverts understanding if your mind clings to words because you give a certain interpretation to the words, which creates a blockage between us. The moment we try to communicate with each other merely at the verbal level, there is agreement or denial. You say, "I am of the same opinion," or "You are wrong, I do not agree with you," and so on. I think this approach is completely false. Understanding is not a matter of agreement and disagreement. Either you understand or you do not understand. The mind that approaches the problem with a set of opinions, conclusions, will agree or disagree, and so there is no perception of the actual.

I would like to talk about action which is not partial, which is not the outcome of knowledge, which is not the product of authority, but something entirely different—which means, really, action without a center. It must have happened to you that you have done something without calculation, without argumentation, without the cunning machinations of thought, without thinking of what has been or what may be, without choice. You must have done something in your life without this whole process taking place. But to understand this kind of action requires a great deal of self-knowledge, which is comprehension of the workings of one's own mind, because it is so easy to deceive oneself and say, "I have acted without a center; I have joined such and such a group without the process of thought"—which is idiotic and immature, for what is functioning is one's own hidden desire. Whereas, action which is total and which has no center requires exploration into oneself—and this means, really, going into the whole process of thinking, into the whole mechanism of the mind, without a limit, without an end in view.

I do not know if any of you have ever seriously gone into yourselves with complete willingness, with wholeheartedness, with joy, without any sense of compulsion, and have tried to discover what you are. Merely to say, "I am this" or "I am not that," is again immature; it has no meaning. To explore, to discover, there must be joy, there must be enthusiasm, vitality, especially when going into this complex thing called the mind. But most of us explore either out of despair or to find something which will give us nourishment, which will give us stability, an assurance of continuity. Real inquiry must be without any of these things. One inquires just to find out what is actually taking place. I do not know if you have ever done that, if you have ever studied yourself as a woman studies her face in a mirror. There is nothing wrong with studying your face in a mirror, which is to see it exactly as it is—straight hair, crooked nose, and so on. You can embellish it, color it, try to make it more beautiful, but that is another matter. Similarly, to study yourself is to see what is actually the state of your mind—why you think and do certain things, why you go to the office or to the temple, why you talk in a certain way to your wife, to your servant, why you read the sacred books, why you attend these talks. You have to know all this from moment to moment, not as accumulated knowledge on the basis of which you function. Learning is a movement of the mind in which there is no accumulation. You can learn only when knowledge is not being gathered from the movement of learning. The moment you gather knowledge, add to what you have learned, you have ceased to learn. A mind that gathers knowledge through learning is driven by the desire for safety, security, or is out for some profit. Whereas, in the movement of learning there is no accumulation—and that is the beauty of learning. To learn is just to see what you are—the hate, the calumny, the vulgarity, the fears, the hopes, the anxieties, the ambitions—without judging,

without evaluating, without condemning or accepting.

Understanding or perception comes when there is a movement of learning which is not additive. If the mind can observe and comprehend itself in this way, you will find that out of such observation and comprehension there is an action which is total, which has no center as the 'I', the self.

Sirs, do try it. Do not attempt to cultivate a particular kind of action, but inquire into the whole problem of action—which you cannot do as long as you are merely seeking an answer to the problem. It is because we give so little thought to these things that our lives are miserable, petty, narrow, sorrow laden. What most of us want is respectability.

A man who would really inquire must first understand his own mind. Without understanding your own mind, you will understand nothing. You may go to church, perform rituals, you may repeat like a gramophone record what you have read in the Scriptures, but that does not make for religion. A religious mind is one that has understood its own processes, its hidden motives, its untrodden paths. It has delved into the profound depths of itself because it is living, moving, functioning, and never coming to a conclusion; it is discovering all the time what is truth. Truth is not static; it is moving, dynamic; it has no abode, and the mind that is incapable of following it swiftly can never understand the quality, the immeasurable nature of truth. That is why self-knowledge is essential—not knowledge of the higher self, the atma, and all that immature stuff, but knowledge of yourself, which is to see how your own mind is conditioned.

Without perceiving the significance of knowledge and authority, it is impossible to know the totality of action in which there is no contradiction. Total action is action without the sense of compulsion and therefore without regret. Surely, such action is wisdom. Wisdom is not to be taught. There can be no school of wisdom. Wisdom is not something that you buy or that comes to you through service, self-sacrifice, and all the rest of it. Wisdom does not come from reading books, or through having many experiences, or through doing what your father or your grandmother or your leaders tell you to do. Wisdom comes only to the mind that perceives what is true and when perception is total. There is no perception without self-knowledge. Wisdom comes only when there is no conflict. You will understand what is total action only when you begin to inquire into the whole process of the mind, and then you will also know how to act in a particular situation, what to do today or any day. Through the part you can never understand the whole, but when you perceive the significance of the whole, out of that comprehension you can understand the part.

To go into all this requires an understanding of the process of one's own thinking. And the beauty of this inquiry lies not in what is achieved, in what is learned or gained, but in the complete innocence of a mind that is free to see anew the skies, the many faces, the rivers, and the rich land. Only a mind that has understood itself is capable of receiving the benediction which has no ending.

November 29, 1959

Fourth Talk in Madras

It must be very difficult to live in goodness, to be humble, to have no anger, not to be envious, not to be acquisitive. To make us somewhat civilized, to keep us within the margin of decency, there are all the various religious sanctions, the taboos, the fears, the promise of heaven, and the threat of hell; and to change without any of these influences, without any compulsion, without reward or punishment—which is to bring about, through comprehension, a radical transformation within the mind—seems to be extraordinarily difficult. To change is apparently one of the most arduous things to do—if we ever change at all. This is not said in any spirit of cynicism. But without understanding the whole process of change, we seek various systems of discipline by which to control or shape the mind. We suppress what we feel should be cast off and thereby hope to sublimate or transcend it.

That is the case with most of us, is it not? When we are angry, we try to suppress our anger; we seek a solution, a way out of it. We never go into the problem and understand it totally, completely—yet this may be the only way of resolving the problem of anger or any other problem that creates conflict in the mind. We live with conflict throughout our lives; from childhood until we die, we are in eternal conflict, both within and without. We are used to exerting will, making an effort to suppress or control ourselves; we practice various methods of discipline, meditation; we read the sacred books and all that sort of thing, hoping to escape from the things which create conflict in our lives. To keep us within the bounds of respectable behavior, there are the various religious sanctions and the moral codes of public opinion, and we try to live in accordance with all that.

So our existence is really a state of contradiction, in which there is a constant effort to be this and not to be that. We are everlastingly trying to become something, to avoid something, to repress, conform, adjust. If you observe yourselves—as one must if one is at all intelligent—you will know that this process goes on in us from day to day, year in and year out until we die. We are making a constant effort to conform, to adjust, to comply, to imitate; this is our life, and from this pattern we hardly ever break away. There is no cessation of that which causes in us a contradiction. We never totally free ourselves from anger, greed, envy, jealousy, although we are forever struggling against these things.

Now, I would like, if I may, to talk about this effort to change and about what is implied in change. I would like to go into it by thinking aloud and talking it over with you because I feel that there must be a fundamental change in the quality of the mind itself, and that the mere outward adjustments of a cunning mind seeking its own profit will lead us nowhere. Such a mind can never really know the quality of peace. It cannot possibly be aware without choice, or be in that state of creative reality.

If one is to go very deeply into this question of change, one must approach it, I think, by understanding what consciousness is—not the consciousness which the books describe, and about which many people have certain theories, conclusions, but the consciousness operating in oneself. That is surely the only point from which one can start. One cannot assume anything; one cannot start with any theory, conviction, or conclusion. I think we must proceed very simply, and not bring in what Shankara and other people have said about consciousness. It is only then that we shall be able to go into this problem as two human beings who are attempting to uncover the ways of our own thinking, to understand our conflicts and why we do certain things.

In trying to understand what we call consciousness, I think we must be aware of certain things. We are not analyzing, we are merely observing—which is quite different from the analytical process, which has a purposive intent, for by its means you hope to get somewhere. So our examination of consciousness is not a process of analysis intended for self-improvement. To me, the desire to improve oneself is a horror; it is a most childish, immature way of thinking. It makes living into a profession; it is on the same level with struggling to get ahead in science, in business, in mathematics, or what you will. We are here not analyzing or trying to improve the self. We are trying to observe the self, to understand this consciousness which is the 'me' in everyday action, in everyday thought and feeling—the desires, the passions, the angers, the brutalities, the cruelties and fears. It is to discover the ways of the 'me' that we are here, not in order to improve the 'me'. There is no improvement of the 'me'. It is only the mediocre mind that says, "I must be much more clever, much more intelligent, much more erudite." However much a petty mind tries to improve itself, it will always be petty.

So please understand from what point of view we are approaching this thing called consciousness. If we do not understand in what manner to look at consciousness, we invariably try to change or control it, and this effort further limits consciousness. It is the very nature of such effort to create a center as the 'me' from which to control consciousness. I do not know if you have noticed that the moment you make an effort, you have already an objective, and this objective limits your vision.

Please come with me in looking at this problem. Do not say, "Is not effort necessary? Is not our very existence—with its pains, pleasures, conflicts, contradictions—a process of effort?" We know all that; you do not have to tell me that, and I do not have to tell you. But I am trying to point out to you something totally different, and that is why you must approach it a little cautiously, hesitantly.

As I was saying, if we do not understand the nature of effort, all action is limiting. Effort creates its own frontiers, its own objectives, its own limitations. Effort has the time-binding quality. You say, "I must meditate, I must make an effort to control my mind." That very effort to control puts a limit on your mind. Do watch this, do think it out with me. To live with effort is evil; to me it is an abomination, if I may use a strong word. And if you observe, you will realize that from childhood on we are conditioned to make an effort. In our so-called education, in all the work we do, we struggle to improve ourselves, to become something. Everything we undertake is based on effort, and the more effort we make, the duller the mind becomes.

So there can be a radical change only when there is the cessation of effort. Most of us are conditioned to make an effort in order to produce the change, and that is why there is no real change at all. Such effort merely produces a modification, with its own limitations.

Please do not accept my word for it, or reject what is being said. It is for you to find out if what I am saying is true. Your whole conditioning is based on the assumption that effort is necessary, but now somebody comes along and says, "Look, that assumption is all wrong." How are you going to find out for yourself what is true? What I am saying may be entirely false, without any reality behind it; it may be born of the idiosyncrasies of a man who is having an easy life and therefore does not want to make any effort. You may think, "It is all very well for you to talk as you do, but we are born with various limitations and in varying degrees of poverty, and we must make an effort; otherwise, we shall be crushed. Besides, our *shastras* all tell us to make an effort, to discipline, control, shape our minds."

So, how will you find out whether what is being said is true? You are used to conflict; it is part of your tradition; you are used to discipline, to control, to adjustment. Public opinion is tremendously important to you. What somebody else says is your "god"—

whether it be Shankara or your neighbor. Do watch your own minds as I am talking; observe how you think. With that mentality how are you going to find out if what is being said is true or false? To find out, surely, you have to question your own ways of thinking and not just question what is being said. You obviously cannot find out what is true and what is false with a mind which from childhood has been taught to conform, to imitate, to follow. So you have to begin by inquiring into the state of your own mind. You have to look into your own consciousness and see why you follow, why you imitate, why you conform. Surely, that is the beginning of any inquiry into consciousness. In such inquiry, there is no analysis, no purposive intent. You are observing to find out if it is possible for the mind to function, to live, to act every day without effort. You see, sirs, a mind that is in a constant state of contradiction, effort, is wearing itself out. It is never fresh, innocent. And surely, you need a fresh mind, an innocent mind, a good, clear mind to perceive the truth or the falseness of anything.

We are inquiring into this thing called consciousness, which should be a total entity, a fully integrated state. But there is a part of consciousness which is in darkness, and a part which is in light—not the spiritual light of Brahma, of Jesus, and all that nonsense which you have been conditioned to believe in. The part which is in light is the superficial mind that goes to the office, that quarrels, that wants a better job—the mind that functions every day. Then there is the hidden mind, the unconscious mind, with its motives, its desires, its intimations of a struggle that is going on below the level of the superficial mind. The whole of that is consciousness. To understand this consciousness, you cannot refer to the books, to what Shankara and others have said about consciousness. If you do, you are lost because you are not aware of what you are, and you merely quote the statements of others. Any fool can quote, and the more foolish he is, the more he quotes. To quote is to stop thinking, to stop inquiring, and therefore the mind becomes dull, insensitive.

I know, sirs, that in listening to me you may say, "It is a good harangue." You do not realize what quoting does to your minds, how dull it makes you. I was talking the other day with a man who was very erudite, who could quote any of the scriptures, whether from the East or from the West, from the North or from the South. But he was totally incapable of thinking for himself. So please do stop quoting and think for yourselves; find out what your own thoughts and feelings are. When you quote you are relying on the authority of another, which is a very easy escape from looking at your own minds and perceiving yourselves as you actually are.

Now you and I, as two human beings, can see that consciousness is everything we think, feel, smell, desire—all the sensations, and behind the sensations, the desires of wanting and not wanting. We cannot go into too many details, but we can see that all of this makes up the totality of consciousness. In this consciousness there is contradiction; though at certain moments we may know a state free of contradiction, it is merely a reaction.

Let us approach it differently. There is the conscious and the unconscious mind. I am not using these words in any special psychoanalytical way; I am just using them as you and I use them in everyday conversation. There is the conscious mind, the mind that is educated in modern society, with all its demands, compulsions, hopes, and fears. If I am born a communist, I generally continue to be a communist. My conscious mind, having been educated in communism, continues to function within that pattern, just as

a Catholic, a Hindu, or a Buddhist functions within his particular pattern. It is the conscious mind that acquires a technique—the technique of how to run a motor or of how to get rid of your unwanted desires. It is the conscious mind that learns from a guru how to imitate virtue, what to do in order to be "spiritual," how to suppress this and cultivate that. It is the conscious mind that acquires knowledge, that adjusts at the superficial level.

Then there is the so-called unconscious. What is the unconscious? How are you going to find out for yourself and not merely quote the psychologist, the expert, the analyst? The unconscious mind is obviously something which most of us have not looked into. And are we capable of looking into it? The only instrument we have for looking into something is the conscious mind, which is learning, acquiring knowledge, and which is always positive in its approach, and can such a mind inquire into the unconscious? I do not know if I am making myself clear. Probably I am not.

I want to know why I am envious—I am taking that as an example. Why am I envious? The conscious mind can understand and explain why it is envious. When it does, it also creates the opposite and says, "I must not be envious." So there is conflict, an effort to be this and not to be that. But envy implies competition, comparison; it implies wanting to be something—to be the prime minister, to be the most famous scholar, to be the biggest lawyer in town, and so on. So envy is very deeply rooted; it is not a thing that can be pushed aside by saying, "I must not be envious."

Now, to inquire into envy, to follow its deep roots requires a mind that is not positive at all. I do not know if you see that. With most of us, the conscious mind has only two approaches: the positive or its opposite, the so-called negative. Either it wants or it does not want. It wants to get rid of envy, or else it wants to keep envy and enjoy it. It says, "Envy has its pain and pleasure; I will try to remove the pain but keep the pleasure of envy." Thus it approaches envy positively, or so-called negatively. But to find the roots of envy requires quite a different state of mind altogether. If envy were a shallow plant, one could simply pull it out and throw it away. But the plant has become a tree with deep roots; it covers the whole of modern civilization, and so the problem continues.

To inquire into envy, to go down into the unconscious where its deep roots are hidden, you require not the conscious mind that has been educated but quite a different mentality, an entirely different state of mind. You do not know the unconscious except through intimations and hints, through dreams and certain moments of clarity; and the unconscious is surely not explorable by the conscious mind. When the conscious mind does try to explore or examine it, there is always the observer watching the observed. That is all the conscious mind can do. It can watch as an observer, as an experiencer, as a thinker apart from the observed, the experienced, the thought. This is still a positive process though it may appear to be negative. The positive process has a negative which is still part of itself.

What we are trying to do, as I said at the beginning of the talk, is to understand effort and to find out if it is possible for the mind to be totally free of effort—free to function integrally, with joy, with delight, without effort.

So what is the conscious mind to do? There are dreams, hints, intimations from the unconscious, but when the conscious mind tries to interpret them, it is still within the field of the positive, with its opposite, the so-called negative. To understand something of which it knows nothing, except vaguely, the

conscious mind must surely be completely silent—if I may use that word. I hope you understand what I mean. The silent mind is not dormant, it is not sluggishly asleep. The conscious mind must be in abeyance, which is to be in that state of attention where there is no positive or negative response.

Look here, sirs, I am trying to tell you something. It is something of which you do not know, except that you have heard of it or read about it in books. You have never felt the beauty of it in your hearts, in your minds. What is the state of a mind that listens? Obviously, an interpretative mind cannot listen. When you interpret what you hear according to your knowledge, you are not listening. In order to explore, to find out, your mind must be in a truly negative state—which is not the opposite of being positive but a wholly different thing. It is the total absence of the positive, with its negative. Your conscious mind must be open, without any purpose, to the intimations of the unconscious; it must be in that state of attention which is really a total negation.

I am sorry if you do not understand all this, but I hope you will. I think every human being can live with dignity, with a sense of freedom, in the state of effortlessness, and it is only in this state of living without effort that there can be creativeness, the perception of reality. The conscious mind must be capable of total attention, which is total negation—and that is the totally positive state. But I won't go into all that now. When the conscious mind is totally attentive, it can look into the unconscious, which is something that it does not know. The unconscious, surely, is the racial inheritance, the traditional values which have been given to you for untold ages. Though you may be ultramodern in the techniques you have learned, in the unconscious you are still a Brahmin, a Vaisya, a Hindu, a Catholic, or whatever because for centuries it has been dinned into your racial unconscious. The unconscious is the accumulated experience not only of the individual but also of the family, the race. It is the result of man's effort to be, to become, to grow, to survive. So consciousness, which is the outcome of effort, is limited. As I said at the beginning, where there is effort, there is an objective; where there is effort, there is a limitation on attention and on action. To do good in the wrong direction is to do evil. Do you understand? For centuries we have done "good" in the wrong direction by assuming that we must be this, we must not be that, and so on, which only creates further conflict.

So the mind has been trained for centuries to suppress, to discipline itself in an effort to overcome its own limitations; and though it may invent the idea of the soul, the atma, the higher self, it is still within the confines of its own thought, within the limits of its own endeavor; therefore, what it calls reality is only a projection of its own delusion. With most of us, this is the actual state of the mind. And how is such a mind to be free? That is the next question.

I recognize that my mind is the result of time, of effort, and I see that effort creates bondage, places a limitation on the extent of consciousness. How is the mind to be free of this limitation? I am not asking "how" in order to find a method by which to free the mind. To ask for a method is a most immature way of thinking, and that is not my purpose. I am asking "how" only to inquire if there is a way out of this bondage of the mind, and it may be that there is no way out at all.

So you are left with the problem: Is there a possibility of freeing the mind totally? This problem, like every other human problem, has no answer. Do you understand, sirs? Here is a problem which, if one really goes into it, is found to be tremendously complex, and it would be silly on my part to say,

"This is the answer." Therefore you are left with the problem. But if you have deeply followed all that has been said, the problem is no longer a problem because you will already have perceived the totality of it; and a mind that perceives the totality of any problem is free of the problem.

You may say this is a very dirty trick I am playing on you—giving you the problem and not showing you a way out. I say there is no way out. But the problem itself is resolved if you see the totality of it. The state of love is entirely different from the feeling that we call love. For most of us, love is a contradiction, full of jealousy, envy, possession, acquisitiveness, despair—you know all that rattling of the mind. But if one hears the noise, if one sees all the implications of so-called love, then the problem itself is resolved. What is required is perception and not this constant trying to find an answer to the problem.

So, effort always limits the mind. If you see the truth of that, it is enough. That very perception will operate; you do not have to do a thing. To see the truth of something is the liberating factor. It is only when you do not see the truth of any problem that you ask, "What am I to do?" If you see how your mind has been conditioned for centuries, and how that conditioning from the past is projecting itself through the present into the future; if you see how your mind is a slave to time, to environment, to the various beliefs which it has inherited and acquired; if you see how you are constantly adding to your conditioning through experience born of that very conditioning—if you see all this very clearly, then liberation comes without your seeking it, and life is then something entirely different.

December 2, 1959

Fifth Talk in Madras

I think it would be profitable and worthwhile to find out for ourselves why the mind is so restless. It is as restless as the sea, never stable, never quiet; though outwardly it may be still, inwardly it is full of ripples, full of grooves and every kind of disturbance. I think it is essential to go into this question rather deeply, and not merely ask how to quiet the mind. There is no way to quiet the mind. Of course, one can take pills, tranquilizers, or follow blindly some system; one can drug the mind with prayers, with repetitions, but a drugged mind is no mind at all. So it seems to me of the utmost importance to go deeply into this question of why the mind is everlastingly seeking something, and having found it, is not satisfied, but moves on to something else—an unceasing movement from satisfaction to disappointment, from fulfillment to pain and frustration. We must all be aware of this endless cycle of pleasure and sorrow. Everything is passing, impermanent; we live in a constant state of flight, and there is no place where one can be quiet, especially inwardly, because every recess of the mind is disturbed. There is no untrodden region in the mind. Consciously or unconsciously we have tried in various ways to bring quietness, stillness, a state of peace to the mind; and having got it, we have soon lost it again. You must be aware of this endless search which is going on in your own mind.

So I would like to suggest that—with hesitance, without dogmatism, without quoting, or coming to conclusions—we try to probe into this restless activity of our minds. And I think we shall have to begin by asking ourselves why we seek at all, why we inquire, why there is this longing to arrive, to achieve, to become something. After all, you are probably here a little bit out of curiosity, but even more, I hope, out of the desire to seek, to find out. What is it that you are seeking? And why do you seek? If we can go deeply into this question by asking ourselves why we are seeking—if we can, as it were, open the door by means of that question, then I think we may perhaps have a glimpse into something which is not illusory and which does not have the transient quality of that which is merely pleasurable or gratifying.

Why is it, and what is it, you are seeking? I wonder if you have ever put that question to yourselves? You know, a challenge is always new because it is something that demands your attention. You have to respond; there is no turning your back on it, and either you respond totally, completely, or partially, inadequately. The incapacity to respond totally to a challenge creates conflict. The world in its present state is a constant challenge to each one of us, and when we do not respond with the fullness, with all the depth and beauty of the challenge itself, then inevitably there is turmoil, anxiety, fear, sorrow. In the same way, this question—what are you seeking, and why do you seek?—is a challenge, and if you do not respond with your whole being but treat it merely as an intellectual problem, which is to respond partially, then obviously you will never find a total answer. Your response to the challenge is partial, inadequate, when you merely make statements or think in terms of definite conclusions to which you have come. The challenge is always new, and you have to respond to it anew—not in your habitual, customary way. If we can put this question to ourselves as though we are considering it for the first time, then our response will be entirely different from the superficial response of the intellect.

What is it that you are seeking, and why do you seek it? Does not this very seeking instigate restlessness? If there were no seeking, would you stagnate? Or would there then be a totally different kind of search? But before we go into the more complex aspects of our inquiry, it seems to me important to find out what you and I as individual human beings are seeking. Obviously, the superficial answer is always to say, "I am seeking happiness, fulfillment." But in seeking happiness, in seeking fulfillment, we never stop to ask ourselves if there is such a thing as fulfillment. We long for fulfillment or satisfaction, and we go after it without looking to see if there is any reality behind the word. In pursuing fulfillment, its expression varies from day to day, from year to year. Growing weary of the more worldly satisfactions, we seek happiness in good conduct, in social service, in being brotherly, in loving one's neighbor. But sooner or later this movement towards fulfillment through good conduct also comes to an end, and we turn in still another direction. We try to find happiness through intellectual pursuits, through reason, logic, or we become emotional, sentimental, romantic. We give to the word *happiness* different connotations at different times. We translate it in terms of what we call peace, God, truth; we think of it as a heavenly abode where we shall be completely fulfilled, never disturbed, and so on. That is what most of us want, is it not? That is why you read the shastras, the Bible, the Koran, or other religious books—in the hope of bringing quietness to the restless mind. Probably that is why you are here.

Seeking implies an object, an end in view, does it not? There can be no search for what is unknown. You can only seek something which you have known and lost or which you have heard of and want to gain. You cannot seek that which you do not know. In a peculiar way, you already know what happiness is. You have tasted the flavor of it, the past has given you the sensation, the pleasure, the beauty of it, so you already know its quality, its nature, and that memory you project. But what you have known is not

what is; your projection is not what you really want. What you have tasted is not sufficient; you want something more, more, more, and so your life is an everlasting struggle.

I hope you are listening to what is being said, not as to a lecture, but as though you were looking at a film of yourself struggling, groping, searching, longing. You are sorrowful, anxious, fearful, caught up in tremendous hope and despair, in the extremes of contradiction, and from this tension there is action. That is all you know. You seek fulfillment outwardly, in the house, in the family, in going to the office, in becoming a rich man, or the chief inspector, or a famous judge, or the prime minister—you know, the whole business of climbing the ladder of success and achievement. You climb that ladder until you are old, and then you seek God. You collect money, honors, position, prestige, and when you have reached a certain age, you turn to poor old God. God does not want such a man, sirs. God wants a complete human being who is not a slave. He does not want a dehydrated human being but one who is active, who knows love, who has a deep sense of joy.

But unfortunately, in our search for happiness, fulfillment, there is an endless struggle going on. Outwardly we do everything possible to assure ourselves of that happiness, but outward things fail. The house, the property, the relationship with wife and children—it can all be swept away, and there is always death waiting around the corner. So we turn to inward things, we practice various forms of discipline in an effort to control our minds, our emotions, and we conform to a standard of good conduct, hoping that we shall one day arrive at a state of happiness that cannot be disturbed.

Now, I see this whole process going on, and I am asking myself: Why do we seek at all? I know that we do seek. We join societies which promise a spiritual reward;

we follow gurus who exhort us to struggle, to sacrifice, to discipline ourselves, and all the rest of it; so we are seeking, endlessly. Why is there this seeking? What is the compulsion, the urge that makes for seeking, not only outwardly, but inwardly? And is there any fundamental difference between the outward and the inward movement of seeking, or is it only one movement? I do not know if I am making myself clear. We have divided our existence into what we call the outward life and the inward life. Our daily activities and pursuits are the outward life, and when we do not get happiness, pleasure, satisfaction in that area, we turn to the inward as a reaction. But the inward also has its frustration and despair.

So, what is it that is making us seek? Do please ask yourself this question; go into it with me. Surely, a happy, joyous man does not seek God; he is not trying to achieve virtue; his very existence is splendid, radiant. So, what is it that is urging us to seek and to make such tremendous effort? If we can understand that, perhaps we shall be able to go beyond this restless search.

Do you know what is the cause of your seeking? Please do not give a superficial answer because then you will only blind yourself to the actual. Surely, if you go deeply into yourself, you will see that you are seeking because there is within each one of us a sense of isolation, of loneliness, of emptiness; there is an inner void which nothing can fill. Do what you will—perform good works, meditate, identify yourself with family, with the group, with the race, with the nation—that emptiness is still there, that void which cannot be filled, that loneliness which nothing can take away. That is the cause of our endless seeking, is it not? Call it by a different name, it does not matter. Deep within one there is this sense of emptiness, of loneliness, of utter isolation. If the mind can

go into this void and understand it, then perhaps it will be resolved.

At one time or another, perhaps while you were walking, or while you were sitting by yourself in a room, you must have experienced this sense of loneliness, the extraordinary feeling of being cut off from everything—from your family, from your friends, from ideas, hopes—so that you felt you had no relationship with anybody or anything. And without penetrating into it, without actually living with it, understanding it, the mind cannot resolve that feeling.

I think there is a difference between knowing and experiencing. You probably know what this feeling of loneliness is from what you have heard or read about it, but knowing is entirely different from the state of experiencing. You may have read extensively, you may have accumulated many experiences so that you know a great deal, but knowledge is not living. If you are an artist, a painter, every line, every shadow means something. You are observing all the time, watching the movement and the depth of shadows, the loveliness of a curve, the expression of a face, the branch of a tree, the colors everywhere—you are alive to everything. But knowledge cannot give you this perception, this capacity to feel, to experience something that you see. Experiencing is one thing, and experience is another. Experience, knowledge, is a thing of the past, which will go on as memory, but experiencing is a living perception of the now; it is a vital awareness of the beauty, the tranquillity, the extraordinary profundity of the now. In the same way, one has to be aware of loneliness; one has to feel it, actually experience this sense of complete isolation. And if one is capable of experiencing it, one will find how really difficult it is to live with it. I do not know if you have ever lived with the sunset.

You know, sirs, there is a radiancy of love which cannot be cultivated. Love is not the result of good conduct; no amount of your being kind, generous, will give you love. Love is both extensive and particular. A mind that loves is virtuous; it does not seek virtue. It cannot go wrong because it knows right and wrong. It is the mind without love that seeks virtue, that wants God, that clings to a system of belief, and thereby destroys itself. Love—that quality, that feeling, that sense of compassion without any object, which is the very essence of life—is not a thing to be grasped by the mind. As I said the other day, when the intellect guides that pure feeling, then mediocrity comes into being. Most of us have such highly developed intellects that the intellect is always corrupting the pure feeling; therefore, our feelings are mediocre though we may be excellent at reasoning.

Now, this sense of loneliness is pure feeling, uncorrupted by the mind. It is the mind that is frightened, fearful, and therefore it says, "I must get away from it." But if one is simply aware of this loneliness, if one lives with it, then it has the quality of pure feeling. I do not know if I am making myself clear.

Have you ever really observed a flower? It is not easy. You may think you have observed it, you may think you have loved it, but what you have actually done is this: You have seen it, you have given it a name, you have smelled it, and then you have gone away. The very naming of the species, the very smelling of the flower causes in you a certain reaction of memory, and therefore you never really look at the flower at all. Just try sometime looking at a flower, at a sunset, at a bird, or what you will, without any interference on the part of the mind, and you will see how difficult it is, yet it is only then that there is the complete perception of anything.

This loneliness, this pure feeling which is a sense of total isolation, can be observed as you would observe the flower—with complete attention, which is not to name it or try to escape from it. Then you will find, if you have gone so far in your inquiry, that there is only a state of negation. Please do not translate this into Sanskrit, or any other language, or compare it with something you have read. What I am telling you is not what you have read. What has been described is not *what is*.

I am saying that if the mind is capable of experiencing this sense of aloneness, not verbally, but actually living with it, then there comes an awareness of complete negation—negation which is not an opposite. Most of us only know the opposites—positive and negative, "I love" and "I do not love," "I want" and "I do not want." That is all we know. But the state of which I am telling you is not of that nature because it has no opposite. It is a state of complete negation.

I do not know if you have ever thought about the quality or the nature of creation. Creativity in the sense of having talent, being gifted, is entirely different from the state of creation. I do not know if it has happened to you that, while walking alone or sitting in a room, you have suddenly had a feeling of extraordinary ecstasy. Having had that feeling, you want to translate it, so you write a poem or paint a picture. If that poem or that picture becomes fashionable, society flatters you, pays you for it, gives you a profit, and you are carried away by all that. Presently you seek to have again that tremendous ecstasy, which came uninvited. As long as you seek it, it will never come. But you keep on seeking it in various ways—through self-discipline, through the practice of a system, through meditation, through drink, women—you try everything in an effort to get back that overwhelming feeling of radiance, of joy, in which all creation is. But you will never get it back. It comes darkly, uninvited.

So it is the state of negation from which all creation takes place. Whether you spontaneously write a poem or smile without calculation, whether there is kindness without a motive or goodness without fear, without a cause, it is all the outcome of this extraordinary state of complete negation, in which is creation. But you cannot come to it if you do not understand the whole process of seeking, so that all seeking completely ceases. The understanding and cessation of seeking is not at the end but at the beginning. The man who says, "Eventually I shall understand the process of seeking, and then I shall no longer seek," is thoughtless, stupid, because the end is at the beginning, which has no time. If you begin to inquire into yourself and perceive why you seek and what it is you are seeking, you can capture the whole significance of it instantaneously; and then you will find that, without any intent, without any causation, there is a fundamental revolution, a complete transformation of the mind. It is only then that truth comes into being.

Truth does not come to a mind that is burdened with experience, that is full of knowledge, that has gathered virtue, that has stifled itself through discipline, control. Truth comes to the mind that is really innocent, fearless. And it is the mind that has completely understood its own seeking, that has gone to the fullest depth of this state of negation—it is only such a mind that is without fear. Then that extraordinary thing which we are all wanting will come. It is elusive, and it will not come if you stretch out your hand to capture it. You cannot capture the immeasurable. Your hands, your mind, your whole being must be quiet, completely still, to receive it. You cannot seek it because you do not know what it is. The immeasurable will be there when the mind understands this whole process of search, not at the end, but at the beginning—which is the continuous movement of self-knowledge.

December 6, 1959

Sixth Talk in Madras

If we are at all thoughtful, we must often have wondered from what source our activities come. We must have examined ourselves, wondering why we do certain things—why we join certain organizations, undertake certain jobs, why we think in a certain manner, hold certain beliefs, why there are the innumerable complex and contradictory desires from which all our actions spring. Some of us, at least, must have watched these contradictory desires operating in ourselves and in others. Just as we have divided the earth into many conflicting parts, calling them by different names—England, India, Russia, America, and so on—so also we are inwardly broken up into many parts, each part in conflict with the others. But the earth is ours, yours and mine; it is not Indian or English, Chinese or Russian, German or American. It is our earth, to be lived on, to be enjoyed, to be nourished, to be looked after and beautified. It is a total thing, not to be broken up. Yet we continue to break up the earth, just as we are broken up in ourselves, and this breaking-up process is a source of constant deterioration.

Now, is there a wholeness, a completeness of being from which total action can take place, instead of this self-contradictory state with which we are so familiar? Let us go into this question together. Why is the mind always broken up in its thinking, in its feeling, in its activity, in the very manner of its existence? If we can go into this problem deeply, perhaps we shall find an action, a way of living, a state of being which is not self-contradictory. But to be free of self-contradiction requires not merely an outward change but a revolution in the quality of the mind itself.

We can see that a fundamental change is necessary at every level of our being and also at every level of society. You and I need to change very drastically because as it is now, our way of life is so fragmentary; it is a self-contradictory process with the various parts of ourselves at war with each other. A revolution in our lives is obviously essential. I do not mean economic revolution—that is a very small thing. What is needed is a revolution in our very being, a crisis in the mind, in consciousness, not just a crisis in society. There must be this inner crisis to bring about a fundamental revolution in our lives.

So, how to change radically is the problem. How is a shallow, petty mind, a mind that is not used to thinking very deeply, a mind that is carried away by outward events, a mind that is caught in a system, whether it be yogic, communistic, religious, or technological—how is such a mind to change fundamentally? I am asking myself, and you, this question; I am thinking aloud about the problem. Is it possible to bring about a radical revolution in the quality of the mind, in the ways of our thinking and feeling? Can one live with one's whole being so that the job, the technique, is not separated from one's daily thoughts and emotions? Is there a way of living which is not fragmentary, not self-contradictory, but which is an integrated whole, like a tree with its many branches, many leaves? Is it possible to live in such a way that every action is a total action, every feeling is whole, every movement of the mind complete? Can you and I live totally, from the very depth of our being, so that there is no self-contradiction? If we can seriously go into this question as two individual human beings, then perhaps we shall find the answer; and that is what I would like to do this evening.

Why is there little or no action in our lives which is not broken up, self-contradictory? I do not know if you have ever asked yourselves this question. You are all in a state of self-contradiction, are you not? And the more you think, the more self-contradictory you become. Being aware of this contradictory state in yourselves, you invoke God, or join some religious society—which merely puts you to sleep. Outwardly you may appear peaceful, calm, but inside there is still contradiction, conflict.

So, is it possible to live with a sense of harmony, beauty, with a sense of never-ending fulfillment—or rather, I won't say fulfillment because fulfillment brings frustration, but is there a never-ending state of action in which there is no sorrow, no repentance, no cause for regret? If there is such a state, then how is one to come to it? One obviously cannot cultivate it. One cannot say, "I shall be harmonious"—it means nothing. To assume that one must control oneself in order to be harmonious is an immature way of thinking. The state of total integration, of unitary action, can come only when one is not seeking it, when the mind is not forcing itself into a patterned way of living.

Most of us have not given much thought to all this. In our daily activities we are only concerned with time, because time helps us to forget, time heals our wounds, however temporarily, time dissipates our despairs, our frustrations. Being caught in the time process, how is one to come upon this extraordinary state in which there is no contradiction, in which the very movement of living is integrated action, and everyday life is reality? If each one of us seriously puts this question to himself, then I think we shall be able to commune with each other in unfolding the problem; but if you are merely listening to words, then you and I are not in communion. We are in communion with each other only if this is a problem to both of us—and then it is not just my problem, which I am imposing on you, or which you are trying to interpret according to your beliefs and idiosyncrasies. This is a human problem, a world problem, and if it is very clear to each one of us, then what I am saying, what I am thinking and feeling, will bring about a state of communion between us, and together we can go to great depths.

So, what is the problem? The problem is that there must obviously be a tremendous change, not only at the superficial level, in one's outward activities, but inwardly, deeply; there must be an inner revolution which will transform the manner of one's thinking and bring about a way of life which in itself is total action. And why doesn't such a revolution take place? That is the problem as one sees it. So let us go deeply into ourselves and discover the root of this problem.

The root of the problem is fear, is it not? Please look into it for yourselves, and don't just regard me as a speaker addressing an audience. I want to go into this problem with you because if you and I explore it together and we both understand something which is true, then from that understanding there will be an action which is neither yours nor mine, and opinions, over which we battle everlastingly, will have ceased to exist.

I feel there is a basic fear which has to be discovered—a fear much more profound than the fear of losing one's job or the fear of going wrong or the fear of outward or inward insecurity. But to go into it very deeply, we must begin with the fears that we know, the fears of which we are all conscious. I do not have to tell you what they are, for you can observe them in yourselves—the fear of public opinion; the fear of losing one's son, one's wife or husband, through the sad experience called death; the fear of disease; the fear of loneliness; the fear of not being successful, of not fulfilling oneself; the fear of not attaining a knowledge of truth, God, heaven, or what you will. The savage has a few very simple fears, but we have innumerable fears, whose complexity increases as we become more and more "civilized."

Now, what is fear? Have you ever actually experienced fear? You may lose your job, you may not be a success, your neighbor may say this or that of you, and death is always waiting just around the corner. All this breeds fear in you, and you run away from it through yoga, through reading books, through belief in God, through various forms of amusement, and all the rest of it. So I am asking: Have you ever really experienced fear, or does the mind always run away from it?

Take the fear of death. Being afraid of death, you rationalize your fear away by saying that death is inevitable, that everything dies. The rationalizing process is merely an escape from the fact. Or you believe in reincarnation, which satisfies, comforts you, but fear is still there. Or you try to live totally in the present, to forget all about the past and the future, and be concerned only with the now; but fear goes on.

I am asking you whether you have ever known real fear—not the theoretical fear which the mind merely conceives of. Perhaps I am not making it very clear. You know the taste of salt. You have experienced pain, lust, envy, and you know for yourselves what these words mean. In the same way, do you know fear? Or have you only an idea of what fear is, without having actually experienced fear? Am I explaining myself?

You are afraid of death, and what is that fear? You see the inevitability of death, and because you do not want to die, you are afraid of it. But you have never known what death is; you have only projected an opinion, an idea about it, so you are afraid of an idea about death. This is rather simple, and I do not quite understand our difficulty.

To really experience fear, you must be totally with it, you must be entirely in it, and not avoid it; you cannot have beliefs, opinions about it. But I do not think many of us have ever experienced fear in this way because we are always avoiding, running away from fear; we never remain with it, look into it, find out what it is all about.

Now, is the mind capable of living with fear, being a part of it? Can the mind go into that feeling, instead of avoiding it or trying to escape from it? I think it is largely because we are always running away from fear that we live such contradictory lives.

Sirs, one is aware, especially as one grows older, that death is always waiting. And you are afraid of death, aren't you? Now, how are you to understand that fear? How are you to be free from the fear of death? What is death? It is really the ending of everything you have known. That is the actual fact. Whether or not you survive is not the point. Survival after death is merely an idea. You do not know, but you believe, because belief gives you comfort. You never go into the question of death itself because the very idea of coming to an end, of entering the totally unknown, is a horror to you, which awakens fear; and being afraid, you resort to various forms of belief as a means of escape.

Surely, to free the mind from fear, you have to know what it is to die while you are physically and mentally vigorous, going to the office, attending to everything. You have to know the nature of death while living. Belief is not going to remove fear. You may read any number of books about the hereafter, but that is not going to free the mind from fear because the mind is used to just one thing, which is continuity through memory, and so the very idea of coming to an end is a horror. The constant recollection of the things you have experienced and enjoyed, everything you have possessed, the character you have built up, your ideals, your visions, your knowledge—all that is coming to an end. And how is the mind to be free of fear?—that is the problem, not whether there is a continuity after death. I hope you are following all this.

If I am to be free of the fear of ending, surely I must inquire into the nature of death; I must experience it, I must know what it is—its beauty, its tremendous quality. It must be an extraordinary thing to die, to enter into something never imagined, totally unknown.

Now, how is the mind to experience, while living, that ending called death? Death is ending; it is the ending of the body and perhaps also of the mind. I am not discussing whether there is survival or not. I am concerned with ending. Can I not end while I am living? Cannot my mind—with all its thoughts, its activities, its memories—come to an end while I am living, while the body is not broken down through old age and disease or swept away by an accident? Cannot the mind, which has built up a continuity, come to an end, not at the last moment, but now? That is, cannot the mind be free of all the accumulations of memory?

You are a Hindu, a Christian, or what you will. You are shaped by the past, by custom, tradition. You are greed, envy, joy, pleasure, the appreciation of something beautiful, the agony of not being loved, of not being able to fulfill—you are all that, which is the process of continuity. Take just one form of it. You are attached to your property, to your wife. That is a fact. I am not talking about detachment. You are attached to your opinions, to your ways of thinking.

Now, can you not come to the end of that attachment? Why are you attached?—that is the question, not how to be detached. If you try to be detached, you merely cultivate the opposite, and therefore contradiction continues. But the moment your mind is free of attachment, it is also free from the sense of continuity through attachment, is it not? So, why are you attached? Because you are afraid that without attachment you will be nothing; therefore, you are your house, you are your wife, you are your bank account, you are your job. You are all these things. And if there is an ending to this sense of continuity through attachment, a total ending, then you will know what death is.

Do you understand, sirs? I hate, let us say, and I have carried this hatred in my memory for years, constantly battling against it. Now, can I instantly stop hating? Can I drop it with the finality of death? When death comes, it does not ask your permission; it comes and takes you, it destroys you on the spot. In the same way, can you totally drop hate, envy, pride of possession, attachment to beliefs, to opinions, to ideas, to a particular way of thinking? Can you drop all that in an instant? There is no "how to drop it" because that is only another form of continuity. To drop opinion, belief, attachment, greed, envy, is to die—to die every day, every moment. If there is the coming to an end of all ambition from moment to moment, then you will know the extraordinary state of being nothing, of coming to the abyss of an eternal movement, as it were, and dropping over the edge—which is death.

I want to know all about death because death may be reality; it may be what we call God—that most extraordinary something that lives and moves, yet has no beginning and no end. So I want to know all about death—and for that I must die to everything I already know. The mind can be aware of the unknown only when it dies to the known—dies without any motive, without the hope of reward or the fear of punishment. Then I can find out what death is while I am living—and in that very discovery there is freedom from fear.

Whether or not there is a continuity after the body dies is irrelevant; whether or not you are born again is a trivial affair. To me, living is not apart from dying because in living there is death. There is no separation between death and life. One knows death because the mind is dying every minute, and in that very ending there is renewal, newness, freshness, innocence—not in continuity. But for most of us, death is a thing that the mind has really never experienced. To experience death while living, all the trickeries of the mind—which prevent that direct experiencing—must cease.

I wonder if you have ever known what love is? Because I think death and love walk together. Death, love, and life are one and the same, but we have divided life, as we have divided the earth. We talk of love as being either carnal or spiritual and have set a battle going between the sacred and the profane. We have divided what love is from what love should be, so we never know what love is. Love, surely, is a total feeling which is not sentimental and in which there is no sense of separation; it is complete purity of feeling, without the separative, fragmentary quality of the intellect. Love has no sense of continuity. Where there is a sense of continuity, love is already dead, and it smells of yesterday, with all its ugly memories, quarrels, brutalities. To love, one must die. Death is love—the two are not separate. But do not be mesmerized by my words because you have to experience this, you have to know it, taste it, discover it for yourself.

The fear of complete loneliness, isolation, of not being anything, is the basis, the very root of our self-contradiction. Because we are afraid to be nothing, we are splintered up by many desires, each desire pulling in a different direction. That is why, if the mind is to know total, noncontradictory action—an action in which going to the office is the same as not going to the office, or the same as becoming a sannyasi, or the same as meditation, or the same as looking at the skies of an evening—there must be freedom from fear. But there can be no freedom from fear unless you experience it, and you cannot experience fear as long as you find ways and means of escaping from it. Your God is a marvelous escape from fear; all your rituals, your books, your theories, and beliefs prevent you from actually experiencing it. You will find that only in ending is there a total cessation of fear—the ending of yesterday, of what has been, which is the soil in which fear sinks its roots. Then you will discover that love and death and living are one and the same. The mind is free only when the accumulations of memory have dropped away. Creation is in ending, not in continuity. Only then is there the total action which is living, loving, and dying.

December 9, 1959

Seventh Talk in Madras

If we could take a journey, make a pilgrimage together without any intent or purpose, without seeking anything, perhaps on returning we might find that our hearts had unknowingly been changed. I think it worth trying. Any intent or purpose, any motive or goal implies effort—a conscious or unconscious endeavor to arrive, to achieve. I would like to suggest that we take a journey together in which none of these elements exist. If we can take such a journey, and if we are alert enough to observe what lies along the way, perhaps when we return, as all pilgrims must, we shall find that there has been a change of heart; and I think this would be much more significant than inundating the mind with ideas because ideas do not fundamentally change human beings at all. Beliefs, ideas, influences may cause the mind superficially to adjust itself to a pattern, but if we can take the journey together without any purpose and simply observe as we go along the extraordinary width and depth and beauty of life, then out of this observation may come a love that is not merely social, environmental, a love in which there is not the giver and the taker, but which is a state of being, free of all demand. So, in taking this journey together, perhaps we shall be awakened to something far more significant than the boredom and frustration, the emptiness and despair of our daily lives.

Most human beings, as they live from day to day, gradually drift into despair, or they get caught up in superficial joys, amusements, hopes, or they are carried away by rationalizations, by hatred, or by the social amenities. If we can really bring about a radical, inward transformation so that we live fully and richly, with deep feelings which are not corrupted by the mutterings of the intellect, then I think we shall be able to act in a totally different way in all our relationships.

This journey I am proposing that we take together is not to the moon or even to the stars. The distance to the stars is much less than the distance within ourselves. The discovery of ourselves is endless, and it requires constant inquiry, a perception which is total, an awareness in which there is no choice. This journey is really an opening of the door to the individual in his relationship with the world. Because we are in conflict with ourselves, we have conflict in the world. Our problems, when extended, become the world's problems. As long as we are in conflict with ourselves, life in the world is also a ceaseless battle, a destructive, deteriorating war.

So the understanding of ourselves is not to the end of individual salvation; it is not the means of attaining a private heaven, an ivory tower into which to retire with our own illusions, beliefs, gods. On the contrary, if we are able to understand ourselves, we shall be at peace, and then we shall know how to live rightly in a world that is now corrupt, destructive, brutal.

After all, what is worldliness? Worldliness, surely, is to be satisfied—to be satisfied not only with outward things, with property, wealth, position, power, but with inward things as well. Most of us are satisfied at a very superficial level. We take satisfaction in possessing things—a car, a house, a garden, a title. Possession gives us an extraordinary feeling of gratification. And when we are surfeited with the possession of things, we look for satisfaction at a deeper level; we seek what we call truth, God, salvation. But we are still moved by the same compulsion—the demand to be satisfied. Just as you seek satisfaction in sex, in social position, in owning things, so also you want to be satisfied in "spiritual" ways.

Please do not say, "Is that all?" and brush it off, but as you are listening, observe, if you will, your own desire for satisfaction. Allow yourselves, if you can, to see in what way you are being satisfied. The intellectual person is satisfied with his clever ideas, which give him a feeling of superiority, a sense of knowing; and when that sense of knowing ceases to give him satisfaction, when he has analyzed everything and intellectually torn to shreds every notion, every theory, every belief, then he seeks a wider, deeper satisfaction. He is converted and begins to believe; he becomes very "religious," and his satisfaction takes on the coloring of some organized religion.

So, being dissatisfied with outward things, we turn for gratification to the so-called spiritual things. It has become an ugly term, that word *spiritual;* it smacks of sanctimoniousness. Do you know what I mean? The saints with their cultivated virtues, with their struggles, their disciplines, their suppressions and self-denials are still within the field of satisfaction. It is because we want to be satisfied that we discipline ourselves; we are after something that will give us lasting satisfaction, a gratification from which all doubt has been removed. That is what most of us want—and we think we are spiritual, religious. Our pursuit of gratification we call "the search for truth." We go to the temple or the church, we attend lectures, we listen to talks like this, we read the Gita, the Upanishads, the Bible—all in order to have this strange feeling of satisfaction in which there will never be any doubt, never any questioning.

It is our urge to be satisfied that makes us turn to what we call meditation and the cultivation of virtue. How virtue can be "cultivated," I do not know. Surely, humility can never be cultivated; love can never be cultivated; peace can never be brought about through control. These things are, or they are not. The person who cultivates humility is full of vanity; he hopes to find abiding satisfaction in being humble. In the same way, through meditation we seek the absolute, the immeasurable, the unknown. But meditation is part of everyday existence; it is something that you have to do as you breathe, as you think, as you live, as you have delicate or brutal feelings. That is real meditation, and it is entirely different from the systematized meditation which some of you so sedulously practice.

I would like, if I may, to go into this question of meditation, but please do not be mesmerized by my words. Don't become suddenly meditative; don't become very intent to discover what is the goal of true meditation. The meditation of which I speak has no goal, no end. Love has no end. Love is not successful; it does not reward you or punish you. Love is a state of being, a sense of radiancy. In love is all virtue. In the state of love, do what you will, there is no sin, no evil, no contradiction; and without love we shall ever be at war with ourselves and therefore with each other and with the world. It is love alone that transforms the mind totally.

But the meditation with which most of us are familiar, and which some of us practice, is entirely different. Let us first examine that—not to justify or condemn what you are doing, but to see the truth, the validity, or the falseness of it. We are going on a journey together, and when on a journey you can take along only what is absolutely essential. The journey of which I am speaking is very swift;

there is no abiding place, no stopping, no rest; it is an endless movement, and a mind that is burdened is not free to travel.

The meditation that most of us practice is a process of concentration based on exclusion, on building walls of resistance, is it not? You control your mind because you want to think of a particular thing, and you try to exclude all other thoughts. To help you to control your mind and to exclude the unwanted thoughts, there are various systems of meditation. Life has been divided as knowledge, devotion, and action. You say, ''I am of such and such a temperament,'' and according to your temperament you meditate. We have divided ourselves into temperaments as neatly as we have divided the earth into national, racial, and religious groups, and each temperament has its own path, its own system of meditation. But if you go behind them all, you will find in every case that some form of control is practiced, and control implies suppression.

Do please observe yourselves as I am going into this problem, and don't just follow verbally what I am saying because what I am saying is not at all important. What is important is for you to discover yourselves. As I said at the beginning, we are taking a journey together into ourselves. I am only pointing out certain things, and if you are satisfied by what is pointed out, your mind will remain empty, shallow, petty. A petty mind cannot take the journey into itself. But if through these words you are becoming aware of your own thoughts, your own state, then there is no guru.

Behind all these systems of meditation which develop virtue, which promise a reward, which offer an ultimate goal, there is the factor of control, discipline, is there not? The mind is disciplined not to wander off the narrow, respectable path laid down by the system or by society.

Now, what is implied in control? Do please observe yourselves because we are all inquiring into this problem together. We are coming to something which I see and which at the moment you do not, so please follow without being mesmerized by my words, by my face, by my person. Cut through all that—it is utterly immature—and observe yourselves. What does control imply? Surely, it implies a battle between what you want to concentrate on, and the thoughts that wander off. So concentration is a form of exclusion—which every schoolboy and every bureaucrat in his office knows. The bureaucrat is compelled to concentrate because he has to sign so many papers, he has to organize and to act; and for the schoolboy there is always the threat of the teacher.

Concentration implies suppression, does it not? I suppress in myself what I do not like. I never look at it, delve deeply into it. I have already condemned it, and a mind that condemns cannot penetrate, cannot understand what it has condemned.

There is another form of concentration, and that is when you give yourself over to something. The mind is absorbed by an image, as a child is absorbed by a toy. Those of you who have children must have observed how a toy can absorb them completely. When a child is playing with a new toy, he is extraordinarily concentrated. Nothing interferes with that concentration because he is enjoying himself. The toy is so entrancing, so delightful, that for the moment it is all-important, and the child does not want to be disturbed. His mind is completely given over to the toy. And that is what you call devotion: giving yourself up to the symbol, the idea, the image which you have labeled God. The image absorbs you, as the child is absorbed by a toy. To lose themselves in a thing created by the mind, or by the hand, is what most people want.

Concentration through a system of meditation offers the attainment of an ultimate peace, an ultimate reality, an ultimate satisfaction, which is what you want. All such effort involves the idea of growth, evolution through time—if not in this life, then in the next life or a hundred lives hence, you will get there. Control and discipline invariably imply effort to be, to become, and this effort places a limit on thought, on the mind—which is very satisfying. Placing a limit on the mind, on consciousness, is a most gratifying thing because then you can see how far you have advanced in your efforts to become what you want to be. As you make effort, you push the frontier of the mind farther and farther out, but it is still within the boundaries of thought. You may attain a state which you call *Ishvara*, God, paramatma, or what you will, but it is still within the field of the mind—the mind which is conditioned by your culture, by your society, by your greed, and all the rest of it.

So meditation, as you practice it, is a process of control, of suppression, of exclusion, of discipline, all of which involves effort—the effort to expand the boundaries of consciousness as the 'I', the self; but there is also another factor involved, which is the whole process of recognition.

I hope you are taking the journey with me. Don't say, "It is too difficult; I don't know what you are talking about," for then you are not watching yourselves. What I am talking about is not just an intellectual concept. It is a living, vital thing, pulsating with life.

As I was saying, recognition is an essential part of what you call meditation. All you know of life is a series of recognitions. Relationship is a process of recognition, is it not? You know your wife or your husband; you know your children, in the sense that you recognize them, just as you recognize your own virtue, your own humility. Recognition is an extraordinary thing, if you look at it.

All thought, all relationship is a process of recognition. Knowledge is based on recognition. So what happens? You want to recognize the unknown through meditation. And is that possible? Do you understand what I am talking about? Perhaps I am not making myself clear.

You recognize your wife, your children, your property; you recognize that you are a lawyer, a businessman, a professor, an engineer; you have a label, a name, a title. You know and recognize things with a mind that is the result of time, of effort, a mind that has cultivated virtues, that has always tried to be or to become something—all of which is a process of recognition. Knowledge is the result of experience which can be recalled, recognized, either in an encyclopedia or in oneself.

Do consider that word *recognize*. What does it signify? You want to find out what God is, what truth is, which means that you want to recognize the unknown, but if you can recognize something, it is already the known. When you practice meditation and have visions of your particular gods and goddesses, you are giving emphasis to recognition. These visions are the projections of your background, of your conditioned mind. The Christian will invariably see Jesus or Mary, the Hindu will see Shri Krishna or his god with a dozen arms, because the conditioned mind projects these images and then recognizes them. This recognition gives you tremendous satisfaction, and you say, "I have found, I have realized, I know."

There are many systems which offer you this sort of thing, and I say none of that is meditation. It is self-hypnosis; it has no depth. You may practice a system for ten thousand years, and you will still be within the field of time, within the frontiers of your own knowledge, your own conditioning. However far you extend the boundaries within which you can recognize your own projections, it is obviously not meditation though you may give it that name. You are merely emphasizing the self, the 'me', which is nothing but a bundle of associated memories; you are perpetuating through your so-called meditation the conflict of the thinker and the thought, the observer and the observed, in which the observer is always watching, denying, controlling, shaping the observed. Any schoolboy can play this game, and I say it has nothing to do with meditation, though the graybeards insist that you must thus "meditate." The yogis, the swamis, the sannyasis, the people who renounce the world and go away to sit in a cave—they are all still caught in this pursuit of their own visions, however noble, which is the indulgence of an appetite, a process of self-gratification.

Then what is meditation? Surely, you are in the state of meditation only when the thinker is not there—that is, when you are not giving soil to thought, to memory, which is the center of the 'me', the self. It is this center that marks the boundaries of consciousness, and however extensive, however virtuous it may be, or however much it may try to help humanity, it can never be in the state of meditation. You can come to that state of awareness, which is meditation, only when there is no condemnation, no effort of suppression or control. It is an awareness in which there is no choice, for choice implies an effort of will, which in turn implies domination, control. It is an awareness in which consciousness has no limits and can therefore give complete attention—which is not concentration. I think there is a vast difference between attention and concentration. There is no attention if there is a center from which you are attentive. You can concentrate upon something from a center, but attention implies a state of wholeness in which there is no observer apart from the observed.

Meditation, as we have gone into it today, is really the freeing of the mind from the known. This obviously does not mean forgetting the way to your home, or discarding the technical knowledge required for the performance of your job, and so on. It means freeing the mind from its conditioning, from the background of experience from which all projection and recognition take place. The mind must free itself from the process of acquisitiveness, satisfaction, and recognition. You cannot recognize or invite the unknowable, that which is real, timeless. You can invite your friends, you can invite virtue, you can invite the gods of your own creation; you can invite them and make them your guests. But do what you will—meditate, sacrifice, become virtuous—you cannot invite the immeasurable, that something about which you do not know. The practice of virtue does not indicate love; it is the result of your own desire for gratification.

So, meditation is the freeing of the mind from the known. You must come to this freedom, not tomorrow, but in the immediate, now, because through time you cannot come to the timeless, which is not a duality. The timeless is whispering round every corner; it lies under every leaf. It is open, not to the sannyasis, not to the dehydrated human beings who have suppressed themselves and who no longer have any passion, but to everyone whose mind is in the state of meditation from moment to moment. Only such a mind can receive that which is unknowable.

December 13, 1959

Eighth Talk in Madras

This is the last talk of the present series.

I think it would be marvelous if, without words, one could convey what one really feels about the whole problem of existence.

Besides the superficial necessity of having a job and all the rest of it, there are the deep, inward urges, the demands, the contradictory states of being, both conscious and unconscious; and I wonder if it is not possible to go beyond them all, beyond the frontiers which the mind has imposed upon itself, beyond the narrow limits of one's own heart, and to live there—to act, to think, and to feel from that state while carrying on one's everyday activities. I think it can be done—not merely the communication of it, but the fact of it. Surely, we can break through the limitations which the mind has placed upon itself because, after all, we have only one problem. As the tree with its many roots, its many branches and leaves, is a totality, so we have only one basic problem. And if, by some miracle, by some grace, by some way of looking at the clouds of an evening, the mind could become extraordinarily sensitive to every movement of thought, of feeling—if it could do that, not theoretically but actually, then I think we would have solved our problem.

As I said, there is essentially only one problem—the problem of "me and my urges," from which all our other problems arise. Our real problems are not how to land on the moon, or how to fire off a rocket to Venus; they are very intimate, but unfortunately we do not seem to know how to deal with them. I am not at all sure that we are even aware of our real problem. To know love, to feel the beauty of nature, to worship something beyond the creations of man—I think all this is denied to us if we do not understand our immediate problems.

So I would like, if I may, to think aloud with you on this question of whether the mind can break through its own frontiers, go beyond its own limitations, because our lives are obviously very shallow. You may have all the wealth that the earth can give you; you may be very erudite; you may have read many books and be able to quote very learnedly all the established authorities, past and present; or you may be very simple, just living and struggling from day to day, with all the little pleasures and sorrows of family life. Whatever one is, surely it is of the utmost importance to find out in what manner the barriers which the mind has created for itself can be swept away. That, it seems to me, is our fundamental problem. Through so-called education, through tradition, through various forms of social, moral, and religious conditioning, the mind is limited, caught up in a moving vortex of environmental influences. And is it possible for the mind to break away from all this conditioning so that it can live with joy, perceiving the beauty of things, feeling this extraordinary sense of immeasurable life?

I think it is possible, but I do not think it is a gradual process. It is not through evolution, through time, that the breaking away takes place. It is done instantly, or never. The perception of truth does not come at the end of many years. There is no tomorrow in understanding. Either the mind understands immediately, or not at all. It is very difficult for the mind to see this because most of us are so accustomed to thinking in terms of tomorrow. We say, "Give me time; let me have more experience, and eventually I shall understand." But have you not noticed that understanding always comes in a flash—never through calculation, through time, never through exercise and slow development? The mind which relies on this idea of gradual comprehension is essentially lazy. Don't ask, "How is a lazy mind to be made alert, vital, active?" There is no "how." However much a stupid mind may try to become clever, it will still be stupid. A petty mind does not cease to be petty by worshiping the god it has invented. Time is not going to reveal the truth, the beauty of anything. What really brings understanding is the state of attention—just to be attentive, even for one second, with one's whole being, without calculation, without premeditation. If you and I can be totally attentive on the instant, then I think there is an instantaneous comprehension, a total understanding.

But it is very difficult to give one's total attention to something, is it not? I do not know if you have ever tried to look at a flower with your whole being, or to be completely aware of the ways of your own mind. If you have done that, you will know with what clarity total attention brings into focus any problem. But to give such attention to anything is not easy because our minds are very respectable; they are crippled with words and symbols, with ideas about what should and should not be.

I am talking about attention, and I wonder if you are paying attention—not just to what is being said, because that is of secondary importance, but are you attentive in the sense of being fully aware of the impediments, the blockages that your mind has created for itself? If you can be aware of these bondages—just aware of them, without saying, "What shall I do about them?"—you will find that they begin to break up, and then comes a state of attention in which there is no choice, no wandering off, because there is no longer a center from which to wander. That state of attention is goodness; it is the only virtue. There is no other virtue.

So, we realize that our minds are very limited. We have reduced the earth and the heavens, the vast movement of life, to a little corner called the 'me', the self, with its everlasting struggle to be or not to be. In what way can this mind, which is so small, so petty, so self-centered, break through the frontiers, the limitations which it has placed upon itself? As I said, it is only through attention, in which there is no choice, that the truth is seen, and it is truth that breaks the bondage, that sweeps away the limitations—

not your effort, not your meditation, not your practices, your disciplines, your controls.

To be in this state of attention requires, surely, a knowledge of the 'me' and its ways. I must know myself; my mind must know the movement of every emotion, every thought. But knowledge is a peculiar thing. Knowledge is cumulative; it is ever in the past. In the present there is only knowing. Knowledge always colors knowing. We are concerned with knowing, and not with knowledge, because knowledge about oneself distorts the knowing of oneself. I hope I am making myself clear. I think there is a difference between knowing myself all the time, and knowledge about myself. When self-knowledge is an accumulation of information which I have gathered about myself, it prevents the understanding of myself.

Look here, sirs. The self, the 'me' is restless; it is always wandering, never still. It is like a roaring river, making a tremendous noise as it rushes down the valley. It is a living, moving thing, and how can one have knowledge about something which is constantly changing, never the same? The self is always in movement; it is never still, never quiet for a moment. When the mind has observed it, it is already gone. I do not know if you have ever tried to look at yourself, to pin down your mind to any one thing. If you do that, the thing you have pinned down is constantly before you—and so you have come to the end of self-knowledge. Am I conveying something? Am I explaining myself?

Knowledge is always destructive to knowing. The knowing of oneself is never cumulative; it does not culminate in a point from which you judge the fact of what is the 'me'. You see, we accumulate knowledge, and from there we judge—and that is our difficulty. Having accumulated knowledge through experience, through learning, through reading, and all the rest of it, from that background we think, we function. We take up a position in knowledge, and from there we say, "I know all about the self. It is greedy, stupid, everlastingly wanting to be superior"—whatever it is. So there is nothing more to know. The moment you take up a position in knowledge, your knowledge is very superficial. But if there is no accumulation of knowledge upon which the mind rests, then there is only the movement of knowing, and then the mind becomes extraordinarily swift in its perceptions.

So it is self-knowing that is important, and not self-knowledge. Knowing the movement of thought, knowing the movement of feeling without accumulation—and therefore with never a moment of judgment, of condemnation—is very important because the moment there is accumulation, there is a thinker. The accumulation of knowledge gives a position to the mind, a center from which to think; it gives rise to an observer who judges, condemns, identifies, and all the rest of it. But when there is self-knowing, there is neither the observer nor the observed; there is only a state of attention, of watching, learning.

Surely, sirs, a mind that has accumulated knowledge can never learn. If the mind is to learn, it must not have the burden of knowledge, the burden of what it has accumulated. It must be fresh, innocent, free of the past. The accumulation of knowledge gives birth to the 'me', but knowing can never do that because knowing is learning, and a mind that is constantly learning can have no resting place. If you really perceive the truth of this, not tomorrow, but now, then you will find there is only a state of attention, of learning, with never a moment of accumulation; and then the problems which most of us now have are completely gone. But this is not a trick by which to resolve your problems, nor is it a lesson for you to learn.

You see, a society such as ours—whether Indian, Russian, American, or what you will—is acquisitive, not only in the pursuit of material things, but also in terms of competing, gaining, arriving, fulfilling. This society has so shaped our ways of thinking that we cannot free ourselves from the concept of a goal, an end. We are always thinking in terms of getting somewhere, of achieving inward peace, and so on. Our approach is always acquisitive. Physically we have to acquire to some extent; we must obviously provide ourselves with food, clothing, and shelter. But the mind uses these things as a means of further acquisition—I am talking about acquisition in the psychological sense. Just as the mind makes use of the physical necessities to acquire prestige and power, so through knowledge it establishes itself in a position of psychological certainty. Knowledge gives us a sense of security, does it not? From our background of experience, of accumulated knowledge about ourselves, we think and live, and this process creates a state of duality—what I am, and what I think I should be. There is therefore a contradiction, a constant battle between the two. But if one observes this process comprehensively, if one understands it, really feels its significance, then one will find that the mind is spontaneously good, alert, loving; it is always learning and never acquiring. Then self-knowledge has quite a different meaning, for it is no longer an accumulation of knowledge about oneself. Knowledge about oneself is small, petty, limiting; but knowing oneself is infinite, there is no end to it. So our problem is to abandon the ways of habit, of custom, of tradition, on the instant, and to be born anew.

Sirs, one of our difficulties in all this is the problem of communion, or communication. I want to tell you something, and in the very telling it is perverted by the expression, the word that is used. What I would like to communicate to you, or to commune with you about, is very simple—total self-abandonment on the instant. That is all—not what happens after self-abandonment, or the system that will bring it about. There is no system because the moment you practice a system, you are obviously strengthening the self. Cannot the mind suddenly drop the anchors it has put down into the various patterns of existence? Some evening when the sun was just going down, when the green rice fields were sparkling, when there was a lone passerby and the birds were on the wing, it must have happened to you that there was all at once an extraordinary peace in the world. There was no 'you' watching, feeling, thinking, for you were that beauty, that peace, that infinite state of being. Such a thing must have happened to you if you have ever looked into the face of the world, into the vastness of the sky. How does it happen? When suddenly there is no worry, when you are no longer thinking that you love someone, or wondering if someone loves you, and you are in that state of love, that state of beauty—what has happened? The green tree, the blue sky, the dancing waters of the sea, the whole beauty of the earth—all this has driven out the ugly, petty little self, and for an instant you are all that. This is surely the state of self-abandonment without calculation.

To feel this sense of abandonment, you need passion. You cannot be sensitive if you are not passionate. Do not be afraid of that word *passion*. Most religious books, most gurus, swamis, leaders, and all the rest of them, say, "Don't have passion." But if you have no passion, how can you be sensitive to the ugly, to the beautiful, to the whispering leaves, to the sunset, to a smile, to a cry? How can you be sensitive without a sense of passion in which there is abandonment? Sirs, please listen to me, and do not ask how to acquire passion. I know you are all passionate enough in getting a good job, or hating some poor chap, or being jealous of someone; but I am talking of something en-

tirely different—a passion that loves. Love is a state in which there is no 'me'; love is a state in which there is no condemnation, no saying that sex is right or wrong, that this is good and something else is bad. Love is none of these contradictory things. Contradiction does not exist in love. And how can one love if one is not passionate? Without passion, how can one be sensitive? To be sensitive is to feel your neighbor sitting next to you; it is to see the ugliness of the town with its squalor, its filth, its poverty, and to see the beauty of the river, the sea, the sky. If you are not passionate, how can you be sensitive to all that? How can you feel a smile, a tear? Love, I assure you, is passion. And without love, do what you will—follow this guru or that, read all the sacred books, become the greatest reformer, study Marx and have a revolution—it will be of no value because when the heart is empty, without passion, without this extraordinary simplicity, there can be no self-abandonment.

Surely, the mind has abandoned itself and its moorings only when there is no desire for security. A mind that is seeking security can never know what love is. Self-abandonment is not the state of the devotee before his idol or his mental image. What we are talking about is as different from that as light is from darkness. Self-abandonment can come about only when you do not cultivate it, and when there is self-knowing. Do please listen and feel your way into this.

When the mind has understood the significance of knowledge, only then is there self-knowing; and self-knowing implies self-abandonment. You have ceased to rest on any experience as a center from which to observe, to judge, to weigh; therefore, the mind has already plunged into the movement of self-abandonment. In that abandonment there is sensitivity. But the mind which is enclosed in its habits of eating, of thinking, in its habit of never looking at anything—such a mind obviously cannot be sensitive, cannot be loving. In the very abandonment of its own limitations, the mind becomes sensitive and therefore innocent. And only the innocent mind knows what love is—not the calculating mind, not the mind that has divided love into the carnal and the spiritual. In that state there is passion; and without passion, reality will not come near you. It is only the enfeebled mind that invites reality; it is only the dull, grasping mind that pursues truth, God. But the mind that knows passion in love—to such a mind the nameless comes.

December 16, 1959

Bombay, India, 1959

✳

First Talk in Bombay

Freedom is of the highest importance, but we place it within the borders of our own conceit. We have preconceived ideas of what freedom is, or what it should be; we have beliefs, ideals, conclusions about freedom. But freedom is something that cannot be preconceived. It has to be understood. Freedom does not come through mere intellection, through a logical reasoning from conclusion to conclusion. It comes darkly, unexpectedly; it is born of its own inward state. To realize freedom requires an alert mind, a mind that is deep with energy, a mind that is capable of immediate perception without the process of gradation, without the idea of an end to be slowly achieved. So, if I may, I would like to think aloud with you about freedom this evening.

Before we go more deeply into this question, I think it is necessary that we be aware of how the mind has become a slave. With most of us, the mind is a slave to tradition, to custom, to habit, to the daily job which we have to do and to which we are addicted. I think very few of us realize how slavish our minds are, and without perceiving what makes the mind slavish, without being aware of the nature of its slavery, we cannot understand what freedom is. Unless one is aware of how the mind is captured and held, which is to comprehend the totality of its slavish-

ness, I do not think the mind can ever be free. One has to understand *what is* before one can perceive that which is other than *what is.*

So let us observe our own minds; let us look at the totality of the mind, the unconscious as well as the conscious. The conscious mind is that which is occupied with the everyday events of life; it is the mind that learns, that adjusts, that acquires a technique, whether scientific, medical, or bureaucratic. It is the conscious mind of the businessman that becomes a slave to the job which he has to do. Most of us are occupied from nine o'clock until five, almost every day of our existence, earning a livelihood; and when the mind spends so much of its life in acquiring and practicing a technique, whether it be that of a mechanic, a surgeon, an engineer, a businessman, or what you will, naturally it becomes a slave to that technique. I think this is fairly obvious. As the housewife is a slave to the house, to her husband, to cooking for her children, so is the man a slave to his job; and both are slaves to tradition, to custom, to knowledge, conclusions, beliefs, to the conditioned ways of their own thinking. And we accept this slavery as inevitable. We never inquire to find out whether we can function without being slaves. Having accepted the inevitability of earning a livelihood, we have also accepted as inevitable the mind's slavishness, its fears, and thus we tread the mill of everyday existence.

We have to live in this world—that is the only inevitable thing in life. And the question is, surely, whether we cannot live in this world with freedom. Can we not live in this world without being slaves, without the everlasting burden of fear and frustration, without all the agony of sorrow? The limitations of the mind, the limitations of our own thinking, make us slaves. And if we observe, we see that the margin of freedom for the individual is getting narrower all the time. The politicians, the organized religions, the books we read, the knowledge and techniques we acquire, the traditions we are born into, the demands of our own ambitions and desires—these are all narrowing down the margin of freedom. I do not know to what extent and to what depth you are aware of this.

We are not talking of slavery as an abstraction, something which you hear about this evening and then return to your old routine. On the contrary, I think it is very important to understand this problem for oneself because it is only in freedom that there is love; it is only in freedom that there is creation; it is only in freedom that truth can be found. Do what it will, a slavish mind can never find truth; a slavish mind can never know the beauty and the fullness of life. So I think it is very important to perceive how the mind, by its own processes, by its addiction to tradition, to custom, to knowledge and belief, becomes a slave.

I wonder if you as an individual are aware of this problem? Are you concerned merely to exist somehow in this ugly, brutal world, muttering on the side about God and freedom, and cultivating some futile virtue which makes you very respectable in the eyes of society? Or are you concerned with human dignity? There can be no human dignity without freedom, and freedom is not easily come by. To be free, one must understand oneself; one must be aware of the movements of thought and feeling, the ways of one's own mind.

As we are talking together, I wonder if you are aware of yourself. Are you aware, not theoretically, but actually, to what depth you are a slave? Or are you merely giving explanations—saying to yourself that some degree of slavery is inevitable, that you must earn a livelihood, that you have duties, responsibilities—and remaining satisfied with those explanations?

We are not concerned with what you should or should not do; that is not the problem. We are concerned with understanding the mind, and in understanding there is no condemnation, no demand for a pattern of action. You are merely observing, and observation is denied when you concern yourself with a pattern of action, or merely explain the inevitability of a slavish life. What matters is to observe your own mind without judgment—just to look at it, to watch it, to be conscious of the fact that your mind is a slave, and no more; because that very perception releases energy, and it is this energy that is going to destroy the slavishness of the mind. But if you merely ask, "How am I to be free from my slavery to routine, from my fear and boredom in everyday existence?" you will never release this energy. We are concerned only with perceiving *what is,* and it is the perception of *what is* that releases the creative fire. You cannot perceive if you do not ask the right question—and a right question has no answer because it needs no answer. It is wrong questions that invariably have answers. The urgency behind the right question, the very instancy of it, brings about perception. The perceiving mind is living, moving, full of energy, and only such a mind can understand what truth is.

But most of us, when we are face to face with a problem of this kind, invariably seek an answer, a solution, the "what to do"; and the solution, the "what to do" is so easy, leading to further misfortune, further misery. That is the way of politicians. That is the way of the organized religions, which offer an answer, an explanation; and having found it, the so-called religious mind is thereby satisfied.

But we are not politicians, nor are we slavish to organized religions. We are now examining the ways of our own minds, and for that there must be no fear. To find out about oneself, what one thinks, what one is, the extraordinary depths and movements of the mind—just to be aware of all that requires a certain freedom. And to inquire into oneself also requires an astonishing energy because one has to travel a distance which is immeasurable. Most of us are fascinated by the idea of going to the moon or to Venus, but those distances are much shorter than the distance within ourselves.

So, to go into ourselves deeply, fully, a sense of freedom is necessary—not at the end, but at the very beginning. Do not ask how to arrive at that freedom. No system of meditation, no book, no drug, no psychological trick you can play on yourself will give you freedom. Freedom is born of the perception that freedom is essential. The moment you perceive that freedom is essential, you are in a state of revolt—revolt against this ugly world, against all orthodoxy, against tradition, against leadership, both political and religious. Revolt within the framework of the mind soon withers away, but there is a lasting revolt which comes into being when you perceive for yourself that freedom is essential.

Unfortunately, most of us are not aware of ourselves. We have never given thought to the ways of our minds as we have given thought to our techniques, to our jobs. We have never really looked at ourselves; we have never wandered into the depths of ourselves without calculation, without premeditation, without seeking something out of those depths. We have never taken the journey into ourselves without a purpose. The moment one has a motive, a purpose, one is a slave to it; one cannot wander freely within oneself because one is always thinking in terms of change, of self-improvement. One is tied to the post of self-improvement, which is a projection of one's own narrow, petty mind.

Do please consider what I am saying, not merely verbally, but observe your own mind, the actuality of your own inner state. As long as you are a slave, your muttering about God, about truth, about all the things that you have learned from sacred books has no meaning; it only perpetuates your slavery. But if your mind begins to perceive the necessity of freedom, it will create its own energy, which will then operate without your calculated efforts to be free of slavery.

So, we are concerned with the freedom of the individual. But to discover the individual is very difficult because at present we are not individuals. We are the product of our environment, of our culture; we are the product of the food we eat, of our climate, our customs, our traditions. Surely, that is not individuality. I think individuality comes into being only when one is fully aware of this encroaching movement of environment and tradition that makes the mind a slave. As long as I accept the dictates of tradition, of a particular culture, as long as I carry the weight of my memories, my experiences—which after all are the result of my conditioning—I am not an individual but merely a product.

When you call yourself a Hindu, a Muslim, a Parsi, a Buddhist, a communist, a Catholic, or what you will, are you not the product of your culture, your environment? And even when you react against that environment, your reaction is still within the field of conditioning. Instead of being a Hindu, you become a Christian, a communist, or something else. There is individuality only when the mind perceives the narrow margin of its freedom and battles ceaselessly against the encroachment of the politician and of the organized beliefs which are called religion, against the encroachment of knowledge, of technique, and of one's own accumulated experiences, which are the result of one's conditioning, one's background.

This perception, this constant awareness of *what is,* has its own will—if I can use that word *will* without confusing it with the will to which you are so accustomed, and which is the product of desire. The will of discipline, of effort, is the product of desire, surely, and it creates the conflict between *what is* and 'what should be', between what you want and what you do not want. It is a reaction, a resistance, and such will is bound to create other reactions and other forms of resistance. Therefore there is never freedom through will—the will of which you know. I am talking of a perceptive state of mind which has its own action. That is, perception itself is action. I wonder if I am making myself clear!

You see, sirs, I realize, as you must realize too, that the mind is a slave to habit, to custom, to tradition, and to all the memories with which it is burdened. Realizing this, the mind also realizes that it must be free because it is only in freedom that one can inquire, that one can discover. So, to perceive the necessity of being free is an absolute necessity.

Now, how is the slavish mind to be free? Please follow this. How is the slavish mind to be free? We are asking this question because we see that our lives are nothing but slavery. Going to the office day after day in utter boredom, being a slave to tradition, to custom, to fear, to one's wife or husband, to

one's boss—that is one's life, and one sees the appalling pettiness, the nauseating indignity of it all. So we are asking this question: "How am I to be free?" And is that a right question? If it is, it will have no answer because the question itself will open the door. But if it is a wrong question, you will find— at least you will think you have found—ways and means of "solving" the problem. But do what it will, the slavish mind can never free itself through any means, through any system or method. Whereas, if you perceive totally, completely, absolutely that the mind must be free, then that very perception brings an action which will set the mind free.

I think it is very important to understand this, and understanding is instantaneous. You do not understand tomorrow. There is no arrival at understanding after thinking it over. You either understand now, or you don't understand at all. Understanding takes place when the mind is not cluttered up with motives, with fears, with the demand for an answer. I wonder if you have noticed that there are no answers to life's questions? You can ask questions like, "What is the goal of life?" or "What happens after death?" or "How am I to meditate?" or "My job is boring, what shall I do?" You can ask, but how you ask is what matters. If you ask with a purpose, that is, with the motive of finding an answer, the answer will invariably be false because your desire, your petty mind has already projected it. So the state of the mind that questions is much more important than the question itself. Any question that may be asked by a slavish mind, and the answer it receives, will still be within the limitations of its own slavery. But a mind that realizes the full extent of its slavery will have a totally different approach, and it is this totally different approach that we are concerned with. You can ask the right question only when you see instantly the absolute necessity of freedom.

Our minds are the result of a thousand yesterdays; being conditioned by the culture in which they live and by the memory of past experiences, they devote themselves to the acquisition of knowledge and technique. To such minds, truth or God can obviously have no meaning. Their talk of truth is like the muttering of a slave about freedom. But you see, most of us prefer to be slaves; it is less troublesome, more respectable, more comfortable. In slavery there is little danger, our lives are more or less secure, and that is what we want—security, certainty, a way of life in which there will be no serious disturbance.

But life comes knocking at our door, and it brings sorrow. We feel frustrated, we are in misery, and there is after all no certainty because everything is constantly changing. All relationships break up, and we want a permanent relationship. So life is one thing, and what we want is another. There is a battle between what we want and what life is, and what we want is made narrow by the pettiness of our minds, of our everyday existence. Our battles, our contradictions, our struggles with life are at a very superficial level; our petty little questionings based on fears and anxieties inevitably find an answer as shallow as itself.

Sirs, life is something extraordinary, if you observe it. Life is not merely this stupid little quarreling among ourselves, this dividing up of mankind into nations, races, classes; it is not just the contradiction and misery of our daily existence. Life is wide, limitless; it is that state of love which is beauty; life is sorrow and this tremendous sense of joy. But our joys and sorrows are so small, and from that shallowness of mind, we ask questions and find answers.

So the problem is, surely, to free the mind totally so that it is in a state of awareness which has no border, no frontier. And how is the mind to discover that state? How is it to come to that freedom?

I hope you are seriously putting this question to yourselves because I am not putting it to you. I am not trying to influence you; I am merely pointing out the importance of asking oneself this question. The verbal asking of the question by another has no meaning if you don't put it to yourself with instancy, with urgency. The margin of freedom is growing narrower every day, as you must know if you are at all observant. The politicians, the leaders, the priests, the newspapers and books you read, the knowledge you acquire, the beliefs you cling to—all this is making the margin of freedom more and more narrow. If you are aware of this process going on, if you actually perceive the narrowness of the spirit, the increasing slavery of the mind, then you will find that out of perception comes energy; and it is this energy born of perception that is going to shatter the petty mind, the respectable mind, the mind that goes to the temple, the mind that is afraid. So perception is the way of truth.

You know, to perceive something is an astonishing experience. I do not know if you have ever really perceived anything—if you have ever perceived a flower or a face or the sky or the sea. Of course, you see these things as you pass by in a bus or a car, but I wonder whether you have ever taken the trouble actually to look at a flower? And when you do look at a flower, what happens? You immediately name the flower, you are concerned with what species it belongs to, or you say, "What lovely colors it has. I would like to grow it in my garden; I would like to give it to my wife, or put it in my buttonhole," and so on. In other words, the moment you look at a flower, your mind begins chattering about it; therefore, you never perceive the flower. You perceive something only when your mind is silent, when there is no chattering of any kind. If you can look at the evening star over the sea without a movement of the mind, then you really perceive the extraordinary beauty of it; and when you perceive beauty, do you not also experience the state of love? Surely, beauty and love are the same. Without love there is no beauty, and without beauty there is no love. Beauty is in form, beauty is in speech, beauty is in conduct. If there is no love, conduct is empty; it is merely the product of society, of a particular culture, and what is produced is mechanical, lifeless. But when the mind perceives without the slightest flutter, then it is capable of looking into the total depth of itself; and such perception is really timeless. You don't have to do something to bring it about; there is no discipline, no practice, no method by which you can learn to perceive.

Sirs, do please listen to what I am saying. Your minds are slaves to patterns, to systems, to methods and techniques. I am talking of something entirely different. Perception is instantaneous, timeless; there is no gradual approach to it. It is on the instant that perception takes place; it is a state of effortless attention. The mind is not making an effort; therefore, it does not create a border, a frontier, it does not place a limitation on its own consciousness. Then life is not this terrible process of sorrow, of struggle, of unutterable boredom. Life is then an eternal movement, without beginning and without end. But to be aware of that timeless state, to feel the tremendous depth and ecstasy of it, one must begin by understanding the slavish mind. Without understanding the one, you cannot have the other.

We would like to escape from our slavery, and that is why we talk about religious things; that is why we read the Scriptures; that is why we speculate, argue, discuss—which is all so vain and futile. Whereas, if you are aware that your mind is narrow, limited, slavish, petty—aware of it choice-

lessly—then you are in a state of perception, and it is this perception that will bring the necessary energy to free the mind from its slavery. Then the mind has no center from which it acts. The moment you have a center, there must also be a circumference; and to function from a center, within a circumference, is slavery. But when the mind, being aware of the center, also perceives the nature of the center, that very perception is enough. To perceive the nature of the center is the greatest thing you can do; it is the greatest action the mind can take. But that requires your complete attention. You know, when you love something without any motive, without any want, such love brings its own results, it finds its own way, it is its own beauty.

So, what is important is to be aware of how one's mind, in the very process of accumulation, becomes a slave. Do not ask, "How am I to be free from accumulation?" for then you are putting a wrong question. But if you really perceive for yourself that your mind is accumulating, that is enough. To perceive requires complete attention; and when you give your whole mind, your whole heart, your total being to something, there is no problem. It is partial attention, in which there is a withholding, that creates the problems and the miseries of our life.

December 23, 1959

Second Talk in Bombay

This evening I would like to think aloud about the question of effort, conflict, and about that limited field of consciousness whose boundaries are laid down by thought and experience. It is rather a complex problem, and I think one has to give a fair amount of attention to comprehend it. We are caught up in conflicts of many types, in varying degrees, and at various depths. Some conflicts are very shallow, mechanical, and easily resolved, but there are others which are much deeper, almost unfathomable. These hidden conflicts invariably produce distorted actions, which in turn create a great deal of misery and sorrow, the ever-increasing problems with which we are all confronted in our daily life.

So, if possible, I would like to talk over this whole question of effort, conflict, and that limited field of consciousness, the boundaries of which have been laid down by thought and experience. You may ask, "When we have so much unemployment, poverty, starvation, degradation, sorrow, fear, and all the other miseries which plague our existence, why discuss the subject of consciousness? What has that to do with our daily living?" I think it has a great deal to do with it. Without understanding the whole process of our own thinking, without being familiar with its ways and movements, I do not quite see how there can be any way out of our difficulties.

In this unfortunate country, you have not only economic, political, and linguistic problems, but you also have individual difficulties arising from the problems which the Western culture has imposed upon the Eastern culture. There are problems of which, perhaps, many of you are unaware—and probably you do not care to be aware of them because you want to live an easy life, a sluggish, indolent life. We are surrounded by many things, both ugly and beautiful. The filth in the city streets, the poverty and squalor of the village, the beauty of the trees against the sky, and our relationship to all these things—most of us are not sensitive to any of this because we want to lead a safe, secure, undisturbed life. But disaster is always just around the corner.

Wherever you are placed, whether you have a great deal of money or are struggling to make ends meet, these problems exist both within and without, and it seems to me of the utmost importance for every serious-minded person to be aware of them. But it is no good merely being aware of the outward problems, and trying to reform the pattern of our physical existence. To bring about clarity in the world, there must first be inward clarity. You cannot put things about you in order without having order inwardly. Order begins with perception, not with the rearrangement of things outside the skin.

So, what we are going to talk about is intimately connected with our daily problems. Please don't shut yourself off by saying, "That does not concern me." It does concern you, terribly. You may not want to be concerned, you may not want to think about it, but it is the job of every human being to be aware of the whole human problem. We cannot concentrate exclusively on a specialized problem, and be occupied only with that. We must be concerned, it seems to me, with the totality of consciousness, and not just with a particular segment of it. You and I must be concerned with the total man because we are responsible for everything that happens in the world, whether it happens in Russia, in America, here in India, or anywhere else. We are closely interrelated, and whatever happens in one place affects us all. No country can be rich while another is stricken with poverty. This is not a political speech, it is merely to point out the responsibility of each one of us as an individual; and that is why I say it is of the utmost importance to be aware of the problem which I am going to talk about this evening.

But before going into it, I think it is important to understand one central issue—that the means is the end. There is no end apart from the means. Do please see the importance of this—but not just intellectually because mere intellectual or verbal comprehension has very little value. Any fool can understand verbally, but to feel the truth of this, to feel that the means and the end are one, is quite another matter.

Through a particular means you cannot reach an end or an object different from that means. There is a right means by which to become an engineer, an architect, a scientist, a surgeon, and so on. There is also a means of working for the utopian goal which the communists and others talk about. We are not concerned for the moment whether the means is right or wrong. But apart from learning a technique, where there is a means to an end, it invariably develops a mechanical attitude towards life, which is really materialistic. The man who puts on a sannyasi's robe, who renounces the world and becomes a monk in order to be "spiritual," is really a materialist because he is dividing the end from the means.

Please understand what I am talking about, and don't say, "You are talking nonsense because all the sacred books, from ancient times up to the present, insist that a system or a method is necessary." That is merely the accepted tradition. You don't know, you just accept and repeat what you have been told. You may say that tradition is the only thing you do know. If that is so, then you must obviously listen fairly intelligently when something is said which is not in accord with tradition. For the time being, at least, you must listen to find out the truth or the falseness of what is being said.

Please see the truth that to use a means to an end develops a mechanical attitude towards life. Using a means to an end implies efficiency. An efficient mind is necessary in the world of engineering, in the world of mechanics, in the world of science; but an efficient mind in the world of thought is a tyrant. Your gurus, your swamis, your religious books are all tyrannical because they are always bound to the pursuit of an end through a means. Therefore the means strangles you; it makes you a slave. There is

no freedom through a means. If the end is freedom, it is no good going through slavery to reach it. If freedom does not lie in the very first step that you take, there will be no freedom at the end. To say that by going through slavery now you will ultimately be free—that is the good old game of the politicians, of the swamis and the yogis.

This is a very important point, so let us be very clear about it. What I am going to uncover and talk over with you does not permit a mind that is in any way mechanical. If, being used to a system, you have come here looking for a new system to replace the old, I am afraid you will be disappointed because I am offering no system, no method, no goal. What we are trying to do together is to uncover, and therefore discover, as we go along. But discovery can take place only when the mind is free, and that is why freedom is so very important. You cannot discover even the common things of life, you cannot see beauty, the lovely shape and color, the newness of things, if you merely look at them habitually. In the very unfolding of a problem lies discovery, but the moment you begin to accumulate what is discovered, you cease to discover. Do please understand this. The discovery or understanding of something new is impossible for the accumulative, mechanical mind.

Look, sirs. You have often heard the crows calling to each other, have you not? What an awful noise they make settling down for the night in a tree! Have you ever listened to their noise, actually listened to it? I doubt that you ever have. You have probably shut it out, saying it is an ugly noise, a nuisance. But if you are really capable of listening, there is no division between that noise and what is said because attention implies the clarity of altogetherness, in which there is no exclusion. And that is what we are trying to do now: to uncover, to unfold the altogetherness of thought, of attention.

So, I hope you are listening to what is being said as you would listen for the first time to something new. Fortunately or unfortunately, but probably most unfortunately, some of you have heard me many times. Your listening has become a habit, and so you say, "I have heard that before; it is nothing new." Sirs, there is nothing new on the earth, but there can be a newness in the way you listen to what you hear. Then everything is new, everything is living; then every movement of the mind is an uncovering, a discovery. So do please listen to me in that way because I am going to touch upon something to which you are not accustomed at all. I want to go into the problem of self-contradiction. Why does it exist, and must one everlastingly bear with it? Or is there a possibility of understanding and going beyond it?

Self-contradiction implies the question of effort, does it not? Our whole life is based on it; from school age until we die, we everlastingly make effort. As a student you were urged to make effort; otherwise, you would not pass the beastly examination. You have to make effort to concentrate at the office; you have to make effort to be reconciled to your boss, to your wife or husband, to your neighbors, with all the ugliness of it; you have to make effort to control, discipline yourself; and some of you make tremendous effort to find what you call God. That is your life, sirs, is it not? From morning till night, you are making effort, with never a moment of quietude, never a moment when the mind is at ease, when it is full, rich, joyous. It is always struggling, struggling, struggling.

To me, such a life is vain, useless; it does not mean a thing; so I would like to examine that whole process. Don't say, "Effort, conflict, is inevitable; it is part of human nature," for then you have stopped listening, you have ceased to inquire. Don't accept anything—either what is being said now, or anything else in the world—because life is not a matter of acceptance and denial. Life has to be lived; it has to be felt and understood. When you merely accept or deny, you have barricaded your mind; you have ceased to feel, to live.

Do please apply this to yourself. You are not just listening to a lot of words that have no meaning in your daily life.

You have accepted the inevitability of effort, and when you are asked why you make effort, you say, "If I did not make effort, I would be torn to pieces by society. If I did not discipline myself, I would be all over the place," and so on. But to find out why you really make effort, you must uncover the source of this urge, must you not, sirs? Throughout your life you make ceaseless effort, and you have never asked yourself why; and at the end of it, what are you? A useless human being, crippled, dehydrated, worthless. So, what is the cause of this constant effort you are making?

Now, when you are inquiring into a cause, mere definition, which is a form of conclusion, has no value. You have to feel it out. You know, there is the intellect, and there is pure feeling—the pure feeling of loving something, of having great, generous emotions. The intellect reasons, calculates, weighs, balances. It asks, "Is it worthwhile? Will it give me benefit?" On the other hand, there is pure feeling—the extraordinary feeling for the sky, for your neighbor, for your wife or husband, for your child, for the world, for the beauty of a tree, and so on. When these two come together, there is death. Do you understand? When pure feeling is corrupted by the intellect, there is mediocrity. That is what most of us are doing. Our lives are mediocre because we are always calculating, asking ourselves whether it is worthwhile, what profit we will get, not only in the world of money, but also in the so-called spiritual world, "If I do this, will I get that?"

So the cause of effort has to be discovered. Don't accept or deny what is being said because I am only helping you to uncover, to look. It is stupid merely to accept or deny, for then one does not look; and we are trying to discover something, to experience it for ourselves.

So, what is the cause of this effort we are always making? Surely, it is self-contradiction. Do you understand? There is contradiction in our thinking, in our living, in our very being; and where there is contradiction, there must be effort—the effort to be or not to be this or that. Contradiction exists in little things, and in big things too. There is contradiction in our various desires; there is the contradiction of what I am and what I think I should be, which is exaggerated by the ideal. Wherever there is an ideal, self-contradiction is inevitable. All ideals perpetuate this inward conflict. However noble the ideal may be, a mind that follows the ideal must be in a continuous state of self-contradiction, and a self-contradictory mind is caught in this net of incessant effort.

Please, sirs, see the truth of this, and do not merely accept or reject what I am saying, for then it will have no value. It is of the utmost importance to see that the ideal perpetuates self-contradiction, and that through self-contradiction there can be no action which is not corrupt. As long as there is self-contradiction, all action is corruption. Sirs, "good" action in the wrong direction is evil, and the "good" action of a mind which is in contradiction with itself is bound to produce misery. That is exactly what is happening in this and every other land.

So, self-contradiction is the cause of this ceaseless effort which most of us are making. Self-contradiction exists because one wants to be something, does it not? I want to be the governor, or the prime minister; I want to be noble, nongreedy; I want to become a saint. Do you follow, sirs? The moment you have an idea of being or becoming something, there must be self-contradiction. Don't say, "Then must I not become something?" That is not the problem. Just see what is implied in becoming something. That is enough.

If you say that you want to become something in the worldly or the so-called spiritual sense, then you must inevitably accept self-contradiction and effort, with all the crookedness that is born of that effort. And as long as there is contradiction within yourself, you will never produce a world in which human beings can be happy. All your saints, all your leaders have been brought up in this tradition of becoming something, and they are seething with self-contradiction; therefore, whatever "good" they may do will only produce evil. You may not like what is being said, but this is a fact.

Self-contradiction does produce action, does it not? And the more determined you are in your self-contradiction, the more energy you pour into action. Do watch this process in yourself. The tension of self-contradiction produces its own action. If you are a clerk and you want to be the manager, or you want to become a famous artist or writer, or a great saint, in that state of self-contradiction you act most vigorously, and your action is praised by society, which is equally in a state of self-contradiction. You are this, which you dislike, and you want to become that, which you like. So, self-contradiction is the cause of your ceaseless effort. Don't say, "How am I to get out of self-contradiction?" That is a most silly question to ask. Just see how completely you are caught up in self-contradiction. That is enough because the moment you are fully aware of the contradiction in yourself, with all its implications, that very awareness creates the energy to be free of contradiction. Awareness of the fact, like awareness of a dangerous thing, creates its own energy, which in turn produces action not based on contradiction.

So, there is contradiction in each one of us, is there not? I hate, and I want to love; I am stupid, and I want to be clever. We are all so familiar with contradiction in ourselves; we live with it day and night. And how is it to be understood—understood, not transcended, suppressed, or sublimated? You know, to understand something, you must have love in your heart. To understand the beauty of a tree trunk, or of a curving branch, or of the sunlight through the leaves, you must look, you must feel, you must love. In the same way, there must be the state of affection, of sympathy, of love, if one is to understand this inner contradiction. And to go deeply into the problem of what creates contradiction, there must be infinite patience. Do you understand, sirs?

I want to know myself, the entirety of myself; I want to know the shallowness, the pettiness of every thought, every feeling; I want to delve deeply into my own consciousness so that I begin to understand its whole process. But to do that, there must be love, there must be patience, there must be a sense of insistency which is not a product of the will, but a spontaneous movement in everyday living. So, with love and patience, and with this sense of insistency, let us try to find out what consciousness is.

Consciousness, surely, is based on contradiction; it is a process of relationship and association. If there is no relationship, there is no consciousness. The relationship of ideas, the association of experiences that one has gathered, of memories that one has consciously or unconsciously stored up, the racial instincts, the traditions that one has inherited, the innumerable influences to which one is subject—all this makes up what we call consciousness. After all, in considering yourself a Hindu, a Parsi, a Buddhist, or a Christian, you are merely the result of certain influences. We are not talking about good or bad influences. All influence limits the mind, and a mind that is limited, narrowed down by influence, is a very effective tool—which is what the organized religions want.

So consciousness, surely, is that state of contradiction, with its ceaseless effort, which lays down the boundaries of the mind; it is the way of thought which creates a center and a circumference.

Look, sirs, let us make it very simple. What are you? You are a businessman, a clerk, a professor, an engineer, or what you will. If you are a professor, your mind is limited by the knowledge you have acquired. That is obvious. If you are a businessman, your experience in the world of acquiring money, with its competition, its cheating, and all the rest of it, limits the field of your thinking. If you are a scientist, your field of inquiry is likewise limited by what you know. If you are a so-called religious man, your consciousness is held within the frontiers of the particular environment in which you were brought up, whether it be Hindu, Buddhist, Muslim, Christian, or any other.

So contradiction, with its effort, limits the mind, and that limited consciousness becomes the 'me'—the 'me' who is an engineer, who has lived so many years and constructed so many bridges, the 'me' who is an inventor or a swami or a businessman, the 'me' who is bound by thought, by experience, by knowledge.

The experiences, the influences, the traditions by which we are bound may be conscious or unconscious. Most of us are probably unaware of all these things that bind us. Being in a state of contradiction, we ask, ''How am I to get out of it?'' or else we accept this inward contradiction as inevitable, and somehow put up with it. But a man who would find out if there is a way of living free of self-contradiction, with all its miseries, must begin to inquire into the nature of his own consciousness, not only at the upper level, but at the deeper levels as well. And if you begin to inquire into yourself, you will inevitably see that your conscious and unconscious conflicts, which produce dreams and various other psychological states, are the result of a deep, inward contradiction. An ambitious man, whether he be a merchant, a politician, or a so-called saint is essentially a self-contradictory human being. So do please see the psychological revolution that will take place when you begin to inquire into this whole problem of self-contradiction.

Self-contradiction is not productive of intelligence but only of cunning. It produces a certain efficiency in adjusting oneself to the environment—and that is what most of us are doing. Self-contradiction, with its ceaseless effort, places a bondage on consciousness; and action born of self-contradiction is fundamentally productive of misery, though on the surface it may seem to be worthwhile. If your mind is in a state of self-contradiction, you may do good superficially, but essentially you are creating further misery. Of course, the streets must be cleaned, and all the rest of it—but we are not talking about that.

Now, seeing that any action born of self-contradiction, with its tension, will invariably produce misery, not only in the individual, but in his relationship with everything, one begins to inquire, "Then what is intelligent action? What is the action which is not born of self-contradiction, which is not the outcome of effort?" Please follow this, sirs. With most of us, idea and action are two separate things. The idea is over there, and our approximation to that idea is what we call action, so there is self-contradiction. Do you follow? The mind which conceives of action as an idea and then shapes its action according to that idea is in a state of self-contradiction, is it not?

So, then, is there an action which is not self-contradictory? We all know the action which is in contradiction with itself—that is our everyday life. The mind is very familiar with it. And seeing the misery, the confusion, the ugliness, the brutality, the fleeting joys that result from such action, the mind is now inquiring if there is an action which does not come out of the womb of self-contradiction. If it exists, what is the nature of that action? Surely, it is a movement which is not divided as idea and action. When you feel something very strongly, you act without calculation, without bringing in the intellect and its cunning reasons, without thinking how dangerous it will be. Out of this pure feeling there is an action which is not self-contradictory. Perhaps I am not making myself clear.

Sirs, when you love something with your whole being, there is no self-contradiction. But most of us have not that wholeness of love. Our love is divided as carnal and spiritual, sacred and profane, and all the rest of that nonsense. We do not know the love which is a total feeling, a completeness of being, which is neither of the past nor of the future, and which is not concerned with its own continuity. That feeling is total; it has no border, no frontier, and that feeling is action free of self-contradiction. Don't say, "How am I to get it?" It is not an ideal, a thing to be gained, a goal you must arrive at. If it is an ideal, throw it out because it will only create greater contradiction in your life. You have enough ideals, enough miseries—don't add another. We are talking about something entirely different: freeing the mind of all ideals, and therefore of all contradiction. If you see the truth of that, it is enough.

So, you see, intelligence is neither yours nor mine, nor is it to be found in any particular book; it is anonymous. When the mind listens to what is being said without accepting or denying, without comparing or evaluating, when it uncovers the truth of everything as it goes along, such a mind is in a state of intelligence, and that intelligence is completely anonymous. Do you understand, sirs? All great things are anonymous, are they not? All the great temples of this country, all the great cathedrals of Europe are anonymous. You don't know who built those structures. No man has left his petty little name on them. Similarly, truth is anonymous, and you must be in a state of anonymity for it to come to you. All creation is anonymous—the creation which comes from nothingness.

If you have diligently followed all that has been said, you will perceive that where thinking is based on experience, it is productive of self-contradiction. What does that word *experience* mean? There is a challenge and a response; the response to the challenge is experience, which becomes memory. Such memory is productive of thought, which says, "This is right, that is wrong. This is good, that is bad. This is what I must do, that is what I must not do," and so on. As long as the mind is thus the residue of experience, as long as there is thought which has its roots in the soil of memory, there must be self-contradiction.

I know this is very difficult to understand, sirs, because for most of us life is based on experience. We move from experience to experience, and each experience, gathered as memory, shapes and conditions all further experience. But I am suggesting that there is a state of mind in which action is entire. There is then no idea apart from action; there is no approximation of action to an idea. If you really begin to inquire into that state of intelligence, you will discover for yourself the astonishing fullness, the entirety, the altogetherness of a mind that has no past, no future; and from that state, action is inevitable. Then living itself is action, and in such action there is no contradiction, but an extraordinary sense of bliss, a quietude which

cannot be repeated, which is not to be imitated or learned from another. It comes darkly, mysteriously, without your asking for it. It comes only when you have gone into yourself very deeply and have torn away the roots of all your conventions, customs, habits, methods, ideals, and superstitions. Then you will find there is love; and with that love there is no evil; neither is there the good, for both are bondages. It is only love that is free.

December 27, 1959

Third Talk in Bombay

I would like, this evening, to talk about knowledge, experience, and time. But before we go into all that very deeply, I think it is important to inquire into the nature of humility; and to explore humility, we have to be clear that it is not something to be acquired, achieved, or cultivated. A virtue that is struggled after, cultivated, gathered by slow degrees, ceases to be a virtue. Surely, this is an important point to understand. Either you are without greed, without envy, or you are not; and if you are greedy, envious, you cannot cultivate nongreed, nonenvy. This is very difficult for most of us to comprehend because we think in terms of time. We conceive of humility as a quality to be gradually acquired, and thereby totally miss the very simple yet extraordinarily profound nature of humility; and without humility one cannot go very far.

The state of humility is essential for all inquiry. It is an "altogether" feeling, without a center from which the mind can say, "I am humble." A person who is positively or negatively determined to be free of any particular problem is not in a state of humility. There is humility only when the mind wishes to see the problem clearly, whatever that exploration may reveal. Such a mind is inquiring. It wishes to know all the implications of the problem, both the pleasant and the unpleasant; it wishes to see things as they are, without the urge to transform, to subjugate, or to sublimate what it sees; and only such a mind is in a state of humility.

As I am thinking aloud, please listen to what is being said with a sense of ease, rather than with effort. The moment you make an effort to listen, you cease to listen. You are listening only when there is a sense of ease, a certain poise of both mind and body, a state of relaxed attention. In that state of relaxed attention the mind will comprehend much more; it will perceive far deeper subtleties than when it says, "I want to understand, and to understand I must make an effort"—which is, I am afraid, what most people do.

I am going to talk about a very simple thing, but its simplicity will not be seen by a complicated mind. Surely, you can see that which is very delicate, which has an astonishingly subtle feeling, only when your mind is at ease, when it is not struggling to get something. I am not talking about anything that you can "get." I want to convey the feeling, the quality of affection, of sympathy, of love—which has no words, which is not a pose, a matter of attitudes and values. I want to communicate with you about the nature of humility, and then to inquire into the process of knowing, with all its implications. But a mind that is merely trying to get or to cultivate that state of humility cannot comprehend its nuances, its significance, its extraordinary quality.

So do please listen with a sense of affection, a sense of easy inquiry, of relaxed attention, because you are not going to get anything from me. I am not going to give you a thing, and you will be wasting your time if you come with the intention of getting something. If there is a giver, and one who takes, then both are in a state of non-humility. To comprehend the nature or to know

the feeling of humility, one must understand this willful determination to be free of, to resolve, one's problems. That is what most of us want, is it not? We want to resolve our problems, to escape from the everyday misery, conflict, strife, from the pettiness, the ugliness, the brutality, and fleeting joy of our daily existence; so we are always groping after something. That is why we follow leaders, join various organized religions, go from one guru to another, hoping to find some means by which to transcend our anxiety, our fear, our lack of love.

We all have problems, there is no getting away from it; and as we live in this world from day to day, our problems are increasing, they are not growing less. The overwhelming weight of so-called civilization is destroying the quality of our own thinking, and we have lost the simplicity with which it is necessary to approach the innumerable problems that confront us. Because the mind desires to transcend or resolve its own problem—whether it is greed, envy, telling lies, being jealous, being lazy, fearful, or what you will—it is determined to find a way, a method, a system by which to do so; and this determination is what destroys humility.

Do please understand this, sirs. It is not something vague or cantankerous, nor is it a particular idiosyncrasy of the speaker. If you observe how your mind thinks in terms of transcending, going beyond, or resolving its problem, in that observation no effort is involved. But where there is effort—the effort to change, to transform yourself—there is no humility, there is essentially vanity. You have the idea that you have changed, that you have gained, that you have gone beyond, all of which gives you a sense of being important; therefore, you never feel the real nature of humility.

What matters is to look at the problem, simply to look at it and be familiar with all its implications. If you study the problem, however painful, ugly it may be, if you look at it, move in it, live with it and—I really mean this—embrace it, take it to your heart, then you will find that you are in a state of humility; and then the problem is quite different from what it was.

All problems are intensely complicated; there can never be an answer of yes or no. To go deeply into a problem, one must have this extraordinary quality of humility, and if you are listening, really listening, you are already in that state. As I said, I have nothing to offer you, I am only pointing out; and when something is pointed out to you, you cannot "get" it, you cannot lay your hands on it—you have to look at it, you have to perceive, feel, touch, smell it. To put away all determination, all effort to change, is not a state of negation; neither is it a positive state. You are just inquiring. It is the impulse to achieve that gives to the mind a sense of its own importance, and achievement is what we call positive action, but such action only brings further confusion and misery. Whereas, if you are inquiring into the problem, which is this state of contradiction with its innumerable urges and influences in which each one of us lives—if you are simply aware of it, then that very awareness is its own action.

Look, sirs. Most of us are envious, are we not? And the problem of envy is quite complex. In envy there is everlasting struggle, comparison, competition, which sharpens the will, the determination to achieve, to go beyond. This is called positive action, and your culture encourages you in it. After all, the desire for fame is based on envy; and being envious, you suffer, you feel frustrated, you are anxious, fearful. Therefore you say to yourself, "I must be free of envy." Your mind is concerned with freedom from envy—which means that it is concerned with getting rid of the pain, the frustration, the transiency of joy which is implicit in envy. So there is

conflict, and where there is conflict, there is inevitably a will which says, "I must go beyond." Such a mind is not in a state of humility.

When the mind is aware that it is envious, when it does not dodge that fact, when it does not cheat itself or assume a hypocritical attitude, but simply says, "It is so, I am envious," such an acknowledgement of the fact brings its own action. But acknowledgement is not acceptance of the fact—there is a difference between the two. When you acknowledge that a thing is so, there is no doubt about it. When you merely accept it, there is always the possibility of not accepting it. So, when you are aware of the fact that you are envious, which means that you see and acknowledge it, then that very acknowledgment, that very self-critical awareness creates an action which is not the action of will. And I say such action comes from the state of humility because it is not accumulative. The moment you accumulate the quality of nonenvy, your mind is no longer in a state of humility—in which alone it can learn.

I do hope I am making myself clear because with an understanding of the nature of humility, I would like to enter into the problem of knowledge, into this extraordinary thing called experience, and into a much more complicated problem, which is that of time. Perhaps your mind is already weary after a long day's work in the office, or you may feel worn out with the family wrangles and adjustments and all the other things that are going on in your life. That is why I suggest that you listen with ease, without strain. You are not learning anything from me, as you would in a school, and there are no examinations to be passed. No guru is going to tell you that you are doing well and that you may go on to the next stage. You are listening to yourself—and listening to yourself is an art. You cannot listen if you are all the time striving to be or to do something. So, I want to talk very casually about experience, and do please listen with a sense of ease. I want to explore, to look into it—and come out of that exploration, perhaps not with experience, but with a mind that is innocent. Because it is only the innocent mind that can perceive what is true, that can understand the fullness, the quality of truth—not the experienced mind. The experienced mind is a dead mind. Whether the mind, being burdened with experience, can dissolve or wipe away all its experiences and be born afresh—that is what I want to go into.

We all have experiences. We experience irritation, jealousy, anger, hatred, violence, and so on. Going through the experience of anger, for example, the mind gathers the residue of that experience; and the residue remains, coloring all further experiencing. We are as easily flattered as we are insulted. Your mind revels in flattery, it is delighted if someone tells you how marvelous you are; and the feeling of pleasure evoked by those words is an experience which remains in your mind. Similarly, if someone insults you, you go through essentially the same experience, but not with pleasure, and the residue of that unpleasant experience also remains in your mind.

So experience leaves a mark on the mind, which is memory. There is memory as the necessary knowledge of mechanics and technique, and memory which is psychological, which is based on the desire to be important, to be this or to be that. Experience is the accumulation of knowledge, whether it be of outward or inward things. The experienced mind says, "I know how to deal with envy, with these wrangles and quarrels," or whatever the problem happens to be. So experience is the soil in which thought grows—the thought of being important, the thought of going beyond, and so on.

Please, sirs, do observe your own minds. I am only describing, and if you are merely listening to the description, you are not living. All descriptions are secondhand, and you are living at firsthand only when you discover for yourself. A hungry man cannot live on descriptions of food, however beautiful, however enticing they may be. So you are listening, not to me, but to yourself. You are observing for yourself how the residue of experience cripples the mind.

If you live on the pleasure of flattery, or on the resentment of insult, surely your mind is dull, crippled. The person who has insulted you, you approach with antagonism, and the flatterer you regard with a feeling of pleasure; therefore, your mind is not fresh to look, to inquire. You go through life gathering impressions, marks, scars, both pleasurable and painful, which remain in the mind and which you call experience; and from experience comes knowledge. So experience as knowledge prevents clarity.

Do please see this point, sirs. Character is not a matter of being obstinate in one's knowledge or strong in one's experience. There is character only when the mind, being fully aware of its accumulated experience, is free of that background and is therefore capable of clarity. Only a mind that is clear has character. Knowledge at one level of human existence is obviously imperative—I must know where I live, I must know how to do my job, I must be able to recognize my wife, and so on. But knowledge at another level prevents the movement of knowing.

So, what is knowing, and what is knowledge? What do we mean when we say we know? Do we know, or are we told, and then say that we know? Please, sirs, do go into this with me, pay a little attention. *To know* is a very interesting word. How do you know, and what do you know? Please ask yourselves, as I am asking myself. Whatever one knows is based on experience, and therefore the mind is already conditioned by it, because all experience is conditioning, is it not? You have a certain experience, you go through some form of sorrow or pleasure, which leaves a mark on your mind, and with that conditioned mind you meet the next challenge. In other words, you translate that challenge in terms of your own limitations, against the background of your own experience, thereby further conditioning your mind. So the mind is more and more conditioned through experience. You don't have to accept this, sirs. If you observe your own minds, you will see it is a fact. The mind can learn only if it is not acquiring, if it is not accumulating, if it is moving. It cannot move, it cannot learn when it has acquired, accumulated, for that is a static state.

So, what is the movement of learning, knowing? I see that knowledge is accumulated through experience. A man may have mechanical or technical knowledge, or he may cleverly have learned how to avoid psychological difficulties and maintain a state of inward comfort for himself; but I see that this knowledge is not the movement of knowing. Surely, the two are entirely different. Knowing is a constant movement; therefore, there is no static state, no fixed point from which to act. I wonder if I am making myself clear?

Look, sirs. Having listened and listening are two entirely different states. Fortunately or unfortunately, some of you have listened to me repeatedly for ten or more years, and having listened, you say, "Yes, I know what he will say." That is not the state of listening. You are listening only when you do not translate what you hear in terms of what you have already heard. The state of listening is entirely different from having listened, gathered, and then listening further. When you listen further to something, you have ceased to listen.

I wonder if you have ever considered the nature of love? Loving is one thing, and having loved is another. Love has no time. You cannot say, "I have loved"—it has no meaning. Then love is dead; you do not love. The state of love is not of the past or of the future. Similarly, knowledge is one thing, and the movement of knowing is another. Knowledge is binding, but the movement of knowing is not binding.

Just feel your way into this, don't accept or deny it. You see, knowledge has the quality of time; it is time-bound whereas the movement of knowing is timeless. If I want to know the nature of love, of meditation, of death, I cannot accept or deny anything. My mind must be in a state, not of doubt, but of inquiry—which means that it has no bondage to the past. The mind that is in the movement of knowing is free of time because there is no accumulation.

Sirs, you see, unless the mind is fresh, new, in a state of innocency, the nature of timelessness, of immortality, cannot be understood. I am not using that word *immortality* in the ordinary sense. I am using it to connote the feeling of immensity, of that which is without measure, the feeling of a mind that has no boundary, no frontier. I am not referring to the immortality that my little mind wants in its desire to live perpetually. That is not immortality at all; it is a bondage, it is enslavement to time. I want to discover the nature of that immortality which is beyond time. To do this, my mind must be in a state of inquiry, that is, in the movement of knowing from moment to moment—not in a state of having known, which puts a stop to knowing. You see, this is the source of misery with most people. You have read your innumerable books; you know what this saint or that guru has said, and when you hear the word *immortality*, you immediately translate it to conform to the pattern of your thinking;

and when you do that, you have stopped the movement of knowing.

Consciously or unconsciously, the mind has gathered many experiences, and can such a mind be in a state of innocency, free to look, to observe, to act without always having this background of the past, this bondage to time? I do not know if it is a problem to you. Probably it is not. But it is bound to be a problem to anyone who inquires into life because all that we know is frustration, misery, and despair, with now and then a fleeting moment of joy. Though there is pleasure in it, with an occasional touch of joy, life for most of us is a dreadful thing, and our eyes are full of tears. Life is something for which there is no answer; it must be understood from moment to moment. But we are always wanting an answer, and the answer we find inevitably conforms to the pattern of what we think we know. And when it turns out—as sooner or later it must—that the answer according to a pattern is no answer at all, again we are in despair.

So, when the mind really begins to inquire into all this, it sees the necessity, if only intellectually, of experiencing a state which is timeless. Time is despair because in time there is only tomorrow. That tomorrow may be stretched to a hundred tomorrows, but at the end of it there is no answer; agony is still there. So our life is chaotic, and there is no end to our misery, however much we may philosophize about it. That is why the inquiry into the nature of timelessness is not a vain, useless thing.

Time is the gathering of experience, and all gathered experience engenders time—the passage of what has been through what is to what will be. Time may solve technical problems; you may presently produce machines in which to go to the moon, and all the rest of it. But our deep human problems are never resolved through time—which means that they cannot be resolved by a mind based on

experience, a mind which is the result of time. When such a mind becomes aware of the impasse, the blank wall before it, there arises a sense of despair. And seeing the nature of this whole timebound process, one must inevitably inquire into what is called the timeless, the eternal—not to speculate on whether there is an eternality, and how to arrive at it, which is a schoolboy approach, but to be in a state of inquiry, in the movement of knowing, never saying, "I know." The man who says he knows does not know.

So the problem is, really, can the mind be free of all its accumulated experience and knowledge and yet not be in a state of amnesia? Can it feel the state of innocency and therefore be free to inquire? Do you understand my question, sirs? As a Hindu, a Parsi, a Buddhist, a Christian, or what you will, you have lived so many years, you have learned so much, acquired so much, suffered so much, and your mind is petty, shallow; though it is full of many things, it is an empty mind, and you go on living that way, accumulating more and more, until you die. Seeing the inevitability of death, you ask if there is something after death. When you are told that there is heaven, and all the rest of it, with that you are satisfied, and still burdened with sorrow, you peacefully pass away.

I feel that what matters is to be in the movement of knowing, that is, in a state of inquiry about oneself. But this requires constant attention—attention, not effort. To pay attention is to be aware of *what is* when you are walking, when you are talking, when you are riding on a bus, or sitting in a cinema, or reading a book. If you can be so aware, then you will discover for yourself the movement of knowing, which is the real state of humility. Only the mind that knows this state of humility is innocent. Then you are no longer a follower, and there is nothing secondhand about you.

At present you are all secondhand; you know only what you have been told about God, about virtue, about almost everything in life. You are what you have read, what you have heard, what your culture has imposed upon you; so you don't know anything except your job, your appetites and anxieties. Being secondhand, you follow, you have authorities, you have gurus, you have all these shoddy gods.

A mind that is in the movement of knowing is in a state of humility, which is innocence, and it is only the innocent that know love. The innocent mind is love; it will do what it will, but it has no ego. So experience is not the teacher. Experience is the teacher of achievement; it is the teacher of mechanical things, as knowledge is. But a mind that is in the movement of knowing is free of knowledge and experience; therefore, it has no past or future, and only such a mind can receive that which is not measurable by the mind.

December 30, 1959

Fourth Talk in Bombay

I would like, if I may, to talk this evening about the unfoldment of energy as desire, fulfillment, and frustration; and perhaps, if our minds can extend so far, we may be able to go into the question of what is beyond the mind. But before we go into all that, I think it is important to be concerned with the problem of change.

For most of us, change in any form is a very disturbing factor. We like the well-worn path of habit and custom, and to bring ourselves to depart from that path, we find almost impossible. For any change in habit and custom, we depend on influence; we think we have to be compelled to change. Circumstances play an important part in bringing about a change in our attitudes, in our

values, as well as in outward things. I think we should go into this matter fairly carefully, so as to uncover for ourselves the ways of our own thinking.

We do change under the influence of propaganda, do we not? Influence in various forms is a very important factor in our lives. The influence of the newspapers; the influence of the books we read, whether sacred or profane; the influence of social, educational, and religious environment; the influence of our neighbors; the influence of the family, of the wife over the husband, and the husband over the wife; the influence of tradition and public opinion; the influence of diet, of climate—these and many other influences are continually shaping our minds. We are never free of these innumerable influences of which we are the result, and there is no denying that we are the creatures of environment. You are a Hindu, a Muslim, a Christian, or whatever it is you are because you have been brought up in a certain culture, with its particular traditions and ways of thinking.

So, influence plays an extraordinarily important part in our lives. We are not discussing what is good influence and what is bad influence. To me, all influence is evil because it conditions and enslaves the mind. If the mind changes under any influence, it is changing only within the circumference of itself, whether that circumference is large or small.

In listening to what is being said, please do not take the attitude of a listener at a talk, but observe your own mind. Observe yourself and your environmental influences, and you will see an extraordinary phenomenon going on within the so-called free mind. I do not think the mind is free, but the mind can be aware of its conditioning and of the innumerable influences by which it is conditioned. You know, certain words have a profound influence on us. Words like *God*, *communism, Chinese, Catholic, Jesus, Buddha,* and so on, have an extraordinarily penetrating influence on our minds, and I think most of us are unaware of it. And unless we really grapple with and understand these influences, any change—whether it be an economic revolution or a change in the outlook of the mind itself—has very little meaning because we are then slaves to propaganda.

You are all listening to me. Why? It would be very interesting to find out. Why do you come here on a hot Sunday afternoon? If you come to be persuaded, to be influenced, to be directed, to be told what to do, then what you hear will be reduced to mere propaganda. And propaganda—whether it be that of the politicians, of the organized religious people, or of the sacred books—has a most destructive effect on the human mind.

So, without understanding the influences to which most of us are such slaves, we shall never find out how to awaken energy, and energy is obviously necessary. I do not mean the energy of a well-read mind, or the energy of a well-fed body—although physical energy is part of it. A neurotic may have tremendous energy, just as an hysterical person may sometimes be very strong. In the same way, a man who is devoted to an ideal often has extraordinary vitality. These are all manifestations of that energy which is the outcome of influence, and if you go into it very deeply, you will find it leads to power. Power in any form is evil, whether it be the absolute power of a dictator, or the power of a wife over her husband, or a husband over his wife, or the power of society over the individual. But before we go into all this, it seems to me that, as human beings living in this mad, monstrous, competitive world, we have to understand the whole question of being influenced.

Why is the mind influenced? And is it possible for the mind to be free of all influences? Surely, a mind held within the field of influence is very limited, though it may be very active. All propagandists are very active, are they not? Yet such a mind is limited, conditioned, and therefore there is bound to be a constant battle within the limitations of itself.

Please observe your own conditioning and see how you are influenced. If you watch this whole process in yourself, you will perceive that everything you think, as well as your actions, your profession, your verbal exchanges, your ideals and beliefs are all the result of the innumerable influences to which you are consciously or unconsciously exposed. The mind is taking in everything, whether you are aware of it or not. The noise of the crows, of the tramcar, the words of the speaker, the movements of the person next to you, and so on—it is all being absorbed by the mind, either consciously or unconsciously.

So, is it not very important to ask ourselves whether the mind can be free of influences? I do not think it can be without first becoming aware of the influences by which it is swayed. Awareness of these influences is part of self-knowledge, is it not? And it is extremely difficult to be so aware because influence is often very subtle. In advertising, they have tried subliminal propaganda—repeatedly flashing an idea on the cinema or television screen so rapidly that the viewer is unaware of it, yet it is absorbed by the unconscious. Similarly, you have been constantly told—it is the tradition of a thousand years—that you are a Hindu. You have been brought up in that tradition, and your job, your profession further conditions the mind; you are influenced, your thought is shaped by what you do, and so on. To be aware of all these influences is not easy. But once you begin consciously, deliberately, incessantly to ask the right question, which is to uncover in yourself these various influences, then the mind becomes extraordinarily alert. So it is necessary, it seems to me, to ask oneself that question.

The past—not only the recent past, but the past of centuries, with all its memories, its psychological wounds, its accumulated experience and knowledge—is influencing the present, the now. The now becomes the passage of the past to the future, so tomorrow is already shaped by yesterday. The present responds to challenge according to the past, and that response shapes the future. This is a very simple process, sirs, if you will observe it in your own life. If you feel that I have insulted you today, when you meet me tomorrow, which is the future, the memory of that insult strengthens your feeling of resentment, and so it goes on and on. Don't translate it as karma. Karma is something entirely different, at least as I see it. For the moment we are just uncovering the problem of influence and change.

When we do change, it is generally through compulsion, through misery, through ambition, or some other form of influence. We change with motives of profit, we change through pain, we change through slavery to some ideology or system of thought. You can see this mechanical process of change operating in the mind, but such change, which is the result of influence, is no change at all—though it gives energy to the mind. The man who has a good job, who is secure in his family, who is building up a large bank account, has an extraordinary sense of energy. The man who has the capacity to talk or to write, to do this or to do that, the man who is gifted in some art or craft, the man who is trying to fulfill himself, to become something—such people have a great deal of energy, but when sooner or later that energy is blocked, there is frustration, a feeling of despair.

Do please follow this, sirs, not just as a talk to which you are listening, but as a description of your own mind, a description of yourself, of your daily existence. In your pursuit of profit you generate energy, but that energy, however cunning, however capable and efficient, always functions from the center towards the circumference. And is that a change? When you change through compulsion, through fear, through motive, through the pursuit of a goal, is there a change?

Take the question of social or economic revolution, with its promised benefits, its plan to create a classless society, and all the rest of it. Is such a revolution a real revolution? Or is it merely a reaction, and therefore a modified continuation of the past? These so-called revolutions have always been only a reaction, and there has always been a reversion to the former state, only modified. So a person who is concerned with total change, with real revolution, which is a transformation in the quality of the mind itself, and not merely a continuation of the modified past—such a person must ask himself, surely, whether it is possible to change without influence, without motive. Change based on motive, on influence, is merely a form of compulsion or imitation; therefore, it is no change at all. Do you understand?

Look, sirs, to restrain oneself from violence by practicing nonviolence is no change at all, though in this country it is glibly talked about every day. Nonviolence with a motive is still violence. The motive is the ideal, which is a projection of the mind, and a mind that conforms to the ideal is imitative; it is still within the field of violence. I wonder if you see this!

Being violent, you say, "I must practice the ideal of nonviolence." Nonviolence is then the projection of your mind as a reaction to violence. Having adopted the ideal of nonviolence, you proceed to discipline yourself, you struggle to conform to that ideal, you go through the painful process of constant adjustment to it—a process which is always superficial, but which is recognized by people as a form of virtue. And that is the strange part of it—we want people to recognize that we are virtuous, that we have become nonviolent, or that we are on the way to nonviolence. Recognition plays an extraordinary part in our lives, does it not? So you see how subtle is the desire for power.

If you examine this whole process very closely and objectively, you will see that the violent mind which has nonviolence as a goal, which is motivated by the desire to change itself and become nonviolent, is still caught in violence. So the question naturally arises: Can the mind which is violent change itself without any motive? Or is it inevitable that all change must come from a motive, from some form of influence? You see the problem, don't you?

We must all change radically, deeply, fundamentally because as we are, we are not real human beings; we are slaves to various forms of influence. And to discover human dignity, to awaken a real sense of freedom, one must surely ask oneself whether it is possible to bring about a radical transformation in the mind without any motive, without any compulsion, without any fear, demand, or influence. If you say that such a thing is not possible, that it is human nature to change with a motive, that for centuries it has been going on, then this is not a problem to you. But the moment you really begin to inquire into the whole question of revolution, of change at any level, you must inevitably ask this question; otherwise, you are thinking very superficially. And it is superficial thinking that has produced this ruthless society with its wars, its so-called revolutions, its concentration camps, its dictatorships, and all the horrors of the police state.

So, if you are deeply concerned with the total transformation of man, then you must be aware of this problem of influence, in which is included seeking inspiration, going to the temple, reading sacred books, repeating mantras—all the monstrously ugly disciplines you go through in order to be free, and which are a denial of real freedom. But if you are merely responding to this talk intellectually, you will go away as empty as you came. The intellect is very superficial. It can invent clever theories; it can argue or counterargue and go on playing that game indefinitely, but it cannot produce change; it cannot bring about a real transformation in the quality of the mind itself.

We are now concerned with real transformation; we are making a real inquiry into the problem of change and revolution. What is revolution? That is the question we are asking ourselves because our times demand it. But this is a perennial problem; it is not just the problem of our times because the human mind is constantly deteriorating. This deterioration is like a wave that is always pounding at our doorstep, and a person who is really serious has to go into the question of whether change can only come about through influence, through fear, through compulsion, or whether there is a totally different kind of change.

The change that is brought about through influence leads to power, does it not? It leads to power, to position—and that is what most of us want. Most of us want to be recognized as being somebody, either in this world or in the so-called spiritual world. Don't you all want that? From the lowest clerk to the highest politician, from the humblest disciple to the greatest guru, each wants to be recognized as a somebody—which is the desire for power. We all want to be important in one way or another—as a stamp collector, as a scientist, as a bureaucrat, as a prime minister, as a good wife, as a good father, or what you will. We want to be recognized, we want to be important, and the moment you want to be important, you have tremendous energy. Look at your own daily existence, sirs; see how this demand to be recognized, this struggle to be important is always going on. A little flattery from a big man, and you purr like a cat. You want to bask in his glory, and you say, "He is my friend; I knew him when he was a boy"—you know all that childish stuff we play about with.

So, when there is change with a motive, that is, when change is brought about by compulsion, by influence, such a change is always towards power, towards being important—important not only in this world but important as a man of God, as a man who has control of his mind, of his body, as a man who is respectable in his virtue, and all the rest of it.

Do please follow this deeply because we are concerned with our lives, not with words. All of us want power, all of us want to be important in some way—even if it is only in the little way of a schoolteacher with ten boys in his class. That is why we have degrees, titles, and all that nonsense.

One can see that where there is a compulsive change, either outwardly or inwardly, there is a sense of power, which ultimately leads to some form of dictatorship, and that this sense of power creates energy. I do not know if you have ever experimented with controlling your mind and your body, but if you have, you will know that it gives you an extraordinary delight to be completely their master. It gives you a great sense of power—much greater than the feeling of power that goes with any worldly position. We are not talking about electric power, and all that. We are discussing the psychological demand for power.

Now, energy as the sense of power seeks its own fulfillment, does it not? That is, I want to fulfill myself through action; I want to be or become something. I want to become the manager, or the chief disciple; I

want to understand, to change; I want to become the most famous politician in town; I want to be the ruler, or to have a degree, or to get a better job so as to earn more money—you know this acquisitive game we play with ourselves, and through which there is fulfillment.

If you observe, you will see that fulfillment is really the demand of a mind which is craving for power. When it is not able to achieve power and is therefore deprived of that fulfillment, it feels frustrated; and to escape from the misery of its frustration, it turns to something else through which it again strives to fulfill itself. If I cannot succeed in this world, I struggle to become a saint, or if I see it is unprofitable to become a saint, I pursue worldly success—and so it goes on and on. The urge to conform to a pattern of change creates energy, which gives a sense of power, and that sense of power seeks to heighten itself through fulfillment.

Watch yourselves, sirs; I am not saying something extraordinary but am merely describing the process of your daily existence. In that process there is immense sorrow because a man who wants to fulfill himself lives inevitably in fear of nonfulfillment, and so the misery begins.

You see, we never ask ourselves whether there really is such a thing as fulfillment at all. A man may see, of an evening, a beautiful formation of clouds and then wish to paint it, but if in painting it he is fulfilling himself, in that very act he has ceased to be a painter. Similarly, you may wish to fulfill yourself through your family, to carry on your name through your son, and you may call it love; but it is not love at all, however much it is recognized as love by respectable society. It is merely the perpetuation of yourself. Sirs, you may laugh it away, but this is a fact.

So, unless the mind is totally dull, utterly insensitive, completely enclosed within itself, it must inevitably inquire to find out whether it is possible to change without motive, because to change with a motive leads only to power and further misery. Is there a way to change which has no motive, which is not based on comparison, which is not a reaction to one's present state? Do let us be very clear on this issue because we are always thinking in terms of duality: good and bad, rich and poor, heaven and hell, and so on. Seeing that change with a motive generates an intense feeling of power, which is a form of fulfillment with all its frustrations, limitations, and sorrow, we want to escape from that by seeking the other; but the other is not to be sought—it is not a reaction, it is not the opposite of our craving for power. To change without motive is something entirely different; it comes unsought, like the change from morning to evening, from darkness to light. The mind sees the destructive and corrupting nature of the desire for power, with its frustration and misery, and its immediate reaction is to try to escape from all that into what is called cosmic consciousness, truth, God—you know all those high-sounding words we use. But that is no change at all. It is merely a continuity of what has been towards the result of what has been, which is what will be.

So, is there a way of inquiry which will help the mind to be in that state of energy, of understanding, which is perpetual change, an eternal movement with no beginning and no end? Do you understand the question, sirs? Please understand the question first, and do not ask how to get it, how to capture that eternality for your own use in your petty little house.

The question is this: You are all familiar with the craving for power, for recognition, for a position of importance, with its fulfillments and frustrations, its sorrows, agonies, and fears. You know how that craving gives an extraordinary energy, without which you could not carry on day after day for fifty years with your jobs, your quarrels, your struggles and miseries. And the greater your capacity is, the wider is your field for the exercise of that energy, and therefore the more evil you create around you. Now, if you see the destructive nature of this craving for power, if you are aware of the whole anatomy of it, then surely you are bound to ask yourself if there is a way for the mind to change which is not an outcome of the craving for power. Do you understand?

We see that this craving for power, with the energy it awakens, is destructive, and that the ambitious mind is ceaselessly being pushed by the wave of deterioration, decay. If you say that all this is natural, inevitable, that human beings can live no other way, then for you it is not a problem. You accept corruption, decay. You are content to live within that framework with your sorrows and passing joys, with your imitated virtues and your invented gods. But if you begin to question, to explore, to discover—not because Shankara or Buddha said so, but through your own endeavor, your own awareness, your own intelligence—then you will find you are unconsciously moving away from all that in a totally new direction. Then there is a change which is not a reaction, not fabricated by the mind.

Sirs, there is a state in which all virtue *is,* and that is the state of attention. To be totally attentive is to be totally virtuous, and therefore to flower in goodness, in beauty. But what do you do now? You find for yourselves a little haven, a placid backwater in the river of life, and there you move, you function, you "change." So perhaps you don't intend to be very serious about these things, but it does not matter. If you have heard only words, what you have heard may remain in your mind because your mind is prone to propaganda, but these talks will then be merely one more noise among many other noises. Whereas, the man who really begins to inquire into all this noise, into the chattering of the mind, must inevitably come to that state of energy which is moving endlessly, and which is not caught in the backwater of his own desires.

So the problem of change, of transformation, is not to be thought of in terms of environmental influences. It is obvious that we need a revolution—an economic revolution, a world revolution—so that there will be one government, for the earth is ours. It is not the rich man's earth or the poor man's earth; it does not belong to Russia or America, to India or China. It is our earth, yours and mine, to be lived on, to be enjoyed, to be cherished, to be loved. But that outward revolution can be brought about only when there is a revolution in your consciousness, a crisis in your own mind—that is, when you have ceased to be a nationalist, when you are no longer an Indian, a Parsi, a communist, or any of those things, when you are a total human being. We do need a world revolution because only such a revolution will solve our economic problem, the problem of starvation. But politicians are concerned not with the problem of starvation but with a particular system, and they quarrel over which system is going to solve the problem. To bring about a revolution outwardly, you have to change inwardly. If you don't change, the challenge destroys you. You have to respond rightly to the challenge; otherwise, you—you as a man, as a culture, as a race—are thrown away.

To inquire into the problem of inward change—which is much more difficult—one must be totally aware of this craving for power which we have. And can the mind, having grasped the significance of this craving, having understood that to change with a motive is a form of power seeking, with all its nuances, its struggles, its pains, its fulfillments and frustrations—being aware of all that, can the mind knowingly, consciously,

without any motive, let go? Do you understand, sirs? That is the real renunciation of the world—not changing gods or becoming a hermit or joining a monastery or putting on different clothes. Real renunciation, which is revolution, is the complete abandonment of power seeking, of wanting to be important, to have recognition—which means, really, entering a world of which we know nothing. To enter a world of which we already know is not renunciation. There is renunciation, revolution, only when we enter a world where the mind has never gone before, where it has not projected itself, where it has no future, no past, but only a sense of attention, of inquiry and perception. Perception has no past; perception is not accumulative; and it is only with the awakening of perception that there is an energy which is not a product of the mind. Don't translate it as ''God''—it has nothing to do with your ugly notions of God. There is an energy which is in itself creative, eternal, and without understanding that, without tasting it, embracing it, knowing the beauty of it, merely to think about God has no value. But it comes darkly, mysteriously, without your asking.

Our lives are not beautiful; our lives are tawdry, shallow, empty; our energy is limited, and it dies. We know hate, jealousy, envy—these are the things with which we are intimate. It is obvious that we have to abandon all that. To be kind without any motive, to be generous without calculation, to share the little that one has, to give with one's heart and mind and hand without asking something in return—that we must do, it is only civilized, decent, but it is not the other. It is like keeping the house in order, polished, spotlessly clean. To keep the house clean and in order is obviously necessary, but if we do it hoping to receive the other, it will never come. Keep the mind clean, alert, watchful; observe every movement of thought, see the significance of every word, but without any motive, without any urge or compulsion. Then you will find an extraordinary thing takes place—there comes an energy which is not your own, which descends upon you. In that energy there is a timeless being, and that energy is reality.

January 3, 1960

Fifth Talk in Bombay

There are several things I would like to go into with you this evening, particularly sensitivity of the mind and meditation. But before we go into these things, it seems to me very important to have a certain clarity of the mind because without this clarity, the mind has not the capacity to think very deeply. Clarity, at whatever level, is completely necessary. If you are not clear about the way to your home, you get confused. If you are not very clear about your feelings, there is self-contradiction. If you do not clearly understand the ways of your own thinking, such lack of clarity leads to illusion. So, clarity in every direction is essential. And it is a most difficult thing, it seems to me, to have a really clear mind because clarity cannot be cultivated, learned; rather, it comes into being through watching, through observing, through perception.

The clarity I am talking about is part of the sense of beauty. I do not know why it is, and I am not judging anyone at all, but there seem to be so few who are sensitive to beauty—to the beauty of a sunset, the beauty of a face, the beauty of a curve, the beauty of a tree or of a leaf fluttering in the breeze, to the beauty of a bird on the wing, or the beauty of a gesture, of a word. I am not referring so much to the expression as to the feeling, the quality, the texture of beauty. I think sensitivity to beauty goes with clarity. Clarity is a state of total being, as beauty is. Beauty is not merely in the face, in the form;

it is the totality of a human being, the totality of a tree, the vastness of the sky, the wholeness of sunlight on a leaf, of moonlight on the water. Beauty is a total thing. In the same way, clarity is not partial. There is no clarity if you are clear about economics or how to get to the moon and totally unclear about the ways of your own thinking, the operations of your own mind. Similarly, you cannot see the beauty of a picture, or hear the loveliness of music, when you are in a state of self-contradiction.

I think clarity is something that pervades the whole mind; it is the feeling of one's total being. Surely, sirs, clarity is simplicity. But most of us think of simplicity in terms of action or behavior; we think it has to do mainly with the manner of our speech, or the nature of our dress. In other words, we look upon simplicity as merely a matter of expression. We say a man is very simple because he has only a couple of loincloths, or because he has renounced this and taken up that. We judge simplicity by the garb, by the outward mode of life. But to me, simplicity is an inward state of being in which there is no contradiction, no comparison; it is the quality of perception in approaching any problem.

Life is becoming increasingly complicated, with more and more experts who are always contradicting each other; and a mind that wants to comprehend life, with all its complexities and problems, must surely approach it very simply. But the mind is not simple when it approaches any problem with a fixed idea or belief, or with a particular pattern of thought. I think simplicity has nothing to do with determination. A mind that is determined is never a simple mind.

Do please listen to all this because unless you understand what I am saying now, you will not understand what I shall try to say about the mind and meditation. Without experiencing this total feeling of clarity, of simplicity, this extraordinary sense of beauty, you cannot possibly comprehend the complex machinery which we call the mind. Most of us have preconceived ideas about the mind. We have come to a conclusion as to what the mind is, or what it should be, and we approach it with that conclusion, with that belief; so it becomes very difficult, if not impossible, for us to understand the mind.

First of all, your mind is not simple, is it? A simple mind, surely, is one that functions, that thinks and feels without a motive.

Do please pay a little attention to what is being said. You may have heard the previous talks, or you may have read what has already been said, but please listen now so as to experience, as you are listening, this feeling, this movement of life in which there is no motive.

Where there is a motive, there must be a way, a method, a practice, a system of discipline. The motive is brought about by the desire for an end, for a goal, and to achieve that goal there must be a way, some form of discipline; and such a mind is not simple, such a mind is not clear because it creates conflict within itself. One has to begin by perceiving for oneself the very simple fact that where there is a motive, there is self-contradiction in living. To me, meditation is a freeing of the mind from all motives, and this requires an astonishing attention to the whole problem of goals, systems, practices, disciplines.

So, I would like to describe the mind, and in listening to the description, please also be aware of the nature of your own mind. The mind is not merely the container of thoughts; it is also the thoughts which it contains, as well as the limitations which time has placed upon it, and it is also something which is not of time. To function smoothly, like a fine machine, is surely one of the qualities of a good mind; so also is the capacity to reason clearly without conclusions, and to discern without prejudice. The mind is likewise the feeling of being distinct, separate; it is also memory, the capacity to experience, and to store that experience as knowledge. The mind is also time—time in the sense of looking back to the things that have been, and looking forward to that which will be—time as before and after. All these elements go to make up the mind.

But the mind is also something covering all this, something which is not merely a word and the recognition of that word. The mind, surely, is like the sky in which everything is contained. A tree is not merely the leaf, the flower, the branch, the trunk, or the root; it is a totality which includes all these things. Similarly, the mind is a totality, and to feel the totality of the mind, to be aware of it is really the beginning of meditation. If we do not feel the totality of the mind, we reduce it to a mere machine—which it is for most of us.

For most of us the mind is a word, a symbol, an image; it is a process of naming out of the background of memory, experience. Having learned a certain job or profession, my mind continues to function automatically; having established a certain relationship with my wife or husband, with my children, with society, I carry on without further thought. My responses to various stimuli are mechanical. My mind does not want to be disturbed; it does not want to question, to be made uncertain, so it establishes a pattern of conduct, of thought, a pattern of relationship to man and to nature, as well as to possessions, things.

This is surely true for most of us, as we know if we are at all observant of the operation of our own minds. Just see how slavish your mind is to words like *love, God, communism, India, Gita.* The mind invents symbols and becomes a slave to the symbols, and then the symbols become far more important than the action of living.

Please, sirs, I am not describing something foreign; I am describing a process which is actually taking place in the daily existence of each one of us. And I do not see how the mind can delve deeply within itself if it is not free of these symbols, of these words whose hold on the mind is the outcome of our experiences, our memories. The mind accumulates knowledge, which is essentially the symbol, the word; and if the mind is unable to free itself from the symbol, from the word, from the memory, which is knowledge, then it can never wander into the wider fields of itself.

Obviously, we cannot forget the things we must know. We cannot forget how to speak; we cannot forget the way home; we cannot forget our various professions, or the techniques which have been developed through science. We must have all this, and we cannot forget it. But there is the other part of the mind which projects itself in time, which creates the future as the goal to be achieved. So the mind as we know it is time; it is the result of time—time as before and after, time as a process of living in the past or in the future, which obviously denies the understanding of the present. I am not talking of chronological time, but of time as a psychological necessity for the unfoldment of the gradual process of achievement which we call evolution. We say we must have time to understand—time being the future.

I hope I am making all this clear and not complicating it. But life is complicated; the mind is complicated. One has to look into all these problems for oneself and not just say, "Help me to be free of time." What one can do, surely, is to be fully aware of all these patterns of the mind and slip through them, as it were, to a state which is not measured by the mind, because whatever the mind does to free itself will always be within the field of time. Any effort the mind makes will further limit the mind because effort implies the

struggle towards a goal, and when you have a goal, a purpose, an end in view, you have placed a limit on the mind; and it is with such a mind that you are trying to meditate.

Do you understand, sirs? First, please see the problem. The problem is not how to meditate, or on what to meditate, but whether the mind is capable of meditation at all. We have been told that we must meditate, and through meditation we hope to achieve a result—happiness, God, truth, or what you will. So we make an effort to meditate, and where there is effort, there is the element of time. We say, "Through discipline, through practice, through control, through the gradual process of time, I shall achieve an understanding of what God is."

To me, that is not meditation at all. It is sheer self-hypnosis, a projection of one's own illusions and experiences—which may give you visions. But to find out what meditation is, surely, you must understand the nature of the mind that approaches the problem. You want to meditate because you have read or been told about the extraordinary nature of meditation. You have heard that there is in it a certain sense of beauty, a certain quality of peace, of silence; so you control, discipline your mind in an effort to meditate, hoping to realize that silence, that peace.

Now, before you can realize that silence, before you can find out what truth is, what God is, you must understand the mind which is meditating; otherwise, whatever it does, the mind will still be playing within the field of its own knowledge and conditioning. You may awaken certain capacities, you may have visions and all the rest of it, but it will all be a form of delusion. If you like to delude yourself, if you accept delusion, then by all means keep on playing with it. But if you really want to find out what meditation is, surely you must begin, not by asking how to meditate, but by inquiring to find out whether the mind which is approaching the problem is capable of understanding the problem.

I do not know if you realize how mechanical the mind is. Whatever it touches becomes mechanical. This evening I see something totally new, and that newness is experienced by the mind, but tomorrow that experience becomes mechanical because I want to repeat the sensation, the pleasure of it. I establish a process, I set up a method through which I seek to recapture that newness, so it becomes mechanical. Everything the mind touches inevitably becomes mechanical, noncreative.

So, the question is: Can my mind realize the nature of its own mechanical habits? Can it just be aware of the fact of *what is*, and not ask how to change it, how to break it down? I think the simple realization of the fact, of the actual fact of *what is*, brings clarity.

Surely, it is important to understand this because most of us try to move away from *what is* towards 'what should be', which creates a great many problems and contradictions. So I just want to know *what is;* that is all, nothing else. I am not interested in 'what should be'. I want to know my mind as it is, with all its contradictions, its jealousies, its hopes and despairs, its aggressiveness, its envy, its capacity to deceive. And the moment I see actually *what is*, there is clarity—clarity which will help me to go much deeper into *what is*.

For most of us, *what is* is not of interest; therefore, it does not open up the capacity to enter into *what is*. We think that by having an ideal we can transform *what is* into 'what should be'—that the ideal, the 'what should be' will awaken the capacity to understand *what is*. But I feel quite the contrary is true—that the capacity to delve into *what is* comes into being when we observe *what is* with undivided attention.

Our whole existence is *what is*, and not 'what should be'. The 'what should be', the ideal, has no reality whatsoever. You may create an ideal, and you may be committed to that ideal, calling it reality; but the ideal is a reaction to *what is*, and reaction is never the real. The real is *what is;* it is our daily existence. The *what is* may be produced by the past, and it may have a future; but the important thing, it seems to me, is for the mind to put aside the past and the future and be wholly concerned with the present, with *what is*—go into it profoundly, and not just remain on the surface by saying, "Well, that is my life, that is the way life goes," and so on. Life is this extraordinary thing which we call the past, the time before, as well as the future, the time after; but life is much wider, much deeper—it has a far more profound significance if the mind can go into it through the present.

To put it differently, all experiencing is conditioned by past experience. If one observes, there is actually only the state of experiencing. But what is experienced is immediately translated into memory, which then conditions further experiencing. The state of experiencing is conditioned by your background as a Hindu, a Muslim, a Christian, or what you will, with all its beliefs and superstitions.

You will get it, perhaps, as I talk about it; but the description is never the real. What is real is seeing the truth instantaneously because truth has no future. You cannot say, "I will see it tomorrow." Truth has no past—it has no continuity, and that is the beauty, the simplicity and clarity of truth.

When the mind which is mechanical investigates to find out what meditation is, it wants to bring meditation into the field of the known. After all, the mind itself is the known; it is nothing else. The mind is not the unknown. And when the mind, which is the known, tries to uncover the unknown, it invents methods, systems, practices, disciplines to that end. I hope you are following, somewhat.

Now, the problem is not how the mind, which is the known, is to uncover the unknown, because it cannot. What it can do is to be aware of its own process, which is the process of the known—and it cannot do anything else. It cannot proceed to uncover the unknown, because it has not that capacity. You may stand on your head, breathe in different ways, practice a discipline, control your thoughts, or do anything else you like; but whatever the mind does, it can never understand, or capture, or feel the unknown.

Then what is meditation?

Now, sirs, as I describe it, please follow the description as though you were meditating. To me, meditation is of the highest importance because all life is meditation—meditation in the sense of a state of living in which the frontiers of the mind are broken down, in which there is no self, no center, and therefore no circumference. Without meditation, life becomes very shallow, mechanical. So meditation is necessary; it is as essential as eating, as breathing. Therefore please follow this, not just verbally, but actually experiencing it as we go along—which means not introducing what you have read or been taught about meditation because then you are not observing, you are not experimentally following.

Meditation, surely, can never be a process of concentration because the highest form of thinking is negative thinking. Positive thinking is destructive to inquiry, to discovery. I am thinking aloud, negatively. Through negation there is creation. Negation is not the opposite of the positive, but a state in which there is neither the positive nor its reaction as the negative. It is a state of complete emptiness, and it is only when the mind is completely empty, in this sense, that there is creation. Whatever is born out of that empti-

ness is negative thinking, which is not confined by any positivism or negativity on the part of the mind itself.

So, concentration is not meditation. If you observe, you will see that concentration is a form of exclusion; and where there is exclusion, there is a thinker who excludes. It is the thinker, the excluder, the one who concentrates that creates contradiction because then there is a center from which there can be a deviation, a distraction. So, concentration is not the way of meditation; it is not the way to the uncovering of that which may be called the immeasurable. Concentration implies exclusion; it implies the thinker who is making an effort to concentrate on something. But the state of attention, which is not concentration, has no frontier; it is a giving of your whole being to something without exclusion.

Now, will you please experiment with something as I am talking? See if you can be in this state of attention, so that not only is your mind functioning but your whole being is awake. Don't say, "What do you mean by my 'whole being'?" It does not matter. Give your whole attention—which means hearing the noise of the bus, of the tramcar, and listening to the silence. If you give your whole attention, you will find that you are also listening to what is being said with an astonishing focus, acumen; but if you merely concentrate, there is exclusion, and therefore no attention.

Concentration is a narrowing down of the mind. To narrow down the mind may be very effective in the case of a schoolboy in a class, but we are concerned with the total process of living, and to concentrate exclusively on any particular aspect of life belittles life. Whereas, when there is this quality of attention, then life is endless; it cannot be measured by the mind.

You have been told that there are different ways to meditate on reality, on God, whatever word you care to use. How can there be ways, methods, systems by which to arrive at something that is living? To that which is static, fixed, dead, there can be a way, a definite path, but not to that which is living. If you want to understand your wife, your neighbor, your friend, there is no "way" to do it; there is no system by which to understand a living human being. Similarly, you cannot go to that which is living, dynamic, through any way or method. But you reduce reality, God, or what name you will, to a static thing, and then invent methods by which to reach it.

So, concentration is not the way of meditation, nor can any method, system, or practice lead you to reality. If you see the truth of this—that no system of any kind, however subtle, however new or well-seasoned in tradition, can lead you to reality—then you will never again enter into that field of delusion, and your mind has already broken loose from its moorings to the past; therefore, it is in a state of meditation.

In meditation there is also the problem of the unknown. The mind, as I said, is the known—the known being that which has been experienced. Now, with that measure we try to know the unknown. But the known can obviously never know the unknown; it can know only what it has experienced, what it has been taught, what it has gathered. So, can the mind—please follow this carefully, sirs—can the mind see the truth of its own incapacity to know the unknown?

Surely, if I see very clearly that my mind cannot know the unknown, there is absolute quietness. Do you understand, sirs? If I feel that I can capture the unknown with the capacities of the known, I make a lot of noise; I talk, I reject, I choose, I try to find a way to it. But if the mind realizes its own absolute incapacity to know the unknown, if

it perceives that it cannot take a single step towards the unknown, then what happens? Then the mind becomes utterly silent. It is not in despair; it is no longer seeking anything.

The movement of search can only be from the known to the known, and all that the mind can do is to be aware that this movement will never uncover the unknown. Any movement on the part of the known is still within the field of the known. That is the only thing I have to perceive; that is the only thing the mind has to realize. Then, without any stimulation, without any purpose, the mind is silent.

Have you not noticed that love is silence?—it may be while holding the hand of another, or looking lovingly at a child, or taking in the beauty of an evening. Love has no past or future; and so it is with this extraordinary state of silence. And without this silence, which is complete emptiness, there is no creation. You may be very clever in your capacity, but where there is no creation, there is destruction, decay, and the mind withers away.

When the mind is empty, silent, when it is in a state of complete negation—which is not blankness, nor the opposite of being positive, but a totally different state in · which all thought has ceased—only then is it possible for that which is unnameable to come into being.

January 6, 1960

Sixth Talk in Bombay

This afternoon I would like to talk with you, if I may, about sorrow, will, and fear. Most of us live in a world of myth, of symbols, of make-believe, which is much more important to us than the world of actuality.

Because we do not understand the actual world of everyday living, with all its misery and strife, we try to escape from it by creating a world of make-believe, a world of gods, of symbols, of ideas and images; and where there is this flight from the actual to the make-believe, there is always contradiction, sorrow. If we would be free of sorrow, surely, we must understand the world of make-believe into which we are constantly escaping. The Hindu, the Muslim, the Buddhist, the Christian—they all have their make-believe world of symbols and images, and they are caught in it. To them, the symbol has greater significance and is much more important than living; it is embedded in the unconscious, and it plays an immense part in the life of all those who belong to one or other of the various cultures, civilizations, or organized religions. So, if we would be free of sorrow, I think it is important, first of all, to understand the make-believe world in which we live.

If you walk down the road, you will see the splendor of nature, the extraordinary beauty of the green fields and the open skies; and you will hear the laughter of children. But in spite of all that, there is a sense of sorrow. There is the anguish of a woman bearing a child; there is sorrow in death; there is sorrow when you are looking forward to something and it does not happen; there is sorrow when a nation runs down, goes to seed; and there is the sorrow of corruption, not only in the collective, but also in the individual. There is sorrow in your own house, if you look deeply—the sorrow of not being able to fulfill, the sorrow of your own pettiness or incapacity, and various unconscious sorrows.

There is also laughter in life. Laughter is a lovely thing—to laugh without reason, to have joy in one's heart without cause, to love without seeking anything in return. But such laughter rarely happens to us. We are bur-

dened with sorrow; our life is a process of misery and strife, a continuous disintegration, and we almost never know what it is to love with our whole being.

One can see this sorrowful process going on in every street, in every house, in every human heart. There is misery, passing joy, and a gradual decay of the mind; and we are always seeking a way out. We want to find a solution, a means or a method by which to resolve this burden of life, and so we never actually look at sorrow. We try to escape through myths, through images, through speculation; we hope to find some way to avoid this weight, to stay ahead of the wave of sorrow.

I think we are familiar with all this. I am not instructing you about sorrow. And it would be absurd if you suddenly tried to feel sorrow as you are sitting here listening—or if you tried to be cheerful; it would have no meaning. But if one is at all aware of the narrowness, the shallowness, the pettiness of one's own life, if one observes its incessant quarrels, its failures, the many efforts one has made that have produced nothing but a sense of frustration, then one must inevitably experience this thing called sorrow. At whatever level, however slightly or however deeply, one must know what sorrow is. Sorrow follows us like our shadow, and we do not seem able to resolve it. So I would like, if I may, to talk over with you the ending of sorrow.

Sorrow has an ending, but it does not come about through any system or method. There is no sorrow when there is perception of *what is*. When you see very clearly *what is*—whether it be the fact that life has no fulfillment or the fact that your son, your brother, or your husband is dead; when you know the fact as it actually is, without interpretation, without having an opinion about it, without any ideation, ideals, or judgments, then I think there is the ending of sorrow.

But with most of us there is the will of fear, the will of discontent, the will of satisfaction.

Please do not merely listen to what is being said, but be aware of yourself; look at your own life as if it were your face reflected in a mirror. In a mirror, you see *what is*—your own face—without distortion. In the same way, do please look at yourself now, without any likes or dislikes, without any acceptance or denial of what you see. Just look at yourself, and you will see that the will of fear is reigning in your life. Where there is will—the will of action, of discontent, the will of fulfillment, of satisfaction—there is always fear. Fear, will, and sorrow go together; they are not separate. Where there is will, there is fear; where there is fear, there is sorrow. By "will" I mean the determination to be something, the determination to achieve, to become, the determination which denies or accepts. Surely, these are the various forms of will, are they not? Because where there is will, there is conflict.

Do look at this and understand not just what I am saying but the implications of will. Unless we understand the implications of will, we shall not be able to understand sorrow.

Will is the outcome of the contradictions of desire; it is born of the conflicting pulls of "I want" and "I don't want," is it not? The many urges, with their contradictions and reactions, create the will of satisfaction or of discontent, and in that will, there is fear. The will to achieve, to be, to become—this, surely, is the will that engenders sorrow.

Sirs, what do we mean by sorrow? You see a child with a healthy body and a lovely face, with bright, intelligent eyes and a happy smile. As he grows older, he is put through the machine of so-called education. He is made to conform to a particular pattern of society, and that joy, that spontaneous delight in life, is destroyed. It is sad to see such things happen, is it not? It is sad to lose someone whom you love. It is sad to realize

that one has responded to all the challenges of life in a petty, mediocre way. And is it not sad when love ends in a small backwater of this vast river of life? It is also sad when ambition drives you, and you achieve—only to find frustration. It is sad to realize how small the mind is—not someone else's, but one's own mind. Though it may acquire a great deal of knowledge, though it may be very clever, cunning, erudite, the mind is still a very shallow, empty thing; and the realization of this fact does bring a sense of sadness, sorrow.

But there is a much more profound sadness than any of these—the sadness that comes with the realization of loneliness, isolation. Though you are among friends, in a crowd, at a party, or talking to your wife or husband, you suddenly become aware of a vast loneliness; there is a sense of complete isolation, which brings sorrow. And there is also the sorrow of ill health.

We know that these various forms of sorrow exist. We may not actually have experienced them all, but if we are observant, aware of life, we know they do exist; and most of us want to escape from them. We do not want to understand sorrow, we do not want to look at it, we do not say, "What is it all about?" All that we are concerned with is to escape from sorrow. It is not unnatural, it is an instinctive movement of desire, but we accept it as inevitable, and so the escapes become far more important than the fact of sorrow. In escaping from sorrow, we get lost in the myth, in the symbol; therefore, we never inquire to find out if there is an ending to sorrow.

After all, life does bring problems. Every minute life poses a challenge, makes a demand; and if one's response is inadequate, that inadequacy of response breeds a sense of frustration. That is why, for most of us, the various forms of escape have become very important. We escape through organized religions and beliefs; we escape through the symbol, the image, whether graven by the mind or by the hand. If I cannot resolve my problems in this life, there is always the next life. If I cannot end sorrow, then let me get lost in amusement; or, being somewhat serious-minded, I turn to books, to the acquisition of knowledge. We also escape through overeating, through incessant talking, through quarreling, through becoming very depressed. These are all escapes, and not only do they become extraordinarily important to us, but we fight over some of them—your religion and my religion, your ideology and my ideology, your ritualism and my antiritualism.

Do watch yourself, and please don't be mesmerized by my words. After all, what I am talking about is not some abstract theory; it is your own life as you actually live it from day to day. I am describing it, but don't be satisfied by the description. Be aware of yourself through the description, and you will see how your life is caught up in the various means of escape. That is why it is so important to look at the fact, to consider, to explore, to go deeply into *what is,* because *what is* has no time, no future. *What is* is eternal. *What is* is life; *what is* is death; *what is* is love, in which there is no fulfillment or frustration. These are the facts, the actual realities of existence. But a mind that has been nurtured, conditioned in the various avenues of escape, finds it extraordinarily difficult to look at *what is;* therefore, it devotes years to the study of symbols and myths, about which volumes have been written, or it loses itself in ceremonies or in the practice of a method, a system, a discipline.

What is important, surely, is to observe the fact and not cling to opinions or merely discuss the symbol which represents the fact. Do you understand, sirs? The symbol is the word. Take death. The word *death* is the symbol used to convey all the implications of the fact—fear, sorrow, the extraordinary sense of loneliness, of emptiness, of littleness and isolation, of deep, abiding frustration. With the word death we are all familiar, but very few of us ever see the implications of that fact. We almost never look into the face of death and understand the extraordinary things that are implied in it. We prefer to escape through the belief in a world hereafter, or we cling to the theory of reincarnation. We have these comforting explanations, a veritable multitude of ideas, of assertions and denials, with all the symbols and myths that go with them. Do watch yourselves, sirs. This is a fact.

Where there is fear, there is the will to escape—it is fear that creates the will. Where there is ambition, will is ruthless in its fulfillment. As long as there is discontent—the insatiable thirst for satisfaction which goes on everlastingly, however much you may try to quench it by fulfilling yourself—that discontent breeds its own will. You want satisfaction to continue or to increase, so there is the will to be satisfied. Will in all its different forms inevitably opens the door to frustration, and frustration is sorrow.

So, there is very little laughter in our eyes and on our lips; there is very little quietude in our lives. We seem unable to look at things with tranquillity and to find out for ourselves if there is a way of ending sorrow. Our action is the outcome of contradiction, with its constant tension, which only strengthens the self and multiplies our miseries. You see this, sirs, don't you?

After all, you are being disturbed. I am disturbing you about your symbols, your myths, your ideals, your pleasures, and you don't like that disturbance. What you want is to escape, so you say, "Tell me how to get rid of sorrow." But the ending of sorrow is not the getting rid of sorrow. You cannot "get rid" of sorrow, any more than you can acquire love. Love is not something to be cultivated through meditation, through discipline, through the practice of virtue. To cultivate love is to destroy love. In the same way, sorrow is not to be ended by the action of will. Do please understand this. You cannot "get rid" of it. Sorrow is something that has to be embraced, lived with, understood; one has to become intimate with sorrow. But you are not intimate with sorrow, are you? You may say, "I know sorrow," but do you? Have you lived with it? Or, having felt sorrow, have you run away from it? Actually, you don't know sorrow. The running away is what you know. You know only the escape from sorrow.

Now, just as love is not a thing to be cultivated, to be acquired through discipline, so sorrow is not to be ended through any form of escape, through ceremonies or symbols, through the social work of the "do-gooders," through nationalism, or through any of the ugly things that man has invented. Sorrow has to be understood, and understanding is not of time. Understanding comes when there is an explosion, a revolt, a tremendous discontent in everything. But, you see, we seek to find an easy way to smother our discontent. We indulge in social work, we get lost in a job, a profession, we go to the temple, worship an image, we cling to a particular system or belief—and all these things, surely, are an avoidance, a way of keeping the mind from facing the fact. Simply to look at *what is* is never sorrowful. Sorrow never arises from just perceiving the fact that one is vain. But the moment you want to change your vanity into something else, then the struggle, the anxiety, the mischief begins—which eventually leads to sorrow.

Sirs, when you love something, you really look at it, do you not? If you love your child, you look at him; you observe the delicate face, the wide-open eyes, the extraordinary sense of innocency. When you love a tree, you look at it with your whole being. But we never look at things in that way. To perceive the significance of death requires a kind of explosion which instantly burns away all the symbols, the myths, the ideals, the comforting beliefs, so that you are able to look at death entirely, totally. But most unfortunately and sadly, you have probably never looked at anything totally. Have you? Have you ever looked at your child totally, with your whole being—that is, without prejudice, without approval or condemnation, without saying or feeling, "He is my child"? If you can do this, you will find that it reveals an extraordinary significance and beauty. Then there is not you and the child—which does not mean an artificial identification with the child. When you look at something totally, there is no identification because there is no separation.

In the same way, can one look at death totally?—which is to have no fear; and it is fear, with its will to escape, that has created all these myths, symbols, beliefs. If you can look at it totally, with your whole being, then you will see that death has quite a different meaning because then there is no fear. It is fear that makes us demand to know if there is continuity after death, and fear finds its own response in the belief that there is or that there is not. But when you can look with completeness at this thing called death, there is no sadness. After all, when my son dies, what is it that I feel? I am at a loss. He has gone away, never to return, and I feel a sense of emptiness, loneliness. He was my son, in whom I had invested all my hope of immortality, of perpetuating the 'me' and the 'mine'; and now that this hope of my own continuity has been taken away, I feel utterly desolate. So I really hate death; it is an abomination, a thing to be pushed aside, because it exposes me to myself. And I do push it aside through belief, through various forms of escape; therefore, fear continues, producing will and engendering sorrow.

So, the ending of sorrow does not come about through any action of will. As I said, sorrow can come to an end only when there is a breaking away from everything that the mind has invented for it to escape. You completely let go of all symbols, myths, ideations, beliefs, because you really want to see what death is, you really want to understand sorrow—it is a burning urge. Then what happens? You are in a state of intensity; you don't accept or deny, for you are not trying to escape. You are facing the fact. And when you thus face the fact of death, of sorrow, when you thus face all the things you are confronted with from moment to moment, then you will find that there comes an explosion which is not engendered through gradualness, through the slow movement of time. Then death has quite a different meaning.

Death is the unknown, as sorrow is. You really do not know sorrow; you do not know its depth, its extraordinary vitality. You know the reaction to sorrow, but not the action of sorrow. You know the reaction to death, but not the action of death, what it implies; you don't know whether it is ugly or beautiful. But to know the nature, the depth, the beauty and loveliness of death and sorrow is the ending of death and sorrow.

You see, our minds function mechanically in the known, and with the known we approach the unknown: death, sorrow. And can there be an explosion so that the known does not contaminate the mind? You cannot get rid of the known. That would be stupid, silly; it would lead you nowhere. What matters is not to allow the mind to be contaminated by the known. But this noncontamination of the mind by the known does not come about through determination, through any action of will. It comes about when you see the fact as it is, and you can see the fact as it is—the fact of death, of sorrow—only when you give your total attention to it. Total attention is

not concentration; it is a state of complete awareness in which there is no exclusion.

So, the ending of sorrow lies in facing the totality of sorrow, which is to perceive what sorrow is. That means, really, the letting go of all your myths, your legends, your traditions and beliefs—which you cannot do gradually. They must drop away on the instant, now. There is no method by which to let them drop away. It happens when you give your whole attention to something which you want to understand, without any desire to escape.

We know only fragmentarily this extraordinary thing called life; we have never looked at sorrow, except through the screen of escapes; we have never seen the beauty, the immensity of death, and we know it only through fear and sadness. There can be the understanding of life, and of the significance and beauty of death, only when the mind on the instant perceives *what is*.

You know, sirs, though we differentiate them, love, death, and sorrow are all the same because, surely, love, death, and sorrow are the unknowable. The moment you know love, you have ceased to love. Love is beyond time; it has no beginning and no end, whereas knowledge has; and when you say, "I know what love is," you don't. You know only a sensation, a stimulus. You know the reaction to love, but that reaction is not love. In that same way, you don't know what death is. You know only the reactions to death, and you will discover the full depth and significance of death only when the reactions have ceased.

So, do please listen to this, not as a lecture, but as something which vitally concerns every human being, whether he is on the highest or the lowest rung of society. This is a problem to each one of us, and we must know it as we know hunger, as we know sex, as we may occasionally know a benediction in looking at the treetops, or at the open sky.

You see, the benediction comes only when the mind is in a state of nonreaction. It is a benediction to know death, because death is the unknown. Without understanding death, you may spend your life searching for the unknown, and you will never find it. It is like love, which you do not know. You do not know what love is, you do not know what truth is. But love is not to be sought; truth is not to be sought. When you seek truth, it is a reaction, an escape from the fact. Truth is in *what is*, not in the reaction to *what is*.

January 10, 1960

Seventh Talk in Bombay

If I may, I would like to explore with you what is the religious mind, the religious spirit, and go into it, if we can, rather deeply. It is a complex problem, as all the problems of human existence are, and I think one must approach it very simply, with a sense of great humility, because to explore such a problem deeply requires a clear mind, a mind that is not burdened with insistent and persistent knowledge. If you would look into any complex human problem, it is no good, it seems to me, bringing in all the knowledge, all the authority that you have accumulated. On the contrary, you must put it aside, and then perhaps you will be able to discover something original, new, something which has not been handed down to you by authority, or which you have accepted because of various demands and compulsions. So, as this problem is somewhat difficult, it is necessary, first of all, to see if one can suspend all one has learned, all the traditions and impressions one has acquired, and discover for oneself what is the religious mind.

Life is getting more and more complex and difficult, not less. The pressures are becoming almost intolerable, and with the pressure, the influences, the ceaseless demands of the modern world, there is increasing envy, hatred, and despair. Hatred is spreading, and despair is much more than the superficial problem of the young man who cannot get a job—that is only part of it. Nor is despair merely the feeling you have when you lose someone by death, or when you want to be loved and are not. Despair, surely, is something much more profound. And to find a way out of despair, to go beyond hatred and this thing called hope—which is merely the reverse of despair, and in which we also get entrammeled—it seems to me that we must inquire into the question of what is really a religious mind, a religious spirit.

To inquire rightly, there can be neither acceptance nor denial. Most of us are either yes-sayers or no-sayers. We have many difficulties, and our response is often an attitude of acceptance, which is to say yes to life, but life is too complex, too vast, merely to say yes to it. The yes-sayers are those who follow tradition, with all its pettiness, narrowness, brutality, who are satisfied with so-called progress, efficiency, who accept things as they are and swim with the current of existence in order not to be too disturbed. Then there are the no-sayers, the people who reject the world, and by rejection they escape into symbology, into all kinds of fanciful myths. They become monks, sannyasis, or join one of the various religious orders. I wonder which attitude we have, to which category each one of us belongs?

There is the saint, and there is the politician. The politician is a yes-sayer; he accepts the immediacy of things and replies to the immediate superficially. The saint, on the other hand, is a no-sayer. He feels that the world is not good enough, that there must be a deeper answer; so he leaves, rejects the world. I suppose most of us neither reject nor accept very deeply, but are satisfied with a verbal yes or with a verbal no.

Now, if we would really explore the question of what is religion, I think we must begin by being very clear in ourselves as to whether we are yes-sayers or no-sayers. There is the no-sayer who intellectually denies the world as it is; he has revolted, but has not explored really profoundly the spirit of religion. Intellectually he has torn everything apart until there is nothing left, as there is nothing left of a flower that is torn apart and thrown by the path, and he is finally driven by his intellectual conclusions, by his despairs and hopes, into the acceptance of some form of religious belief.

Please, sirs, watch your own minds and your own lives. As many of us are not too intellectual or aggressive, we are satisfied with the easy, mediocre life; and though we may say no to the world—to the world of progress and prosperity, to the world of things—nevertheless we are caught in it. So, actually, we are neither yes-sayers nor no-sayers in any vehement sense; we are neither hot nor cold. I do not think such a mind is capable of discovering in its exploration what is the religious spirit; and without that discovery, it is impossible to answer any of the vital problems of life because progress, prosperity, the multiplication of things only make us more and more slavish. It is fairly obvious that we are fast becoming slaves to machines, to things, and we do not have to go into it very deeply to see that the superficial mind is satisfied with its own slavish state. It is satisfied with property, with position and power; it is satisfied in its superficial, imitative activity.

Now, as the mind becomes increasingly a slave, the margin of freedom naturally gets more and more narrow—and that is our actual position, is it not? That is our life. Being bored with certain things, we want more things or more action, or we seek power. When these ends are not gained, we feel frustrated, we are in despair, and so we escape through a religious belief, through the church, the temple, through symbolism, rituals, and all the rest of it. If it is not that, then we become angry with the world—and anger has its own action. Anger is very productive of action, is it not? When you are angrily in revolt, it gives you energy, and that energy awakens capacity, all of which is regarded as something new, original. But anger, cynicism, despair, and bitterness—surely, these feelings are not necessary to a real understanding of the problems of our existence. We know neither what is the good life nor what our daily living is all about—this extraordinary process of misery and strife, of pettiness, ugliness, calumny, avarice, this everlasting struggle until we die. So we invent a goal, a purpose, an end; and whether that end is immediate or projected far away as God, it is the outcome of a mind that is really in despair, in misery, in chaos. Surely, this is fairly obvious the moment you begin to think clearly, objectively, and not merely in terms of what you can get out of life for yourself.

Sirs, this question of whether there is a reality, whether there is God, whether there is something permanent, original, new, is not just our own immediate demand. Man has sought it for centuries. Thirty-five thousand years ago, on the walls of a cave in North Africa, man painted the struggle between good and evil; and always, in those pictures, evil is victorious. We are still looking for an answer—but not some stupid, gratifying answer of a schoolboy, of an immature mind, but an answer which will be really true, a total response to a total demand. I think we do not ask totally, and that is our difficulty; there is no total demand. It is only when we are in despair that we look, we ask, we hope. But when we are in full vigor, in the full stream of our existence, there is no total demand; we say, "Leave me alone to fulfill myself."

You know, this total demand arises only when there is complete aloneness. When you have explored everything about you; when you have looked into all the religions, with their symbols, their stupidities, their organized dogmatism; when you are no longer held by explanations, by words, by books, by ideas, by all the things the intellect invents, and have rejected them all, but not because you cannot find satisfaction in them—only then are you really alone. It is too immature to accept or reject things out of satisfaction or dissatisfaction. But when you are in serious doubt; when you observe, examine; when you ask questions and there are no answers except those offered by the dead ashes of tradition, of conditioning; and when you deeply and totally reject all this, as you surely must—then you are alone, completely alone, because you cannot depend on anything; and that aloneness is like a flower that grows in the wilderness.

I do not know if you have ever been in a desert in springtime. There has been no rain, just moisture, and not very much of it. The ground is very dry and hard; the sun is brilliant. There is a sense of ruthlessness, of nakedness, of emptiness. And in the springtime, a flower comes up, a lovely thing—perhaps more beautiful than all the cultivated flowers in the rich man's garden. It has a perfume of its own, and a color which is not the color of the well-nourished flower in a lovely garden. It is a thing of extraordinary beauty, and it has flowered in a desert. And I think there is in complete aloneness a flowering of the mind, which is surely religious.

But, you see, that is tremendously arduous; it is hard work, and you do not like hard work. You prefer an easy, indolent existence—earning a livelihood, accepting what comes, and just drifting along through life. Or, if you don't do that, you practice some system, some form of compulsion, discipline. You get up every morning at four o'clock to meditate—by which you mean forcing yourself to concentrate, compelling your mind to conform to a particular pattern. You drill yourself incessantly, day after day, and that you consider hard work. But that, it seems to me, is a most childish way of working; it is not the work of a mature mind. By hard work I mean something totally different. It is hard work to examine every thought and feeling, every belief, without bringing in your own prejudices, without shielding yourself behind an idea, behind a conclusion, an explanation. It requires hard, clear thinking—which is real work. And most of us do not want to tackle that kind of work. We would rather accept a senseless belief, belong to an organized religion, go to the temple, the church, or the mosque, repeat some words and get a little sensation; and with these things we are satisfied.

A man who goes every day to the temple, to the mosque, to the church—him you call a religious person. Or you say that the people who worship Masters, saints, gurus are very religious. Surely, they are not religious people; they are frightened people. They are the yes-sayers; they don't know and they don't explore, they have not the capacity; therefore, they rely on something outside, on an image graven by the hand or by the mind. Seeing all this, and being aware of the misery, the cruelty, the unutterable squalor both within and without, surely, if we are to find a sane, rational way out of all this mess, we must inquire into the question of what is a religious mind.

Now, how does one inquire? Do please pay a little attention. What is the way of inquiry? How does one set about it? Does the state of inquiry exist when there is a positive approach, or only when there is a negative approach? By a positive approach I mean looking at the problem with a desire to find an answer. When I am frustrated, in despair, and I want to find an answer, there is a motive for my exploration, is there not? My search is the result of my desire to find a way out. So I will find a way out, but it will be very shallow and empty; I will rely on some authority or follow a system, which will give me despair again tomorrow. Being unhappy, miserable, sorrow laden, in a state of incessant conflict, I want to escape from this whole business; so there is a motive, and that motive creates a positive action; and such positive action, which is search with the demand for an answer, is very limited; it does not open the door to the heavens.

Do please understand this; otherwise, you will not discover for yourself what is a religious mind, and the beauty of it.

So, that which you can never know through a positive action cannot be approached with a motive, with a compulsion born of despair. That is a false approach. If you see the truth of this for yourself, then you can find out what is the other approach—which is not a reaction, not the opposite of the positive. Do you understand? I hope I am making myself clear.

One sees very clearly what the positive approach is. It is the approach which most of us indulge in. Being miserable, I want a way out, so I take a tranquilizer or go to a guru or to a church or do some other foolish, ugly thing and am satisfied. That is the positive approach. It is the approach of a mind that is in conflict, that is in a state of sorrow, confusion, and that wants an answer, a way out—which it seeks through the practice of a method, a system, or through some other positive activity.

Now, if the mind sees the truth of that positive approach, which is to see the falseness of it, then the negative approach is not a mere reaction to it. That is, I want to find out what is true, not what I would like to be true, so I do not bring my personality into it; I put aside my beliefs, my conclusions, my desire to escape from this intolerable misery. I want

to discover for myself what is the meaning of this whole existence—but not according to my pleasure, or according to my fancy, or according to my tradition, which are all such stupid, silly, and conditioned things. I want to find out the truth of the matter, whatever it is. So, for me there is no method, there is no authority, there is no guru, there is no system. And it is only such a mind—do please pay a little attention, sirs—it is only such a mind that can find out: a mind which has torn everything apart, which is not seeking any form of satisfaction or gratification, which has no end in view.

I wonder if you have noticed something in life. Life has no beginning and no end—in the beginning is the end. To a man who wants an answer, life is very limited. For him there is yesterday, today, and tomorrow, and in those terms he thinks of life. But life does not answer him in those terms. Life is endless, and therefore in life there is no death. There is a death only when we say, "What about me?"—'me' being the entity who has thought in terms of yesterday, today, and tomorrow. As the 'me' who is in misery, you want to find a state of salvation where you will not be disturbed; you want to sit quietly and everlastingly in your own backwaters of ugliness. But have you not noticed that where the sky and the earth meet, there is no end, no division? It is all one movement. It is the mind that divides life from death, that struggles and creates problems.

So, if one can approach negatively this problem of what is the religious spirit, that negation is not a reaction to the positive. If it is a reaction to the positive, as communism is a reaction to capitalism, then it is merely the same thing in a different form. To change within the field of conditioning is not to change at all. But the negative approach is something entirely different, and it is only through the negative approach that the mind can explore and discover.

I hope, as I am talking, that you are perceiving for yourself, as a direct experience, the truth—that is, the falseness—of the positive approach. Just as you have everyday experiences of hunger, thirst, sex, the demand for position, power, prestige, and all the rest of it, so the experience of the positive approach to your problems is always going on, whether you are conscious of it or not. But if you clearly see the truth of it, if you actually perceive the falseness of the positive approach, and the limitations, the pettiness of a mind that demands an answer for its own satisfaction, then your mind is in a state of negation, which is really creative; for such a mind can explore and discover.

I hope you are not merely listening to explanations, to words, because the word is not the thing; it is merely a symbol, and the symbol is never the real. A man who is satisfied with the symbol is living with the ashes of life, with the aridity of existence. So I hope you are actually perceiving and experiencing the truth. And to such a mind, what is the question?

The question is: What is the religious spirit? You do a great many things in the name of religion which are not religion. Having seen the truth of it, all that is out; it is finished, put away. Then what is the religious spirit? Surely, the religious spirit is a kind of explosion in which all attachment is broken, utterly destroyed.

There is only attachment; there is no such thing as detachment. The mind invents detachment as a reaction to the pain of attachment. When you react to attachment by becoming "detached," you are attached to something else. So that whole process is one of attachment. You are attached to your wife or your husband, to your children, to ideas, to tradition, to authority, and so on; and your reaction to that attachment is detachment. The cultivation of detachment is the outcome of sorrow, pain. You want to escape from the

pain of attachment, and your escape is to find something to which you think you cannot be attached. So there is only attachment, and it is a stupid mind that cultivates detachment. All the books say, "Be detached," but what is the truth of the matter? If you observe your own mind, you will see an extraordinary thing—that through cultivating detachment, your mind is becoming attached to something else.

Now, the religious spirit is an explosion which shatters all attachment so that the mind is not attached to anything. Surely, that is the nature of love. Love is not attached. Desire is attached, memory is attached, sensation is an abyss of attachment; but if you observe, in love—whether it be for the one or the many—there is no attachment. Attachment implies the past, the present, and the future. Do you understand, sirs? Whereas, love has neither past, present, nor future. It is only memory that is time-bound—the memory of what you consider to be love.

So, the mind that is exploring, probing into what is called religion is really a mind that is totally in revolt. You know, it is fairly easy to revolt against a particular thing—against poverty, against one's family, against tradition, or against a particular religion. And when we revolt against a particular religion, we generally join some other religion; we revolt against Hinduism and join Christianity, or Buddhism, or what you will. Such revolt is merely a reaction; it is not total revolution, complete transformation.

Sirs, are you just listening to me, or are you watching your own minds? My words are the reflection of your own thoughts, of which you may be conscious or unconscious. I am describing your own minds, and if you are merely listening to words and are not observing your own minds, then you will continue to be in sorrow and turmoil.

The revolt which I am talking about is against every form of attachment—but not as a reaction. You see the truth that your attachment to certain intellectual explanations has left you dry, arid. There have been minor explosions or reactions in your life which have left their marks on your mind, and you are attached to these marks. You may have withdrawn from this organization, joined that movement, followed a different leader, and so on. All these minor explosions and responses have left marks on your mind, and thus marked, your mind has become hard. This hardness is really attachment to what you have done, to the memory of your own experiences. And the total revolution of which I am talking is the complete perception of the truth of all this; it is the very state of explosion itself.

Perhaps this is rather difficult for most of us to understand because we are used to thinking of revolution in terms of changing from one form of conditioning to another. Today I am this, and tomorrow I want to change into that. Seeing poverty under capitalism, I say communism is the answer; therefore, there must be a revolution. Surely, any such revolution is only partial and therefore no revolution at all. Most alert and so-called intelligent people have played with communism, with this and that, with ten different things. Having played with all that, their minds are cluttered up, confused, hard; and when such a mind asks, "What is truth? What is God?" it has no meaning whatsoever. What has meaning is to break all that, to shatter it completely without any motive, without any urge or compulsion. This explosion, in which there is no place for satisfaction or for any system, is the only real revolution. Then you will find, when the mind is in this state of explosion, that there is creativeness—not the creativeness which is expressed in a poem or in carving a piece of stone or in painting, but a creativeness which is always in a state of negation.

Now, sirs, this becomes purely theoretical for you; and theory, speculation, or living on the words of another has very little meaning. But the mind that has really gone into all this, that has entered upon a pilgrimage of inquiry from which there is no return, that is inquiring, not only now, during this hour, but from day to day—such a mind will have discovered a state of creation which is all existence. It is what you call truth or God. For that creation to take place, there must be complete aloneness—an aloneness in which there is no attachment, no companionship, either of words or thoughts or memories. It is a total denial of everything which the mind has invented for its own security. The complete aloneness, in which there is no fear, has its own extraordinary beauty; it is a state of love because it is not the aloneness of reaction; it is a total negation, which is not the opposite of the positive. And I think it is only in that state of creation that the mind is truly religious. Such a mind needs no meditation; it is itself the eternal. Such a mind is no longer seeking—not that it is satisfied, but it is no longer seeking because there is nothing to seek. It is a total thing, limitless, immeasurable, unnameable.

January 13, 1960

Eighth Talk in Bombay

Most of us, whatever our position in life, are in great turmoil—at least we should be if we are not—because the various pressures of the world events and of the uncontrollable historical processes that are taking place around us are pushing us all into a narrow groove where the margin of freedom is growing less and less. And as each one of us is invariably seeking a way out of this turmoil, this confusion and misery, we join various movements, either political or religious, and we follow their leaders in the hope of finding a solution for the numerous problems which burden our lives. We are confused, and in our confusion we try to find someone who will lead us out of this turmoil and misery. It seems to me that we are very reluctant to go into ourselves and examine the problem directly. We want someone to provide a solution; we want a system, a philosophy, a guru, a leader to resolve our problems and lead us to peace, to inner quietude. As that is not possible, I would like, if I may, to talk over with you this going within oneself, this unraveling of the process of self-knowledge.

We know that the scientists have conquered many problems and that whatever is needed, they are able to produce. If the scientists and the politicians would get together, they could also solve the problem of starvation, the problem of food, clothing, and shelter for all, and stop the destruction of man by man. It could be done, but they are not going to do it as long as their thinking is based on nationalism, on motives of their own personal profit. And even if this far-reaching outward change were brought about, it seems to me that the problem is much deeper. The problem is not merely starvation, war, the brutality of man to man; it is the crisis in our own consciousness. Fundamentally, the problem lies within. But however intent and capable we may be, most of us are unwilling to go into ourselves very deeply. We want to change, to transform the world, but the real revolution, the total change is within, and not so much without. We find it extremely difficult to go within, and so we try to escape intellectually or sentimentally, devotionally.

Intellectually we spin a lot of theories, we get caught up in words, in ideas. I wonder if you have noticed how eager we are to discuss theories, how quickly we get lost in words. When we play this game, we think we are being very intelligent, but it is really nothing at all; it is empty verbalism, it has no meaning. Sentimentally, emotionally, we

cling to a system of belief, or we go from one system to another. We also get lost in so-called devotion to an idea or to a leader. There is in all this a certain satisfaction, a temporary alleviation of our struggle, but sooner or later we find ourselves back in the same old position, with its many problems.

All these devices, it seems to me, are so futile; they are not solutions to our problems at all. It is only an immature mind, a mind that has not tasted love, that has not breathed deeply the perfume of sorrow—it is only such a mind that escapes into all these trivial things, which are mere entertainments. You find a guru, or you go to the temple, worship an image, which gives you temporary relief. Unfortunately, you are very easily satisfied by these temporary measures, and you try to make them permanent by setting up a habit of devotion, of following—following a guru, a political leader, or some other authority. Whether you follow politically or religiously, all following, surely, is evil because following implies a desire for security, and the mind that seeks security is denying the impermanency of life. Life is obviously impermanent. Nothing in the world is permanent, and there is nothing permanent inwardly, inside the skin, except habit—habit of thought, habit of ideas. We are caught in these habits, and if we break one habit, we form another, which again takes on a certain permanency. So it seems to me that we are always evading the central issue, which is ourselves.

In referring to ourselves, I mean, not just the egocentric entity of whom we are more or less aware every day, but the entity who is the result of society, the result of a particular culture or civilization, of climate and tradition. And unless the individual is deeply transformed, one cannot see how there can be a way out of all this chaos. I am talking of the individual who is not in opposition to the collective. At present there is only collective thought, from which our action takes place. This collective thought—whether it be that of communism, of capitalism, of fascism, or what you will—denies the individual; and all creation in life, all understanding arises from the individual, not from the mass. Actually, there is no such thing as the mass, except in thought, in idea, to which we are slaves.

So, to understand this whole process of existence, it is necessary for the individual to shake himself free from the mass, from tradition. To do this one must go into oneself—there is no other means, no other way to open the door of life. What you are, society is. Society is not different from you. Though you may have a distinctive name, some property, a private bank account, and so on, you are part of society; you are not separate from it. When you say you are a Hindu, a communist, or whatever it may be, it means that you are part of that culture, part of that particular society, which has helped you to think in a certain way. So you are a slave to various influences, and it is necessary, surely, to understand these influences or pressures if you are to understand yourself, who are the result of them.

You are the result, not only of your father and mother, but of a thousand yesterdays, a thousand generations; you are the result of the whole of humanity. If you don't understand this, life becomes extraordinarily boring, an endless struggle with very little significance, giving rise to the philosophy of despair, or the philosophy of being satisfied with things as they are, which is the mere acceptance of existence. All this seems so obvious.

So, you have to see the fact that you are the world, and that without a transformation in yourself, without a total revolution in the mind, in the ways of your own thinking, you cannot bring about a fundamental change in the world. Especially in an overpopulated country like this, you have to start with your-

self; there has to be a revolution in the world of your relationships. Sirs, goodness flowers in your relationship with another, and without understanding that goodness, all your social reforms and innumerable outward changes are only going to lead to further misery in a very superficial existence.

So, it seems to me of the utmost importance to understand oneself, but in this matter there is a tremendous reluctance on your part because you say, "What is there to understand about myself? I know my own reactions very well."

Now, before we enter into that, I think it is important to understand the significance of the word *verb*. The verb implies, surely, an unbroken movement, an active present; though it has a time element in it, embracing the past and the future as well as the present, the verb implies a total state, does it not? "I was," "I am," and "I will be"—if one goes into this rather deeply, one finds it to be a total state, an active present which is timeless. But most of us are caught in the "I was" and the "I will be"; there is no active present. The "I was" is memory, and the "I will be" is also memory—a projection of the past through the present to the future. We say, "I have been angry, and I shall not be angry," so there is a lag, a gap, and this gap is used as a means to a future state. For most of us the verb implies not just one state but three separate states, "I have been greedy," "I shall not be greedy," and the lag between them, which is the effort to become non-greedy.

Now, I think it is very important to understand that the verb implies a total action, not a broken-up action. It has within it not only the overtones of what has been, and of what ultimately should be, but it also contains that which is happening now. But most of us are unaware of what is actually happening now; we are concerned with the "what has been" or the "what will be." If you observe your own mind, you will see this fact, which is an extraordinary discovery—that you are never concerned with being, but only with having been, and becoming. Unless we perceive this fact rather carefully, intelligently, and widely, we shall not be able to understand all that is implied in self-knowledge; and I think it is because most of us lack this understanding that we become so superficial in what we call our self-knowledge.

I am going to play a little bit with the implication of that word *verb*—and I mean play because unless one can play, one will never find out. Do you understand? Unless you are capable of laughter, real laughter, you don't know what sorrow is, you don't know what it is to be really serious. If you don't know how to smile, not merely with your lips, but with your whole being—with your eyes, with your mind and heart—then you don't know what it is to be simple and to take delight in the common things of life.

Surely, the verb, as well as the name of a thing, is dual. The name is never the thing. The tree and the word *tree* are totally different. The symbol is never the fact, never the truth, but to most of us, the symbol has become more important than the fact. We never look at the tree without the word, and the word destroys our perception of the tree.

Do please listen to what I am saying, sirs. The word *crow* is not the living thing which disturbs us with its noise. But we get lost in the word and thereby never examine the truth behind the word. So one has to separate the word, the name, from the thing; and one has also to understand the verb—which is much more complex and vital.

Take the verb *to love*. If you look at it very closely, you will see that you are not loving. All you can say is, "I have loved," or "I must love." You think in terms of what has passed, and of what is to happen, or should happen—the "before" and the "after." You are never in the state of being, which is a living thing, the active present. This active present, which is implied by the verb, has no future, no past; and it seems to me of the utmost importance to understand this.

As I said, most of us are never in the state of being; we have always been, or we hope to be, so time as a process of becoming is a very important factor in our life. But there is an active present in which the "what has been", the *what is,* and the "what will be" are all included, they are not separate, and one has to understand this extraordinary state of being, this living, active present. Existence is not what has been or what will be; existence is the now, in which all time is contained. And the important thing in listening to what is being said, is to comprehend, if you can, this state of being in which all time is included—to be aware of it without effort, to capture its significance without saying, "I must understand."

Sirs, goodness is not of the past or of the future; it is a present state of which the mind must be totally unconscious. The moment you feel that you are good, you are no longer good. The man who strives to cultivate humility is vain and stupid because humility cannot be cultivated. Humility is a state of being; it is not a virtue to be cultivated—which is a horror. Cultivated virtue is always a horror, for when you cultivate a virtue, you have ceased to be virtuous. When you are trying to be nonviolent, you are full of violence.

So, with this understanding of the verb, in which "being," "have been," and "will be" are all part of the active present, let us examine the nature of the self.

The self, the 'me', is a center of thought, a center which is conditioned by experience, by knowledge. As the motor of the bus that brought you here, like every other complex machine, is a result of the knowledge and experience of many people, so the self is the expression of a collection of experiences, memories, and therefore it is essentially mechanical. I think this is important to understand. The self is not a spiritual entity at all; it is purely the result of habits, experiences, memories, influences, an expression of the collective tradition, and all the rest of it. It is a process of thinking based on memory, on knowledge, on experience, and therefore it is mechanical. Whatever it thinks—whether it thinks of God or of a piece of machinery or of a job—it is still within the confines of its own limitations. When you talk about the higher self, the atma, the soul, the indwelling God, and so on, it is merely a habit; you are repeating what you have been taught. The communist has been taught not to believe in all this religious rot, so he will say there is no such thing as God or the soul; it is all rubbish, a capitalistic invention.

So the self, the observer, the thinker, the experiencer, is not a spiritual entity; it is the mechanism of memory centralized as the 'me' with its various limitations. This is a fact. But you object because you say, "Is there not a spiritual world, something permanent beyond all this?" When, being caught in the actual fact of mechanical habit, the mind speculates about something beyond, such a mind is obviously stupid. That is why it is very important to understand this mechanism of memory, of habit, which we call the self, the 'me'.

Knowledge is mechanical. If you happen to be an engineer, your knowledge of engineering is something which you have acquired, and what you have acquired, learned, becomes a habit. Whether you are an engineer, a scientist, a bureaucrat, or an officeworker, you establish a series of habits, and in those habits you are caught; your mind is held in the machinery of habit—in a habit of relationship, in a habit of thinking, in a habit of action.

Please, sirs, do watch your own minds. You are not merely listening to me; that is not important at all, but in listening to me, you are observing yourselves. And if you are in fact observing yourselves, you will see how the mind is caught in the machinery of habit. This is nothing to shudder or be anxious about; it is simply a fact, and the problem is to free the mind completely from habit, so that it does not continue in the old pattern, or establish a new set of habits in the process of relinquishing or destroying the old.

Habits, surely, imply a mind that does not want to be disturbed. As long as the mind wants to be secure—it does not matter whether it is an engineering mind, a mathematical mind, a scientific mind, a political mind, or the mind of a seeker after truth, whatever that means—it inevitably falls into the groove of habit and is unaware that it is running in a groove. So one has to become conscious of the fact that one's mind, because it is seeking pleasure, security, a sense of nondisturbance, falls into a groove. Just to be conscious, aware of this fact, is what matters—not how to break down a particular habit. The very desire to break down a habit produces another habit.

Now, who is it that is aware? Who is the observer, the one who watches the operation of these habits? That is the question you will invariably ask, is it not? If you look very closely, you will see that there is no observer at all; it is merely one habit observing another habit.

Look, sirs: When you are in the very movement of an action, there is neither the observer nor the observed. When, for instance, you are very angry, in the full intensity of that feeling there is no separate entity who observes and tries to alter what is observed. Do you understand? The actual fact is that in the moment of experience, there is neither the observer nor the thing observed.

Now, that state of experiencing, in which there is no observer and no observed, is the active present. So the question, then, is this: Knowing that one's mind is caught in habit, how is one to bring about that state of awareness in which there is no observer? I do not know if I am making the problem clear. Let us approach it differently.

Where there is the observer and the observed, inevitably there is contradiction and conflict, is there not? When I observe somebody who is rich, and I want to be as rich, as comfortable, as free as he is, there is in me a conflict, a contradiction, an effort to be like that. So where there is the observer and the observed, there is a contradiction, a conflict, an effort to be or to become, which places a limitation on consciousness.

Sirs, this may sound rather difficult, but it is not. What is difficult is the word, the phrase, but the actual feeling, the actual experiencing of it, is entirely different.

Take knowledge, for instance. All knowledge is in the past. What the engineer or the scientist has learned is in the past, put away in his mind. What you have learned is always in the past, which you use in the present towards a future. Now, if you observe, you will see there is a movement of knowing, which is different from knowledge. When you are in that movement, there is neither the observer nor the observed; there is only the movement of knowing. So, self-knowing is more important than self-knowledge. What you have stored up as knowledge about yourself becomes a habit which prevents you from knowing the self as it actually is from moment to moment.

Look, sirs: I want to know myself, and the 'myself' is a most extraordinary thing, if you observe it. It is never still; it is always seeking, wanting, denying, accumulating, accepting; it takes so many different forms of desire; it has so many thoughts, so many pursuits, so many frustrations, fears, hopes. The whole of that is the self, the 'me'—the 'me' that establishes a goal, the 'me' that hopes or

is in despair, the 'me' that lusts after something, the 'me' that loves, that feels sexual. It is a living thing, it is not static. And when the mind that is static with knowledge approaches this living thing, either it says, ''I must not be like that,'' and tries to change it, or it says, ''Yes, that is me, but what can I do about it?'' This denial or acceptance, which is based on knowledge, becomes a habit. Whereas the movement of knowing, which is the active present, is a process of discovery, of learning about oneself from moment to moment. Do you see the difference, sirs?

You say, ''I know my wife,'' but do you? What you mean is that you have an image of her based on certain ideas, on what you have learned, observed. So what has happened? You have established this knowledge as a habit, and you say, ''I know my wife.'' Do examine it, sirs. Can you ever say that you know a living human being who, like yourself, is constantly undergoing a change, who is full of anxieties, fears, apprehensions, uncertainties? You can say that you know how to run a diesel engine, or what a piston is, or how the jets work, because they are all mechanical. But you reduce all your relationships—with human beings, with nature, with ideas—to mechanical habits because you find it very convenient to live in that state; you are far less likely to be disturbed. You say, ''I know my wife''—and relegate her to the category of mechanical things. In the same way, when you say, ''I know myself,'' it means that you have knowledge about yourself which has become a pattern or habit of thought. Whereas, if you really see the significance of the word *knowing*, which implies the active present in which the past and the future are included, then there will never be either condemnation or mere acceptance of *what is*.

You see, I am trying to convey to you something which you have never thought about, and that is where our difficulty lies. Communication is always difficult, but more so when one is trying to say something to which very few have given any thought. Surely, you are learning something, are you not? In the very act of listening, you are learning. It is not a matter of collecting words, thinking about them later, and drawing a lesson from that in order to learn. Learning is an active process. As you are listening, you are learning; you are not accumulating knowledge.

Sirs, to learn about love, in the sense of understanding the meaning, the whole significance of it, you cannot approach it by saying, "I have had the experience of love, and I know what it is," because love is never still. The mind tries to make love into a habit, to reduce it to a memory—and thereby destroys it. You cannot acquire knowledge about love. It is a living thing, and you can only be in it, learn about it every second, and therefore there is never a point at which you can say, "I know what love is." Such love is dead. Memories and recollections of love are ashes; they have no meaning at all.

In the same way, the mind can be in the movement of knowing about itself. In that movement there is no entity as the observer, the censor, and hence no contradiction, no effort to be or to become; therefore, there is a living understanding of the mind as it is. There is no atma, no censor who chooses, no approximation to a pattern, which creates authority. Do you understand, sirs? At one stroke you remove all that nonsense; therefore, you free the mind from effort, from conflict. There is choiceless awareness. The mind is in a state of knowing, learning, being, which is the active present.

You see, sirs, our difficulty is that very few of you have really gone into this. Probably you are feeling sentimental and are being mesmerized by my words. But all this requires very precise thinking; it requires a certain clarity, great simplicity; and you can have that clarity, that simplicity, with its extraordinary vitality, only when you begin to understand that there is only a movement of knowing. All fixed knowledge about oneself is purely mechanical habit, which creates the censor, and therefore there is contradiction, conflict. Whereas, in the movement of knowing, the mind goes within itself, but not in terms of time; and this timeless movement brings about a quietness, a sense of peace. It is not the peace of imagination nor the tranquillity of an intellectual mind that has built an ivory tower for itself, nor the quietude of a devotee who has handed himself over to some image, belief, or ideal. All such "peace" is dead, it is a form of stagnation. But if you begin to understand this living thing called the self, which is merely a centralized collection of various influences, then in that movement of knowing, which is the active present, you will find that the mind, being free of the censor, is also free of contradiction and conflict. To such a mind there comes a sense of total silence, complete peace, and it is only such a mind that is creative. Such a mind is not functioning merely from memory; it is completely empty of mechanical habit, and to such a mind there comes that which is truth, the immeasurable. Truth never comes to a mind that is caught in its own cleverness, nor to a mind that is disciplined, desiccated, burned up; nor does it come to the saints, to the leaders, to the merely virtuous. Truth, reality, which is the flowering of goodness, that sense of love, comes only to a mind that has entered into the understanding of itself.

January 17, 1960

Banaras, India, 1960

✳

First Talk at Rajghat

It seems to me very important to think fundamentally and to feel deeply about the major problems of life. To think fundamentally is not to think theoretically or speculatively but rather to free the mind from the circles that it has woven around itself, and also from the circles that the world—circumstances, tradition, so-called knowledge—has woven around it. But most of us think theoretically; we are satisfied with facile answers and explanations, lulled to sleep by quotations, by satisfactory words, and however difficult our problems may be, we generally manage to slither through them rather contentedly and superficially.

So, to those who are listening seriously and not just passing the time of day because they have nothing else to do, I would like to suggest that we go together, if we can, into our various problems, into the many conflicts and contradictions which burden our lives. By "going together" into our problems, I do not mean mere verbalization, or the offering of explanations, but rather to find out if we cannot actually experience what is being said by examining our own minds and our own lives, so that we come out of it with clarity, precision, and understanding. Otherwise we are merely indulging in words. You will come to these talks and gather a few more explanations, collect a few more ideas, and then slip back into the traditional way of life, or into a comfortable, secure way of life which you have established for yourself.

That is why I would suggest that those who are really serious about these matters should not only listen to what is being said, but, in the very process of listening, should observe their own minds, explore their own ways of thinking, uncover their own habits and activities in daily life. Unless we are willing to do this, it seems to me that these talks will not be worthwhile at all. I have been here often, and some of you have heard me repeatedly, fortunately or unfortunately, for the last ten years; and most of us change very little. We are established in our positions and have gained prestige. We are growing old, and we shall soon be in the grave without having solved any of our problems.

So, may I suggest that while listening to these talks you do not accept or reject, which would be immature, but rather explore with me the problems that each one of us has. To explore is not merely to describe and be satisfied but actually to uncover the conflicts, the confusions, the trivialities of our lives.

One can see, through reading the newspapers and being observant of the events that are going on in the world, that freedom is getting less and less; the margin of freedom is narrowing down. Do you know what I mean? The mind has very little chance to be free; it is not able to think out, to feel out, to discover because organized religions throughout the world, with their dogmatic beliefs, have crippled our thinking; superstitions and traditions have enclosed the mind, conditioned the mind. You are a Hindu, a Christian, a Muslim, or you belong to some other organized belief which has been imposed upon you from childhood, and you function within that circle of limitation, narrow or wide. When you say you are a Hindu, a Muslim, or what you will, please observe your own mind. Are you not merely repeating what has been told to you? You do not know, you merely accept—and you accept because it is convenient. Socially, economically, it gives you security to accept and live within that circle. So freedom is denied—not only to the Hindu, to the Christian, to the Muslim, but to all who are held within the enclosure of an organized religion.

And if you observe you will see that whatever profession you belong to is also enslaving you. How can a man be free who has spent forty years in a particular profession? Look what happens to a doctor. Having spent seven years or so in college, for the rest of his life he is a general practitioner or a specialist, and he becomes enslaved by the profession. Surely, his margin of freedom is very narrow. And the same is true of the politicians, of the social reformers, of the people who have ideals, who have an objective in life.

So, if you are observant, you will see that everywhere in the world the margin of freedom and human dignity is getting less and less. Our minds are mere machines. We learn a profession, and forever after we are its slaves. And it seems to me that it requires a great deal of understanding, real perception, insight, to break this circle which the mind and society have woven around each one of us. To approach these enslavements anew, to

tackle them fundamentally, deeply, radically, I think one has to be revolutionary—which means thinking, feeling totally, and not just looking at things from the outside. And one must have a sense of humility, must one not?

I do not think humility is a cultivated virtue. Cultivated virtue is a horror because the moment you cultivate a virtue, it ceases to be a virtue. Virtue is spontaneous, timeless; it is ever active in the present. A mind that merely cultivates humility can never know the fullness, the depth, the beauty of being really humble; and if the mind is not in that state, I do not think it can learn. It can function mechanically, but learning, surely, is not the mechanical accumulation of knowledge. The movement of learning is something entirely different, is it not? And to learn, the mind must have a sense of great humility.

I want to know what freedom is—not speculative freedom, which is self-projected as a reaction to something. Is there such a thing as real freedom—a state in which the mind is actually freeing itself from all the traditions and patterns which have been imposed upon it for centuries? I want to know what is this extraordinary thing after which people have struggled through the ages; I want to find out, learn all about it. And how can I do that if I have no sense of humility? Humility has nothing whatsoever to do with the self-protective humbleness which the mind imposes upon itself. That is an ugly thing. Humility cannot be cultivated, and it is one of the most difficult things to experience, surely, because we have already established ourselves in certain positions. We have certain ideas, values; we have a certain amount of experience, knowledge, and this background dictates our activities, our thoughts. An old man who has accumulated knowledge through his own experiences and through the experiences of others, and who is driven by his urge to be important, to establish for himself a position of power, prestige—how can such a man be in a state of humility and thereby learn about his own trivialities? So it seems to me that we have to be tremendously attentive and deeply aware of this sense of humility.

The world is in an extraordinary confusion, is it not? Look at your leaders, swamis, gurus, friends—they are all in a state of self-contradiction; they do not know what to do. Some of us have had minor explosions within ourselves and have responded accordingly. When, for example, we see poverty, starvation, all the social misery that is going on around us, there is a minor explosion within ourselves. We want to act, to do something, not sit around and everlastingly talk, speculate; so the minor explosion brings the minor response. We join a movement of some kind and work, work, work. But that does not satisfy, it has no depth, it does not include the vast expanse of life, so we throw it aside and look to something else; again we join a movement, an organization. And so we go on throughout our life, joining, discarding, having minor explosions and responding with equal triviality.

Sirs, may I suggest that you listen to what is being said, not as a mere lecture, but as a description of yourself and of your own existence; for if we are not aware of our own lives, if we are not vitally conscious of what is actually taking place within and around us, these talks become empty, utterly futile. So, please relate what is being said to your own life, and do not merely throw it aside as something very nice in theory, but not practical. After all, it is practical to think very clearly and not to deceive oneself. To know what the problems are, and to find out how you respond to them, is extraordinarily important, is it not? Otherwise you merely wend your way through life, or create still greater confusion because you happen to get more votes and hold an important position. The mind is anyhow lethargic, very slow,

sluggish; it needs a great shaking up because it has settled down in a comfortable, secure position and does not want to be disturbed. That is the case with most of us. And from that isolated position of security, the mind moves, acts, and thinks. And life demands, surely, not only at the present time but always, a totally different response.

So it seems to me that to learn, humility is essential. Life is impressing certain things on the mind, and if we are at all aware, we are learning all the time. But most of us learn merely as a process of accumulation. I do not know if you have ever thought about learning—what it means to learn. I am not talking about schoolboy learning, which is merely the cultivation of memory, an additive process of gathering information. That kind of learning is mechanical, and it is a necessary part of existence, but I am talking about learning in an entirely different sense. Surely, the mind cannot learn if it has already accumulated. From that background of accumulation, it cannot look at anything anew, can it?

I wonder if you have ever noticed what happens in your mind when you look at a sunset or the river. You have knowledge about the river, you know its name, its so-called spiritual significance, and this knowledge prevents you from really looking at the river. Sirs, am I talking of something foreign to all of you? I do not feel you are moving with me.

There are many problems in life, and how do you look at them? How do you look at the problem of power? How do you regard the tyranny of a few people over the majority? How do you look at the power of a very learned mind and the power of the word to sway the multitude? What is your reaction to the Gita, to the Vedas, to all the spiritual books? If your reactions are merely trivial, if they are the traditional reactions which you have picked up from your environment, surely you cannot learn.

To me, learning is a constant, timeless movement; it is never cumulative. The mind that has accumulated knowledge has ceased to learn, though it may go on adding to its knowledge. Surely, learning is something entirely different from the acquisition of knowledge because learning can never be an additive process.

I am so sorry, but I do not feel that you understand this at all. I have no communion with you. It is too bad.

Sirs, the mind—your mind—is the result of time, is it not? It is the cumulative outcome of many centuries, of many yesterdays. Now, that mind wants to learn, it wants to understand something. But can it understand anything with all this accumulation? It can interpret what it sees, saying it is good or bad, pleasant or unpleasant, worthwhile or not worthwhile; but a mind that wants to learn, to understand something, must surely be free from the past.

So, if the mind is to learn, to understand what freedom is, it must begin by perceiving to what an extent, to what depth it is a slave. One cannot merely say, "My mind is a slave," and regard freedom as a goal that one must seek. A slavish mind cannot seek freedom because it does not know what freedom means. Whatever it seeks, it will still be slavish. But if the mind begins to learn to what extent it is a slave, if it is constantly observing the actual fact of its own enslavement, then it also begins to see where freedom lies. But most of us are not concerned with learning about ourselves. We are concerned with superficial activities, with escaping from ourselves through temples, through knowledge, through books, through social work, and all the rest of it.

I am concerned, as everyone in the world must be, with what is freedom because freedom is getting less and less. Governments, even the democratic governments, do not give you freedom; they only talk about it.

We can sit here and criticize the government, but this is freedom only in a very limited sense. Under the tyrannical governments, there is no freedom at all; they do not allow people to talk with each other like this. So the margin of freedom is getting more and more narrow, which means that human dignity is wearing very thin. Please do see the importance of this. It is only in freedom that you can be creative, and to find out what freedom is, to learn about it, you must first know to what extent your mind is slavish. And being aware of its slavishness, can the mind break through it?

Look, sirs, we are all aware of tradition—the tradition of the family, of the group, of the nation. How much is your mind made up of that tradition? To what extent is your mind a slave to it? You must find out, surely. And to find out, you cannot say that tradition is right or wrong, good or bad; you cannot ask what to do about tradition, whether the mind can function without tradition, or bring up any of the superficial questions that one puts in superficially examining something.

I really want to know to what extent my mind is a slave to tradition—the tradition of centuries, and also the tradition of yesterday, which I have created for myself. Tradition is habit. To what extent is my mind a slave to habit? And is it possible to free the mind from habit? This is not a superficial question—it is the fundamental question. Until I know how to answer it—and I can answer it only by learning about myself—my inquiry into social problems, my discussion of economic and religious problems, will always be very superficial because I shall merely respond according to the tradition which society has imposed upon me. Most of us are satisfied with this kind of superficial thinking, and that is why it is very difficult for us to be serious in examining ourselves, to learn about ourselves and find out to what extent we are slaves.

And to learn about ourselves, humility is necessary, is it not?

I do not know if you have ever felt the strange quality of humility. Humility implies love, does it not? It implies a chastened approach to problems. Humility implies an absence of all conclusions, all goals which the mind has projected.

Look, sirs, we, the older generation, always talk about the new generation transforming the world. But those very people who talk so hopefully about the new generation impose their patterned way of thinking on the younger people. They really do not want a new generation; they want the perpetuation of their own exact pattern of existence. And if the mind is to learn, surely humility is essential, is it not? I am laboring this point because most of us are conceited—we think we know. Actually, what is it that we know? Have you ever looked at the process called "knowing"? Have you ever inquired into this question of "I know"? What you know is what you have gathered; it depends on what your experiences have been, and those experiences are part of your conditioning. Do you understand, sirs? If you are a rich man, your experiences are shaped according to the pattern of your riches. If you are a poor man, your experiences are limited to the state of your poverty. If you are a scholarly person, your experiences are largely determined by the books you read. If you have been a bureaucrat for forty years, it is obvious that your experiences are mostly confined to that field; yet you say, "I know," and from that conceit you want to shape the course of other lives. That is what we all do. The politician, the so-called religious person, the scholar, the professor, the husband, the wife—everybody does this. It is a curse.

So, what is the problem for those who are really serious? The people who are pursuing some goal, who are lost in some activity, or in getting what they want are not serious at all. That is only vanity. A serious man is one who wants to find out, to discover for himself, and not repeat what umpteen people have said. And surely such a man, being really serious, must explore all these things.

Take, for example, the whole question of nonviolence. In this country we talk a great deal about nonviolence, and we have made a philosophy of it. To me it is all rubbish, if you will forgive my saying so. The fact is that we are violent. Being violent, we make an ideal of nonviolence, and thereby establish a contradiction within ourselves; and with that contradictory mind we invent a philosophy—which is so utterly silly. What matters, surely, is to see that I am violent and begin to understand this whole problem of violence—not try to be nonviolent. I do not know what it means to be nonviolent. How can I know what it means? I can only speculate about it, which is worthless. What I can do is to learn about violence in myself, watch it, see all its implications, its significance, its neurotic, contradictory states; and thus to learn about violence in myself requires a great deal of humility. But a mind which seeks to be nonviolent is a conceited, speculative mind; it is escaping from violence and thereby creating a contradiction within itself; and a self-contradictory mind can never understand and be free of violence. However much it may discipline itself to be nonviolent, it will always be in a state of contradiction, and a self-contradictory mind is a violent, destructive mind. Please do see this simple fact.

The difficulty with most of us is that we refuse to see the fact that we are violent because we are committed to the ideal of nonviolence, whatever that may mean. But if I see that I am violent, and I want to understand my violence, go into it totally, with my whole being, then I must abandon the contradiction, I must see the falseness of the ideal of nonviolence. What is the good of my talking about nonviolence when my whole being is violent, though I may cover it up? So I have to perceive my violence, I have to go into it, understand it; and to do that, my mind must obviously be in a state of humility. Do you understand, sirs?

So it seems to me that we must think out all these problems rather fundamentally. The important thing is not to find an answer that is immediately satisfactory, or for the moment applicable, but rather to have an overall feeling about all these problems.

I am afraid I am not at all communicating to you what I want to convey. It may be my fault; it may be the cold morning or perhaps one did not sleep properly or has overeaten.

You see, most of us do not want to be disturbed. Have you ever noticed a man in a good position who gets exceptional benefits out of his job? He does not want to be disturbed, he will not let go, he will not allow others to have a chance at it. The same situation is endlessly repeated throughout the world, and it is the same in different ways with each one of us. We need a shaking that will loosen us and ultimately, of course, there is death. Is this a problem to you, sirs? The mind is always seeking security, a haven in which it will never be disturbed, and therefore it becomes a slave to a particular pattern of living, thinking, feeling. How can such a mind be broken loose from its moorings? How can such a mind learn?

Our problem is, first of all, to know ourselves—which is not a mere idealistic pursuit because it is only in knowing ourselves that we can know what action is. Knowing ourselves is the basis of real action—action which is worthy, significant. Most of us do not want to know ourselves; it is too much of a bore, an exercise; we would rather be told what to do. But to uncover the ways of our own thinking, to see the motives which lie behind our activities, is surely one of the fun-

damental issues, is it not? If we know how to uncover ourselves, we shall break the pattern of slavery, and we shall then know what freedom is—which is of the utmost importance because the margin of freedom is everywhere becoming very narrow. The more progress we make in the world of things and in the world of ideas, the less freedom there is. In America, where there is prosperity such as the world has never known, people are becoming slaves to prosperity. That is one of the major issues there now. Here there is poverty and we want prosperity. We want more food, more clothes, more things; and we are becoming slaves to the very idea that we must be prosperous.

So do please examine yourself to find out to what extent, to what depth your mind is enslaved. It may not be enslaved to the routine of an office, it may not be caught in the mechanical slavery to things, but it may be that you are a slave to knowledge. And without seeing all this, without really inquiring into it, without uncovering and discovering it for yourself, I do not see how you can live in freedom.

You know, there are many people for whom life is a despair. Having worked all their lives trying to bring about social reforms or what you will, suddenly there is an end, and they are frustrated; all the established philosophies, religions, ideals have come to an end, and they are in despair. I wonder if any of you know that state at all? But people who are very clever, when they face that despair, invent a philosophy of their own, which is what is happening in the world at the present time; they say, "Accept life as it is, and make the best of it."

Now, when you have examined all the avenues of escape, the clever theories, the quotations from the Gita, and all the rest of it, and when your mind refuses to be tricked by any explanation or facile adjustment so that you have no answer, then you must surely come to a state of despair which is not the opposite of hope. Most of us hope for something, big or small—for a better job or to find a way out of a difficult problem—and when our hopes are not fulfilled, we are in a state of despair, which is merely a reaction from hope because we are still wanting something. I do not mean that kind of despair, which is really quite immature. I am talking of a mind that has examined all these things and has not found an answer. Such a mind is not a hopeful mind; it is not seeking or wanting to find a final answer. It is in a state of complete not-knowing, complete despair, and there is no way out. Surely, only then one finds that which is truth.

Truth, or God, or what you will—the thing we all talk about so easily—is not so easy to come by. One has to work very hard—but not through disciplines and practices, which are all meaningless because they contain the seed of hope and despair. To uncover and see what one is actually thinking, and why one is thinking it; to perceive the influences of tradition, the motives, the habitual patterns of thought—all this is very hard work. One has to be attentive all the time. If, being sluggish, the mind is inattentive, it may discipline itself to be attentive, but that only makes the mind still more sluggish. A disciplined mind is essentially a sluggish mind. If you think about this, you will see how true it is. An alert, active mind, a mind that looks into, examines everything, needs no discipline. Discipline is in the very process of examination, the process of understanding.

Sirs, I think it is very important that all that is said be applied to oneself. If you are capable of really examining yourself, going very deeply within yourself, then you will find there is a freedom which is not the opposite of slavery, and in the light of this freedom, all the problems of your life have a different meaning altogether. It seems to me

that the only important thing in life is to find this freedom because in this freedom there is creativity, there is that reality which human beings are everlastingly seeking.

January 24, 1960

Second Talk at Rajghat

Perhaps this morning, after I have talked a little, it might be worthwhile to discuss what I have talked about. By discussion I mean that you and I should think the problem out together, that we should inquire, not only verbally, but see how far our minds can penetrate into the problem. To discuss in that way might be more worthwhile than merely to listen—though listening is an extraordinary thing in itself. But very few of us listen. We are surrounded by our own words, by our own explanations, by our own experiences, and we scarcely if ever listen to another to find out what he really thinks. After I have talked a little, perhaps we could go into this question more intimately and deeply through exchanging thoughts and verbally clearing the field, as it were.

What I want to talk about this morning is a problem which I think confronts not only those of us who are here but also the rest of the world. We are all concerned with the problem of working together, cooperation, getting things done together. This problem of working together has been approached in various ways, has it not?—coercively, compulsively, and persuasively. Working together has become important, not only in society, in commercial production, but also ideologically—which I am not sure is working together at all. The whole question of working together has many implications, and everyone who is concerned with a radical change in society is also concerned, surely, with this question. We generally work together through fear of punishment, or through hope of reward, or through the desire to gain position, prestige, power, do we not?

Please, may I suggest that we do not merely listen to the words but actually apply to ourselves what is being said.

We sometimes work together because we are influenced intellectually, emotionally, by a cunning person or by one who has assumed spiritual authority as a saint, as a guru, and so on. That is one way of bringing about our so-called working together. Another is the political way. A certain piece of work has to be done, a party is formed opposing another party with a different plan, and there is a campaign for the getting of votes. In that is implied a great deal of cunning, scheming, chicanery, an enormous amount of propaganda and persuasion.

We are considering the problem, so please follow this a little bit closely.

Then there is the working together for an idea, for a belief, which may be social or so-called spiritual. An idea is put forward by someone, and we cooperate with that person because we think the idea is excellent, worthwhile, or significant. That is also called working together. So we work together for an idea, through persuasion, through compulsion, through fear of punishment or hope of reward, and that is all we know. That is how we come together to do something. You may say that our working together is not so brutal and superficial, that we work together for love of the country, love of an idea, love of the poor. Surely, when there is love, there is no sense of compulsion or persuasion, is there? There is no vote getting, no forming of parties, no sense of the 'mine' and the 'yours'.

To work together for something which is not a self-projected idea, which is not profitable for oneself, for one's family or relations, and so on—such working together has quite a different significance. But before we can find out what it is to work together in

that way, surely we must eliminate in ourselves the various forms of compulsion.

Am I capable of working with others in an endeavor which is not based on authority, either mine or yours or his, and in which there is no personal profit, however subtle? A true working together comes about, surely, only when you and I both understand the problem, really understand it, for it is this very understanding that creates the necessity of working together. Our cooperation is then not self-imposed; it is not the outcome of so-called tolerance or of any form of persuasion. The moment you and I both see that a certain form of education must be brought about, there is no 'you' and no 'I'—what is important is the new education. When you and I both see that starvation must be rooted out, when we see the absolute necessity of it, not merely intellectually, but when we feel it deeply, totally, with a great deal of affection, sympathy, love, then in that state of understanding, surely, you and I work together to eliminate starvation. But if you have a pet system by which to wipe out starvation, and I have another, then the system becomes all-important; so you gather votes, and I gather votes, and we fight each other, dissipating our creative thought and energy in an endless struggle to bring about a system that will solve the problem.

Do please examine this. Though it is not possible to go into many details, one can see that working together implies a great deal. There can be a true working together in every department of life—political, social, economic, religious, educational—only when we free our minds from every form of fear, from every form of influence and reward; and for most of us this is a very difficult thing to do because we want something at the end of it. We want a position, a certain prestige, or we think, "This is the right thing to do," and we work, sweat for it, gathering votes and pushing others aside; so there is contention, conflict. And to me, every form of conflict, at whatever level of our existence, is a most destructive, deteriorating factor in life.

So, it seems to me that the solution to this problem of working together lies in bringing about a radical change in ourselves—a change which is not the result of any form of influence. Sirs, we do change through persuasion, do we not? It may be the communist form of persuasion, or the socialist form of persuasion, or the democratic form of persuasion, or the persuasion of the mother saying, "Do this for me"; whichever it is, we do change a little. I wonder if you have ever looked at your own lives to see whether you have changed at all? If you have changed, how has this change in your life been brought about? Has it been through persuasion, through compulsion, through a motive in some form? Or has the change come about without any motive? Surely, a change brought about through a motive is really no change at all, is it?

Look, sirs, revolution is obviously necessary—revolution in the school, in society, in religion. Things must be broken up, however uncomfortable it may be; they cannot go on as they are. Where a few privileged people rule; where tradition, dogmatism, and stupidity reign; where the few have educational and other advantages which the many have not; where there is immense poverty, starvation, degradation, and at the same time extraordinary prosperity—things cannot remain as they are. Something must break, and it is breaking, however much you may like your present mode of existence and want it to continue. So, revolution—economic, social, religious—there must be. But unfortunately, most people resist it. The bank clerk, the family man who has a house, a little property, the man in a position of power—everybody resists change, in little things and in big things. Have you not noticed this in your own lives? When you have to eat a different kind of food, something which is not the highly-spiced food you are used to, your body rebels. That also is a form of the desire not to change.

Please search your own minds, not my speech. Don't merely listen to a talk. It is a clear morning; there is the lovely river, the beautiful sky. It is much better to look at all those things than be crowded in this room with people who have no intention of examining themselves. It is much better to enjoy life, to feel the richness of the earth, to be aware of poverty, to see the river flowing by, than to sit here and speculate. Speculation is the most stupid form of intellectual amusement.

As I was saying, we always resist change, but change is going to take place whether we like it or not. Those who rule and resist will be broken the moment the thing they have built up begins to crack; whereas the wise man knows that change is inevitable, and yields in himself when revolution is shattering the things he has been building. But such people are few.

So the problem is how to bring about a radical change in ourselves—which is so obviously necessary—without persuasion. If you are persuaded to change, you are merely reacting to a certain form of compulsion, whether it is the Indian form, or the communist form, or the Western form; and to change through any form of compulsion is no change at all. If you change because you are offered a reward or because you are threatened, no real change has taken place. You have merely conformed to another pattern. Revolution which is a reaction to what has been is not a revolution because it merely establishes a new pattern, which is a modified form of the old; that is all. Am I talking too fast?

One sees that if there is to be a real change in the world, there must first be a radical transformation in the quality of the mind itself because people change very easily from the totalitarian to the democratic state, or from democracy to totalitarianism, whether it be the Nazi kind or the communist kind. Give them more food, offer them better opportunities for earning a livelihood, excite them in the stupidities of nationalism, and they will all "change," one way or the other. But one sees that any such change is only a reaction, and a mind that merely reacts can again be influenced to change in another direction—today I am a communist, and if that does not pay, I become a socialist, or a capitalist, and so on. Seeing this process going on throughout the world, one asks oneself what it all means. Where is the change to take place? Is change merely a matter of dropping one pattern and conforming to another? Do you see the problem, sirs?

What is implied in the word *change*? Being greedy, I want to change the moment greed is painful, but I don't want to change as long as I find a great deal of pleasure in greed. So when I try to get rid of greed, I am changing with a motive; my desire to change is a reaction, and that reaction can again be modified. I do not know if you are following all this.

Can there be a change, a total revolution—not an economic revolution or a social revolution or a religious revolution, which are all superficial, but an inward revolution which is total, in which my whole consciousness, my whole being is shattered, and a new thing comes up? You see, sirs, change for most of us is a modified continuity of the past, and that is no change at all. Seeing this difficulty, and realizing how complex is this whole process of revolution, change, one inevitably asks: Is it possible to change at all within the field of consciousness?

Is this all too difficult, sirs?

Question: May I speak?

KRISHNAMURTI: Just a moment. I have not yet finished what I want to say. First see the problem, sir. If one really goes into it, one sees it to be a problem of thought versus being. For most of us, thought is a means to change. Through thought we hope to change, through ideas we hope to transform ourselves. I persuade you, through ideas, to drop your nationalism, to take up a particular form of religious practice, or what you will. I manage to persuade you because I am very clever; I show you the absurdity of this or that, and you are persuaded by my intensity, by my words, and you change—or at least you think you have changed.

Now, what has actually taken place in that process? You have changed your ideas, you have changed your thought, but thought is always conditioned. Whether it is the thought of Jesus, Buddha, X, Y, or Z, it is still thought, and therefore one thought can be in opposition to another thought; and when there is opposition, a conflict between two thoughts, the result is a modified continuity of thought. In other words, the change is still within the field of thought, and change within the field of thought is no change at all. One idea or set of ideas has merely been substituted for another.

Seeing this whole process, is it possible to leave thought and bring about a change outside the field of thought? All consciousness, surely, whether it is of the past, the present, or the future, is within the field of thought; and any change within that field, which sets the boundaries of the mind, is no real change. A radical change can take place only outside the field of thought, not within it, and the mind can leave the field only when it sees the confines, the boundaries of the field, and realizes that any change within the field is no change at all. This is real meditation. To go into it requires a great deal of work, thought, energy—the energy which we now dissipate on practices of various kinds, which are all so childish. Really to investigate the field of thought and to see the limitations of consciousness is of the utmost importance. After all, these limitations are the result of effort, of contradictions, of conflicts and the desire to change. It is seeing this limited field totally, understanding it completely, that the radical change of which I am talking comes about—not through any form of persuasion, compulsion, or authoritative influence; and I think this is the only way to function, to live and work together.

Yes, sir?

Comment: I feel that the changes you are talking about—social, economic, and political—are all the expressions of one unifying principle.

KRISHNAMURTI: That is a theory.

Comment: I feel there is a unifying principle working in the world, in the whole of creation.

KRISHNAMURTI: It may be. I don't know.

Comment: Changes will come, and nobody can resist them.

KRISHNAMURTI: Are we not resisting changes, each one of us? To see that is what matters. If we were not resisting change, we would not talk about a unifying principle. Then life would be a constant revolution.

Comment: The unifying principle rests on the revolution.

KRISHNAMURTI: Why bring the term *unifying principle* into this problem at all?

Question: If changes are inevitable, what makes us resist them?

KRISHNAMURTI: That is very simple to answer. The man who has a good position—politically, economically, in the school, or anywhere else—resists changes. He says, "For God's sake, keep things as they are." The people in authority resist any change because they do not want to be disturbed. Right through life it is the same, from the prime minister to the small-town politician. The man who is discontented with things as they are—it is he who wants to find out about change. Being disturbed, dissatisfied in himself, he accepts a particular form of change which satisfies him; and once established in that habit, he also does not want to be disturbed.

Comment: Dissatisfied people can very easily be caught in any kind of change which is made to appear the opposite of what they dislike.

KRISHNAMURTI: Yes, sir, that is what we were saying.

Question: You say that real change must be outside the field of thought. But must we not first know all the possible facts that can be collected by the mind about something, and then let that information influence us until our feelings tell us that it is right?

KRISHNAMURTI: I don't quite see how it can work that way. You are saying that through analysis and deduction one must collect information, see the importance of this collected information, transform it into feeling, and then act from that feeling. That is what most of us do, consciously or unconsciously. I say that a certain political or religious way of living is right. How do I know? Because I have read about it, people and my own experience have persuaded me, and I feel it is worthwhile, that it will improve the lot of man, so I commit myself to the party, and I am against other parties. That is what most of us do all the time. Now, in engendering that feeling, surely what is implied is a sense of judgment based on experience, is it not? And experience is obviously conditioned. My experience as a communist, as a democrat, or what you will, is the outcome of various influences, persuasions, compulsions, fears, rewards. From that conditioning there is feeling, and I act.

Comment: I think feeling is more or less unconscious. We should use our conscious thoughts to influence our unconscious feeling, which is the unconscious mind.

KRISHNAMURTI: Is there a real division between the conscious and the unconscious, or is it an unnatural division created by our social, environmental influences? The conscious mind is the mind that has learned, that has acquired knowledge; it is a superficial collector of information. It goes to the office every day, does certain routine things, and so on. Then there is the unconscious, and can the conscious mind influence the unconscious? If you really examine it, you will see that it is the unconscious that is influencing the conscious mind, fortunately or unfortunately; there is an interplay between the two all the time. But to discuss this question of the conscious and the unconscious requires a great deal of penetration and time. We would have to start right at the beginning, not at the end of the hour. Perhaps we can do it another time.

Question: How is one to bring about a change outside the field of consciousness?

Comment: That is possible only when we can forget the division between you and me.

KRISHNAMURTI: I do not think you have listened at all. A gentleman asks how to change outside the field of consciousness. He wants to know what the method is, how to do it. You know, it is one of the odd things about us that we are so slavish to methods—as though any method is going to solve our human problems. Sir, there is a method for putting something together. If I want to be a mechanic, I learn how to deal with mechanical things. That is very simple. I go to school and they teach me the method. But we are not talking of mechanical things, and therefore there is no method. You have to think it out. Sir, do look at it this way, if I may suggest: Is there a method by which to love people?

Comment: No.

KRISHNAMURTI: Why do you say no to that question, and yet ask for a method to change?

Question: Isn't it true that we think of change as something tangible, something that can be felt, experienced?

KRISHNAMURTI: Think it out, sir, don't ask me. The problem is so vast. You cannot say, "Tell me what is the method to change"; it has no meaning. If you are concerned about change, not just theoretically so that you go back home and continue in the old way, but if you see the necessity of it and realize that you have got to change, then this problem arises—the problem of persuasion, influence, punishment, reward, and your own reactions of which you are not aware; so it is meaningless to get up and say, "Please tell me in a few minutes all about change outside the field of consciousness."

What is a man to do who is really interested in this question?—and human beings must be vitally interested in it because it is the problem throughout the world. It is the problem not just of this school, or of the man round the corner, but of humanity itself. Can a change be brought about in the quality of the mind, which is now becoming so mechanical, slavish? If this is a vital problem to you and me, we won't casually ask for a method; we will discuss factually, not theoretically. I feel all theoretical discussion is valueless, hot air, a waste of time. We will discuss factually if we really see the necessity of a fundamental change. I see that I am greedy, and I want to know if it is possible to be free of greed; I see that I am envious, and I want to find out if I can break that envy. I am not looking for a method, but I say, "Let me examine the problem of envy." If a man who is in a position of power says, "Look, I am a great man; I like being in this position, and don't disturb me," then for him there is no problem. I go away from such a man; I don't play up to him because I want nothing from him. But as ordinary human beings, you and I are concerned with this problem. It is not my problem, which I am thrusting on you; it is your problem. If you sit there and say, "Tell me all about it," then you and I have no relationship. But if a few of us can think it over together, then that is a totally different thing.

Question: There is a staircase, and we reach the roof by its means. We do not know what type of roof it is until we get there. Can we say that the roof is something external to the staircase? Will there be a roof if there is no staircase?

KRISHNAMURTI: Sir, the house is the floor, the walls, the windows, the roof, and the staircase. You cannot separate the staircase or the roof from the house. There is no such thing as a roof hanging without the walls. The house is a total thing. Now, any change within the house—going from one room to another, decorating each room in a different way, and so on—is a limited change; it is conditioned, narrow. It is obviously not freedom. So, can there be a total change, a change which is not within the house? Do you say that such a change is impossible, that any change is always within the house? Do you say it is nonsense to talk about a change outside the house? What is it that you think? Is all change within the house, or is it possible to bring about a change outside—or rather, not a change but a way of action? After all, change means action—a way of action which is not confined to the house.

Look, sir, let us say I am a Hindu, and I see how stupid, squalid, ugly it all is, so I join Catholicism. That is an action, is it not? And I think I have changed. But my "change" is still within the house, within the cage; it is still within the field of human misery. I have only exchanged one state of slavery for another. Seeing this fact, I say, "Is it possible to act without this limitation, without this house, without Hinduism, Catholicism, or any other system? Vast numbers of people, including the Catholics and the communists, say it is not possible. That may be so, but then you have to admit that the mind is everlastingly a slave.

Comment: You say the change from Hinduism to Catholicism is no change. But when we climb the staircase, we are at a different level.

KRISHNAMURTI: In other words, you are saying that through the gradual process of going step by step up the staircase, you reach the roof, where you have a different outlook on life. In saying this, you are inviting time, are you not? When you go step by step up the ladder until you reach the roof, that process, from the first step to the last, implies gradualness; the distance from one point to another must be traversed, which means time, does it not? All this is still within the field of thought, within the field of the mind.

Comment: A man going up the stairs has not seen the roof; he does not know what the roof is like until the last step, and then it is a spontaneous thing.

KRISHNAMURTI: Similes are most misleading, and that is why one hesitates to use them. Let us not get lost in similes and examples. Don't try to find a way out—just see the problem. Though I am putting all this into words, be aware of the problem for yourself, sir. The problem is that we must change. You may say, "Don't disturb me, let things remain as they are," but things will not remain as they are. Life is going to shatter that which has become crystallized. Whether it is life in the form of a soldier with a gun, or life as a man like me with the word, something is going to shatter you. And when you are shattered by an outward event, through some form of compulsion or influence, is that a change? Is it a change if there is a motive of any kind? And is it possible to change without a motive? Don't say it is possible, or it is not possible. We are thinking it out. We are not coming to any conclusion. It is a terrible thing to come to a conclusion because then you have stopped thinking. The problem is enormous, and one has to be very tentative about it; one has to inquire, to find out for oneself through watching, through constant awareness, if there is a change which is not induced, which is not the result of influence.

Sirs, another difficulty is that the mind likes to function in habit. Habit is the desire to be secure. If I am a so-called great man, used to having power, I like to function in that habit. The mind establishes various habits which give it a certain sense of security, and it resists any movement that disturbs those habits. When we do want to break a habit into which the mind has fallen, we say that we must have an ideal, that we must practice, that we must do this or do that; and I say, is that a change? Or is change something entirely different—something which awakens the extraordinary feeling of creation? Surely, that is the only real change. Creation is not the creative faculty of a cunning mind, nor is it the creativity of a mind that has a gift or a talent; it is the sense of complete release from the house of the self, and from acting within that house.

January 26, 1960

Third Talk at Rajghat

I would like, if I may this morning, to talk about what to do in life, which is what some people philosophically call action. We have divided action from life, have we not? And I wonder if action can be divided from life? There is what we call social action, political action, reformatory action, the action of education, the action of a businessman, the action of a swami, a yogi, a philosopher, and so on. There are these various forms of action, and the question of what to do, as if the thing that has to be done were apart from life. It is like digging a hole on the bank of the river, barricading oneself in that hole, and then saying, "How shall I flow with the river?" First we divide action from life, and then we try to find a way of bridging the gap between them. If you have observed, is this not what we are doing most of our lives? We have a pattern of action, whether it be the socialistic, religious, philosophic, educational, or commercial, and most of us are satisfied with that particular pattern of action.

Take the reformer, for example. He has a certain pattern of action with which he is satisfied, for he thinks it will transform the world, so he works, pushes, sacrificing everything for the sake of that pattern, and he never breaks away from it.

That is the difficulty with most of us, is it not? We don't seem to be able to appreciate the whole of life. Do you know what I mean by that word *appreciate?* To appreciate is to be sensitive to, to be aware or take cognizance of the whole of life; and if we can be aware, cognizant of the whole of life, then I think we can discuss more profitably what is action. Action is not separate from life but stems, or is born, from this very sensitivity which is a deep appreciation of life as a whole. I do not know if I am making myself clear.

Let us suppose that you are an educational expert. You think you know all about education. You have put up a few buildings, and you function in a very limited educational field. You don't regard the whole of life, which includes politics, religion, social reform, philosophy, sorrow, joy, love, anger, the appreciation of something beautiful; you leave all that alone. You concern yourself only with the narrow field which you call education, and you don't want anybody to touch it, to break it up, because it has given you a sense of security; you have a position, a certain prestige, and you don't want it disturbed. But like the river, life is flowing on all the time; it is battering at what you call education, and it won't leave you alone. So there is a conflict between the living, the moving, the dynamic, and that which is static. The static is that which you have carved out of your own thought, and which has become established as your professorial or bureaucratic status, or the status of the practical man, as he is called.

Then there are those who regard religio-social reform as of primary importance, and if you examine it objectively, clearly, without any personal bias, you will see that here too

the mind establishes a pattern of activity, a way of life with a great many defenses and taboos. It says, "I must do this and not that; I must get up at a certain hour, live in a certain way, work for the whole of mankind," and so on and so on. Do you understand? Just as there is supposed to be an American way of life, or an English way of life, so the religio-social reformer says, "This is the way of life for me." Life itself is so immense, so vast, so incredibly complicated and beautiful, yet he ignores all that. He may verbalize, philosophize about it, indulge in explanations, but he does not want anything to interfere with the pattern which he has established for himself. Yet that extraordinary thing called life comes and batters him, so there is a contradiction within and without, and sooner or later he is in misery. He does not know why, but he is miserable, frustrated, burdened with a constant sense of apprehension.

Or take the so-called religious man. He says, "I have nothing to do with the world; I am seeking God," and he becomes a monk or assumes the robe of renunciation. He observes certain ascetic practices; he remains a bachelor and denies, sacrifices, suppresses, desiccates, dehydrates himself. He too has set a pattern, a way of life for himself. In the extraordinary movement of life, there is love, there is joy, there is the whole complex relationship of sex, there is the fellowship of man, there is music, there are sorrows, despairs, hopes, and fears. But he denies life; he has cut himself off from the movement of life in a kind of graven cathedral of ideas. He is a Christian, a Buddhist, a Hindu, or what you will.

This process goes on all the time with most of us. If you have examined your own thinking, if you are aware of yourself at all, you will have noticed how you carve for yourself a niche, a shelter, a haven of ideas, of beliefs, of relationship, and then you don't want to be disturbed. Is this not the manner of our lives? There is this intense urge to take shelter in something—in nationalism, in a particular religion or philosophy, in a way of life—and we deny the extraordinary movement of life in which there is beauty, sensitivity, freedom, in which there is no beginning and no ending. It is a movement that has no form, in which there is no Christ, no Buddha, no X, Y, or Z. It is life itself, and it is battering at us all the time, pounding at the walls of our isolated existence.

So there is a contradiction in our lives, a self-contradiction of which we are consciously or unconsciously aware. There is a deep, inward sense of frustration, and from this contradiction, from this frustration, from this schizophrenic cleavage in our existence, we act. The battle is outward as well as inward. You are a socialist, and I am a so-called religious man; or you are an educational expert, and I concern myself only with business; or you are a politician, and I am the poor voter whom you can trick into almost anything; or you are an extraordinarily intellectual person, and I am stupid; or you are the saint, and I am the sinner. You try to convince or convert me, but I don't want to be disturbed, so I say, "Leave me alone"; or if it suits me because I see that I can get some advantage out of it spiritually, physically, or politically, I say, "You are perfectly right, I will follow you."

So, from this contradiction within and without, our activity is born. I do not know if you have noticed people who are extraordinarily active, who are always doing something, always reforming, preaching, moralizing, telling others what they should do. If you have talked to such people, if you have observed them, lived with them, you will know in what a state of contradiction, in what inward misery they are. They don't know what it means to love, and I don't think you know. If you love, that is enough; you don't have to do anything else. If you

love, do what you will, it is always good. Love is the only source of action in which there is no contradiction.

I know all this sounds pleasant; it is a nice thing to listen to on a lovely morning, but you don't know what that love is. You cannot know that love if you hold on to your particular pattern of existence and say, "I will carry this with me." To find the other, you have to shatter the pattern.

Sirs, I wonder if you have ever given any thought to the question of what is false and what is true? Any person can say without much thought, "This is false, that is true." But to inquire into, to be sensitive to and appreciate what is false and what is true is extraordinarily difficult because to find out what is true, one has to see the false and forever put it away, and not merely follow the pattern of what others have said to be true.

Please, sirs, do listen to me.

To find out what is true and not follow another who tells you what is true, or arbitrarily assert what is false and what is true, you must see that which is intrinsically false and put it away. In other words, one finds out what is true, surely, only through negation. Say, for instance, you realize that you cannot have a quiet mind as long as there is greed, so you are concerned, not with quietness of the mind, but with greed. You investigate to see if greed can be put away completely—or avarice, or envy. There is a constant purgation of the mind, a constant process of negation.

Sirs, if I want to understand the whole of this extraordinary thing called life, which must be the totality of all religions; if I want to be sensitive to it, appreciate it, and I see that nationalism, provincialism, or any limited attitude is most destructive to that understanding, what happens? Surely, I realize that I must put away nationalism, that I must cease to be a Hindu or a Muslim or a Christian. I must cease to have this insular, nationalistic attitude and be free of the authority of organized religions, dogmas, beliefs. So, through negation, the mind begins to perceive what is true. But most of us find it very difficult to understand through negation because we think it will lead us nowhere, give us nothing. We say it will create a state of vacuum—as though our minds were not in a state of vacuum now!

To understand this immensity, the timeless quality of life, surely you must approach it through negation. It is because you are committed to a particular course of action, to a certain pattern of existence, that you find it difficult to free yourself from all that and face a new way, a new approach. After all, death is the ultimate negation. It is only when one dies now, while living, which means the constant breaking up of all the habit patterns, the various attitudes, conclusions, ideas, beliefs that one has—it is only then that one can find out what life is. But most of us say, "I cannot break up the pattern, it is impossible; therefore, I must learn a way of breaking it; I must practice a certain system, a method of breaking it up"; so we become slaves to the new pattern which we establish through practice. We have not broken the pattern but have only substituted a new pattern for the old.

Sirs, you nod your heads, you say this is so true, logical, clear—and you go right on with the pattern, old or new. It seems to me that the real problem is the sluggishness of the mind. Any fairly intelligent mind can see that inwardly we want security, a haven, a refuge where we shall not be disturbed, and that this urge to be secure creates a pattern of life which becomes a habit. But to break up that pattern requires a great deal of energy, thought, inquiry, and the mind refuses because it says, "If I break up my pattern of life, what will become of me? What will this

school be if the old pattern is broken? It will be chaos"—as if it were not chaos now!

You see, we are always living in a state of contradiction from which we act, and therefore we create still more contradiction, more misery. We have made living a process of action versus being. The man who is very clever, who convinces others through his gift of the gab or his way of life, who puts on a loincloth and outwardly becomes a saint, may inwardly be acting from a state of contradiction; he may be a most disastrously torn entity, but because he has the outward paraphernalia of a saintly life, we all follow him blindly. Whereas, if we really go into and understand this problem of contradiction within and without, then I think we shall come upon an action which is not away from life. It is part of our daily existence. Such action does not spring from idea but from being. It is the comprehension of the whole of life.

I wonder if you are ever in the position of asking yourself, "What am I going to do?" If you do put that question to yourself, do you not always respond according to a pattern of thought which you have already established? You never allow yourself to ask, "What shall I do?"—and stop there. You always say, "This must be done, that must not be done." It is only the intelligent mind, the awakened mind, the mind that sees the significance of this whole process—surely—it is only such a mind that asks, "What shall I do, what course of action shall I take?" without a ready-made answer. Having through negation come to that point, such a mind begins to comprehend, to be sensitive to the whole problem of existence.

I wonder, sirs, if we can discuss all this? It is very difficult to discuss in the sense of exposing oneself. We may intellectually, verbally exchange a few ideas. But it is quite another matter to really expose ourselves, to be aware of the fact that we have committed ourselves to something, to a particular course of action, to see the limitations of that pattern, and to find out by discussing, thinking it out together, how to break it up. Such a discussion would be highly worthwhile, and I hope we can do it.

Comment: Every human being must sometime or other have expressed an action which has not broken the unitive feeling for life. Out of deep feeling a man acts, without any sense that his action springs from a separate center. But even in such a case, where there is the spontaneous, original feeling of action which enriches life, the very momentum of that action seems to create a separate center.

KRISHNAMURTI: A gentleman suggests that it may not be possible to act with one's whole being, without having that action again bring about a separate center from which other actions take place. Do you understand the problem? That is, have you ever known an action which involved your whole being, intellectual, physical, emotional—an action in which there was no motive, no thought of reward or fear of punishment? In such an action, you just do something as though for the first time, without any calculation, without thinking, "Is this right? Is this wrong?" Have you ever known such an action, such a state? We do occasionally experience it, do we not? And then what happens? After having acted in that state, we realize what an extraordinary experience it was—action with a sense of complete freedom, in which there was no resultant burden of repentance or self-glorification. It was a total action, without residue. But then we say, "I must make that experience real, lasting; I must perpetuate that state; I must always act in that way." So we have again established a center, a platform, a memory which we want to continue. There was a moment when we acted without calculation, with all our

being—not even with all our being, but out of the fullness of something. That experience has left a mark on the mind as memory. We pursue this memory, thereby establishing another series of actions according to a pattern of thought; so there is a contradiction between that which was done spontaneously, totally, and the patterned or habitual action, which is always partial. And we never realize the contradiction, but say, "At least through memory I shall get back to the other."

Comment: Because otherwise our life is empty. But this very effort to get back to the other state only makes the center stronger.

KRISHNAMURTI: Most of us have very rarely experienced that total action, if at all. What we know is partial action, which is so satisfying, so safe, and as we don't really know anything else, we hold on to it. Now, is it possible—please follow this next question—is it possible for you and me to break up the partial? Do you understand?

Question: Is it possible not to have the memory of total action? Can you give us some clue to that?

KRISHNAMURTI: Is it ever possible not to have memory?

Comment: We have never had that experience.

KRISHNAMURTI: To deny all memory is an impossibility, is it not, sir? Can you forget, remove from your consciousness the memory of where you live? Such a thing would be absurd, would it not? But if where you live is all-important to you, then the memory of it shadows your whole existence.

Look, sir, let us suppose I have had an experience of total action—action without thought, without the calculation of a cunning, purposeful mind. It has left a memory. I cannot forget that experience; the mind cannot say it did not happen. I know very well it happened. Now, how did it happen? It did not happen through any calculation, through any practice or determined effort. It just took place. Now, can I see the fact that it just took place, and also see that any cunning thought, any future purpose as a means to get it back is the very denial of it?

I will explain again.

Let us say I am walking along the bank of this river, and the sunset is over the city. It is rather a beautiful sight and it leaves an imprint on the mind, so the next evening I go again to the river, hoping to capture that same feeling, but it does not happen, that experience does not take place. Why? Because I have gone the second time with the desire to experience it. The first time there was no desire; I was just walking, watching the sunset, seeing the swallows skim along the water's edge, and suddenly there was that extraordinary feeling. But the next evening I went with the special intent of capturing that feeling; it was a calculated act, while the other was not.

So, our problem is: Can the mind be in a state of noncalculation? The experience has taken place, one cannot deny it, and is it possible not to pursue the memory of it in order to prolong that experience, in order to increase it? That is the question. Having had the experience, with its memory, is it possible to look at that memory and not let it take root in the mind?

Question: That is my question, which has not been answered. Is it possible not to cling to the memory of that experience?

KRISHNAMURTI: The memory of it has afforded me a great deal of pleasure, so I give it importance. I don't just say it is part of

life, and move on. Unpleasant memories we put away very quickly, or they are washed away psychologically because for various reasons we don't want to retain them. But we cling to pleasant memories. Why? Because they delight us, they give us a sense of well-being, and all the rest of it. So the mind has allowed itself to give soil for the pleasant memories to take root. It does not say, "Pleasant memories are the same as unpleasant memories; let me not cling to either of them." You may say that you don't want to cling to pleasant memories, but you really do; so you see how the mind plays tricks on itself.

Also, sir, please look at the strange fact that we always want an answer. Do you think there is an answer to anything in life? To mechanical things there is an answer. If a motor goes wrong and I don't know how to put it right, I call a mechanic who does. But is life like that? Is there an answer to any problem life has created? Or is there only the problem—which I have to understand, and not ask how to answer it?

Here is a fact—the mind clings to pleasant memories and takes shelter in them. And I must understand, surely, why the mind holds on to the particular experience which it calls pleasure; I must see the complex machinery of this desire to hold on to the pleasant and let go of those things which are not pleasant; I must perceive the extraordinary subtlety of the mind which says, "I will let go of this and hold on to that." What is important is this perception, not what to do.

Question: Will this not also become a practice?

KRISHNAMURTI: When you are studying something living, it is not a practice. You can practice a mechanical skill in handling something static. But if you want to understand a child, can that become a practice?

The child is living, moving, changing, mischievous, and to understand him, your mind must be as alive and as quick as he is. You see, sir, one of our problems is why the mind becomes so mechanical. I know that this question of practice arises everywhere. Should we not practice this or that in order to realize God?—as though God, life, truth, that extraordinary something, were static! You think that if you do certain things day after day, year in and year out, you will ultimately get the other. But is the other, whatever you may call it, so cheap as that?

Comment: You said something about our difficulty being a certain intrinsic sluggishness which prevents us from keeping pace with the flow of life. I wish you would go into that sluggishness a little bit.

KRISHNAMURTI: The fact is that the mind is sluggish. How are we to awaken it? How is the mind to shed its sluggishness? That is the question. Now, is there a method? Please follow this carefully. Is there a method to throw off sluggishness? Let us keep it very simple. If I say I must not be sluggish, and I force myself to get up every morning at six o'clock, and all the rest of it, will my mind be less sluggish? Will it, sir? Actually, you think it will; otherwise, you would throw aside your various practices, would you not? Now, can a sluggish mind be awakened through any practice? Or does practice merely further its sluggishness? The mind in itself is generally not sluggish; it has become sluggish through something. Take a child's mind, a young mind. It is not sluggish, is it?

Comment: But we are grown-up people with established habits.

KRISHNAMURTI: The young mind is active, curious, inquiring; it is never satisfied; it is always moving, moving, it has no frontiers. Now, why have we grown-up people become sluggish? Why, sir? Surely one of the major causes of this sluggishness is the fact that we have established a pattern of existence for ourselves; we want to be secure, do we not? Put it in different ways: economically, socially, religiously, in the family—in everything we want to be secure. Do you think a young mind wants to be secure? Later on it will make itself secure, and therefore become sluggish. So one of the major factors in our sluggishness, it seems to me, is this fact that the mind wants to be secure; and where there is a desire to be secure, there must be fear, anxiety, apprehension. Look at it, follow the chain of cause and effect. The mind desires to be secure, and thereby breeds fear. Having bred fear, it wants to escape from fear, so various forms of escape are established: belief, dogma, practices of different kinds, turning on the radio, gossiping, going to the temple, and a hundred other things. All these escapes are the causes of our indolence, of our sluggishness of mind. But once the mind sees the futility, the falseness of the urge to be secure in any way, then it is always active.

Question: What is the state of mind of a child of three, who has no memory?

KRISHNAMURTI: Sir, is there such a thing as a mind without memory? Even modern electronic computers have memories, and they remember, like the human brain, by association, and so on. Our minds function mechanically, and if we are satisfied with that, there is no problem; but the moment you begin to question whether it is possible for the mind to be free from this mechanical or habitual way of working, then this whole problem arises. Most of us are satisfied with the pleasantly mechanical operation of the mind, but if you say, "That is not good enough; I want to break up this mechanical habit,'' then you enter a field where there is no authority, and you have constantly to inquire, push, drive.

Question: Is it possible for a man whose consciousness is full of experiences to analyze himself?

KRISHNAMURTI: What is involved in this question? What does it mean to analyze, to look into, to explore the complicated machinery of one's own mind? In that process there is the censor and the object which he examines, is there not? Please follow this a little, if you are not too tired. In analysis there is always the observer and the observed, the analyzer and the analyzed. Now, who is the analyzer, and what does he analyze? Has not that which is analyzed produced the analyzer? That is, sir, to put it differently, there is the thinker and the thought. The thinker says, "I am going to analyze thought," but before he begins to analyze thought, should he not consider who is the thinker? Has not thought produced the thinker? Therefore he is part of thought. Right, sir? The thinker is part of thought, he is not separate from thought; therefore, as long as there is the thinker, the censor, the entity who evaluates, condemns, identifies, and so on, analysis will always produce a contradiction, will it not? Are you interested in going into this?

As long as there is a thinker apart from thought, all analysis can only produce further contradiction. So the problem is: Is it possible to observe thought without the thinker? Can the mind look at something without bringing into existence the looker, the censor, the observer, the experiencer? Can I look at a flower without the observer who says, "That is a daisy, I don't like it," or "That is a yellow marigold, I like it"? Now, when the mind is capable of looking without the cen-

sor, then there is no need for analysis because in that state of observation there is a total comprehension. You see, sir, where there is a censor and that which he observes, there is a conflict; where there is a thinker apart from thought, there is a contradiction; but when the mind can free itself from this dualistic, contradictory process, then there comes a state of perception in which there is total comprehension.

So the problem is: Can I look at myself without conflict? Can I see things in myself as they actually are, without the watcher who says, "How ugly I am," or "How good I am"? Can I just observe myself without introducing the censor?

Question: Why do we want security?

KRISHNAMURTI: Why does the mind want security? The whole social structure is based on the demand for security, is it not? Religiously, and in the everyday life that we know, the mind dreads the sense of negation, the feeling of complete isolation, which is fear. This is the beginning of the complex desire to be secure. One feels much safer if one has a secure relationship, doesn't one? When I feel perfectly safe in my job, I can go on mechanically, and I do not want to be disturbed. If my gods, my traditions, my beliefs give me safety, again I do not want to be disturbed—all of which means that one's mind is very sluggish. Realizing this, we say, "What shall I do; what practice shall I undertake in order to break up my sluggishness?" And so we enter the whole field of stupidity and illusion.

January 31, 1960

Fourth Talk at Rajghat

I think it is important to see the implications of agreement and disagreement, and also of conviction. All three imply a certain form of influence, do they not? Most of us can be persuaded by reason, by explanation, either to agree or to disagree with something, and there can be awakened in us a sense of conviction. But it seems to me that neither conviction nor disagreement can ever bring about understanding, and it is understanding alone that radically changes the nature of one's commitments and one's way of life.

So I think we ought to be very clear that here we are not concerned with persuading each other to adopt any particular form of thought, way of action, or pattern of belief. We are concerned primarily with understanding. This means that you and I must be very clear that in these talks there is no propaganda, that I am not out to convince you of anything, and that therefore there can be no question of agreement or disagreement. A mind that agrees now can also disagree later on, just as a mind that disagrees now will later on probably agree; and such a mind is not capable of understanding. Understanding is not born of agreement or disagreement, or of conviction; it is something entirely different. Understanding is the state of mind, surely, when there is complete attention, that is, when the mind sees totally, perceives comprehensively the whole problem; and in that state of mind there is neither agreement nor disagreement.

I think we ought to understand this fact very clearly because the lives of most of us are guided, shaped by agreement, disagreement, or conviction. Today you are completely convinced of something, and ten years later you are equally convinced of something quite the reverse. You agree now, and later disagree. Surely, this process of conviction, agreement, and disagreement breeds a state of contradiction, and a mind in a state of contradiction does not understand anything at all. Most of us live contradictory lives because our beliefs, our thoughts, our activities

are based on the pattern of conviction, agreement, and disagreement. But, as I said a little while ago, we are not here to persuade each other to think in any particular way or to adopt a certain course of action; therefore, we ought to be able to listen to each other without the desire to resist or to shape our lives according to what is being said. As I am not trying to break down your pattern of living, or shake you loose from your beliefs and dogmas, or change the course of your action, our relationship is entirely different. We are trying to understand each other, and therefore there is no barrier, no resistance, and hence a sense of intimate communion. At least, that is what I feel there should be in these talks—a sense of intimate communion with each other about the ways of the mind, and about the heart that is conditioned by the ways of the mind.

So, listening itself becomes very important, and not agreement or disagreement, or saying, "I must be convinced before I can act." To me, that is all sheer nonsense because it reflects very shallow thinking. In our relationship of listening, we are trying to understand, and that is much more difficult, much more arduous; it requires far greater attention than mere agreement or disagreement. With that clearly in mind, let us look at custom, which is called morality, and at goodness, which is called virtue.

Goodness is not the result of a culture, whereas custom or morality is. Morality which has become a custom is a cultivated habit in which the mind is pursuing a particular pattern of thought or experience, either self-imposed or imposed by society, and such a course of moral rectitude has nothing to do with goodness. The mind cannot flower in custom, in habit, however long it may continue in that pattern; it can only decay. Custom is a withering process, and goodness is the only state in which the mind can flower and know the meaning of compassion. The mind may cultivate morality, discipline itself in rectitude, but such a mind is not compassionate. It is a bourgeois, respectable mind, a mind that is the result of adjustment to society, which demands a certain pattern of thought and activity.

In a habit of thought, in a pattern of belief, there is no joy, no flourishing of the mind, whereas if you will consider goodness, you will see that in goodness there is a never-ending sense of being without contradiction. I think it is very important to understand this because, most unfortunately, our lives are guided by custom and habit; therefore, our lives are very narrow and shallow, however much we may decorate them with a pattern of glory or speculative delight. The mind which is a slave to a particular conditioning, to a pattern of routine or custom, is surely not a good mind. However difficult, however disciplinary, however respectable a custom may be, it is still only a pattern which the mind is following. But most of us are greatly concerned with respectability and recognition. We want to be recognized as respectable because in that respectability we feel secure, both economically and inwardly. We like to fit into the pattern which custom has established as being right. If you go into it very deeply, you will see that custom is the door to safety, security; for when the mind has passed through that door, it can never go wrong in the sense of not being recognized as respectable.

I do hope that you are not merely listening to the words, or being mesmerized by them, but are self-critically aware, and that what is being said is therefore self-applicable. As I said at the beginning, we are intimately communing with each other about the complexities, the intricacies, the subleties of our own minds; and to fathom the mind one needs not a defensive attitude but a certain relaxed attention.

So, most of us are committed to a certain course of action, to a certain pattern of thought and behavior, which is recognized as respectable; and the morality which comes out of that desire to be secure, to be recognized as the right kind of man, has surely nothing whatsoever to do with goodness. Custom is national, sectarian, limited, whereas goodness has no nationality; it is not recognizable to a respectable mind. And that brings us to a very important point, which is—why does the mind have this compulsion, this urge to belong to something? Why does the mind wish to commit itself to a course of action, a way of life, a pattern of belief? Why? I wonder if you have thought about it? Why does the mind wish to commit itself to something, belong to something?

You know, many intellectual people, writers, and so-called thinkers have committed themselves to various organizations or activities. They become communists, and because that movement is not satisfying or is found to be destructive, they drop that and join something else. The desire to commit the mind to something exists, not only among the high-brow intellectual people, but also in each one of us. You belong to a club, to a group, to such-and-such a society, to a particular religion or social activity—why? If you say, "I don't belong to anything, but I like to be with the members of this party or group," that is merely a way of avoiding the issue. We want to find out, surely, why there is in us this intense compulsion to belong to something—to a school of thought, to a particular philosophy, to this or that church or party. If we can understand why human beings at all levels have this craving to belong to something, then I think we shall be able to break down totally this constant formation of groups and sects, of conflicting nationalities and political parties, which is so destructive.

Do please pay a little attention to this. I know most of you belong to something or other, and I can imagine the sort of things you belong to. You form part of a group opposed to other groups, and each group seeks new members—you know that whole game, the racket of proselytizing and propaganda. But if you and I can find out—genuinely, with intelligence, with awareness—why the human mind has this extraordinary urge to belong to something, to commit itself to something, then we shall cease to be Hindus, Muslims, Christians, communists, and all these absurd divisions will be swept away. Then we shall be human beings with the dignity of freedom, individuals who do not belong to a thing, and who therefore have a human relationship which is not based on the exclusiveness of family or community, of nation, race, or organized religion.

Why is it that we have this urge to commit ourselves to something? One cause of this urge, surely, is that we see confusion, misery, degradation, and we want to do something about it; and there are people who are already doing something about it. The communist, the socialist, the various political parties and religious groups—they all claim to be doing something to save the poor, to bring food, clothing, and shelter to the needy. They talk about the welfare of the people, and they are very convincing. Many of them sacrifice, practice austerities, work from morning till night at something or other; and seeing them we say, "What extraordinary people they are." Because we want to help, we join them—and so we have committed ourselves. Just follow the sequence of it. After having committed ourselves to a party or a movement, we look at everything through that particular window, in terms of that particular course of action, and we don't want to be disturbed. Previously we were disturbed; but now, having committed ourselves, we are in a state of comparative tranquillity,

and we don't want to be disturbed again. But there are other parties and movements, all claiming the same thing, each with a clever leader who manifests an extraordinary, recognizable rectitude.

So the desire, the urge to do something makes us commit ourselves to a particular course of action. We don't look to see whether that course of action includes the totality of man. Do you understand? I will explain what I mean. Any particular course of action is exclusive, and is therefore concerned only with a part of man. It is not concerned with the whole man—with his mind, his human quality, his goodness, and all that. It is a partial, not a total, concern.

And we commit ourselves, not only to a particular course of action, but also to a particular belief or way of life. The man who becomes a sannyasi, a monk, a saint, has taken a vow to be celibate, to live in poverty, to offer prayers, to be this and not to be that; he has committed himself to that pattern. Why? Because it is a marvelous escape, a way of resolving all his problems by avoiding the constant lapping of life on the banks of his mind. He does not understand this movement of life, he does not know what it is all about, but at least his self-discipline and his belief give him a sense of safety, security; and there is always Jesus or Buddha or God at the end of it, so the man who is committed to such a course is perfectly happy. He says, "What is there to doubt? It is all quite clear. Come and join us, and you too will know all about it." He has become respectable because it is recognized that he is doing the right things.

All this I have not said cynically or harshly. I am just pointing out, not criticizing, and you are just looking.

We also commit ourselves in order to gain personal and satisfactory ends, do we not? Committing myself to a society, or to a particular course of action, gives me a sense of permanency, a sense of security. Please, sirs, watch yourselves; do not just listen to what I am saying.

You all belong to these various things, and you never say, "Why do I belong, why do I commit myself to anything?" And I think that it is very important to understand why we commit ourselves to something because many people have committed themselves to one thing after another, and at the end of their life, they are completely disillusioned, miserable, frustrated, unhappy. Belonging, committing oneself to something, is the cultivation of that rectitude which is based on custom, and which has nothing whatsoever to do with goodness. It is a subtle form of hypocrisy. I don't have to commit myself to an ideal. I am what I am. Being envious, why should I introduce a contradictory factor which I call the ideal? My concern is to understand envy, go into it, see all its implications; and through that understanding of envy, goodness comes. Goodness is not a pattern of action—for God's sake, do see that the two have nothing to do with each other whatsoever. A man who has no love in his heart may follow a pattern of gentleness, but such a mind is corrupt, it is a disintegrating mind. That is why it is very important to understand this process of belonging to something, of committing, dedicating oneself to something.

You see, behind all this belonging to something, there is the intense desire to be secure, and strangely, that sense of security depends on social recognition. If I join a recognized political party, or belong to a recognized religious order, or take up a recognized course of activity, in that recognition I feel safe, both economically and inwardly, and it also gives me certain personal advantages. So one begins to see very clearly that a mind which is committed to something—to Jesus, to Buddha, to any particular way of life according to which it is disciplin-

ing itself—can never know goodness. It can never know what love is, and love, after all, is the only solvent for all our problems. A mind that does not know what love is, that is not aware of the quality of that feeling, may pursue any course of action however respectable, however right, but it will lead only to further misery and destruction for others and for itself.

So one sees that custom, or the cultivation of habit as virtue, has inherent in it a destructive, disintegrating element. And if one sees this process clearly, if one understands it and does not cut it off volitionally, it drops away as a withered leaf drops from the tree; and in that dropping away there is a new budding of goodness, a new sense of unfoldment, and therefore a way of life which is entirely different from the other. That, it seems to me, is the only religious life—not all the things which you practice, which is not the religious life at all; it is just a matter of convenience, a ceremonial robe which you put on. It is not the mind that is ridden by custom, by habit, or committed to a course of action, but it is the good mind which can receive what is not measurable. The good mind does not want anything. In itself it is a movement, it is a state of bliss in which there is no demand. It is only when the mind ceases to demand, ceases to ask, to search— it is only then that reality comes into being.

I have talked for forty minutes, and now perhaps we can discuss a little. But what do we mean by a discussion? It is not a schoolboy or college debate in which you put forward one set of ideas, and I another, and we wrangle about it to see who comes out victorious. If that is all you are interested in, then you are victorious already; you have already won. But if we want to understand the problems of life, then we must not be in a debating mood, we must not discuss in an argumentative or contentious spirit. Life is a problem to most of us, and words will not solve it, explanations will not heal our wounds. We have to understand it, and to understand requires a great deal of love, gentleness, hesitancy, humility, not argumentation as to who is right and who is wrong.

Question: What is the difference between the spirit and the body?

KRISHNAMURTI: Is there such a division? I don't know why we ask such questions, first of all. Generally we have been told this or that, and we want to find out what is true. Now, to find out, to discover, to uncover the truth of anything demands a mind which does not want a conclusion, and which does not start from a conclusion, either negative or positive, but says, "I don't know. Let us inquire." When such a mind asks a question, its meaning is quite different from that of the mind which says, "Tell me, I want to know the answer." Life being immense, vast, immeasurable, how can you hold it in your fist and say, "I have found the answer"?

So, with our minds in that state of inquiry, let us ask: Is there a division between the mind and the body? Is the spirit or the soul different from the mind? Or is it all one, a unitary process which man breaks up into several parts for his own convenience, saying, "This is spirit, this is matter; this is the body, this is the soul," and then tries to unify them again? And when he can't unify them, he talks about the atma and escapes through that idea. Surely, each one of us is a total human being. Though the body is separate from the mind, man is a total entity; and to perceive, to understand this totality, to feel it, to relish it, to see the beauty of it is much more important than to say there is a soul apart from the ugly little mind, and garland the soul with your words.

What is your question, sir?

Question: You said there is a pattern of life based on agreement and disagreement, and that a mind which conforms to this pattern is not a good mind. It is only a good mind that is capable of understanding, and a good mind never conforms to a pattern. But is there anybody, in any mode of existence, who does not conform to a pattern? You also conform to a pattern, sir, in saying, "This is a good mind, and that is a bad mind."

KRISHNAMURTI: Sir, I am afraid you did not listen to the talk. I was just pointing out a fact—which does not mean that I condemn or approve of it. It is so. I did not say, "This is a good mind, and that is a bad mind." It was never in my mind to create this division between the two.

Comment: But, sir, you did.

KRISHNAMURTI: You win, sir.

Question: I have a question. So long as I am egoistic, my life must be spent in pursuing one thing after another. Can I think myself out of it?

KRISHNAMURTI: Sir, you can think yourself out of anything. To think yourself out of something is to create illusion, but that illusion may seem extraordinarily real. Living here in Banaras with all the filth, the poverty, the ugliness, the brutality, the starvation, the callousness, I can live in a tower of isolation and say these things do not exist. I have thought myself out of something, but that is obviously not facing the fact.

The fact is that most of us are extraordinarily self-centered, only we don't want to admit it. It is this center that has committed itself to a course of action which looks generous, noble, religious, and all the rest of it; but the center is still there. This center, with its self-interested activities, has to be understood; and to understand is not to condemn it but to see it as clearly as one sees one's face in a mirror. One has to pursue it right through, in both the conscious and the unconscious; one has to uncover it, see all its ways, however subtle; and in the understanding of it, there is a withering away of that thing which is the center.

Question: How is one to understand the unconscious mind?

KRISHNAMURTI: That is rather a difficult problem, and the question is put by a young student. As we all know, there is the conscious mind and the unconscious mind. The river is not only the shining, sparkling surface which we see, but also the dark, hidden, living waters below. In the same way, consciousness is the hidden as well as the surface mind. And just as the river, with its surface and its hidden depths, is a total thing, so also is consciousness, only we have divided it for convenience into the conscious and the unconscious mind. In actual fact, there is no such division; there are no gates which shut you off from the unconscious while you function on the conscious level.

The conscious mind is superficially adjusting, reflecting, learning, acquiring information, is it not? You are learning modern physics. You are adjusting on the surface to a certain course of action which is foreign to the ancient culture in which you were born. That is very necessary because you have to earn a livelihood, adjust yourself to the modern world, and all the rest of it. But there is also the deeper part of consciousness, the hidden or unconscious mind, which is the racial inheritance, the residue of all the past, of custom, of tradition, of what your ancestors have been, or what you have repeatedly been told. So there is a contradiction between the thing below, the residue of the past, and that

which on top is adjusting itself to the modern world. Do you follow?

Below the surface you are a Hindu, a Muslim, or what you will; on top you are studying to be an engineer or a scientist. The thing below is much stronger than the thing on top, which has barely scratched the surface. Unless we understand the totality of this movement, which is made up of the surface as well as the residue of the past which is below the surface, life becomes a state of contradiction.

Now, how is one to understand that which is below the surface? That is your point. In other words, how is the conscious mind to understand something with which it is not familiar? The conscious mind starts by analyzing, dissecting; and with this positive approach, can you observe that which is essentially negative? Do you understand? I will go into it, but not much, because it would take too long.

Let us suppose you are grown-up and married, with children of your own. Your conscious mind is occupied all day long with going to the office, with your money, with your customs, your gossip; it is eternally chattering. But when you go to sleep at night, the conscious mind becomes somewhat quiet. Then the unconscious gives you a hint in the form of a symbol, and when you wake up in the morning, you say, "I have had a marvelous dream." The unconscious mind is trying to convey something through a hint, a symbol, a dream, which it wants the conscious mind to understand. Because it is not capable of understanding, the conscious mind has to interpret that dream, so you have the further complication of the interpreter, who may interpret it wrongly, and again there is a conflict.

Now, to understand the total movement of the mind, of the unconscious as well as the conscious, one must be aware of every thought, of every feeling during the day. It is neither difficult nor easy. It requires a mind that says, "I really want to understand this whole process." Then you are watchful, attentive, awake to everything that is going on all day, aware of every movement, every hint, every flutter of the mind and the heart. And when your mind is thus attentive—not concentrated, but attentive—then when you do go to sleep, the unconscious as well as the conscious mind is quiet; it is no longer giving you hints. The whole mind is quiet, not just because it is tired, but it is quiet in a different way altogether. And in that real quietness, in that deep stillness, there is a new flowering, a new state of being.

Question: How can we be revolutionary when we are not?

KRISHNAMURTI: You know, the young mind, the innocent mind is always revolutionary—revolutionary in the sense of never accepting, always inquiring, exploring, seeking, wanting to know. Such a mind has no frontiers, no boundaries. But through so-called education and respectability, through adjustment to society, through its own ambitions, vanities, and all the rest of it, the young mind becomes an old mind, a sterile mind which functions only within the field of habits, customs, and commitments.

Now, most people think that being revolutionary is a matter of committing oneself to a so-called revolutionary organization or activity. They become socialists, or communists, or Trotskyites, or Stalinites; they belong to this or that movement of the ultra-left, to various forms of tyranny, and they call that being revolutionary. But when one observes, one sees that that is no revolution at all. It is merely a new commitment, the substitution of one pattern for another. If I cease to be a Hindu and become a Christian, and I say there has been a tremendous revolution in my life, it is sheer nonsense. I have merely left one cage and entered another. A revolutionary mind has no cage, no pattern. It is a mind that is truly religious because it has no authority, and therefore it is a really good mind—not opposed to the bad mind, as that gentleman suggested. You see, revolution means a real change, a mutation or transmutation of the center.

February 7, 1960

New Delhi, India, 1960

--- ✳ ---

First Talk in New Delhi

If I may, I would like to talk over with you some of the problems which all of us are confronted with. In talking over these problems with each other, we must clearly understand that any form of influence or persuasion is very temporary, affecting only the conscious mind, and does not bring about a radical change at all. And a radical change is necessary. Some form of revolution in the quality of our thinking is obviously essential, and we can bring about a fundamental change in the mind only when there is a sensitivity to the problems, and not mere acceptance or denial either of the problems or their so-called solutions. If you and I do not clearly understand this, we shall be merely wasting our time. I do not want to influence you in any way whatsoever. It is not my intention to persuade you to act in any particular direction, nor do I wish to determine a course of action for you to pursue. To me, all such forms of persuasion or influence are a denial of freedom. There is neither good influence nor bad influence; there is only influence. Influence is propaganda, and propaganda always destroys the capacity to think clearly.

If this is very well understood between us—that there is no intention on my part to persuade you to think in any particular direction—then let us try to think over together the many problems that we have; let us con-sider them clearly, dispassionately, so that the mind is no longer bound, no longer a slave to any pattern of behavior or thought, because negative thinking is the highest form of thinking.

By "negative" I do not mean the opposite of the positive. Most of us think positively, in terms of do and don't, which is adjustment to a conclusion, to a pattern of thought or action. The pattern may be the result of a great deal of experience, it may be the outcome of research and many experiments, but it is still a pattern; and thinking according to a pattern, however conclusive, satisfactory, is a process of conformity which always conditions the mind.

But it seems to me that to deny such positive thinking, and merely to revolt against the pattern, will in no way create thinking which is of the highest quality. The highest form of thinking is negative thinking—that is, just to be aware of the fallacies of positive thinking, to see the conflicts it creates, and from there to think clearly, dispassionately, without any prejudice or conclusion.

Perhaps, this evening, we can go into all that because we have many problems, and I think no problem is isolated. Every problem is related to every other problem, and the individual problem is obviously the problem of the world. When we divide problems as individual and global, individual and social, individual and political, individual and communal, I think such dividing is fallacious and does not bring about comprehension at all. What brings about comprehension is this awareness or perception of the total, undivided problem.

Some of you may be hearing all this for the first time, and your difficulty will be to understand what the words are meant to convey. Words are symbols, and merely to adhere to symbols stops all thinking. Whereas, if we can slip through the symbols, through the words and definitions—not denying them, but seeing their limitations and going beyond them—then, perhaps, we shall be able to understand the problem.

So, what is the central problem for each one of us, for the mind? In putting this question, I am not preparing to point out the problem so that you can either accept or deny it. We are trying to understand—which means there can be neither denial nor acceptance. The moment you deny or accept, all investigation ceases, all inquiry into the problem comes to an end. And it is also very important to be able to listen to the question, is it not? Most of us, I think, do not listen at all. We hear a great deal, but we do not listen, just as we do not see anything without interpretation.

If I may, I would like to explain a little what it means to listen. Listening is an art. To listen, you must give total attention, and you cannot give total attention when your mind is interpreting what it is hearing, translating it in terms of what you already know or have experienced. A mind that listens in the true sense of the word does not interpret what it hears according to its own experiences. It is not interpreting at all—it is totally attentive. Such listening without interpretation gives to the mind a temporary focus in which there is that strange quality of total attention.

I wonder if you have ever listened to anything with total attention? To most of us, at-

tention implies the effort to concentrate, but where there is an effort to concentrate, there is no listening and therefore no understanding. Listening implies, surely, a mind that is completely relaxed and yet attentive. If you will kindly experiment with this state of relaxed attention, which is listening, we can proceed to inquire—and inquiry will then be neither yours nor mine. Such inquiry is not conditioned, it is not in response to any demand or necessity; therefore, such inquiry begins to free the mind.

It seems to me the central problem for all of us is the fact that we are slaves—slaves to society, slaves to public opinion, slaves to our professions, slaves to our religious dogmas and beliefs. And a mind that is slavish obviously cannot perceive what is true. A man who spends thirty, forty, or fifty years in his profession as an engineer, a bureaucrat, a politician, a physicist, becomes a slave to that profession, does he not? He may mutter on the side about reality, God, goodness, virtue, and all the rest of it, but such a mind is obviously not a free mind. And surely it is only a free mind that is capable of inquiry, of search, of finding and unfolding.

The problem is not what to do about being a slave but to understand the depth of our slavery. To me, that word *understanding* does not mean merely grasping a problem intellectually; it has quite a different meaning. Intellectually, verbally, one may comprehend all the arguments, all the reasons and deductions, and come to some kind of conclusion, but surely that is not understanding. Understanding demands a comprehensive perception of the whole process of existence, not just a sectional or fragmentary grasp of one problem. Life covers everything, it has no beginning and no end; life is the good and the bad; life is the communist, the socialist, the capitalist, the imperialist; life is that total something in which dwell the painter, the musician, the man of sorrows. If I want to understand this extraordinary thing called life with all its vastness—and not only the vastness but also the particular, the limited, the life of a person in a small village or in a town—if I want to understand this extraordinary thing called life, I must have the capacity to approach it totally. It seems to me that we cannot approach it totally because our minds are so very limited, and from that limitation we respond to the challenge of life; therefore, there is everlasting conflict, misery, strife. So the problem is, surely, whether the mind is capable of a total response so that it does not create problems and is not in constant conflict with itself.

Most of us do not seem to realize to what an extent the mind is a slave, both outwardly and inwardly; and I do not think it is possible for the mind to free itself from this slavery until it is aware of its own slavishness. The mind is a slave to tradition, to experience, to habit, and without understanding the whole process of how habit enslaves the mind, merely trying to free the mind from a particular habit has no value at all.

Do please listen to this a little attentively, at least for the time being, because we shall tackle as we go along the many questions that will inevitably arise in your minds in the course of these talks. Unless we grasp from the very beginning the importance of seeing *what is,* which is to perceive the actual state of one's own mind, merely to ask questions and try to find answers is utterly futile. There are these many problems—the problem of starvation, the problem of freedom, the problem of relationship, the problem of whether truth, reality, exists or does not exist, the problem of meditation, and the extraordinary problem of creation, the movement of life. All these problems do affect us, superficially or most profoundly, and we cannot find an answer to any of them if we do not understand the actual fact of *what is.* Most of us

are unwilling to face the fact of *what is;* we want to escape from it, and there are many escapes which have become traditional. So, the important thing is not how to free the mind—what is the means, the method, the discipline, and all the rest of it—but to understand the fact of one's own slavery to habit. It is the perception of this fact that is going to bring freedom to the mind, and not the resolution or determination to free the mind.

Most of us would be horrified if we were really aware of what slaves we are to habit. We want to get into good habits, which are called virtues, but habit is mechanical, and a virtue ceases to be a virtue when it becomes habitual. A mind that practices humility, and makes a habit of it, has ceased to be humble; it has lost the quality of that strange thing called humility. And yet, if you observe very carefully the movements of your own mind, you will see that the mind almost invariably creates for itself a pattern of habit, and then functions mechanically in that habit.

We divide habit into the good and the bad, the good being the respectable, that which is recognized as virtue by society; but virtue which is recognized by society, which has become respectable, is no longer virtue. The mind is everlastingly seeking a mode of activity which is purely mechanical, and when it finds such a state, it is satisfied because in that state of mechanical functioning, mechanical thinking, there is a minimum of friction, of conflict. That is why habit becomes very important to the mind, and why the mind becomes a slave to habit.

Actually, habit is the mind, just as time is the mind. After all, we are the result of time, not only in the chronological sense, but inwardly, psychologically we are the result of time, of many centuries. We are slaves to tradition, not only to the tradition of a thousand years, but to the tradition of yesterday. Again, if you go into yourself, observe your own mind, you will see that such functioning in accordance with tradition is always mechanical, whether the tradition is ancient or recently set going by the demands of the present, the immediate.

Sirs, may I suggest that you do not just listen to the talk but actually be aware of yourselves. The talk is useful only as a mirror to reflect the functioning of your own minds. If the description becomes all-important, and you are merely accepting or denying the description, then you are not observing your own minds; and if you are not observing your own minds, then these talks are utterly futile and a waste of time. The description, the symbol is never the real. The word *mind* is not the mind, and if you merely cling to the word, then the extraordinary quality, the subtlety, the deep movement of the mind will pass you by.

So, what is it you are actually doing? You are listening, surely, in order to observe your own mind in action, and to be aware of the nature of your own thought. In thus being aware of your mind and its activities, you neither accept nor deny. There is no conviction, one way or the other. You are merely observing the fact, and the observation of a fact does not demand any previous conclusion.

As I said, our minds are the result of time. Our minds are the result of influence, whether it be the communist influence or any other. Our minds are bound by tradition, which is a form of influence. Our minds are the result of experience, and experience has become tradition. To all this our minds are slaves. Through so-called progress, culture, and education, through political activities, through propaganda, through various forms of adjustment and conformity, the margin of freedom is getting narrower and narrower. I do not know if you are aware of how little freedom we have. The politicians, the specialists, the various professions, the radio and television, the books and newspapers we read—all these things are influencing, conditioning the mind, and so depriving us of this extraordinary feeling of freedom. That is the fact, and we are concerned with the fact, not with what we should do in order to be free. We shall understand what is to be done when we are sensitive to *what is,* and sensitivity to *what is* depends on the quality of the mind that gives attention to *what is.* One may say, "Yes, I am a slave, but I cannot change because I am tied to my job; my whole existence is committed." Surely, that is a very superficial observation. Or one may say, "To live in this way is natural, inevitable." Again, such a statement is very superficial. So, on the sensitivity of your mind depends the depth to which you understand the fact of *what is.*

Look, sirs, let us suppose that I have been trained from my youth to be a bureaucrat. I now function somewhat easily but mechanically in that profession—and I have been a slave to it for the past forty years. Most of us are in that position, and very few of us are aware of our slavery. A doctor who practices as a specialist is a slave to his specialty; that is his haven to which he has given many years of his life. We are slaves to what we have been educated to do. We are slaves to our occupations, our professions. That is the actual fact, and the mind rebels against looking at the fact. If you observe your own mind, you will see how it wants to push the fact aside. Now, I am suggesting that you merely look at the fact, which is to be aware that you are a slave, and then you will find that such awareness, such perception, brings its own action.

But that raises another issue. Most of us, when we are confronted with a problem, want to do something about it. In other words, there is a thinker who acts upon the problem. But the thinker is himself the problem.

I wonder if I am making myself clear?

You see, sirs, I feel that freedom is absolutely necessary—not a conditional freedom, but a total freedom. For only a free mind is creative; only a free mind will know what love is; only a free mind is in that state of goodness which is not a cultivated virtue. So freedom is essential. But if you observe, you will see that freedom is being denied to every human being through knowledge, through experience, through habit, through the various functions that we perform.

Now, is it possible for the mind to be free?—which is not the opposite of slavery. Do you understand? The opposite is always a reaction, is it not? The opposite of violence is nonviolence. It is a reaction; therefore, it has the quality of violence. But if the mind understands its own violence, then it is free of violence, which is a state entirely different from nonviolence. Similarly, when the mind goes into this whole process of slavery, when it understands in what way and to what extent it is a slave, then there is no reaction because that very understanding brings a freedom which is not the opposite of slavery.

Sirs, let me put the problem differently. Surely, love is not the opposite of hate. In love there is no jealousy, no competition. Where there is ambition, there is no love; where the mind is seeking power, position, prestige, there is no love. One can comprehend the quality of love only through negation of what is called the positive. In other words, the state of love can be found, understood, felt, or that state is, only when the mind is not ambitious, no longer caught in the conflict of jealousy. And if we would understand what it is to be free, or to be in that state of perception which is freedom, then we must comprehend, we must totally aware of the implications of slavery.

Sirs, I am afraid we are not in communion with each other. Do you know what it means to commune with another? Between two people who love each other, words are often unnecessary. When they look at each other, there is a common attention at that moment which is total; words are unnecessary because there is instant communion at the same level, at the same time. Now, you and I are not in that state of communion because you do not really see that this problem is your problem. It is not something I am imposing on you. I am merely pointing it out. Some of you may be aware of your slavery, but most of you don't want to look at it, so there is a separation, a cleavage; there is a distance between the speaker and yourself because freedom to you means something entirely different. You translate it in your own terms, according to the tradition in which you were brought up, and thereby you completely miss the significance of what is being said. If there were communion between us with regard to the problem, then the mind would be in a state of attention all the time at its profoundest depth.

Do you understand what I mean?

Look, sirs, our lives are very petty, very narrow, full of strife and misery. Whatever we touch, with the hand or with the mind, is destroyed, perverted, corrupted. Everything about us indicates corruption. Being small, our minds are struggling, struggling, struggling all the time. To understand this problem, you must give it your full attention; you must be earnest, not just at this moment, but right through life. I think there is a difference between earnestness and seriousness. A man with a conclusion, with a dogmatic belief, is very serious, and so is a man who is somewhat unbalanced. But I am talking about the earnestness of a mind which wants to penetrate as deeply as possible into every problem of life, and therefore cuts off all the escapes. Surely, to such a mind, this question of freedom and slavery is very important.

On every side, governments are destroying our freedom. Education is conditioning us, and so-called progress, with its mass production, is also reducing us to slavery. Though you may not regard this as a problem, the problem exists. There are tyrannies in the world, dictators, rulers who are out to control the mind of man. This is a problem which is confronting each one of us every day. The question of how to interpret the Gita or the Upanishads is no problem at all. It is not a problem to an earnest mind. What somebody has said—whether it be Marx or the Buddha or the Christ—is not important. What is important is to understand for ourselves the things we are faced with, and not translate them in terms of the past; and that requires our attention, our complete earnestness.

This question of freedom is an immense problem that is actually confronting each one of us; it is not a mere theoretical problem to be discussed by the philosopher or by the politician who is everlastingly talking about freedom and peace. It is a problem to the earnest mind that is seeking to disentangle itself from sorrow, but you cannot give your attention to it if you are not deeply aware of it, if it is not a direct challenge to you.

I do not know, sirs, if you realize in what a state of despair man is. He has tried everything; he has committed himself to various activities, to various movements, to various philosophies, religions, and at the end of it he has found nothing. He may believe, he may speculate, but that is all without understanding, so there is despair. Do you understand, sirs? There is despair when the mind sees the spread of tyranny, when it is aware that politics have become all-important, when it perceives that organized religion is controlling the thought of man. Turn where you will, you are bound to come upon this sense of despair. Those who have their backs to the

wall invent philosophies, and by their cleverness capture other people in their net of despair.

So, being aware of this whole process which is life, as a human being you have to face it; you cannot say, "It is not my problem." It is your problem, and you can resolve the problem totally only when you begin to understand the quality, the movement, the extraordinary activity of your own mind. If you do not understand yourself, whatever you are—consciously or unconsciously—you are in a state of despair; and the more intellectual you are, the deeper and wider is your despair. Of course, shallow minds very quickly forget their despair by going to the temple or reading a book or turning on the radio or repeating certain futile words, but the despair is still there.

Now, can the mind confront this enormous problem without despair? Surely, despair arises only when the mind clings to the hope of resolving the problem. I think it is possible, without going through the process of hope and despair, to understand the problem—that is, to understand the mind, to understand oneself, but that is exactly what most of us do not want to do because it entails work, it demands attention, a constant perception of every thought and every feeling. Yet without self-knowledge, do what you will, there can be no freedom. By self-knowledge I mean an awareness and understanding of every movement of thought and feeling from moment to moment. I am not referring to the higher self and the lower self, to the atma, the self that is supposed to be supreme, and all that business. I am talking about the mind that functions in everyday life, the mind that is enslaved, that is envious, ambitious, cruel, the mind that knows joy and sorrow, that is caught in a method, in a symbol, in an illusion. What matters is to understand your own mind, the mind that is functioning in you at every moment of the day because only through the clarity of that understanding is there freedom. I say the mind can be totally free, and it is only the totally free mind that knows if there is reality, if there is God, a state which cannot be measured by the mind.

February 14, 1960

Second Talk in New Delhi

Most of us must be aware that a fundamental change is necessary. We are confronted with so many problems, and there must be a different way—perhaps a totally different way—to approach all these problems. And it seems to me that unless we understand the inward nature of this change, mere reformation, a revolution on the surface, will have very little significance. What is necessary, surely, is not a superficial change, not a temporary adjustment or conformity to a new pattern, but rather a fundamental transformation of the mind—a change that will be total, not just partial.

To understand this problem of change, it is necessary, first of all, to understand the process of thinking and the nature of knowledge. Unless we go into this rather deeply, any change will have very little meaning, because merely to change on the surface is to perpetuate the very things we are trying to alter. All revolutions set out to change the relationship of man to man, to create a better society, a different way of living; but through the gradual process of time, the very abuses which the revolution was supposed to remove recur in another way with a different group of people, and the same old process goes on. We start out to change, to bring about a classless society, only to find that through time, through the pressure of circumstances, a different group becomes the new upper class. The revolution is never radical, fundamental.

So, it seems to me that superficial reformation or adjustment is meaningless when we are confronted with so many problems, and to bring about a lasting and significant change, we must see what change implies. We do change superficially under the pressure of circumstances, through propaganda, through necessity, or through the desire to conform to a particular pattern. I think one must be aware of this. A new invention, a political reformation, a war, a social revolution, a system of discipline—these things do change the mind of man, but only on the surface. And the man who earnestly wants to find out what is implied in a fundamental change must surely inquire into the whole process of thinking, that is, into the nature of the mind and knowledge.

So, if I may, I would like to talk over with you what is the mind, the nature of knowledge, and what it means to know, because if we do not understand all that, I do not think there is any possibility of a new approach to our many problems, a new way of looking at life.

The lives of most of us are pretty ugly, sordid, miserable, petty. Our existence is a series of conflicts, contradictions, a process of struggle, pain, fleeting joy, momentary satisfaction. We are bound by so·many adjustments, conformities, patterns, and there is never a moment of freedom, never a sense of complete being. There is always frustration because there is always the seeking to fulfill. We have no tranquillity of mind, but are always tortured by various demands. So, to understand all these problems and go beyond them, it is surely necessary that we begin by understanding the nature of knowledge and the process of the mind.

Knowledge implies a sense of accumulation, does it not? Knowledge can be acquired, and because of its nature, knowledge is always partial, it is never complete; therefore, all action springing from knowledge is also partial, incomplete. I think we must see that very clearly.

I hesitate to go on because if we are to understand as we go along, we must commune with each other, and I am not sure there is any communion between us. Communion implies understanding, not only the significance of the words, but also the meaning beyond the words, does it not? If your mind and the speaker's mind are moving together in understanding, with sensitivity, then there is a possibility of real communion with each other. But if you are merely listening to find out at the end of the talk what I mean by knowledge, then we are not in communion. You are merely waiting for a definition, and definitions, surely, are not the way of understanding.

So the question arises: What is understanding? What is the state of the mind that understands? When you say, "I understand," what do you mean by it? Understanding is not mere intellection; it is not the outcome of argumentation, it has nothing to do with acceptance, denial, or conviction. On the contrary, acceptance, denial, and conviction prevent understanding. To understand, surely, there must be a state of attention in which there is no sense of comparison or condemnation, no waiting for a further development of the thing we are talking about, in order to agree or disagree. There is an abeyance or suspension of all opinion, of all sense of condemnation or comparison; you are just listening to find out. Your approach is one of inquiry, which means that you don't start from a conclusion; therefore, you are in a state of attention, which is really listening.

Now, is it possible, in such a large crowd, to commune with each other? I would like to go into this problem of knowledge, however difficult, because if we can understand the problem of knowledge, then I think we shall be able to go beyond the mind; and in going beyond or transcending itself, the mind may be without limitation, that is, without effort, which places a limitation on consciousness. Unless we go beyond the mechanistic process of the mind, real creativeness is obviously impossible, and what is necessary, surely, is a mind that is creative so that it is able to deal with all these multiplying problems. To understand what is knowledge and go beyond the partial, the limited, to experience that which is creative requires not just a moment of perception but a continuous awareness, a continuous state of inquiry in which there is no conclusion—and this, after all, is intelligence.

So, if you are listening, not merely with your ears, but with a mind that really wishes to understand, a mind that has no authority, that does not start with a conclusion or a quotation, that has no desire to be proved right, but is aware of these innumerable problems and sees the necessity of solving them directly—if that is the state of your mind, then I think we can commune with each other. Otherwise you will merely be left with a lot of words.

As I was saying, all knowledge is partial, and any action born of knowledge is also partial, and therefore contradictory. If you are at all aware of yourself, of your activities, of your motivations, of your thoughts and desires, you will know that you live in a state of self-contradiction—"I want" and at the same time "I do not want; this I must do, that I must not do," and so on and so on. The mind is in a state of contradiction all the time. And the more acute the contradiction, the more confusion your action creates. That is, when there is a challenge which must be answered, which cannot be avoided, or from which you cannot escape, then your mind being in a state of contradiction, the tension of having to face that challenge forces an action; and such action produces further contradiction, further misery.

I do not know if it is clear to each one of us that we live in a state of contradiction. We talk about peace, and prepare for war. We talk about nonviolence, and are fundamentally violent. We talk about being good, and we are not. We talk about love, and we are full of ambition, competitiveness, ruthless efficiency. So there is contradiction. The action which springs from that contradiction only brings about frustration and further contradiction. Knowledge being incomplete, any action born of that knowledge is bound to be contradictory. Our problem, then, is to find a source of action which is not partial—to discover it now, so as to create an immediate action which is total and not say, "I will find it through some system, at some future time."

You see, sirs, all thought is partial; it can never be total. Thought is the response of memory, and memory is always partial because memory is the result of experience, so thought is the reaction of a mind which is conditioned by experience. All thinking, all experience, all knowledge is inevitably partial; therefore, thought cannot solve the many problems that we have. You may try to reason logically, sanely about these many problems, but if you observe your own mind you will see that your thinking is conditioned by your circumstances, by the culture in which you were born, by the food you eat, by the climate you live in, by the newspapers you read, by the pressures and influences of your daily life. You are conditioned as a communist, or a socialist, as a Hindu, a Catholic, or what you will; you are conditioned to believe or not to believe. And because the mind is conditioned by its belief or nonbelief, by its knowledge, by its experience, all thinking is partial. There is no thinking which is free.

So we must understand very clearly that our thinking is the response of memory, and memory is mechanistic. Knowledge is ever incomplete, and all thinking born of knowledge is limited, partial, never free. So there is no freedom of thought. But we can begin to discover a freedom which is not a process of thought and in which the mind is simply aware of all its conflicts and of all the influences impinging upon it.

I hope I am making myself clear.

After all, what is the aim of education as we have it now? It is to mold the mind according to necessity, is it not? Society at the present time needs a great many engineers, scientists, physicists; so through various forms of reward and compulsion, the mind is influenced to conform to that demand, and this is what we call education. Though knowledge is necessary, and we cannot do without being educated, is it possible to have knowledge and not be a slave to it? Being aware of the partial nature of knowledge, is it possible not to allow the mind to be caught in knowledge so that it is capable of total action, which is action not based on a thought, an idea?

Let me put it this way. Is there not a difference between knowledge and knowing? Knowledge, surely, is always of time, whereas knowing is not of time. Knowledge is from a source, from an accumulation, from a conclusion, while knowing is a movement. A mind that is constantly in the movement of knowing, learning, has no source from which it knows. Am I only making it more complicated?

Sirs, let us try another way. What do we mean by learning? Is there learning when you are merely accumulating knowledge, gathering information? That is one kind of learning, is it not? As a student of engineering, you study mathematics, and so on; you are learning, informing yourself about the subject. You are accumulating knowledge in order to use that knowledge in practical ways. Your learning is accumulative, additive. Now, when the mind is merely taking on, adding, acquiring, is it learning? Or is learning something entirely different? I say the additive process which we now call learning is not learning at all. It is merely a cultivation of memory, which becomes mechanical; and a mind which functions mechanically, like a machine, is not capable of learning. A machine is never capable of learning, except in the additive sense. Learning is something quite different, as I shall try to show you.

A mind that is learning never says, "I know," because knowledge is always partial, whereas learning is complete all the time. Learning does not mean starting with a certain amount of knowledge, and adding to it further knowledge. That is not learning at all; it is a purely mechanistic process. To me, learning is something entirely different. I am learning about myself from moment to moment, and the 'myself' is extraordinarily vital; it is living, moving; it has no beginning and no end. When I say, "I know myself," learning has come to an end in accumulated knowledge. Learning is never cumulative; it is a movement of knowing which has no beginning and no end.

Sirs, the problem is this: Is it possible for the mind to free itself from this mechanistic accumulation called knowledge? And can one find that out through the process of thinking? Do you understand? You and I realize that we are conditioned. If you say, as some people do, that conditioning is inevitable, then there is no problem; you are a slave, and that is the end of it. But if you begin to ask yourself whether it is at all possible to break down this limitation, this conditioning, then there is a problem; so you will have to inquire into the whole process of thinking, will you not? If you merely say, "I must be aware of my conditioning; I must think about it, analyze it in order to understand and destroy it," then you are exercising force. Your thinking, your analyzing is still the result of your background, so through your

thought you obviously cannot break down the conditioning of which it is a part.

Just see the problem first, don't ask what is the answer, the solution. The fact is that we are conditioned, and that all thought to understand this conditioning will always be partial; therefore, there is never a total comprehension, and only in total comprehension of the whole process of thinking is there freedom. The difficulty is that we are always functioning within the field of the mind, which is the instrument of thought, reasonable or unreasonable; and as we have seen, thought is always partial. I am sorry to repeat that word, but we think that thought will solve our problems, and I wonder if it will.

To me, the mind is a total thing. It is the intellect; it is the emotions; it is the capacity to observe, distinguish; it is that center of thought which says, "I will" and "I will not"; it is desire; it is fulfillment. It is the whole thing, not something intellectual apart from the emotional. We exercise thought as a means of resolving our problems. But thought is not the means of resolving any of our problems because thought is the response of memory, and memory is the result of accumulated knowledge as experience. Realizing this, what is the mind to do? Do you understand the problem?

I am full of ambition, the desire for power, position, prestige, and I also feel that I must know what love is; so I am in a state of contradiction. A man who is after power, position, prestige, has no love at all, though he may talk about it; and any integration of the two is impossible, however much he may desire it. Love and power cannot join hands. So what is the mind to do? Thought, we see, will only create further contradictions, further misery. So, can the mind be aware of this problem without introducing thought into it at all? Do you understand, or am I talking Greek?

Sirs, let me put it in still another way. Has it ever happened to you—I am sure it has—that you suddenly perceive something, and in that moment of perception you have no problems at all? The very moment you have perceived the problem, the problem has completely ceased. Do you understand, sirs? You have a problem, and you think about it, argue with it, worry over it; you exercise every means within the limits of your thought to understand it. Finally you say, "I can do no more." There is nobody to help you to understand, no guru, no book. You are left with the problem, and there is no way out. Having inquired into the problem to the full extent of your capacity, you leave it alone. Your mind is no longer worried, no longer tearing at the problem, no longer saying, "I must find an answer"; so it becomes quiet, does it not? And in that quietness you find the answer. Hasn't that sometimes happened to you? It is not an enormous thing. It happens to great mathematicians, scientists, and people experience it occasionally in everyday life. Which means what? The mind has exercised fully its capacity to think, and has come to the edge of all thought without having found an answer; therefore, it becomes quiet—not through weariness, not through fatigue, not by saying, "I will be quiet and thereby find the answer." Having already done everything possible to find the answer, the mind becomes spontaneously quiet. There is an awareness without choice, without any demand, an awareness in which there is no anxiety; and in that state of mind there is perception. It is this perception alone that will resolve all our problems.

Again, let me put the problem differently. When we are concerned with the mind, we have to inquire into consciousness, have we not, because the mind is consciousness. The mind is not only intellect, feeling, desire, frustration, fulfillment, despair, but also the totality of consciousness, which includes the unconscious. Most of us function superficially on the conscious level. When you go to the office day after day from 10 to 5, or whatever it is, year in and year out, with a terrible sense of boredom, you are functioning automatically, like a machine, in the upper layers of consciousness, are you not? You have learned a trade or a profession, and your conscious mind is functioning at that level, while below there is the unconscious mind. Consciousness is like a deep, wide, swift-flowing river. On the surface many things are happening, and there are many reflections, but that is obviously not the whole river. The river is a total thing; it includes what is below as well as what is above. It is the same with consciousness, but very few of us know what is taking place below. Most of us are satisfied if we can live fairly well, with some security and a little happiness on the surface. As long as we have a little food and shelter, a little puja, little gods and little joys, our playing around on the surface is good enough for us. Because we are so easily satisfied, we never inquire into the depths; and perhaps the depths are stronger, more powerful, more urgent in their demands than what is happening on top. So there is a contradiction between what is transpiring on the surface and what is going on below. Most of us are aware of this contradiction only when there is a crisis because the surface mind has so completely adjusted itself to the environment. The surface mind has acquired the new Western culture, with its parliamentarianism, and all that business, but down below there is still the ancient residue, the racial instincts, the silent motivations that are constantly demanding, urging. These things are so deep down that we do not ordinarily feel them, and we do not inquire into them because we have no time. Hints of them are often projected into the conscious mind as dreams—which I am not going into for the time being.

So, the mind is that whole thing, but most of us are content to do no more than function on the surface. It is only in moments of great crisis that we are aware of this deep contradiction within ourselves, and then we want to escape from it, so we go to the temple, to a guru, or we turn on the radio, or do something else. All escapes, whether through God or through the radio, are fundamentally the same.

There is, then, a contradiction in consciousness; and any effort to resolve that contradiction, or to escape from it, places a further limitation on consciousness.

Sirs, I am talking about the same thing all the time in different ways. We are concerned with the mind, and how the mind, being educated in knowledge, in the partial, is to be aware of the total, because only when the mind is aware of the total is there a comprehension in which the problem ceases.

Am I explaining it sufficiently clearly, so that we can proceed without further laboring the point?

All thinking is limited because thinking is the response of memory—memory as experience, memory as the accumulation of knowledge—and it is mechanistic. Being mechanistic, thinking will not solve our problems. This does not mean that we must stop thinking. But an altogether new factor is necessary. We have tried various methods and systems, various ways—the congress way, the socialist way, the religious way—and they have all failed. Man is still in misery; he is still groping, seeking in the torture of despair, and there is seemingly no end to his sorrow. So there must be a totally new factor which is not recognizable by the mind. Do you follow?

You don't understand, sirs, so please don't nod your heads.

Surely, the mind is the instrument of recognition, and anything that the mind recognizes is already known; therefore, it is not the new. It is still within the field of thought, of memory, and hence mechanistic. So the mind must be in a state where it perceives without the process of recognition.

Now, what is that state? It has nothing to do with thought; it has nothing to do with recognition. Recognition and thought are mechanistic. It is, if I may put it this way, a state of perception and nothing else—that is, a state of being.

Am I only complicating it further?

Look, sirs, most of us are petty people, with very shallow minds, and the thinking of a narrow, shallow mind can only lead to further misery. A shallow mind cannot make itself deep; it will always be shallow, petty, envious. What it can do is to realize the fact that it is shallow, and not make an effort to alter it. The mind sees that it is conditioned and has no urge to change that conditioning because it understands that any compulsion to change is the result of knowledge, which is partial; therefore, it is in a state of perception. It is perceiving *what is*. But generally what happens? Being envious, the mind exercises thought to get rid of envy, thereby creating the opposite as nonenvy, but it is still within the field of thought. Now, if the mind perceives the state of envy without condemning or accepting it, and without introducing the desire to change, then it is in a state of perception; and that very perception brings about a new movement, a new element, a totally different quality of being.

You see, sirs, words, explanations, and symbols are one thing, and being is something entirely different. Here we are not concerned with words, we are concerned with being—being what we actually are, not dreaming of ourselves as spiritual entities, the atma and all that nonsense, which is still within the field of thought, and therefore partial. What matters is being what you are—envious—and perceiving that totally, and you can perceive it totally only when there is no movement of thought at all. The mind is the movement of thought—and it is also the state in which there is complete perception, without the movement of thought. Only that state of perception can bring about a radical change in the ways of our thinking, and then thinking will not be mechanistic.

So, what we are concerned with is, surely, to be aware of this whole process of the mind, with its limitations, and not make an effort to remove those limitations—to see completely, totally *what is*. You cannot see totally *what is* unless all thinking is in abeyance. In that state of awareness there is no choice, and only that state can resolve our problems.

February 17, 1960

Third Talk in New Delhi

If I may, I would like to think aloud about the "what to do," not only in the present, but also in the future, and to consider with you the whole significance of action. But before going into that, I think we must be very clear that I am not trying to persuade you to take any particular form of action, to do this or to do that; for all persuasion, which is propaganda, whether it be considered good or bad, is essentially destructive. So let us keep very clearly in mind that you and I are thinking out the problem together, and that we are not concerned with any particular form of action, either with what to do tomorrow or with what to do today; but if we can understand the total implication of action, then perhaps we shall be able to work out the details.

Without understanding comprehensively the full significance of action, merely to be concerned with a particular form of action

seems to me very destructive. Surely, if we are concerned only with the part and not with the whole, then all action is destructive action. But if we can understand action as a total thing, if we can feel our way into it and capture its significance, then that understanding of total action will bring about right action in the particular. It is like looking at a tree. The tree is not just the leaf, the branch, the flower, the fruit, the trunk, or the root. It is a total thing. To feel the beauty of a tree is to be aware of its wholeness—the extraordinary shape of it, the depth of its shadow, the flutter of its leaves in the wind. Unless we have the feeling of the whole tree, merely looking at a single leaf will mean very little. But if we have the feeling of the whole tree, then every leaf, every twig has meaning, and we are sensitive to it. After all, to be sensitive to the beauty of something is to perceive the totality of it. The mind that is thinking in terms of a part can never perceive the whole. In the whole the part is contained, but the part will never make up the whole, the total.

In the same way, let us see if we can rather diligently and with a sense of humility go into this whole question of what is action. Why does action create so much conflict? Why does action bring about a state of contradiction? And what is the totality of action? If we can sensitively and with hesitancy begin to understand the nature of total action, then perhaps we shall be able to come down to the particular.

But very few of us are sensitive—sensitive to the sunset, sensitive to a child in the street, sensitive to the beauty of a face, sensitive to an idea, to a noise, to everything in life. Surely, it is only a humble mind, a mind which does not deny or accept—it is only such a mind that is sensitive to the whole. The mind is not sensitive if it has no humility, and without humility there is no investigation, exploration, understanding. But humility is not a thing to be cultivated. Cultivated virtue is a horror; it is no longer a virtue. So, if we can, with that natural feeling of humility in which there is sensitivity, go into this whole question of action, then perhaps a great deal will be revealed of which we are now unaware.

You see, the difficulty with most of us is that we want a definition, a conclusion, an answer; we have an end in view. I think such an attitude prevents inquiry. And inquiry into action is necessary, surely, because all living is action. Action is not departmental or partial; it is a total thing. Action is our relationship to everything: to people, to nature, to ideas, to things. Life cannot be without action. Even though you retire to a monastery, or become a sannyasi, or a hermit in the Himalayas, you are still in action because you are still in relationship.

And action, surely, is not a matter of right and wrong. It is only when action is partial, not total, that there is right and wrong.

Sirs, don't accept or deny this. We are going into it.

So-called right action belongs to the respectability of society, and society is always in a state of corruption. What it considers good is partial; and what it considers evil is also partial.

I do not know if you have ever considered energy. All life is energy, is it not? Thinking, feeling, hunger, lust, ambition, the desire to fulfill with its shadow of frustration and sorrow—all this is the process of energy. There is energy from a center, and energy which has no center. What we call action is always in the form of energy expanding from a center—the center being a bundle of ideas, knowledge, experiences, memories, conclusions, definitions, and patterns of action; the "I will" and "I will not." For most of us, action is from that center—which is one of our basic problems.

And why is it that, however active we are—planning, writing, probing, exploring, creating new ideas, bringing about new inventions—the mind is in a state of constant deterioration? And if the mind is in a state of deterioration, then any action springing from that state is inevitably destructive. So why is the mind always caught in this wave of deterioration?

I do not know if you have thought about this problem, or if you have examined your own mind. When you are very young, full of vitality, eagerness, innocence, there is a delight in everything; all the common things have meaning. But as you grow older your mind becomes dull because it has been educated to accept life in terms of society and to adjust itself to that pattern. We all know this. Very few of us ever stop to look in silence at a tree or at the evening sky. Our minds are chattering, deteriorating all the time. Why? Why is there no innocence—not the cultivated innocence of a clever mind that wants to be innocent, but that state of innocence in which there is no denial or acceptance, and in which the mind just sees *what is?* In this state of innocence there is moving, unbounded energy. But we grow old in the pattern of society, with its ambitions, frustrations, joys, sorrows; our minds become more and more dull, and when old age comes upon us, we are destroyed. Why?

Now, we are not asking why in order to find an answer, but we shall find the truth when we examine the problem. The problem is never apart from the answer; the problem is the answer. If I examine the problem, if I am sympathetic, sensitive to the problem, if I look into it, explore it, I begin to understand it; and the understanding of the problem is the dissolution of the problem. But when the mind seeks an answer, it moves away from the problem—which is what most of us do. Then the answer is merely an escape from the problem, and therefore the problem pursues us. So, when we ask why, it is merely to inquire into the problem, which is to study the mind in movement.

Why is it that the minds of most of us are constantly in a state of decay? Any fine machine that is well-oiled and highly tuned functions with a minimum of friction and does not soon wear out. But where there is friction, where there is conflict, struggle, there is deterioration. Conflict is deterioration, and it is because most of us are in a state of contradiction, which is conflict, that we are always caught in a wave of deterioration. And is it possible to live without this conflict, this deterioration? If you say conflict is natural, human, and therefore inevitable, there is no problem; you accept conflict and go on deteriorating. But the moment you question it, there is a problem into which you are beginning to inquire.

As we have seen, all life is action; living is action, thinking is action, and not-thinking is also action. And we also see that any action from a center creates conflict. When the mind is tethered to a center, naturally it is not free; it can move only within the limits of that center.

Sirs, the function of these talks is not to enable you to gather new ideas—because I do not think new ideas ever fundamentally change man—but to point out the importance of observing your own minds. If you are constantly aware of the way you are thinking, the way you are feeling, the manner of your whole being, whatever it is, then that very observation is enough. Do you know what I mean? If you see and understand something totally, there is no real problem. It is like studying a map. Once you know where all the roads are and the distance to a particular village or town, then getting there is a secondary problem. But it requires that you do look at the map, that you study it with close attention. In the same way we should regard what we are discussing because mere intellectual acceptance or denial of what is being said does not alter the fact that, for most of us, action springs from a center to which we

are committed and is therefore productive of everlasting contradiction, conflict.

I wonder if we have ever considered why most human beings want to belong to something, why they want to commit themselves to something, or be part of something? There is in most of us this compulsion to belong to an organization or group, to follow a particular philosophy or pattern of action. Have you ever examined this compulsion in yourself? Are you at all aware of why it exists, why you have the desire to commit yourself to something? For example, you all think of yourselves as Indians, and you are committed to that idea. Why? Or you say you are a Christian, a Buddhist, a Muslim, a communist, or something else. Why? Why this urge to be committed to something—to a philosophy, to a discipline, to a belief? Is it not based on the desire to be secure? Please do not deny or accept it; just look at it. Belonging to something, committing yourself to something gives you an activity in which you feel safe, secure, because others are also taking part in that activity; it makes you feel that you are not in a state of isolation. So that is part of the center from which you are acting.

As we can see if we observe, all our activity springs from a center. As I pointed out just now, one is acting from a center in committing oneself to a group, to a cause, to a belief or ideology; and there is also the center of action which is knowledge—knowledge as experience, knowledge of what has been and of what one thinks will be.

I wonder if you are following this, not just the words, but are you actually seeing that you have committed yourself to something, and that from that commitment all your action springs? That commitment invariably creates contradiction, conflict, because you are limiting energy. Life is relationship, and relationship is action. There is no human being who is isolated. If he is isolated, he is dead; he is paralyzed within the fortress of his own ideas. As all relationship is action, and action is the movement of life, why is it necessary to have a center from which to act? Do you follow, sirs, what I mean? I think it is important to understand this.

We generally act from an idea, do we not? Let us examine that a little bit. We act from an idea. First there is the idea, and then action in conformity with that idea; or rather, there is an effort to approximate action to the idea, or to bridge the gap between them—the idea being a reaction, a response from the background of experience, of knowledge, of tradition, and so on.

Now, we are asking ourselves: Is it possible to act without an idea? Please, it sounds quite crazy—but I am not at all sure that the man acting with an idea is not crazy because he creates conflict, and that which is in conflict brings about its own destruction. When you have an idea from which you are acting, there is a contradiction because the idea is separate from action. Your mind is in a state of conflict, and a mind in conflict is in the process of deterioration. And yet most of us spend our whole life approximating action to an idea, which is called the ideal.

So, if you examine it closely, you will see that the ideal is a factor of deterioration—which none of you are willing to see because you have been trained from childhood to accept an ideal. But merely to deny the ideal is still within the field of the opposites, and that also is action arising from an idea.

I do not know if you are following this. Surely, a mind that is pursuing an ideal, however noble or ridiculous, is actually pursuing its own projection. Such a mind is in contradiction with itself, and a mind in contradiction with itself is fundamentally in a state of deterioration.

Now, can you look at this fact quite dispassionately? Can you perceive the truth that a self-contradictory mind, a mind caught up in conflict, is in a state of deterioration? That is obviously a fact, though you may translate or explain it in different ways. And can the mind, having been trained to accept and approximate itself to an ideal—which creates conflict, a contradiction—see that it is in a state of deterioration? Can you look at that fact and perceive the truth of it?

Surely, all conflict, at any level, in any form, is destructive, whether it be conflict between people, between desires, or between ideas. And it is of the utmost importance that the mind, which has grown into the habit of conflict, should see the truth of this because the liberating factor is the perception of what is true, and not the practice of what is true. Perceiving the truth is one thing, and practicing the truth is another. The practicing of what is true will never liberate the mind from deterioration because such a practice is a mechanical process in which action is approximating itself to an idea—which is the very cause of conflict. But if you perceive the truth that all conflict at any level is destructive, then quite a different process is taking place; then there is no center from which you are acting according to an idea.

I do not know if we are meeting. I think it is very important for you and me to commune with each other about this matter, and understand it. Our education, our morality, our virtue, our seeking God, and all the rest of it, is based on effort, discipline, control, subjugation, which is a process of torturing oneself; and a mind that is tortured, distorted by discipline, corrupted by the effort to be or to become, cannot receive or understand that immense energy which is without effort, which has no beginning and no end.

So it is very important for each of us to perceive what is true. And what does it mean to perceive the truth of something? I wonder if you have ever seen anything without giving it a name. I wonder if you have ever watched a bird on the wing without saying that it is a parrot or a sparrow. I wonder if you have ever looked at a face without saying that it is your wife, or your friend, or your uncle. I wonder if you have ever observed yourself without attributing to yourself a quality, without saying, "I am in I.C.S., a big man," or "I am a little man, and I must be something else."

Surely, beauty and the perception of beauty is that state of mind in which there is a total absence or abnegation of the center. When you see a beautiful mountain in all its majesty against the sky, for a moment the center is driven away, and you are face to face with something tremendous, magnificent, which has no word. In that state there is a vast appreciation of what is beautiful. It is a state of perception in which all meaning, all virtue, everything is. The mind perceives totally, and that is liberation—that is the very essence of intelligence.

But the mind cannot perceive totally if there is either acceptance or denial, either condemnation or identification. Do listen to what I am saying, not merely verbally, but give your heart to it so that you are listening with your whole being, for only then will you understand the significance of perception in the sense in which I am using the word. The mind that has not committed itself to any pattern of behavior, to any political party, to any country, to any tradition, but is totally outside of all these things—it is only such a mind that can perceive what is true. It is not a question of how an unperceiving mind can learn to perceive; there is no practice, no method, no system by which to awaken perception. All that the mind can say is, "I do not perceive," full stop. If you know you are unperceiving, then the question is: Why? Not that you are trying to find an answer, but you are giving your full attention; that is all. You are giving your full attention, which means that your mind is alive, open to everything.

So you begin to see that your mind is conditioned to ideals, conditioned to think, to act, to feel from a center. Living in this way does create a state of contradiction, conflict, and such a mind inevitably deteriorates. Now, if you see that to be a fact, then the fact itself is sufficient. You know, having an opinion about a fact is very different from understanding a fact. The mind that understands a fact has no opinion about it—it is so. But a mind that has an opinion about a fact will never understand the fact.

Take what is happening in this country: starvation, appalling poverty, complete degradation, the utter lack of human dignity. All the politicians belonging to the various parties say they want to solve these problems, and each party has its own method, its own leaders who say, "We will solve these problems in our way." To them the system is much more important than the fact of starvation. They are committed to the system, and from that commitment they act. The party, the system being their center of action, they are incapable of forgetting their ugly, corruptive ambitions and all the horrors which prevent the solution of the problem of starvation. If all of us get together and say, "Let us solve this problem," it can be solved. But we are nationalists, Europeans, Asiatics, communists, capitalists, and so starvation goes on.

So, if we can look at the fact without the screen of what we are committed to, then the fact itself awakens the intelligence which will bring about right action. We cannot look at the fact with a mind that is committed to an ideal, and is therefore in conflict, in a state of corruption. To look at the fact, we must have no commitments, and then perception is intelligence; and intelligence will act in its own way, at the right time, with the right method.

So, we are concerned with action. When action is from a center, energy is limited, and therefore in a state of contradiction. When action is without a center, energy is limitless, unchanging, immortal; it is the movement of that reality which has no beginning and no end. What matters is to be aware of the center without any choice, that is, simply to be aware of our commitments—our commitments to the political party, to knowledge, to experience, to desire—without any struggle, without any denial of what we are committed to. I assure you, just to be aware of the center from which one is acting has much more significance and is much more potent than the desire to get rid of or to modify it. You see, the mind which is not in a state of contradiction is an innocent mind because it does not have any sense of a center. Surely, innocency is the quality of a mind in which the 'me', the self, the accumulative factor is not; and only such a mind can receive that energy which has no beginning and no end, that extraordinary something—call it reality, God, or what you will, the name does not matter very much.

Our problem, then, is to understand how energy gets caught in a center from which all action takes place, thereby creating contradiction and misery. The understanding of the problem is the resolution of the problem. And then you will find, as you go deeply into it, that there is action without an idea, an action which is born of perception; and the beauty of it is that it has no before or after; it is a timeless, immeasurable state.

February 21, 1960

Fourth Talk in New Delhi

If I may, I would like to think aloud with you about authority, fear, pleasure, and love, and try to go into it all rather deeply and comprehensively. Perhaps in this process each one of us will be aware of his own fears and pleasures, and of what he calls love, so that together we can find out what is implied in these things and whether it is at all possible to be free of fear. Because fear, of which one may be conscious or unconscious, is really a dreadful thing; it is most destructive, enervating, and leads to constant misery.

But before we go into that, I think we should be very clear in ourselves with regard to the approach we are going to take in examining these things. The approach is very important—how we look at a problem, how we understand it. Surely, true examination, true exploration is possible only when we go beyond mere verbalization. If we are limited to words, we are not really capable of exploring, and words then prevent full comprehension.

So we must examine what we mean by the word, must we not? The word is only a symbol; it represents an object, or something which we think and feel. The word and the object are two different things, but for most of us the word unconsciously becomes the thing. A word like *Hindu* or *Muslim* is a symbol which represents in your mind a certain type of human being, and for you the word is not separate from the person; like his name, that word awakens in your mind an image of the person, with certain qualities and characteristics, and the word becomes the person.

Now, I think it is essential to understand that the word is not the thing. The word *tree* is not the tree; it is only a symbol which conveys the idea of the tree. But for most of us, the word is the thing, and therefore the word has assumed great importance. We think in terms of words, of symbols; and I wonder if we ever think without words, without symbols?

If we are to examine this problem of fear and find out whether the mind is capable of being really free from fear—which means going most profoundly into the untrodden recesses of the mind where fear lurks—we must begin, it seems to me, by understanding that the word is not the thing. The word *fear,* or *love,* or *authority* is not the thing it represents.

Most of us have an intense urge to follow, and either we are unaware of this urge or we think it is natural, inevitable. In any case, it has become an extraordinary factor in our lives, and unless we are following something or somebody, we feel lost. We follow a guru, an ideal, a leader, or a political party, and this urge to follow is the basis of authority, is it not? "I do not know, but you know, so I will follow you. To me you are the embodiment of what I consider to be knowledge or wisdom, and therefore I follow you." Or I want power, position, prestige—political or religious—so I join the group which offers me these things and follow its leader, who is going to help me achieve what I want in the name of peace, and all the rest of it. So, unless we understand this urge—the urge to follow, to be right, to be successful, to achieve a result—we shall not understand fear; and the urge is different from the word.

Sirs, unless you really apply this to yourselves, you won't be able to penetrate very deeply into the problem of fear.

Now, how does one look at a fact about oneself? Have you at any time really faced a disturbing fact about yourself? Or have you denied it, covered it up, found excuses for it, run away from it? Have you ever said to yourself, "I am a liar," or "I am quite a stupid person," without bringing into it extraneous excuses, justifications, or condemnations? To say to oneself, "This is what I am," and stop there—surely, that is facing the fact of what one is. But to most of us that is completely unacceptable because we live in a state of idealization, romanticism, of trying to become something which we are not. So, to face a disturbing fact about ourselves becomes an extraordinarily difficult problem.

You know, we are living in a monstrously stupid society and seeing a desperately poor man when you yourself have just put on a good suit of clothes, you must feel, if you are at all sensitive, a sense of guilt. And the more sensitive you are, the more acute is that feeling. Now, is it possible to be aware of that sense of guilt, to face the fact and see all its implications, and not look away or try to do something about it? Because any action with regard to the fact is an avoidance of the understanding of the fact.

Please, this is important to understand. I do hope you are following it and that I am making myself clear. Because, unless we are able to look at a fact, there is no possibility of that fact bringing about its own right action. You know, as we said this morning when a few of us were discussing, a material has its own discipline. Do you understand? When you are working with a material, that material has its own discipline. You may make a pot, but you cannot paint a picture with clay. In the same way, if you do not understand the fact, but try instead to do something about it, you are introducing a factor which is not inherent in the fact. We will see it more clearly as we go along.

To most of us, following somebody or something—an ideal, a precept, a goal, a political or religious leader—has become very important. We follow thoughtlessly, and we never find out why we follow. Without looking at the fact, we say, "It is natural, it is human, it is inevitable to follow; it leads me to success. Besides, what would become of me if I did not follow somebody, or some ideal? I would be lost." Such explanations prevent us from looking simply at the fact that we follow. But if we do look at the fact that we follow, without justifying or condemning it, then the fact, which is the material, has its own discipline and its own action.

Sirs, I feel that the mind can be totally free from fear. And fear is a most destructive, corrupting element, is it not? I am merely stating it as a fact, not as a condemnation. When the mind is afraid, it is not capable of thinking clearly, feeling deeply; it is not capable of perception. It sets going various inhibitions, conflicts, and destructive responses. If the mind is not really free from fear, then the urge to follow, which is the demand for authority, is established; therefore, the mind becomes a slave to something—to a leader, to a political organization, to a religious belief, and so on.

Sirs, unless you are alertly observing your own minds, what is being said will sound very complicated and very difficult; but it is not. The real difficulty is that most of us are not at all sensitive. We live on the surface—going to the office, quarreling over sex, pursuing the casual pleasures—and with that we are satisfied. But if we want to find out how to free the mind from fear, we have got to understand this question of authority—authority at every level, whether it is the authority of the policeman who asks you to keep to the left, or the authority of the government, or the authority of the priest, or the authority of your own mind, which has accumulated experience and knowledge, and acts according to the dictates of that background. As long as the mind is a slave to authority, imposed or self-created, it is incapable of understanding the full depth of fear and being free of it.

Now, what is fear? Let us explore it a little bit. I am not talking of any one particular fear—fear of darkness, fear of losing one's job, fear of a snake, fear of tradition, of public opinion, fear of death, fear of pain, and so on. These fears are all in relation to some particular thing, are they not? But I am talking of fear in relation to everything, not in relation to just one particular thing. If we understand profoundly the central fact of fear, we can then be free of fear in relation to everything and thereby bring about a mind that is intelligent.

Most people are afraid of death, are they not? And the older we grow, the more there is this nightmare of fear. I am not discussing death—we will talk about that some other time. But fear of the fact of death is not something that you can analyze and be free of. Do you understand what I mean?

I do not know if you have ever analyzed yourself, analyzed your own feelings and ideas. If you have, you will know what is implied in analysis—not the analysis done by a professional psychiatrist or psychologist, but self-analysis. In the process of analyzing yourself, as you will have found if you have ever done it, there is always the analyzer and the analyzed, with the analyzer assuming a position of authority as the one who knows.

Is all this becoming rather complicated? I hope not. But if we would understand this nightmare—this dark shadow of fear—I am afraid we have to go through all this. It isn't child's play to be free of fear; it's not just a matter of saying, "I won't be afraid." You have to observe and understand the extraordinary complications of the thing called fear, and I am only pointing out that analysis is not the way. I may analyze myself and see that I want to follow because, without following somebody or something, I am afraid that I shall go astray. But the fear of going astray is much stronger than the process of analysis, and after analyzing myself, I find that I am still afraid. So analysis, whether done by oneself or by another, merely maintains fear at a deeper or a different level. Analysis, then, is not the way to resolve fear.

Now, what is fear? Surely, fear is always within the field of time. I am afraid of dying—dying the next moment, or ten years later. The thought of tomorrow, with its uncertainty, and the thought of yesterday, with its pleasures and its pains, creates a web of fear. Sirs, have you ever noticed that you are not afraid of something with which you are instantly faced? If in going round a corner you suddenly meet a snake, the body responds immediately, it instinctively jumps away; there is no fear because there is no time to think. But the moment you begin to think, fear comes into being.

Most of us, surely, have experienced lying, not telling the truth—and we do it because we don't want to be found out, we don't want to expose ourselves to criticism, so fear is at the bottom of our inaccurate statement. That is, the mind foresees what it is going to be asked and is prepared and willing to lie in order to cover up what it is afraid to acknowledge. If you observe yourself you will see that fear always, under all circumstances, involves time, yesterday and tomorrow—the thing that may happen tomorrow, or the thing that was done yesterday, which may be discovered and condemned at any moment. So, fear is essentially a process of time.

Sirs, instead of taking notes, or memorizing words, I wish you would actually watch your own minds in operation. You are all afraid, aren't you? If you were not, you wouldn't be sitting here. I do not know if you have ever thought about it, but a really happy man is not afraid—not the man who is happy because he has a few things, but a supremely happy man who is inwardly rich with the eternal virtues, who never seeks God, never goes to a temple. But most of us, unfortunately, are not in that position. Most of us are afraid in one way or another, at a superficial level or very deeply. And may I suggest that you look at your own fear, whether it is the fear of your boss, of your wife or husband, of public opinion, of losing your job or your health, of death, of not being one of the important ministers, or what you will. Just watch your own fear and you will see, if you observe very carefully, that it

involves time—the feeling that you might not be or become something, that you must change and might not be able to, and so on. So time is the factor of fear: time as yesterday, today, and tomorrow; time as the past functioning in the present and bringing about the future; time by the clock, as well as time inwardly, psychologically.

So, the mind can be free of fear only when it is capable of freeing itself from time—which is to see the fact, to face the fact, and not try to change the fact. Please, this is important to understand because if you can at the end of this talk get up with that sense of freedom from fear, then you will know what love is. Then you will know what joy is, and you will be a human being mature with dignity and clarity and character. Character is clarity. A mind that is afraid is never clear. That is why it is important to understand how to look at a fact, and to find out what makes the mind give to the fact the quality of time. The fact is you are afraid, and you see that fact, but you have introduced the quality of time by saying, "I must change the fact, I must do something about it, I must be courageous." All such thinking introduces the factor of time because change is in time. So, to look at a fact without explanations, justification, or condemnation implies the cessation of time.

Do please listen to this. It is not complicated. It demands attention, and attention has its own discipline. You don't have to introduce a system of discipline. You know, sirs, what this world needs is not politicians, or more engineers, but free human beings. Engineers and scientists may be necessary, but it seems to me that what the world needs is human beings who are free, who are creative, who have no fear; and most of us are ridden with fear. If you can go profoundly into fear and really understand it, you will come out with innocency, so that your mind is clear. That is what we need, and that is why it is very important to understand how to look at a fact, how to look at your fear. That is the whole problem—not how to get rid of fear, not how to be courageous, not what to do about fear, but to be fully with the fact.

Sirs, you want to be fully, totally with the wave of pleasure, don't you? And you are. When you are in the moment of pleasure, there is no condemnation, no justification, no denial. There is no factor of time at the moment of experiencing pleasure; physically, sensually, your whole being vibrates with it. Isn't that so? When you are in the moment of experiencing, there is no time, is there? When you are intensely angry, or when you are full of lust, there is no time. Time comes in, thought comes in only after the moment of experiencing, and then you say, "By Jove, how nice," or "How terrible." If it was nice, you want more of it; if it was terrible, fearful, you want to avoid it; therefore, you begin to explain, to justify, to condemn, and these are the factors of time which prevent you from looking at the fact.

Now, have you ever faced fear? Please listen to the question carefully. Have you ever looked at fear? Or, in the moment of being aware of fear, are you already in a state of flight from the fact? I will go into it a little bit, and you will see what I mean.

We name, we give a term to our various feelings, don't we? In saying, "I am angry," we have given a term, a name, a label to a particular feeling. Now, please watch your own minds very clearly. When you have a feeling, you name that feeling—you call it anger, lust, love, pleasure. Don't you? And this naming of the feeling is a process of intellection which prevents you from looking at the fact, that is, at the feeling.

You know, when you see a bird and say to yourself that it is a parrot or a pigeon or a crow, you are not looking at the bird. You have already ceased to look at the fact because

the word *parrot* or *pigeon* or *crow* has come between you and the fact.

This is not some difficult intellectual feat but a process of the mind that must be understood. If you would go into the problem of fear or the problem of authority or the problem of pleasure or the problem of love, you must see that naming, giving a label prevents you from looking at the fact. Do you understand?

You see a flower and you call it a rose, and the moment you have thus given it a name, your mind is distracted; you are not giving your full attention to the flower. So, naming, terming, verbalizing, symbolizing prevents total attention towards the fact. Right, sirs? Shall we go on? All right. We are continuing what we were talking about at the beginning. We are still asking ourselves if it is possible to be choicelessly aware of a fact, and the fact is fear.

Now, can the mind—which is addicted to symbols and whose very nature it is to verbalize—stop verbalizing and look at the fact? Don't say, "How am I to do it?" but put the question to yourself. I have a feeling, and I call it fear. By giving it a name I have related it to the past, so memory, the word, the symbol, is preventing me from looking at the fact. Now, can the mind—which in its very thought process verbalizes, gives names—look at the fact without naming it? Do you understand? Sirs, you have to find this out for yourselves, I cannot tell you. If I tell you and you do it, you will be following, and you won't be free of fear. What matters is that you should be totally free of fear, and not be half-dead human beings—corrupt, miserable people who are everlastingly afraid of their own shadow.

To understand this problem of fear, you have to go into it most profoundly because fear is not merely on the surface of the mind. Fear is not just being afraid of your neighbor, or of losing a job; it is much deeper than that, and to understand it requires deep penetration. To penetrate deeply you need a very sharp mind, and the mind is not made sharp by mere argumentation or avoidance. One has to go into the problem step by step, and that is why it is very important to comprehend this whole process of naming. When you name a whole group of people by calling them Muslims, or what you will, you have got rid of them; you don't have to look at them as individuals, so the name, the word has prevented you from being a human being in relationship with other human beings. In the same way, when you name a feeling, you are not looking at the feeling, you are not totally with the fact.

You see, sirs, where there is fear there is no love. Where there is fear, do what you will—go to all the temples in the world, follow all the gurus, repeat the Gita every day—you will never find reality, you will never be happy, you will remain immature human beings. The problem is to comprehend fear, not how to get rid of fear. If you merely want to get rid of fear, then take a pill which will tranquilize you, and go to sleep. There are innumerable forms of escape from fear, but if you escape, run away, fear will follow you everlastingly. To be fundamentally free of fear, you must understand this process of naming, and realize that the word is never the thing. The mind must be capable of separating the word from the feeling, and must not let the word interfere with direct perception of the feeling, which is the fact.

When you have gone so far, penetrated so deeply, you will discover there is buried in the unconscious, in the obscure recesses of the mind, a sense of complete loneliness, of isolation, which is the fundamental cause of fear. And again, if you avoid it, if you escape from it, saying it is too fearful, if you do not go into it without giving it a name, you will never go beyond it. The mind has to come face to face with the fact of complete inward loneliness and not allow itself to do anything about that fact. That extraordinary thing called loneliness is the very essence of the self, the 'me', with all its chicaneries, its cunningness, its substitutions, its web of words in which the mind is caught. Only when the mind is capable of going beyond that ultimate loneliness is there freedom—the absolute freedom from fear. And only then will you find out for yourself what is reality, that immeasurable energy which has no beginning and no end. As long as the mind spawns its own fears in terms of time, it is incapable of understanding that which is timeless.

February 24, 1960

Fifth Talk in New Delhi

I would like this evening to talk about several things, especially about effort, discipline, and meditation. But, unfortunately, most of us are satisfied with theories; we are not concerned with being. We would rather talk about compassion than be compassionate. We would rather talk about goodness and explain why we are not good than flower in goodness. We are so easily satisfied with symbols, with ideals and cunning explanations which, when examined closely, are found to be mere words in the air.

I think it would be a great mistake if we now merely resorted to words and explanations, because what we are going to discuss is a rather complex issue. Our lives at present are very shallow, empty, and we are making a lot of noise philosophizing about that shallowness, that emptiness. We read books about it—books by well-known modern philosophers, or our own traditional books, the Gita, the Upanishads, and all the rest of it—and think we have understood the whole significance of life, with all its vastness, its beauty, its complexities. We think we are marvelously free when we have only read about freedom—which all indicates a childish sense of verbal satisfaction.

So I would like to suggest this evening that we try to uncover, if we can, some of the problems which confront us in our daily lives. We are concerned with effort, everyday effort—the ceaseless battle within ourselves, the struggle to be or not to be something, the effort involved in going to the office every day, the conflict in relationship, and the various other contradictions in our lives. To say that everyday effort does not concern us, that it is not part of a religious life, seems to me utterly wrong. So I think we must be concerned with effort, which we shall discuss presently.

There is also this whole problem of discipline—the discipline demanded by the communists and by the various other political parties, the discipline that you impose upon yourself if you are lazy, the discipline of learning a technique, and the discipline insisted upon by the books, the teachers, the gurus. All that is part of our life.

And it is also part of our life, surely, to find out what is the state of the mind that contemplates, meditates. Without knowing for ourselves the quality of a mind that meditates, that is in a state of contemplation, we miss an enormous part of life, because this contemplative state of mind is, in its very essence, sensitivity to beauty, sensitivity not just to a part but to the whole process of existence.

And we should be concerned with the whole of life, not just with a part, should we not? Politics deals only with a part; social revolution concerns itself only with a segment of the whole. In all our activities, whether bureaucratic, scientific, or what you will, we are concerned with the part and not with the whole. And if we do not understand the whole, we shall be in everlasting conflict with others and with ourselves. So it seems to me very important and most urgent that we should find out what is the quality of the mind that is in a state of meditation.

Now, we are not going to explore the so-called steps to meditation because all practice is mechanical. We are not going to say what meditation is, and what it is not. First we have to understand the mind as a whole, and then we shall come upon or discover the nature of meditation; we shall find out whether a discipline is necessary or not, and what is true effort. All this will be clear if we can understand what is the way of thinking. Because that is really our problem, is it not?—how to think. Thinking is possible, surely, only when there is room in the mind for observation. We must have space to think. The mind must be wide open in order to function freely in thought. For a limited mind cannot think freely. A mind that is free can think freely, but not the other way around. When there is open space in the mind for observation, there is contemplation. But our minds are limited, tethered to various techniques and experiences, bound to knowledge, and our space for observation is very narrow. So it is very important, surely, to understand the nature of consciousness—not only the conscious mind, but also the unconscious, which is the world of symbols. Without understanding this world of symbols, of words, of instincts, the mind is not free to observe, and therefore there is no space for contemplation.

If I may turn aside for a moment, I think it is important to understand what it means to listen, for then, perhaps, what is being said will have a meaning beyond the words. It seems to me that very few of us ever do listen. We do not know how to listen. I wonder if you have ever really listened to your child, to your wife or husband, or to a bird. I wonder if you have ever listened to the mind as it watches a sunset, or if you have read a poem with an attitude of listening. If we know how to listen, that very listening is an action in which the miracle of understanding takes place. If we know how to listen to what is being said, we shall discover whether it is true or false. And what is true, one does not have to accept—it is so. It is only when there is contention between the false and the false that there is acceptance and rejection, agreement and disagreement.

So it is important to find out how to listen. You have certain ideas about discipline, about effort, about meditation; you have various images based upon the traditional or the modern approach, and upon the experiences which you have had; and all these, surely, prevent you from listening. When the mind is comparing what is being said with what is said in the Gita, the Bible, or by another person, there is no real listening. When there is comparison, there is no understanding at all because a mind that is comparing ceases to see the fact.

So listening is quite an art—listening with your whole being. And you do listen in that way when you are tremendously interested in something. If it is a matter of getting more money or becoming famous, you listen with all your being, don't you? When you hope to get something for yourself, you are so eager that you put all comparison aside. So you do listen when it is profitable to you—and you are probably listening in that way now. But then, unfortunately, you will be listening in vain because what is being said is not profitable to you; you are not going to make money out of it, either in this world or in the next. All you have to do is to find out, uncover, discover; and that requires not only listening but an attention which is not mere concentration.

Do you know the difference between attention and concentration? A concentrated mind is not an attentive mind, but a mind that is in the state of attention can concentrate. Attention is never exclusive; it includes everything. If you are attentive as you are listening to what is being said, you are also aware of the sound of the birds, of the noise on the road, of your own posture, your own gestures, as well as of the movements of your own mind. But if you are concentrating—which involves strain, exclusion—in order to pay attention, you will find that such concentration is not conducive to understanding. I am not going to go into all that at present.

What I want to convey is that the mind is the field of symbols, the field of memory, the field of knowledge; and as long as the mind remains within its own field, it cannot function in freedom. So it seems to me that meditation is the whole process of discovering and understanding for oneself the limitations placed upon consciousness by effort, by discipline, and through this process of meditation, giving the mind space to function widely, deeply, without the boundaries of its own anxieties and fears.

We have to begin, surely, by seeing that life is infinitely wide, that it has no beginning and no end. Life has a beginning and an end only when it is 'yours', that is, when you function from a center. This center is the 'you' that pursues pleasure, the 'you' that quarrels, that is ambitious, vain, stupid, the 'you' that was born and is going to die. The mind that functions from this center is like a man who has carved out for himself a little space on the bank of a wide, deep-flowing river, and for the rest of his life remains in this little space—which is what most of us do. In this little space we meet, in this little space we cultivate virtue, in this little space we are lustful, we are vain, and all the rest of it, and we never enter into the full stream of life. All our ambitions, ideals, disciplines, controls, adjustments are in this little haven which we call our life—and just beyond it is the real life, the life which is in constant movement, which has no beginning and no end.

Now, we have to see that life as a fact, and not regard it as a theory, or say, "It sounds awfully nice, but it is not practicable." We have got to contemplate, live it every day; otherwise, we shall continue to be in a state of misery in which we now are. We are in a state of contradiction, we are confused, we are full of sorrow, inwardly poor; our joys are so empty because we have separated ourselves from that extraordinary movement of life, and we have very little touch with it. This is not a poetic simile, and what is being said is not romantic sentimentalism. I am talking about a fact which we must directly experience in our everyday life, and not regard as something which we have to strive after. So we have to understand effort.

What is effort? I do not know if you have ever thought about it. We make constant effort, do we not? In the morning you feel lazy, but when the bell rings you make an effort and get out of bed. A little later you go to the office, where again you make effort. The schoolboy makes an effort to pass a beastly examination. There is the effort to be virtuous, the effort to control one's mind, the effort to adjust in relationship, the effort to achieve an aim, and so on. For most of us, life is a process of striving, striving—a ceaseless conflict. Why? Have you ever thought about it?

Surely, most of us make effort because we are afraid that if we don't we shall become more lazy, or lose our jobs, or stagnate. So at the back of effort there is fear. Watch your own efforts, observe yourselves and you will see there is this fear of going to sleep—physically, mentally, inwardly—if you don't make effort. And we say that it is natural, that it is part of our existence to live like this. Everything around us makes effort. The tree has to make an effort to grow, and so on; therefore, effort is inevitable. But let us

go a little further into it and find out whether effort really is inevitable.

Effort implies conflict, does it not? If there were no conflict, would you make an effort? Do please consider this, go into it with me, because I want to uncover a state in which the mind functions without effort and in which it is much more alive, vastly more intelligent than a mind that makes effort. Effort implies, surely, a conflict within and without. Conflict arises because of a contradiction in oneself. If there were no self-contradiction, you would be what you are: stupid, petty, violent, envious. The discovery of what you are never creates a conflict. It is only when you want to change what you are into something else that there is self-contradiction and therefore conflict. Effort invariably implies duality, does it not?—the good and the bad, pleasure and pain, and all the rest of it. Duality is contradiction, and as long as the mind is in contradiction with itself, there must be conflict, which shows itself in effort. So our problem is not whether one can live without effort but whether it is possible to eradicate totally this state of self-contradiction. That is one problem, which we shall come to a little later.

Now, what do we mean by discipline? From childhood we are disciplined to conform, to obey the elders, to follow tradition, to imitate an example, a hero, to adjust ourselves to the established pattern. And the pattern, the hero, the tradition is always respectable—the respectable being that which is recognized as worthwhile by society.

Please do follow this, because it is a description of your own life.

Every political or religious organization inevitably contains the seed of reaction, and you can see why. The leaders have a vested interest; they are somebodies in their organization or party, and they do not want it to be broken up. They are fulfilling their ambitions in the name of peace, in the name of brotherhood, and all the rest of the nonsense that they talk. So, religious and political organizations of every kind are invariably hotbeds of reaction. They want things to go on as they are, with only slight modification.

Similarly, a mind which is organized, disciplined—discipline being suppression, conformity, imitation, fear—whether in the political or so-called religious field, is a reactionary mind. It is afraid of change, it is anxious about new ideas setting in. But this does not mean that a disorganized mind is a free mind. If you oppose the organized mind with the disorganized mind, you will not understand what I am talking about. I am talking about only one thing, which is the organized mind, the disciplined mind—the mind that imitates, conforms, follows—not its opposite. Such a mind inevitably invites fear and therefore resists every form of change, transformation, revolution. I am not using the word *revolution* in the economic, social, or political sense. Revolutions at that level are only partial; therefore, they are not revolutions at all. Revolution cannot be partial; it is something total. It has nothing whatsoever to do with religious or political beliefs, or with economic upheavals. Revolution, which is always total, is in the mind, in the quality of thinking, in the quality of being.

Most of us have been disciplined, made to conform. If you belong to a political party, the whips, the leaders make you conform to the party line. If you criticize, out you go. It is the same with religious organizations if you criticize the Pope or Shankaracharya or any of the big, influential religious leaders. So a disciplined mind resists freedom because its thought is organized to conform, to function within a pattern. A disciplined mind is incapable of inquiry because it has not the space, the freedom to find out. Your inquiry about God within the framework of discipline is no inquiry at all; it is just the muttering of

tradition. But if you would find out whether or not there is reality, that energy which has no beginning and no end, which does not belong to any belief or organized religion—if you would find that out, then your mind must understand this process of being disciplined to conform. You will also have to understand why conflict exists between the thinker and the thought.

If you observe your own mind, you will see that there is a conflict between the experiencer and the experienced, between the thinker and the thought. The thinker is the censor, the judge who says, "I must not be this, I must be that; that is pleasurable, and I must pursue it; this is painful, and I must avoid it." So there is a division between the thinker and the thought. This is an everyday fact which you know and accept, is it not? The thinker is always trying to dominate, to change the movement of thought, and this division, with its conflict, you say is an inevitable part of existence.

Now, what we are concerned with is the total elimination of conflict because a mind in conflict is a silly mind. It is like a machine that functions badly. It may be very clever in its conflict, it may produce great books, make eloquent speeches, write poems that reflect its struggle and tension, but it is not a mind that flowers in goodness; it flowers in contradiction and pain. So, we are concerned with the total elimination of conflict. It is only when the mind is free of conflict that it can be what it is, and then it is capable of an extraordinary sense of creation—which we will not go into at present.

As long as there is a thinker apart from thought, there is conflict. This division, with its conflict, you have accepted as inevitable; but is it? You say, "That is my practical experience." But even though Shankara, Buddha, and all the rest of them have said so, may I suggest that you put aside these authorities, as well as the authority of your own experience, and examine it.

Is there a thinker apart from thought? Or is there only thought, which creates the thinker? If there is no thought, there is obviously no thinker.

Please, sirs, this is not a verbal trick; it is not an argument for you to accept or reject. If you think in terms of acceptance or rejection, you are living in a false world. I am asking a question, which is: If there is no thought, where is the thinker? Because thought is fleeting, transient, in a constant state of flux; it demands a permanent entity, so thought creates the thinker. Don't you want everything to be permanent? Your job, your property, your bank account, your relationship with your wife or husband—don't you want these things to be permanent, lasting? You want your soul to continue in the hereafter; you want your way of thinking, your way of living, your comforts, your vanities to go on everlastingly. So your thought creates a permanent entity which you say is the thinker, and you give to the thinker various qualities, calling it the atma, the higher self, and all the rest of it. But it is all within the field of thought, and thought is time because thought is the reaction of memory—memory as knowledge or experience.

So thought creates the thinker, the censor, the observer. And is it possible to think without the censor? Do you understand? Is it possible to observe without the observer? Don't agree or disagree, sirs. Please, you have to find out. One direct experience of your own is worth more than all the books put together. If you can find out for yourself what is true, you can burn all the Vedas, the Upanishads, the Gita, and the Bible; they are not worth looking at.

Now, you have to find out directly for yourself whether it is possible to be in that state of thinking without the thinker, ex-

periencing without the experiencer. Please, sirs, it is not complicated. In the moment of your intense anger, is there an observer? It is only after the emotional upheaval has taken place that you say, "By Jove, I was angry." Then comes identification, and the condemnatory process begins; there is contradiction, conflict, an effort to conform to the pattern recognized by society as being respectable. Do you understand, sirs? The pattern is recognized as being respectable; otherwise, you would not try to conform to it. And respectability is a horror, an ugly thing because it opens the door to mediocrity.

So, our problem is to understand the state of the mind which is in meditation because meditation is essential—but not the meditation that most people practice sitting in a room and repeating a lot of words; that is not meditation. Repetition merely puts the mind to sleep, and you can do that very easily by taking a tranquilizer. I know you will dislike what is being said because you have found that your traditional repetition of certain words and names for ten minutes or so gradually makes your mind quiet, but it has only gone to sleep, and that is what you call meditation. You also call it meditation when you solicit, pray, beg for something for yourself, for your country, for your party, or for your family. You put forth the begging bowl of inward poverty and ask somebody to fill it. That is not meditation. Meditation is something entirely different, as you will see. The state of meditation is possible only when there is space in the mind for observation, and that space is denied to a mind which is suppressed, disciplined to conform to a pattern. A mind in the state of meditation, contemplation, is not striving to be anything.

Sirs, I am only trying to convey in different words what has been said previously. If you have not followed the talk for the last forty minutes or more, you won't understand what is being said now.

A mind in contemplation is free of symbols; it has no visions because visions are projections of that background in which it has been conditioned. A mind in contemplation is no longer making effort, as effort is generally understood; therefore, there is no observer, there is no censor. A mind in contemplation, which is the state of meditation, is completely silent, and that silence is not induced. You can discipline your mind to be silent, but that is merely conformity to a pattern in the hope of getting what you desire; therefore, it is not silence. A mind in meditation is absolutely silent, and that silence is not projected, not wished for, not cultivated. That silence is from moment to moment, it has no continuity; therefore, it cannot be practiced, it cannot be developed any more than you can develop humility. Do you understand? If you cultivate, develop humility, you are no longer humble; you don't know what humility means. Leave the cultivation of humility to the saints, to the leaders, who are full of vanity and therefore cultivate the opposite, hoping thereby to become still more respectable. The cultivation of virtue is effort in limitation, so this quality of silence is not something to be cultivated.

The mind in meditation is in a state where there is no movement of thought, and therefore no projection of the background in which it has lived. Only the mind which has understood all that we have been talking about—understood in the sense of having perceived the fact, not merely having accepted the words, the explanations, which are ashes—and is therefore completely silent with a silence that is not induced by breathing or any other trick—it is only such a mind that can know the immeasurable, the eternal, that which has no beginning and no end.

February 28, 1960

Sixth Talk in New Delhi

Before inquiring into revolution and religion, which is what I would like to talk about this evening, I think we should understand what we mean by learning. It is only when we look at facts as they actually are that we can learn about them. But most of us are incapable of looking at facts as they are without trying to interpret or do something about them. When we are confronted with a fact, most of us approach it with prejudice, with a temperamental bias, with our particular knowledge or experience, whether it be scientific, bureaucratic, business, religious, or what you will; so we never do look at the fact. And it seems to me that we can learn about anything in life only when we cease to approach the fact with conclusions, ideas, and opinions, for it is only then that the fact begins to reveal its own significance.

So I would suggest this evening that we approach the problem of religion and the problem of revolution with the intention of seeing, first of all, what the facts are, which means that we must look at them without our conditioning. This is going to be very difficult because we are so heavily conditioned—conditioned as Hindus, as Muslims, as Christians, conditioned politically, technologically, and in other ways. But if we can put aside our various conditionings and look at the facts, then I think we shall be able to learn immeasurably.

This extraordinary movement which we call life is a thing to be learned about, and in learning there is no beginning and no end. We cease to learn only when we approach life with our narrow prejudices and predilections. Life is vast, is it not? With all its beauty, its sorrows, miseries, and contradictions, its poverty, degradation, and fear, its anxieties, hopes, and despairs, life is really immeasurable; and to understand all that, we must surely have a mind that is capable of immeasurable comprehension. But unfortunately, most of us have no such comprehension, and when we are confronted with a vital problem, our response is always determined by our conditioning, by our prejudices, and so on.

So, this evening let us see if we cannot seriously, with full intent, put aside all that we know or think we know, all the things with which we are familiar, and look at the actual facts. Then, perhaps, we shall be able to learn, and learning is action. Action and learning are not separate. The movement of learning implies comprehension, seeing the significance of the problem—its width, its depth, its height. The very perception of the problem is action. Action and perception are not separate. But when we have an idea about the problem, the idea is separate from action, and then the further problem arises of how to approximate action to the idea. So, what matters is to look at the problem without fear, without anxiety, without our temperamental evaluations, for then we shall be able to learn, and that very movement of learning is action.

I think we should see this very clearly before we proceed because we must act, we must bring about a tremendous revolution in our thinking, in our morality, in our relationships. There must obviously be a radical transformation, a total revolution in all the ways of our life. But we cannot be in that state of revolution if we do not see the fundamental fact that where there is understanding there is action. Action is not separate from understanding or perception. When I understand a problem, that very understanding includes action. When I perceive deeply, that very perception brings an action of itself. But if I merely speculate, if I have an idea about the problem, then the idea is separate from action, and the further problem arises of how to carry out the idea. So let us bear very clearly in mind that understanding

is action, that understanding is not separate from action.

Now, what are the facts? One of the major facts is that, all over the world, the religious and political leaders are as confused as their followers. The religious leaders may say, "We are not confused; we have our faith, our belief; we know, we perceive what is true." But the religious leaders are Christians or Hindus or Muslims; their minds are shaped according to a pattern, conditioned by the culture in which they happen to have been brought up. Dislodge them from their conditioning, and they are completely lost. Each religious leader has a group of followers who accept his authority, and that authority is based on their mutual conditioning. No Hindu will follow the Pope, and no Catholic will follow a Hindu guru—though a Hindu who is disturbed, disillusioned, may take shelter in Christian authority, and vice versa.

So, like the political leaders, the religious leaders are fundamentally confused. They are all in a state of contradiction. Though the political leaders may talk about peace, world unity, and trot out all the rest of those easy words which they employ to exploit people, they are in confusion, in a state of contradiction. That is one fact. Another fact is that you who follow them are also confused. You choose your leaders out of your confusion, and those whom you choose out of your confusion are bound to be equally confused. The mind that is very clear in itself, that sees everything totally, in true proportion, does not follow and does not become a leader.

It is a major fact that we are all confused. Very few of us are aware of this total confusion—total in the sense that our whole being is confused. Most of us say, "We are only partially confused. There are areas in us which are very clear, and by means of this light we are trying to bring about the cessation of our partial confusion." But a confused mind can think only in terms of confusion. It may project ideas of clarity, but it is still confused, and where there is confusion, there is bound to be deterioration. You may have better agricultural methods, rockets that will go to the moon, and all the rest of it, but inwardly there is a sense of deterioration. We have tried various methods of approach to the problem of existence, and they have all failed. Religion has failed, education has failed, and politics really makes very little sense because the politician always deals with the partial, never with the totality of man. The politician is concerned with the immediate, and not with the whole of time. So there is confusion and a sense of deterioration; there is unexpressed sorrow and immense, unfathomable despair.

I do not know if you are at all aware of this fact of despair, the feeling that there is no way out. Man has tried in various ways. He has tried knowledge, he has tried organized religion, he has tried various systems of philosophy, and after all this he has come to a blank wall, so there is a feeling of despair. Man has reached the end of his tether. I wonder if you are at all aware of this! Perhaps you know despair only in terms of your own life. There is despair when you want something very badly and cannot get it; there is despair when your wife or husband, your son or brother dies. If you are a little man who longs to be rich and famous, you may despair of ever achieving what you want. All this is part of a wider, deeper despair in which action has lost its meaning, in which temples, philosophies, gurus have ceased to have any significance. There is, of course, the world of entertainment, amusement, superficiality, the world of escape; but with that we do not have to deal because those of us who are at all serious have already seen through it.

So, faced as we are with confusion, deterioration, with corruption and an over-whelming sense of despair, what do we do? Most of us turn to faith as a means of solving our problems—faith in religious authority, or faith in the authority of the state.

Do please follow all this because we have to bring about a new quality of mind; a fundamental revolution, a deep mutation has to take place, and it cannot take place if we are not aware of all these facts.

As I was saying, being faced with the present crisis, most of us turn to faith—faith in the idea of God, or faith in the state, or faith in a future utopia, a marvelous new world to be created by the communists, the socialists, the politicians. Faith is an extraordinary thing, if you observe it, because it indicates that we want to cling to something which has been created for us by a leader, by an expert, by the politician or the priest. That is, being confused, uncertain, in a state of despair, we want something to which we can cling, so either we turn to the revival of a dead religion or we dream of creating a new state with the help of the politician, with the help of the economist, the scientist, and so on. By worshiping God through the priest, through an organized religion, or by working to bring about a so-called new society, we hope to have something on which we can rely to solve all our problems. So, faith invariably implies authority, does it not?—the authority which hope creates.

Do please follow this—not just the words, but, if you will, observe your own minds. Because what is it we are doing this evening? We are trying to commune with each other. In thinking aloud, I am not moralizing—that is a terrible, an ugly thing to do. Nor am I laying down the law, which is another horror of the so-called leaders. We are trying to commune with each other about these difficulties. So you have to watch your own mind, you have to observe your own life, you have to be aware of your own conditioning. I am merely describing, and if you are satisfied with mere description, then what is being said will have very little meaning.

Now, most of us, when we are confused, in despair, want to follow someone, so we have faith in a leader, whether religious or political. But when a confused, despairing mind follows another, it only creates greater misery, greater confusion. You choose a leader out of your confusion, so the leader himself is confused; therefore, your following has no value at all. Seeing the truth of this, what is one to do?

Religion as we know it, the religion to which we have been conditioned, is not the real solution, though real religion is the solution. Let us go into that. We see that, like our own lives, the world is in a state of chaotic misery, and we do not understand it; therefore, we turn to religion in the hope of understanding life, in the hope of understanding truth, God, or what you will, and what happens? Religion, with all its superstitions, with its beliefs and sanctions, tells us that there is a God, that we must be this, we must not be that, and so on and so on. In other words, we are conditioned by the religion in which we have been brought up, or to which we turn in the hope of finding a solution. This conditioning is not a conscious process; it is generally unconscious, but the moment we become conscious of our conditioning, we see that religion, as it is, is not the answer.

Religion, as it is, is essentially based on ideas, on faith, on authority. A man who goes every day to the temple, who reads the Gita, the Bible, or the Namaz, who performs certain ceremonies, who everlastingly repeats certain words, the names of Krishna, Rama, this one or that, who wears the so-called sacred thread and aspires to go on some pilgrimage—him you consider a religious man. But surely, that is not religion. It is an ugly, dreadful, stupid thing. But most of us are caught in it and we cannot get out. To

get out, to break through our conditioning requires a great deal of energy, which we do not have because our energy goes into earning a livelihood and resisting any form of change. To change demands going against society, does it not? And if in a Hindu society you were not a Hindu, or if you were not a Brahmin in a Brahmin society, or a Christian in a Protestant or Catholic society, you might find it difficult to get a job.

So, one of our difficulties is that to bring about a revolution in oneself requires tremendous energy, which very few of us have because energy, in this sense, implies perception. To see anything very clearly, you must give to it your whole attention, and you cannot give your whole attention if there is any shadow of fear—economic fear or social fear, which is fear of public opinion. Being in a state of fear, we think of reality or God as something far away, unearthly, something which we have to struggle after, grope for—you know all the tricks we use to escape from the conflict of our daily life to something which we call peace, goodness, God. That is our actual state, is it not?

We see, then, that organized religion, with its superstitions, beliefs, and dogmas is not religion at all, and never has been. We have merely been educated, conditioned from childhood to accept these things as religion, so organized religion is actually a detriment to the discovery of what is the true religious life.

Then there is the organized revolution, which is supposed to bring about a new and marvelous state on earth—but which is actually a reactionary movement because the people who organize it are themselves as conditioned as the priests. They are the Marxists, the communists, the socialists; they too belong to something, and they too have a pattern of thought and action to which they want you to conform.

Do you realize, sirs, what is happening in the world? Man is losing his freedom, and he is willing to lose his freedom in the hope of having a better economic society. Tyranny in the guise of communism or some other form of so-called socialism is spreading, and you don't care because you say, "At least my children will be better off than I am, and the poor will have something to eat." You don't mind being slaves as long as you have food, clothing, and shelter; so you live a very superficial life, and with that you are content. But man is not all on the surface; he is an extraordinarily complex entity, and without understanding this complex entity, merely to bring about a reformation on the surface has no meaning because it will only create still more misery, still more confusion and slavery. Do please understand this. We are now in a worldwide crisis, and you cannot meet this crisis by saying that we must go back to Hinduism, or to Islam, or to Christianity. That is a silly answer; it is not a mature response.

Seeing the truth of all this, what is one to do? Please put that question to yourself. What is one to do? You cannot join any organized religion, you cannot belong to any social reform group, to any political party, because they are all dealing only with the partial. There is no leader, religious or political, who is going to save you. By following a leader you may have bread, but you are not going to be satisfied with bread. You too are ambitious, you want power, position, prestige. To be free, you have to understand the whole complex entity which is yourself and not accept the partial response of a political or religious leader.

So, what is one to do? Being in despair, being confused and in a state of misery, being appallingly apprehensive of both living and dying, what is one to do? I wonder if we have ever asked ourselves this question? We have all had minor challenges in our lives, with correspondingly minor responses. But this challenge is not a minor one. Do you understand what I mean? Seeing poverty, you say, "I must do something about it," and your action is then the minor response to a minor challenge. Or, being in despair, you turn to some hope which is again a minor response. We have all had these minor challenges and minor responses in our lives. And seeing the futility of all that, we are now putting to ourselves the question: What is one to do? So this is a major challenge to which we cannot respond in a minor way. Do you understand?

Sirs, we have lost our smile, we have lost our laughter, we no longer see beauty. Our world is split up into Indian and Chinese, capitalist and communist, German and English, Russian and American, Hindu and Islamic. But the earth is ours; it does not belong to the communists or the capitalists, to the Hindus or the Christians. It is our earth, yours and mine, to live upon, to enrich. The earth is wide and beautiful, a lovely thing to behold—and we have divided it. Through politics, through possessiveness, through ambition and religious bigotry, we have made it narrow. We think in terms of the North and the South, the East and the West, in terms of your country and my country, your property and my property; and we are all seeking power, position, prestige.

Now, when one sees all this horror, this misery, this degradation, corruption, and violence, what is one to do? I think there is a total answer, and a total answer is necessary because partial answers are no good any more. The guru, the so-called religious person says, "Seek God, and you will have all the answers." That is sheer nonsense because you have got to live in this world. You can no longer run away to the Himalayas or to a monastery or lose yourself in the Cross or the Crescent or in any other symbol. Those days are over. You will have to find out for yourself what to do because there is no escape. Reason cannot open the door to you any more; no amount of intellectual cunning will bring you quietness, peace, a sense of love. Intellect has become barren, and all that is born of intellect is sterile. You cannot rely on knowledge, you cannot rely on the Gita, on the Bible, or on any other book because to rely on authority has no meaning. Do please realize this. You have relied on authority all your life, and you are still miserable, ridden by fear, by anxiety, despair.

So, what is one to do? As I said, I think there is a total answer, but first we must be very clear that no partial answer can ever meet the total challenge. Through exclusive concentration on a part, you can never understand the whole. The whole is the true. Life is not only joy, nor is it just the beauty of a sunset, or of the evening star, or of a bird on the wing. Life is also ugliness and despair; it is this fearful anxiety and frustration which we all know. So we have to put a question to ourselves that will awaken the total answer to the whole of this. Do you understand, sirs? If you ask, "What am I to do?" only because you have quarreled with your boss or your wife has run away, that is a very superficial question which will find a superficial answer. There is a complete answer to that and every other question only when we approach the problem totally—which is to understand our own immense loneliness and poverty of being. That is why we must be very clear as to the manner in which we are putting this question to ourselves.

If an answer is not total, it is no answer at all; and I say there is a total answer to all these problems. There is a complete way of looking at life, with all its problems, and that is with a mind that has understood itself. When there is no self-knowledge, no understanding of the ways of thought—not somebody else's thought, but your own—then all your responses to the demands of life are bound to be partial, self-contradictory, and therefore productive of further misery. By self-knowledge I mean the understanding of yourself, the understanding of your own behavior, your own motives, prejudices, fears. I do not mean your ideas about the atma, the higher self, and all that business, which is still within the field of thought, within the field of your conditioning.

Now, knowledge is one thing, and knowing is another. Please, this may be a little difficult, but just follow it. Knowledge is of time. Knowledge, being cumulative, is always partial; it has a beginning and an end. Knowledge, or accumulated experience, is memory; and the response of that memory is what we call thought—thought expressed in words, or thought without words. This whole process is knowledge.

Then there is the state or movement of knowing. A mind that is in the movement of knowing, learning, has no beginning and no end—it is timeless. So we have to be very clear about the difference between knowledge and knowing.

Knowledge is of time. I know, and I shall know more; I am violent, and I shall be nonviolent. That implies an additive process in time. The man who says, "I know," is always within the field of time. But knowing is timeless. Do please comprehend this; otherwise, you won't understand what follows.

All knowledge is within the field of time, so knowledge is not the answer. It is knowledge that has created the people who say, "We know, you don't know. We have heard the voice of God. We are the leaders, you follow us." Such people belong to time, which is knowledge, and knowledge is obviously not the way out of our mess.

Now, I think there is a movement of knowing, learning, which has nothing to do with time. When you are learning, there is no time, is there? In that movement there is no beginning and no end. You don't know; you are learning. I wonder if you see the difference! When you are in the movement of learning, there is no entity who is accumulating knowledge and thereby creating the differences of accumulation and the conflict between them.

Look, sirs, when you are learning, there is no time involved at all, is there? Because learning or knowing is infinite; it has no beginning and no end. In that same way, without any sense of accumulation, there must be the knowing of oneself. Words are extraordinarily difficult. I am knowing you, I am knowing myself. In knowing, there is never a moment of contradiction, never a moment of conflict. When the mind is in the movement of knowing, it has removed the source of conflict; and when you remove the source of conflict, you are then able to respond totally to life.

So, knowing about oneself is the beginning of freedom because it brings about a mind which is not caught in time. The mind that has this quality of timelessness can answer all our human problems because it is in a state of creation; and only such a mind is open to receive that which is not measurable by knowledge.

March 2, 1960

Seventh Talk in New Delhi

I would like this evening to talk about time and death, but it seems to me that it is important, first of all, to understand what we mean by listening. You are listening to what is being said, obviously, and what is being said is a challenge. But are you listening in order to find an answer, or are you listening to the challenge itself? I think there is a difference between listening to the challenge, and trying to find out how to respond to the challenge. Most of us, when we are confronted with a challenge, with a problem, im-

mediately start looking for an answer, for a way out of the problem, so the problem is never important. For most of us, what is important is the solution, but the solution is in the problem—it is not away from the problem.

So, we must be very clear that we are not merely trying to find an answer, a solution, but are listening to the challenge, to the issues involved in time and death. If you are merely concerned with finding an answer, then I am afraid you will go away disappointed because it is not the purpose of these talks to provide answers. But what we are trying to do is to explore the problem together, and in any exploration, how one explores is of the highest importance. If you explore in order to find an answer, then your exploration becomes merely a means to an end, and therefore exploration has no value in itself. The moment your attention is diverted to finding a solution for the problem, exploration and discovery cease to have very much significance.

Please do listen to this a little attentively, if you will. When we are faced with a problem, the immediate reaction of most of us is to try to slip out of it; we want to find an answer, and we say, "What shall I do?" But time and death are an immense problem, are they not? They are an extraordinarily complex problem, in which there is a sense of magnificence, a certain splendor and beauty. But if we do not appreciate or are not sensitive to the problem, merely to seek a solution is so empty, a routine matter that has very little significance.

So, it matters very much how you are listening. As I said, there is a great difference between listening to find an answer, and listening to the problem, to the challenge itself. If you are looking for an answer, your mind is distracted, but if you are trying to understand the problem, then your whole mind is giving attention to it; and surely that is the way you must inquire into time and death because these two factors play an extraordinarily important part in our lives. But whether you seek a solution or give your full attention to the challenge depends entirely on yourself.

When someone whom you love dies and you are enveloped in a cloud of sorrow, your only concern is to find a way of being free from this grief, from this burden of tears; you are generally not interested in understanding the extraordinary thing called death. Isn't that so? And there is this problem of time, in which each one of us is involved—not only chronological time, but also inward time, the psychological sense of time that is developed by a mind which says, "I was, I am, and I shall be." All of us are concerned with time in one way or another. There is the necessity of catching a train, or arranging for what one will do or where one will go tomorrow. Time is also involved in the cultivation of a virtue—which of course is totally absurd—in fulfilling an ambition, in trying to think out a problem, and so on.

Now, to understand time, you have to understand the operations of the mind as a whole, and in that understanding you will perceive the altogetherness of time.

Sirs, may I point out that you are not only listening to my words. Words are mere symbols, they have very little meaning in themselves. You are also observing your own mind—or rather, the mind is observing itself, which means that it is aware of how it is listening to what is being said. Please, I am laboring this point because if we do not lay the right foundation, our structure will be superficial and very shoddy. But if we know how to lay the foundation deeply, rightly, then we can build truly. What we are trying to do now is to lay the right foundation so that the process of inquiry will be right, and that inquiry depends on you, not on me. In listening to these words, you have to be aware of all the operations of your own

mind. I am using words to describe the operations of the mind, but if you hear only the words and do not listen to the mind itself in operation, then the words will convey very little.

The altogetherness of time is the active present. A verb is in its essence the active present, is it not? The verb *to be* includes "has been," "being," and "will be"—that which was, that which is, and that which is to be. But most of us are concerned with the progression of what has been, through what is, to what will be. That is our life, and we are functioning, acting in those terms—the past flowering in and being modified by the present, thereby creating the future. Our action, which is already determined by yesterday, is modified by today and shapes what will be tomorrow. In other words, for most of us the cause and the effect are separated by an interval, a gap in which the cause inexorably becomes the effect, and which by Indians is generally called karma.

Now, if you examine very closely this chain of cause-and-effect, you will find that our action is not so completely dependent on the original cause but may arise from something entirely different. That is, a mango seed will always produce a mango tree, never a palm or a tamarind. The cause is fixed in the very nature of the mango seed, and it produces a fixed effect. It cannot do otherwise than produce a mango tree. But with us the situation is quite different because what was an effect becomes a cause, which is constantly being modified in the present through various influences and may therefore produce an effect entirely different from the original cause. So, with human beings the cause is never fixed; it is always undergoing a change, and that change is reflected in future action. The understanding of this fact is the total comprehension of action.

Time, for most of us, is this progression of the past through the present to the future, the feeling that I have been and that I am; and because I have been and I am, I shall be. In this field of time we function.

Now, time is knowledge, is it not? Yesterday I did or thought or experienced such and such a thing, and with the knowledge of what I did or thought or experienced, I meet the present challenge—the anger of my wife or husband, the condemnation of the political bosses, or whatever it is. I live in the present with what I have known, and the known, in response to the present challenge, creates the future. So the mind is always working within the field of time, within the field of the modified known. The possibility of functioning beyond time is merely a theory, a matter of faith or belief, which is itself a projection of the known within the field of time. That is one aspect of it.

Then there is the aspect of time which the mind creates as memory. Every experience that you have, however small or great, however petty or magnificent, takes root in the soil of the mind as memory, does it not? The mind becomes the soil in which experience takes root.

I do hope you are following all this so that, at the end of the talk or even now, we can all feel the extraordinary quality of time and death. To a mind that understands, that is not afraid, death must be something astonishing, colossal; it must be as magnificent, as beautiful as life is. But, you see, we do not know what death is; it is the unknown, and therefore it becomes something to be thought about, to be speculated upon. Sirs, as long as the mind does not understand its own operations, death will have very little meaning.

So it is very important for each one of us to go through this process of inquiry, not theoretically, but actually, so that the mind comes out of it with a clarity of perception. Most of us are asleep and tortured by the nightmare of our own demands, urges, com-pulsions, ambitions. We are always functioning within that field of tyranny, of conflict, which is the field of all the things that we go through every day. And the problem, the challenge is: Can the mind really disentangle itself from the known and be in a state to receive the unknown, which is death? Do you understand, sirs?

For most of us, death is despair. Death is finality, which is a terrible thing for a man who is full of vitality, who is ambitious, creative, who is working, acquiring, doing. At the end of all this—death. What for? And being full of despair, such a man invents a philosophy or turns to a belief—belief in resurrection or in reincarnation—that satisfies him, gives him hope.

As I was saying, every experience that you have takes root in the mind as memory. If I flatter you or insult you, that experience takes root in your mind, does it not? You never forget it. So the mind has become the soil in which experiences, thoughts continually take root—the mind being the unconscious as well as the conscious—and from that background of memory, of accumulated thought and experience, we act, we think, we are. That background is the factor of the known, it is the creator of the known. I wonder if you are following this?

Look, sirs, you go to the office every day because you have learned a certain technique by which you earn your livelihood. That technique has become a mechanical memory. You know what to do and how to do it, and from that background you act, from that background you are. So what you are and what you do is essentially mechanical, repetitious, with little modifications here and there. It is the same with almost all of us. Experience as knowledge has taken root in the mind, and we function always within the field of the known, for from the known we create the opposite and act from that opposite, which is still within the field of the known, the field of time.

So, there is time as yesterday, today, and tomorrow; and time as memory, which is the factor of the known. Time is the verb *to be*— that which has been, that which is, and that which will be. Now, if you consider that verb, you will see that the state it represents, while embracing what has been, what is, and what will be, is always actively present. Similarly, there is only a state of mind which is actively present, though we translate it as yesterday, today, and tomorrow.

Now, the problem, the challenge is this: Is it possible for the mind which is aware of this whole process of time, which has explored and understood it, to grasp the significance of death? Death is the unknown; it is not merely the disintegration of the body, and our fear of death is the fear of there being no continuity, which is naturally the psychological reaction of memory, whose urge is to continue in time. Let me put it differently.

What is it about death we are afraid of? Essentially it is fear of not being, isn't it? I have been, and I am; but when death comes, I may cease to be. That is what I am afraid of because I want to continue. Though different names are given to it by different people, to continue in one form or another is the urge of everyone, and continuity is always within the field of time. Without time, without memory, there is no continuity as ''I was'' and ''I will be.'' But the factor of fear comes in when there is any doubt about this continuity of being, and so the mind begins to invent or cling to comforting theories, which it then tries to bolster up by saying, ''There is a great deal of evidence for human continuity after death,'' and so on and so on.

Thought is continuity; thought is time. There is no thinking, no verbalizing without memory. Memory functions essentially within the field of time, and therefore memory is mechanical. If I ask you something with which you are thoroughly familiar, you respond immediately. But if the question is more complex, you take a little more time; there is an interval between the challenge and the response. In that interval the mind is in operation, searching the corridors of memory, or thinking out what the answer should be. So, thinking has continuity.

Sirs, this is really important, and if you will, please go into it a little bit with me. Let us take the journey into it together because if we do not understand the process of thinking, we shall not know what it is to die. To most of us, death is a finality to be feared because we want to continue. But if we can investigate and understand the whole process of thinking, then death is not a fearsome finality because there is no longer any sense of wanting to continue. We will go into it, think it out together.

Factually, what are you? Please do not respond theoretically, saying that you are the atma, that you are a son of God, and all the rest of it. Factually, what are you? You are the result of your environmental influences, are you not? You are the result of the culture, the education, the social environment in which you were brought up. I know you don't like to think that, but it is a fact. You like to think of yourself as an extraordinary spiritual entity who is not influenceable. But the fact is that you are what you have been taught. You are the embodiment of tradition, of superstition. You are the entity who has learned a technique and who functions like a machine in a certain pattern of action. You are sorrowful, you are lustful, you are seeking power. All that is what you actually are, and on top of it you superimpose the concept of an extraordinary spiritual state which is still the result of the culture in which you were brought up, whether it be Hindu, Buddhist, Muslim, Christian, or what you will.

Now, essentially you want that bundle of conditioning to continue, with little modifications here and there. You don't want too much sorrow, you don't want to be in a constant battle with yourself, you would like to have a little more peace, but you want to continue in essence as you are. What you are is thought—thought being the result of accumulated experiences, which is memory. You function from the background of the known, and that background is what you want to continue. Therefore death is to you a finality, a fearful door to go through, so you say to yourself, "There must be some form of continuity."

Now, that which has continuity is mechanical. Sirs, do please listen to this. That which has continuity is mechanical. If you know how to oil it properly, a machine will continue running for a very long time. If you can create a machine without friction, it will continue to function indefinitely, as the satellites are doing. But it will be entirely mechanical. And you are frightened of not continuing to function in this mechanical sense. I think you are frightened because that is all you know—how to function mechanically in time. The idea of ceasing to function mechanically, in a world you do not know, which is death, is frightening to you, and being frightened, you say that there must be reincarnation or some other form of continuity—you know all the speculative, hopeful theories which the mind invents.

Please bear in mind that we are not discussing whether there is a form of continuity or not. That is totally irrelevant. It is a stupid mind that says, "I must continue," and it will remain stupid. It may continue, but it will still be mechanical.

So, our problem, surely, is this: Is it inevitable that we function within the field of time, within the field of the known? And is it possible to die to the known? Is it possible to die to one's pleasure? We all want to die to our pains. But is it possible to die to one's pleasure? Is it possible to die to everything that one has known so that the mind is not merely a machine? Do you follow?

That which has continuity functions in time as yesterday, today, and tomorrow. It is being modified each minute, but it has a continuity, and whatever has a continuity is mechanical; therefore, it cannot be creative. A machine can never be creative. These electronic brains can function with incredible speed, but they cannot invent, they can never be in a state of creation. For most of us, life is machine-like, one long series of mechanical actions, and therefore we are bored with it, and from this terrible routine of existence, we seek to escape through God, through going to temples, churches, through turning on the radio and pursuing every other form of distraction.

As I said at the beginning of the talk, we are not seeking an answer because in serious matters life has no answer. Life, which is vast and profound, has little ripples which cause disturbances, and from these superficial disturbances we try to escape through an answer. If you are seeking an answer because you are disturbed, you may think about God, you may play games with the idea of truth, eternity, but your mind will still be shallow, stupid, petty. So, is it possible to die to the things one has known, the things the mind is rooted in? If one can, then there is only a state of dying, and not the finality of death.

Sirs, through human endeavor, human continuity, the mind has become mechanical. We are not even fully operative machines but half-dead machines; our brains are functioning at only twenty-five percent of capacity, or not even that. We are not functioning totally, wholly. We are caught between the communist, with his Marxist theories, and the so-called religious person, with his beliefs, with his dogmas, and we are creating a monstrous world. Though every politician has on his tongue that word *peace,* his actions and his very existence deny it. We are living in a terrible world, and we need a new mind—not an old mind modified, but a totally new mind. And you cannot have a new mind, a mind that is young, innocent, fresh, as long as there is any desire for continuity.

So, is it possible to die to the whole of yesterday? Please listen to this. It is not my problem, it is your problem. Can you die to the whole of yesterday? Now, that is a challenge, isn't it? And are you listening to the challenge—or listening to find out how to die to yesterday? The miseries, the pleasures, the fleeting joys, the routine, the ugly brutality of your existence, the appalling shallowness of your thinking—can you die to all that? If you are listening to find out how to die, trying to decide how much to keep and how much to discard, then you won't find an answer. But if you are listening to the challenge, then that very listening is the experiencing of dying.

As I said, we need a new mind because the old mind has created terrible problems for which it has no answers. Whatever it reforms creates another misery; whatever it builds produces another shadow, a further conflict. So, a fresh mind is essential if we are to create a new generation, a different world.

Now, can your mind die to everything it has known—known in terms of continuity or ambition? Can you die to all that—and not ask what will happen if you die to it? To ask what will happen is not to listen to the challenge but only to seek an answer to the problem with which you are confronted. The challenge is: Can you die to your ambition, to your corruption, to your envy, to your acquisitiveness? And if you listen to the challenge, then that very act of listening is the experiencing of dying to that which has continuity.

Don't you see, sirs? You need an innocent mind, a fresh mind, a mind which is not cluttered up with the known. An innocent mind is a mind which functions in the unknown, and dying to the known is the door to the unknown. The unknown is not measurable by the known. Time cannot measure the timeless, the eternal, that immensity which has no beginning and no end. But our minds are bound to the yardstick of yesterday, today, and tomorrow, and with that yardstick we try to inquire into the unknown, to measure that which is not measurable. And when we try to measure something which is not measurable, we only get caught in words.

So it is only a mind that has listened to and understood the challenge of death—it is only such a mind that can die to its own miseries and therefore be in a state of innocency; and from that state of innocency there is a totally different action altogether. Such action is always in the present; it is the active present. An innocent mind does not think in terms of having been something yesterday, which it is modifying today in order to gain something tomorrow. I feel it is urgently important for each one of us to find this out for himself. Because, as we are now, we are creating a dreadful world for the generations to come. We cannot bring into being a new generation unless we ourselves die to the old. As long as the mind lives and functions within the field of time, do what it will—go to innumerable temples, worship strange gods, repeat every kind of prayer, perform sacrifices, mumble a lot of words—it can never know that which is eternal, immeasurable. Only the mind that lives completely in the silence of the active present is open to receive the unknowable, and it is only such a mind that can bring about a new world because only such a mind is in a state of creation.

March 6, 1960

Eighth Talk in New Delhi

This is the last talk, and I would like this evening, if I may, to think aloud with you about virtue, sensitivity, and what we call love and beauty. I do not know if we have ever asked ourselves, at any time, why it is that we lose our sensitivity, not to any particular thing, but this extraordinary sensitivity to everything—to the open skies, to the rain on the road, to the vast, moving clouds, to the moonlight on the waters, to the smile on a face, to the weary bullock drawing a cart. Why is it that we lose this quality of nearness to things? Why is it that, as we grow up, we lose all sense of innocency, which is the very essence of sensitivity? Why do we lose the appreciation of what is beautiful, the sense of astonishment, of amazement, of wonder at the whole process of living?

I think it would be good if we could approach this problem very attentively and hesitantly, so as to find out for ourselves why our minds become dull. Fundamentally, it seems to me, one cause of this dullness of the mind is its cultivation of virtue—please listen, I am going to explain. And dullness also comes about when the mind has committed itself to a course of action, when one belongs to a particular group and must act within the framework of that commitment. The mind is likewise made dull by the desire to possess power, to dominate. I think these are three of the principal causes of the mind's dullness.

Surely, what is essential is a very sensitive, alert mind—a mind that, being intense, creates its own efficiency—and that sensitivity, that intensity is denied to a mind that is merely cultivating virtue. There is a virtue which is not the product of the mind. What we generally call virtues—the moral sanctions, the professional ethics, the codes of righteous behavior, and so on—are all creations of a particular society, are they not?

Whereas, virtue in the true sense is not a product of the mind, and it is not recognizable as virtue by society.

I think one has to see very clearly that when a mode of conduct becomes respectable and is therefore recognizable as being virtuous, it is no longer virtuous. A virtue like being nonviolent, being kindly, being humble, and so on, when recognized as virtue by society, or by oneself, ceases to be a virtue and becomes mere respectability. When the mind struggles to acquire a particular quality, be it humility, sympathy, nonviolence, or what you will, it is surely not virtue; it is merely a form of resistance in which the mind is approximating itself to a pattern.

Please do feel your way into what is being said—but not in order to accept or deny because a mind that merely accepts or denies is really an unreasoning mind; it is not a thoughtful, intelligent mind because it has already taken a stand from which it judges, and it is therefore incapable of exploration, inquiry.

We are inquiring into the nature of virtue. The mind must obviously be virtuous because only a virtuous mind is orderly, sensitive, capable of acting out of its own clarity. But the mind that is induced, influenced, disciplined to be virtuous is not a virtuous mind because it knows only resistance, a constant adjustment to the demands of respectability. Any effort to be virtuous, to be moral, any endeavor to be something other than what one is naturally creates a resistance to what one is, and this resistance prevents the understanding of what one is; yet such effort, which is really an avoidance, an escape from what one is, is generally regarded as virtue.

Take a very simple thing. In this country there is a great deal of talk about nonviolence. All the political and so-called religious leaders talk about nonviolence, but the fact is that man is violent. You are violent, and your violence is expressed, not only through everyday ambition, but through this tremendous effort you make to control, to discipline yourself, to force yourself to conform to a particular pattern. There are various kinds of violence, are there not? There is violence as cruelty to others, and the very essence of self-fulfillment is also violence. The cultivation of non-violence is a form of violence. This is a fact, and yet you cultivate nonviolence as though it were a tremendous virtue. The acceptance of non-violence as an ideal is a process by which you become respectable through being recognized by society as a virtuous person. To be respectable, you must have the earmarks of nonviolence; you must show that you are nonviolent, your virtue must be recognizable by the people around you, by society.

So, recognition plays an immense part in what we call virtue. But virtue which is cultivated by the mind, which is recognized and accepted by society and has therefore become respectable, is not virtue at all. I think this is very important to understand because it is one of the major factors which is making the mind dull. What matters, surely, is to see the fact that one is violent, to go into it, understand it, and not resist it—which does not mean that you must become violent and hit somebody! The important thing is to understand deeply the feeling of violence, which expresses itself in so many ways. If you begin to understand that every form of so-called virtue which is brought into being through effort, through resistance, through suppression, is destructive to sensitivity, then you will see that there is a virtue which is entirely different because it is not the product of a cunning mind.

I wonder if you have ever felt a sense of humility? Most of us, I am sure, have felt respect, and where there is respect, there is also disrespect. You are respectful to your

boss, to the great of the land, to the people who have power, position, authority. You show respect in order to get something in return; you give a garland in order to receive a blessing. You bow very low to the man above you and push aside others who don't matter to you—they are the servants, the underlings, the underdogs. Now, there is a quality which has no element either of respect or disrespect, and that is the sense of humility. The mind in a state of humility is neither respectful nor disrespectful. But the mind that wants something in return is full of respect and disrespect. Having disrespect, it cultivates respect, which is a resistance to disrespect, so disrespect goes on festering like a wound in the mind, and respect also. But the mind that has a sense of humility is in an entirely different state.

Now if we, as we are listening this evening, can be sensitive to and directly experience that state of humility, we will have touched something which cannot be recognized. Do you understand? You cannot say, "Well, my mind is humble, and I know what it means." The moment the recognizing process takes place, there is no longer a state of humility. Please understand this. Love is not recognizable. When we say that we love someone, we are using a word to communicate a feeling, but the moment we have recognized and expressed that feeling, the quality of it has already changed. What we can do, surely, is to see for ourselves that as long as the mind is in a state of respect and disrespect, it has not the quality of humility.

As I was saying, the quality of humility is not recognizable. Anything that is recognized by the mind as humility is not humility. So one has to be aware of the manner of one's speech, the manner of one's being; one has to discover what is behind the words, the gestures, the actions. Through negation one comes to the positive, which is humility. Though humility is not recognizable, not describable, as respect and disrespect are, it has a positive quality which can be felt when the other state is not. A mind that is conscious of itself as being virtuous is really an immoral mind, and however much it may cultivate virtue, morality, it is still immoral. Now, just leave it at that.

Let us go on to the next thing, which is: Why do most of us have an urge, a compulsion to commit ourselves to something? We belong to a party, to a group, to a sect; we commit ourselves to a framework of ideas, to a set of beliefs, to a system of philosophy; we regard ourselves as communists, socialists, imperialists, capitalists, as followers of a particular guru, and all the rest of it. Why? Please, I am going to answer the question, but if you who belong to something find out, as I am talking, why you belong, then my explanation will have a meaning, a significance.

Now, the politicians all over the world talk about peace, and we all want peace. A mind in conflict, like war, is obviously destructive, and we realize that there must be peace. So what do we do? We immediately begin to join organizations, we commit ourselves to the communists or to some other group which says it is going to bring about world peace. And what happens? You are committed to one group, and I to another, so inevitably we are in conflict with each other. If I am in the capitalists' camp, I say the communists' talk about world peace is double-talk, and vice versa. So, the moment we belong to a group which promises peace, we are already in conflict with another group which promises peace in a different way, and the result is that we all talk about peace while perpetuating conflict.

Surely, we have to begin by understanding why we commit ourselves, why we belong to something or other. Why do you call yourself an Indian, a Muslim, a Buddhist, a Christian, or a communist? Obviously, for a very

simple reason. You desire to be identified with a group, to belong to something because it gives you a sense of security. You say, "Action is necessary; therefore, we must join together." And the moment you join together and form a group, you are battling with another group which wants to act in the same way. In other words, the action which comes from commitment to a party, to a political or religious group, to a particular society, guru, culture, or way of life invariably leads to conflict—which is fairly obvious in the world at the present time.

Now, I think there is a totally different kind of action when the mind does not belong to anything, is not committed to any group. But first let us investigate why we have this compulsion to belong.

It is not only the little man who has this compulsion, but also the great intellectual, the saint—they all want to belong to something. Why? Observe yourself and you will see that if you do not belong to something, you feel insecure. Insecurity means fear, insecurity means economic loss, and belonging to something gives to the self a feeling of expansion. Being a communist, or a Catholic, or belonging to any other big, widespread organization—with all the implications involved in it—gives you an immense feeling of security. It also gives you a sense of importance, and from this sense of importance there springs action which invariably produces conflict with others.

Do please look at the phenomenon that is going on in the world. First we create this ugly thing called nationalism, thereby dividing ourselves into conflicting groups; and then, still holding on to our nationalism, we say there must be internationalism, brotherhood, and all that nonsense. What will bring peace to the world is really comprehensive action, that is, action outside the patterns which divide people and create conflict. When you and I do not belong to a thing, when we are not Indians, Americans, Christians, Buddhists, when we have put aside all these political and religious divisions which are destroying people—it is only then that we can meet as human beings, with dignity, and set about solving our many problems. The communists are not going to solve our problems; nobody can solve them except you and me—when we have not committed ourselves to any group, to any pattern of action. Then there is an action which is much more dynamic, much more creative, much more vital. Most of us have committed ourselves, we belong to something, and that is one of the major reasons for our minds being so stupidly dull—a fact which we do not see, though it is right under our noses.

Sirs, do think it out, don't just agree with me. Your agreement or disagreement has very little significance. What has significance is to purge your thought, your whole system, of the urge to belong to something. You cannot be free of that urge unless you are aware of it in yourself, unless you examine it, go into it, understand it. If you do not condemn or justify it, if you do not say it is natural, that everybody wants to belong to something, and so on, but understand it, really grasp the truth of it, then you will find that you are entirely free of it instantaneously. That is one of the strange things about truth. The perception of what is true in a problem frees the mind from the problem. You don't have to do a thing.

In the same way, one has to see the fact that to belong to any group, to be committed to any religious or philosophical system, to any pattern of action is destructive because it divides men and makes the mind dull. When you are committed, when you belong to something, you cease to think beyond the prescribed pattern because the moment you do, you become critical, and then you are thrown out, you are made insecure. Belonging to a group may make for very effective, efficient action, but that action is destructive. You resist seeing this fact because you do not know an action which is not the outcome of commitments, of belonging to something. But it is only when you don't belong to anything, to any organization, to any group, that there is a possibility of discovering, through that sense of negation, a positive action which is total. Do please understand this.

So one sees that virtue, as we know and cultivate it, is one of the factors that makes the mind dull, mechanical. Another factor that makes the mind dull is the feeling of belonging to something. And there is a third factor which makes the mind dull—the desire for power.

I do not know if you have ever noticed in yourself this desire for power. You want to be prominent, famous; you want your opinion to be known, whether it is to a small circle of people or on a worldwide scale. There is in each one of us this intense urge to be somebody, to be recognized by society as a successful person. If you watch your own mind, you will see how, in a small way or in a big way, you crave recognition.

Please, sirs, this is very important to understand because, as you will see, a mind that is established in power is an evil mind. All power is evil, whether it be political power or so-called religious power. The moment you have achieved power, position, success, your mind has already lost its suppleness, its alertness, its quickness, its extraordinary quality of natural growth, of gentleness.

You know, it is a most difficult thing to be anonymous. Many of us have a craving for anonymity, reach a point when we want to be anonymous, because there is beauty in complete anonymity, and invariably one feels extraordinarily free. So what do we do? We put on a loincloth or enter a monastery or take another name, but inwardly we are still full of ambition, only of a different kind. We now want to be known as a spiritual man, so we have only discarded one cloth and taken another, gotten rid of one name and assumed another. Outwardly we are putting on a show of anonymity, but inwardly we are burning with vanity and pursuing power. Our "humility" consists in putting on a loincloth, or a robe, or taking only one meal a day, all of which is recognizable by society as being respectable.

I know you all smile and agree, but you are all after exactly the same thing. (Laughter) Don't laugh it away, sirs. You all want power, you all want position, prestige, though there may be one or two exceptions. And the mind that is seeking power, thinking it will do good, is a very destructive mind because it is concerned with itself. Sirs, truth cannot be found unless the mind is totally anonymous. I wonder if you have noticed that love is anonymous! I may love my wife, my children, but the quality of that love is anonymous. Like the sunset, love is neither yours nor mine.

So there is evil, corruption, when the mind is immersed in power, and the desire for power is one of the most difficult things to wipe out. It is not easy to be nobody, to be inwardly anonymous. You may say, "In sitting on the platform and talking, are you not expressing yourself?" Outwardly one may be talking, but inwardly one can be totally anonymous. And when there is this sense of complete anonymity, then you will find that there comes a comprehensive action which has nothing to do with the past, or with the thirst for power that creates such animosity and evil in the world. All power is evil, whether it be the power of nations, the power of leaders, the power of a wife over her husband, or of the husband over his wife and children. If you observe yourself when you are not posing, you will see, in the secret recesses of your own mind, that you too want power to dominate, to be known, to have your name appear in the newspapers; and

when a mind is seeking power, it is a destructive mind, it can never bring about peace in the world.

So, these are factors that make the mind dull: the virtue which is cultivated by the mind and recognized by society as being virtuous, the thought and the action of a mind which is committed to a particular pattern of ideas, and the search for power, position, prestige. All these imply a self-centered activity, a self-importance, a self-expansion, do they not? It is this process that makes the mind dull, and a dull mind loses all its sensitivity.

Now, I do not know if you have ever considered what is beauty. I am not suddenly talking about something entirely different because it is related to all that has been said this evening. I wonder if you have ever stopped of an evening to look at the sky? On your way here, did you notice the stormy clouds, their shape, their darkness, their depth, the extraordinary sense of power behind them? If you saw all that beauty, did you have a reaction to it, or was there only a sense of total perception in which there was no reaction?

Please, I am afraid this is going to be rather difficult, in the verbal sense, but if you have ever felt the quality of beauty, you will be instantaneously aware of the significance of what is being said. Most of us are insensitive to the sky, to the road, to the passerby, to death. But I am talking of a mind which is sensitive; I am inquiring into the nature of a mind that perceives beauty. Surely, when you perceive something totally, there is no reaction. You may express it in words, saying, "What a lovely sunset it is," but the moment of total perception is a moment when your whole being is in a state of nonidentification through memory.

Sirs, I am not talking apart from you; I am thinking aloud with you, and to go beyond, you must move with me, playing with the words. A mind that is not sensitive to beauty is a very sordid mind. It may build great dams; it may help to carry out any number of five-year plans. It may do this and that, but a mind that is insensitive to beauty is essentially a stupid mind, and it cannot create anything except that which is mechanical.

We are talking of beauty. Where there is a complete experiencing of something, there is no reaction of memory, and hence no furthering of memory through reaction. Such a mind is in a state of beauty, and beauty is related to love. Sirs, love is a passion.

Now, one has to be clear in the use of words. Most of us dread that word *passion* because we live in a society which considers passion to be ugly, not respectable. But lust is different from passion. Love invariably goes with passion, not with lust. You have destroyed passion, carefully rooted it out because you have said that passion is an ugly thing, and you are not passionate human beings. You may be lustful, and probably you are—sexually lustful and lustful after power, position—but you are not passionate human beings. And you cannot be passionate if there is no self-abandonment.

Do you understand? There must be that inward sense of austerity which in its very nature is simplicity. But you cannot cultivate austerity. If you do, it becomes a virtue which is recognizable and therefore respectable—a horrible thing. You know, sirs, without passion, there is no passionate action. Mostly, action that we have at present is not passionate; it is a calculated, cunning action.

Intensity, or passion, is the outcome of self-abnegation—not the abnegation which is a denial of this and that, but the total self-abnegation which brings about a state of austerity. In this state of austerity, the mind is simple, and such a mind is a passionate mind. Only the passionate mind knows love, and only the mind that knows love can perceive what beauty is—not the artist who paints a picture and is full of his own egocentricity. Love is passionate; therefore, love is beauty. Without beauty there is no love, and without love there is no beauty. Only the mind that perceives the everlasting to everlasting—it is only such a mind that can act without creating misery.

Do please listen with your heart to what is being said, and do not regard it as a talk being given on a topic. It is your own mind of which you have to be aware. It is your own action that matters, not the action of the political or religious leaders. It is what you are, what your mind is, that counts. The mind that has not committed itself, that does not belong to anything, the mind that is not strengthening its own egocentricity through the cultivation of virtue, the mind that is no longer seeking power—it is only such a mind that knows love and therefore beauty. Such a mind, surely, is totality; it has no beginning and no end, and its action is a blessing, not a curse. Only such a mind can receive the real, that which is immeasurable.

March 9, 1960

Ojai, California, 1960

--- ✳ ---

First Talk in The Oak Grove

I think from the very first we should be quite clear why we gather at these meetings. I feel that it would be an utter waste of time if you treated these talks as a form of entertainment, as something to do of an afternoon or of a morning when you have nothing better to do. And I feel it would also be a waste of time, yours and mine, if you merely listened as though you were trying to gather some information. Because these meetings, I feel, are not merely for the communication of ideas but rather for an inquiry into the very process of thinking and that requires, on your part, a great deal of attention. I do not mean by attention mere concentration, but an attentive mind which is willing to explore, to examine, and to discover.

As these meetings are not entertainment in any form whatsoever, I think it would be very profitable if we could also dispense with the idea that we are doing any kind of propaganda. I am not trying to convince you of anything—of any particular way of thinking or of a new way of living, a new pattern of action, because I do not believe in propaganda. Ideas do not fundamentally change the quality of the mind. We are trying to discuss, to explore the quality of the mind, the nature of thinking—and to go beyond, if possible, into spheres, into realms where thought cannot penetrate. For after all,

thought is very limited. All reasoning has its own conditioning. One must reason, one must think clearly, definitely, positively; but thinking, however wide, however deep, however expansive, is still limited. All thinking begins with knowledge, or the accumulation of knowledge; it arises from the background of knowledge; and knowledge, surely, is very limited.

So, if we can explore together our own minds, then I think these meetings will be very worthwhile. But to inquire into oneself is very arduous, very difficult, for most of us are not used to it. Most of us are used to being told what to do, what to think; we are used to pursuing a certain series of ideas, a rule of conduct, but it is quite another matter to explore the total process of consciousness, to investigate the whole of this entity which we call the mind. So I think it would be very important if, without any persuasion, without any direction or influence, we could together investigate our own minds.

However much progress we may make in this world, however far we may go into the skies—visit the moon, Venus, and all the rest of it—the lives of most of us are still very shallow, superficial; they are still outward. And it is much more difficult to go inward; there is no technique for it, no professor to teach it, no laboratory where you can learn to travel within. There is no teacher who can guide you—and please believe me—there is no authority of any kind that can help you to investigate this complex entity called the mind. You have to do it entirely by yourself, without depending on a thing. And as modern civilization is becoming more and more complex, more and more outward, progressive, there is a tendency for all of us to live still more superficially, is there not? We attend more concerts, we read more clever books, we go endlessly to the cinema, we gather together to discuss intellectually, we investigate ourselves psychologically with the help of analysts, and so on; or, because we live such superficial lives, we turn to churches and fill our minds with their dogmas, both unreasonable and reasonable, with beliefs that are almost absurd; or we escape into some form of mysticism. In other words, realizing that our everyday living is shallow, most of us try to run away from it. We engage our minds in speculative philosophies or in what we call meditation, contemplation, which is a form of self-hypnosis; or, if we are at all intellectual, we create a thought-world of our own in which we live satisfied, intellectually content.

Seeing this whole process, it seems to me that the problem is not what to do, or how to live, or what is the immediate action to be taken when we are confronted with war, with the catastrophes that are actually going on in the world, but rather how to inquire into freedom. Because without freedom, there is no creation. By freedom I do not mean the freedom to do what you like—to get into a car and zip along a road, or to think what you like, or to engage yourself in some particular activity. It seems to me that such forms of freedom are not really freedom at all. But is there a freedom of the mind? As most of us do not live in a creative state, I think it is imperative for any thoughtful, serious man to inquire very profoundly and very earnestly into this question.

If you observe, you will see that the margin of freedom is getting very, very narrow; politically, religiously, technologically our minds are being shaped, and our everyday life is diminishing that quality of freedom. The more civilized we become, the less there is of freedom. I do not know if you have noticed how civilization is making us into technicians, and a mind that is built around a technique is not a free mind. A mind that is shaped by a church, by dogmas, by organized religion is not a free mind. A mind that is darkened by knowledge is not a free mind. If we observe ourselves, it soon becomes obvious that our minds are weighed down by knowledge—we know so much. Our minds are bound by the beliefs and dogmas which organized religions throughout the world have laid upon them. Our education is largely a process of acquiring more technique in order to earn a better livelihood, and everything about us is shaping our minds, every form of influence is directing, controlling us.

So, the margin of freedom is getting narrower and narrower. The terrible weight of respectability, the acceptance of public opinion, our own fears, anxieties—all these things, surely, if one is at all aware of them, are diminishing the quality of freedom. And this is what, perhaps, we can discuss and understand during the talks that are to follow: How can one free the mind, and yet live in this world with all its techniques, knowledge, experiences? I think this is the problem, the central issue, not only in this country, but in India, in Europe, and all over the world. We are not creative, we are becoming mechanical. I do not mean by creativeness merely writing a poem or painting a picture or inventing a new thing. Those are merely the capacities of a talented mind. I mean a state which is creation itself.

But we shall go into all that, if we may, when we understand the central issue—that our minds are becoming more and more conditioned, that the margin of freedom is getting less and less. We are either Americans, with all the emotional, nationalistic quality behind the flag, or we are Russians, Indians, this or that. We are separated by frontiers, by dogmas, by conflicting ways of thinking, by different categories of organized religious thought; we are separated politically, religiously, economically, and culturally. And if you examine this whole process that is taking place around us, you will see that as individual human beings we count for very little; we are almost nothing at all.

We have many problems, individually as well as collectively. Individually, perhaps, we shall be able to solve some of them, and collectively we shall do what we can. But all these problems, surely, are not the main issue. It seems to me that the main issue is to free the mind, and one cannot free the mind, or the mind cannot free itself until it understands itself. Therefore self-knowledge is essential—the knowing of oneself. That requires a certain quality of awareness because if one doesn't know oneself, there is no basis for reasoning, for thought. But knowing and knowledge are two different things. Knowing is a constant process, whereas knowledge is always static.

I do not know if that point is clear; if not, perhaps I can make it clear as we go along. But what I want to do this evening is merely to point out certain things, and later on during the talks that are to follow, we can investigate them. We have to begin by seeing the overall picture—not concentrating on any particular point, on any particular problem or action, but looking at the whole of our existence, as it were. Once having seen this extraordinary picture of ourselves as we are, we can then take the book of ourselves and go into it chapter by chapter, page by page.

So, to me the central problem is freedom. Freedom is not from something; that is only a reaction. Freedom, I feel, is something entirely different. If I'm free from fear, that is one thing. The freedom from fear is a reaction which only brings about a certain courage. But I'm talking of freedom which is not from something, which is not a reaction, and that requires a great deal of understanding.

I would like to suggest that those who are coming regularly to these meetings should give some time, when they are away from here, to thinking over what we have been discussing. We are not refuting or accepting anything because I am not in any way your authority; I am not setting myself up as a teacher. To me, there is no teacher, there is no follower—and please believe me, I mean this very earnestly. I am not your teacher, so you are not my followers. The moment you follow, you are bound, you are not free. If you accept any theory, you are bound by that theory; if you practice any system, however complicated, however ancient or modern it may be, you are a slave to that system.

What we are trying to do is to investigate, to find out together. You are not merely listening to what I point out, but in listening you are trying to discover for yourself so that you are free. The person who is speaking is of no value, but what is said, what is uncovered, what one discovers for oneself is of the highest importance. All this personal cult, this personal following, or the putting up of a person in authority is utterly detrimental. What is of importance is what you discover in your investigation of how to free the mind, so that as a human being you are creative.

After all, reality, or that which is not expressible in words, cannot be found by a mind that is clogged, weighed down. There is, I think, a state—call it what you will—which is not the experience of any saint, of any seeker, of any person who is endeavoring to find it because all experience is really a perpetuation of the past. Experience only strengthens the past; therefore, experience does not free the mind. The freeing element is the state of the mind that is capable of experiencing without the entity who experiences. This again requires a certain explanation, and we shall go into it in the coming talks.

What I do want to say this evening is that there is a great deal of disturbance, a great deal of uncertainty, not only individually, but also in the world; and because of this disturbance, this uncertainty, there has arisen every kind of philosophy—the philosophy of despair, the philosophy of living in the immediate, of accepting existence as it is. There is a breaking away from traditions, from acceptance, and the building of a world of reaction. Or, leaving one religion, you go to another; if you are a Catholic, you drop Catholicism and become a Hindu or join some other group. Surely, none of these responses will in any way help the mind to be free.

To bring about this freedom, there must be self-knowledge—knowing the way you think and discovering in that process the whole structure of the mind. You know, fact is one thing and symbol is another; the word is one thing and what the word represents is another. For most of us, the symbol—the symbol of the flag, the symbol of the cross—has become extraordinarily important, so we live by symbols, by words; but the word, the symbol, is never important. And to break down the word, the symbol, to go behind it is an astonishingly difficult task. To free the mind from the words—you are an American, you are a Catholic, you are a democrat, or a Russian, or a Hindu—is very arduous. And yet, if we would inquire into what is freedom, we must break down the symbol, the word. The frontier of the mind is laid down by our education, by the acceptance of the culture in which we have been brought up, by the technology which is part of our heritage; and to penetrate all these layers that condition our thinking requires a very alert, intense mind.

I think it is most important from the very beginning to understand that these talks are not meant in any way to direct or control your thinking or to shape your mind. Our problem is much too great to be solved by belonging to some organization, or by hearing some speaker, by accepting a philosophy from the Orient, or getting lost in Zen Buddhism, by finding a new technique of meditation, or by having new visions through the use of mescaline or some other drug. What we need is a very clear mind—a mind that is not afraid to investigate, a mind that is capable of being alone, that can face its own loneliness, its own emptiness, a mind that is capable of destroying itself to find out.

So, I would point out to all of you the importance of being really serious; you are not coming to these talks for entertainment, or out of curiosity, or just because I happen to have come back after five years. All that is a waste of time. There is something much deeper, wider, which we have to discover for ourselves: How to go beyond the limitations of our own consciousness. Because, all consciousness is a limitation and all change within consciousness is no change at all. And I think it is possible—not mystically, not in a state of illusion, but actually—to go beyond the frontiers which the mind has laid down. But one can do that only when one is capable of investigating the quality of the mind and having really profound knowledge of oneself. Without knowing yourself, you cannot go far because you will get lost in an illusion, you will escape into fanciful ideas, into some new form of sectarianism.

The more we advance in worldliness and the more progress there is, the greater is our enslavement—which doesn't mean that there must be no progress. The more we are so-called educated technologically, and the more we cripple ourselves with knowledge, which darkens the mind, the narrower grows our freedom. The more there is knowledge, the more there is fear; there is no lessening of fear because knowledge darkens the mind, as experience burdens the mind.

So, considering all these many aspects of our living, our main problem, as the speaker sees it, is this question of freedom. Because it is only in freedom that we can discover; it is only in freedom that there can be the creative mind; it is only when the mind is free that there is endless energy—and it is this energy that is the movement of reality.

To conclude this first talk, I would suggest that until we meet tomorrow morning, you consider, observe, and be aware of the enslavement of your own mind. And perhaps we can, during one of these meetings, discuss, exchange ideas. As I said, this first talk is merely an outline of the contents of the book, and if you are content with the outline, with the headlines, with a few ideas, then I'm afraid you will not go very far. It is not a matter of acceptance or denial, but rather of inquiry into yourself—which does not demand any form of authority. On the contrary, it demands that you should follow nobody, that you should be a light unto yourself; and you cannot be a light unto yourself if you are committed to any particular mode of conduct, to any form of activity which has been laid down as being respectable, as being religious. One must begin very near to go very far, and one cannot go very far if one does not know oneself. The knowing of oneself does not depend on any analyst. One can observe oneself as one goes along in every form of relationship, every day; and without that understanding, the mind can never be free.

May 21, 1960

Second Talk in The Oak Grove

I would like, if I may this morning, to talk about authority, knowledge, and freedom. It seems to me that the more mechanical the mind becomes, the greater is our desire to feel strongly, to perceive deeply, to have wider perceptions, intuitions, and insights. And most of us resort to various forms of stimulation in order to have these intense feelings, these intense experiences, perceptions. I think one must have observed this fact, quite casually even. The more shallow and mechanical the mind becomes, and the more it is bound to a routine, the greater is its demand for wider, deeper, more profound feelings. So you resort to every form of stimulation: to drink, to sex, and to various other forms of outward and inward stimulation. You go to church to enjoy the Mass, which is a form of stimulation, or you resort to certain drugs, to mescaline, LSD, so that you can perceive more profoundly the beauty of a flower, see more intensely its color, feel more deeply the beauty of the hills and the quietness of an evening. And I think this dependence on stimulation is inevitable as long as the mind is being conditioned by the process of civilization.

Before I go into all that, I would like to say that it is very important that you and I establish right communication between ourselves because, after all, the purpose of these talks is to communicate with each other, and not to impose upon you a certain series of ideas. Ideas never change the mind, never bring about a radical transformation in the mind. But if we can individually communicate with each other at the same time and at the same level, then perhaps there will be an understanding which is not merely propaganda. It is not my intention to persuade you to think in any direction, along any particular line, because the more we are persuaded by the influences of propaganda, the less we are capable of feeling, and the less intense we are. So these talks are not meant to dissuade or to persuade you in any way, either actually or subliminally.

To communicate, we must have the opportunity to listen to each other. To listen is an art in itself. Very few of us listen—to the winds, to the silent operations of our own minds. We never really listen to another, or to the hints, the intimations of the unconscious. We are so occupied with the daily activity, the daily routine, with our anxieties, worries, angers, jealousies, that there is no space left in which the mind can be quiet to listen, to find out, to understand.

So I would suggest that you listen, not in any way to deny or accept, but as though you were listening to some facts, because the very listening to a fact is in itself action. If I know how to listen, that very listening is an action in itself. But if I do not know how to listen, and listen only partially, there is then the idea that needs to be put into action. Listening itself is a form of harmonious action in which there is no interval between the idea and the action. If you think this out, you will see how true it is.

Bearing in mind that in no way do I intend to persuade you to any particular philosophy, to any particular form of meditation or course of action, let us, in communicating with each other, see for ourselves very definitely and distinctly how the mind is becoming more and more mechanical, how modern civilization is making the mind more limited with knowledge, with authority. Our lives being mechanistic, we invariably turn to some form of stimulation, either religious or superficial, and these stimulations inevitably further deaden the mind.

So I would like to explore, to talk over with you the question of authority, because authority does corrupt the mind. Authority limits the depth of the mind. Authority cripples all thought; it lays a frontier to the mind. The solution does not lie in merely breaking away from authority but in understanding the complex problem of authority. The understanding of authority is freedom from authority.

As we can see in the case of all governments, as well as in education and in science,

there is the exercise of authority, the demand that you copy, imitate, follow, obey. All organized religions with their dogmas, with their beliefs, demand obedience, not only in the monasteries, but also from the layman; they exercise their influence to make you conform to an established pattern. And the mind seeks authority—not only the authority of the specialist, of the doctor, of the technician, but also of the priest, of the teacher, of the guru, of the Master; or it seeks the authority of a book, whether it be the Bible, the Gita, or the latest book on health.

Why does the mind seek authority? I do not know if you have gone into it, if you have thought it out. I think the mind seeks authority because it wants to be secure. We abhor the idea of being uncertain—uncertain in our relationships, uncertain of our ability to arrive, to succeed, to discover; so we put aside the fear that uncertainty creates, the anxiety of a mind that is not sure, by seeking some form of authority.

Please do follow what is being said, not merely verbally or intellectually, but see this fact operating in your own mind—the demand to be secure, to do the right thing, to copy, to imitate in order to succeed, in order to be safe, in order to arrive, to fulfill. So authority is built up.

The understanding of authority is quite complex because authority takes many forms. There is the authority of the policeman, of the laws of society; there is the authority of a community, of public opinion; there is the authority of nature, and so on. Where is authority right, and where is authority totally wrong? To find out requires a great deal of investigation and understanding. To follow the laws of society, to keep to the right side of the road is necessary. But where does authority make the mind mechanistic? Surely, it is only when the mind is free, clear, unhindered by authority, by imitation, by the desire to be secure—it is only then that the mind, being free, can feel intensely without stimulation, without drugs.

So there is this complex process of authority—the authority of the church, of the book, of the law, of the specialist; and unless we understand authority, with its imitation, its corrupting influence, there is no freedom. And it is only when the mind is free that there is a state of creation.

I wonder if you have ever experienced what it is to create, or to be in the state of creation? Because I feel that God, or what name you will, is that state of creation; and only a free mind can discover that absolute state. That is why it is necessary to understand the whole problem of authority. Understanding itself brings its own fruit. There is no understanding first, and freedom afterwards. When you understand the complex problem of authority, that very understanding is a process of freeing the mind from authority. Understanding frees the mind from effort. Effort implies conformity, does it not? There is effort to be or to live according to a particular pattern of thought, and such effort implies, essentially, the whole question of authority. The action and the very desire of a mind that is caught in effort, in trying to be something, demands authority and conformity. Though we cannot go into all the details, one can grasp immediately, if one's mind is given to it, what is basically implied in this question of authority.

Then there is the problem of knowledge. I know it is now the fashion, and always has been, probably, to think that the more learned you are, the more books you have read, the more knowledge you have accumulated, the freer you are. And I wonder if knowledge does free the mind? I am not advocating ignorance; I am not saying that you should not read. But I want to question this whole problem of knowledge.

What do we mean by knowledge? Surely, knowledge implies the process of recognition, and the process of recognition is based on experience, is it not? So experience is the beginning of knowledge, and does experience free the mind? Experience may give you a technique in action, and probably it is necessary. If you are an engineer or a potter or a violinist or a writer or a technician of some kind or other, knowledge is necessary. But when does knowledge darken the mind? Where is the demarcation between knowledge and darkness? When is the mind crippled by knowledge? And when is the mind made free? When does knowledge no longer cripple the mind?

To understand this question, we must go into the problem of experience, must we not? We think that the more experience we have, the freer, more enlightened, and more capable we are. The more experience we have, the more capable we are in a certain direction, obviously. The better our technique, the more skilled we are with our hands, the more perfect we are in our mechanistic, technical knowledge, the greater is our capacity in earning a livelihood. That is obvious, we don't have to discuss it. But we do have to find out, surely, if the mind is darkened by knowledge, by experience. That is, does not the mind, through knowledge, make itself secure? Do you understand? The more knowledge I have, the more secure I am. In its accumulation of knowledge, the mind builds itself a shelter, makes itself secure; and a mind that is secure is a dead mind. Haven't you noticed the people who are very religious, who are clothed in righteous behavior, who are absolutely sure of their dogma, of their belief—how dead they are, though they call themselves religious, mystical, and all the rest of it? It is the desire to be completely secure that breeds darkness through knowledge, and such a mind can never be free.

So, if you go into it very deeply, you will find that knowledge is really a very complex thing, involving the whole of our consciousness—not only the consciousness with which we are familiar, the consciousness which is occupied daily in going to the office, learning a technique, and so on, but also the unconscious, the hidden part of the mind. If you go into this whole process of consciousness, which includes the unconscious, you will find there is no corner of it which knowledge has not penetrated and conditioned. Either as racial inheritance, or through the acceptance of modern education, knowledge has made our consciousness a vehicle of the known; and the mind may function brilliantly, very intellectually, but so long as it does not understand the operation of knowledge, it is still functioning in darkness. If you examine experience, you will see that every experience is a strengthening of recognition.

I wonder if I am conveying anything at all? You see, we are considering the liberation of the mind so that the mind can be in that state of creation which is not concerned with expression, though expression may come from it. A creative mind is never concerned with expression; it is not concerned with action, with reform. Creation is a timeless movement—a movement which is never concerned with the immediate, and only the immediate is concerned with reform.

I do not know if, while walking alone in the woods or along a street, you have ever noticed a moment when everything in you is silent, completely still. There is an unexpected, uninvited moment in which the mind, with all its anxieties, with all its worries and pursuits and compulsions, has completely come to an end. In that unexpected, spontaneous moment, time has totally ceased. And if you happen to be gifted as a painter, as a writer, or as a housewife, you may express that moment in action; but the action is

not that moment. The action of painting may give you fame, money, position, prestige; and man, seeking these things, goes after the technique and loses the other. That moment must have happened to most of us at sometime or other in our lives, and then we wish to capture, to hold, to continue in that moment. So, the experience of that moment darkens the mind with its knowledge of that moment and thereby prevents further experiencing. That is why experience as knowledge is destructive to the new.

Please, this is not just my special way of looking at life. These are facts. The more experience you have, the more the mind is made dull; there is no innocency of the mind; there is never a moment when the mind is not caught in knowledge, which is essentially of time. So, if you observe, you will see that knowledge—to know, to practice, to hold—darkens the mind; and the mind, being darkened, seeks greater, wider stimulation, so it turns to religions, to philosophies, theologies, speculations, or to the latest drugs.

The mind which is concerned with freedom must explore the question of authority, as well as that of knowledge, for knowledge and authority go together. Unfortunately, most of you are probably listening to me because you think I have some kind of authority. You probably think I know what I'm talking about. (Laughter) No, no, sirs, please don't laugh it away; do listen. There is this absurdity of reputation, fame, and all that; but you are actually listening to find out for yourself the truth of the matter, are you not? And if you examine this whole problem of experiencing, you will see that every form of experience which takes root in the soil of the mind is detrimental because it destroys the freedom of the mind; it breeds a sense of security, and therefore there is no innocency, no freshness to the mind. Such a mind cannot renew itself, except in further experience—

which is the process of recognizing; it is the result of the past and therefore a continuation of the past, however modified.

So, a mind that is concerned with the understanding of freedom must not inquire superficially but delve deeply within itself to discover the anatomy and the structure of authority. A mind that merely follows authority can never know what it is to be creative. A mind that has disciplined itself to a pattern of action is not a free mind. Through discipline the mind can never be free. The mind can be free only by understanding this whole problem of discipline—not at the end, but at the very beginning of the practice of discipline.

You see, to understand a problem like knowledge requires complete attention, and that attention is its own discipline. I do not need a discipline to understand knowledge. The moment I begin to explore the problem, that very exploration demands that the mind discipline itself. Do you understand? Any material has within it its own discipline. To do anything with a piece of wood, you must work in a certain way. The nature of the material imposes its own discipline. Similarly, in the very understanding of this problem of knowledge and authority, in which are implied discipline, experience, and time, there is a discipline which is not imposed. In that discipline there is no conflict or contradiction.

So, the very process of understanding is its own discipline and its own freedom. The mind that has not investigated, that has not discovered for itself the truth of knowledge and authority, can never be free. It may go to all the churches, it may read innumerable books, it may discipline itself from morning till night, but it is not a free mind.

I am talking of the mind as a total thing, not just as the machinery of thought—the mind that succeeds, that fails, that loves, that remembers, that recognizes, that suffers, that knows pity, enjoyment. I am talking of that totality. And that totality of the mind cannot be perceived through any part. You must perceive it as a whole, feel it entirely; and then you can consider the individual things of the mind. The mind is the unconscious as well as the conscious; there is no division between the two, and it is essential to feel the whole nature of the mind, the quality of that totality, if you would understand what it is to be free and what it is to be in that state of creation which has no beginning and no end.

This is not a silly, frustrating sense of mysticism. It demands a great deal of attention and the application of thought—or rather, not thought, but an insistent inquiry into the very process of thinking, feeling, being. And as one begins to understand, one will discover for oneself—naturally, without any compulsion, without any urge—what it is to be free, and what is that state which is not of time and which is not measurable by the mind.

May 22, 1960

Third Talk in The Oak Grove

When I came to give this series of talks, I had the full intention to go through with eight talks; but unfortunately, I can't do it. I can only give these four—and so the last talk will be tomorrow morning. As many of you have come from great distances to listen to them, I regret very much that physically I can't go on with all the talks. I'm sorry.

I would like, this evening, to talk over with you a rather complex problem—that of consciousness, revolution, and religion. Throughout life, however wide our learning, however intelligent we may be, we do have accidents, we do make mistakes; life doesn't run smoothly, as we would like. And we make great effort to alter, to change our lives; we try to reform ourselves, to conform to a certain mold of conduct, to fit into a groove of moral action. But it seems to me that, however necessary, such effort does not bring about a radical transformation within oneself. However much we may struggle individually to do the right thing, to behave rightly, to lead a simple, moral life, these activities, though necessary, seem so futile, so empty when the world as a whole is in such a dreadful, catastrophic state; and I'm sure most of you must have asked yourselves, what can one individual do about this whole awful mess? I think that is a wrong question altogether, and a wrong question will not find a right answer. I think one has to put the right question, and the right question is not whether the transformation of an individual will affect society, the whole mass of humanity. There is now a tremendous crisis, not economically, socially, intellectually, or even religiously, but there is a crisis in consciousness itself. I think that is the real issue, and not the mere transformation of the individual. One has to understand totally, if one can, this crisis in consciousness; and to do that, one must examine the whole process of consciousness.

I am going to talk about consciousness in very simple terms, using ordinary words, not psychological, metaphysical, or complicated words. I am using the word *consciousness* to mean all the levels of our thinking, feeling— the totality of our being, not only the totality of the individual being, but also the totality of the collective, the human. And I hope that you will not just listen to the words, which would be merely an intellectual process, but will think it out with me as we go along. The art of listening is very important—to understand what it is to listen. I feel that very few of us really listen. When we do listen, we translate or interpret what we hear according to the pattern of our own thinking, or we reject it altogether. To listen totally is to listen without accepting, rejecting, comparing,

or contradicting; and I feel that if one can listen totally, then the very act of listening brings about an instantaneous perception, understanding. So, if you are at all serious about these things, may I suggest that you listen in this manner.

We must all be aware of this extraordinary crisis in the world—by which I do not mean the conflict between Russia and America, or between the East and the West, because that is not a crisis at all. That is merely a political upheaval, maintained by the politicians throughout the world. The politicians have not created the crisis of which I am speaking, and the politicians do not make for peace, any more than the so-called religious people do. If we would deeply understand the real, fundamental crisis, it seems to me that we have to inquire afresh into this whole question of what is consciousness because the revolution has to take place, not at the economic, social, or moral level, or at the level of ideas, but in consciousness itself. I feel the crisis is there.

So, what is this thing that we call consciousness, the mind? I do not know if you have ever experienced the totality of consciousness, which is rather difficult—the totality, not just the segment of consciousness which is aware of the various experiences that one has every day, and which interprets, reacts, responds to those experiences. That is only a part of consciousness. There is the world of dreams, and the interpretation of those dreams, which is still part of consciousness. Then there is the whole world of thought, of knowledge, of experience, of things remembered—the past in conjunction with the present, which creates the future. That too is part of consciousness. There is also the influence of the family, of the group, that unconscious conditioning which is racial inheritance, however young the race may be, or however old—surely, all that is part of this consciousness of which the psychologists speak, and of which we also speak, rather easily and facilely, in referring to our own minds. So, consciousness is the known and the unknown—that part of the mind which has never been delved into.

Now, most of us live at the superficial level of consciousness, carrying on from day to day rather wearily, with a certain amount of boredom, frustration, with here and there a touch of joy and fulfillment, with sorrow, travail, misery, and all the conflicts that we are heir to; and within that field of consciousness, we make effort to change. When we get angry, we try not to be angry; when we are jealous, envious, greedy, we try to control, to reform ourselves. But this is all within the field of the known, and a problem of the known has an answer which is already known. I think this is important to understand. When the mind puts to itself any problem, the mind already knows the answer because the problem is known. That is, when you know the problem, whether it is in the economic field, in the field of electronics, or wherever else, the answer is also known. The moment you put a problem into words, that problem has an answer which is already known, though you may take time to discover it. You can see the truth of this for yourself, if you have thought about it.

So, all our endeavor to change, to bring about a radical revolution inwardly and outwardly, is within the field of consciousness; and consciousness, as you will see if you really go into it, is a world of symbols. We live by symbols. The symbol is a word; the symbol is the cross for the Christian; the symbol is the image which the mind creates out of its own experiences, and from which it projects visions, ideas. We live in a world of symbols, and the symbol is always the known. The symbol is the known representing the unknown, which the mind cannot feel out for itself.

Please, I am only putting into words what we already know. If we have given any thought to these matters, we already know all this. And we also know, very deeply for ourselves, that any change within this field of consciousness, the field of the known, is not a revolution; it is only a change in the pattern of behavior, in the pattern of thought. A man may give up Christianity and become a Zen Buddhist, or give up Hinduism and become a Catholic, but his action is still within the field of consciousness; it is merely a change in the pattern which holds him within the cage. And that is what we are all doing—we are always moving within the field of the known.

Do consider what is being said; don't reject it, saying, "I don't understand." It is very simple to understand. I'll try to make it clear by putting it differently.

As I said, the moment we are capable of putting any problem into words, bringing it into focus, into the field of consciousness, such a problem—whether it be economic, social, technical, or moral—has already an answer; therefore, it is no longer a problem. The moment you have an answer, it is not a problem. The answer may take several months to investigate and work out, but the mind knows the answer because it has been able to put the problem into words. I think this is important to understand, especially if you would follow what I am going to say. The mind already knows the answer to any problem it can put into words, however complex, however subtle, however delicate; therefore, it is not a problem at all. The mind thinks it is a problem, but it is not. If you understand that, then the next question I would like to put forward is this: Is there a problem which the mind—because it is always functioning within the field of the known—has never been able to put into words, consciously or even unconsciously, and therefore cannot possibly answer? I feel there is such a problem—a problem which the mind cannot tackle, for which consciousness has no answer. Therefore, that is the real problem.

Do please give a little attention, if you will, to what I am trying to convey.

As I said, the crisis is in consciousness; the revolution is not, as we all think, at the economic, social, or intellectual level. If there is a "revolution" there, it is merely a change of pattern, a change of ideas, the building up of new theories. If the crisis is within the field of the known, we will answer it according to our conditioned minds, as Americans, Russians, Hindus, or what you will. But a mind that has been through this so-called revolution, that has understood all these various problems, with their answers—such a mind is confronted with quite a different issue because it sees there is no possibility whatsoever of a fundamental change within the field of the known. Then where is the revolution to take place?

Am I making this thing somewhat clear? Please don't agree with me because it is not a matter of agreement or disagreement; it is not something you can reject because you don't understand it, or accept because you understand a few words during an hour's talk. It is a problem that must really be gone into, and this requires profound thinking, or meditation, contemplation.

So there must be a revolution, a tremendous revolution—but not within the field of the known because that has no meaning any more. Whether you are a communist, a socialist, a democrat, a republican, an American, a Hindu—oh, who cares? If you happen to be a communist, you are more brutal, more ruthless in seeking power; but you do mischief, one way or the other. And if you belong to any particular organized religion, you are equally dictated to by the bosses in the name of God, Christ, the church, and all the rest of it. The older the organized religion, the more clever it is in adapting itself to the present conditions and the new ways of dominating the mind.

We know all this. But unfortunately, though we know it, most of us belong to something or other, or we change from this to that, thinking we are thereby making tremendous progress. And when we have finished with that whole process—I am not in any way talking patronizingly about it—when we have finished with all that, then the question arises: What is one to do? Do you understand? You have changed. You don't belong to any organized religion. You have given up this belief, that belief—if you have. You are no longer an American or a Hindu or a Russian or a German—you are a human being. You do not belong to any one country. You belong to the world; the world is yours, though the politicians have divided this beautiful earth as American, Russian, Chinese. You have been through all that, and yet the mind, consciousness, is still struggling within the field of its own frontiers. You understand what I'm talking about, I hope?

Realizing this, what is one to do? I think that is the problem, that is the crisis, though we don't know how to articulate it, put it into words. That is the problem, not only of the intellectuals, but of the religious person who is more or less serious. The people who go to church, who perform a few rituals, join a monastery, or hold certain beliefs—they are not religious people at all. We'll come to that presently.

So, how is the mind to bring about that energy which is not contaminated by consciousness? Do you understand?

Let me put it this way. All of us, most unfortunately, look to something greater than ourselves; we all want leaders to tell us what to do. When we are fed up with the political leaders, we turn to the religious leaders, or we retire to a monastery to meditate, so religion has become, for most of us, an escape from the reality of existence—not an escape from consciousness, but an escape from the reality of everyday existence. Your creeds and dogmas, your churches and organized beliefs are simply a means for the mind to take comfort. Your belief in God is as meaningless as another's nonbelief in God. There is no essential difference between the two. You have been taught to believe, and the other has been taught not to believe; or you believe because you rationalize, depending on your conditioning.

Now, when you have seen through all this illusion of symbols, ideas, and words, you may become cynical or bitter, like the angry young men in England and the beatniks in this country, which is fairly easy to do; but when you are no longer cynical, bitter, despairing, then you must inevitably ask, "Where is the religious mind to find the answer?" Books cannot give you the answer; there is no book that can show you a thing. Books can explain, they can give you knowledge, but knowledge only darkens the mind, and for the mind to seek the answer through knowledge has no meaning. So, when you have discarded all religions, all the behavior patterns which society calls morality, what are you to do? I am not saying there is no moral action—that is not the point. When you see how the mind becomes a slave to ideas, a slave to prosperity—when the mind is fully aware of all this, what is it to do to bring about a real revolution, not within the field of consciousness, but a revolution which is not contaminated by the known? In putting it differently, am I helping to make it clear, or am I only making it more complicated?

Look, sirs, let me put it another way. You see, life for most of us is a terrible bore. Our lives are routine. We try to fulfill, at whatever level, and every fulfillment has its own shadow of despair; every joy, every bursting forth has its own misery and its own degradation. We know all this, but knowing it doesn't prevent us from going on in the same way, in the same direction. And we also know, as we begin to examine this struggle within, that all individual effort to be good, to be noble, to pursue the right ideal, and all the rest of it is invariably a process of egotistic salvation, which creates endless conflict. If you examine this effort, in which most of us are caught, you will see that it is essentially born of self-contradiction. A mind which is not in a state of self-contradiction doesn't make an effort—it is. Effort is the state of a mind, of a heart that is in conflict with itself because it is everlastingly struggling to become something, and what it becomes is the result of its own contradiction, and therefore breeds still further contradiction.

So, all our effort—intellectual, moral, economic—is very restrictive, limiting, time-bound, and there is no way out of it. Seeing this fact, one begins to ask oneself: Where is the revolution which is new? Where is the state of mind which is not contaminated by the old? Where is there innocency which is not a mere denial or intellectual formula? Where is there a mind which has been through this whole process, which has traveled through all these fields of limitation, and which knows what it is to be creative in the ultimate sense of that word? Creativity is not painting pictures or writing poems—I don't mean that. I am referring to that state of creation which is energy without a beginning and without an end, which does not demand an expression—which *is*.

You must have asked yourself all these questions. But you always want to find an answer, you want to achieve that state, so you are putting a wrong question, and inevitably you will have a wrong answer. You can't achieve that state. Do what you will—go to all the monasteries, read all the books, attend all the talks, including these, seek out every teacher—you can never achieve that state of creation. It can come into being only when you have understood or felt out all the dark recesses of your own mind, so that the mind is completely still and not demanding anything. Don't you see what you are doing within yourself, and therefore outwardly too? You are seeking a state of mind in which you will be capable of understanding, in which you will have no problem; you want to be in a perpetual state of ecstasy, where you will know what love is, and all the rest of it. You are always asking. Your problems are known, and your answers are also known; therefore, you have created a picture, a symbol of what you should or should not be.

So, the mind has the power to remember, to discard, to know and to use that knowledge; it has the power to decide, to compare, to condemn, to evaluate. This mind is in constant operation; it is always judging, weighing, observing, interpreting; and I feel the crisis is there. If, being aware of this crisis, the mind puts its question within the field of the known, it will have an answer according to its own knowledge; therefore, the problem continues. Whereas, can one confront the problem without a motive? Can one see for oneself—actually, not merely verbally—that the crisis is there, without knowing how to answer it? Do you understand? Because you really don't know how to answer it, do you? You have been through this or that religion, you have tried yoga or some other system of meditation, you have read the usual books, attended this talk, that talk, and have done all the things that every human being does in search of the answer—and you have not found it. Perhaps the problem itself has not been clear to you because you have never felt the totality of consciousness; you have only known certain parts of it. But this evening you may have been able to feel the totality of this enormous thing.

You know, when you suddenly see something extraordinarily beautiful—a mountain, a stream in the shade of a tree, or the face of a child—your whole being becomes quiet, does it not? You don't say, "Why is it so beautiful?" Your mind, your whole being is, for a moment at least, completely still because there is no answer. But that is merely an imposition. The beauty of something has momentarily knocked out your mind. It is like depending on a drug to make you quiet, taking LSD so that you will have marvelous visions.

What we are talking about has no answer, so we have only the crisis without the answer. But you have never faced the crisis in those terms. You have never lived in that crisis without seeking an answer—because there is no answer. The fields of the known may be traversed in one swift perception, or it may take many years to cross the fields of the known. But when you have come to that point where you are really faced with the crisis which has no answer, and the mind is silent with a silence that is not imposed, then you will see, if you have the patience, that there is a revolution—a tremendous revolution in which the mind is made innocent through death of the known; and only such a mind can discover that which is everlasting.

May 28, 1960

Fourth Talk in The Oak Grove

I am afraid this will have to be the last talk of the present series. I had intended to give another four talks, but unfortunately my physical condition will not allow me to go on. So this will be the last talk, and would you kindly tell your friends also that there will be no more talks here after today.

If I may, I would like this morning to talk about time, death, and meditation. I would like to go into these rather complex questions with you, but not just intellectually or verbally, because intellectually to grapple with these problems is of very little importance. It may amuse the intellect, but if we merely play with words, we are left with ashes. As most of us are intimately concerned with these problems, we should consider the fact and not be content with the word. The fact is much more important than the word. Time is an extraordinary fact, and it would be of great interest and significance if we could understand the whole process of time. All our life depends on time, and for the majority of us, death has tremendous significance. Either we are frightened of death or we rationalize it, or we cling to certain beliefs which give us hope and nullify our fears and despairs. Meditation is also very important. A mind that does not know what it is to meditate has not lived at all; it is a dull, stupid, irrelevant mind.

So, I would like to discuss these things with you. I will do the verbalizing, if you will kindly give your attention to what is being said and follow it right through to the end. By attention I do not mean enforced concentration, because a mind that is forced to concentrate is not capable of understanding. But if the mind can flow with the ideas, without accepting or denying, without correcting or translating, then perhaps our thinking will transcend mere verbalization.

Most of us think from a conclusion, from the background of experience, from a remembered past. Our thinking arises as a reaction from the past. All our thinking is the response of memory. If we had no memory, there would be no thinking. One of the faculties of the mind is to remember and to coordinate as knowledge all the things it has experienced, and from that state of conditioning, from that background of experience as knowledge, the mind responds to any challenge, to any question, to any problem. This response is what we call thinking, and our thinking, as you will see if you observe it very carefully, is the very process of time. I will go into that presently.

Unless we understand the mechanical response of thinking, it seems to me that we shall not be able to grasp the significance of time. Our thinking is not merely the everyday reactions and responsibilities, the routine of work, and so on, but it is also the process of thinking abstractly, inwardly, comprehensively, the correlating of every form of experience, knowledge, in order to bring about a decision.

So, it is important to understand the mechanism of thinking and to see its limitations. All thinking is limited thinking; there is no freedom in thinking. Thinking is the process of a mind which has accumulated knowledge and responds from that background; therefore, thinking can never be free, it is always limited. And if we respond to any human problem, however deep or superficial it may be, merely through the process of thinking, we shall not be able to resolve it, but on the contrary, we shall create more problems, more confusion, more misery. That is why it is absolutely essential to understand the mechanism of thinking.

When you are asked a familiar question, your response is immediate, is it not? If you are asked where you live, or what is your name, or what is your profession, your response is immediate because you are very familiar with these things. But if you are asked a more serious or complicated question, there is a lag between the question and your response. In that time interval your mind is furiously at work, looking into its accumulated memories to find the answer; and later on, as every schoolboy knows, the answer comes. If you are asked a much more complex question, involving a great deal of memory and the mechanism of inquiry, there is a still greater interval, a greater lag of time before the mind answers. And if a question is asked to which your mind, having searched the corridors of memory, can find no answer, then you say, "I don't know." But the "I don't know" is merely the state of a mind which is waiting, expecting, still trying to find an answer.

I hope you are following this because the next statement is important to understand. You see these three steps, do you not? There is the mind's immediate response to a question, its response within a certain period or lag of time, and finally, having searched without finding an answer in the corridors of memory, it says, "I don't know." But when the mind says, "I don't know," it is waiting, expecting, looking for an answer. With most of us, that is the state of the mind. Having thought, searched, inquired, we say, "I don't know." But in saying "I don't know," the mind is waiting, expecting. Now, there is a state in which the mind says, "I don't know," but it does not expect, is not waiting for an answer. There is no answer, there is no searching—it is in a state of complete not-knowing. Do you see the difference?

Sirs, may I say something? Please, don't take notes, for goodness' sake. This isn't a lecture. You and I are trying to discover, experience as we go along; we are trying to feel our way through. You are not capturing a phrase here and there to think over when you go home. You are doing it now—which means that you are really listening, and thereby actually experiencing what is being said. This is not a suggestion; you are not being influenced one way or the other. It is merely the statement of a fact. I am going to talk on the same subject in different ways from the beginning to the end, and if you are taking notes, or otherwise not giving your full attention, you are not going to be able to follow it right through. You have to give your whole, unenforced attention. The moment you force attention, you are blocking perception because anything that is forced is

unnatural, it is not spontaneous. So please, those of you who are serious, do give your full attention, and don't be distracted by taking down a few scattered words that have very little meaning.

As I was saying, thinking is the response of memory. The response may be immediate, or it may take time; and the mind may ultimately say, "I don't know." But when the mind says, "I don't know," it is waiting for an answer, either from its own deep-rooted experiences in the unconscious or from a source beyond its own cognition. And there is the mind which has been through and recognizes this whole mechanical process of knowing, and responding according to that knowledge, with the time-lag involved in it. When such a mind says, "I don't know," it is not waiting for an answer or expecting a solution; it has wholly stopped searching, and therefore it is in a state of not-knowing.

So, all thinking is the response of memory, the response of experience as knowledge, whether that knowledge be of the individual or of the collective. Knowledge or experience implies accumulation, and accumulation implies time—the thing that has been and the thing that will be, the before and the after, yesterday moving through today to tomorrow, time which is static and time as movement. Time is static as the experience of many thousands of yesterdays, and though it moves through the present, fulfilling itself in tomorrow as the future, it is still static, only modified. That is, what has been, has been added to. It is an additive, accumulative process; and that which has accumulated, and is accumulating, is always within the field of time. From this accumulative center we function mechanically. All electronic brains function as we do, only much faster, much more brilliantly, much more accurately; but it is essentially the same process as our thinking. So our thinking is mechanical; we function from conclusion to conclusion, from the known to the known, and always within the field of time—which is fairly obvious when you begin to examine it unemotionally, as you must, because anything that we examine emotionally is distorted. This demands mere perception of the fact; whether you like or dislike the fact is irrelevant. To perceive the fact as it is requires a state of mind in which there is no emotion, no sentiment—and then there is perception which is of the highest intensity.

So, thinking, being mechanical, is not the way to a life which is not mechanical. Life is not mechanical, energy is not mechanical. But we want that energy to be mechanized so that our minds may function happily, easily, comfortably within the field of time as convenience; therefore, we reduce life, with all its extraordinary vastness and depth, to a process of thinking, which is mechanical or intellectual; and then, not being able to find an answer to our problems, we become cynical, fearful, or we are in a state of despair. The more intellectual we are, the more despairing is our existence, and out of despair we invent philosophies; we say that we must accept life as it is and make the best of it, that we exist now, and it is only the now that matters. Not being able to understand the totality of time, we try to cut away the past and the future and live only in the present—which cannot be done because there is no present. There is existence, but not an isolated present; and to create a philosophy out of this formula of the present is so utterly immature, materialistic, limiting.

One begins to see that the mechanical process of thinking, which involves time, is not the answer; and yet all our days, our nights, our dreams—everything about us and within ourselves is based on thought. We never come to that state in which the mind, having been through all this, says, "I don't know." That is the state of innocency; it is a state in which the mind can discover some-

thing new, something which is not projected by its own desires, ambitions, fears, longings, despairs.

So, one perceives very clearly that thinking, however clever, however intelligent, however cunning, however philosophical, speculative, or theological it may be, is still essentially mechanistic. Theologians the world over start from some conclusion— "Jesus is the Savior," full stop—and from there build the whole structure of speculative philosophy. Similarly, the mind builds a vast intellectual superstructure based on the concept of existence as the now, or gets lost in speculative theories about the hereafter. And when we realize for ourselves the mechanistic nature of thinking, then arises the problem of how to put an end to it—how to die to the past. Do you understand the question?

I do not know if you have ever thought about death. You may have thought about it, but have you actually faced death? Do you understand the difference? To think about death is one thing, and actually to confront death is another. If you think about death, invariably there arises fear with its sense of frustration in the coming to an end of things irrevocably, irremediably. But if you are confronted with death, there is no answer, there is no way out, there is no measure which will give you comfort, security—it is a fact. Death in the sense of total cessation, physically and psychologically, has to be faced. It is not to be denied, accepted, or rationalized—it is there. And it must be an extraordinary experience to die, as it must be an extraordinary experience to live totally. As we do not understand what it is to live totally, without conflict, without this everlasting inward contradiction, perhaps we shall never know what it is to experience the totality of death. The older we grow, the more fearful we are of death. Being afraid of death, we go to doctors, try new medicines, new drugs, and perhaps we may live twenty or thirty more years; but there it is , inevitably, round the corner. And to face that fact—to face it, not to think about it—requires a mind that is dead to the past, a mind that is actually in a state of not-knowing.

The future, after all, the tomorrow, is still within the field of time. And the mind is always thinking and functioning between yesterday and tomorrow, with today as a connecting passage. That is all it can do—prepare for the future through the present, depending on the past. We are caught between what has been and what will be, the before and the after, and we function mechanically in that field. And is it possible to die to that whole sense of time—actually to die, and not ask how to die? Death doesn't ask you if you are willing to die. You can't compromise with death, you can't ask it questions. Death is one of the most absolute things, a finality. You can't bargain with it. I know most of us would like to. We would like to ask of it gifts, favors, the boon of escape; but death is indomitable, incorruptible.

So, can the mind die to its many yesterdays, to both the pleasant and the unpleasant memories of experience as knowledge? Can it die to the things it has gathered—die as it goes along? I do not know if you have ever experimented with that—to die to all your worries—not so that you can lead a more peaceful life or do more business or arrive fresh at your office with a dead past, and thereby get a greater advantage over somebody else, or over a situation. I don't mean that kind of nonsense. To die without any future; to die without knowing what tomorrow is—after all, that is death. And that requires a mind which is very sharp, clear, capable of perceiving every thought, conscious or unconscious, a mind which is aware of every pleasure and does not allow that pleasure to take root as memory. And is it possible so to die that there is no tomorrow?—which is not a state of despair. The moment you think in terms of hope and despair, you are again within the field of time, of fear. To go through that very strange experience of dying, not at the ultimate moment of physical death when one becomes unconscious, or one's mind is dull, made stupid by disease or drug or accident, but to die to the many yesterdays in full consciousness, with full vitality and awareness—surely that does create a mind which is in a state of not-knowing, and therefore in a state of meditation.

I would like to talk about this subject of meditation rather extensively, if there is time. Meditation is one of the most important things in life, as love is, as death and time are. But I do not think many of us know what it is to meditate. We know how to concentrate, as every schoolboy and schoolgirl does, how to focus our attention on something; and we also know that when something is vitally interesting, it absorbs the mind, as a child is absorbed with a new toy. The mind is then in a state of concentration, which is a state of complete absorption and exclusion, but that is not the way of meditation.

Meditation is important because it opens the door to self-knowledge. But self-knowledge becomes very superficial and rather boring if it is merely information about yourself which you have gathered and held in your mind. You may say, "Well, I know myself, and there is nothing much to know." There isn't. One is greedy, ambitious, violent, sexual, and all the rest of it; so you say, "Yes, I know myself." But to go beyond that is the knowing of oneself, not the knowledge of oneself. I hope I am making it clear.

The knowing of oneself is entirely different from the process of acquiring knowledge about oneself, because knowing is a constant movement. There is no end to knowing, to learning, and therefore there is never a moment which is not extraordinarily vital and unfolding. But if, having read a few books and having watched yourself a little here and there, now and then, you say, "I know myself," that knowledge is merely additive, accumulative; and it is stifling, deadly, it brings only darkness. Whereas, knowing is an indefinite movement.

So, meditation is the process of knowing oneself, and that is the door through which you will know the universe, because you are not just you, with a name and a bank account, or a profession. You are a result of the whole of man, whether he lives in Russia or America, in India or China. We are human beings, not labels, and within each human being is this total consciousness of humanity, of suffering, of thoughts, of ambitions—here as in India or China. Circumstances vary, conditions differ, but people have the same misery, the same joy, the same platitudes, the same use of slogans, and the same happy moments.

To meditate is to inquire into the process of the mind without an object. The moment you have an object which you are seeking, your search is the result of a cause, and that cause brings about the accumulation which you call knowledge, and therefore there is the darkness of knowledge.

I do not know if you have ever observed that there is a strength which has no cause. Most of our strength is the result of a cause, which is determination, the will to be or not to be something. This urge to be or not to be is in turn the result of one's various contradictory desires, ambitions, fulfillments, miseries. Every urge to be something has its roots in a cause, and it is that cause which projects, creates, or develops a certain strength in the form of resistance, determination. When you remove the cause, the determination is gone, but another cause soon comes into being, and a different determination arises. Whereas, if the mind has examined and understood this whole process and there-

fore knows the meaning of meditation, then it will discover a strength that has no cause, a strength which is not of time.

So, meditation is essential—but not the so-called meditation of following a particular system. That is mere self-hypnosis; it is too immature, too silly altogether. Meditation is to be in a state of total awareness so that the mind is emptying itself every moment of the day and therefore constantly discovering, because only that which is empty can receive. It is only the empty mind that has space to contemplate—not a mind that is making ceaseless effort to be or not to be, to arrive, to guard itself, to escape. Such a mind cannot be empty. It is only when the mind is empty of yesterday, of time, and is aware of that extraordinary thing called death—it is only then, being thus empty, that it can receive—not receive what you want. A mind that wants and seeks is not an empty mind. An empty mind is not just empty, it is not just blank—it is a very active mind. It has been through this whole process about which I have talked, and therefore it is vital, clear, without any sense of acceptance, denial, expectation, or rejection. And without this vital emptiness of the mind, our life is very drab. You may be very clever, you may be able to write books, paint pictures, or you may be a very skillful lawyer or politician, but without knowing what it is to meditate, life becomes extremely superficial, dull; and a dull mind is always seeking a way out of its dullness, and thereby creating further dullness for itself.

Seeing this chaotic state of things within and without, one has to purge oneself of the known, not verbally, intellectually, but actually; one has to die to everything. And when the mind is empty—which is really not a good word—but when the mind is empty, as the sky is empty, then that which is not measurable by man comes into being.

May 29, 1960

Questions

Banaras, 1960

Index